Building an Enriched Vocabulary

Joseph R. Orgel, Ph. D.

Sadlier-Oxford
A Division of William H. Sadlier Inc.
New York

About the Author

In the course of his long career as a teacher of English and as a writer, JOSEPH R. ORGEL has exercised a significant influence in helping to upgrade, modernize, and enliven the English curriculum in American schools.

A product of the public schools of New York City, and of the College of the City of New York, Dr. Orgel did graduate work at Columbia University and New York University. From the latter institution he obtained his Ph.D. degree in English and Comparative Literature.

Dr. Orgel served for many years in the New York City school system as classroom teacher, administrator, and special lecturer. He also held the position of Reader for the Educational Testing Service, Princeton, New Jersey.

Dr. Orgel is the author or coauthor of more than forty books in the field of English, including works on grammar and usage, vocabulary, reading comprehension, literature and pedagogy. His titles include: *Words, Words, Words*; *Graded Units in Vital English*; *Comprehensive English in Review*; *Macbeth Workshop*; *Succeeding in College Entrance Tests*; and *Handbooks in English*. These books have been widely used in secondary schools and colleges in all parts of the United States, and in various foreign countries as well. Dr. Orgel has also served as feature writer on education and as a book reviewer for various metropolitan journals and for *Scholastic*.

Copyright © 1995 by
Oxford Book Company, Inc.
A Division of
William H. Sadlier, Inc.

ISBN: 0-87105-510-4

17 18 19 20 /987

Home Office: 9 Pine Street
New York, NY 10005

Editor
Calvin A. Roeder, Jr.

Cover Photos
FPG International/Color Box - telephone;
Gary Buss - computer;
Telegraph Colour Library - diary;
Tom Campbell - pen

Photo Research
Jim Saylor

Illustrators
Tom Huffman
Denise Mickalson

Contents

The Structure and Organization of BUILDING
  AN ENRICHED VOCABULARY   v

Learning Words: An Introduction for the Student   1

  I.   The Vocabulary of Vocabulary   1

  II. The Tools of Vocabulary Building   5

  III. The Development of Our Vocabulary   8

Basic Word List   21

Pronunciation Key   26

Lesson 1
  1. abdicate — 10. addiction   27
Lesson 2
  11. adjourn — 20. agile   38
Lesson 3
  21. alienate — 30. anecdote   49
Lesson 4
  31. anomaly — 40. assimilate   60
Lesson 5
  41. astute — 50. authentic   71
Lesson 6
  51. avarice — 60. bland   82
Lesson 7
  61. bleak — 70. brusque   93
Lesson 8
  71. bungle — 80. catholic   104
Lesson 9
  81. caustic — 90. clandestine   115
Lesson 10
  91. coerce — 100. conjecture   126
Review
  1. abdicate — 100. conjecture   137

Lesson 11
  101. connoisseur — 115. cynical   141
Lesson 12
  116. dapper — 130. dexterous   157
Lesson 13
  131. dilapidated — 145. duplicity   175

Lesson 14
146. eclectic — 160. enigma   192

Lesson 15
161. entice — 175. exigency   209

Lesson 16
176. exodus — 190. fetish   226

Lesson 17
191. fiasco — 205. futile   243

Lesson 18
206. gape — 220. harbinger   257

Lesson 19
221. haughty — 235. incense   273

Lesson 20
236. inception — 250. justify   291

Review
101. connoisseur — 250. justify   306

Lesson 21
251. kudos — 265. medium   311

Lesson 22
266. mercenary — 280. nuance   328

Lesson 23
281. obscene — 295. pensive   345

Lesson 24
296. peremptory — 310. premise   363

Lesson 25
311. prerogative — 325. quixotic   378

Lesson 26
326. raze — 340. resilient   398

Lesson 27
341. reticent — 355. satellite   414

Lesson 28
356. scapegoat — 370. syndrome   432

Lesson 29
371. tacit — 385. venal   448

Lesson 30
386. veneer — 400. zenith   464

Review
251. kudos — 400. zenith   481

Cumulative Review (Words 1–400)   486
Index   494

The Structure and Organization of BUILDING AN ENRICHED VOCABULARY

BUILDING AN ENRICHED VOCABULARY is a fusion and updating of two of Joseph R. Orgel's most successful works, NEW BUILDING WORD POWER and ENRICHING YOUR VOCABULARY. Accordingly, its overall aim is essentially the same as that of the earlier books: to prepare college-bound 11th- and 12th-graders to meet the challenges ahead by familiarizing them with the vocabulary of Modern English.

In BUILDING AN ENRICHED VOCABULARY, this goal is achieved in three ways:

* in-depth study of 400 key words (the Basic Word List)

* intensive preparation for specialized question-types frequently used on standardized vocabulary tests assessing college readiness

* supplementary survey of a broad but varied segment of the vocabulary students will meet at the college level or on standardized vocabulary tests

In this revision, every effort has been made to profit from the criticisms, advice, and suggestions of a wide variety of people who have used Dr. Orgel's earlier books, and it is hoped that teachers and students will see BUILDING AN ENRICHEDVOCABULARY as a worthy companion to those two outstanding textbooks.

The Introductory Chapter   An introductory chapter entitled "Learning Words" (pages 1–20) is the first item that meets the student's eye in BUILDING AN ENRICHED VOCABULARY. It reviews key technical terms or concepts relating to the study of vocabulary; it introduces the dictionary and the thesaurus; and it surveys the chief stages in the development of the vocabulary of Modern English. The historical survey has been included in order to supply the student with enough background information to make effective use of the various exercises and other materials relating to etymology or word origins that are interspersed throughout the book. Each of the three subsections of the introductory chapter concludes with a short but practical reinforcement exercise.

The Basic Word List.   The key element in the structure of BUILDING AN ENRICHED VOCABULARY is the Basic Word List of 400 essential vocabulary items (pages 21–25). This list was developed from many sources, including traditional and contemporary literature, newspapers, magazines, films, and radio-TV programs. Due attention was also paid to the spelling and vocabulary lists which have gained wide recognition as valid bases for teaching language skills on the secondary level. Current subject-area textbooks and glossaries were also examined, and the standard word-frequency studies by Dolch, Thorndike–Lorge, Dale–O'Rourke, Johnson, Hillerich, Harris, Jacobson, Carroll–Davies–Richman, and others were used to evaluate and revise the tentative word list.

The criterion for the selection of entries on the Basic Word List was their frequent appearance in printed materials (essays, magazine articles, business and social letters). The words were also chosen for their frequency on standardized vocabulary tests. In this connection, there is an unavoidable element of subjective judgment. Accordingly, the author and editor have had to rely to some extent on their "feel" for the language and for the words that are likely to be most useful to, and rewarding for, students preparing to enter college.

Lesson Format.   The 400 key words on the Basic Word List have been put in alphabetical order into 30 lessons, each containing 10 or 15 words. Each of these lessons consists of the following parts:

- A set of *word entries*, in the form dictionaries adopt

- "*Using the Words*," a set of exercises providing practical reinforcement of the material presented in the word entries

- "*Dissecting the Words*," a section on word origins, or "*Completing Verbal Analogies*," a section dealing with the type of analogy questions usually found on standardized vocabulary tests

- "*Working with Context Clues*," a section introducing the student to the type of word-omission question commonly found on standardized vocabulary tests

- "*Enriching the Lesson*," a set of advanced dictionary/thesaurus exercises that enrich the material presented in the word entries and round out the presentation

The Word Entries.   Each lesson in BUILDING AN ENRICHED VOCABULARY begins with a set of dictionary-like word entries of a standardized pattern consisting of three parts:

- the *headline*, which includes the key word in syllabicated form, the part of speech of the key word, the pronunciation and a brief etymology

- the *body* of the entry, containing the definition or definitions; one or more illustrative sentences or passages; related forms of the key word; phrases showing the range of applicability of the key word; and usage notes regarding tone, connotation, look-alikes, and so forth

- the *supplement* to the entry, consisting of a group of synonyms and antonyms of the key word or its related forms; a selection of phrases involving these synonyms and antonyms or in some way relating to the general idea expressed by the key word; and appropriate usage notes referring to these items

The following remarks explain more fully the nature of the word entries:

- The *pronunciation* is indicated by means of a simple set of diacritical marks explained at the beginning of the book (page 26). Usually the commonly accepted pronunciation is indicated, though alternate pronunciations may be sanctioned by some dictionaries. However, exceptions to this general rule do occur occasionally when a word changes its pronunciation upon becoming a different part of speech.

- The *etymology* has been kept as simple as possible. Usually it attempts to account only for the present spelling of the key word (insofar as that is possible) and to break the word up into its basic component parts without indicating intermediate stages in its development. It is believed that this schematic representation of the word's origin will prove more useful to students than a fuller treatment would.

- The *definitions* provided are for the most part brief and clear. Usually only the common meaning is given. Additional meanings may be given if they are of equal value, or if the key word is used as more than one part of speech. If there is any uncertainty as to what a given word means, students should be encouraged to consult an unabridged dictionary.

- The *illustrative sentences or passages* have been especially designed to show how the key word is normally used in a "typical" context. Where more than one illustrative sentence accompanies a single definition, a literal use of that meaning is given in the first sentence and a figurative or "extended" application in the second. The illustrative sentences involve situations that are familiar to the average high-school student while at the same time selectively introducing college-level subject matter or sentence structure.

- For the most part, only a selection of appropriate *synonyms* and *antonyms* of maximum usefulness has been provided. Students should be encouraged to consult a thesaurus or other "word-finder" for more complete listings.

- *Usage notes and phrases* have been kept to a minimum so as not to overload the entry or confuse the student with too much detail.

- The items included in the supplement ("Synonyms," "Antonyms," "Phrases") are normally not defined or explained. This was done in part to provide material for Exercise V in "Using the Words" (see below). Accordingly, students should be instructed to make use of a dictionary when studying this section of the word entry. (The items in the headline and body of a word entry are, of course, self-explanatory, and no dictionary work is required for them.)

Using the Words.   Immediately after the last word entry in each lesson you will find a varied group of practical exercises entitled "Using the Words." These exercises review and reinforce the material presented in the word entries in a brief but highly effective way. Since they call on the student to use and reuse the key words in a variety of situations, the exercises extend and supplement the discussion contained in the word entries themselves.

Each of the exercises contained in "Using the Words" deals with one part of the preceding set of word entries. Nonetheless, the particular type of exercise that is included varies somewhat, depending on whether the section appears in an odd- or even-numbered lesson, as the following chart indicates:

Odd-Numbered Lesson	Even-Numbered Lesson
I. Syllabication and Pronunciation	I. Parts of Speech
II. Words Out of Context	II. Words in Phrases
III. Completing Sentences	III. Completing Sentences
IV. Synonyms and Antonyms (First Format)	IV. Synonyms and Antonyms (Second Format)
V. Word Roundup	V. Word Roundup
VI. Framing Sentences	VI. Framing Sentences

A careful examination of this sequence against a typical word entry will show that Exercise I relates to the headline, Exercises II and III to the body, and Exercises IV and V to the supplement. (See above for definitions of these terms.) Exercise VI acts as a final check on the learning experience by asking students to use the key words or their related forms in sentences of their own devising.

The following comments may prove helpful when trying to make effective use of "Using the Words":

- The sentences in Exercise III, "*Completing Sentences*," require the student to choose a word that fits logically and meaningfully into a given blank. If students have a good grasp of the meanings of the key words, they should have no trouble making the correct selections. Context clues of one type or another have been carefully "sewn" into the sentences to insure that the correct word is selected. In the earlier lessons the literal meanings of the key words are all that is involved in the sentences. Note that Exercise III makes use of only those words that have not already been used in Exercise II, so that Exercises II and III form a complementary pair of tests covering all the key words in the lesson.

- The activities in Exercise V, "*Word Roundup*," are designed to cover the diverse materials contained in the "Usage Notes" and "Phrases" sections of the word entry. Since many of these items are not explained in the text, the student may have to consult a dictionary or thesaurus to answer the questions about them. Thus, Exercise V acts as a simple dictionary/thesaurus exercise that is in part designed to lead up to the more advanced and complicated dictionary/thesaurus exercises contained in "Enriching the Lesson."

"Dissecting the Words." The reader will no doubt have noticed that the etymological material contained in each word entry is not covered by any of the exercises in "Using the Words." That is because a special section, entitled "Dissecting the Words," has been provided. This concentrated presentation should meet the practical needs of the average college-bound student than a more piecemeal approach would have done.

"Dissecting the Words" appears immediately after "Using the Words" in *odd-numbered* lessons. Important word elements occurring in the key words—prefixes, roots, and suffixes—are analyzed to show what each means, where it comes from, and how it is employed in other useful words not on the Basic Word List.

A short but lively exercise involving the use of a dictionary or thesaurus concludes each of the etymology sections, so that the learning exercise is reinforced in as effective a manner as possible.

"Completing Verbal Analogies." Earlier it was remarked that BUILDING AN ENRICHED VOCABULARY in part attempts to prepare students for the type of standardized vocabulary test that is frequently used to assess college readiness. The next two sections of the lesson—"Completing Verbal Analogies" and "Working with Context Clues"—have this practical aim.

"Completing Verbal Analogies," appears immediately after "Using the Words" in all *even-numbered* lessons. As the teacher is well aware, analogy questions are valuable and revealing, not merely as a kind of mental gymnastics but also as a means of pinning down the exact meanings of words and of remedying misconceptions or uncertainties about how they are used. For that reason, analogy questions serve as both a functional as well as an effective pedagogical tool.

The treatment of analogy questions in BUILDING AN ENRICHED VOCABULARY is organized but succinct, and a wealth of examples has been provided to give students adequate practice in handling these verbal brainteasers. Two different kinds of analogy-completion questions frequently met with on standardized tests are analyzed in detail (see pages 68 and 168), and about 15 basic word relationships (e.g., "A means the same as B," "A is an example of B," and "If a person is A, he/she lacks B") are highlighted. Each analogy section is divided into three parts in order to reinforce and help master the style or the kind of analogy taught in the lesson. Starting in Lesson 20, special review exercises not only recapitulate the kinds of word relationships that the students are already familiar with but also introduce a few others that they have not been formally taught to recognize. (The latter were included in order to provide the teacher with a useful check of student mastery of the material under real testing conditions.)

The analysis of a representative set of analogy situations in BUILDING AN ENRICHED VOCABULARY is to be considered as introductory to the whole field of verbal logic. The teacher may feel it pedagogically necessary to simplify the concepts or upgrade the level of the exercises in order to meet the special needs of the students. In any event, the study of analogies as presented in this book is certain to provide a practical test of the challenges students will confront on college-entrance aptitude tests and other such vocabulary situations.

"Working with Context Clues." The other special section in the lesson that aims at preparing students for standardized vocabulary tests is called "Working with Context Clues." It first appears in Lesson 11 and occurs in every lesson thereafter.

"Working with Context Clues" has been designed to familiarize students with the type of word-omission question that frequently appears on standardized vocabulary tests. In this type of question the student is given a short passage of connected prose from which (usually) two words have been removed and replaced by blanks. The passage is followed by four or five pairs of words from which the student is to select the pair that correctly completes the passage. Context clues are provided within the passage to guide students to the correct choice.

BUILDING AN ENRICHED VOCABULARY addresses the problem of preparing students for this type of testing device by providing a systematic pedagogical program based on the recognition of three broad categories of context clues. These may be conveniently described as *restatement clues* (page 171), *contrast clues* (page 205), or *inference clues* (page 238). Each of these clues is first introduced and explained in the context of a *one-word* omission question and then extended to the type of *two-word* omission questions that the student can expect to meet on an actual test. Extensive exercise materials have been provided to reinforce the learning experience at every stage, and a wide variety of review items has been included.

Many of the basic words taught in BUILDING AN ENRICHED VOCABULARY appear as the answers in the exercises accompanying the "Working with Context Clues" sections. This was intentionally done to tie these sections more closely to the rest of the lesson.

Though the present treatment of two-word omissions cannot be considered exhaustive, the coverage is certainly as full an introduction as the teacher is likely to find in any comparable vocabulary book. Indeed, in many ways it is fuller and more thorough than what is currently available.

Thus, "Working with Context Clues" helps make BUILDING AN ENRICHED VOCABULARY a unique educational tool.

"Enriching the Lesson." The final section of every lesson is called "Enriching the Lesson." It contains a group of advanced dictionary/ thesaurus exercises that "spin off" from something that has been noted in the word entries, and is intended to enrich and round off the lesson. For example, Lesson 1 contains the word *academic*, which is derived from an ancient Greek place name. Accordingly, the "Enriching the Lesson" section that concludes Lesson 1 contains an exercise relating to other place names that have become familiar, everyday words in Modern English.

The material included in the exercises in this section of the lesson is drawn from every phase of the development of the vocabulary of Modern English, from the first Latin borrowings in the Old English period to the most recent coinages.

The material is organized around a number of important "themes" which throw light on the character and history of our vocabulary. These themes include the technical vocabulary of English (e.g., The Language of the Mind, page 242), the sources of our vocabulary (e.g., Words from Faraway Places, page 241, and Eponyms, page 102), word formation (e.g., Curious Compounds, page 125), advice on the use of words (e.g., Clichés, page 91), humor (e.g., the various "Verbal Diversions" included in the text), and others. Though no single lesson contains an exercise relating to each of these themes, they nonetheless weave in and out of the overall presentation and contribute liveliness and variety to what might otherwise have been dull and monotonous.

The Reviews. The treatment of vocabulary contained in the 30 lessons is rounded out by the inclusion of three *periodic reviews* (after Lessons 10, 20, and 30, respectively) and one *final cumulative review* (at the end of the book). Each of these items covers the material presented in the word entries and "Dissecting the Words" sections only and does not draw upon the specialized features dealing with standardized vocabulary tests or the advanced dictionary/thesaurus exercises in "Enriching the Lesson." For use as either review or testing devices, these supplementary sections combine familiar testing techniques with some new and interesting question types.

Illustrations. Ample use of photographs and other visuals has been made to illustrate and enrich the text. Two groups of illustrative materials deserve special notice: The *"Wordsmiths,"* which focus on some of the people who have made significant contributions to the development of the modern dictionary and thesaurus; and *"Careers for Word Buffs,"* which highlights some of the careers that a person who is good at vocabulary might profitably pursue. These items and the other illustrations in the text make a unique contribution to the particular pedagogical approach taken in BUILDING AN ENRICHED VOCABULARY.

Supplementary Materials. For the convenience of the teacher using BUILDING AN ENRICHED VOCABULARY in the classroom, a *Teacher's Annotated Edition* of the student text and a 96-page *Supplementary*

Exercise and Testing Program have been prepared. The former provides answers to all questions in both the student edition and the supplementary testing program; the latter supplies additional exercise materials that can be used for review or testing. The Teacher's Annotated Edition offers a ready resource in one easy-to-use product.

Using the Program. It is believed that the program presented here can be used with profit and enjoyment by the vast majority of students in our secondary schools. The rate of progress will depend, naturally, on both the grade and ability levels of particular classes or students. The book may be used as a regular class text, as a supplementary resource, or as a self-teaching text by individual students.

Building an Enriched Vocabulary

Learning Words

An Introduction for the Student

I. The Vocabulary of Vocabulary

Before you begin learning the words presented in this book, it might be useful to review what you know about the "vocabulary of vocabulary." Accordingly, a number of key concepts or technical terms relating to the study of words are discussed below. Some of these items—*synonyms*, for instance—will no doubt be familiar, but the discussion may help to bring their meaning and use into sharper focus. Others—*connotation*, for example—may be entirely new to you.

Denotation and Connotation. It would be fair to say that words basically convey meaning in two distinct ways, for which the terms *denotation* and *connotation* have been devised.

The **denotation** of a word is its specific meaning, as given in a dictionary. For example, the denotation of the adjective *scholarly* is "learned." Similarly, the denotation of the adjective *grasping* is "overly eager for material gain," and the denotation of the verb *travel* is "make a journey." The verb corresponding to *denotation* is *denote*.

Connotation, on the other hand, relates to the tone of a word—that is, the emotions or associations that the word arouses in the listener or reader. If a word—*scholarly*, for instance—arouses positive emotions, its tone or connotation is said to be favorable or positive. If it arouses negative emotions (the way *grasping* does), its tone or connotation is said to be negative, unfavorable or pejorative (pronounced pə-jôr´-ə-tĭv). A word that does not arouse any strong feeling, either good or bad, is said to be neutral. The verb *travel* is such a word. The verb corresponding to *connotation* is *connote*.

Literal and Figurative Meaning. It would also be fair to say that, generally speaking, words may be used on two quite distinct planes of meaning, which for convenience can be termed *literal* and *figurative* (or *metaphorical*).

When a word is being used in a **literal** sense, it is being employed in its strict or primary dictionary meaning in a situation (or context) that "makes sense" from a purely logical point of view. For example, if someone says that there are logs floating in the river, he or she is using the verb *float* literally because logs can actually float in water.

If, however, the person says that a famous actress "floated" into the room, he or she is using *float* in a non-literal way and in a context that does not "make sense" from a purely logical point of view. People can't really float into a room, except by artificial means. In other words, the person has applied the verb *float* to an unusual context in order to create a vivid and forceful image of the grace and elegance with which the actress *walked* into the room. Notice that now *float* no longer means "be buoyed up by," but something closer to "move gracefully or as if on air." We call this "extended" or non-literal application of a word a **figurative** or **metaphorical** usage.

Another example may help clarify this distinction. If you read an old tale about a knight who slew a fire-breathing dragon, the word *fire-breathing* in this context is being used quite literally. Dragons were indeed believed to breathe real fire. If, however, your best friend says that her father rushed into the room "breathing fire," the expression *breathing fire* is being used figuratively or metaphorically in order to convey a vivid picture of the man's state of mind. In other words, your friend is simply saying that her father was very angry or upset, but she is saying it more colorfully and dramatically than the words "in a very angry/upset frame of mind" could possibly convey. It is this added dimension that makes the figurative use of language so striking and appealing.

One final note: Though all words, of course, have literal meanings and can be used literally, only a fraction of the vocabulary can normally be applied figuratively. Such words are often referred to as "resonant." One must be careful, therefore, not to try to use "non-resonant" words in a figurative way.

Parts of Speech. Lexicographers (dictionary writers) and grammarians classify the words and other expressions that make up our language as different parts of speech, depending upon the function or functions they perform. Knowing what these classifications are and what they signify helps a person use a word correctly. For that reason, it might be well at this point to review some of the more common classifications that appear in this book.

A **noun** is a word or phrase that names a person, place, thing, or idea. Examples include *astronaut, library, trowel,* and *justice.* Nouns are usually divided into *common nouns* (e.g., *girl, day*) and *proper nouns* (e.g., *Jane, Wednesday*). All of the nouns on the Basic Word List in this book (see pages 21–25) are common nouns.

An **adjective** is a word that is used to describe a noun (or pronoun). It changes (or modifies) the meaning of the word to which it refers by answering such questions as: How many? Which one? What kind? Examples include *yellow, old, first,* and *many.* As with nouns, adjectives are divided into *common adjectives* (e.g., *tall, earliest*) and *proper adjectives* (e.g., *Spanish, Elizabethan*). All of the adjectives on the Basic Word List in this book (see pages 21–25) are common adjectives.

A **verb** is a word that expresses some kind of action or indicates some state of being. Examples include *run, think, enjoy, remain,* and *be*. Verbs are further subdivided into those that can take an object (*transitive* verbs) and those that cannot (*intransitive* verbs). *Shoot* is an example of a transitive verb; *sleep*, an illustration of one that is intransitive.

An **adverb** is a word that modifies a verb, an adjective, or another adverb. Adverbs usually answer such questions as: Where? When? How? How much? How long? Examples include *there, sometimes, badly, forever*, and *almost*.

One final note: Some words perform a number of different functions and are, therefore, classified as more than one part of speech. For example, *hope* is both a noun and a verb, *exact* is both a verb and an adjective, and *consular* is both a noun and an adjective.

Synonyms and Antonyms. Over the centuries English has absorbed a great many words that mean more or less the same thing as other words in the language. Two words that are similar in meaning are called **synonyms**. For example, *fragile* and *delicate* are more or less synonyms. So are *thief* and *robber*. The adjective form of *synonym* is *synonymous*.

Of course, no two words in English ever really convey exactly the same meaning, have exactly the same tone or connotation, or apply to exactly the same situations. They may be very close to one another, but they are rarely identical twins. That is because usage over a long period of time has shaped and molded a special character for most words, and it is this character that makes a word unique. For example, *hate* and *detest* mean much the same thing, except that *detest* conveys a stronger or more intense feeling of loathing than *hate* does. Accordingly, a person who says that he or she "detests" spinach is registering a stronger dislike of the vegetable than is the person who merely says that he or she "hates" it. Usually a dictionary provides much useful information about such fine distinctions of meaning and usage, but it cannot cover everything. For that reason, the student must often learn such subtleties by observation—that is, by noticing how and when other people use a given word, both in speaking and writing.

Just as some words mean more or less the same thing, others indicate opposites. A word that means the opposite of another word is called its **antonym**. For example, the verbs *relish* and *detest* are antonyms. So are the adjectives *wet* and *dry*. The adjective form of *antonym* is *antonymous*.

Frequently, the term *antonym* is used not so much for the opposite of a given word as for its *counterpart*. For example, *doctor* doesn't really have an opposite, but it does have a counterpart—*nurse*, also *patient*. Similarly, *actor* doesn't have an opposite, but it does have a counterpart—*actress*. These are the items that people mean when they speak of the "antonym" of *doctor* or the "antonym" of *actor*, and the student should bear this in mind when dealing with antonym questions on various kinds of standardized tests.

The Parts of a Word. As you probably already know, words are made up of various parts or elements, for each of which a general name has been devised. The most important of these are:

prefix—a syllable or syllables placed at the beginning of a word. Examples include *in* (as in *inspect*), *pre* (as in *predict*), and *post* (as in *postpone*).

root or **base**—the main part of a word to which prefixes and suffixes (see below) are attached. Examples include *spect* (as in *inspection*), *dict* (as in *prediction*), and *pone* (as in *postponement*).

suffix—a syllable or syllables placed at the end of a word. Examples include *or* (as in *inspector*), *ion* (as in *prediction*), and *ment* (as in *postponement*).

Exercise

The following questions are designed to help you apply your knowledge of the "vocabulary of vocabulary" to real situations.

1. With or without the aid of a dictionary, supply the *denotation* of each of the following adjectives. Then indicate whether its *connotation* is favorable, unfavorable, or neutral. (There are two examples of each.)

a. valiant	**c.** sudden	**e.** enchanting
b. malevolent	**d.** puritanical	**f.** parallel

2. Indicate whether the connotation of the *italicized* word in each of the following sentences is *positive, negative (pejorative)*, or *neutral*. (There is one example of each.)

    a. Though his answers are technically correct, they are invariably routine and *mechanical*.

    b. We are looking for students with outstanding *scholastic* records.

    c. The candidate's *rugged* honesty made a strong appeal to the voters.

3. Indicate whether the *italicized* word in each of the following sentences is being used in a *literal* or a *figurative* way. (There are two examples of each.)

    a. Dawn *tiptoed* silently across the meadow and drummed her rosy fingers on my windowpane.

    b. I *danced* with the most beautiful girl in the class last night.

    c. Stella *tiptoed* across the room so as not to disturb her sleeping brother.

    d. All kinds of delightful images *dance* across the pages of that wonderful novel.

4. In each of the following groups, select the *synonym* of the lettered word. Consult a dictionary, if necessary.

   a. petty
      unusual slight foreign dry visible

   b. neat
      sloppy strong tidy foolish loud

   c. rebellion
      failure defeat uprising change courtesy

   d. conceal
      burn show plunge answer hide

   e. quarrel
      doubt work order excite argue

5. In each of the following groups, select the *antonym* of the lettered word. Consult a dictionary, if necessary.

   a. cheerful
      noisy soft sad pleasant dangerous

   b. graceful
      awkward polite colorful anxious hard

   c. fix
      disturb please enjoy reply break

   d. bravery
      intelligence cowardice wealth beauty strength

   e. amateur
      beginner pupil farmer professional volunteer

6. With or without the aid of a dictionary, divide each of the following words into its component parts. Some of the words may lack one or more of these parts.

	Prefix	Root	Suffix
a. reporter	_____	_____	_____
b. interrupt	_____	_____	_____
c. confusion	_____	_____	_____
d. description	_____	_____	_____
e. mindful	_____	_____	_____

II. The Tools of Vocabulary Building

The Dictionary. The dictionary is the most important reference book and guide for the student who wishes to increase his or her vocabulary and acquire the ability to use words accurately and effectively. An entry in a good dictionary provides a wide range of information about the word being considered. Though the treatment is usually concise, the information is reliable. For that reason, you should regard the dictionary as your "bible" of the English language and its vocabulary.

Of course, most dictionaries come in two basic versions: a large *unabridged* edition designed for scholarly use, and a smaller *compact* edition designed to meet everyday needs. The difference between the two does not lie so much in the fact that words have been left out of the smaller book, but in the fact that the entries are much briefer and more succinct in the compact edition.

Thus, a typical entry in an unabridged dictionary provides the reader with the following information:

- the spelling and syllabication of the word involved
- its pronunciation
- an indication of the part of speech of the word
- information regarding inflectional endings
- the etymology or origin of the word
- its definition or definitions, both past and present
- illustrative phrases utilizing the word
- idiomatic expressions involving the word (when applicable)
- special or technical uses of the word
- related or derivative forms of the word
- a selection of synonyms and antonyms, often with explanatory notes clarifying subtle distinctions of meaning, tone, or usage

Study the following example of a typical entry from an unabridged dictionary. It is taken from the Unabridged Edition of *The Random House Dictionary of the English Language* (New York: Random House, 1967). Try to determine where each of the items listed above appears in the entry.

a·bate (ə bāt′), v., a·bat·ed, a·bat·ing. —v.t. 1. to reduce in amount, degree, intensity, worth, etc.; lessen; diminish: *to abate a tax; to abate one's enthusiasm.* 2. *Law.* a. to put an end to or suppress (a nuisance). b. to suspend or extinguish (an action). c. to annul (a writ). 3. to deduct or subtract: *to abate part of the cost.* 4. to omit: *to abate all mention of names.* 5. to remove, as in stone carving, or hammer down, as in metalwork, (a portion of a surface) in order to produce a figure or pattern in low relief. —v.i. 6. to decrease or diminish in intensity, violence, amount, worth, etc.: *The storm has abated. The pain in his shoulder finally abated.* [late ME ⟨ MF *abat(re)*, equiv. to *a-* A-⁵ + *batre* ⟨ LL *batere* for L *batuere* to beat] —a·bat′·a·ble, *adj.* —a·bat′er; *Law.* a·ba′tor. *n.*
—Syn. 6. subside. —Ant. 1, 6, increase, intensify.

Here is the way a compact dictionary treats the same word. The entry is taken from the College Edition of *The American Heritage Dictionary* (Boston: Houghton Mifflin Company, 1982). Which of the items listed above appear in both the unabridged and the compact dictionaries? Which appear only in the unabridged dictionary?

a·bate (ə-bāt′) v. a·bat·ed, a·bat·ing, a·bates. —tr. 1. To reduce in amount, degree, or intensity; lessen. 2. To deduct from an amount; subtract. 3. *Law.* a. To put an end to. b. To make void. —intr. 1. To subside. 2. *Law.* To become void. [ME *abaten* ⟨ OFr. *abattre*, to beat: *a-*, to (⟨ Lat. *ad-*) + *batre*, to beat ⟨ Lat. *battuere*.]

For the vast majority of the exercises in this vocabulary book, you will need to make use of a compact dictionary. Occasionally you will also need to consult an unabridged dictionary or other reference book, such as a thesaurus.

The Thesaurus. Do you own a thesaurus? No student should be without this useful reference book.

The word *thesaurus* is derived from the Greek *thesauros,* meaning "treasure" or "treasury." Although the word is sometimes used in the general sense of "dictionary" or "encyclopedia" —as a "thesaurus of quotations"—it more commonly denotes a special kind of wordbook. The words are presented (not defined) in groups of related-idea categories according to a distinctive logical pattern. An index tells the reader, by a system of reference numbers, where a certain word, together with its associative words, is to be found in the main part of the thesaurus.

Writers have found this kind of reference book to be a valuable memory prodder. And the word *writer,* as used here, means not a professional author or journalist but anyone who is trying to use English with force and precision and who needs help in finding the "right word."

How to Use a Thesaurus. Before you can make effective use of the thesaurus, you will need to do the following things:

1. Read the Preface or Introduction. It discusses in detail the special principles on which the thesaurus is based.

2. Read the Synopsis of Categories, which will give you an idea of the order and general range of the various related categories.

3. Read the introductory section, "How to Use the Book," which tells the reader, among other things, how to find:
    a. the most fitting word for a given idea
    b. the correct word for something vaguely remembered in its associations
    c. words suggestive of new ideas on a given subject

4. Always *turn first* to the Index Guide, which lists alphabetically the words you are looking for in the book.

Exercise

The following activities have been designed to help you improve your ability to use a dictionary or thesaurus.

1. Using the unabridged dictionary entry for *abate* that is printed on page 6, answer the following questions.
    a. Define *abate.*
    b. Give one phrase that illustrates its meaning.
    c. Give the etymology of *abate.*
    d. Give three special meanings *abate* has when used as a legal term.
    e. Give one synonym and two antonyms for *abate.*
    f. Syllabicate *abate,* and place the major stress mark (') after the syllable that is accented when the word is pronounced.

2. Read the Preface (Introduction), Synopsis of Categories, and Index Guide in your thesaurus. Then answer the following questions.

    a. In what specific writing situations or problems can the thesaurus serve as a helpful reference book?

    b. In what respects is the thesaurus different from an ordinary dictionary?

    c. Give five different cleaning devices listed under "Cleanliness."

    d. Give five synonyms suggested in the category under the word *corrective*.

    e. From the sections captioned "Obedience" and "Disobedience," select three adjective synonyms for *revolt*, and three verb synonyms for *disobey*.

    f. The thesaurus lists more than twenty forms of government. Define five such terms.

III. The Development of Our Vocabulary

Since many of the exercises contained in this book relate to the origins or sources of the vocabulary of present-day English, it might be wise at this point to review what you know about the development of the language. Doing this will help you "make sense" out of much of the isolated information scattered throughout the pages of this book. It may even give you a few new insights into the character and history of the language.

The "Family Tree" of English. English belongs to the Indo-European family of languages. **Indo-European** is thought to have developed 5000 or more years ago somewhere in central Europe or Western Asia. Quite a few modern English words appear to have their origins in Indo-European. Examples include *wolf* and *snow*.

Eventually, the people who spoke this "parent" language or group of related languages split up and went off in different directions. From these separate groups of people, a number of related "branches" of Indo-European developed. These branches include Celtic (now chiefly represented by Welsh, Irish, and Scottish Gaelic), Hellenic (that is, Greek), Italic (Latin and its Romance off-shoots—French, Italian, Spanish, Portuguese, etc.), and Germanic.

It is to the **Germanic** branch of Indo-European that English specifically belongs. Germanic, however, is divided into three large groups of related languages. These are North Germanic (that is, the Scandinavian languages except Finnish), East Germanic (which consists only of an extinct language called Gothic), and West Germanic (to which a number of languages, including English, belong).

The **West Germanic** group of languages is usually further subdivided into High and Low German. High German includes

Modern German and Yiddish. **Low German** (named for the relative lowness of the area in which it is spoken) consists of Frisian (spoken in parts of Holland), Dutch and Flemish (also spoken in the Low Countries), Plattdeutsch (spoken in northern Germany), and English. Note, however, that English and Frisian are sometimes grouped separately between High German and the other Low German languages.

Angles, Saxons, Jutes, and Old English. The history of the English language and its vocabulary can be said to start around A.D. 450. About then, a number of Germanic tribes (the Angles, the Saxons, the Jutes, and probably some Frisians) began to invade and conquer the island of Britain.[1] For more than a century, these peoples poured in from Denmark, north Germany, and the Low Countries. Eventually they occupied all of present-day England, a bit of Wales, and part of southern Scotland.

The newcomers brought with them a number of closely related West Germanic dialects, out of which **Old English** (sometimes called Anglo-Saxon) developed. Old English is the earliest form of English that can be documented. In use until perhaps 1150, Old English represents the basic Germanic foundation upon which Modern English has been built.

[1] Previously, Britain had been occupied by Celtic-speaking peoples (from ca. 900 B.C.). In A.D. 43, the Romans conquered the island and made it part of their empire. However, they withdrew in 410, before the first Germanic settlers arrived. Thus, the population that these settlers found in Britain was basically a mixture of romanized and unromanized Celts. From this population, however, the Germanic settlers picked up very little in the way of vocabulary, except for place names (e.g., *Avon*).

Alfred the Great (849–899), the most famous Anglo-Saxon king of England, was an influential patron of the language and literature of the Old English period.

Many Old English words have survived into Modern English. For example, *man, wife, child, house, ship, sheep, wrath, mirth, strong, good, well, drink, fight, to, after, and, if, we, us*, and many other common words derive from Old English. Nonetheless, these "survivors" constitute only a fraction of the vocabulary of Modern English. That is because much of the Old English element has long since dropped out of the language in favor of words from other sources.

Christianity, Latin, and Greek.   In 597, the Church of Rome began to convert the Anglo-Saxon peoples of England to Christianity. This was one of the most important events in English history for the development of vocabulary. The adoption of Christianity paved the way for the introduction of a good many **Latin** words into English.[2] Most of these borrowings related, of course, to religion (e.g., *altar, mass, creed*). Still, others referred to household items (*candle*), clothing (*cap*), food (*radish*), medicine (*fever*), and a host of other things. These words and others like them represent the beginning of Latin's influence on English. It would be hard to overemphasize this influence. Modern English probably owes more of its vocabulary, either directly or indirectly, to Latin than to any other language.

[2] While still on the continent, the Germanic peoples of England had already picked up a few Latin words. For the most part, these relate to military, commercial, or culinary matters (e.g., *wall, street, pound, cheap, kitchen, cup, wine, cheese*), though other areas of life are also represented. Before the advent of Christianity, a few Latin words may also have come into Old English via Celtic (e.g., *port* and the place-name element *-c(h)ester* or *-caster*).

The Christian missionary St. Augustine of Canterbury lands in Kent in southeast England in 597.

In addition, these "naturalized" Latin words represent the first installment in a long series of borrowings from many languages—French and Greek, to name only two. Over the centuries, such borrowings (called **loan words**) have greatly altered and enriched the vocabulary of English. Indeed, without them, English would not be what it is today.

With the coming of Christianity, a number of words that Latin had borrowed from **Greek** also entered Old English, usually in their Latin forms. These include *monk, deacon, psalm, oyster, chest,* and *school.* Earlier, when the Germanic peoples of England were still on the continent, they had borrowed a few other Greek expressions via Latin. These include *bishop, anchor, dish, copper, chalk,* and *pepper.*

Vikings and Old Norse. In 787, Viking bands from Denmark, Norway, and other areas of Scandinavia began to raid Anglo-Saxon territory. This was the start of what proved to be a large-scale, long-term invasion. By 878, much of northern and eastern England (to say nothing of Scotland) had been overrun. In 1014, the king of Denmark seized the English throne, and Danish kings ruled the country until 1042.

The upshot of all this turmoil was the permanent settlement of large numbers of Scandinavians (mostly Danes and Norwegians) in Britain. These newcomers spoke Old Norse dialects—that is, early forms of the modern Scandinavian languages. **Old Norse** (sometimes called Scandinavian) was Germanic. For that reason, it was fairly closely related to Old English. Culturally, the Anglo-Saxons and the Vikings were also similar. Thus, it was almost a foregone conclusion that, as the two peoples fused, large numbers of Old Norse words should begin to filter into English. Of course, much of this borrowing can't actually be documented until somewhat later, in what is called the Middle English period (see page 15).

Surprisingly, most of the Old Norse vocabulary that entered English referred to everyday things, for which there were usually Old English words already. Every part of speech in the language was affected. For example, the following nouns all derive from Old Norse: *axle, birth, dirt, egg, fellow, gap, girth, leg, loan, outlaw, rift, score, slaughter, snare, thrift, window.* The same is true of the following verbs: *call, cast, crawl, droop, gape, gasp, glitter, kindle, lift, nag, ransack, scare, sprint, thrust.* The same is also true about these adverbs or adjectives: *akimbo, aloft, athwart, both, flat, ill, loose, low, muggy, odd, rotten, rugged, same, weak.* The same is true of the conjunction *though* and the pronouns *they, their, them.* Even something as basic to the language as the verb *to be* was affected, since *are* derives from Old Norse.

In some instances, the Old Norse word drove the corresponding Old English word out of the language. For example, *take* displaced *niman,* and *sky* superseded *wolcen.* In other cases, the Old English word survived but took on the meaning of its Old Norse counterpart. Examples include *dream, dwell,* and *bread,* which in

Old English meant "joy," "lead or go astray," and "fragment," respectively. In still other cases, both words remained in the language, but with somewhat different meanings or uses. Examples include *craft* and *skill, hide* and *skin, rear* and *raise*, and *shirt* and *skirt*. Even a few "mixed forms" (or **hybrids**) were created—for example, *screech* and *shriek*, which technically should be something like *shreech* and *scriek*.

Normans and Old French.　Directly across the English Channel from Britain lies the French province of Normandy. In the 9th and 10th centuries, Vikings (called Normanni, or "Northmen," in Latin) occupied the area. Subsequently, these Scandinavians converted to Christianity and adopted an early form of French as their official language.

In 1066, William, Duke of Normandy, defeated Harold, the last Anglo-Saxon king of England, at the Battle of Hastings. As a result, Duke William became the first Norman king of England. Norman monarchs ruled the country until 1154, when they were succeeded by other French-speaking kings.

The Norman Conquest of England was probably the most important event in English history for the development of the language. For one thing, Norman French became the official language of the royal court and upper classes. This state of affairs lasted for about 200 years, during which time English was pushed well into the background. (Of course, English remained the language of the common people and middle classes throughout the period.)

The Battle of Hastings, 1066.

In addition, the use of an early form of French at the upper levels of society led to the introduction of many **Old French** words into English. This was just the beginning of the tremendous influence that French has exerted on the language. This influence has subsequently been reinforced by later borrowings from Modern French. French and Old Norse are, after Latin, the two most important sources for the vocabulary of Modern English.

Old French altered almost every aspect of the vocabulary, and more of the Old English element dropped out of the language. For example, Old French words relating to the following broad topics entered the language during the Middle Ages:

Topic	Borrowed Word
government	*realm, royal, govern, mayor*
social rank	*prince, duchess, baron, peasant*
land and property	*manor, demesne, estate, chattels*
law	*justice, suit, jury, pardon*
religion	*saint, mercy, charity, preach*
defense	*war, peace, battle, lieutenant*
wearing apparel	*costume, robe, cape, lace, jewel*
food	*beef, gravy, cream, peach, jelly, vinegar, spice, mince, roast*
household	*chair, couch, chamber*
art and literature	*beauty, paint, treatise*

Of course, a great many other common words also derive from Old French. Here are some examples:

nouns	*city, courtesy, virtue, grace, joy, marriage, people, point, reason*
adjectives	*able, brief, chaste, debonair, fine, gay, petty, puny, rich*
verbs	*chafe, embrace, enjoy, force, pay, reply, trace*

Even the wording of many common idiomatic expressions was influenced by the corresponding French phrase—for example, *by heart* and *in vain.*

Finally, a number of hybrids were created. These "mixed" forms usually fused an Old English (that is, Germanic) suffix onto a French (or Latin) root. Examples include *courtship, faintness, dukedom, artless, princely,* and *powerful.*

Learning, Latin, and Greek.   Old French is a Romance language derived from Latin. Thus, many of the words given above can be traced back beyond Old French to Latin. During the Middle Ages, Latin (in its medieval form) was the language of the university, the church, some types of law, and many official documents. So it shouldn't be surprising that, between 1066 and 1485, many words entered English directly from Latin. Examples include *adjacent, genius, index, inferior, intellect, lucrative, limbo, minor, necessary, ornate, picture, prevent, stupor*, and *tract*. As these items indicate, many of the new Latin words were abstract or technical terms. Thus, they may have first been used by professionals and only later achieved a wider circulation.

More Greek words also came into English during the Middle Ages, usually through Latin or French. Examples include *tyrant, scepter, theology, schism*, and *heresy*. As with the new Latin words, many of these Greek borrowings were technical terms that educated people may have introduced.

The Crusades and Arabic.　In 1095, the First Crusade to recover the Holy Land from the Moslems got under way. Subsequently, eight other crusades were launched. These expeditions brought Europe into contact with the Arabs (who held Palestine) and Arabic civilization. The Arabs also held much of Spain during the Middle Ages.

As a result of these contacts, a few **Arabic** words began to creep into English. Most of these words relate to science and mathematics (e.g., *alchemy, alkali, elixir, zenith, algebra, cipher, zero*). Others refer to food (e.g., *orange, sherbet, spinach, syrup*), clothing (e.g., *sash*), rooms and furniture (e.g., *alcove, sofa, mattress*), and many other things (e.g., *admiral, tariff, salaam*). Not all of these words, of course, came into the language during the Middle Ages; some appeared later. Also, none of them entered English directly from Arabic, but through intermediary sources (e.g., Spanish, French, Medieval Latin). By the way, some of these words can be recognized by the presence of the Arabic definite article *al* ("the") at the beginning of the English form.

The launching of the First Crusade, 1095.

Trade and the Low German Languages. During the Middle Ages, England traded extensively with the Low Countries and north Germany, especially in wool. These commercial relations continued to be close until well into the 18th century.

As a result, a good many **Dutch**, **Flemish**, and other **Low German** words filtered into English, either during the Middle Ages or later. Some of these words relate to shipping (e.g., *yacht, schooner, sloop, cruise, skipper, mate, swab, deck, dock*), commerce (e.g., *freight, smuggle, roster, dollar*), and textiles (e.g., *nap, ravel, cambric*). Others refer to military matters (e.g., *furlough, tattoo, plunder, beleaguer*), painting (e.g., *easel, sketch, etching, stipple, landscape*), and a good many other things (e.g., *measles, pickle, plump, poppycock, rant, slurp, snoop, spook, sputter, squirt, tattle, wiseacre, wriggle*). The Dutch settlers of North America were also responsible for some new terms (e.g., *cookie, cruller, patroon, Yankee*). And, much later, *veldt, trek*, and *apartheid* were contributed by **Afrikaans**, the form of Dutch spoken in South Africa.

Synonyms and Middle English. By the end of the Middle Ages, the process of word acquisition had provided English with a rich and varied assortment of synonyms. Often there were three or more words for the same thing. Each of these words had entered the language from a different source and at a different time. Usually the elements involved were Germanic, French, and Latin (or Greek). Here are a few examples: *kingly—royal—regal; climb—mount—ascend;* and *ask—question—interrogate.*

The vocabulary developments since 1066 and some technical changes relating to sounds and grammar resulted in the creation of **Middle English**. Roughly in use from 1150 to 1500, Middle English is the earliest form of the language that is unmistakably English. Accordingly, a speaker of Modern English can read many

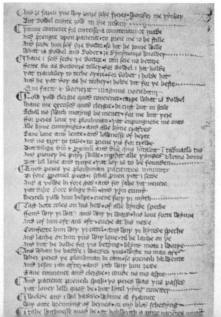

A sample of Middle English. A page from *The Vision of Piers Plowman*, probably by William Langland (1332–1400), one of the greatest works of Middle English literature.

Middle English texts, especially those written in the 1400's, without a great deal of difficulty. For example, college students frequently study the poems of Geoffrey Chaucer (died 1400) in the original language. To do this, they receive relatively little special training.

During the early years of its existence, Middle English was not the dominant language in England. Norman French held that position and kept it for about 200 years after 1066. Still, Middle English made steady advances during this period and by the mid-1300's was well on its way to becoming the dominant language of the country, a position it finally secured in the 1400's.

Neither Old nor Middle English was a single, monolithic language, but a group of related dialects. For that reason, there was nothing in either period that could be called "standard" English. Toward the end of the Middle Ages, however, London English had moved a long way in this direction. Still, a standard form of the language wasn't completely achieved until later.

Early Modern English, 1500–1660.   The 16th and 17th centuries were an eventful period in the history of English. The invention of printing from movable type, the tremendous revival of interest in classical Greece and Rome that occurred during the Renaissance, the Protestant Reformation, and other developments helped to introduce the use of English into fields of learning where Latin had formerly reigned supreme and also did much to establish a more uniform spelling of the language. The great voyages of discovery and the creation of British colonies in North America and elsewhere spread the language beyond the confines of England and enriched it by introducing new words from all sorts of faraway places.

As a result of these developments, together with a number of technical changes relating to the sounds and grammar of the language, **Modern English** was born. Modern English, of course, is the form of the language that is used today throughout the English-speaking world. It is with this form of the language that this vocabulary book is concerned and in which it is written.

The creative genius that shaped events during the early modern period also affected the vocabulary of English. During the 16th and 17th centuries, thousands of new words entered the language. Most of them were from Latin (e.g., *create, dexterity, notorious, transition, vindicate*), but others came from Greek (e.g., *atmosphere, anachronism*), French (e.g., *essay*), Italian (e.g., *argosy, charlatan, gala*), and Spanish or Portuguese (e.g., *palisade, desperado, armada*). Purely English resources were also called on in the coining of new words—for example, *freshman.*

Some of the new words that entered the language at this time retained their original form (e.g., *climax. epitome*); others underwent some modification or simplification. Often this took the form of dropping a foreign ending—for example, *consult* from Latin *consultare.* Sometimes a word that had already been borrowed was borrowed a second time with a slightly different form or meaning. Examples include *dish* and *disc*.

Since so many strange new words were entering English, the first dictionaries began to appear. These were usually very modest publications that confined themselves to the hard new words in the language. For example, *The Table Alphabeticall of Hard Words*, by Robert Cawdry, published in 1604, contained only about 3000 entries and did not deal with everyday words that even a child would understand. Also, most early dictionaries only defined the words they included and did not contain the other useful information that a modern dictionary provides.

Finally, it was during this period that **American English**, the particular brand of Modern English used in the United States, had its beginnings. While this was happening, a number of words from the languages used by the American Indians began to filter into English. Examples include *hickory, moccasin, opossum, powwow, skunk, tomahawk, totem,* and *wigwam.*

The language of the early English settlers in America also absorbed a good many words from the languages used by other colonizing nations, notably Dutch (e.g., *cookie, waffle, boss, Yankee*), French (e.g., *chowder, prairie, buccaneer*), and Spanish (e.g., *banana, cockroach*). Words from the African languages used by the black slaves who were brought to America from 1619 on also probably began to enter American English at this time, though most of these contributions (e.g., *voodoo, gumbo, cooter*) cannot be documented until much later. The foregoing examples and others like them reflect the English colonists' need for new words to describe what was unfamiliar to them.

The Founding of Philadelphia by William Penn, 1681.

Developments Between 1660 and 1800. Between 1660 and 1800, the spirit of creativity that had marked the early modern period gave way to a desire for system, regularity, and conformity to a standard based upon reason and buttressed by authoritative example from the classical past. This led to efforts to standardize, refine, and "fix" the English language. Thus, for the first time grammar books laying down "rules" for the proper use of English (e.g., William Loughton's *Practical Grammar of the English Language* [1734]), style manuals (e.g., George Campbell's *Philosophy of Rhetoric* [1776]), and a dictionary in the modern sense of the word (Dr. Samuel Johnson's *A Dictionary of the English Language* [1755]) began to appear.

Despite somewhat misguided attempts to purify and control the language during the 18th century, the vocabulary of English continued to grow. Since France was at the height of her power as a cultural force, more French expressions came into the language. Examples include *ballet, champagne, coiffure, connoisseur*, and a host of other familiar words.

At the same time, Great Britain was building up a vast overseas empire in such places as North America, Australia, and India. This development not only led to an expansion of the use of English

A scene from Tchaikowsky's ballet *Swan Lake. Ballet* is one of the words that English has borrowed without change from French. French, of course, had originally borrowed the word from Italian.

throughout the world, but also encouraged many "exotic" words to enter the language. For example, India contributed such items as *bungalow, cashmere, jungle, thug,* and *verandah;* the West Indies supplied *barbecue, hurricane,* and *tobacco;* and Australia provided *boomerang* and *wombat.* The influence of Great Britain's overseas territories continued through the 19th century, when some of the items listed above came into the language, and it is still felt today.

The period also saw significant developments in American English. All kinds of new expressions were being introduced to fill the needs of life in colonial America and later the United States. Examples include *bullfrog* (which appeared around 1705), *buckshot* (from 1775), *sidewalk* (1765), *cent* (coined by Thomas Jefferson around 1785), *harmonica* (invented by Benjamin Franklin about 1765), and a huge number of other familiar terms. Noah Webster's *American Spelling Book* appeared toward the end of this period, and his *American Dictionary* somewhat later.

From 1800 to the Present.   The 19th and 20th centuries witnessed the rise of an industrialized society in both Europe and America. The various technological advances that accompanied this development contributed (and continue to contribute) greatly to the enrichment of our vocabulary. Scarcely any phase of life or language was untouched. Not only were new words and phrases relating to technological progress invented (e.g., *automobile, telephone, television, computer*), but a good many old expressions took on new meanings (e.g., *park* a car, a radio *broadcast*).

The growth of science during the 19th and 20th centuries also had a tremendous impact on the vocabulary. Thousands of new technical or scientific terms entered the language (e.g., *stethoscope, carbohydrate, psychoanalysis*), and new concepts appeared on the scene (e.g., *relativity, evolution, automation*). Though much of this new scientific vocabulary is used only by specialists, a good part of it has filtered into the everyday language, usually as the result of popularization by our greatly improved means of mass communication. Startling new scientific developments, such as the exploration of space, have also channeled some of the vocabulary of science into the popular language. For example, even children know what is meant by *countdown* or *astronaut.*

A new science devoted to the study of language appeared on the scene during the 19th century. It is called **linguistics** (or sometimes **philology**). The contributions that philologists have made during the last 150 years or so have greatly increased our knowledge of language and also furnished new and improved tools for its study—for example, the multivolume *New (Oxford) English Dictionary.* As a result, popular interest in language has never been as great as it is today.

New social, political, or economic philosophies (e.g., communism) have left their mark on our language, and the two great world wars of the 20th century have also enriched it (e.g., *blitz-krieg, camouflage, Iron Curtain*). The same is true of countless social, political, economic, and cultural developments in our country. For example, we all know what *consumerism* or *an environmentalist* or *integration* is.

Finally, the tremendous influx of immigrants to our shores during the late 19th and early 20th centuries also made our language richer. Certainly it would be hard to do without the contributions of these new Americans—for example, the "yiddishisms," listed on page 81 of this book.

Into the Future. English will certainly continue to grow as it enters the 21st century. New developments, new problems, and new needs will require new terminology. Keep your eye peeled for new items coming in our vocabulary. It is an exciting and rewarding pastime.

Exercise

The following questions will help you review what you have learned about the development of our vocabulary.

1. To which branch of the Indo-European family of languages does English belong?

2. Define each of the following terms relating to the development of English, and state when this phase of our language was in use.

   a. Old English   b. Middle English   c. Modern English

3. Give **one** example of a word or phrase that English has borrowed from each of the following foreign languages. Then define your example, and use it in a short illustrative sentence.

   a. Latin   c. Old Norse   e. Arabic
   b. Greek   d. Dutch   f. French

4. Explain how each of the following historical events contributed to the growth of the vocabulary of English.

   a. conversion to   c. Norman conquest of
      Christianity   England
   b. Viking invasions of   d. colonization of North
      England   America

5. Briefly explain the impact of each of the following on the growth of our vocabulary.

   a. industrialization   b. science

Basic Word List

Lesson 1
1. abdicate
2. abet
3. abhor
4. abject
5. absolve
6. abstain
7. academic
8. accede
9. acclimate
10. addiction

Lesson 2
11. adjourn
12. adverse
13. advocate
14. aesthetic
15. affable
16. affectation
17. affluent
18. agenda
19. aggregate
20. agile

Lesson 3
21. alienate
22. allege
23. allude
24. ambience
25. ambivalent
26. amnesty
27. anachronism
28. anarchy
29. anathema
30. anecdote

Lesson 4
31. anomaly
32. apathy
33. appall
34. apprehend
35. arbitrary
36. arbitrate
37. array
38. articulate
39. askew
40. assimilate

Lesson 5
41. astute
42. asylum
43. atone
44. atrocity
45. atrophy
46. attrition
47. augment
48. augur
49. austere
50. authentic

Lesson 6
51. avarice
52. avid
53. badger
54. baffle
55. banal
56. belligerent
57. benign
58. bicker
59. bizarre
60. bland

Lesson 7_____

61. **bleak**   64. **boisterous**   68. **brash**
62. **blight**   65. **bombastic**   69. **bravado**
63. **blithe**   66. **boorish**   70. **brusque**
                       67. **boycott**

Lesson 8_____

71. **bungle**   74. **cajole**   78. **cantankerous**
72. **bureaucracy**   75. **callous**   79. **captious**
73. **buttress**   76. **calumny**   80. **catholic**
                       77. **candid**

Lesson 9_____

81. **caustic**   84. **chagrin**   88. **circumspect**
82. **censor**   85. **charlatan**   89. **circumvent**
83. **censure**   86. **chronic**   90. **clandestine**
                       87. **circuitous**

Lesson 10_____

91. **coerce**   94. **collaborate**   98. **condone**
92. **cogent**   95. **compatible**   99. **confrontation**
93. **cohere**   96. **complacent**   100. **conjecture**
                       97. **concise**

Lesson 11_____

101. **connoisseur**   106. **corpulent**   111. **crucial**
102. **consensus**   107. **corroborate**   112. **culpable**
103. **construe**   108. **counsel**   113. **cursory**
104. **consummate**   109. **credibility**   114. **curtail**
105. **copious**   110. **criterion**   115. **cynical**

Lesson 12_____

116. **dapper**   121. **delineate**   126. **desultory**
117. **defect**   122. **delinquent**   127. **deviate**
118. **defer**   123. **delude**   128. **devoid**
119. **dejected**   124. **demure**   129. **devout**
120. **delete**   125. **denouement**   130. **dexterous**

Lesson 13_____

131. **dilapidated**   136. **discourse**   141. **divulge**
132. **dilatory**   137. **discriminate** 142. **docile**
133. **diligent**   138. **disparage**   143. **dormant**
134. **dire**   139. **disparity**   144. **drastic**
135. **discomfit**   140. **distraught**   145. **duplicity**

Lesson 14

146. eclectic
147. effete
148. efficacious
149. effrontery
150. elicit
151. elite
152. emaciated
153. emanate
154. embellish
155. eminent
156. empathy
157. emulate
158. enclave
159. endemic
160. enigma

Lesson 15

161. entice
162. entreat
163. envisage
164. epithet
165. equanimity
166. equitable
167. erudite
168. esoteric
169. ethical
170. ethnic
171. euphemism
172. exacerbate
173. exalt
174. exemplary
175. exigency

Lesson 16

176. exodus
177. exotic
178. expedient
179. exploit
180. expound
181. fabricate
182. facetious
183. facsimile
184. fallacy
185. fathom
186. fatuous
187. feasible
188. feign
189. felicitous
190. fetish

Lesson 17

191. fiasco
192. fickle
193. filch
194. finesse
195. flagrant
196. flaunt
197. flout
198. fluctuate
199. foible
200. forestall
201. formidable
202. fortuitous
203. frugal
204. fulsome
205. futile

Lesson 18

206. gape
207. garble
208. gloat
209. goad
210. graphic
211. gratuitous
212. gregarious
213. grimace
214. grope
215. grueling
216. gruesome
217. gullible
218. haggard
219. harangue
220. harbinger

Lesson 19

221. haughty
222. heinous
223. ignominy
224. illicit
225. immaculate
226. immunity
227. immutable
228. impasse
229. impediment
230. impervious
231. implacable
232. implicit
233. impugn
234. incarcerate
235. incense

236. **inception**	241. **instigate**	246. **irony**
237. **indigent**	242. **insuperable**	247. **jeopardize**
238. **ingenious**	243. **intervene**	248. **jettison**
239. **inherent**	244. **intrepid**	249. **judicious**
240. **innovation**	245. **inveigh**	250. **justify**

251. **kudos**	256. **litigation**	261. **malapropism**
252. **lackadaisical**	257. **lucid**	262. **malice**
253. **legacy**	258. **lucrative**	263. **mammoth**
254. **liability**	259. **lurk**	264. **mandatory**
255. **libel**	260. **lush**	265. **medium**

266. **mercenary**	271. **myriad**	276. **nomadic**
267. **moot**	272. **narcissistic**	277. **nominal**
268. **morass**	273. **nebulous**	278. **nostalgia**
269. **motley**	274. **negligible**	279. **novice**
270. **mundane**	275. **nepotism**	280. **nuance**

281. **obscene**	286. **ominous**	291. **paradox**
282. **obsequious**	287. **opportune**	292. **paraphrase**
283. **obsession**	288. **ostensible**	293. **parochial**
284. **obsolete**	289. **ostracize**	294. **parody**
285. **officious**	290. **pandemonium**	295. **pensive**

296. **peremptory**	301. **phobia**	306. **precarious**
297. **perjure**	302. **plagiarism**	307. **precocious**
298. **permeate**	303. **plaintive**	308. **predatory**
299. **pernicious**	304. **plethora**	309. **prelude**
300. **persevere**	305. **poignant**	310. **premise**

311. **prerogative**	316. **promulgate**	321. **pseudonym**
312. **probity**	317. **propensity**	322. **purge**
313. **procrastinate**	318. **propitiate**	323. **pusillanimous**
314. **prodigious**	319. **protracted**	324. **quell**
315. **prolific**	320. **prowess**	325. **quixotic**

Lesson 26

326. raze
327. recalcitrant
328. recant
329. reciprocate
330. recrimination
331. redundant
332. relent
333. reminiscence
334. remorse
335. renegade
336. repercussion
337. replenish
338. reprisal
339. rescind
340. resilient

Lesson 27

341. reticent
342. retribution
343. retroactive
344. reverberate
345. revere
346. ritual
347. rudiment
348. ruminate
349. ruse
350. sabotage
351. sacrilegious
352. salient
353. sanctimonious
354. sanguine
355. satellite

Lesson 28

356. scapegoat
357. schism
358. scrutinize
359. secular
360. senile
361. solace
362. sordid
363. stamina
364. stereotype
365. stigmatize
366. stipulate
367. strategy
368. strident
369. surveillance
370. syndrome

Lesson 29

371. tacit
372. taciturn
373. tangible
374. tenable
375. tentative
376. thwart
377. tranquil
378. traumatic
379. trenchant
380. turbulent
381. ubiquitous
382. urbane
383. usurp
384. vagary
385. venal

Lesson 30

386. veneer
387. venerable
388. veracity
389. versatile
390. veto
391. vie
392. vindictive
393. vitiate
394. volatile
395. wane
396. wrath
397. yoke
398. zany
399. zeal
400. zenith

Pronunciation Key

The authorities used for the pronunciation of words in the Basic Word List include the *Random House Dictionary, Webster's Third New International Dictionary*, and the *American Heritage Dictionary*. In the relatively few cases where these authorities are not in agreement, the author and the editor have chosen the pronunciation that appears to be representative of the actual preference of most educated people in the American speech community. In some instances, several equally acceptable pronunciations are given.

Diacritical Marks. The following diacritical marks are used in this book to indicate the pronunciation of all the vowel sounds and one consonant in the words of the Basic Word List:

ā as in face
ă as in mat
ä as in father
â as in care

ē as in fever
ĕ as in send
ē̆ as in perfect
ə as in alone

ī as in bite
ĭ as in bill
î as in pier

ō as in code
ŏ as in cod
ô as in for
o͞o as in spoon
o͝o as in look
ou as in out or cow

yo͞o as in pure
ŭ as in up
û as in lurk

th as in clothe
th as in cloth

The Schwa. In a great many English words, the vowel sounds of unstressed syllables are faint or indistinct. These "neutral" vowel sounds, for all practical purposes, are identical, regardless of the letter that may be used to represent them. In most modern dictionaries, the pronunciation of such vowel sounds is indicated by the symbol ə (an inverted e). This is designated by the term *schwa*—pronounced *shwa* or *shva*.

The schwa should be used to indicate the pronunciation of the unstressed vowel sound (*italicized*) in each of the following words: form*a*l, p*a*rtner, vis*i*ble, hum*o*r, circ*u*s, paral*y*sis. A schwa is usually pronounced as the *a* in *a*lone or the *u* in *u*p.

Lesson 1

1. abdicate — 10. addiction[1]

---

1. **ab-di-cate** *verb* ăb´-dĭ-kāt
[*ab* (Latin), "away" + *dicare, dicatus* (Latin), "proclaim"]

Definition: To give up formally, as an office, duty, power, or claim.

The first Romanov czar of Russia was crowned in 1613; the last was forced to **abdicate** in 1917.

However heavy the burden may be, you cannot **abdicate** your responsibilities as the head of this household.

Related Form: (*noun*) abdication

Synonyms: (*verbs*) resign, renounce, relinquish, divest oneself of; (*nouns*) resignation, renunciation, relinquishment

Antonyms: (*verbs*) retain, hold on to

Phrases: renounce a claim or title, relinquish (or waive) a right, resign from a job, divest oneself of power

Usage Note:
Relinquish implies that a person is giving up something regretfully or unwillingly; *resign* suggests that a feeling of hopelessness has led to the decision.

2. **a-bet** *verb* ə-bĕt´
[*a*, from *ad* (Latin), "to" + *beter* (Germanic), "bait or incite"]

Definition: To encourage or assist, especially in wrongdoing.

Anyone who intentionally **abets** Tom's starry-eyed scheme to run away from home to join a traveling circus is clearly misguided.

"Failing to provide adequate recreational facilities in the community **abets** juvenile delinquency," the speaker declared.

Phrase: to aid and abet

Synonyms: (*verbs*) egg on; promote, further, advance, help, aid

Antonyms: (*verbs*) dissuade, discourage, deter, restrain, curb, inhibit, hinder, block, frustrate, thwart (Word 376)

Phrases: with the connivance of, in league with

---

[1] For a full listing of the basic words in each lesson, see the Basic Word List, pages 21–25.

3. ab-hor *verb* ăb-hôr´

[*ab* (Latin), "from; at" + *horrere* (Latin), "shiver, shudder"]

Definition: To regard with horror and loathing; to hate intensely.

Religious prejudice is something decent people **abhor**.

Related Forms: (*adjective*) abhorrent; (*noun*) abhorrence

Usage Note:

Because *abhor* implies strong *moral* condemnation, it should properly be reserved for attitudes or actions that really do offend a person's sense of right and wrong (*e.g.*, racism, child abuse). This, of course, is not to say that the word *cannot* be applied to other things. On the contrary, it is frequently used of trifling matters that normally would not be thought to grate on one's *moral* sensibilities—for example, spinach or TV game shows.

Synonyms: (*verbs*) loathe, despise, detest, abominate

Antonyms: (*verbs*) like, fancy, relish, love, cherish, delight in, be fond of, dote on

Phrases: look askance at, make a wry face at, turn up one's nose at, turn thumbs down at

Usage Note:

Do not confuse the verb *loathe*, meaning "dislike intensely," and the adjective *loath*, meaning "reluctant, disinclined." Note the following pair of sentences:

The human vice I *loathe* most deeply is insincerity.

I am *loath* to sign your petition.

4. ab-ject *adjective* ăb´-jĕkt *or* ăb-jĕkt´

[*ab* (Latin), "down; from" + *jacere, jactus* (Latin), "throw"]

Definition:

a. Wretched, miserable; degrading, humiliating.

Many people around the world live in such **abject** poverty that they cannot afford even the most essential items of food and clothing.

b. Mean-spirited, base; despicable, contemptible.

Only an **abject** coward would stand idly by as a defenseless old woman was mugged.

c. Complete and unrelieved.

At the slightest sound of thunder, my dog dives under the bed in a state of **abject** terror.

Phrases: an abject flatterer, an abject liar, an abject imitator, abject surrender, abject apologies

Synonyms: (*adjectives*) disheartening, debasing, hopeless, helpless; vile, shameless, ignoble, craven; utter, sheer, downright, thoroughgoing

5. ab-solve   *verb*   ăb-sŏlv′

[*ab* (Latin), "from" + *solvere* (Latin), "loosen; release"]

Definition: To clear of guilt or blame.

"The evidence I will present," the lawyer told the jury, "clearly **absolves** my client of any complicity in the crime."

The most effective way we can **absolve** our society of the charges of racism and prejudice is to remedy the injustices of the past.

Related Form: (*noun*) absolution

Usage Note:
In a religious sense, *absolve* and *absolution* refer to granting a pardon, especially for a sin.

Synonyms: (*verbs*) acquit, exonerate, exculpate, vindicate; (*nouns*) acquittal, exoneration, vindication

Antonyms: (*verbs*) incriminate, inculpate; indict, impeach; convict, condemn; (*nouns*) indictment; conviction, condemnation

6. ab-stain   *verb*   ăb-stān′

[*abs*, a form of *ab* (Latin), "from" + *tenere* (Latin), "hold; keep"]

Definition: To refrain completely and voluntarily.

Only ten members of the Security Council voted on the resolution; the others **abstained**.

If you want to lose some weight, you'll have to **abstain** from eating those rich desserts you love so much.

Related Forms: (*nouns*) abstinence, abstention; (*adjective*) abstinent

Usage Note:
Abstain and *abstinence* are often used in reference to strong drink, with the meaning "refrain completely from drinking." A common synonym for *abstinence* in this sense is *temperance*. Persons who never drink intoxicating beverages are sometimes referred to as *teetotalers*.

Synonyms: (*verbs*) forgo, forbear, avoid, shun, eschew; (*nouns*) self-restraint, self-denial, forbearance, abstemiousness; (*adjectives*) abstemious, forbearing, temperate, sparing, moderate; ascetic

Antonyms: (*verbs*) indulge (in), partake (of); (*noun*) indulgence; (*adjectives*) self-indulgent, intemperate, immoderate

Usage Notes:
a. *Abstemious, forbearing, temperate,* and *sparing* all indicate moderation in indulging one's appetites. *Abstinent,* on the other hand, indicates a total avoidance of the thing in question.

b. Be careful not to confuse the verb *forbear*, meaning "to restrain oneself," with the noun *forebear*, meaning "ancestor." The noun, which is usually plural, has a slightly different pronunciation, with the accent on the *first* syllable (fôr′-bâr).

7. ac-a-dem-ic   *adjective*   ăk-ə-děm′-ĭk

[From *Akademia*, the name of the ancient Greek philosopher Plato's school outside Athens. It was located in a grove or park dedicated to the hero Akademos.]

Definition:

    a.   Pertaining to a college or other institution of learning; scholarly.

        The role of a scholar in modern society is a subject of abiding concern in **academic** circles everywhere.

    b.   Theoretical rather than practical; unrealistic.

        What we need to do is develop a solid plan of action, not engage in **academic** debates over purely theoretical questions.

Related Forms: (*nouns*) academy, academician; (*adverb*) academically

Phrases: academic freedom, the halls of academe; an academic question

Synonyms: (*adjectives*) scholastic; speculative

An academic procession during the graduation exercises at an American university; Plato (*inset*)

From the Halls of Academe

Academy applies to institutions of higher learning, secondary schools, or any place where special subjects, arts, and skills are taught (*e.g.*, military academies, riding academies). The word is also used to refer to societies of learned men who have united to advance learning, literature, the arts and sciences (*e.g.*, the National Academy of Sciences, the Academy of Motion Picture Arts and Sciences).

    The phrase *academic freedom* refers to the freedom of a teacher or student to discuss or express his or her views on political, social, or economic issues without interference from public or school officials.

    An *academician* is a member of a learned society.

    An *academic question* is one that is purely theoretical and has little or no bearing on practical problems or "real" situations.

8. **ac-cede** *verb* ăk-sēd´

[*ad* (Latin), "to" + *cedere* (Latin), "go; yield"]

Definition:
   a. To yield to; to agree to.

> It took no little persuasion to get my parents to **accede** to my plan for a hitchhiking trip to California.

   b. To enter upon an office or dignity.

> Queen Elizabeth II **acceded** to the throne of Great Britain upon the death of her father, George VI, in 1952.

Related Forms: (*nouns*) access, accession, accessory; (*adjective*) accessible

Synonyms: (*verbs*) agree, assent, consent, concur, acquiesce, comply

Antonyms: (*verbs*) dissent, demur, balk at

9. **ac-cli-mate** *verb* ə-klī´-mĭt *or* ăk´-lə-māt

[*acclimater* (French), "get used to"]

Definition: To get used to (usually an environment or situation).

> Coming from the Pacific Northwest, we found it difficult to **acclimate** ourselves to the heat and humidity of a New York summer.

Related Forms: (*verb*) acclimatize; (*nouns*) acclimation, acclimatization

Synonyms: (*verbs*) adjust, adapt, orient, orientate, familiarize, accustom, habituate; (*noun*) orientation

10. **ad-dic-tion** *noun* ă-dĭk´-shən

[*addictus* (Latin), "given over to"; from *ad* (Latin), "to" + *dicere, dictus* (Latin), "say"]

Definition: A habit-forming practice or pursuit, usually one that is bad for a person's health or morally objectionable; habitual use of, or devotion to, something.

> Cigarette smoking is an **addiction** that may prove difficult to overcome.

> The speaker at last Thursday's assembly discussed a number of problems relating to young people, including drug **addiction**.

Related Forms: (*noun*) an addict; (*adjectives*) addictive, addicted to

Usage Note:
Addiction and addicted to are much used today in connection with drugs, but neither expression is limited to that area alone. One may, for example, be addicted to gambling, television, or coffee. In addition, both terms may be employed semi-humorously, as in "addicted to detective stories" or "an addiction to chocolate marshmallow sundaes."

Using the Words

Exercise I. Syllabication and Pronunciation

Syllabicate the following words correctly, and place the major stress mark (') after the syllable that is accented when the word is pronounced. Two answers are correct in some instances.

Example: a–bet'

1. addiction
2. abject
3. academic
4. acclimate
5. accede
6. absolve

Exercise II. Words Out of Context

In each of the following groups, select the item that best expresses the meaning of the numbered word at the left.

1. abstain
   a. transfer b. refrain c. indulge
   d. vote

2. abhor
   a. relish b. release c. frustrate
   d. detest

3. abet
   a. encourage b. initiate c. deplore
   d. hamper

4. accede
   a. offer b. renew c. demur
   d. yield

5. abject
   a. proud b. temperate c. wretched
   d. scholarly

Exercise III. Completing Sentences

Complete each of the following sentences by selecting the most appropriate word from the group of words preceding the sentences. Make whatever adjustments are necessary to fit the words into the sentences properly.

absolve   academic   acclimate

abject   addiction   abdicate

1. I chose an _____ career rather than business because I felt that I was better suited to the life of a teacher and scholar.

2. Convinced by the evidence presented by the defense, the jury _____ the defendant of all wrongdoing.

3. Long accustomed to their own traditional way of life, the refugees found it difficult to _____ themselves to a new language and strange customs.

4. Many a crime is committed by someone who has developed an
_____ to drugs and must have large sums of money to
support this habit.

5. "I'd rather resign from my job," Professor Harris declared,
"than _____ my right to speak out publicly on such an
important social problem."

Exercise IV.   Synonyms and Antonyms

Classify each of the following pairs of words as **S** for **synonyms** or
A for **antonyms.**

1. absolve—convict
2. familiarize—acclimate
3. relinquish—retain

4. accede—consent
5. abet—encourage
6. relish—abhor

Exercise V.   Word Roundup

1. What is the difference between an *abstemious* person and a
person who is *abstinent*? Complete each of the following with
one of these words.

    a. Henry takes a drink once in a long while. He is _____.
    b. Henry never touches liquor. He is _____.

2. Define each of the following phrases. Consult a dictionary or
other reference book if necessary.

    a. academic robes
    b. a riding academy

    c. academic freedom
    d. an academic question

3. Explain the difference in meaning between the terms in each
of the following word pairs.

    a. forbear—forebear
    b. loathe—loath

Exercise VI.   Framing Sentences

A. Use each of the following words in a short illustrative sentence.

1. abet
2. abject

3. accede
4. addiction

B. Give a **noun** form of each of the following words, and use it in a
short illustrative sentence.

1. abdicate
2. abhor

3. absolve
4. abstain

5. academic
6. acclimate

Dissecting the Words

At this point in half the lessons in this book, there is a section devoted to etymology. **Etymology** is the study of where words come from and how they are formed or change. Accordingly, each of these sections focuses attention on some of the prefixes, roots, and suffixes that make up the bulk of the words on the Basic Word List. The reason for studying these word elements is simple: they form the backbone of a substantial proportion of the English words in current use. For that reason, one effective way to expand your word power is to learn the meanings of such word elements and to use them as "keys" to a wider understanding of new words that crop up in your reading and school studies.

Prefix

The Latin prefix **ab**, **abs**, meaning "away from, off," is found in numerous English words. A few of them, including *abdicate* and *abject*, appeared in this lesson. Here are some more:

abduct (literally, "to lead away")—to take away by force

abscond—to depart secretly

abrupt—(literally, "broken off")—sudden or hasty

abstract—to draw from. The noun *abstract* means "a brief summary or a shorter form of the original."

Other English words containing this prefix include *abrasion*, *absent*, *abrogate*, and *absurd*.

Sir James A. Murray (1837–1915), the editor of the multivolume *New (Oxford) English Dictionary*, probably the most authoritative and certainly the most complete English dictionary in existence.

1. **Ced** is a Latin root meaning "go" or "yield." It provides the core meaning of many English words, including *accede*, studied in this lesson. (Note that this root appears as **ceed** in some English words.) Here are some other words from the same root:

concede—to grant or admit. Noun: *concession*

secede—to break away from; to withdraw from membership in. Noun: *secession*

exceed—to go beyond what is necessary or proper. Noun: *excess*; adjective: *excessive*; adverbs: *exceedingly, excessively*

recede—to go back, to withdraw. Noun: *recession*

proceed—to go forward. Noun: *procession*

antecedent—going before. A person's *antecedents* are his ancestors or forerunners.

procedure—the regular, definite order by which something is done.

Other words from this root are *intercede, precedent, cession*.

2. The root **dic, dict**, which is found in the Latin verb *dicere*, "to say," and in the related verbs *dicare*, "to proclaim; to give up," and *dictare*, "to declare; to order," is the basis of the words *abdicate* and *addiction*, studied in this lesson. Note the following English words also formed from this root:

contradict (literally, "to speak against")—to oppose, to deny

valedictory (literally, "saying *be well*")—farewell

indict (literally, "to declare against")—to charge with guilt

interdict (literally, "to say between")—to prohibit

dictum (literally, "a thing said")—an authoritative statement

Other English words containing this root include *edict, dedicate, benediction, predict, ditty* (a little song), *malediction* (a curse), *predicament, indicate, dictionary*, and *dictator*.

Exercise

1. Select the word that does not contain the prefix *ab*.
    a. abhor b. abscond c. abide d. abject

2. Give **three** English words that are derived from the same root as *accede*. Use each in a short illustrative sentence.

3. Explain the origin of each of the following words: *indict, dictum, contradict, ditty, benediction*.

4. Explain the meaning of each of the following phrases, with particular reference to the etymology of the word in *italics*. Consult a dictionary or other reference book if necessary.
    a. the class *valedictorian*
    b. a *receding* hairline
    c. *abstract* art
    d. the *antecedent* of a pronoun

Enriching the Lesson

Lesson 1 includes a number of legal terms, such as *absolve* and *accessory*. The following exercise may help you widen your knowledge of the language of the law. Consult a dictionary or other reference book for the meanings of the words indicated; then do the exercises.

A. Match the legal term in Column A with the phrase that defines it in Column B.

Column A	Column B
1. indictment	a. a law passed by a duly authorized law-making body
2. subpoena	b. one who is guilty of a crime
3. statute	c. a formal written accusation of a crime
4. culprit	d. a temporary delay in carrying out a sentence
5. affidavit	e. a written order summoning a person to a court to give testimony
6. plaintiff	f. to call before a court to answer a formal charge
7. reprieve	g. to expel from the practice of law
8. arraign	h. a written statement under oath
9. contraband	i. the person who makes the complaint in a lawsuit
10. disbar	j. smuggled goods

B. Now complete each of the following.

1. What is the difference between an *accessory before the fact* and an *accessory after the fact*?

2. What is a *quitclaim*? Show how *quit* in this word is related etymologically to *acquit*.

3. Why would a respected lawyer object to being called a *shyster*? In which country is the term *barrister* used?

4. What is a *writ*? Define *writ of habeas corpus* and *writ of mandamus*.

5. What is the difference between *impeach* and *convict*? Which branch of Congress has the power to *impeach* a President of the United States? Which is authorized to *try and judge* him?

6. What is a *plea*? Define *plea–bargaining* and *to cop a plea*.

7. Legally speaking, what is a *misdemeanor*? a *felony*? What is the difference between the two? Define *tort*.

8. If the defendant in a criminal case is seeking a *change of venue*, what is he or she asking for? Why might a judge grant such a request?

9. Define the following: *petit jury, grand jury, hung jury*.

10. What principle of constitutional law is usually referred to by the phrase *double jeopardy*?

Exercise II. Place Names in Common Use

A fair number of common English words—for example, *academic*, studied in this lesson—are derived from the names of places. Some of these expressions are listed below. With or without the aid of a dictionary, define each as it is used in present-day English. Then give the place name from which the word is derived. Finally, choose any **five** of the items, and for each compose an original sentence that clearly illustrates the expression's meaning.

1. limerick	6. hackneyed	11. blarney
2. varnish	7. limousine	12. mayonnaise
3. mecca	8. bedlam	13. gasconade
4. cologne	9. sybaritic	14. tawdry
5. bunkum	10. donnybrook	15. sardonic

Exercise III. Expanding Your Word Power

The words listed below are not on the Basic Word List, but they were mentioned in passing in Lesson 1. All of them would make useful additions to your working vocabulary. Define each, give its etymology, list **two** synonyms and **two** antonyms (where possible), and use in a short sentence that clearly illustrates its meaning.

1. waive	5. connive	9. acquiesce
2. deter	6. incriminate	10. orientation
3. aversion	7. ascetic	11. indulge
4. ignoble	8. eschew	12. demur

Lesson 2

11. **adjourn** — 20. **agile**

---

11.   **ad-journ**   *verb*   ə-jûrn´
[*a*, from *ad* (Latin), "to" + *diurnum* (Late Latin), "day"]

Definition:
   a.   To close formally.

     Congress is scheduled to **adjourn** in two days, but pressing business will probably delay its closing for at least a week.

   b.   To put off to another time; to move to another place.

     "This meeting is **adjourned** until ten o'clock tomorrow morning," the chairwoman declared, rapping her gavel smartly on the table.

     In view of clear community prejudice against the defendant, the judge **adjourned** the trial to another county.

     After dinner we **adjourned** to the living room for a quiet chat.

Related Form: (*noun*) adjournment

Synonyms: (*verbs*) conclude, terminate; defer (Word 118), postpone; suspend; transfer

12.   **ad-verse**   *adjective*   ăd´-vûrs *or* ăd-vûrs´
[*ad* (Latin), "to; against" + *vertere, versus* (Latin), "turn"]

Definition: Hostile in purpose or effect; unfavorable.

     Although the novel received much **adverse** criticism in the press, it became a national best seller.

Related Forms: (*adverb*) adversely; (*nouns*) adversary, adversity

Usage Note:
     Do not confuse *adverse* with the related adjective *averse*, meaning "opposed" or "disinclined." *Adverse* (with the *d*) is used of things to indicate that they have gone contrary to a person's wishes. *Averse* (without the *d*), on the other hand, indicates opposition on the part of the person himself. Note the following pair of sentences:

     The Supreme Court handed down an *adverse* decision on censorship.

     The Supreme Court showed itself *averse* to censorship laws.

Synonyms: (*adjectives*) unfavorable, unfriendly, negative, antagonistic, antipathetic, inimical

Antonyms: (*adjectives*) favorable, friendly, propitious

38

13. ad-vo-cate   *verb:* ăd′-və-kāt   *noun:* ăd′-və-kĭt

[*ad* (Latin), "to" + *vocare, vocatus* (Latin), "call"]

Definition:

a. (*verb*) To speak or argue in favor of; to give active public support to.

> In his TV address to the nation, the President **advocated** a series of measures that he believed would curb inflation.

b. (*noun*) A person who pleads in the interest of a cause or individual.

> I have become her **advocate** because I honestly believe in her ideas.

Related Form: (*noun*) advocacy

Synonyms: (*verbs*) champion, support, espouse, uphold, recommend; (*nouns*) proponent, backer, defender, spokesman

Antonyms: (*verbs*) denounce, condemn, oppose, attack; (*nouns*) critic, opponent, adversary, antagonist

A scene from *The Devil's Disciple* (1897), a play about the advocates and opponents of the American Revolution by George Bernard Shaw (*inset*).

Devil's Advocate

In the Roman Catholic procedure of canonization, by which a person is elevated to sainthood, arguments are heard pro and con regarding the proposed measure. A church official is selected to pick flaws in the record or character of the candidate—to present arguments against the canonization. This official is given the title *advocatus diaboli*, "devil's advocate." The idea is that any candidate who can survive the onslaughts of a skilled devil's advocate probably does have authentic credentials for sainthood.

The expression has been widened to embrace anyone who expresses the "opposition" point of view as a means of arriving at the truth, even though, in fact, he may not be in disagreement with his opponent. Thus one might say: "I am not necessarily in disagreement with your plan, but I am going to serve as a *devil's advocate* and point out its possible flaws."

14. aes-thet-ic   *adjective*   ĕs-thĕt´-ĭk

[*aisthetikos* (Greek), "perceptible to the senses"]

Definition: Pertaining to a sense of beauty; artistic.

From an **aesthetic** point of view the painting did not appeal to me; however, it was a souvenir of my childhood, and I decided to keep it.

Related Forms: (*adverb*) aesthetically; (*nouns*) aesthete, aesthetics

Usage Notes:
- a. *Aesthetic* is sometimes spelled *esthetic*. Do not confuse the word with *ascetic*.
- b. An *aesthete* is a person who is sensitive to, or has a love of, the beautiful in art or nature. However, the term is often used with an unfavorable tone to indicate someone who makes overmuch of his or her sensitivity to beauty.
- c. *Aesthetics* is a branch of philosophy dealing with theories and principles of beauty in art and literature.

15. af-fa-ble   *adjective*   ăf´-ə-bəl

[*ad* (Latin), "to" + *fari* (Latin), "speak" + *abilis, abile* (Latin), "able to"]

Definition: Courteous and agreeable in manner; easy to talk to or approach.

It's fun to spend an hour or two chatting with old Señora Rivera because she is one of the most **affable** people in the neighborhood.

Related Forms: (*adverb*) affably; (*nouns*) affableness, affability

Synonyms: (*adjectives*) sociable, genial, amiable, friendly, good-natured

Antonyms: (*adjectives*) unsociable, surly, testy, ill-tempered

16. af-fec-ta-tion   *noun*   ăf-ĕk-tā´-shən

[*affectare, affectatus* (Latin), "strive after"]

Definition: A pretentious display of manners or sentiments that are not genuine; a peculiar habit of dress or behavior that has been adopted to impress others.

Beneath his **affectation** of elegance and refinement, I could easily recognize the crude and awkward youth I had known years ago.

Sue Ellen's so-called "Southern" accent is just an **affectation**; actually, she was born and raised in Brooklyn.

Related Forms: (*adjective*) affected; (*verb*) affect

Phrases: an affected style of speaking; to affect an air of sophistication

Synonyms: (*nouns*) pose, pretense; mannerism

Phrase: to put on airs

17. af-flu-ent   *adjective*   ăf′-loo-ənt

[*ad* (Latin), "to" + *fluens, fluentis* (Latin), "flowing," from *fluere* (Latin), "flow"]

Definition: Prosperous, wealthy.

The Internal Revenue Service maintained that the income the man had reported on his tax form was not sufficient to support his **affluent** lifestyle.

Related Forms: (*noun*) affluence; (*adverb*) affluently

Synonyms: (*adjectives*) flourishing, well-to-do, opulent

Antonyms: (*adjectives*) indigent (Word 237), destitute, penniless, poverty-stricken

Phrases:

living high off the hog—This phrase of rural American origin suggests that a person is in good circumstances because he or she is eating the more desirable cuts of meat from a slaughtered hog.

as rich as Croesus—This phrase goes back to Croesus, King of Lydia, an ancient country in western Turkey. Croesus had a reputation among the Greeks for being extremely rich, and he became the personification of limitless wealth.

to serve Mammon—The word *mammon* means "riches" in Aramaic, an ancient Semitic language related to Hebrew. Among the Hebrews of Biblical times, *mammon* was personified as the god Mammon, who represented not merely wealth but materialism and an excessive concern with acquiring riches.

The Affluent Society

This phrase was popularized as the result of the publication in 1958 of a book with this title by the noted American economist, John Kenneth Galbraith. The title referred to the relatively high standard of living enjoyed by most (but by no means all) Americans, with a profusion of such things as automobiles, television sets, air conditioners, etc. When the phrase is used today, however, it is often with a strong suggestion that too many people are excluded from the benefits of such living standards.

18. **a-gen-da**   *noun*   ə-jĕn′-də

[*agere* (Latin), "do"]

Definition: A list or program of things to be done or acted upon.

There are several important items on the **agenda** for today's meeting, and each will probably require a good deal of discussion before it can be disposed of.

Poland had top priority on Adolf Hitler's **agenda** of military conquest in the fall of 1939.

Usage Note:
Agenda was originally a Latin plural noun meaning "things to be done" (singular, *agendum*). However, it is generally treated in English today as a collective noun taking a singular verb, as in the following example:

The *agenda* includes the question of raising money for the dance.

On the other hand, it is certainly not wrong—although it may seem a bit pedantic—to treat *agenda* as a plural form. In that case, the Latin singular form *agendum* may be used to indicate one particular item among several included in the agenda.

Synonyms: (*nouns*) schedule, docket

Usage Note:
A *docket* is literally a list of cases awaiting action in a court of law, but the word is often used figuratively of any list of things to be done.

19. **ag-gre-gate**   *noun and adjective:* ăg′-rə-gĭt
                      verb: ăg′-rə-gāt

[*ad* (Latin), "to" + *grex, gregis* (Latin), "herd"]

Definition:
a. (*noun*) The total amount or sum total of the individual parts.

The United Nations is no more than a loose **aggregate** of nations, each of which retains full sovereignty.

b. (*verb*) To gather or merge into a single whole; to amount to.

The merger of the two great banks **aggregated** working capital totaling several billion dollars.

c. (*adjective*) Total, collective.

The **aggregate** effect of the various treaties was to produce a new balance of power among the major nations of the world.

Related Form: (*noun*) aggregation

Usage Note:
Perhaps the widest current use of *aggregate* as a noun occurs in the prepositional phrase *in the aggregate*, meaning "collectively."

Synonyms: (*nouns*) mass, assemblage, amalgamation, conglomeration, cluster; (*verbs*) amalgamate, consolidate; (*adjectives*) net, composite

20. agile   *adjective*   ăj´-əl

[*agilis* (Latin), "busy; active," from *agere* (Latin), "do"]

Definition: Swift and light in action, movement, or thought.

Despite his sixty-odd years, the circus clown was as energetic and **agile** as any of the younger members of the troupe.

It certainly takes a very **agile** mind to do some kinds of crossword puzzles.

Related Form: (*noun*) agility

Synonyms: (*adjectives*) nimble, limber, alert, brisk, supple, lithe, spry

Antonyms: (*adjectives*) torpid, sluggish, lethargic; awkward, clumsy

Phrases: to limber up one's muscles, to look chipper

Usage Note:

Some distinctions should be drawn among the synonyms listed above: *alert* refers to quickness of mind; *brisk* suggests liveliness; *supple* means "pliant" or "bending and twisting easily"; and *spry* indicates agility despite age or infirmity.

Using the Words

Exercise I.   Parts of Speech

Indicate the part of speech of each of the following words. Two answers are possible in one instance; three in another.

1. agenda	3. advocate	5. affluent
2. adjourn	4. agile	6. aggregate

Exercise II.   Words in Phrases

In each of the following groups, select the item that best expresses the meaning of the *italicized* word in the introductory phrase.

1. *adjourned* the meeting promptly at three o'clock
   a. planned   b. opened   c. suspended   d. attended

2. very *agile* for her age
   a. ignorant   b. clumsy   c. popular   d. spry

3. *advocated* changes in the tax laws
   a. considered   b. rejected   c. supported   d. ignored

4. came from a very *affluent* family
   a. obscure   b. poverty-stricken   c. brilliant   d. wealthy

5. the *aggregate* opinion of the jury
   a. collective   b. informed   c. far-reaching   d. mistaken

Exercise III. Completing Sentences

Complete each of the following sentences by selecting the most appropriate word from the group of words preceding the sentences.

aesthetic	advocate	agenda
affectation	adverse	affable

1. We are determined to succeed in spite of all the _____ conditions affecting this project.

2. The first item on the _____ at the convention was the selection of a temporary chairman.

3. Our personnel manager is a very _____ woman, whose friendly, informal manner immediately puts a person at ease.

4. While the Romans were essentially practical in their approach to building design, the Greeks were deeply concerned with beauty for its own sake and worked hard to produce structures of high _____ appeal.

5. Throwing an obscure French expression into the middle of an English sentence just to show that you've been to Paris is an _____ that really irritates me.

Exercise IV. Synonyms and Antonyms

A. Match each word in Column A with its **synonym** in Column B.

Column A	*Column B*
1. terminate	a. amiable
2. nimble	b. consolidate
3. opulent	c. pretense
4. pose	d. conclude
5. fuse	e. luxurious
	f. spry

Now indicate which of the basic words taught in this lesson (Words 11–20) is most nearly **synonymous** with each of the words in Column A.

B. In each of the following groups, select the **two** words that are most nearly **antonyms**.

1. a. agile b. filthy c. hostile d. sincere e. awkward

2. a. civilian b. opponent c. foreigner d. advocate e. aesthete

3. a. ascetic b. sluggish c. propitious d. adverse e. neat

4. a. artificial b. testy c. penniless d. aesthetic e. affable

5. a. wealthy b. insincere c. indigent d. lithe e. illegal

1. Explain the derivation of *agenda*. Give the singular form of the word. How do you explain the fact that *agenda* itself may be used as a singular form?

2. Define each of the following phrases.
   a. a devil's advocate
   b. to live high off the hog
   c. the affluent society
   d. to put on airs
   e. to serve Mammon
   f. in the aggregate

Exercise VI. Framing Sentences

Use each of the following words in an original sentence that clearly illustrates its meaning.

1. adjourn
2. adverse
3. advocate
4. affable
5. affluent
6. agenda
7. agile
8. affectation
9. aesthetic

Completing Verbal Analogies

What Is a Verbal Analogy?   Today, practically every standardized test in vocabulary contains at least one section dealing with verbal analogies. A **verbal analogy** is a kind of equation that uses words, rather than numbers. This equation indicates that the relationship between two words or expressions is the **same** as the relationship between two other words or expressions.

Here is a simple verbal analogy:

boy : man = girl : woman

This is to be read, "The word *boy* is to the word *man* as the word *girl* is to the word *woman*"—or, more simply, "*Boy* is to *man* as *girl* is to *woman*." What the analogy is saying is that the relationship between the word *boy* and the word *man* is the same as the relationship between the word *girl* and the word *woman*.

And what is that relationship? Well, a boy grows into a man. In other words, the word *boy* refers to the immature version of the male human being, while the word *man* indicates the fully adult specimen.

In the same way, a girl grows into a woman. In other words, the word *girl* refers to the immature version of the female human being, and the word *woman* indicates the adult.

Now, if the four words in the original analogy are replaced by what they mean (as indicated above), the new analogy will read:

immature male : adult male = immature female : adult female

This makes it clear that the relationship between the pair of words on each side of the equals sign is the same. That relationship can be expressed as "A boy becomes a man, just as a girl becomes a woman." This is essentially what the analogy is saying.

In the analogy sections of standardized tests, students are asked to complete analogies just like the one given above. They are to do this by selecting one or two (or a group of two) items from a possible four or five choices. The format varies a bit from test to test, and, of course, the number of word relationships involved is as infinite as a human being's capacity to manipulate words and ideas.

Exercise I

Three common word relationships that occur in analogy questions on standardized tests are listed below. (In this list, A means the first word or expression in the analogy, B the second, and so forth.)

  a. A means the same as B; C means the same as D.

  b. A means the opposite of B; C means the opposite of D.

  c. A is an example of B; C is an example of D.

And here are five complete analogies taken from typical standardized tests. The four expressions that make up each have been marked A, B, C, and D. Look at each analogy carefully. Then indicate which of the three word relationships on the list it illustrates.

　　　A　　B　　　C　　　D
1. up : down = north : south

　　　A　　　B　　　C　　　　D
2. orange : fruit = potato : vegetable

　　　A　　　　B　　　　C　　　　D
3. Oriental : Eastern = Occidental : Western

　　　　A　　　　B　　　C　　　D
4. Columbus : discoverer = Edison : inventor

　　　　A　　　　B　　　　C　　　D
5. renounce : relinquish = abhor : loathe

Exercise II

Below are five complete analogies. Three of them are correctly constructed; the other two are not. Read each analogy carefully. Then indicate which **three** are correctly constructed. Explain why the other two are not.

1. affluent : indigent = wealthy : poor

2. advocate : support = accede : dissent

3. Judy Garland : singer = Marilyn Monroe : actress

4. fire : hot = ice : cold

5. abet : deter = fuse : merge

Enriching the Lesson

Exercise I.   Specialized Knowledge

There are many terms in English that indicate specialized skills or knowledge and the people who possess them—for example, *academician* (studied in Lesson 1) and *aesthete* (studied in Lesson 2). A number of these terms are listed below. With or without the aid of a dictionary, define each. Then choose any **five**, and for each compose an original illustrative sentence.

1. conjurer	8. podiatrist	15. ophthalmologist
2. chiropractor	9. comptroller	16. nutritionist
3. virtuoso	10. astrologer	17. optometrist
4. therapist	11. anthropologist	18. acrobat
5. environmentalist	12. sociologist	19. neurosurgeon
6. consumer advocate	13. pediatrician	20. geologist
7. urbanologist	14. obstetrician	

Exercise II.   Portmanteau Words

A **portmanteau word** (sometimes called a **blend**) is a word that has been coined by combining elements of two other words. For example, the portmanteau word *brunch* is made up of *breakfast* and *lunch*.

Read the following excerpt from Lewis Carroll's *Through the Looking-Glass*. It deals with portmanteau words.

"You seem very clever at explaining words, Sir," said Alice to Humpty Dumpty. "Would you kindly tell me the meaning of the poem called 'Jabberwocky'?"

> 'Twas brillig, and the slithy toves
>   Did gyre and gimble in the wabe;
> All mimsy were the borogoves,
>   And the mome raths outgrabe.

"That's enough to begin with," Humpty Dumpty interrupted. "There are plenty of hard words there. *Brillig* means four o'clock in the afternoon—the time when you begin broiling things for dinner."

"That's very well," said Alice—"and *slithy*?"

"Well, *slithy* means *lithe* and *slimy*. *Lithe* is the same as *active*. You see, it's like a portmanteau [a kind of large suitcase]—there are two meanings packed up into one word."

Below are a number of portmanteau words. Define each, and indicate the elements that went into its formation.

1. chortle	6. flurry	11. autobus
2. splatter	7. telecast	12. cablegram
3. simulcast	8. smog	13. telethon
4. happenstance	9. motel	14. sitcom
5. squawk	10. guesstimate	15. Amerind

Exercise III. Exploring the Dictionary

1. What is a business *conglomerate*? How does it differ from an ordinary business organization?

2. Consult a dictionary or other reference book for the specific meaning of each of the following "group words." Then use each in a sentence that clearly illustrates its meaning.

   a. federation
   b. confederation
   c. cabal
   d. bloc
   e. cartel
   f. coalition
   g. consortium
   h. alliance
   i. junta

3. Define *federalism*. What does the term *world federalism* mean?

4. Explain the meaning of each of the following expressions involving the word *devil*.

   a. in a devil-may-care mood
   b. giving the devil his due
   c. deviled eggs
   d. between the devil and the deep blue sea
   e. a devilish expression
   f. a printer's devil
   g. a devil's-food cake
   h. bedeviled by misfortune

Exercise IV. Expanding Your Word Power

The words listed below are not on the Basic Word List, but they were mentioned in passing in Lesson 2. All of them would make useful additions to your working vocabulary. Define each, give its etymology, list **two** synonyms and **two** antonyms (where possible), and use in a short sentence that clearly illustrates its meaning.

1. adversary
2. adversity
3. inimical
4. espouse
5. surly
6. genial
7. destitute
8. amalgamate
9. composite
10. lethargic
11. antipathetic
12. nimble

Lesson 3

21. **alienate** — 30. **anecdote**

---

21. al-ien-ate   *verb*   āl′-yə-nāt *or* ā′-lē-ə-nāt

[*alienare, alienatus* (Latin), "estrange," from *alius* (Latin), "other"]

Definition: To cause hostility or indifference where love, friendliness, or interest formerly existed.

> During the years before the Russian Revolution, the increasingly rigid and oppressive policies of the czarist government **alienated** many of those who formerly supported it.

Related Forms: (*noun*) alienation; (*noun and adjective*) alien; (*adjectives*) alienable, inalienable

Usage Note:
Alienation denotes a state of estrangement, disaffection, or isolation. In psychology, the word is used in a special sense to indicate a state of estrangement between a person and the outside world, or between the different parts of the personality.

Synonyms: (*verbs*) estrange, disaffect, antagonize

Antonyms: (*verbs*) befriend; captivate

Phrases: sever (or break off) relations with; the generation gap; catch someone's fancy, ingratiate oneself with

22. al-lege   *verb*   ə-lĕj′

[*ad* (Latin), "to; toward" + *legare* (Latin), "charge"]

Definition: To claim that something is true but without offering any proof.

> The men now being held in police custody are **alleged** to have robbed eight supermarkets in the last year.

> As an excuse for refusing to lend me the money, she **alleged** that she had financial troubles of her own.

Related Forms: (*noun*) allegation; (*adjective*) alleged

Usage Note:
The use of the word *allege* often implies that there is some doubt about the truth of a statement—for example, in the second sentence above. At other times, the word *allege* is used because the speaker wishes to disclaim all responsibility for the truth of whatever follows—for example, in the phrases "an alleged miracle" or "the alleged visitor from Mars."

Synonyms: (*verbs*) claim, contend; declare, assert, affirm, avow, asseverate, aver

23. al-lude   *verb*   ə-lo͞od′ *or* ăl-yo͞od′

[*ad* (Latin), "to" + *ludere* (Latin), "play"]

Definition: To refer to indirectly.

> During the course of the evening, he **alluded** to the fact that he had attended Harvard.

Related Forms: (*noun*) allusion; (*adjective*) allusive

Usage Note:
Take care not to confuse the following words:

> *allude* (refer indirectly to) and *elude* (evade, escape)
> *allusion* (an indirect reference) and *illusion* (a false perception or impression)
> *allusive* (containing allusions; suggestive) and *illusory* (tending to deceive) or *elusive* (difficult to find or grasp)

Synonyms: (*verbs*) hint at, suggest, insinuate, intimate

24. am-bi-ence   *noun*   ăm′-bē-əns

[*ambi* (Latin), "around" + *iens* (Latin), "going," from *ire* (Latin), "go"]

Definition: The surrounding or pervading atmosphere; the tone and spirit of an environment.

> In the 1920's, the literary and artistic **ambience** of the Latin Quarter in Paris attracted many young American writers, such as Ernest Hemingway and F. Scott Fitzgerald.

Related Form: (*adjective*) ambient

Synonyms: (*nouns*) surroundings, milieu, setting; character, flavor

25. am-biv-a-lent   *adjective*   ăm-bĭv′-ə-lĕnt

[*Ambivalenz*, a German word coined by Sigmund Freud from *ambi* (Latin), "both" + *valens, valentis* (Latin), "worth"]

Definition: Wavering or uncertain because of an inability to make a choice between two contradictory feelings or viewpoints in regard to a person, a thing, or a course of action.

> My parents have **ambivalent** feelings about the college I have chosen. On the one hand, they are favorably impressed by its academic standards; on the other, they are unhappy about its great distance from our home.

Related Form: (*noun*) ambivalence

Phrases: ambivalent emotions, an ambivalent position

Synonyms: (*adjectives*) contradictory, opposing, conflicting, equivocal; vacillating

Antonyms: (*adjectives*) definite, firm, unwavering, steady; clear-cut, unequivocal

26. **am·nes·ty**   *noun*   ăm´-nəs-tē

[*a* (Greek), "not" + *mnasthai* (Greek), "remember"]

Definition: An official pardon granted to offenders against the government, especially for political offenses.

> At the end of the Civil War, Abraham Lincoln wanted to grant a general **amnesty** to all Southerners who would take an oath of loyalty to the Union. Congress, however, was firmly opposed to the idea.

Synonyms: (*nouns*) forgiveness, immunity (Word 226), remission (of punishment), absolution (of sin)

27. **a·nach·ro·nism**   *noun*   ə-năk´-rə-nĭz-əm

[*ana* (Greek), "backwards" + *chronos* (Greek), "time"]

Definition: The misplacing of an object or event in a period to which it cannot possibly belong; anything out of its proper time frame.

> Cassius's reference to mechanical clocks in Shakespeare's *Julius Caesar* is an **anachronism** because such devices were unknown in Roman times.

> Fifteen years ago a young man wearing long hair and a beard would have been in the height of fashion. Today he would be considered something of an **anachronism**.

Related Forms: (*adjective*) anachronistic

Synonyms: (*nouns*) incongruity, inconsistency, contradiction; throwback

28. **an·ar·chy**   *noun*   ăn´-ər-kē

[*anarchia* (Greek), "anarchy," from *an* (Greek), "without" + *archos* (Greek), "ruler"]

Definition: Absence of governmental authority; general political and social disorder.

> We all want the greatest possible individual liberty, but our society will lapse into **anarchy** unless we voluntarily accept certain basic restraints and controls on what we do.

Related Forms: (*nouns*) anarchism, anarchist

Usage Note:
Anarchism is a political doctrine that advocates the abolition of all forms of government as being oppressive and undesirable. The word is also used in an extended sense to indicate active resistance to the state, including terrorism and guerrilla warfare. An *anarchist* is a person who favors the ideas of anarchism or engages in activities aimed at the violent overthrow of an existing government.

Synonyms: (*nouns*) disorder, chaos, lawlessness, pandemonium (Word 290), turmoil

29. **a-nath-e-ma** *noun* ə-năth´-ə-mə

[*anathema* (Late Latin), "a curse," from *anathema* (Greek), "a votive offering"]

Definition:
 a. A curse or strong denunciation.

  Let us direct our **anathemas**, not against individual evils, but against the society that allows them to exist.

 b. The person or thing cursed; more generally, any object of intense dislike.

  The word "capitalism" is **anathema** to a Communist.

Usage Note:
When *anathema* occurs without modification after the verb *to be* (as in the second example above), it functions more as an adjective than as a noun. For that reason, it may properly be replaced by such adjectives as *repugnant* or *abhorrent*, rather than by the corresponding nouns (*repugnance, abhorrence*). Thus, the second example above could also read:

 The word "capitalism" is *repugnant/abhorrent* to a Communist.

One of the few nouns that can replace *anathema* in this situation is *abomination* (with the indefinite article).

 The word "capitalism" is *an abomination* to a Communist.

Related Forms: (*verb*) anathematize; (*noun*) anathematization

Synonyms: (*nouns*) malediction, execration, imprecation; abomination

Antonyms: (*nouns*) blessing, benediction, eulogy, encomium; (*verbs*) bless, glorify, praise, extol, cherish

30. **an-ec-dote** *noun* ăn´-ĭk-dōt

[*anekdota* (Greek), "unpublished things," from *an* (Greek), "not" + *ek* (Greek), "out" + *dotos* (Greek), "given"]

Definition: A brief account of some interesting or amusing incident, especially one containing biographical or historical details.

 The early 19th-century English critic Isaac D'Israeli once observed that a well-chosen **anecdote** can reveal a person's true nature more vividly than an elaborate character analysis.

Related Forms: (*adjective*) anecdotal; (*nouns*) anecdotist, anecdotage

Usage Note:
Anecdotal means "containing anecdotes." An *anecdotist* is a person who tells anecdotes, especially as a hobby or profession. *Anecdotage*, a blend of *anecdote* and *dotage*, indicates the kind of old age that is accompanied by a tendency to ramble on endlessly about the past.

Synonyms: (*nouns*) tale, story, vignette, sketch, narrative, reminiscence, memoir; episode; storyteller, raconteur

An Amusing Anecdote

Frank Knox, United States Secretary of the Navy from 1940 to 1944, was noted for his emphasis on tight security with respect to official information.

One day, an old friend asked him an extremely indiscreet question regarding the movements of United States ships in the Pacific.

Knox said nothing for a few moments, and then, with a confidential gesture, whispered, "Look here. Can you keep a secret?"

"Of course, of course," the friend answered.

"Well," said Knox, "so can I."

Frank Knox

Using the Words

Exercise I. Syllabication and Pronunciation

Syllabicate the following words correctly, and place the major stress mark (') after the syllable that is accented when the word is pronounced.

Example: al–lege'

1. amnesty
2. allude
3. ambience
4. alienate
5. anarchy
6. anecdote

Exercise II. Words Out of Context

In each of the following groups, select the item that best expresses the meaning of the numbered word at the left.

1. ambience — a. formula b. concern c. atmosphere d. schedule
2. ambivalent — a. discourteous b. imaginary c. wealthy d. conflicting
3. anathema — a. a throwback b. an abomination c. a champion d. an illusion
4. anarchy — a. chaos b. poverty c. fear d. danger
5. amnesty — a. assemblage b. gap c. mannerism d. pardon

Exercise III.   Completing Sentences

Complete each of the following sentences by selecting the most appropriate word from the group of words preceding the sentences. Make whatever adjustments are necessary to fit the words into the sentences properly.

allege   anachronism   alienate

anecdote   allude   anarchy

1. In the account he gave of his war experiences, he didn't once _____ to the three decorations he had received for outstanding valor.

2. Since the American Indians didn't have cigarettes, it would be an _____ to portray Sitting Bull or Crazy Horse puffing on a Marlboro.

3. I know the Senator is _____ to have accepted bribes and other favors in return for his political support, but so far none of these accusations has been proved.

4. In the late 17th century an Englishman named Samuel Pepys kept a diary that is full of amusing stories and _____ involving people who were prominent at the time.

5. "If you treat the people around you badly," Anita observed, "you will eventually _____ every last one of them."

Exercise IV.   Synonyms and Antonyms

Classify each of the following pairs of words or phrases as **S** for **synonyms** or **A** for **antonyms**.

1. alienate—antagonize
2. milieu—ambience
3. anathema—blessing
4. anecdote—yarn
5. claim—allege
6. unequivocal—ambiguous
7. allude to—hint at
8. order—anarchy
9. anachronism—throwback
10. immunity—amnesty

Exercise V.   Related Forms

A.   Give a **noun** form for each of the following words, and use it in an original sentence that clearly illustrates its meaning.

1. alienate
2. allude
3. allege
4. ambivalent

B.   Give an **adjective** form of each of the following words, and use it in an original sentence that clearly illustrates its meaning.

5. anecdote
6. anarchy
7. anachronism
8. allege

Explain the difference in meaning between the words in each of the following groups.

1. allude—refer
2. allusion—illusion
3. allusive—elusive
4. elusive—illusory

Dissecting the Words

Prefixes

1. The Latin prefix **ad**, meaning "to, toward," appears in countless English words. Sometimes it is disguised when it precedes a root beginning with a consonant. In such cases, the d in ad is often dropped, and the following consonant doubles. For example, *affluent*, meaning "prosperous," studied in Lesson 2, comes from *ad* and the Latin verb *fluere*, meaning "flow." When the two parts are joined, the d of *ad* is replaced by an *f* (because *fluere* begins with an *f*). Similarly, *ad* and *knowledge* merge to become *acknowledge*; *ad* and *grandize* become *aggrandize*, meaning "to increase in power or rank."

Thus, *ad* may appear in an English word as **ac-, af-, ag-, al-, an-, ap-, ar-, as-,** or **at-**. This merging, or fusion, of consonants is technically called **assimilation**.

2. The Greek prefix **a, an**, meaning "not," "without," or "opposed to," is found in two words studied in this lesson: *anarchy* and *anecdote*. (Note that the prefix takes the form **an** before a root beginning with a vowel and usually before *h*.) Other words derived from this prefix include:

anonymous (from *an*, "without" + *onuma*, "name")—of unknown authorship

atypical—not typical

amorphous (from *a*, "without" + *morphe* "form")—shapeless, formless

asymmetrical—not symmetrical

amoral—without moral quality (that is, neither moral nor immoral); lacking a sense of morals

Roots

1. The Greek root **arch** (the *ch* is pronounced as a *k*) has a variety of meanings. One of them is "government" or "ruler." It appears in *anarchy*, studied in this lesson. Other English words containing *arch* with the same meaning include:

monarchy (from *monos*, "sole" + *archos*, "ruler")—a government in which one person is the sole and absolute ruler

oligarchy (from *oligos*, "few" + *arche*, "rule")—a government which is entirely in the hands of a small group of people or families

patriarch (from *pater*, "father" + *archos*, "ruler")—a father who is the head of a family or tribe

As a prefix, **arch** (here the *ch* is pronounced *tch*) means "principal" or "of the highest rank." English words in which this meaning of **arch** appears include:

archbishop—bishop of the highest rank

archenemy—chief enemy

archduke—a nobleman whose ceremonial or social status is the same as that of a reigning monarch

archfiend—chief fiend (a name for the devil)

Be careful not to confuse the Greek prefix/root **arch** with the English word *arch*, which means "sly" or "mischievous" (as in "an *arch* smile").

2. The Latin root **voc**, **voke**, meaning "call," forms the basis of the word *advocate*, studied in Lesson 2. Other words containing this root include:

vocation—a profession, trade, or calling

avocation—a hobby (that is, something that a person pursues for pleasure in addition to his or her regular job)

revoke (literally "to call back")—to withdraw. Noun form: *revocation*

convoke (literally "to call together")—to assemble. Noun form: *convocation*

invoke—to call upon ("*invoke* God's blessing") or ask for ("*invoke* aid"). Noun form: *invocation*

provoke—to stir up or cause. Noun form: *provocation*; adjective form: *provocative*. An *agent provocateur* is a person who deliberately stirs up trouble or dissension.

vociferous—loud-voiced

evoke—to call forth or elicit

A sample of Old English. A page from the only surviving manuscript of the great Anglo-Saxon epic poem *Beowulf*, which was probably written in the 8th century. (The manuscript, however, only dates from around A.D. 1000.) *Beowulf*, which blends both Christian and pagan elements, gives a remarkable picture of the life and customs of the early Germanic peoples.

Exercise

1. How does the prefix *ad* change when added to a root beginning with a consonant? What is the technical name for this phenomenon? Give **six** words studied in Lessons 1–3 that illustrate it.

2. Complete the following activities relating to *arch.*

   a. What is an *archdiocese*? What church official resides in an archdiocese? Give the adjective form of *archdiocese.*

   b. What is a *patriarch*? Name the three patriarchs mentioned in the Bible.

   c. What does the word *arch* mean in such phrases as *an arch smile*? What does the prefix *arch* mean in such phrases as *an archenemy*?

   d. Add *arch* to each of the following, and explain how the addition adds stature or dimension to the original word: *angel, duke, duchess, priest, deacon.*

   e. Match the word in Column A with its meaning in Column B.

Column A	Column B
1. monarchy	a. government by the few
2. hierarchy	b. rule by a single sovereign
3. oligarchy	c. a ruling body arranged into a series of grades

3. In place of the blank space in each of the following sentences, supply a word or phrase that clearly shows that you know the meaning of the Latin root *voc, voke.*

   a. To deliver the *invocation* at the beginning of your school's graduation exercises is to _____ upon God for divine favor.

   b. If something you have done has *provoked* an argument with your kid brother, it has _____.

   c. If your bus pass has been *revoked*, it has been _____.

   d. If a statement by the President of the United States has *evoked* a lot of comment, it has _____.

   e. If you attended a *vocational* school, you would expect the school to prepare you for your _____ in life.

4. For each of the following definitions, supply a word beginning with the Greek prefix *a, an.*

   a. shapeless or formless
   b. the condition of a country without an effective government
   c. of unknown authorship
   d. lacking a sense of morals
   e. a short narrative, often containing biographical details

5. Occasionally *ad* appears in a Latin phrase that English has borrowed without change. A few such phrases are listed below. Define each.

   a. ad libitum (*or* ad lib, *for short*) d. ad nauseam
   b. ad hoc   e. ad infinitum
   c. ad hominem   f. ad valorem

Enriching the Lesson

Exercise I. Parlez-Vous Français?

The word *milieu*, mentioned in this lesson, is taken wholly and without change from French. English has many other such words and phrases. A few of them are listed in Column A below. With or without the aid of a dictionary, match each of these expressions with its meaning in Column B.

	Column A		*Column B*
1.	carte blanche	a.	appetizers
2.	fait accompli	b.	an object of strong dislike
3.	savoir-faire	c.	a meeting or meeting place
4.	chef d'oeuvre	d.	a small specialty shop
5.	bête noire	e.	full power to act as one sees fit
6.	faux pas	f.	knowing the right or proper thing to do
7.	hors d'oeuvres	g.	something that cannot be reversed
8.	boutique	h.	a blind alley or dead end
9.	rendezvous	i.	a social blunder
10.	cul-de-sac	j.	a masterpiece

Exercise II. Stating the Case

1. Lesson 3 contains two words, *allege* and *allude*, that indicate particular ways of giving information in speech or writing. A number of other such terms are listed below. With or without the help of a dictionary, define each in such a way as to bring out its distinctive meaning.

   a. intimate *(verb)*   e. assert   i. avouch
   b. expatiate   f. declaim   j. aver
   c. avow   g. enunciate   k. cite
   d. insinuate   h. asseverate   l. imply

2. What is the distinction between a *soliloquy* and a *colloquy*? What is a *colloquium*? a *monologist*? *dialogue*?

3. Each of the following colloquial expressions has to do with talking or keeping silent. Define each.

   a. rap   d. talk back   g. badmouth
   b. chew the fat   e. spiel   h. talk big
   c. clam up   f. gab   i. blurt out

Exercise III. Telling a Story

1. What is a *fable*? How does it differ from an *anecdote*? an *allegory*? Give the names of two authors who are famous for writing fables. In a short paragraph, retell a fable by one of these authors. Why do you think these stories are called fables?

2. Define the following: *tall story, memoir, yarn, parable, allegory*. How does each differ from the other? Recount a *yarn* you have heard; a *parable* from the Bible; a *tall story*.

3. What is a *quip*? *retort*? *bon mot*? Define each of these words, and, if possible, supply an anecdotal illustration of the definition.

4. The noted American painter James McNeill Whistler is as famous for his witty retorts as for his artistic achievement. The following anecdote shows Whistler in top form:

   > At a dinner attended by Oscar Wilde and Whistler, Whistler is said to have remarked: "People will forgive anything but beauty and talent. So I am doubly unpardonable." Everybody roared at this observation, except Wilde. Wilde, a noted wit in his own right, looked rather chagrined at Whistler's "score" and muttered, "I wish I'd said that." To this, Whistler retorted, "You will, Oscar—you will!"

   Now recount another Whistlerian anecdote; a witticism by Oscar Wilde; an example of repartee by George Bernard Shaw; an anecdote about George S. Kaufman. To do this, you will probably have to consult biographies and other books dealing with these witty writers.

5. What does the Latin word *fabula* mean? How does the Latin word contribute to the meaning of the English word *fabulous*? Explain what *fabulous* means in the following phrases: *a man of fabulous wealth, fabulous exploits, a fabulous party*.

Exercise IV. Expanding Your Word Power

The words listed below are not on the Basic Word List, but they were mentioned in passing in Lesson 3. All of them would make useful additions to your working vocabulary. Define each, give its etymology, list **two** synonyms and **two** antonyms (where possible), and use in a short sentence that clearly illustrates its meaning.

1. alien	5. chaos	9. vignette
2. estrange	6. encomium	10. episode
3. vacillate	7. affirm	11. extol
4. contend	8. proscribe	12. excommunicate

Lesson 4

---

31. **a-nom-a-ly** *noun* ə-nŏm´-ə-lē
[*an* (Greek), "not" + *homalos* (Greek), "even," from *homos* (Greek), "same"]

Definition: A deviation from what is normal or expected.

Charles Darwin wrote that there was no greater **anomaly** in nature than a bird that could not fly.

Related Form: (*adjective*) anomalous

Phrases: an anomalous situation, in an anomalous position; an anomaly in the world of politics

Synonyms: (*nouns*) abnormality, peculiarity, oddity, freak, misfit; incongruity; (*adjectives*) abnormal, irregular, freakish, deviant, atypical; incongruous

Antonyms: (*noun*) the norm; (*adjectives*) normal, usual, commonplace, ordinary, regular, typical; congruous

32. **ap-a-thy** *noun* ăp´-ə-thē
[*a* (Greek), "without" + *pathos* (Greek), "feeling; suffering"]

Definition: Lack of feeling, emotion, or interest.

I hoped that my idea for the class project would be greeted with some enthusiasm. Instead, it met with complete **apathy**.

Fewer people turned out to vote this year. This is indicative of the growing **apathy** with which the general public seems to regard political campaigns.

Related Forms: (*adjective*) apathetic; (*adverb*) apathetically

Synonyms: (*nouns*) indifference, unconcern, aloofness, detachment, impassivity; (*adjectives*) indifferent, uninterested, aloof, detached, stolid, impassive, unfeeling, emotionless

Antonyms: (*nouns*) enthusiasm, ardor, fervor, zeal (Word 399); concern, interest; (*adjectives*) interested, concerned; ardent, fervent, keen, zealous, passionate

Usage Note:
Be careful not to confuse *uninterested* and *disinterested*. A person is said to be *uninterested* when he or she takes no interest in something; a person is said to be *disinterested*, however, when he or she has no self-interest involved in the matter. Thus, *uninterested* is a synonym of *apathetic*, but *disinterested* means the same as *impartial*.

33. ap-pall   *verb*   ə-pôl´

[*ap(p)alir*, (Old French), "grow pale," from *ad* (Latin), "at" + *pallere* (Latin), "be pale"]

Definition: To fill with intense horror, fear, or dismay.

The huge number of soldiers killed during the bloody battle of Antietam **appalled** the entire nation, both North and South.

I was **appalled** to learn that a fistfight had broken out on the floor of the State Senate yesterday.

Related Form: (*adjective*) appalling

Phrases: an appalling sight; appalling disclosures

Usage Note:
Appall, also spelled *appal*, implies a strong sense of helplessness in the face of something truly enormous or monstrous.

Synonyms: (*verbs*) horrify, shock, astound, stupefy, stun, dismay; (*adjectives*) horrifying, shocking, stunning, horrific, frightful, dreadful, fearful

Antonyms: (*verbs*) please, cheer, gladden, exhilarate, elate; (*adjectives*) cheering, gratifying, exhilarating

Phrase: be aghast at

34. ap-pre-hend´   *verb*   ăp-rĭ-hĕnd´

[*ad* (Latin), "to" + *prehendere* (Latin), "seize"]

Definition:
   a.   To arrest or take into custody.

The police **apprehended** the escaped convict about three blocks from the prison.

   b.   To perceive or understand the meaning of.

One cannot fully **apprehend** the principles of our Constitution without studying the Federalist Papers.

   c.   To look forward to with fear or anxiety.

The doctor assured his patient that there was nothing to **apprehend** in the forthcoming operation.

Related Forms: (*nouns*) apprehension, apprehensiveness; (*adjective*) apprehensive

Usage Notes:
   a.   The noun *apprehension* has several meanings: (*1*) anxiety about the future; (*2*) an arrest; (*3*) understanding. *Apprehensiveness*, on the other hand, indicates merely uneasiness about the future.

   b.   *Apprehensive* means "fearful of what may be coming."

Synonyms: (*verbs*) seize, capture, nab, collar; grasp, comprehend, discern, fathom (Word 185); dread, fear, have misgivings about, anticipate the worst, have a foreboding of

35. **ar·bi·trar·y** *adjective* är′-bə-trĕ-ē *or* är′-bĭ-trâr-ē

[*arbiter* (Latin), "judge" + -*arius* (Latin), "connected with"]

Definition:
    a. Subject to or determined by one's judgment; random.

        "The example I have used is purely **arbitrary**," the speaker told her audience. "I'm sure all of you could come up with others that would be just as illuminating."

    b. Arrived at by an exercise of the will, personal preference, or whim, as opposed to being based on reason or justice.

        The sentence a judge hands down should be based firmly on accepted principles of law and justice. It should not be a purely **arbitrary** decision.

    c. Given to willful decisions or demands; tyrannical or dictatorial.

        He wouldn't make a good supervisor because he is so **arbitrary** and overbearing in his dealings with others.

        During the reign of Czar Nicholas I (1825–55), the Russian government became increasingly **arbitrary** and repressive.

Related Forms: (*adverb*) arbitrarily; (*noun*) arbitrariness

Synonyms: (*adjectives*) judgmental, discretionary; capricious, irrational; prejudiced, partial; unreasonable; highhanded, overbearing, despotic, autocratic, authoritarian

Antonyms: (*adjectives*) objective, fair, just, equitable (Word 166)

Phrase: a judgment call

36. **ar·bi·trate** *verb* är′-bə-trāt

[*arbitrari, arbitratus* (Latin), "give judgment," from *arbiter* (Latin), "judge"]

Definition: To act as an impartial judge in a dispute; to settle.

Both the union and the employer have confidence in Mr. Donelli's fair-mindedness and knowledge of the industry. That is why he was chosen to **arbitrate** the contract dispute.

Related Forms: (*nouns*) arbitration, arbitrament; arbitrator, arbiter; (*adjectives*) arbitrational, arbitrable

Phrases: submit to arbitration, binding arbitration; an arbiter of taste, *arbiter elegantiae* (or *elegantiarum*)

Usage Note:
An *arbitrator* (or *arbiter*) is the person who is chosen to settle a dispute. *Arbitration* is the process by which a settlement is reached. *Arbitrament* is the act of settling the dispute or the settlement that is finally made. *Arbitrable* means "open to arbitration." For example, if the president of a union says that certain demands are not arbitrable, he/she means that they are not negotiable. An *arbiter elegantiae* is a judge of what's tasteful and what isn't.

Synonyms: (*verbs*) adjudicate, mediate

A collective bargaining session under the direction of a federal mediator.

37. ar-ray   *verb and noun*   ə-rā´

[*arayer* (Old French), "arrange," possibly from *arredare* (Vulgar Latin), "arrange"]

Definition:

  a. (*verb*) To line up; to dress up.

     "I looked up from my wagon," the old pioneer said, "and saw a band of hostile Indians **arrayed** along the top of a nearby hill."

     We set out for the prom **arrayed** in the finery that we had worked so hard to acquire.

  b. (*noun*) An imposing grouping; rich and beautiful attire.

     The reputed head of the underworld syndicate entered the courtroom with an impressive **array** of attorneys and other legal advisers.

     Soldiers in full battle **array** patiently awaited inspection by their commanding officer.

Usage Note:

Originally *array* meant "to ready for battle," though the word is rarely used in this sense today. Nonetheless, something of this association with the military still clings to the word's more modern usages. A careful inspection of the examples given above will reveal this.

Synonyms: (*verbs*) align; assemble, draw up, marshal, muster; deploy; adorn, deck out, doll up, gussy up; equip, outfit, accouter; (*nouns*) alignment, line-up; finery; equipment, accouterments

Antonyms: (*verbs*) disperse, disband, dismiss

38. **ar-tic-u-late**   *verb:* är-tĭk´-yə-lāt   *adjective:* är-tĭk´-yə-lĭt

[*articulare, articulatus* (Latin), "say clearly," from *articulus* (Latin), "division; part"]

Definition:

    a. (*verb*) To pronounce distinctly; to express well in words.

         The speaker couldn't be understood because he slurred and mumbled his words instead of **articulating** them clearly.

         One of the duties of a President is to **articulate** the policies and programs of his administration in a forceful and convincing way.

    b. (*adjective*) Expressed clearly and forcefully; able to employ language easily and fluently.

         The President's statement in defense of his economic program was unusually **articulate** and effective.

         Helen was chosen to present our petition to the Mayor because she is the most **articulate** speaker in the class.

Related Forms: (*nouns*) articulation, articulateness

Synonyms: (*verbs*) enunciate; clarify, expound (Word 180), elucidate, explicate; (*adjectives*) fluent, eloquent, silver-tongued, glib

Antonyms: (*verbs*) mumble, mutter, maunder, swallow one's words; (*adjectives*) slurred, unintelligible, garbled; inarticulate, incoherent

---

39. **a-skew**   *adjective and adverb*   ə-skyōō´

[Derivation uncertain but probably *a* (Middle English), "on" + *skew*]

Definition:

    a. (*adjective and adverb*) Out of line or position; turned to one side.

         The drawers had been pulled out of the bureau, the lamps had been knocked over, and every picture on the wall was **askew**.

    b. (*adverb*) Disapprovingly; scornfully.

         "Why is that dreadful old dowager looking **askew** at me?" I wondered. "Do I have my shirt on backwards or something?"

Synonyms: (*adjectives*) crooked, cock-eyed, uneven, unsymmetrical, awry; (*adverbs*) disdainfully, contemptuously, askance, derisively

Antonyms: (*adjectives*) straight, symmetrical; (*adverbs*) approvingly, benignly

Usage Notes:

    a. Note the somewhat subtle difference in the use of *askew* and *awry* (pronounced ə-rī´). *Askew* is usually reserved for concrete objects like lampposts and hats. *Awry*, on the other hand, is generally used of more abstract things, like plans, arrangements, or actions.

    b. Also note the distinction between *askew* and *askance*, meaning "sideways" or "oblique(ly)." *Askew* usually implies simple disapproval or scorn. *Askance* (variant, *askant*), however, implies mistrust and suspicion, as well as disapproval.

40. **as-sim-i-late** *verb* ə-sĭm´-ə-lāt

[*ad* (Latin), "to" + *similis* (Latin), "like; same"]

Definition:

a. To absorb fully or make one's own; to adopt as one's own.

It took Joe a long time to **assimilate** all the technical information that a first-rate computer programmer must possess.

America has **assimilated** the cultural traditions of many different peoples, and this process has greatly enriched our national life.

b. To adapt fully.

The foreign-born worker quickly **assimilated** her manner of speaking to that of her native-born colleagues.

Related Form: (*noun*) assimilation

Usage Note:

The word *assimilation* is much used by sociologists to indicate the process by which individuals belonging to a minority group adopt the living habits and standards of the dominant group in the society. The process is also called *acculturation*. (For the use of *assimilation* in linguistics, see page 55.)

Here we see a group of modern immigrants becoming full-fledged citizens of the United States.

Synonyms: (*verbs*) integrate, homogenize; fuse, merge; naturalize, acculturate; digest; incorporate, appropriate; adjust, transform

Antonyms: (*verbs*) segregate, isolate, insulate

Phrases: a process of naturalization; in the mainstream; a separatist movement, a standoffish attitude

Using the Words

Exercise I. Parts of Speech

Indicate the part of speech of each of the following words. Two answers are possible in some instances.

1. apathy
2. askew
3. array
4. arbitrary
5. apprehend
6. articulate

Exercise II. Words in Phrases

In each of the following groups, select the item that best expresses the meaning of the *italicized* word in the introductory phrase.

1. *apprehended* the suspect
    a. accused **b.** protected **c.** caught **d.** released **e.** tried

2. an *articulate* proponent of the plan
    a. long-standing **b.** unexpected **c.** well-known
    d. eloquent **e.** self-appointed

3. an *anomaly* in today's world
    a. adage **b.** issue **c.** element **d.** ideal **e.** abnormality

4. with the bedclothes all *askew*
    a. crooked **b.** faded **c.** clean **d.** torn **e.** neat

5. a totally *arbitrary* group of numbers
    a. meaningless **b.** random **c.** unlikely **d.** useful
    e. unworkable

Exercise III. Completing Sentences

Complete each of the following sentences or pairs of sentences by selecting the most appropriate word from the given group of words. Make whatever adjustments are necessary to fit the words into the sentences properly.

appall	apathy	arbitrate
assimilate	anomaly	array

1. "Randy must be totally uninterested in politics," Tony observed. "Lately I've noticed that an expression of profound _____ and boredom comes over his face every time the subject comes up."

2. In the face of my opponent's formidable _____ of facts and figures, I was forced to concede that I was wrong.

3. "The only practical way to settle this dispute," the attorney remarked, "is to call in an impartial third party to _____ it."

4. Some people can absorb large masses of data with great speed. Others require a great deal of time to _____ even the smallest bit of information.

5. The devastation and suffering wrought by a series of earthquakes in southern Italy in 1980 _____ the entire world.

Exercise IV.   Synonyms and Antonyms

A.   Match each word in Column A with its **synonym** in Column B.

Column A	*Column B*
1. comprehend	a. askance
2. mediate	b. horrify
3. disapprovingly	c. despotic
4. dismay	d. referee
5. tyrannical	e. grasp

   Indicate which of the basic words taught in this lesson (Words 31–40) is **synonymous** with each of the words in Column A.

B.   In each of the following groups, select the **two** words that are most nearly **antonyms**.

1. a. adorn b. surround c. muster d. fulfill e. disband
2. a. inarticulate b. ordinary c. typical d. eloquent
   e. askew
3. a. boredom b. freak c. judgment d. norm e. umpire
4. a. keen b. dreadful c. apathetic d. partial e. straight
5. a. equip b. appall c. assemble d. elate e. seize

Exercise V.   Word Roundup

1. Explain the difference in meaning between *disinterested* and *uninterested*.

2. What special meaning does the word *assimilation* have for a sociologist? for a linguist? Give a synonym for *assimilation* as used in sociology and one for the word as used in linguistics.

3. What is an *arbiter*? an *arbiter elegantiae* (or *elegantiarum*)?

Exercise VI.   Framing Sentences

Use each of the following words in an original sentence that clearly illustrates the word's meaning.

1. anomalous	4. apprehensive	7. array
2. apathetic	5. arbitrary	8. articulate
3. appall	6. arbitration	9. askew

Completing Verbal Analogies

Analogy Question Type I. Perhaps the simplest type of analogy question used on standardized tests (and also the easiest word relationship met with) is shown below. For convenience, the four elements involved in this sample have been labeled *A, B, C,* and *D.*

Type I

    A   *B*   *C* |——————*D*——————|
absolve : exonerate = abstain : (*indulge, acquit, forgo, impeach, abet*)

What the student is being asked to do in this type of question is complete an analogy that is three-quarters finished. The student is to do this by selecting one of the five choices offered under *D.* Note that these choices are italicized within a pair of parentheses.

Completing Type-I Analogy Questions Correctly. There are three basic steps involved in the correct completion of Type-I analogy questions.

Step 1: Look at items *A* and *B,* and determine the relationship between them. *A* and *B* represent the two words that are in the **key** or **given relationship**. The key or given relationship usually comes before the equals sign (or before the word *as*) in an analogy question. It indicates which word relationship is being used on both sides of the equals sign in the particular analogy under consideration. (In this book the words in the key or given relationship are printed in **boldface type** so they can be spotted easily.)

In the sample analogy given above, the relationship between *A* and *B* (*absolve, exonerate*) is clearly sameness. *Absolve* and *exonerate,* as indicated in Lesson 1 (page 29), are synonyms; they mean the same thing.

This means that the relationship between *C* and *D* must also be one of sameness. In other words, the answer selected from the group of five choices given under *D* must mean the same as *C.*

Step 2: Now look at *C,* and determine what it means. In the sample, *C* is *abstain,* which, as indicated in Lesson 1 (page 29), means "refrain."

Step 3. Finally, look at the group of choices offered under *D,* and select the word that means the same as *abstain.* This is the item that is needed to complete the analogy correctly.

And what is the word wanted? It is *forgo,* which was listed as a synonym of *abstain* on page 29.

The other choices offered under *D* are clearly wrong. *Indulge* means the opposite of *abstain,* and the other words (*acquit, impeach,* and *abet*) bear no relation whatsoever to it. (Note, however, that *acquit* is a synonym of *absolve* and *exonerate,* while *impeach* means the opposite of these two words. These items were intentionally included in the group in order to confuse the student. When doing analogy questions, always keep an eye out for such traps.)

"A Means the Same as B." Thus, the complete analogy reads:

absolve : exonerate = abstain : forgo

Note that the word relationship involved in this sample is *sameness.* We can express this relationship in abstract terms as "*A* means the same as *B;* *C* means the same as *D.*" This relationship is one of the most frequently used on standardized tests.

Exercise I

Complete the following analogies.

1. **agenda : schedule** = affectation : (*sincerity, adversity, mannerism, conclusion, aesthetics*)

2. **ambivalent : uncertain** = equivocal : (*illusory, abominable, eventful, ambiguous, unanimous*)

3. **advocate : champion** = critic : (*accessory, opponent, teetotaler, flatterer, bystander*)

4. **anomaly : misfit** = anarchy : (*setting, freak, chaos, denunciation, yarn*)

5. **academic : theoretical** = opulent : (*civil, destitute, natural, unsociable, luxurious*)

Exercise II

Write **three** complete analogies of your own to illustrate the word relationship "*A* means the same as *B*; *C* means the same as *D*." In **two** of your original analogies, use at least **one** of the basic words studied in Lessons 3–4 (Words 21–40).

Noah Webster

In 1828, Noah Webster (1758–1843), America's first scientific lexicographer, published a two-volume *American Dictionary of the English Language.* This work and its successors down through the years have made the name Webster synonymous with *dictionary* in American households for over a century and a half. What got Webster started on the dictionary project was his profound dismay over the continued use of British textbooks and dictionaries in American schools after the United States had become independent from Great Britain. Thus, Webster began his great work in a spirit of national pride. When he was finished, his dictionary contained more than 12,000 words that were not listed in any other dictionary then available. Many of these new items were "Americanisms"—that is, expressions coined and used by Americans. Sales of the dictionary were tremendous, and the work did much to shape and standardize American English, its spelling and pronunciation. Webster produced a second edition of his dictionary in 1840, and the work has been revised and updated many times since then. Indeed, Webster's dictionary (in its revised form) is still a staple item in the library or book collection of almost every household in the United States.

Enriching the Lesson

Exercise I. Our Greek Heritage

The words *apathy* and *anarchy*, studied in this lesson, are but two of the numerous English words based on Greek originals. Some other words of the same type are listed below. With or without the aid of a dictionary, define each, and indicate what the original Greek word or word elements meant.

1. archaic
2. cacophony
3. neophyte
4. paragon
5. phobia
6. stratagem
7. misanthropic
8. philanthropy
9. dogmatic
10. dynamic
11. epidemic
12. panegyric
13. sophistry
14. monopoly
15. cataclysm
16. dynasty
17. pedantic
18. pedagogy
19. didactic
20. orthodox

Exercise II. Order and Chaos

1. In Lesson 3 you learned that *anarchy* denotes the chaos resulting from a lack of effective government. The following words indicate different types of government. (An anarchist is opposed to them all.) Define each term in such a way as to bring out the distinctive characteristics of the type of government involved.

   a. democracy
   b. theocracy
   c. socialism
   d. communism
   e. fascism
   f. oligarchy

2. Answer the following questions, or supply the information requested.

   a. What is a *nihilist? nihilism?*

   b. What is a *subversive* interested in doing? Give a verb related to this word, and tell what it means.

   c. What is meant by *sedition?* Give an adjective related to this word, and tell what it means.

Exercise III. Expanding Your Word Power

The words listed below are not on the Basic Word List, but they were mentioned in passing in Lesson 4. All of them would make useful additions to your working vocabulary. Define each, give its etymology, list **two** synonyms and **two** antonyms (where possible), and use in a short sentence that clearly illustrates the word's meaning.

1. stolid
2. indifference
3. aghast
4. elate
5. discernment
6. misgiving
7. capricious
8. adjudicate
9. deploy

Lesson 5

41. **astute** — 50. **authentic**

---

41. **a-stute** *adjective* ə-stōot′ *or* ə-styōot′
[*astutus* (Latin), "cunning," from *astus* (Latin), "craftiness"]

Definition: Keen of mind and judgment, especially in practical matters; cunning.

The novelist Jane Austen was an **astute** observer of life and manners in the English countryside at the beginning of the 19th century.

The financier amassed a tremendous fortune by **astute** speculations in the stock market.

Related Forms: (*noun*) astuteness; (*adverb*) astutely

Phrases: an astute analysis, an astute criticism; astute advertising

Synonyms: (*adjectives*) shrewd, perceptive, sharp, acute; sagacious, judicious (Word 249); far-sighted, perspicacious; quick-witted, clever; wily, cagey; (*nouns*) perceptiveness, discernment, acumen, sagacity

Antonyms: (*adjectives*) obtuse, unperceptive, undiscerning; empty-headed, stupid, foolish, doltish, vacuous, inane

Phrases: sharp practice; acute perceptions; cunning as a fox; shrewd insights into human nature; a shrewd investor

42. **a-sy-lum** *noun* ə-sī′-ləm
[*asulon* (Greek), "place of refuge," from *a* (Greek), "without" + *sulon* (Greek), "right of seizure"]

Definition:
a. An institution that shelters and cares for mentally unbalanced, aged, or homeless persons.

The English word *bedlam* derives from the name of an infamous insane **asylum** in medieval London, the Hospital of St. Mary of Bethlehem.

b. Any place offering protection or security.

At every stage in its short history, the United States has served as an **asylum** for the persecuted and downtrodden of the world.

c. Protection against a legal or social penalty.

After weeks in hiding, the ousted President of Iran escaped to France, where he was granted political **asylum**.

Synonyms: (*nouns*) sanctuary, refuge, haven

Phrases: seek sanctuary; take refuge; protective custody; a safe house

71

Sanctuary

Literally, the word *sanctuary* (from *sanctus* [Latin], "sacred") denotes a holy place, usually the most sacred part in a church, often referred to as "the holy of holies" In Biblical times, the sanctuary sheltered the Ark of the Covenant.

The word *sanctuary* is imbedded in historical tradition. In ancient and medieval times, churches and monasteries served as a place of asylum or sanctuary for persons fleeing violence or penalties of the law. Once inside such a refuge, a fugitive would claim "the right of sanctuary"—that is, immunity from arrest or injury. To injure such a protected person or to remove him by force was regarded as a sacrilege. Eventually the abuse of the privilege led to its general abolition, though it survives in modern times in certain situations.

43. a-tone   *verb*   ə-tōn′

[from the English phrase "to be *at one* with," the idea being that a person who atones for a misdeed is brought back together with God and made whole (or one with himself) in conscience]

Definition: To make up for or repent.

"You made an honest mistake," Wanda said. "Don't feel that you have to **atone** for it."

The plot of the novel is awfully contrived, but the wonderfully vivid descriptions of the setting do much to **atone** for this weakness.

Related Form: (*noun*) atonement

Synonyms: (*verbs*) expiate, redeem, offset; (*nouns*) penance, expiation; compensation, reparation, restitution, redress

Phrases: make amends for; do penance for; Day of Atonement

Usage Note:

The *Day of Atonement* (from the Hebrew *Yom Kippur*) is a day set aside by Jews for fasting and prayer as penance for sins and misdeeds committed during the year just past.

72

44. **a-troc-i-ty** *noun* ə-trŏs′-ə-tē

[*atrox, atrocis* (Latin), "cruel," from *ater, atris* (Latin), "dark" + *-ox, -oc-* (Latin), "looking"]

Definition: A savagely cruel, brutal, or inhuman deed; a monstrosity.

For days after the city had fallen to the enemy, bands of drunken soldiers wandered the streets, committing one **atrocity** after another on the helpless and terrified population.

"*You* may call that thing a hat," Al exclaimed. "*I* call it an **atrocity**."

Related Forms: (*adjective*) atrocious; (*noun*) atrociousness

Usage Note:
Atrocious (pronounced ə-trō′-shəs) means not only "extremely cruel or brutal" (as in the phrase "an atrocious crime") but also "extremely poor or bad" (as in the phrases "atrocious behavior" and "atrocious taste"). *Atrociousness*, the noun form, is used in exactly the same way.

Synonyms: (*nouns*) enormity, outrage; (*adjectives*) barbarous, barbaric, sadistic; grisly, gruesome (Word 216), ghastly; heinous (Word 222), outrageous; horrible, dreadful, abominable

Antonyms: (*nouns*) kindness, good deed, act of charity; (*adjectives*) clement, benevolent, kindhearted, merciful, humane; impeccable, flawless, irreproachable, unimpeachable

Phrases: war crimes, a crime against humanity

45. **at-ro-phy** *noun and verb* ă′-trə-fē

[*a* (Greek), "without" + *trophe* (Greek), "nourishment"]

Definition:
a. (*noun*) A failure to develop normally; a progressive wasting away or decline.

Medical experts state that almost every case of muscle and tissue **atrophy** is the result of changes in cell nutrition, disease, or prolonged disuse.

The tremendous influx of wealth, luxuries, and slaves that resulted from the acquisition of foreign lands was in part responsible for the moral **atrophy** of the Roman ruling class.

b. (*verb*) To waste away.

"Well, here I am," Mr. Kravitz thought to himself sadly on the morning of his 40th birthday, "a middle-aged man whose talents are beginning to **atrophy**."

Related Form: (*adjective*) atrophic

Synonyms: (*nouns*) deterioration, degeneration, decay; (*verbs*) decay, deteriorate, degenerate, shrivel, wither, shrink, rot, stunt

Antonyms: (*nouns*) growth, development, maturation; (*verbs*) grow, develop, mature, flourish, prosper

46. **at·tri·tion** *noun*   ə-trĭsh´-ən

[*attritio, attritionis* (Latin), "a rubbing against," from *ad* (Latin), "against" + *terere* (Latin), "rub"]

Definition:

    a. A gradual wearing down or weakening of resistance resulting from constant friction, pressure, or harassment.

        Guerrilla warfare achieves its ends through a slow but steady process of **attrition**, rather than by victory in a quick, winner-take-all campaign.

        "A heavyweight boxing match is not so much a pitched battle as a war of **attrition**," the sportscaster observed. "For that reason, the winner is usually the fighter who is not too battered and exhausted to go on."

    b. A gradual, often natural decrease in size, strength, or number as a result of resignation, retirement, death, or the like.

        "The sales department is a bit overstaffed," the firm's personnel manager remarked. "However, the normal rate of **attrition** around here should solve that problem fairly quickly."

Synonyms: *(nouns)* abrasion, erosion; exhaustion, enervation; reduction, diminution

Antonyms: *(nouns)* increase, augmentation, expansion, enlargement

47. **aug·ment** *verb*   ôg-mĕnt´

[*augmentum* (Latin), "an increase," from *augere* (Latin), "to increase"]

Definition: To make greater; to become greater.

    If we are to contend with the population explosion, we must **augment** the world's food supply.

    Traffic noises in the street outside my window **augment** appreciably during rush hour.

Related Form: *(noun)* augmentation

Synonyms: *(verbs)* increase, enlarge, expand, extend, magnify

Antonyms: *(verbs)* decrease, lessen, reduce, curtail (Word 114), diminish; contract, shrink, shrivel, abate, slacken, dwindle

48. **au·gur** *noun and verb*   ô´-gûr

[*augur* (Latin), "soothsayer, diviner"]

Definition:

    a. *(noun)* Someone who can forecast the future by spotting various signs or indications of what is to come.

        "I know you claim to be a reliable **augur** of future trends and developments in the economy," Mike remarked. "Still, your predictions are usually no more accurate than other people's."

b. (*verb*) To predict or foretell through signs; to point to or be an omen of.

> The Aztec Indians of Mexico believed that comets **augured** impending disaster, even the end of the world.

> The enthusiasm with which our candidate has been greeted all over the country certainly **augurs** well for success in the upcoming election.

Related Form: (*noun*) augury

Usage Note:
The noun *augury* (pronounced ô´-gyə-rē) means a number of things: (1) "the art of forecasting the future"; (2) "a prophecy"; and (3) "a sign or omen." Accordingly, words that mean the same thing include both *divination* and *prediction*, as well as *portent, premonition,* and *harbinger.*

Synonyms: (*nouns*) soothsayer, diviner, prophet, seer; (*verbs*) prophesy, divine, prognosticate; portend, forebode, presage, bode, foreshadow

The inauguration of George Washington, April 30, 1789.

Augur

In ancient Rome, the *augurs* were a group of priests who sought to discover, by observing certain signs, whether or not the gods approved of a proposed policy or action. The sign most often used for this purpose was the flight of birds, although the augurs also depended on such phenomena as lightning, comets, and the appearance of the entrails of animals. The "taking of the auguries" preceded every important public action, and, especially in the early days of Rome, was widely used by private individuals.

From *augur*, we get the word *inaugurate*, meaning "to begin formally; to induct into office," and the corresponding noun, *inauguration*. The hope is, of course, that the omens will be favorable for such an important beginning.

A specialist among soothsayers or diviners in ancient Rome was the *auspex*, who depended specifically on the flight of birds. From this title, we get the word *auspicious*, meaning "favorable, under good omens," and its opposite, *inauspicious*.

49. aus·tere *adjective* ô-stēr´

[*austeros* (Greek), "dry, withered"]

Definition: Rigidly severe; severely simple or bare.

My grandfather was an **austere** man whom I never knew to laugh or smile.

During World War II, living conditions in England were extremely **austere** because of severe shortages of food, fuel, and consumer goods.

The Puritans practiced an **austere**, cheerless form of religion.

Caesar's simple, even **austere**, style of writing contrasts greatly with the complicated and ornate manner of Cicero.

Related Forms: (*nouns*) austereness, austerity, austerities; (*adverb*) austerely

Phrases: austere surroundings, an austere manner, an austere diet; a life of austerity; the austerities imposed by want

Synonyms: (*adjectives*) stern, strict, strait-laced; abstemious, sober, puritanical, ascetic; solemn; harsh, forbidding; somber, gloomy; plain, unadorned, undecorated

Antonyms: (*adjectives*) gentle, mild, kindly; affable (Word 15), tolerant; self-indulgent; elaborate, involved; orotund, florid; gaudy, flamboyant

50. au·then·tic *adjective* ô-thĕn´-tĭk

[*authentikos* (Greek), "genuine"]

Definition: Genuine, trustworthy.

"The painting the salesman showed you has to be a fake," Vera informed me. "You can't buy an **authentic** Rembrandt for five dollars."

Related Forms: (*noun*) authenticity; (*verb*) authenticate

Phrases: an authentic record, an authentic document, an authentic account

Synonyms: (*adjectives*) real, true, actual, veritable, bona fide, legitimate, kosher; indisputable, indubitable

Antonyms: (*adjectives*) counterfeit, fraudulent, fake, forged, spurious, phony, bogus, apocryphal; dubious, untrustworthy, fishy

Usage Notes:
   a. The synonyms and antonyms listed above include a number of colloquial or slang terms, including *fake, phony, bogus*, and *fishy. Kosher*, a colloquial term meaning "legitimate or proper," has come into English (via Yiddish) from the Hebrew word *kasher*, meaning "in accordance with Jewish dietary laws and, therefore, clean or proper."
   b. *Bona fide*, literally meaning "in good faith," is one of a large group of words and phrases that English has borrowed without change from Latin. In English it means "genuine" or "sincere."

Using the Words

Exercise I. Syllabication and Pronunciation

Syllabicate the following words correctly, and place the major stress mark (') after the syllable that is accented when the word is pronounced.

1. astute
2. atone
3. atrocity
4. attrition
5. augment
6. authentic

Exercise II. Words Out of Context

In each of the following groups, select the item that best expresses the meaning of the numbered word at the left.

1. asylum
   a. prison b. booth c. arena d. haven e. office

2. atrocity
   a. natural talent b. inhuman act c. outstanding accomplishment d. grievous fault e. kind deed

3. augment
   a. imagine b. solidify c. belittle d. curtail e. enlarge

4. augur
   a. accumulate b. bode c. expiate d. compensate e. refine

5. authentic
   a. phony b. gross c. kosher d. cagey e. rotten

Exercise III. Completing Sentences

Complete each of the following sentences by selecting the most appropriate word from the given group of words. Make whatever adjustments are necessary to fit the words into the sentences properly.

| atone | attrition | austere |
| astute | atrophy | augment |

1. The reason why pre-med programs have such a high rate of _____ is simple: A great many students find the course of study too demanding and turn to something easier.

2. Protestant churches in New England tend to be _____ structures with little or no architectural adornment.

3. It was never clear whether the defendants had been acquitted because they were innocent or because they had an _____ lawyer who found a clever way to get them off the hook.

77

4. I have heard it said that many Americans no longer know right from wrong and have, in effect, sunk into a profound state of moral _____.

5. Paying for the repairs that are necessary seems to be an effective way to _____ for the damage you have done.

Exercise IV. Synonyms and Antonyms

Classify each of the following pairs of expressions as **S** for **synonyms** or **A** for **antonyms**.

1. erosion—attrition
2. gaudy —flamboyant
3. perceptive—dense
4. seer—prophet
5. bona fide—bogus

6. sanctuary—refuge
7. flourish—wither
8. magnify—minimize
9. impeccable—flawless
10. humane—barbaric

Exercise V. Framing Sentences

A. Use each of the following words in an original sentence that clearly illustrates its meaning.

1. asylum
2. atrocity
3. atrophy
4. attrition
5. augment
6. augur

B. Give a **noun** form of each of the following words, and use it in an original sentence that clearly illustrates its meaning.

1. astute
2. atone
3. authentic
4. austere

Dissecting the Words

Roots

1. The Greek root **auto(s)**, meaning "self" or "same," is found in numerous English words, including *authentic*, studied in this lesson. Here are some other words in which this root appears:

autocrat (literally "self-ruling")—a ruler with unlimited or unrestricted power; a tyrant or despot. Noun: *autocracy*; adjective *autocratic*

autopsy (literally "seeing with one's own eyes")—the examination of a dead body to determine the cause of death

autonomy—independence; self-government. Adjective: *autonomous*

autograph—a person's own signature or handwriting

autodidact—a person who is self-taught

automatic—self-operating; running or working by itself

2. The Latin root **ag, act** (as in the Latin verb *agere, egi, actus*) means "act, drive." It occurs in such words as *agent* and *agile*, mentioned earlier in this book. Other words derived from the same root include:

exigency—a driving need

agitate—to stir up

coagulate—to form into a compact mass; to congeal

enact—to make into law; to act out on the stage. Noun: *enactment*

cogent—forceful; convincing

cogitate (literally "drive about in one's mind") —to ponder or consider
intently

Suffix

The suffix **-ize** (British variant, **-ise**) has the general meaning of "make or make into." It has proved to be a handy tool for making a verb out of a noun or an adjective. For example:

popular + ize = *popularize*— to make popular

deputy + ise = *deputise* to make into a deputy

Sometimes, of course, the spelling of the form to which *-ize* is attached is modified in some way in the new word. For example:

pole + ize = *polarize* (not *polize!*)—to concentrate around two conflicting
or contrasting positions

fraternity + ize = *fraternize* (not *fraternitize!*)—to be sociable with

Exercise

1. Answer the following questions regarding words containing the root *auto(s)*.

    a. The word *autointoxication* may be used in both a physical and a psychological sense. Explain the two senses in which the word may properly be used.

    b. Explain the italicized word in this sentence: "The few remaining colonies in Africa are demanding *autonomy*."

    c. What part of the human nervous system is referred to as *autonomic*? Why is this word appropriate?

    d. What does *autosuggestion* mean? Explain its origin.

2. With or without the aid of a dictionary, define each of the nouns or adjectives listed below, and convert it into a related verb form by adding *-ize*. (Make any spelling changes that are necessary.)

a. victim	f. eulogy	k. social
b. dogma	g. civil	l. plagiarism
c. politics	h. legitimate	m. theory
d. trauma	i. proselyte	n. radical
e. deputy	j. tyranny	o. normal

Enriching the Lesson

Exercise I.   Latin Phrases in English

As indicated earlier in this lesson, *bona fide* is just one of a large group of phrases that English has borrowed without change from Latin. Some other examples are listed below. What does each mean in present-day English? What is its literal meaning in Latin?

1. alter ego
2. quid pro quo
3. de facto
4. persona non grata
5. obiter dictum
6. amicus curiae
7. de jure
8. status quo
9. pro tempore (*often shortened to* pro tem.)
10. prima facie
11. modus operandi (*often shortened to* m.o.)
12. ex officio
13. alma mater
14. sub rosa
15. in absentia
16. vice versa
17. casus belli
18. non sequitur
19. sine qua non
20. deus ex machina

Exercise II.   "Newsworthies"

A number of the basic words studied in this lesson, including *atrocity, attrition*, and *asylum*, frequently crop up in newspaper and magazine articles and on radio-TV news programs. Each has gained a currency that makes it "newsworthy." A number of other examples of "newsworthy" expressions are listed below. With or without the aid of a dictionary, explain what each of these items means. Then use it in a phrase or sentence of your own.

1. détente
2. an activist
3. deficit spending
4. elitist
5. a police state
6. racial balance
7. a pluralistic society
8. a welfare state
9. a civil libertarian
10. permissiveness
11. a status symbol
12. urban renewal
13. double-digit inflation
14. a reactionary
15. sexist
16. the establishment
17. gentrification
18. the Moral Majority
19. rapprochement
20. a conservative
21. Marxist-Leninist
22. the mass media
23. a grass-roots movement
24. open diplomacy
25. software
26. a third-world nation
27. the feminist movement
28. a liberal
29. the inner city
30. human rights

Can you think of any others to add to this list?

Exercise III. Yiddish in English—Is It Kosher?

Yes, today it certainly is kosher (a Yiddish word meaning "clean" or "proper") to use the word *kosher* colloquially. All the latest dictionaries sanction such usage. A word or phrase that is Yiddish in origin and has been assimilated into our daily language is called a **yiddishism**.

Many of us use yiddishisms without being aware of their origin. Here are a few familiar expressions that are actually translations from Yiddish: *O.K. by me! How come? He knows from nothing. It shouldn't happen to a dog. What's with the jokes?*

It should be noted that since many of these adopted expressions are identified as either *slang* or *informal* by the dictionaries, they must be handled with care. One should not use them in formal writing, nor too freely in many other situations, since not everyone will understand them. However, with nationwide exposure via films, television, and other media, these and other expressions are becoming rapidly assimilated into English. Some of the words fill a language need. For example, we have no equivalent English word or phrase to pinpoint the kind of annoying meddler that the yiddishism *kibitzer* denotes.

Recently, Leo Rosten, a well-known American writer, made a comprehensive study of Yiddish in English. Two of the words that he analyzes in detail are *chutzpah* ("unbelievable gall") and *megillah* ("a long, boring, over-detailed account"). The yiddishism *shtik*—meaning "a stylized or arch piece of acting overused by a performer"—is rapidly coming into wide circulation, especially among actors and theater people generally.

The yiddishisms listed below have been culled from recent national broadcasts. How many of them can you define?

1. yenta	5. schlock	9. cockamamie
2. nudge	6. kvetch	10. nosh
3. schnook	7. schlemiel	11. schlep
4. klutz	8. schmooze	12. maven

Can you suggest any other words or phrases that would be appropriate for a lexicon of yiddishisms?

Exercise IV. Expanding Your Word Power

The words listed below are not on the Basic Word List, but they were mentioned in passing in Lesson 5. All of them would make useful additions to your working vocabulary. Define each, give its etymology, list **two** synonyms and **two** antonyms (where possible), and use in a short sentence that clearly illustrates the word's meaning.

1. acumen	5. redress	9. clement
2. obtuse	6. impeccable	10. foreshadow
3. enormity	7. deteriorate	11. flamboyant
4. grisly	8. enhance	12. spurious

Lesson 6

51. avarice — 60. bland

---

51. av·a·rice   *noun*   ăv′-ə-rĭs

[*avarus* (Latin), "greedy," from *avere* (Latin), "desire"]

Definition: An excessive desire to acquire and possess wealth; a combination of greed and stinginess.

> Few novels portray the dehumanizing effects of **avarice** as vividly and forcefully as George Eliot's *Silas Marner*.

Related Forms: (*adjective*) avaricious; (*noun*) avariciousness

Synonyms: (*nouns*) acquisitiveness, cupidity, covetousness, rapacity; miserliness, parsimony, niggardliness; (*adjectives*) acquisitive, greedy, covetous, rapacious, grasping; stingy, miserly, niggardly, tightfisted

Antonyms: (for the miserly side of *avarice*): (*nouns*) generosity, liberality, openhandedness; (*adjectives*) generous, liberal, openhanded

52. av·id   *adjective*   ăv′-ĭd

[*avidus* (Latin), "craving; greedy," from *avere* (Latin), "desire"]

Definition: Extremely eager, anxious, or enthusiastic.

> **Avid** baseball fans like Martha, Harry, and Cal found the players' strike of 1981 extremely hard to endure.

Related Forms: (*noun*) avidity; (*adverb*) avidly

Phrases: an avid sportsman, an avid reader, avid for adventure

Synonyms: (*adjectives*) zealous, ardent, keen, fervent, fervid, voracious, insatiable, rabid, fanatical, passionate, gung ho

Antonyms: (*adjectives*) indifferent, apathetic, unresponsive; (*nouns*) apathy (Word 32), indifference

53. badg·er   *verb*   băj′-ĕr

[Origin uncertain, possibly from the name of the animal]

Definition: To tease; to annoy with a constant string of petty torments.

> The older children had **badgered** and baited the younger child until he was on the point of tears.

> "Getting at the truth is one thing," the judge reminded the overly aggressive attorney. "**Badgering** the defendant out of his wits is quite another."

82

Synonyms: (*verbs*) harass, torment, pester, plague, vex, irritate, hassle, bait, harry

Antonyms: (*verbs*) leave in peace; soothe, calm, pacify

54. baf-fle   *verb*   băf´-əl

[Origin uncertain]

Definition:

a. To puzzle completely.

"How you manage to do well on tests when you never seem to crack a book completely **baffles** me," Jerry remarked.

b. To prevent from achieving a goal.

Despite several clues that at first seemed promising, the police were eventually **baffled** in their attempt to solve the murder.

Related Forms: (*adjective*) baffling; (*noun*) bafflement

Synonyms: (*verbs*) perplex, mystify, bewilder, nonplus, confound; thwart (Word 376), foil, balk, frustrate, stymie, stump; (*adjectives*) mystifying, bewildering, enigmatic; perplexed, mystified, quizzical

Antonyms: (*verbs*) understand, comprehend, fathom (Word 185); help, aid, assist

55. ba-nal   *adjective*   bā´-nəl *or* bə-näl´

[*banal* (French), "commonplace," from *ban* (Old French), "summons to military service"]

Definition: Made stale by constant use or repetition.

I expected dialogue by such a well-known writer to sparkle with wit. Unfortunately, it proved to be **banal** and flat.

Related Forms: (*noun*) banality; (*adverb*) banally

Synonyms: (*adjectives*) trite, hackneyed, stereotyped, prosaic, commonplace, pedestrian, insipid, vapid, fatuous (Word 186), jejune, corny; (*nouns*) triteness, insipidity; cliché, platitude, bromide

Antonyms: (*adjectives*) novel, fresh, original, innovative, provocative, striking, sparkling, scintillating, piquant; (*nouns*) novelty, originality

Usage Note:

a. *Trite* and *hackneyed* indicate staleness or dullness due to overuse. *Stereotyped* suggests a lack of originality and an overheavy reliance on conventional ideas, images, or forms. *Pedestrian* and *prosaic* simply indicate that something is quite ordinary. *Vapid* and *fatuous* suggest a lack of substance or perceptivity. *Jejune* adds to this the idea of childishness. *Corny* is a slang expression that can designate anything from triteness to oversentimentality.

b. Do not confuse *banal* with *baneful*, which means "harmful" or "destructive."

56. bel-lig-er-ent   *adjective and noun*   bə-lĭj´-ər-ĕnt

[*bellum* (Latin), "war" + *gerens* (Latin), "waging," from *gerre* (Latin), "wage"]

Definition:
   a. (*adjective*) Warring, actually engaged in a war; warlike or hostile.

> Between 1915 and 1917, Italy, Bulgaria, Romania, Greece, Turkey, and the U.S.A. all entered World War I. This increased the total number of **belligerent** nations to a dozen, though that many were never involved in the conflict simultaneously.

> How can we hope to arrive at a fair settlement, or even discuss the situation calmly, when your attitude is so **belligerent**?

   b. (*noun*) A party (for example, a nation or organization) engaged in a war.

> The Security Council called upon the **belligerents** to halt all military operations and send representatives to an emergency peace conference.

Related Forms: (*nouns*) belligerence, belligerency; (*adverb*) belligerently

Synonyms: (*adjectives*) martial, combative, bellicose, quarrelsome, contentious, militant, pugnacious, hawkish

Antonyms: (*adjectives*) pacific, peaceable, conciliatory, dovish

Usage Note:
Though *belligerent* and *bellicose* are often used interchangeably, they are really quite different. Both words of course mean "warlike or hostile," but only *belligerent* also means "warring" or "actually engaged in a war." In addition, *bellicose* tends to be used of a natural or inborn inclination toward aggressiveness, whereas *belligerent* tends to be reserved for a hostile attitude that is not innate, but rather the result of some quite specific external cause.

Mars and Martial

Mars was the Roman god of war. His name is the source of our word *martial*, meaning "warlike" or "military," and also of the name of the month of March, during which the chief festivals of Mars occurred. The planet Mars is also named after this deity.

57. be-nign   *adjective*   bǐ-nīn′

[*bene* (Latin), "well" + *genus* (Latin), "birth; race"]

Definition:
   a.   Gentle and kindly.

       Though he may look friendly and **benign**, he is really quite nasty and foul-tempered.

   b.   Wholesome or favorable.

       Shirley credits her sunny disposition to the **benign** influence of a happy childhood and loving parents.

Related Forms: (*noun*) benignity (pronounced bǐ-nǐg′-nə-tē; (*adjective*) benignant (pronounced bǐ-nǐg′-něnt); (*adverb*) benignly

Usage Note:
In medicine, *benign* means "not a threat to a person's health or life"—for example, in the phrase "a benign tumor." Its opposite is *malignant*.

Synonyms: (*adjectives*) benevolent; favorable, auspicious, beneficial, salutary, salubrious

Antonyms: (*adjectives*) malevolent; pernicious (Word 299), deleterious, injurious, inimical, noxious, detrimental

58. bick-er   *verb*   bǐk′-ẽr

[*bikeren* (Middle English), "thrust; attack"]

Definition: To engage in petty quarreling.

       The conference soon degenerated into an ugly dispute as the participants began to **bicker** over minor details of procedure.

Related Form: (*noun*) bickering

Synonyms: (*verbs*) squabble, wrangle, haggle, dicker

Antonyms: (*verbs*) agree, concur

59. bi-zarre   *adjective*   bǐ-zär′

[*bizarre* (French), "strange," originally "gallant"; from *bizarro* (Spanish), "handsome, manly"; from *bizar* (Basque), "beard"]

Definition: Weird or fantastic.

       For some fans of punk rock, the more **bizarre** the performers' costumes, make-up, and antics, the more enjoyable the performance.

Related Form: (*noun*) bizarreness

Synonyms: (*adjectives*) grotesque, outlandish, freakish, odd, queer, singular, far-out, unconventional, eccentric

Antonyms: (*adjectives*) normal, conventional, orthodox, straight, square; sedate, conservative, sober, staid

60. **bland**   *adjective*   blănd

[*blandus* (Latin), "smooth; soft-spoken"]

Definition:

   a. Mild or gentle. (When used in this sense, the word is usually neutral in tone.)

      The doctor prescribed a **bland** diet for the patient suffering from ulcers.

   b. Lacking interest or liveliness; flat. (When used in this sense, the word is distinctly pejorative.)

      He expressed his opinion in language so ordinary and **bland** that he made little or no impression on his audience.

Related Forms: (*noun*) blandness; (*adverb*) blandly

Phrases: bland food, a bland personality, a bland smile, a bland style

Synonyms: (*adjectives*) calming, soothing, nonirritating; dull, boring, unexciting, insipid, lifeless; nondescript, mediocre, run-of-the-mill

Antonyms: (*adjectives*) irritating, harsh; spicy, pungent, piquant, racy, colorful, florid, scintillating, lively, sprightly

Using the Words

Exercise I. Parts of Speech

Indicate the part of speech of each of the following words. In one case, two answers are correct.

1. benign	**3.** avid	**5.** avarice
2. bicker	**4.** belligerent	**6.** bizarre

Exercise II. Words in Phrases

In each of the following groups, select the item that best expresses the meaning of the *italicized* word in the introductory phrase.

1. a *benign* countenance
    a. beautiful b. scarred c. kindly d. surly

2. motivated by *avarice*
    a. vengeance b. fear c. greed d. ambition

3. *bizarre* behavior
    a. weird b. aggressive c. laudable d. ordinary

4. a *bland* writing style
    a. curious b. nondescript c. florid d. original

5. *badgered* me with questions
    a. thrilled b. puzzled c. flattered d. pestered

Exercise III. Completing Sentences

Complete each of the following sentences by selecting the most appropriate word from the given groups of words.

banal   avarice   belligerent

baffle   bicker   avid

1. Though Queen Victoria sympathized deeply with the Southern cause, she had no intention of allowing Great Britain to become a(n) _____ in the American Civil War.

2. "We will never be able to present a united front in the upcoming election if we continue to _____ among ourselves about matters of no importance," the politician warned.

3. Ordinary detectives are often unable to solve the crimes they're investigating, but no mystery—no matter how complicated or puzzling—ever seems to _____ the great Sherlock Holmes.

4. "I've been a(n) _____ sportsman all my life," the movie star told the reporter, "and I rarely miss a day on the golf links or tennis court."

5. Some of the incidental ideas expressed in the film are novel and interesting, but the overall handling of the theme is terribly _____ and flat.

Exercise IV. Synonyms and Antonyms

A. Match each of the words in Column A with its **synonym** in Column B.

Column A
1. mediocre
2. beneficial
3. pester
4. foil
5. outlandish

Column B
a. harass
b. fantastic
c. run-of-the-mill
d. salutary
e. frustrate

Now indicate which of the basic words in this lesson (Words 51–60) is **synonymous** with each of the words in Column A.

B. In each of the following groups, select the **two** words that are most nearly **antonyms.**

1. a. terminate b. squabble c. concur d. atrophy

2. a. triteness b. bafflement c. miserliness d. generosity

3. a. piquant b. freakish c. swift d. vapid

4. a. quarrelsome b. conciliatory c. typical d. inane

5. a. fervent b. peaceful c. orderly d. apathetic

Exercise V. Word Roundup

1. Explain the difference in meaning and usage between *bellicose* and *belligerent*. Use each in an original sentence that clearly shows its meaning.

2. By means of illustrative sentences, show how *bizarre* may be applied to each of the following.

   a. human behavior

   b. physical objects

   c. ideas or points of view

3. What is a *benign* tumor? Give an antonym for *benign* in the medical sense.

4. A number of the expressions mentioned in the Synonyms and Antonyms sections of the word entries in Lesson 6 are *slang*. Make a list of these items.

Exercise VI. Framing Sentences

Use each of the following words in an original sentence that clearly illustrates its meaning.

1. avaricious
2. avidity
3. badger
4. baffling
5. banality
6. belligerence
7. benignly
8. bickering
9. bizarre
10. blandness

Completing Verbal Analogies

"A Means the Opposite of B." Analogy questions involving opposites (antonyms) occur frequently on standardized vocabulary tests. This type of analogy can be expressed in abstract terms as "*A* means the opposite of *B*; *C* means the opposite of *D*." Look at the following example of such an analogy question, and try to figure out the answer.

  A   *B*   *C* ─────────── *D* ───────────
affluent : indigent = equitable : (*florid, destitute, arbitrary, opulent, bland*)

The answer is *arbitrary*. Here's why: The words in the key relationship (*A, B*) are *affluent* and *indigent*. They are opposites or antonyms. So, an antonym for *C*, *equitable*, is needed to complete the analogy correctly. The only word available for this purpose from among the five choices given is *arbitrary*. Hence, *arbitrary* is the correct answer.

Note, however, that *destitute* is both an antonym of *affluent* and a synonym of *indigent*. Similarly, *opulent* is both an antonym of *indigent* and a synonym of *affluent*. In addition, *florid* is something of an antonym of *bland*. All these words were included among the five choices in order to confuse the student and make selecting the right answer more difficult.

Note also that in analogy questions involving opposites (antonyms) the positive or desirable quality often comes first.

A commercial artist "pastes up" an advertisement that was written by a copywriter. Being a copywriter in an advertising agency is an excellent career goal for someone who can use words well.

Exercise I

Complete each of the following analogies.

1. **augment** : **decrease** = wax : (*polish, wane, declare, frustrate, accelerate*)

2. **piquant** : **bland** = generous : (*ardent, dull, amiable, miserly, liberal*)

3. **absolve** : **incriminate** = acquit : (*liberate, mystify, convict, resolve, exclude*)

4. **conciliatory** : **belligerent** = astute : (*passionate, sagacious, indifferent, bellicose, obtuse*)

5. **authentic** : **spurious** = austere : (*flamboyant, bogus, puritanical, reliable, wily*)

6. **relish** : **abhor** = agile : (*lithe, contradictory, clumsy, zealous, commonplace*)

Exercise II

Write **three** original analogies involving opposites (antonyms). In your analogies use at least **three** of the basic words presented in Lessons 1–6 (Words 1–60).

The following items review what you have so far learned about analogy questions. Complete each.

1. **anarchy** : **chaos** = avarice : (*indulgence, mannerism, provocation, cupidity, encouragement*)

2. **hackneyed** : **innovative** = pedestrian : (*original, quarrelsome, auspicious, prosaic, grisly*)

3. **badger** : **harass** = abstain : (*pester, indulge, pacify, champion, forbear*)

4. **haven** : **sanctuary** = aggregate : (*anomaly, pretense, cluster, refuge, misdemeanor*)

5. **malevolent** : **benign** = adverse : (*noxious, weird, mediocre, favorable, covetous*)

6. **assiduous** : **indolent** = diligent : (*inconsolable, lethargic, abstemious, charitable, rapacious*)

Enriching the Lesson

Exercise I. Fighting Words

With or without the aid of an unabridged dictionary, complete the following exercises.

1. Define the following expressions.

a. war of nerves	i. mobilization
b. amphibious operation	j. guerrilla
c. blitzkrieg	k. armistice
d. pacification	l. skirmish
e. preemptive strike	m. hostage
f. pacifist	n. ordnance
g. hostilities	o. broadside
h. maneuvers	p. hold out the olive branch

2. What is an *Armageddon*? Explain the story behind this word, and indicate where it comes from.

3. What is a *Pyrrhic victory*? Explain the story behind this phrase.

4. What is *martial law*? When is it usually imposed? Give an instance when martial law was recently imposed, and explain why. What are *martial arts*?

5. The Latin word *bellum* means "war." What does *ante-bellum* mean? In what connection is this Latin phrase used in American history?

Exercise II. Clichés

A **cliché** is simply an expression that has grown stale and flat as a result of overuse. Some good examples of clichés are *enjoy the fruits of one's labor, wolf down one's food, go like a house afire*, and similar hand-me-down metaphors and similes. Every cliché was presumably once fresh and original, but such expressions have been so overworked that today they strike us as being trite and "corny."

This, however, is not to say that clichés should be avoided altogether. Countless clichés, like *bend over backwards, cut corners*, and *turn a new leaf*, are still serviceable, even if they are overly familiar. In fact, it would be hard, if not impossible, to carry on a conversation or otherwise communicate without calling on clichés.

For that reason, a sound principle to follow in regard to clichés is this: Don't be a fanatic about avoiding them, but don't overuse them either. Also, bear in mind the literal meaning of the cliché, and try to use it only where it will be appropriate and effective. For example, a 12th-grader who has just mailed out a batch of college applications might sum up his or her hopes for them by using a familiar cliché in this novel way: "Well, I've cast my bread upon the waters," the student might observe. "Now all I can do is pray that some of it comes back sandwiches!"

Now complete the following group of exercises involving clichés.

1. Some of the sentences below contain clichés; others have a measure of freshness and originality in them. Write the identifying letter of each sentence containing a cliché. Then replace the cliché with language that is more distinctive and effective.

   a. On that hot summer afternoon the garden sizzled with bees.

   b. When we arrived back at camp, we were as hungry as bears.

   c. Her mere presence on the platform turned a routine gathering into a once-in-a-lifetime event.

   d. She left no stone unturned in her search for the missing papers.

   e. The news we received this morning was like a bolt from the blue.

   f. The fullback drove through the line like a knife going through soft cheese.

2. Substitute a fresher, more original expression for each of the clichés listed below.

   a. worked like a Trojan
   b. a sumptuous repast
   c. slept like a log
   d. prostrate with grief
   e. lost his shirt at the track
   f. paint the town red

3. Draw up a list of **twenty** clichés that you have heard or seen in the last week.

4. Complete each of the following comparisons with a word or phrase that is not a cliché.

   a. as fat as _____
   b. as mad as _____
   c. as old as _____
   d. as pretty as _____
   e. as quiet as _____
   f. as big as _____

Exercise III. A Verbal Diversion

Modern English is rich in colloquial expressions involving the names of members of the animal kingdom. Two such expressions are *chicken feed* (meaning "a woefully insufficient sum of money") and *to smell a rat* (meaning "to suspect that something is not quite as it should be"). A number of similar items, all of them widely used today in informal speech and writing, are listed below. With or without the aid of a dictionary or other reference book, define each. Then choose any **five**, and use each in a short sentence that clearly illustrates the expression's meaning.

1. a red herring
2. a round robin
3. a stool pigeon
4. a loan shark
5. an eager beaver
6. to dovetail
7. to play possum
8. a white elephant
9. to handle with kid gloves
10. a dark-horse candidate
11. a kangaroo court
12. a lame-duck session of Congress
13. a bookworm
14. to let the cat out of the bag
15. to go to the dogs
16. a harebrained scheme
17. to throw to the wolves
18. a paper tiger
19. to take the bull by the horns
20. a sacred cow
21. to get one's goat
22. a wild-goose chase
23. a sheepish grin
24. to have a frog in one's throat

Can you add to this list from your own knowledge?

Exercise IV. Expanding Your Word Power

The following words are not on the Basic Word List, but they were mentioned in passing in Lesson 6. All of them would make useful additions to your working vocabulary. Define each, give its etymology, list **two** synonyms and **two** antonyms (where possible), and use in a short sentence that clearly illustrates the word's meaning.

1. niggardly
2. voracious
3. bait
4. quizzical
5. platitude
6. insipid
7. grotesque
8. foil
9. haggle
10. militant
11. sedate
12. eccentric

Lesson 7

61. **bleak** — 70. **brusque**

---

61. **bleak**　　*adjective*　　blēk

[*ble(i)kke* (Middle English), "pale," from *bleikr* (Old Norse), "white; pale"]

Definition:

　a.　Desolate, windswept, and bare.

　　Much of the coast of northern Alaska is **bleak** and uninviting.

　b.　Cold and gloomy; unpromising.

　　The funeral cortege moved off slowly and silently through the chill air of the **bleak** November day.

　　Unless we can raise fresh capital, the outlook for the survival of this company is exceedingly **bleak**.

Related Form:　(*noun*) bleakness

Synonyms:　(*adjectives*) barren; raw, harsh, chilling, forbidding; dour; dismal, dreary, drab, somber, grim, cheerless, depressing

Antonyms:　(*adjectives*) lush (Word 260), verdant; balmy, mild, rosy, temperate; cheerful, blithe (Word 63), joyful, joyous; positive, upbeat; promising, encouraging, bright, sunny

62. **blight**　　*verb and noun*　　blīt

[Origin unknown]

Definition:

　a.　(*verb*) To check or destroy the growth of.

　　According to the paper, an unexpectedly early frost has **blighted** a sizable part of the Florida citrus crop.

　　High interest rates **blighted** the manufacturer's plans to borrow the capital he needed to modernize his operation.

　b.　(*noun*) Something that impairs growth or causes ruin.

　　A truly nationwide effort is needed if we are going to check the **blight** that is slowly destroying our inner cities.

Phrases:　blighted hopes, urban blight

Synonyms:　(*verbs*) nip, wither, shrivel; blast, ruin, devastate; frustrate, foil, dash; (*nouns*) bane, scourge, plague; eyesore

Antonyms:　(*verbs*) foster, nourish, promote, stimulate; (*nouns*) stimulus, stimulant

Phrases:　dry rot; put a damper on; urban renewal

63. **blithe** *adjective* blīth *or* blĭth

[*blithe* (Old English), "sweet; happy"]

Definition:

a. Merry and carefree.

Anita's **blithe** and sunny disposition is clearly the product of a happy childhood spent amid pleasant surroundings.

b. Overly unconcerned; reckless.

I am deeply disturbed by his **blithe** lack of regard for the rights and feelings of others.

Related Forms: (*noun*) blitheness; (*adverb*) blithely

Synonyms: (*adjectives*) lighthearted, jolly, jocund, jovial, buoyant, sprightly, mirthful, happy-go-lucky; light-minded, heedless, indifferent, nonchalant, blasé

Antonyms: (*adjectives*) morose, saturnine, gloomy, despondent, morbid, melancholy; pensive (Word 295); solemn, dour

64. **bois-ter-ous** *adjective* boi′-stər-əs *or* boi′-strəs

[*boistres* or *boistous* (Middle English), "violent; fierce"]

Definition: Noisy and rowdy.

As the heckling from the audience became more **boisterous**, the speaker found that he had to shout to be heard.

Related Forms: (*noun*) boisterousness; (*adverb*) boisterously

Phrases: boisterous students, boisterous laughter

Synonyms: (*adjectives*) loud, obstreperous, vociferous, clamorous; unruly, disorderly, riotous, uproarious, disruptive, turbulent (Word 380), tempestuous

Antonyms: (*adjectives*) quiet, peaceful, tranquil (Word 377), halcyon; calm, orderly; muted, hushed, muffled, sedate

Halcyon

The adjective *halcyon* (hăl′-sē-ən), meaning "calm and peaceful" or "prosperous," has an interesting history. It comes from the Greek word *halkuon*, meaning "kingfisher" (a kind of sea bird; see drawing). In Greek mythology, the kingfisher was reputed to have the power to calm the wind and the waves while it nested on the sea during the winter solstice (December 22). Accordingly, "halcyon days" are the days of fine weather that occur about that time and, by extension, any period of peace or tranquility.

65. bom-bas-tic   *adjective*   bŏm-băs′-tĭk

[*bombax* (Late Latin), "cotton (often used for padding)," related to *pambuk* (Turkish), "cotton"]

Definition: Pompous or inflated in language.

Lincoln's short, subdued address at Gettysburg is far more moving than Hale's lengthy and **bombastic** oration on the same occasion.

Related Form: (*noun*) bombast

Synonyms: (*adjectives*) grandiloquent, grandiose, hyperbolic, high-sounding, high-flown, highfalutin, extravagant; swollen, bloated, turgid; (*nouns*) fustian, rant, claptrap

Antonyms: (*adjectives*) plain, direct, straightforward; lean, spare; unvarnished, unembellished; artless, unpretentious; terse, succinct; muted

Usage Note:
Bombast indicates overly padded and pretentious language. *Fustian* applies to inflated language that is absurdly out of keeping with its quite ordinary content. *Rant* (also a verb) emphasizes the expression of strong emotions, together with extravagance of language and violence of delivery. *Claptrap* is pretentious, insincere, or empty language designed to attract applause.

66. boor-ish   *adjective*   boŏr′-ĭsh

[*boer* (Dutch), "farmer"]

Definition: Rude or unrefined.

Fortunately, the loud and generally **boorish** behavior of a few of the guests did not spoil the party for the rest of us.

Related Forms: (*nouns*) boor, boorishness

Usage Notes:
a. Do not confuse a *boor* (that is, a rude or unrefined person) with a *bore* (that is, a dull or tedious person). An easy way to keep the two straight is to remember that *bore* is related to *boring* and *boredom*.

b. Also keep *boor* separate from the proper noun *Boer*. You may recall from your study of history that the Boers were South Africans of Dutch descent who engaged in an unsuccessful war with Great Britain from 1899 to 1902. Their descendants are the *Afrikaners* of today.

Synonyms: (*adjectives*) vulgar, uncouth, gauche, crude, crass, churlish, ill-bred, low-bred, ill-mannered, unmannerly; (*nouns*) vulgarian, lout, yahoo

Antonyms: (*adjectives*) urbane (Word 382), suave, polished; tactful, discreet, diplomatic; (*nouns*) savoir-faire, social savvy, finesse (Word 194), "class," style

67. boy-cott   *verb and noun*   boi´-kŏt

[After Charles C. Boycott, a land agent in County Mayo, Ireland, who was subjected to this form of treatment in 1880 for refusing to lower rents on the lands he managed]

Definition:

    a. (*verb*) To refuse to buy, use, or deal with as a way to protest (or force acceptance of) some form of behavior.

       During the civil rights movement of the 1950's and 1960's, both blacks and whites **boycotted** segregated lunch counters, bus depots, schools, and the like.

    b. (*noun*) An instance of such treatment.

       Many forms of nonviolent protest, including sit-ins, picket lines, and **boycotts**, have become common in today's United States.

Synonyms: (*verbs*) ban, proscribe, ostracize (Word 289), blacklist, blackball; (*nouns*) ban, embargo

Antonyms: (*verbs*) patronize, fraternize with, support; endorse, sanction, approve

Charles C. Boycott

In 1873, a retired English army officer, Captain Charles C. Boycott (1832–1897), became the rent collector on the estates of an aristocrat called Lord Erne. These estates were in Country Mayo, Ireland, and the tenants on them were Irish small farmers who paid an annual rent for the use of the land. Unfortunately, Captain Boycott took his job too seriously, and, as a result, a new word, *boycott*, entered the language.

This is what happened. A series of poor harvests in the late 1870's caused widespread suffering among Lord Erne's tenants. Accordingly, in 1880 they asked for a 25% reduction in their rents. To these pleas Captain Boycott turned a deaf ear. As a matter of fact, he attempted to evict some of the tenants for nonpayment of their rent. In reply, the tenants and other people who sympathized with them decided to have nothing whatsoever to do with the captain. He was refused lodgings when he traveled, frequently did not receive his mail, and had to make special arrangements to get food and other necessities. These tactics worked so well that Captain Boycott was forced to give up his job and return to England. He left Ireland late in 1880, and shortly thereafter the verb *boycott*, meaning "refuse to deal with as a means of protest," first appeared in English.

68. brash   *adjective*   brăsh

[Origin unknown, possibly *brisk* + *rash*]

Definition: Overly bold, hasty, and thoughtless.

Nature and experience have a way of turning a **brash** and tactless youngster into a thoughtful and considerate adult.

Related Form: *(noun)* brashness

Phrases: a brash comedian, brash behavior

Synonyms: *(adjectives)* rash, reckless, foolhardy, impetuous, precipitate; impudent, saucy, impertinent, brazen, shameless; tactless, gauche

Antonyms: *(adjectives)* cautious, prudent, circumspect (Word 88), wary; tactful, considerate

69. bra-va-do   *noun*   brə-vä´-dō

[*bravada* (Spanish), "boastfulness," from *bravo* (Spanish), "brave; boastful"]

Definition: A boastful or swaggering show of false bravery; false courage in general.

His challenge to fight was pure **bravado**; inwardly he hoped that no one would take him on.

Synonyms: *(nouns)* braggadocio, swagger, bluster, cockiness, bluff

Antonyms: *(nouns)* fearlessness, intrepidity, gallantry, audacity, bravery, valor, pluck, daring, stoutheartedness, dauntlessness

Phrases: put up a bold front; call someone's bluff; Dutch courage

70. brusque   *adjective*   brŭsk

[*brusque* (French), "fierce; harsh," from *brusco* (Italian), "sharp; sour"]

Definition: Overly short or abrupt.

He is so courteous and affable that I was totally taken aback by his unaccountably **brusque** answer to my question.

Related Form: *(noun)* brusqueness

Phrases: a brusque reply, a brusque tone, a brusque manner

Usage Notes:
 a. *Brusque* is also spelled *brusk*. This applies to *brusqueness* as well.
 b. Do not confuse *brusque (brusk)* with *brisk*, meaning "lively or energetic."

Synonyms: *(adjectives)* curt, blunt, terse; gruff, rough, sharp, harsh; uncivil, impolite

Antonyms: *(adjectives)* civil, polite, cordial, affable (Word 15); voluble, effusive

Using the Words

Exercise I. Syllabication and Pronunciation

Syllabicate the following words correctly, and place the major stress mark (′) after the syllable that is accented when the word is pronounced.

Example: a–bet′

1. boycott
2. bombastic
3. bravado
4. brusque
5. boisterous
6. boorish

Exercise II. Words Out of Context

In each of the following groups, select the item that best expresses the meaning of the numbered word at the left.

1. brusque   a. pompous b. curt c. energetic
   d. obscure e. unwieldy

2. bombastic   a. fearful b. reckless c. mild
   d. sprightly e. inflated

3. boisterous   a. tranquil b. bloated c. dismal
   d. rowdy e. exhausted

4. blight   a. bluster b. merriment c. eyesore
   d. claptrap e. curiosity

5. brash   a. overly sensitive b. overly forward
   c. overly critical d. overly tired
   e. overly stingy

Exercise III. Completing Sentences

Complete each of the following sentences by selecting the most appropriate word from the given group of words. Use the words exactly as they are printed in this list.

bleak	blight	boorish
boycott	bravado	blithe

1. Tanya is usually somewhat solemn and gloomy, but today she's in an uncharacteristically _____ and bubbly frame of mind.

2. Benito Mussolini's speeches were full of the kind of bluster and _____ that one associates with a braggart, a bully, and a coward.

3. I know they think they're being suave and sophisticated, but I consider their conduct downright _____.

4. They are depressing people to be around because their attitude to life is so _____ and cheerless.

5. Since most of the country continued to buy the product to which the small group of protesters objected, the _____ failed.

Exercise IV. Synonyms and Antonyms

Classify each of the following pairs of words as **S** for **synonyms** or **A** for **antonyms**.

1. bleak—rosy
2. lighthearted—blithe
3. boycott—patronize

4. halcyon—tempestuous
5. reckless—brash
6. brusque—civil

Exercise V. Word Roundup

1 Distinguish between the words in each of the following pairs.

    a. brusque—brisk   b. boor—bore

2. Explain the meaning of the *italicized* element in each of the following phrases.

    a. *bleak* prospects
    b. urban *blight*
    c. *boisterous* laughter

    d. *blighted* hopes
    e. a *brash* comedian
    f. a *brusque* reply

3. Define each of the following terms.

    a. bombast
    b. claptrap

    c. rant
    d. fustian

    What do these words have in common?

4. Explain the story behind the phrase *halcyon days*. Then retell the myth of Alcyone and Ceyx, and relate it to the history of the phrase. (If you don't know the myth, look it up in Robert Graves's *The Greek Myths*, Volume One, or *Bulfinch's Mythology*.)

Exercise VI. Framing Sentences

A. Use each of the following words in an original sentence that clearly illustrates its meaning.

1. blight
2. blithe

3. boycott
4. bravado

B. Give a **noun** form of each of the following words, and use it in an original sentence that clearly illustrates its meaning.

1. bleak
2. boisterous
3. bombastic

4. boorish
5. brash
6. brusque

Dissecting the Words

1. The Latin prefix **ambi** means "both" or "around." It occurs in *ambience* and *ambivalent*, studied earlier in this book. Other words using this prefix include:

ambidextrous (literally, "with a right hand on both sides")—able to use both hands equally well

ambient (literally, "going around")—surrounding or encompassing

ambiguous (literally, "going in both directions at once")—unclear or uncertain

ambition (literally, "a going around [to canvass for votes]")—a strong desire to achieve some goal

The corresponding Greek prefix is **amphi**. It occurs in the following English words:

amphitheater—a kind of theater or stadium that has seats going all around the stage or arena

amphibious (literally, "living both lives")—able to live or operate on land *and* in the water

2. The prefix **be**, meaning "thoroughly" or "completely," is of Germanic origin. It appears in many words that have come down to us from Old and Middle English. Today it is used for the following purposes:

a. To give greater force or thoroughness to an action.

be + smirch = *besmirch*—to soil thoroughly

b. To make an intransitive verb (*i.e.*, one that cannot take a direct object) transitive.

be + moan = *bemoan*—to moan and groan about

c. To form a verb or participial adjective from a noun.

be + witch = *bewitch*—to enchant; *bewitching*—enchanting; *bewitched*—enchanted

Samuel Johnson

The eminent 18th-century writer and critic Samuel Johnson (1709–1784) published his two-volume *Dictionary of the English Language* in 1755. It surpassed earlier dictionaries in the precision of its definitions and the wealth of its examples of usage. Though the work had its flaws and revealed much about Johnson's personal prejudices, it soon became a staple item in most private libraries.

The Latin root **vert**, **vers** means "turn." It is found in many English words, including *adverse*, studied earlier in this book. Here are a few other words from this root.

advert—to refer to

animadversion—a strong criticism; a hostile remark

averse—disinclined, reluctant, or opposed to

avert—to turn away from; to prevent. Noun: *aversion*

divers—several

diverse—varied. Another adjective with the same meaning is *diversified*.

invert—to turn over or in on itself. Noun: *inversion*

convert—to transform, exchange, or adopt. A *convert* is a person who adopts (turns to) a new religion or other doctrine. Noun: *conversion*

revert—to turn or go back to. Noun: *reversion*

subvert (literally, "turn from under")—to overthrow; to seek to undermine (as, for example, a government or institution). Adjective: *subversive;* noun: *subversion*

vertigo (literally, "a turning about")—a sensation of dizziness and a feeling that one is about to fall

Exercise

1. Define each of the following words using the prefix *be*, and use the word in a short sentence that clearly illustrates its meaning. Then give the etymology of the word, and explain the function that *be* performs.

a. beseech	f. betroth	k. bereave
b. bespeak	g. beguile	l. befall
c. bedizen	h. berate	m. belittle
d. belie	i. begrudge	n. befriend
e. beleaguer	j. behoove	o. belabor

2. Complete each of the following sentences by supplying a word or phrase which clearly shows that you know the meaning of the underscored root or prefix.

   a. To di<u>vert</u> a person is to _____ his or her mind aside from the business at hand.

   b. A sub<u>vers</u>ive movement is one that seeks to _____ the existing government or social order.

   c. An <u>amphi</u>bious military operation is one that will take place _____.

   d. In an <u>amphi</u>theater the seats go all _____ the stage or arena.

Enriching the Lesson

Exercise I. Eponyms

A good many English words derive from the names of the people who were originally associated with the object, practice, or attitude that the word indicates. Such words are called **eponyms**. A good example of an eponym is *boycott*, studied in this lesson.

Below are listed a number of other useful eponyms. With or without the aid of a dictionary or other reference book, define each, and give the name of the person from whom the word comes. Then choose any **five** items on the list, and for each write a short sentence that clearly illustrates its meaning.

1. bowdlerize	6. maverick	11. silhouette
2. quisling	7. sadistic	12. galvanize
3. shrapnel	8. gerrymander	13. martinet
4. mesmerize	9. chauvinist	14. nicotine
5. lynch	10. sandwich	15. masochistic

Exercise II. Classical Contributions to English

A. *"O Ye Immortal Gods!"*   Surprisingly, the names of a number of Roman (or sometimes Greek) gods live on in present-day English words. Some of these words are listed below in Column A. With or without the aid of a dictionary, match each with its meaning in Column B. Then give the name of the god from which the modern English word derives, and explain how the deity in question is connected with the current meaning of the word.

Column A	*Column B*
1. jovial	a. warlike or military
2. bacchanalian	b. sullen and gloomy
3. mercurial	c. jolly or merry
4. saturnine	d. riotous and drunken
5. martial	e. fickle or changeable

B. *Gifts from the Greeks.*   The geography, history, and mythology of ancient Greece have contributed much to the richness and variety of modern English. Below are listed a few samples of this remarkable heritage. Define the *italicized* item in each of the following phrases, and explain its connection with the ancient Greeks.

1. a *titanic* struggle	6. an *Achilles' heel*
2. a *herculean* task	7. a *spartan* lifestyle
3. a *laconic* reply	8. a *tantalizing* glimpse
4. to run in a *marathon*	9. an *atlas* of the world
5. a *colossal* mistake	10. to deliver a *philippic*

Exercise III. Spanish Borrowings

Present-day English contains a number of words borrowed with little or no change from Spanish. *Bravado*, studied in this lesson, is a good example of such a word. A number of others are listed below. Define each as it is used in English today. Then use it in an original sentence that clearly illustrates its meaning.

1. aficionado
2. bonanza
3. peccadillo
4. macho
5. embargo
6. armada
7. desperado
8. cargo
9. incommunicado

Exercise IV. Short, Sturdy Words

According to an old saying, "the shorter the word, the harder the push." This lesson has presented a number of short, sturdy words with a lot of "push" (e.g., *blight, bleak, blithe*). These items, of course, do not exhaust the list. On the contrary, English abounds in forceful, one-syllable expressions. Many of them have come down to us from Old and Middle English; others are derived from Old Norse, the language of the Vikings.

1. With or without the aid of a thesaurus, list **ten** forceful, one-syllable synonyms for the humble and rather bland word *hit*. Then define each of your choices so as to bring out its distinctive qualities, and use it in an original sentence. (Hint: You might do well to start with *thwack* or *cuff*.)

2. With or without the aid of a dictionary, define the following words that were in use long before Chaucer died in 1400 and are still alive today. Then use each in an original sentence.

   a. goad
   b. bliss
   c. meek
   d. quake
   e. shirk
   f. throng
   g. craft
   h. wail
   i. scrimp
   j. bleat
   k. gloat
   l. rend
   m. grim
   n. skulk
   o. cram

Exercise V. Expanding Your Word Power

The words listed below are not on the Basic Word List, but they were mentioned in passing, in one form or another, in Lesson 7. All of them would make useful additions to your working vocabulary. Define each, give its etymology, list **two** synonyms and **two** antonyms (where possible), and use in a short sentence that clearly illustrates the word's meaning.

1. dour
2. stimulus
3. blasé
4. obstreperous
5. hyperbole
6. turgid
7. sanction
8. impertinent
9. crass
10. jocund
11. efface
12. voluble

Lesson 8

---

71. **bun-gle**   *verb*   bŭn´-gəl
[Origin unknown, perhaps from *bangla* (Swedish), "work poorly"]

Definition: To mismanage or make a mess of.

They **bungled** the job so badly that it took me days to straighten out the mess.

Related Form: (*noun*) bungler

Synonyms: (*verbs*) botch, butcher, mangle, mar, spoil, foul up, bollix up; (*nouns*) butcher, klutz; (*adjectives*) incompetent, inept; clumsy, awkward

Antonyms: (*nouns*) expert, whiz, ace; (*adjectives*) competent, workman-like, skillful, adroit, deft, dexterous

Usage Note:
Some of the items included among the synonyms for *bungle*—for example, *bollix up* and *klutz*—are slang expressions that should be avoided in formal speech and writing. The same is true for the antonyms provided. For example, neither *ace* nor *whiz* would be considered appropriate in formal contexts.

72. **bu-reauc-ra-cy**   *noun*   byŏŏ-rŏk´-rə-sē
[*bureau* (French), "desk; office" + *kratia* (Greek), "rule"]

Definition: A complicated system of administrative agencies and officials; the officials themselves.

"I don't know whether the people being helped by our federally-funded social programs are eating up too much of the taxpayer's money," the Senator remarked. "However, the **bureaucracy** that administers such programs may be."

Related Forms: (*noun*) bureaucrat; (*adjective*) bureaucratic

Usage Note:
Today *bureaucracy, bureaucrat,* and *bureaucratic* are used most frequently of government, especially the federal government, to suggest too much formalism or "red tape." As a result, the terms are almost always pejorative (unless, of course, the context indicates otherwise). Note, too, that all three expressions may properly be used of nongovernmental institutions, since private organizations are run in much the same way as the government. Indeed, *bureaucracy* and its derivatives can justly be applied to any administrative setup that has become overgrown or that insists upon following complex rules and procedures that seem to hinder or stifle quick and effective action.

Charles Dickens

Thomas Carlyle

Red Tape

The term *red tape* is used critically to describe bureaucratic procedures that are considered unnecessarily rigid, complicated, and time consuming. When we say that "something is tied up in red tape," we mean that there are so many regulations, so many papers to be filled out, so many technicalities to observe that it is difficult to get anything done.

The term is said to have been introduced by Charles Dickens and popularized by Thomas Carlyle, the English historian. It originated from the common use of pieces of red tape to tie together bundles of legal papers in English courts and governmental offices.

Today, official papers are more likely to be processed by a computer than tied together by a clerk, but people still complain about the delays and frustrations caused by too much "red tape."

---

73. but-tress   *noun and verb*   bŭt′-rĭs

[*bo(u)terez* (Old French), "thrusting," from *bo(u)ter* (Old French), "strike against, butt"]

Definition:

   a. (*noun*) A support or reinforcement.

      The towering walls of many medieval cathedrals are prevented from falling down by hugh "flying" **buttresses** on the outside of the building.

   b. (*verb*) To support or reinforce.

      The speaker **buttressed** her arguments with a solid presentation of relevant facts and figures.

      At present, Congress is considering a number of measures designed to **buttress** and protect the economy against the ravages of inflation.

Synonyms: (*nouns*) prop, brace; mainstay, cornerstone, pillar; (*verbs*) prop up, brace, bolster, shore up, strengthen

Antonyms: (*verbs*) weaken, impair, undermine

74. ca-jole   *verb*   kə-jōl′ *or* kă-jōl′

[*cajoler* (French), "chatter like a jay in a cage"]

Definition: To persuade or obtain by flattery or deceit.

Like most people, I enjoy flattery, but I can't be **cajoled** into doing something that I know in my heart is foolish.

He's so tight with his money that it's just about impossible to **cajole** a nickel out of him, no matter how worthy the cause.

Related Forms: (*nouns*) cajolery, cajoler

Synonyms: (*verbs*) wheedle, inveigle, coax, beguile, induce, flatter

Antonyms: (*verbs*) dissuade, deter, discourage

Phrases: soft-soap, sweet-talk; curry favor with; apple-polishing

75. cal-lous   *adjective*   kăl′-əs

[*callosus* (Latin), "thick-skinned," from *callus* (Latin), "hard skin"]

Definition: Unfeeling or insensitive.

The sight of children starving slowly and horribly to death brought tears of rage and indignation to the eyes of even the most **callous** and thick-skinned observer among us.

Related Forms: (*noun*) callousness; (*adverb*) callously

Usage Note:
Do not confuse the adjective *callous* with either the noun *callus*, meaning "a hardened or thickened part of the skin" (*e.g.*, "had a callus on his hand"), or the adjective *callow*, meaning "untried or inexperienced" (*e.g.*, "a callow youth").

Synonyms: (*adjectives*) indifferent, unresponsive, unsympathetic; thick-skinned, hardhearted, hardboiled, hardnosed

Antonyms: (*adjectives*) compassionate, tenderhearted, softhearted, kindhearted; thin-skinned, sensitive

76. cal-um-ny   *noun*   kăl′-əm-nē

[*calumnia* (Latin), "trickery; slander"]

Definition: A false statement deliberately made up to injure a person.

"It is one thing to make honest criticisms of my administration and its methods," the President observed. "It is quite another to repeat **calumnies** and slanders that simply have no basis in fact."

Related Forms: (*verb*) calumniate; (*adjective*) calumnious

Synonyms: (*nouns*) lie, falsehood; slander, libel; slur, aspersion

Antonyms: (*nouns*) flattery, adulation

Phrases: do a hatchet job on, hurl brickbats at; mudslinging

77. can-did   *adjective*   kăn´-dĭd

[*candidus* (Latin), "white; pure," from *candere* (Latin), "glisten"]

Definition:

   a.   Fair and impartial.

> "Only a disinterested observer of the accident can give you a **candid** account of what actually happened," the police officer told the reporter.

   b.   Frank or outspoken.

> "Diplomats are supposed to be cautious and tactful," LeVar said. "That's why you can't expect their public statements to be as **candid** and forthright as you might wish."

   c.   Informal or unposed.

> "Why do I always look like the Incredible Hulk in **candid** photos?" my little brother asked plaintively.

Phrases: a candid opinion, a candid interview, a candid critic

Related Forms: (*nouns*) candor, candidness; (*adverb*) candidly

Synonyms: (*adjectives*) objective, disinterested, unbiased, unprejudiced, balanced; forthright, unreserved, straight-from-the-shoulder; spontaneous, impromptu

Antonyms: (*adjectives*) partial, biased, prejudiced; reserved, reticent (Word 341); disingenuous, artful; evasive, equivocal, ambiguous

Candidate

In ancient Rome a man who wished to be elected to public office wore a white robe or toga while canvassing for votes. That way, he could be recognized more easily wherever he went. Since the Latin word for "white" is *candidus*, the would-be official came to be known as a *candidatus*, meaning "one clothed in white." From this we get our English word *candidate*.

78. can-tan-ker-ous   *adjective*   kăn-tăng´-kĕr-əs

[Probably *contekour* (Middle English), "brawler," from *contek* (Norman French), "strife"]

Definition: Foul-tempered and quarrelsome.

"Having to put up with a surly and **cantankerous** boss can sometimes make life pretty miserable," Betty Lou said. "Still, I like working in an office."

"When I was a young man I tried to be as agreeable as possible," dad remarked. "But now that I'm getting on in years, I find that I have become surprisingly **cantankerous**."

Related Forms: (*noun*) cantankerousness; (*adverb*) cantankerously

Usage Note:
Though *cantankerous* is normally used of people who are determined to be nasty or disagreeable (*e.g.*, "the cantankerous leader of the opposition party"), the word may also be applied to animals or things. In that case, it means "irritating or difficult to deal with." Examples of such usage include "a cantankerous washing machine" and "a cantankerous camel."

Synonyms: (*adjectives*) peevish, contrary, cross-grained, irritable, irascible, perverse, choleric, bearish, testy, crabby, grouchy, cranky; intractable, unamenable, ornery; (*nouns*) curmudgeon, grouch

Antonyms: (*adjectives*) good-natured, sweet-tempered, amiable, lovable, affable (Word 15), genial; even-tempered, unexcitable, imperturbable, equable; docile (Word 142), tractable, amenable

79. cap-tious   *adjective*   kăp´-shəs

[*captieux* (French), "hypercritical," from *captio* (Latin), "seizure; deception"]

Definition:
   a.   Quick to find petty faults or raise trifling objections; overly demanding or fussy.

     Though they found a lot to disagree with in my plan, most of their objections were **captious** and niggling.

   b.   Intended to trap, confuse, or show up.

     "A President has to be pretty alert when talking to the press," the aide observed. "After all, a careless answer to a **captious** question could land him in a great deal of political hot water."

Phrase: a captious critic

Related Forms: (*noun*) captiousness; (*adverb*) captiously

Synonyms: (*adjectives*) hypercritical, caviling, carping, censorious; niggling, pettifogging, hairsplitting, picky, picayune, nit-picking; artful, tricky, loaded

Antonyms: (*adjectives*) unexacting, uncritical, undiscriminating; straightforward; laudatory, complimentary

80. **cath-o-lic**   *adjective*   kăth´-ə-lĭk *or* kăth´-lĭk

[*katholikos* (Greek), "general," from *kata* (Greek), "according to + *holos* (Greek), "(the) whole" + *ikos* (Greek), "pertaining to"]

Definition:

a. Broad or widely inclusive.

Painting and sculpture, architecture and engineering, mathematics and music—these were just a few of Leonardo da Vinci's truly **catholic** interests.

b. General or universal; worldwide.

Even though living standards in many parts of the world have noticeably improved since 1900, poverty, hunger, and unemployment are still **catholic** concerns for mankind in the last quarter of the 20th century.

Related Form: (*noun*) catholicity

Usage Note·

Be sure to distinguish carefully between *catholic* (with a *c*) and *Catholic* (with a *C*). The word with the capital letter is a proper adjective that refers to the ancient universal (that is, undivided) Christian church or to its present-day representatives. Frequently, of course, *Catholic* is used as an abbreviation for *Roman Catholic*—that is, in reference to the Church of Rome, its beliefs and practices, or its members.

Synonyms: (*adjectives*) comprehensive, wide, liberal; ecumenical, global

Antonyms: (*adjectives*) narrow, provincial, parochial (Word 293)

Using the Words

Exercise I. Parts of Speech

Indicate the part of speech of each of the following words. In one case, two answers are correct.

1. bungle
2. buttress
3. callous
4. cajole
5. calumny
6. catholic

Exercise II. Words in Phrases

In each of the following, select the item that best expresses the meaning of the *italicized* word in the introductory phrase.

1. an outright *calumny*
   a. trick b. fool c. mistake d. coward e. falsehood

2. a *cantankerous* engine
   a. wasteful b. ornery c. complicated d. expensive
   e. dirty

3. unusually *candid* comments
   a. learned b. tactful c. sour d. frank e. amusing

4. *catholic* tastes in music
   a. broad b. strange c. ordinary d. austere e. narrow

5. tried to *buttress* her position at the office
   a. undermine b. clarify c. strengthen d. eliminate
   e. utilize

Exercise III. Completing Sentences

Complete each of the following sentences or pairs of sentences by selecting the most appropriate word from the given group of words.

callous	captious	bureaucracy
buttress	bungle	cajole

1. If you focus your attention too single-mindedly on trifles, as some overly _____ critics do, you may lose sight of the more important aspects of the thing you are considering.

2. "I'd hoped that my proposal for reducing our overgrown federal _____ would have passed the House by now," the Representative told the press. "Unfortunately, it is still all tied up in Congressional red tape."

3. "If you keep telling your uncle what a superb driver he is," Marv advised me, "you may be able to _____ him into giving you driving lessons in his new car."

4. Anyone who can look at photos from Auschwitz or Buchenwald and not be moved deeply is indeed _____ and insensitive.

5. "Just how am I supposed to get quality work out of a staff that manages to _____ the simplest job?" the production chief asked ruefully.

Exercise IV. Synonyms and Antonyms

A. In each of the following numbered groups, select the **two** words that are most nearly **synonyms**.

1. a. discourage b. butcher c. mangle d. attend e. retain

2. a. bolster b. impair c. pretend d. brace e. convene

3. a. patronize b. magnify c. inveigle d. boycott
   e. wheedle

4. a. mannerism b. libel c. chaos d. slander e. order

5. a. objective b. grisly c. spurious d. lethargic
   e. impartial

Now, for each of the pairs of synonyms that you have selected, supply a word from the Basic Word List for this lesson (Words 71–80) that means the **same** or **almost the same** thing.

B. In each of the following numbered groups, select the **two** words that are most nearly **antonyms**.

1. a. cantankerous b. penniless c. genial d. authentic
   e. workmanlike

2. a. spry b. captious c. illegal d. chipper e. unexacting

3. a. deft b. inept c. academic d. collective e. inimical

4. a. illusory b. atrocious c. catholic d. narrow e. gaudy

5. a. smooth-talking b. glib c. brand-new d. callous
   e. tenderhearted

Exercise V. Word Roundup

1. Two groups of expressions with related meanings are given below. Indicate the items in each that would be classified as *slang* or *overly colloquial*.

A. Ability

a. expert   c. competent   e. klutz
b. inept   d. ace   f. adroit

B. Persuasion

a. coax   c. inveigle   e. wheedle
b. sweet-talk   d. cajole   f. soft-soap

2. Define *callous, callus,* and *callow*. Use each in an original illustrative sentence.

3. What is the difference between *catholic* and *Catholic*? Use each in a sentence that clearly illustrates its meaning.

4. Define *red tape*, and use the phrase in an original sentence.

5. Explain the story behind the word *candidate*. How is the word related to *candid*?

Exercise VI. Framing Sentences

Use each of the following words in an original sentence that clearly illustrates its meaning.

1. bungle   6. calumniate
2. bureaucrat   7. candor
3. buttress   8. cantankerous
4. cajole   9. captious
5. callously   10. catholic

Completing Verbal Analogies

"A Denotes the Lack of B." Another word relationship frequently encountered on standardized vocabulary tests may conveniently be expressed as "*A* denotes the lack of *B*." An example of an analogy question utilizing this word relationship is given below. See if you can figure out the correct answer.

$$A \qquad\qquad B \qquad\qquad C \; \overline{\qquad\qquad\qquad D \qquad\qquad}$$

cowardly : courage = awkward :(*fear, honor, grace, kindness, intelligence*)

The answer, of course, is *grace*. An *awkward* person lacks *grace* (or gracefulness), just as a *cowardly* person lacks *courage*.

Exercise I

Complete the following analogies based on the word relationship "*A* denotes the lack of *B*."

1. **biased : objectivity** = callous : (*ambition, experience, compassion, malice, humor*)

2. **boorish : manners** = blithe : (*skills, morals, funds, friends, cares*)

3. **indigent : money** = lethargic : (*wisdom, energy, talent, family, schooling*)

Exercise II

Write **three** original analogies based on the relationship "*A* denotes the lack of *B*." In your analogies use at least **one** of the basic words studied in Lessons 1–8 (Words 1–80).

Exercise III

The following items review what you have so far learned about analogy questions. Complete each.

1. **affable : cantankerous** = catholic : (*liberal, genial, critical, provincial, abnormal*)

2. **bungle : botch** = defame : (*flatter, slander, ignore, praise, persuade*)

3. **bleak : warmth** = brash : (*caution, frankness, pride, greed, enthusiasm*)

4. **grasping : rapacious** = generous : (*miserly, ardent, liberal, bellicose, grotesque*)

5. **buttress : undermine** = foster : (*sanction, foreshadow, promote, redress, blight*)

Enriching the Lesson

Exercise I. The Language of Government and Politics

The word *bureaucracy*, studied in this lesson, often comes up in discussions of government and politics. A number of other words and phrases connected with the workings of our government or political system are listed below. Define each.

1. checks and balances
2. political machine
3. revenue-sharing
4. civil rights
5. merit system
6. pocket veto
7. favorite son
8. separation of powers
9. lobby *or* interest group
10. reapportionment
11. referendum
12. party platform
13. executive order
14. popular sovereignty
15. regulatory agency
16. due process of law
17. judicial review
18. civil service
19. bipartisan
20. franchise
21. eminent domain
22. senatorial courtesy
23. logrolling
24. conflict of interest
25. filibuster
26. political patronage

Can you think of any others? List and define them.

Exercise II. Gobbledygook

Gobbledygook is the name by which people commonly refer to the inflated, involved, and unnecessarily obscure language that is characteristic of bureaucratic pronouncements. The word was coined by Maury Maverick, chairman of the Smaller War Plants Corporation during World War II. As head of this government agency, Maverick was subjected to a seemingly endless flow of trite, tortured, or pompous language, for which he devised the name *gobbledygook*. Here is an example of the kind of writing (and speaking) that Maverick had in mind. It is taken from an administrative order issued a few years ago by the Federal Food and Drug Administration.

> References in this order to any order shall be construed as referring to that order as amended by any subsequent order, whether made before or after the making of this order, and if any order referred to in this order is replaced by any such subsequent order, the references shall be construed as referring to that subsequent order.

As you know, the purpose of language is to communicate ideas and information clearly and concisely. Needless to say, this sentence and the kind of writing it represents defeat that purpose. To begin with, the sentence is oppressively long (58 words) and involved. This makes it almost impossible for the reader to grasp what is being said without rereading the sentence several times.

113

(A simple way to begin correcting this problem would be to break the sentence in two just before the words *and if.*)

In addition, the phrasing is awkward and unnatural. Notice, for instance, the number of passive constructions, the use of the single word *order* to indicate several different sets of instructions issued at different times, and the presence of clumsy or tortured expressions (*e.g.*, "shall be construed as referring to," "the making of this order," "any such subsequent order"). These items add to the difficulties the reader already faces in trying to make something meaningful out of this muddle.

By now the point of this discussion should be clear to you: Write as clearly, simply, and concisely as you can. Don't let your sentences become unduly long and involved. Don't overload them with highfalutin expressions or bizarre turns of phrase. Use the active voice of the verb rather than the passive. And, finally, try not to string together too many Latinate words, because such expressions tend to "weigh down" a sentence and produce a ponderous effect. As Maury Maverick wrote to his staff in a now-famous memo about writing style: "Say what you're talking about" as clearly and directly as possible.

One final note: Needless to say, gobbledygook is not the exclusive preserve of government. Indeed, anyone who has been in the armed forces, tried to make "sense" out of the fine print in an insurance policy, or had occasion to inspect business documents knows just how pervasive it can be.

1. Read the following statement from an official report issued by one of the administrative departments of the government of New Zealand. The statement concerns the possible use of a certain piece of land for recreational purposes. Then try your hand at rephrasing the statement in comprehensible English.

   It is obvious from the difference in elevation with relation to the short depth of the property that the contour is such as to preclude any reasonable development potential for active recreation.

2. A federal agency that was considering the accuracy of a label used on a certain brand of bottled beer said that the label "*retained a tendency to mislead.*" Rephrase the *italicized* words in intelligible English.

Exercise III. Expanding Your Word Power

The words listed below are not on the Basic Word List, but they were mentioned in passing, in one form or another, in Lesson 8. All of them would make useful additions to your working vocabulary. Define each, give its etymology, list **two** synonyms and **two** antonyms (where possible), and use in a short sentence that clearly illustrates the word's meaning.

1. deft	4. adulation	7. irascible
2. impair	5. impromptu	8. amenable
3. cavil	6. disingenuous	9. curmudgeon

Lesson 9

---

81. **caus-tic**   *adjective*   kôs´-tĭk
[*kaustikos* (Greek), "burnt"]

Definition:

a. Able to dissolve or eat away by chemical action.

Substances with highly **caustic** or corrosive properties are widely used in present-day commercial processes, such as the manufacture of cloth and yarn.

b. Sharp and biting.

Why is it that so many successful theater critics seem to possess sharp tongues and **caustic** wits?

Phrases: a caustic substance, a caustic agent, a caustic reply

Related Forms: (*noun*) causticity; (*adverb*) caustically

Synonyms: (*adjectives*) corrosive; keen, cutting, stinging, tart, pungent, trenchant, mordant, astringent, acidulous, sarcastic, sardonic, acrimonious, venomous; (*nouns*) asperity, acrimony, mordancy, acerbity; sarcasm

Antonyms: (*adjectives*) mild, bland (Word 60), amiable, good-natured, charitable; sweet, sugary, honeyed, saccharine

82. **cen-sor**   *noun and verb*   sĕn´-sər
[*censor* (Latin), from *censere* (Latin), "estimate, assess"]

Definition:

a. (*noun*) An official who examines works of literature, films, and the like for things considered to be immoral, offensive, or dangerous, and who is empowered to prohibit or remove this material; anyone who acts as an arbiter of morals or reading/viewing matter.

"If it were always easy to distinguish art from obscenity," the official remarked, "the job of a **censor** wouldn't be so difficult."

b. (*verb*) To examine for and remove objectionable material.

Many parents believe that prime-time TV programs should be carefully **censored** in order to protect children from accidental exposure to "adult" material.

Related Forms: (*adjectives*) censorial, censorious; (*noun*) censorship

Synonyms: (*nouns*) expurgator, bowdlerizer; comstockery, Grundyism; (*verbs*) expurgate, bowdlerize; excise, delete (Word 120), expunge

115

Anthony Comstock (*left*);
Cato the Censor (*above*)

Censors and Censorship

English has borrowed a good many words and phrases without change from Latin. One such word is *censor*. In ancient Rome there were two magistrates with this title. Their functions included taking the census of citizens (which was necessary for tax purposes), filling vacancies in the Senate (Rome's governing body), and supervising public morals and behavior. One Roman censor, Cato the Elder (234–149 B.C.), became especially well known for his stern and unyielding standards of behavior and for the overly aggressive way in which he sought to impose them on the Roman people.

The word *censor* and the powers connected with the office or the act have passed down to present-day society. Various public officials in the United States possess a limited power of censorship over moving pictures, written materials, TV programs, etc., although the word itself is likely to be avoided. Of course, censorship is limited by the First-Amendment guarantees of freedom of expression.

English has a number of interesting expressions connected with censorship. One of these is *Grundyism*. Grundyism is a rigid insistence upon strict conformity to the accepted moral or social code. The word derives from Mrs. Grundy, an overly proper character in the English playwright Thomas Morton's comedy, *Speed the Plough* (1798).

Another useful expression is *comstockery*, which indicates zealous but narrow-minded (and often unfair) censorship of art, literature, or the like. The word is derived from Anthony Comstock (1844–1915), an American author and an aggressive, if somewhat bigoted, crusader against what he considered immorality.

83. **cen-sure**   *noun and verb*   sĕn´-shər

[*censura* (Latin), "censorship"]

Definition:

a.   (*noun*) Open and strong criticism or disapproval (often taking the shape of a formal reprimand by someone in authority).

Perhaps my actions were hasty and ill-advised, but they certainly did not merit the kind of harsh public **censure** they received.

The 18th-century English satirist Jonathan Swift wrote that "**censure** is the tax a man pays to the public for being eminent."

What do you think Polonius means when he advises his son, Laertes, to "take each man's **censure** but withhold thy judgment"?

b.   (*verb*) To criticize severely; to disapprove strongly.

I am very wary of anyone who is too quick to **censure** and too slow to forgive.

Phrases: a letter of censure, a vote of censure, a resolution of censure

Related Forms: (*noun*) censurer; (*adjective*) censurable

Synonyms: (*nouns*) rebuke, reprimand, reproof; (*verbs*) rebuke, reprimand, reprove, reprehend, condemn, upbraid, chastise; (*adjectives*) reprehensible, blameworthy

Antonyms: (*nouns*) praise, commendation; approval, approbation; (*verbs*) praise, commend, laud, extol, applaud; (*adjectives*) laudable, praiseworthy, meritorious, admirable, creditable

Phrases: (*expressing strong disapproval*) take to task, call on the carpet, dress down, bawl out; (*expressing mild disapproval*) let off with a slap on the wrist; (*expressing approval*) give a pat on the back

84. **cha-grin**   *noun and verb*   shə-grĭn´

[*chagrin* (French), "sadness"]

Definition:

a.   (*noun*) Irritation, embarrassment, or humiliation caused by disappointment or frustration.

"I didn't particularly want to go to the party," Alex admitted. "Still, I felt a deep sense of **chagrin** when I realized that I wouldn't be invited."

b.   (*verb*) To cause such a feeling.

Since Marsha prides herself on her skill as a politician, her failure to win election to the Student Council **chagrined** her deeply.

Synonyms: (*nouns*) vexation, annoyance, mortification; (*verbs*) vex, annoy, mortify, abash

Antonyms: (*nouns*) jubilation, exultation, delight, exhilaration, elation; (*verbs*) exult, delight, exhilarate, elate

85. char-la-tan   *noun*   shär´-lə-tən

[*ciarlatano* (Italian), a variant of *cerretano* (Italian), "an inhabitant of Cerreto," a village near Spoleto in central Italy. The place was famous for its quacks.]

Definition: Anyone who claims to have skills or knowledge that he or she doesn't possess.

> "Don't be too eager to accept the claims of every fad diet that comes along," my physician warned me. "Some of these programs may have been concocted by **charlatans** whose recommendations could do you great harm."

Related Forms: (*nouns*) charlatanism, charlatanry

Synonyms: (*nouns*) impostor, quack, mountebank, humbug, fraud, faker

Two famous charlatans and their modern impersonators: Burt Lancaster as Elmer Gantry and Fernando Corena as Dr. Dulcamara ("Sweet and Sour"), the quack doctor in Gaetano Donizetti's comic opera *The Elixir of Love* (*inset*).

Quacks and Other Charlatans

A *quack* (from *quacksalver*) is a person who makes false claims about the salves and other medications that he or she sells. By extension, the word indicates anyone who makes false or exaggerated claims about his or her medical knowledge, skills, or techniques. A *mountebank* (literally, a person who "climbs on a bench") is a charlatan who uses clownish or flamboyant techniques to sell his or her wares. By extension, the word is applied to any boastful or unscrupulous salesman. A *humbug* is a self-important fraud. An *impostor* is simply someone who assumes another person's identity for the purposes of fraud or deception.

86. **chron-ic**   *adjective*   krŏn´-ĭk

[*chronikos* (Greek), "pertaining to time," from *chronos* (Greek), "time"]

Definition: Continuing over a long period of time or recurring often.

The poor woman suffers terribly from **chronic** arthritis.

His inability to arrive anywhere on time, at first an amusing weakness, has become a **chronic** problem.

For as long as I can remember, our economy has been plagued by **chronic** inflation.

Phrases: chronic insomnia, chronic attacks of asthma, chronic financial problems, chronic unemployment, a chronic complainer

Related Form: (*adverb*) chronically

Usage Note:
When used as a medical term, *chronic* indicates the kind of ailment or disease that develops slowly over a very long period of time and only gradually becomes serious or fatal—for example, heart disease. The opposite is *acute*, which indicates the kind of medical problem that comes on a person suddenly or unexpectedly and takes only a short time to become critical— for example, appendicitis.

Synonyms: (*adjectives*) long-lasting, prolonged, continual, constant; habitual, inveterate, confirmed, deep-rooted, ingrained; perennial, recurrent

Antonyms: (*adjectives*) transitory, transient, evanescent, ephemeral; sporadic, occasional

Phrases: a hardened criminal, a lingering illness, a confirmed bachelor, sporadic fighting

87. **cir-cu-i-tous**   *adjective*   sẽr-kyo͞o´-ĭ-təs

[*circu(m)* (Latin), "around" + *ire, itus* (Latin), "go"]

Definition: Indirect or roundabout; long-winded.

"If I have a little time on my hands after school, I take the long way home," Marta said. "It's a **circuitous** route, but the scenery is just beautiful!"

His style of writing is so **circuitous** and diffuse that I often get lost halfway through one of his paragraphs.

Phrases: circuitous logic or reasoning, circuitous procedures

Related Forms: (*nouns*) circuitousness, circuit

Synonyms: (*adjectives*) winding, meandering, rambling, sinuous, devious, oblique; circumlocutory, periphrastic, digressive

Antonyms: (*adjectives*) direct, undeviating, unswerving, straightforward, unveering

Phrases: veer off at a tangent, sidetrack a discussion, as the crow flies, beat around the bush

88. **cir-cum-spect** *adjective* sûr'-kəm-spĕkt

[*circum* (Latin), "around" + *specere, spectus* (Latin), "look"]

Definition: Cautious or prudent, especially in regard to the consequences of actions or statements; tactful.

Since you don't know most salespeople personally, always be as **circumspect** as possible in your dealings with them.

Phrases: a circumspect investor, circumspect behavior

Related Forms: (*noun*) circumspection; (*adverb*) circumspectly

Synonyms: (*adjectives*) careful, watchful, vigilant, guarded, wary, chary, leery; discreet, politic, diplomatic, judicious

Antonyms: (*adjectives*) careless, imprudent, incautious, heedless; rash, reckless, foolhardy; brash (Word 68), precipitate; indiscreet, tactless

89. **cir-cum-vent** *verb* sûr-kəm-vĕnt'

[*circum* (Latin), "around + *venire, ventus* (Latin), "come"]

Definition: To get around or avoid, especially by trickery or deception.

We planned our route so as to **circumvent** heavily congested urban areas that might slow down our progress.

If people are not in agreement with a given law, they may attempt to ignore or **circumvent** it.

Related Form: (*noun*) circumvention

Synonyms: (*verbs*) by-pass, skirt, evade, sidestep, dodge, duck

Antonyms: (*verbs*) obey, observe, comply with, respect, abide by

90. **clan-des-tine** *adjective* klăn-dĕs'-tĭn

[*clandestinus* (Latin), "secret," from *clam* (Latin), "in secret"]

Definition: Concealed from view so as to hide one's purpose.

Try as they might, federal agents were unable to locate the **clandestine** printing press that had turned out the counterfeit $100 bills.

Related Forms: (*noun*) clandestineness; (*adverb*) clandestinely

Phrases: a clandestine meeting, clandestine broadcasts, clandestine activities

Synonyms: (*adjectives*) surreptitious, covert, furtive, stealthy, under-hand(ed)

Antonyms: (*adjectives*) open, undisguised, overt, manifest, obvious, avowed

Phrases: deep cover, behind closed doors, cloak-and-dagger, an under-cover agent

Using the Words

Exercise I. Syllabication and Pronunciation

Syllabicate the following words correctly, and place the major stress mark (´) after the syllable that is accented when the word is pronounced.

Example: **a-bet´**

1. charlatan
2. circumspect
3. censor
4. chagrin
5. circuitous
6. circumvent

Exercise II. Words Out of Context

In each of the following groups, select the item that best expresses the meaning of the numbered word at the left.

1. charlatan
   a. officer b. immigrant c. fraud
   d. critic

2. clandestine
   a. sharp b. secret c. savage
   d. sensible

3. censure
   a. rebuke b. remove c. relax
   d. restore

4. circuitous
   a. electrical b. collective c. indirect
   d. foolhardy

5. caustic
   a. expensive b. final c. responsible
   d. biting

Exercise III. Completing Sentences

Complete each of the following sentences or pairs of sentences by selecting the appropriate word from the given group of words. Use each word only once.

censor	chagrin	circumvent
charlatan	chronic	circumspect

1. The novelist felt a deep sense of _____ when the book he had worked on so long and hard received unfavorable reviews in the press.

2. "A person never knows where a friendship will lead," mom observed. "That's why it's always best to be as _____ as possible in choosing one's companions."

3. Unemployment is a _____, rather than an occasional, problem for some members of our society.

121

4. I thought we should meet the problem head-on; Tom thought we should try to _____ it.

5. During a war, a government will often _____ all kinds of documents in order to keep sensitive or classified material from falling into the hands of the enemy.

Exercise IV. Synonyms and Antonyms

Classify each of the following pairs of words as **S** for **synonyms** or **A** for **antonyms**.

1. caustic—corrosive
2. bowdlerize—expurgate
3. commend—censure
4. chagrin—delight
5. charlatan—mountebank

6. covert—overt
7. habitual—chronic
8. circuitous—straightforward
9. imprudent—circumspect
10. circumvent—dodge

Exercise V. Word Roundup

1. Explain the difference between a *chronic* illness and an *acute* illness.

2. Give **two** colloquial phrases that mean "censure strongly." Use each in an original sentence.

3. Define each of the following.

    a. a humbug
    b. a quack
    c. a pat on the back
    d. cloak-and-dagger

    e. an undercover agent
    f. as the crow flies
    g. a hardened criminal
    h. a confirmed bachelor

4. What is the source of the term *Grundyism*? the word *comstockery*? What does each of these words mean?

5. Give **three** synonyms for each of the following. Consult a thesaurus if necessary.

    a. praiseworthy

    b. blameworthy

Exercise VI. Framing Sentences

A. Use each of the following in an original sentence.

    1. clandestine
    2. censor
    3. charlatan
    4. chagrin

    5. circuitous
    6. censure
    7. circumvent
    8. caustic

B. Give an **adverb** form of each of the following, and use it in an original sentence.

    1. chronic

    2. circumspect

Dissecting the Words

Prefix

The Latin prefix **circum**, meaning "around" or "about," occurs in a number of English words, including *circuitous, circumspect,* and *circumvent,* all of which were studied in this lesson. Here are some other examples:

circumference (literally "a carrying around")—the boundary of a circle

circumlocution—a roundabout way of saying something. Adjective: *circumlocutory*

circumnavigate—to sail around (for example, the globe)

circumscribe (literally, "to write around")—to encircle; to confine or restrict within limits

circumstance (literally, "a standing around")—a fact or condition that accompanies an event or has some bearing on it. The related adjective *circumstantial* means "relating to the circumstances involved" or, by extension, "incidental, nonessential."

In some English words *circum* loses its *m* and becomes **circu**. Good examples of this include *circuitous* and *circuit.*

Finally, note that *circum* itself comes from the Indo-European root **(s)ker**, which means "bend" or "turn." Words from this root include *circus, circle, circulate, curvature,* and, surprisingly, *search* and *crown.*

Roots

1. The Greek root **chron(o)** means "time." It is found in a small number of English words, including *chronic* and *anachronism.* Here are some other words using this root:

chronology—the arrangement of events in time; a list of events in the order that they happened. Adjective: *chronological*

chronicle—a year-by-year record of historical events; to record events in this way. Noun: *chronicler*

synchronize—to occur at the same time; to cause to coincide in time.

2. English words ending in *-cracy* are derived from the Greek root **kratia** meaning "rule" or "power." One such word is *bureaucracy,* studied in Lesson 8. Here are a few more:

democracy (*demos* [Greek] "people" + *kratia,* "rule")—rule by the people

plutocracy (*ploutos,* [Greek] "wealth" + *kratia,* "rule")—rule by the wealthy class of society. Noun: *plutocrat;* adjective: *plutocratic*

aristocracy (*aristos* [Greek] "best" + *kratia,* "rule")—rule by the upper or privileged classes. Noun: *aristocrat;* adjective: *aristocratic*

theocracy (*theos* [Greek] "god" + *kratia,* "rule")—a government controlled solely by the religious authorities. Adjective: *theocratic*

ochlocracy (*ochlos* [Greek], "mob" + *kratia,* "rule")—mob rule

thalassocracy (*thalassa* [Greek], "sea" + *kratia,* "rule")—domination of the sea; naval supremacy. Noun: *thalassocrat*

Exercise

1. Define the following terms or phrases, and indicate what part the prefix *circum* plays in each.

   a. circumstantial evidence   c. a circuit court
   b. a circuit breaker   d. a circumlocution

2. Two of the books of the Bible are called *Chronicles*. Judging by this name and your knowledge of the meaning of the root *chron(o)*, what do you think these books contain?

3. One of the most common forms of Elizabethan drama is called the *chronicle play*. Judging by this name and your knowledge of the root *chron(o)*, what do you think such a play would be about and how would it be organized?

4. What is a person's *chronological age*? *mental age*?

5. Name an example, past or present, of each of the following forms of government. For instance, *Great Britain* is a good example of a *constitutional monarchy*.

   a. aristocracy   c. autocracy
   b. democracy   d. theocracy

Enriching the Lesson

Exercise I. "Time on My Hands"

With or without the aid of a dictionary, define each of the following expressions involving the word *time*. Then choose any **five** of the items, and for each compose an original sentence that clearly illustrates the expression's meaning.

1. timeserver
2. timely
3. time-honored
4. behind the times
5. time deposit
6. time bomb
7. in good time
8. for the time being
9. time-out
10. timetable
11. make time
12. high time
13. timepiece
14. time clock
15. keep time

Now, using a thesaurus, supply the following information:

16. List and define **five nouns** that relate in one way or another to the concept of time. For instance, you might begin with *duration* or *infinity*.

17. List and define **five verbs** that have to do with time. For example, you might begin with *tarry* or *abide*.

18. List and define **five adjectives** involving the concept of time. For instance, you might begin with *retroactive* or *transient*.

19. List and define **five phrases** connected in some way with the concept of time. For instance, *the ravages of time* or *tide over* might top your list.

Exercise II. Our Latin Heritage

A good number of words commonly used in modern English come with little or no change from Latin. One such word, *censor*, was studied in Lesson 9. Some other words of this kind are listed below. With or without the aid of a dictionary, define each. Then choose any **five**, and for each compose an original sentence.

1. alias
2. quorum
3. propaganda
4. bonus
5. gratis
6. onus
7. affidavit
8. opprobrium
9. consensus
10. alibi
11. animus
12. caveat
13. ultimatum
14. verbatim
15. imprimatur

Can you think of any others? Make a list of them.

Exercise III. Curious Compounds

The way English forms compound words is fascinating. **Compound words** are words that are made up of two (or more) separate words or word elements (e.g., *standoff, takeover, kingless, fearful*). One curious group of compound words is made up of a short, usually monosyllabic verb plus its object, usually a noun, in that order. A good example of this kind of compound is *scarecrow*, which, as you already know, is a dummy set up in a field to *scare* (the verb) off *crows* and other birds (the object) looking for food.

Below are listed a number of other compound words made up of a verb and its object. The first ten items are given out of context; the others are *italicized* in a representative phrase. Define each item, and indicate which part of the word contains the verb and which its object. Then choose any **five**, and for each supply an original sentence that illustrates the word's meaning.

1. scofflaw
2. pickpocket
3. turncoat
4. spendthrift
5. breakwater
6. tattletale
7. scapegrace
8. spoilsport
9. daredevil
10. cutthroat
11. at a *breakneck* pace
12. a *telltale* odor
13. a *makeshift* arrangement
14. a *lackluster* performance
15. a *stopgap* measure

Exercise IV. Expanding Your Word Power

The words listed below are not on the Basic Word List, but they were mentioned in passing in Lesson 9. All of them would make useful additions to your working vocabulary. Define each, give its etymology, list **two** synonyms and **two** antonyms (where possible), and use in a short sentence that clearly illustrates the word's meaning.

1. sarcasm
2. saccharine
3. sporadic
4. abash
5. manifest
6. inveterate
7. ephemeral
8. oblique
9. periphrastic
10. diplomatic
11. approbation
12. trenchant

125

Lesson 10

91. coerce — 100. conjecture

---

91. co-erce   *verb*   kō-ûrs′

[*co*, a form of *cum* (Latin), "together" + *arcere* (Latin), "confine"]

Definition: To force someone to do something against his or her will by using undue pressure, threats, intimidation, or physical violence.

> There are far more subtle ways of **coercing** a person into doing what you want than twisting his or her arm.

> "Though my parents frequently advise me about how to act in a particular situation," Rhoda said, "they never try to **coerce** me into doing what they think best."

> When he realized that he couldn't attain his objectives by flattery or persuasion, he resorted to **coercion**.

Related Forms: (*nouns*) coercion, coerciveness; (*adjectives*) coercive, coercible; (*adverb*) coercively

Synonyms: (*verbs*) constrain, compel, pressure, bulldoze, dragoon; hector, browbeat, cow

Phrases: strong-arm tactics; high-pressure someone, bring pressure to bear, railroad someone into; under duress

---

92. co-gent   *adjective*   kō′-jĕnt

[*cogens, cogentis* (Latin), "driving together"; from *co*, a form of *cum* (Latin), "together" + *agere* (Latin), "drive; force"]

Definition: Forceful and convincing; to the point.

> "The objections that Gloria raised to my plan were not only **cogent**," Frank admitted candidly, "they were totally unanswerable!"

> One of the articles in yesterday's paper had some **cogent** and perceptive things to say about our troubled economy.

Phrases: a cogent argument; a cogent criticism, a cogent account, a cogent description, a cogent analysis, at her most cogent and compelling

Related Forms: (*noun*) cogency; (*adverb*) cogently

Synonyms: (*adjectives*) powerful, potent, effective, telling; persuasive, compelling; valid, sound; relevant, pertinent, apposite, germane, apropos

Antonyms: (*adjectives*) weak, ineffective, unconvincing, frivolous, inane; invalid, untenable; irrelevant

93. co-here   *verb*   kō-hēr′

[*co*, a form of *cum* (Latin), "together" + *haerere* (Latin), "stick, cling"]

Definition: To hold or stick together; to fit together into an orderly, logical, and unified whole.

> Add just enough water to the mixture of sand and cement to produce a gritty substance that **coheres** like oatmeal.

> If all the elements in your essay don't **cohere** properly, you won't achieve a single overall effect.

Related Forms: (*nouns*) coherence, coherency, cohesion, cohesiveness; (*adjectives*) coherent, cohesive

Usage Note:

In spoken and written English, *coherence* is the principle that requires the parts of a sentence or a longer composition to be so worded and arranged that they "stick together" in an orderly, logical relationship. Errors that usually produce incoherence, especially in student writing, include "dangling" or misplaced modifiers, faulty pronoun reference, lack of an overall focus, puzzling shifts in thought, the inclusion of irrelevant details, the illogical arrangement of facts or events, and the omission of essential information.

Synonyms: (*verbs*) coalesce, combine, gel

Antonyms: (*verbs*) separate, fall apart, come apart, come asunder; diverge, disperse, dissipate, diffuse, scatter; (*noun*) incoherence; (*adjectives*) incoherent, disjointed

94. col-lab-o-rate   *verb*   kə-lăb′-ə-rāt

[*col*, a form of *cum* (Latin), "together" + *laborare, laboratus* (Latin), "work"]

Definition:

a. To work together on some kind of joint project. (In this sense the tone of the word is neutral.)

> Though Shakespeare usually worked by himself, other Elizabethan dramatists frequently **collaborated** on plays.

b. To cooperate with the enemy in some kind of treasonable activity. (In this sense the tone of the word is definitely pejorative.)

> "Make no mistake," the leader of the resistance movement declared. "A frightful punishment awaits any citizen who willingly **collaborates** with the foreign power that has occupied our country."

Related Forms: (*nouns*) collaboration, collaborator

Synonyms: (*verbs*) cooperate, team up, join forces, pool one's efforts; intrigue, collude, conspire; (*nouns*) partner, colleague, coworker; quisling, fifth-columnist, fellow traveler; partnership, team effort, joint effort

Antonyms: (*verbs*) work by oneself; dissociate oneself from, part company with, take leave of

Phrase: in cahoots with

In the 1930's Vidkun Quisling (1887–1945) was a respected Norwegian serving in various political and diplomatic posts. By 1945, however, he had become Norway's most notorious traitor, and his surname had supplied English with a new word for *turncoat* or *traitor*.

Trained at Norway's only military academy, Quisling became a major in the Norwegian army. After that, he served as an official at the League of Nations and was responsible for the handling of refugees fleeing Stalin's Russia.

While acting as Norway's Minister of Defense from 1931 to 1933, Quisling developed a great admiration for the Germans. When World War II broke out, Quisling helped the German military plan the invasion of his native land, and when the Nazis arrived, he used his influence to hasten Norway's collapse. Somewhat later, the Nazis appointed Quisling Premier of Norway, a position he held until the war ended. In May 1945, Quisling was arrested, tried, and executed for high treason. It was from Quisling's part in the betrayal of Norway that his name has come to be synonymous with treachery.

---

95. com-pat-i-ble   *adjective*   kəm-păt′-ə-bəl

[*com*, a form of *cum* (Latin), "together" + *pati* (Latin), "feel; endure" + *abilis* (Latin), "able to"]

Definition:
a. Capable of use with some other brand or model.

A cassette made for a Betamax video recorder won't work on VHS equipment because the two recording systems aren't **compatible**.

b. Capable of living or getting along together.

I'm surprised that those two people work so well together because their personalities don't seem at all **compatible**.

Related Forms: (*nouns*) compatibility, compatibleness; (*adverb*) compatibly

Synonyms: (*adjectives*) harmonious, agreeable, like-minded; consistent, congruous; parallel

Antonyms: (*adjectives*) incompatible, antagonistic; inconsistent, incongruous

Phrases: in sync, in keeping with, in line with

96. com-pla-cent   *adjective*   kəm-plā´-sĕnt

[*com*, a form of *cum* (Latin), "with; very" + *placens, placentis,* from *placere* (Latin), "please, be satisfied"]

Definition: Overly self-satisfied; smug.

"If you had achieved as much this year as he has," I replied, "you'd be a little **complacent**, too!"

Related Forms: (*nouns*) complacence, complacency; (*adverb*) complacently

Phrases: a complacent attitude, a complacent look

Usage Note:
Do not confuse the adjective *complacent*, meaning "self-satisfied," with the related adjective *complaisant*, meaning "eager to please" or "cheerfully obliging."

Synonyms: (*adjectives*) content(ed), self-content(ed), pleased with oneself

Antonyms: (*adjectives*) dissatisfied, discontent(ed), malcontent, displeased with oneself

Phrase: to rest on one's laurels

97. con-cise   *adjective*   kən-sīs´

[*concidere, concisus* (Latin), "cut up"; from *con*, a form of *cum* (Latin), "very" + *caedere, caesus* (Latin), "cut"]

Definition: Saying a lot in a few words.

Since there is a charge for every word you use in a telegram, always make your message as **concise** as possible.

Phrases: a concise account, a concise statement

Related Forms: (*nouns*) conciseness, concision; (*adverb*) concisely

Synonyms: (*adjectives*) brief, compact, succinct, terse; laconic, summary; pithy

Antonyms: (*adjectives*) wordy, prolix, verbose, garrulous, loquacious, long-winded

98. con-done   *verb*   kən-dōn´

[*condonare* (Latin), "forgive"; from *con*, a form of *cum* (Latin), "completely" + *donare* (Latin), "give away"]

Definition: To overlook or disregard an offense, thereby implying forgiveness, acceptance, or possibly approval of it.

"I'm perfectly willing to wink at a harmless practical joke," mom remarked, "but I refuse to **condone** outright vandalism."

Today it is considered permissible for children to behave in ways that earlier generations of parents would not have **condoned**.

Related Forms: (*nouns*) condonation, condoner

Synonyms: (*verbs*) ignore, close one's eyes to, turn a blind eye to; accept, countenance, stomach, put up with, tolerate

Antonyms: (*verbs*) condemn, denounce, disapprove, deprecate, castigate, decry, revile

99. con-fron-ta-tion   *noun*   kŏn-frən-tāˊ-shən

[*confrontare, confrontatus* (Latin), "have a common border"; from *con*, a form of *cum* (Latin), "together" + *frons, frontis* (Latin), "forehead"]

Definition: A face-to-face encounter, usually (but not always) suggesting a hostile or defiant attitude.

> "Our two countries must make every effort to settle our differences peacefully," the ambassador said. "An all-out **confrontation** might ruin us both."

Related Form: (*verb*) confront

Synonyms: (*nouns*) showdown, face-off, shoot-out

Phrases: stand up to, square off against, throw down the gauntlet, take up the gauntlet, on the brink

Drawing by Lorenz: © 1975, The New Yorker Magazine, Inc.

"Mea Culpa, I'd like you to meet J'Accuse."

Brinkmanship

Brinkmanship (brink + man + ship) is a term sometimes used today in connection with crucial international disputes. The word denotes a political or military maneuver in which a country pushes a dangerous situation to the *brink* or extreme limit of safety before withdrawing. The purpose of creating such a crisis is to give the impression that the country has made a life-or-death decision, and that it is prepared to go "beyond the brink" to all-out war rather than make any concession. The coinage of words like *brinkmanship* illustrates the degree to which new words are invented to fill a language need.

130

100. **con-jec-ture**   *noun and verb*   kən-jĕk´-chər

[*conjectura* (Latin), "conclusion"; from *con*, a form of *cum* (Latin), "together" + *jacere, jactus* (Latin), "throw"]

Definition:

   a.   (*noun*) A conclusion based on inadequate evidence; a guess.

   Since the coroner's findings were inconclusive, the exact cause of the child's death remains for the present a matter of **conjecture**.

   b.   (*verb*) To conclude from inadequate evidence; to guess.

   "I haven't enough hard evidence at hand to say for sure," the detective declared. "I can only **conjecture**, based on past experience, that this was an inside job."

Related Forms: (*adjective*) conjectural

Synonyms: (*nouns*) surmise, supposition, presumption, suspicion, inference; speculation, theory; (*verbs*) surmise, suppose, presume, suspect, infer; speculate, theorize

Antonyms: (*nouns*) fact, certainty; (*verbs*) demonstrate, substantiate

Phrases: an educated guess, a shot in the dark, a ballpark estimate

Using the Words

Exercise I.   Parts of Speech

Indicate the part of speech of each of the following words. In one case, two answers are correct.

1. confrontation
2. compatible
3. conjecture
4. coerce
5. cogent
6. complacent

Exercise II.   Words in Phrases

In each of the following groups, select the item that best expresses the meaning of the *italicized* word in the introductory phrase.

1. a particularly *cogent* argument
    a. forceful   b. bizarre   c. elaborate   d. weak   e. silly

2. *compatible* interests
    a. unusual   b. conflicting   c. deep   d. parallel   e. scholarly

3. *condone* wrongdoing
    a. point at   b. flinch at   c. aim at   d. rail at   e. wink at

4. find someone with whom to *collaborate*
    a. chat   b. team up   c. disagree   d. sit down   e. sympathize

5. an interesting *conjecture*
    a. fact   b. situation   c. guess   d. development   e. history

Exercise III. Completing Sentences

Complete each of the following sentences or pairs of sentences by selecting the most appropriate word from the given group of words.

concise   confrontation   cohere
coerce   conjecture   complacent

1. Though it omitted many details, her spare and _____ account of the accident left us in no doubt as to exactly what had happened.

2. Some chemical compounds _____ readily; others are highly unstable and separate easily.

3. "I don't understand why you are walking around with that _____ grin on your face," I exclaimed. "Exactly what have you done to make you so pleased with yourself?"

4. The bitter rivals for public office met in a dramatic _____ on TV to debate the issues of the campaign.

5. "No, dummy!" I exclaimed. "If you're trying to _____ *me* into doing something *I* don't want to do, you hold the gun to *my* head, not to your own!"

Exercise IV. Synonyms and Antonyms

A. In each of the following numbered groups, select the **two** words that are most nearly **synonyms**.

1. a. gel b. rebuke c. separate d. coalesce
2. a. disregard b. overlook c. redress d. compel
3. a. circumvent b. blight c. pressure d. bulldoze
4. a. put-on b. showdown c. time-out d. shoot-out
5. a. terse b. succinct c. frivolous d. incongruous

Now, for each of the pairs of synonyms you have selected, supply a word from the Basic Word List for this lesson (Words 91–100) that means **the same** or **almost the same** thing.

B. In each of the following numbered groups, select the **two** words that are most nearly **antonyms**.

1. a. cogent b. agreeable c. unique d. frivolous
2. a. campaign b. conjecture c. certainty d. chagrin
3. a. awry b. faulty c. discontent d. complacent
4. a. collaborate b. border c. dissociate d. recognize
5. a. joyful b. compatible c. frequent d. antagonistic

Exercise V.   Word Roundup

1. With or without the aid of a dictionary, define or explain each of the following expressions.

    a. strong-arm tactics
    b. fifth-columnist
    c. in cahoots with
    d. in sync
    e. rest on one's laurels
    f. throw down the gauntlet
    g. brinkmanship
    h. a shot in the dark
    i. an educated guess
    j. turn a blind eye to

2. Explain what principle of good writing (and speaking) is indicated by the term *coherence*. What are some of the characteristics of *incoherent* writing?

3. Explain the difference between *complacent* and *complaisant*. Use each in a sentence that clearly illustrates the word's meaning.

Exercise VI.   Framing Sentences

A. Use each of the following words in an original illustrative sentence.

    1. conjecture
    2. cogent
    3. collaborate
    4. compatible
    5. confrontation
    6. condone

B. Give an **adjective** form of each of the following, and use it in an original illustrative sentence.

    1. cohere
    2. conjecture
    3. coerce

C. Give an **adverb** form of each of these words, and use it in an original illustrative sentence.

    1. cogent
    2. complacent
    3. concise

Henry W. Fowler

Henry W. Fowler (1858–1933) was an English philologist and lexicographer who was educated at Rugby and Oxford. He taught at a school in Scotland for some years, then moved on to London, where he worked as a free-lance journalist. Together with his younger brother Francis, he wrote a guide to correct English called *The King's English* (1906) and *The Oxford Concise Dictionary* (1911). His most outstanding work, however, was *A Dictionary of Modern English Usage*.

In the courtyard of the Bodleian Library at Oxford, where Fowler did some of his research.

Completing Verbal Analogies

"A Indicates the State of Being B."   Another important word relationship that turns up on standardized vocabulary tests may conveniently be expressed as "*A* indicates the state of being *B*." An example of an analogy question involving this word relationship is given below. See if you can figure out the correct answer before you read the explanation of it given below.

A   B   C   D

chagrin : mortified = candor : *(careless, vexed, frank, reserved, hungry)*

The answer, of course, is *frank*. *Candor* indicates the state of being *frank* or open about one's knowledge, thoughts, or feelings, just as *chagrin* indicates the state of being *mortified* or humiliated by some kind of disappointment or frustration.

Note that, as usual, the wrong choices offered under *D* include some traps for the unwary. For example, *vexed*, which is something of a synonym of *mortified*, indicates how a person feels when overcome with *chagrin*, but it has nothing to do with *candor*. Similarly, *reserved* indicates a trait that is the opposite of the one suggested by *candor*.

Exercise I

Complete the following analogies based on the word relationship "*A* indicates the state of being *B*."

1. **complacence : smug** = vigilance : *(sweet, quarrelsome, generous, watchful, jolly)*

2. **conciseness : brief** = cogency : *(terse, forceful, elaborate, bizarre, childish)*

3. **prudence : careful** = apathy : *(indecisive, indignant, indigent, indiscreet, indifferent)*

Exercise II

Write **three** original analogies based on the relationship "*A* indicates the state of being *B*." In your analogies use at least **two** of the basic words studied in Lessons 1–10 (Words 1–100).

Exercise III

The following items review what you have so far learned about analogy questions. Complete each.

1. **anarchy : order** = apathy : *(influence, ignorance, income, interest, intelligence)*

2. **callous : compassionate** = caustic : *(forthright, bland, callow, myopic, pungent)*

3. **clandestine : openness** = compatible : *(conflict, direction, sympathy, meaning, unity)*

4. **coerce : constrain** = cohere : *(circumvent, censure, compel, commend, coalesce)*

5. **affluence : rich** = captiousness : *(hypercritical, hyperbolic, hyperactive, hypothetical, hypocritical)*

Enriching the Lesson

Exercise I. Look-Alikes

English has a great many duos or even trios of words that look alike but mean quite different things. Some of these items are paired off below. With or without the aid of a dictionary, explain the difference in meaning between the members of each pair.

1.	abrogate—arrogate	11.	affect—effect
2.	human—humane	12.	flaunt—flout
3.	resound—redound	13.	fallible—fallacious
4.	envious—enviable	14.	noisy—noisome
5.	official—officious	15.	founder—flounder
6.	laudable—laudatory	16.	ceremonious—ceremonial
7.	judicial—judicious	17.	fortunate—fortuitous
8.	ferment—foment	18.	contemptible—contemptuous
9.	ingenious—ingenuous	19.	progeny—prodigy
10.	martial—marital	20.	depredation—deprivation

Now, choose any **five** of the pairs of words listed above. For each, compose a set of **two** sentences, each of which illustrates the meaning and use of **one** of the words in the pair.

Exercise II. By the Sweat of Your Brow

Some terms and expressions used in connection with working in general and labor-management relations are listed below. With or without the aid of a dictionary or other reference book, define each.

1.	labor force	11.	seniority
2.	skilled worker	12.	real wage
3.	unskilled worker	13.	minimum wage
4.	blue-collar worker	14.	cost-of-living increase
5.	white-collar worker	15.	craft union
6.	journeyman	16.	industrial union
7.	apprentice	17.	right-to-work laws
8.	injunction	18.	automation
9.	collective bargaining	19.	featherbedding
10.	equal employment opportunity	20.	productivity

Exercise III.   Ships That Have Never Seen the Sea

Below you will find a group of "ship" words. Some of these words are familiar or traditional, while others form a newly launched "squadron." With or without the aid of a dictionary, define each. Then illustrate its meaning by using it in an original sentence or by telling an anecdote that conveys its basic idea.

1. statesmanship
2. gamesmanship
3. horsemanship
4. wordsmanship
5. sportsmanship
6. one-upmanship
7. leadership
8. lifemanship
9. guardianship

Exercise IV.   A Verbal Diversion

A.   *Doublets*   A good many common English phrases are made up of two elements connected by the word *and* or the word *or* (or sometimes a preposition). Such phrases are often called **doublets**. A good example of a doublet is *aid and abet*, mentioned in Lesson 1. Below are listed a number of other doublets. Define each.

1. flotsam and jetsam
2. null and void
3. sackcloth and ashes
4. kith and kin
5. rank and file
6. spick and span
7. by hook or crook
8. raise a hue and cry
9. cut and dried
10. in dribs and drabs

B.   *Triplets*   There is also a small group of common phrases made up of three elements. Such phrases are sometimes called **triplets**. A good example of a triplet is the phrase *ready, willing, and able*.

Below you are given the first two elements of a number of other common triplets. Supply the missing third element. Also, define any of these phrases that is not immediately intelligible to you.

1. lock, stock, and _____
2. hook, line, and _____
3. bell, book, and _____
4. healthy, wealthy, and _____
5. tall, dark, and _____
6. any Tom, Dick, or _____
7. signed, sealed, and _____
8. beg, borrow, or _____
9. rag, tag, and _____
10. blood, sweat, and _____

Exercise V.   Expanding Your Word Power

The words listed below are not on the Basic Word List, but they were mentioned in passing in Lesson 10. All of them would make useful additions to your vocabulary. Define each, give its etymology, list **two** synonyms and **two** antonyms (where possible), and use in a short illustrative sentence.

1. potent
2. relevant
3. inane
4. valid
5. incongruous
6. diffuse
7. intrigue
8. malcontent
9. substantiate

Review

1. abdicate — 100. **conjecture**

Exercise I. Syllabication and Pronunciation

Syllabicate the following words correctly, and place the major
stress mark (') after the syllable that is accented when the word is
pronounced. Two answers are correct in some instances.

1. acclimate
2. augur
3. banal
4. bombastic
5. chagrin
6. coerce

Exercise II. Parts of Speech

Indicate the part of speech of each of the following words. In some
cases, two answers arc correct.

1. advocate
2. atrophy
3. bicker
4. brash
5. censure
6. conjecture

Exercise III. Words Out of Context

In each of the following groups, select the lettered item that best
expresses the meaning of the numbered word at the left.

1. abdicate
   a. serve b. retain c. delete d. beg
   e. resign

2. appall
   a. propose b. determine c. horrify
   d. cover e. attract

3. anarchy
   a. chaos b. hostility c. support
   d. ignorance e. effort

4. boisterous
   a. greedy b. cowardly c. ugly d. noisy
   e. lazy

5. bleak
   a. mindless b. fearless c. aimless
   d. timeless e. cheerless

6. baffle
   a. nurture b. puzzle c. aid d. relish
   e. conclude

7. captious
   a. favorable b. destitute c. hypercritical
   d. collective e. clumsy

8. clandestine
   a. opulent b. sarcastic c. furtive
   d. vigilant e. laudable

9. caustic   a. cutting   b. frivolous   c. occasional
                    d. indirect   e. lofty

10. cogent   a. loathsome   b. innocent   c. theoretical
                   d. compelling   e. endless

Exercise IV. Words in Phrases

In each of the following groups, select the lettered item that best expresses the meaning of the *italicized* word in the introductory phrase.

1. *adjourned* the meeting
   a. suggested   b. suspended   c. convened   d. arranged
   e. attended

2. *chronic* financial problems
   a. occasional   b. unexpected   c. severe   d. recurrent
   e. temporary

3. *badger* a witness
   a. call   b. find   c. harass   d. question   e. excuse

4. a *brusque* reply
   a. curt   b. puzzling   c. detailed   d. timely   e. written

5. a *complacent* attitude
   a. nasty   b. foolish   c. hostile   d. dangerous   e. smug

Exercise V. Completing Sentences

Complete each of the following sentences by selecting the most appropriate word from the given group of words. Use each word only once. Make any adjustments that are necessary to fit the words into the sentences properly.

asylum	boycott	concise
collaborate	affluent	bungle

1. Though I can occasionally afford some of life's more expensive luxuries, I'd hardly describe myself as _____.

2. "Usually I don't make a mess of things," I thought in dismay as I looked at the burned muffins, "but this time I've really _____ the job."

3. Traditionally, refugees from all sorts of oppression have sought _____ in the United States.

4. Since there isn't much space to write on a postcard, you must make your messages as _____ as possible.

5. When two famous dramatists _____ on the script for a new play, the result is likely to be extraordinary.

Exercise VI. Synonyms and Antonyms

Classify each of the following pairs of words as **S** for **synonyms** or **A** for **antonyms**.

1. hostile—belligerent
2. abhor—relish
3. augment—reduce
4. amnesty—pardon
5. bland—piquant
6. estrange—alienate
7. circuitous—roundabout
8. reckless—circumspect
9. affable—surly
10. deter—abet

Exercise VII. Framing Sentences

Use each of the following words in a short illustrative sentence of your own devising.

1. addiction
2. agile
3. boycott
4. buttress
5. cantankerous
6. charlatan

Exercise VIII. Related Forms

A. Give a **noun** form of each of the following words.

1. abstain
2. allege
3. cajole

B. Give a **verb** form of each of the following words.

1. authentic
2. confrontation
3. calumny

C. Give an **adjective** form of each of the following words.

1. apathy
2. bureaucracy
3. avarice

Exercise IX. Word Roundup

1. Explain the difference between the words in each of the following pairs.

   a. loathe—loath
   b. averse—adverse
   c. aesthetic—ascetic
   d. callow—callous
   e. allusion—illusion
   f. forbear—forebear

2. Explain what each of the following means.

   a. academic freedom
   b. halcyon days
   c. red tape
   d. live high off the hog

3. Explain the story behind each of the following expressions.

   a. Grundyism
   b. candidate

4. What principle of good writing and speaking is indicated by the term *coherence*? What are some of the characteristics of *incoherent* writing?

5. Give the singular form of the word *agenda*. Explain the fact that *agenda* itself may be used as a singular form.

Exercise X. Etymology

1. Give **three** English words that derive from the Latin root *ced* or *ceed*. What does this root mean?

2. What does the Greek prefix *a* or *an* mean? For each of the following definitions, supply an English word beginning with this prefix.

   a. shapeless or formless   b. of unknown authorship

3. How does the prefix *ad* change when it is added to a root beginning with a consonant? What is the technical name for this phenomenon?

4. Convert each of the following nouns or adjectives to a verb by adding the suffix *ize*. Make any spelling changes that are necessary. Then define the verb you have created.

   a. social   b. proselyte   c. maximum

5. Define each of the following words using the Germanic prefix *be*, and explain what function the prefix performs.

   a. bemoan   b. bewitch   c. besmirch

Lesson 11

---

101. **con·nois·seur**   *noun*   kŏn-ə-sûr´

[*connoisseur* (obsolete French), "expert"; from *connoistre* (Old French), "know"; from *co*, a form of *cum* (Latin), "thoroughly" + *(g)noscere* (Latin), "know"]

Definition: Someone with informed and discriminating judgment, especially in matters of art, literature, or taste.

> Though the exhibition was by no means a popular success, it caused a sensation among **connoisseurs** and scholars.

> I don't know anything about quiches or souffles, but I'm a true **connoisseur** when it comes to pizza.

Synonyms: (*nouns*) expert, authority, specialist, pundit, savant, maven, devotee; judge, critic, arbiter; (*plural noun*) cognoscenti

Antonyms: (*nouns*) beginner, novice, neophyte, greenhorn, tenderfoot, tyro; amateur, dilettante

Usage Note:
Amateur and *dilettante* both refer to someone who studies or practices an art for his or her own amusement. *Dilettante* also suggests the idea of dabbling or not being very serious about the pursuit. A *connoisseur*, on the other hand, has sufficient knowledge or expertise to serve as a competent judge or critic.

102. **con·sen·sus**   *noun*   kən-sĕn´-səs

[*consensus* (Latin), "general agreement"; from *con*, a form of *cum* (Latin), "together" + *sentire, sensus* (Latin), "feel"]

Definition: Collective uniformity of opinion; general agreement in feeling or belief.

> Though everyone in our club agreed that we had a problem, there was no group **consensus** on how to solve it.

Usage Note:
Adding the phrase "of opinion" to *consensus* is frowned upon by most authorities because the idea that these words express is already included in the meaning of *consensus*.

Synonyms: (*nouns*) unanimity, like-mindedness, concord, harmony, accord, unity, concurrence

Antonyms: (*nouns*) discord, disagreement, disunity, disharmony, dissent, conflict, diversity, dissidence

Phrases: in accord with, in unison, of the same mind

103. con-strue   *verb*   kən-strōō´

[*con*, a form of *cum* (Latin), "together" + *struere* (Latin), "heap up"]

Definition: To analyze, explain, interpret, or understand.

As you have already learned, the word *agenda* may be **construed** as either singular or plural.

"Am I to **construe** your silence as an admission of guilt?" dad asked.

Related Forms: (*verb*) misconstrue; (*adjective*) construable; (*nouns*) construction, misconstruction

Synonyms: (*verbs*) deduce, infer, translate, gather, take to mean

Antonyms: (*verbs*) misinterpret, misunderstand

104. con-sum-mate   *adjective:* kən-sŭm´-ĭt   *verb:* kŏn´-sə-māt

[*con*, a form of *cum* (Latin), "together" + *summare, summatus* (Latin), "add up"]

Definition:
   a. (*adjective*) Complete or perfect in the highest degree.

     The soprano may lack the **consummate** artistry of a great singing actress like Callas or Sills, but she is still a remarkable performer.

   b. (*verb*) To bring to completion or perfection.

     Though there are still a few minor details to iron out, we expect to **consummate** the deal sometime this week.

Related Forms: (*noun*) consummation; (*adverb*) consummately

Synonyms: (*adjectives*) superlative, supreme; transcendent, surpassing, matchless; finished, total; masterful, virtuoso; (*verbs*) clinch, conclude

Antonyms: (*adjectives*) mediocre, indifferent, run-of-the-mill, ordinary; inept, incompetent, inadequate; (*verbs*) begin, start, initiate, launch

105. co-pi-ous   *adjective*   kō´-pē-əs

[*copiosus* (Latin), "plentiful," from *copia* (Latin), "plenty"]

Definition: Large in number or quantity; full.

In no time at all, the guests reduced the **copious** supply of edibles to a mere memory.

A long epic poem like Dante's *Divine Comedy* is equally the product of a **copious** mind and a fertile imagination.

Related Forms: (*nouns*) copiousness, copiosity; (*adverb*) copiously

Synonyms: (*adjectives*) abundant, plentiful, ample, bountiful, bounteous, profuse, lavish, numerous; extensive, comprehensive

Antonyms: (*adjectives*) meager, scanty, scarce, sparse; inadequate, insufficient; empty, vacant, vacuous, barren

Cornucopia

A Greek myth tells how Zeus, having been nursed in infancy by the nymph-goat Almathea, showed his gratitude by a gift of a miraculous horn. This horn, or *cornucopia* (Latin, *cornu*, "horn" + *copiae*, "of plenty") furnished the possessor with an inexhaustible supply of food and other good things. A horn overflowing with fruits and ears of grain has come to be used as an emblem of plenty in the decorative arts, as well as a general symbol of abundance and prosperity.

106. cor-pu-lent   *adjective*   kôr´-pyə-lĕnt

[*corpulentus* (Latin), "fat," from *corpus* (Latin), "body"]

Definition.   Fat and bulky.

"I know I've grown somewhat **corpulent** lately," I remarked. "Still, I think it's awfully cruel of them to refer to me as 'The Incredible Bulk.'"

On paydays my wallet becomes pretty **corpulent**; the rest of the week it looks as if it's on a very stringent diet.

Related Forms: (*nouns*) corpulence, corpulency

Synonyms: (*adjectives*) chubby, plump, husky, burly, portly, stout, rotund, obese

Antonyms: (*adjectives*) lean, lanky, thin, wiry, scrawny, gaunt

107. cor-rob-o-rate   *verb*   kə-rŏb´-ə-rāt *or* kô-rŏb´-ô-rāt

[*corroborare, corroboratus* (Latin), "strengthen"; from *cor*, a form of *cum* (Latin), "thoroughly" + *robur, roboris* (Latin), "oak; strength"]

Definition: To confirm the truth or accuracy of.

"My client's testimony may sound far-fetched," the lawyer told the jury, "but reliable witnesses will **corroborate** every last word of it."

"Recent economic developments simply do not **corroborate** your rosy view of this company's future," one executive remarked to another.

Related Forms: (*nouns*) corroboration, corroborator; (*adjectives*) corroborative, corroboratory

Synonyms: (*verbs*) verify, substantiate, support, back up, bear out

Antonyms: (*verbs*) contradict, refute, rebut, confute, discredit, impugn

108. coun-sel   *noun and verb*   kaun´-səl

[*conseil* (French), "advice," from *consilium* (Latin), "deliberation"]

Definition:

   a. (*noun*) Advice secured through consultation.

> At first I ignored my grandmother's advice, but as I grew older, I came to appreciate the wisdom of her **counsel**.

   b. (*noun*) An adviser, especially a legal adviser.

> Under a landmark Supreme Court ruling, every defendant in a criminal case is assured of representation by legal **counsel**.

   c. (*verb*) To advise or recommend as a course of action.

> "Before you make your final choice," my faculty adviser **counseled**, "visit each of the colleges to which you've applied."

Usage Note:
Do not confuse *counsel* with either *council* (a group assembled to give advice or exchange opinions) or *consul* (an official appointed to represent a government in a foreign country, especially in commercial matters).

Related Form: (*noun*) counselor

Phrases: keep one's own counsel, on advice of counsel, a camp counselor

Synonyms: (*nouns*) guidance, direction, recommendation; attorney, lawyer; (*verbs*) guide, instruct, urge, exhort, admonish, caution

109. cred-i-bil-i-ty   *noun*   krĕd-ə-bĭl´-ə-tē

[*credibilis* (Latin) "believable," from *credere* (Latin), "believe" + *abilis, abile* (Latin), "able to"]

Definition: The ability to inspire belief or trust.

> "The Secretary's public statements are often at odds with official pronouncements," the reporter observed. "This has seriously impaired his **credibility** as a reliable spokesman for the administration."

Related Forms: (*noun*) credibleness; (*adjective*) credible; (*adverb*) credibly

Usage Notes:

   a. Do not confuse *credibility,* which indicates the ability to inspire belief or trust, with *credence,* which indicates the belief or trust that has been inspired.

   b. Note too the difference between *credible,* which means "worthy of belief," and *creditable,* which means "worthy of *praise.*"

   c. The phrase *credibility gap* refers to a general public skepticism about the truth or accuracy of official claims or statements.

Synonyms: (*nouns*) reliability, believability, plausibility, trustworthiness, dependability

Antonyms: (*nouns*) unreliability, undependability

110. cri·te·ri·on   *noun*   krī-tîr´-ē-ən

[*kriterion* (Greek), "means of judging," from *kritein* (Greek), "judge"]

Definition: A standard or principle on which to base a judgment or decision.

> Usefulness is not the only **criterion** for including words in this book, but it is the primary one.

Usage Note:
The plural of *criterion* is *criteria* (or sometimes *criterions*). Under no circumstances is the form ending in *a* acceptable as the singular.

Synonyms: (*nouns*) yardstick, touchstone, guideline, gauge, canon, rule

111. cru·cial   *adjective*   kroo´-shəl

[*crucial* (Old French), "cross-shaped," from *crux, crucis* (Latin), "cross"]

Definition: At a point that will determine the final outcome; of supreme importance.

> "The next few months are **crucial**," President Harry S. Truman once said. "What we do now will affect our American way of life for decades to come."

Related Form: (*adverb*) crucially

Synonyms: (*adjectives*) critical, decisive, momentous, pivotal, vital

Antonyms: (*adjectives*) insignificant, unimportant, inconsequential

Phrases: the crux of the matter, reach the crisis point

112. cul·pa·ble   *adjective*   kŭl´-pə-bəl

[*culpabilis* (Latin), "blameworthy," from *culpa* (Latin), "guilt; fault"]

Definition: At fault; blameworthy.

> "I should have kept a closer eye on the project," the supervisor confessed. "In this regard, I'm as **culpable** as those who actually botched up the job."

Phrases: culpable stupidity, culpable neglect (or negligence)

Related Forms: (*nouns*) culpability, culpableness, culprit

Usage Note:
Culpable is stronger than *blameworthy*, but less severe than *guilty*. As the example above indicates, it is usually reserved for a fault that is the result of an error of omission, lack of sound judgment, negligence, or ignorance, rather than actual criminal intent.

Synonyms: (*adjectives*) guilty, delinquent, peccant, wanting; blamable, censurable, reprehensible

Antonyms: (*adjectives*) innocent, blameless; laudable, commendable, meritorious, praiseworthy

113. cur-so-ry *adjective* kûr´-sə-rē

[*cursorius* (Late Latin), "pertaining to running," from *currere, cursus* (Latin), "run"]

Definition: Hasty and superficial.

"I was so pressed for time that I couldn't give the lengthy report more than a **cursory** reading," the busy executive confessed.

Phrases: a cursory examination, a cursory report, in a cursory fashion

Related Forms: (*noun*) cursoriness; (*adverb*) cursorily

Synonyms: (*adjectives*) hurried, perfunctory, quick, summary, careless, unmethodical, casual, slapdash

Antonyms: (*adjectives*) thorough, exhaustive, comprehensive, in-depth, systematic, painstaking, careful, meticulous

114. cur-tail *verb* kər-tāl´

[from obsolete English *to make a curtal of* (a *curtal* being a horse with shortened ears and tail); from *curtus* (Latin), "shortened"]

Definition: To shorten or reduce.

When problems arose at the office, I was forced to **curtail** my vacation and hurry back to the city.

Over the centuries, the powers of the British monarch have been greatly **curtailed**.

Related Form: (*noun*) curtailment

Synonyms: (*verbs*) abridge, abbreviate, truncate, lessen, diminish, cut short, cut back, dock, pare down, trim

Antonyms: (*verbs*) increase, enlarge, augment, amplify, expand, extend

115. cyn-i-cal *adjective* sĭn´-ĭ-kəl

[*kunikos* (Greek), "doglike, currish," from *kuon* (Greek), "dog"]

Definition: Inclined to doubt or deny the virtuousness or honesty of human motives; sneeringly bitter or negative.

"As you say, my view of the world may be far too rosy," I admitted. "On the other hand, yours is perhaps a bit too **cynical**."

Related Forms: (*nouns*) cynic, cynicism; (*adverb*) cynically

Synonyms: (*adjectives*) skeptical, suspicious, doubtful; pessimistic, misanthropic; derisive, scornful; caustic (Word 81), sardonic, acerbic

Antonyms: (*adjectives*) optimistic, sanguine, positive; naive, starry-eyed, romantic, idealistic

Phrase: view the world through rose-colored glasses

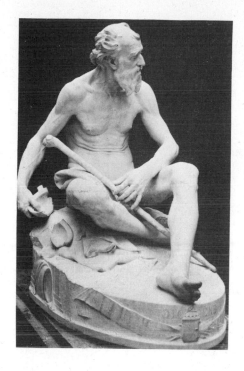

Diogenes of Sinope (*left*);
Alexander the Great (*above*)

Cynic

The Cynics were a group of ancient Greek philosophers who followed the teachings of Antisthenes of Athens (ca. 444–ca. 371 B.C.). Antisthenes, a pupil of Socrates, believed that virtue was the only good, and that human happiness consisted in trying to be virtuous. In order to become virtuous, he argued, a person must reduce his or her dependence on the outside world. That meant living in poverty, scorning pleasure, and ignoring social conventions. As you can see, this was a high-minded, but essentially negative, program.

Of course, it wasn't long before the Cynics were sneering at people and their motives as well as at things. For instance, Diogenes of Sinope (ca. 412–323 B.C.), a pupil of Antisthenes, showed his contempt for worldly goods by living naked in a tub. He expressed his disdain for the average human being (and his or her motives) in an equally dramatic way. During the daytime, he went around Athens shining a lantern in people's faces and looking at them intently. When asked why he did this, he replied haughtily that he was looking "for a man."

Diogenes even sneered at Alexander the Great and his achievements. For instance, once Alexander asked Diogenes, "Can I do anything for you?" "Only get out of my sunshine!" Diogenes sarcastically replied.

It is from such contemptuous attitudes toward people and their motives that our modern words *cynic* and *cynical* take their meanings.

By the way, the ancient Greeks probably nicknamed these philosophers *Kunikoi* (that is, "doglike") because of the bad manners they displayed. The name was ironically appropriate because the gymnasium at which Antisthenes taught happened to be named the *Kunosarges*. To the Greeks, the first syllable of this name appeared to contain a form of the Greek word for *dog* (*kuon*).

Using the Words

Exercise I. Syllabication and Pronunciation

Syllabicate the following words correctly, and place the major stress mark (′) after the syllable that is accented when the word is pronounced. Two answers are correct in one instance.

1. connoisseur
2. consensus
3. consummate
4. corroborate
5. counsel
6. credibility
7. culpable
8. cursory
9. cynical

Exercise II. Words Out of Context

In each of the following groups, select the item that best expresses the meaning of the numbered word at the left.

1. connoisseur
   a. bystander b. expert c. foreigner
   d. advocate e. beginner

2. copious
   a. some b. few c. no d. one
   e. many

3. counsel
   a. advise b. refuse c. order
   d. control e. question

4. criterion
   a. needle b. thimble c. pincushion
   d. yardstick e. scissors

5. culpable
   a. in unison b. on target c. at fault
   d. by heart e. off guard

6. consummate
   a. complete b. plump c. empty
   d. reliable e. mediocre

7. cursory
   a. positive b. different c. innocent
   d. hasty e. abundant

Exercise III. Completing Sentences

Complete each of the following sentences or pairs of sentences by selecting the most appropriate word from the given group of words. Use each word only once. Make any adjustments that are necessary to fit the words into the sentences properly.

corpulent	consensus	corroborate
construe	cynical	credibility
connoisseur	curtail	crucial

1. The country is so deeply divided over the issue that no national _____ on how to handle the matter appears likely, or even possible.

2. "The facts of the matter don't appear to _____ your suspicions," Grace said. "Can you offer any evidence to back up your ideas?"

3. The official's absurd excuses for covering up his involvement in the unsavory affair have completely destroyed his _____, even among his warmest supporters.

4. "I don't know what to make of their recent behavior," Jack admitted. "How should it be _____?"

5. Selling arms to both sides in a civil war strikes me as a heartless and _____ exploitation of an unfortunate situation.

6. "I realize that this decision is by no means inconsequential," mom told me. "Still, I don't believe it is as _____ as you make out."

7. I'd describe some of my classmates as lean or lanky; others I'd call a bit _____.

8. Though her job responsibilities have been greatly enlarged this year, mine have by no means been _____.

Exercise IV. Synonyms and Antonyms

Classify each of the following pairs of words as **S** for **synonyms** or **A** for **antonyms**.

1. disprove—corroborate
2. copious—plentiful
3. crucial—insignificant
4. unanimity—consensus
5. untrustworthiness—credibility
6. culpable—blameless
7. portly—corpulent
8. connoisseur—novice
9. cynical—starry-eyed
10. infer—construe
11. truncate—curtail
12. cursory—thorough
13. lawyer—counsel
14. consummate—clinch

Exercise V. Word Roundup

1. What is the difference between a *dilettante* and *connoisseur?*

2. Why shouldn't the phrase *of opinion* be added to the word *consensus?*

3. What is the difference in meaning between *burly* and *husky? chubby* and *obese?*

4. Briefly explain the background behind the words *cornucopia* and *cynic.*

5. Tell the difference between the words in the following pairs.

   a. counsel—council
   b. counsel—consul
   c. credibility—credence
   d. credible—creditable

6. Give the plural of *criterion*. (Two forms are possible.)
7. Define each of the following words or phrases.

   a. greenhorn
   b. credibility gap
   c. in unison
   d. the crux of the matter
   e. view the world through rose-colored glasses

Exercise VI.   Framing Sentences

A. Use each of the following words in an original illustrative sentence.

1. connoisseur
2. consensus
3. construe
4. counsel
5. criterion
6. credibility
7. consummate
8. cursory
9. curtail

B. Give a **noun** form of each of these words, and use it in an illustrative sentence.

1. corpulent
2. corroborate
3. culpable

C. Give an **adverb** form of each of these words, and use it in an original sentence.

1. cynical
2. crucial
3. copious

Culprit

When a prisoner was brought before the bar of justice during the Middle Ages, the presiding judge would ask him (or her) how he (or she) pleaded. If the defendant replied, "Not guilty," the prosecutor would step forward and signify that he was ready to prove the opposite. He would do this by saying in Norman French: "Culpable! Prit d'averrer..."—that is, "(The defendant is) guilty! (I am) ready to prove...." Eventually, the first two words of the prosecutor's reply were shortened to "culprit." By the 17th century, this new word had become a standard part of the judge's formal question, which ran, "Culprit, how will you be tried?" From this technical usage, our word *culprit* has developed its modern meaning of "an offender."

Dissecting the Words

Co, col, com, con and **cor** are all combining forms of the Latin preposition **cum**, meaning "with," "together," or "completely." These elements appear in all the basic words studied in Lesson 10 and many of those studied in Lesson 11. Note how each is used.

a. **Co**, a shortened form of **com**, occurs before Latin words beginning with *h, gn*, or (usually) a vowel. It is also used to coin new words, in which case it may be attached to words beginning with other consonants.

   coherent (*co*, "together" + *haerere*, "stick")—sticking together

   cognizance (*co*, "completely" + *gnoscere*, "know")—conscious knowledge or recognition of something

   coalesce (*co*, "together" + *alescere*, "grow")—to fuse or merge

   coeducational (*co*, "together" + *educational*)—attended or participated in by both male and female students

   cobelligerent (*co*, "with" + *belligerent*)—a partner in a war

b. **Col** is used before Latin words beginning with *l*.

   colloquial (*col*, "together" + *loqui*, "speak")—acceptable only in familiar conversation

   collusion (*col*, "together" + *ludere*, "play")—cooperation, usually secret, in some fraudulent or evil enterprise

c. **Com**, the basic combining form of **cum**, appears before Latin words beginning with *b, m, p*, and sometimes *i*.

   combat (*com*, "together" + *battere*, "fight")—battle

   commemorate (*com*, "completely" + *memmorare*, "mention, be mindful of")—to serve as a memorial of

   commiserate (*com*, "together with" + *miserari, miseratus*, "pity")—to sympathize with; to feel pity or sorrow for

   compete (*com*, "with" + *petere*, "strive")—to vie or contend with

d. **Con** is used before all consonants except *b, h, l, m, r*, and *w*.

   contagious (*con*, "together" + *tangere*, "touch")—transmitted by direct or indirect contact

   construct (*con*, "together" + *struere*, "pile up")—to build or erect

   conjugal (*con*, "together" + *jugum*, "yoke")—relating to marriage

   conform (*con*, "together" + *formare*, "shape")—to have the same form or character; to act in the same way

e. **Cor** is used before Latin words beginning with *r*.

   corrode (*cor*, "completely" + *rodere*, "gnaw")—to dissolve or wear away by chemical action

   correlate (*cor*, "together" + *relatus*, "carried back")—to show a logical relationship among different elements

Exercise

1. For each of the following definitions, give an English word that contains a form of the Latin preposition *cum*.

    a. work together
    b. meet together
    c. draw close together
    d. fall down completely
    e. unite into a compact mass

    f. existing at birth
    g. stick together
    h. agree together
    i. squeeze together
    j. destroy the virtue of

2. With or without the help of a dictionary, give the meanings of the component parts of the words listed below. Then, define each word, and use it in a short illustrative sentence.

    a. coauthor
    b. commutation
    c. compatible
    d. corrugate

    e. coordinate
    f. commingle
    g. confederate
    h. coexistence

    i. compunction
    j. concurrent
    k. constrain
    l. contemplate

H. L. Mencken

H. L. Mencken (1880–1956) was one of the most colorful and influential figures in the history of American linguistics. Though Mencken was a working journalist and magazine editor all of his life, he found time to compile a monumental study of American English called *The American Language*. First published in 1919 and subsequently revised or expanded on several occasions, *The American Language* deals with all aspects of American English from its beginnings in the 17th century to the most recent developments in the 1930's and 1940's. The lively, often caustic style in which this and other works were written influenced such notable 20th-century American writers as Theodore Dreiser, Sinclair Lewis, and Sherwood Anderson. Indeed, the word *Menckenese*, coined to describe Mencken's pungent, vigorous style, has found a lasting place in our language.

Working with Context Clues

Sentence-Completion Exercises. Today, practically every standardized vocabulary test contains at least one section involving sentence-completion exercises. A **sentence-completion** exercise (sometimes called a **cloze exercise**) asks a student to complete a sentence or group of sentences from which one or two words have been removed. The student is to do this by selecting one of the four or five possible "answers" that are supplied. Here is a sample sentence-completion exercise. See whether you can figure out which word belongs in the blank.

> Faithfully reading a weekly news magazine like *Time* or *Newsweek* not only broadens my knowledge of current events but also _____ my vocabulary.
>
> **a.** decreases **b.** fragments **c.** expands **d.** demolishes **e.** contains

Sentence-completion exercises test a student's ability to perceive a meaningful connection between the words in a sentence or between the sentences in a paragraph. They also test a student's knowledge of the meanings of specific words and the proper use of these words in an appropriate context. Thus, sentence-completion exercises are excellent tools for ascertaining a student's knowledge of the vocabulary of Modern English.

Of course, every sentence-completion exercise provides the student with enough information to make the correct choice without going beyond what is actually given. This is done through the use of context clues. As their name implies, **context clues** are verbal or logical hints that have been carefully "sewn" into the context that surrounds the blank for the missing word. Sometimes these hints are quite concrete—a word or a phrase that "gives away" the correct answer. Other times, they depend more on an appreciation of the whole situation that is outlined in the passage. In either case, context clues point the student unmistakably toward the correct choice. Here, for example, are the context clues in the sample sentence-completion exercise given above. They have been underlined so you can spot them easily.

> Faithfully reading a weekly news magazine like *Time* or *Newsweek* <u>not only</u> <u>broadens</u> my knowledge of current events <u>but</u> <u>also</u> _____ my vocabulary.

Now can you figure out which of the five choices given above belongs in the blank? The answer, of course, is Choice *c, expands.* Here's why.

If you look at the part of the sentence that follows the word *but*, you will realize that a verb is missing. This tells you that the kind of word you want is a verb.

Next you may notice that the sentence contains the phrase *not only. . . but also.* This is the type of conjunction that binds two parallel or similar parts of a sentence together. Accordingly, the verb that is missing after the words *but also* must mean something like the verb that follows the words *not only.* And what is the verb that follows *not only?* It is *broadens.*

Now you know that you need a verb that means more or less the same as *broadens.* And what is that verb? It is *expands,* which is the only one of the choices that means anything close to *broadens.*

As you can see, completing this type of exercise successfully boils down to a search for the context clues that point to the correct choice. This, in turn, involves knowing what general types of clues are usually employed in such exercises. These general types will be discussed in the "Working with Context Clues" sections of the next few lessons.

Exercise I

Three sample sentence-completion exercises are given below. The context clues that each contains have been underlined. Using these context clues as guideposts, choose the word that correctly completes each exercise.

1. There is only one word that can adequately describe the disorder now prevailing on the convention floor: _____!

   a. harmony b. chaos c. apathy d. bureaucracy
   e. tranquility

2. Jonathan Swift once said that he didn't like people in the aggregate, but that he could put up with them as _____.

   a. machines b. humans c. individuals d. animals
   e. creatures

3. "Don't take the laundry off the line yet," mom said. "It is still _____ to the touch."

   a. dry b. dirty c. dull d. dense e. damp

Exercise II

Three more sample sentence-completion exercises are given below. The correct answer has been underlined in each case. Using the answer as a guidepost, underline the context clues that each of the samples contains.

1. "Glenda is in a particularly _____ mood today," I observed. "I've not seen her in such a lighthearted and carefree frame of mind for a long time."

   a. bleak b. blithe c. belligerent d. brusque e. boorish

2. Although Josh is not an especially able public speaker, the address he gave on Parents' Day was surprisingly _____.

   a. chronic b. prompt c. inseparable b. articulate
   e. scarce

3. No one believes a word he says simply because his long record of deceptions and half-truths have completely destroyed his _____.

   a. credence b. affluence c. censure d. ambience
   e. credibility

Enriching the Lesson

Exercise I.   The Greeks Had a Word for It

Even though you have probably never studied Greek, you may actually know some. That is because English has borrowed quite a few words and phrases with little or no change from Greek (allowing, of course, for the difference in alphabets). One of these items is *criterion*, studied in this lesson. Some others are listed below. With or without the aid of a dictionary, define each. Then choose any **five**, and, for each, compose a short illustrative sentence.

1.	pathos	11.	dilemma	21.	dogma
2.	aroma	12.	climax	22.	antithesis
3.	plethora	13.	diagnosis	23.	catharsis
4.	ethos	14.	psyche	24.	hubris
5.	panacea	15.	crisis	25.	trauma
6.	genesis	16.	catastrophe	26.	hypothesis
7.	phenomenon	17.	stigma	27.	apotheosis
8.	aegis	18.	acme	28.	charisma
9.	hoi polloi	19.	metamorphosis	29.	iota
10.	synopsis	20.	nemesis	30.	paralysis

Exercise II.   Linguistic Shortcuts

A. *Abbreviations.*   A good many abbreviations for Latin phrases commonly turn up in written English. Some of these items are listed below. With or without the help of a dictionary, define each, and give the full Latin phrase for which the abbreviation stands. Then, choose any **five** of the items, and use each in a short illustrative sentence.

1.	etc.	7.	op. cit.	13.	ca. *or* c.
2.	et al.	8.	e.g.	14.	A.D.
3.	q.v.	9.	i.e.	15.	cf.
4.	ibid.	10.	N.B.	16.	viz.
5.	loc. cit.	11.	A.M.	17.	fl.
6.	P.S.	12.	sc.	18.	vs.

B. *Acronyms.*   Another type of linguistic shortcut is called an acronym. **Acronyms** are pronounceable words that are made up of the initial letters (or sometimes syllables) of a multiword phrase. Since so many of our modern-day organizations, agencies and products have fairly long formal names, acronyms are usually devised for them. This saves people the time and trouble of saying or writing the full name. For example, *NATO* (pronounced nā´-tō) is an acronym for the *N*orth *A*tlantic *T*reaty *O*rganization. Similarly, *Nabisco* (pronounced nə-bĭ´-skō) is an acronym for the *Na*tional *Bisco*mpany. Good acronyms become so common that soon everybody understands what is meant, and the long formal name may become quite scarce in everyday usage.

   Below are listed a number of common acronyms. With or without the help of a dictionary, define each. Then give the phrase or formal name for which the acronym stands.

1.	NASA	7.	MIRV	13.	SALT
2.	CORE	8.	SHAPE	14.	radar
3.	NOW	9.	WASP	15.	scuba
4.	SEATO	10.	AWOL	16.	sonar
5.	VISTA	11.	ZIP Code	17.	laser
6.	UNESCO	12.	OPEC	18.	posh

Exercise III.   Philosophical and Religious Positions

The word *cynical*, studied in this lesson, suggests a philosophical position or a general attitude toward life. English is rich in such words. Some of them are listed below. With or without the aid of a dictionary, define each. Then choose any **five**, and use each in a short illustrative sentence.

1.	materialist	11.	romantic	21.	skeptic
2.	hedonist	12.	stoic	22.	monotheist
3.	idealist	13.	humanist	23.	heretic
4.	empiricist	14.	egotist	24.	altruist
5.	atheist	15.	mystic	25.	racist
6.	agnostic	16.	optimist	26.	pessimist
7.	pragmatist	17.	realist	27.	latitudinarian
8.	epicurean	18.	egalitarian	28.	utilitarian
9.	freethinker	19.	misogynist	29.	fundamentalist
10.	misanthrope	20.	humanitarian	30.	iconoclast

Exercise IV.   Expanding Your Word Power

The words listed below are not on the Basic Word List, but they were mentioned in passing in Lesson 11. All of them would make useful additions to your working vocabulary. Define each, give its etymology, list **two** synonyms and **two** antonyms (where possible), and use in a short illustrative sentence.

1.	tyro	6.	profuse	11.	canon
2.	discord	7.	plausible	12.	pivotal
3.	deduce	8.	gaunt	13.	meticulous
4.	derisive	9.	rebut	14.	abridge
5.	initiate	10.	admonish	15.	acerbic

Lesson 12

116. **dapper** — 130. **dexterous**

---

116. dap-per   *adjective*   dăp´-ĕr

[*dapyr* (Middle English), "elegant," probably from *dapper* (Low German), "agile"]

Definition: Neatly and stylishly dressed.

Some of the boys I know always look as if they've slept in their clothes; others are very **dapper** dressers.

Related Form: (*adverb*) dapperly

Usage Note:
As the example given above suggests, *dapper* is normally reserved for men. Accordingly, a stylishly dressed woman would probably be called *chic* (pronounced shek), not *dapper*.

Synonyms: (*adjectives*) natty, smart, spruce, stylish, chic

Antonyms: (*adjectives*) unkempt, sloppy, slovenly, shabby, seedy; dowdy, blousy, frowsy, frumpy

117. de-fect   *noun:* dē´-fĕkt   *verb:* dĭ-fĕkt´

[*deficere, defectus* (Latin), "fail; remove from"; from *de* (Latin), "away from" + *facere, factus* (Latin), "do; make"]

Definition:
  a. (*noun*) A flaw or shortcoming.

   "It shouldn't be hard to punch holes in their theory," I said. "After all, its **defects** are fairly obvious."

  b. (*verb*) To desert one country, cause, or the like for another.

   Over the years, a good many Russian intellectuals and artists, dissatisfied with life in their own country, have **defected** to the West.

Related Forms: (*nouns*) defectiveness, defection, defector; (*adjective*) defective

Usage Notes:
  a. Something that is *defective* is faulty. For example, a piece of machinery or a copy of a book may be defective. Do not confuse the word with *deficient*, which means "lacking." For example, a person may be deficient in good judgment.

  b. Someone who defects from one country or cause to another is called a *defector*, and the act of defecting is called a *defection*.

Synonyms: (*nouns*) blemish, fault, imperfection, weakness, failing, bug, kink; (*verbs*) abandon, forsake, bolt; repudiate, disown, abjure

157

118. de-fer   *verb*   di-fûr´

[*de* (Latin), "away" + *ferre* (Latin), "carry"]

Definition:
   a. To put off or postpone.

> In a hurry to adjourn for the holidays, the legislators decided to **defer** consideration of the bill until after the recess.

   b. To yield courteously to the wishes or judgments of someone else.

> "Mom and dad know more about life than I do," Carol said. "That's why I usually **defer** to their better judgment."

Related Forms: (*nouns*) deferment, deferral, deference; (*adjectives*) deferential, deferent

Usage Note:
The nouns *deferment* and *deferral* denote a temporary postponement of, or exemption from, something (for example, induction into the army). The noun *deference* indicates a willing or courteous submission to another person's wishes or ideas, usually out of respect for the latter's age, wisdom, or experience. The adjectives *deferential* and *deferent* mean "respectful," as in "a deferential attitude."

Synonyms: (*verbs*) delay, table, shelve, hold off on, put on ice, put on a back burner; bow to, give way to, accede to (Word 8)

Antonyms: (*verbs*) expedite, facilitate, hasten; spurn, disdain, reject

119. de-ject-ed   *adjective*   dĭ-jĕk´-tĭd

[*dejicere, dejectus* (Latin), "cast down"; from *de* (Latin), "down" + *jacere, jactus* (Latin), "cast, throw"]

Definition: In very low spirits.

> When I saw that **dejected** look on his face, I sensed that things hadn't quite worked out as he had hoped.

Related Forms: (*noun*) dejection; (*verb*) deject; (*adverb*) dejectedly

Synonyms: (*adjectives*) sad, blue, depressed, gloomy, despondent, melancholy, morose, downcast, dispirited, disheartened

Antonyms: (*adjectives*) happy, merry, elated, exultant, jubilant

Phrases: on top of the world; down in the dumps

120. de-lete   *verb*   dĭ-lēt´

[*delere, deletus* (Latin), "wipe away"; from *de* (Latin) "away" + *lere, letus* (Latin), "wipe; blot"]

Definition: To strike out or remove.

> One clause in the proposed law was **deleted** because most committee members felt that it was unsound.

Related Form: (*noun*) deletion

Do not confuse the adjective *deleterious* with forms of the verb *delete*.
Deleterious means "physically or morally harmful."

Synonyms: (*verbs*) cancel, expunge, omit, efface, excise

Antonyms: (*verbs*) retain, include; add, insert

121. de-lin-e-ate   *verb*   dĭ-lĭn´-ē-āt

[*delineare, delineatus* (Latin), "draw lines"; from *de* (Latin), "completely" + *linea* (Latin), "thread; line"]

Definition: To make an accurate line drawing or diagram of; to portray or describe in detail.

The artist's pen-and-pencil sketch not only **delineated** the model's features accurately but also captured something of her personality.

Few writers have J. D. Salinger's remarkable ability to **delineate** the emotions, aspirations, and troubled confusion of the average teenager.

Related Forms: (*nouns*) delineation, delineator

Usage Note:
As a technical term, *delineate* and *delineation* indicate a drawing or engraving that consists of lines, as opposed to one that employs shading or tints. Note too that both words stress fullness and accuracy of detail.

Synonyms: (*verbs*) picture, depict, set forth, sketch, etch

122. de-lin-quent   *adjective and noun*   dĭ-lĭng´-kwĕnt

[*delinquens, delinquentis* (Latin), "leaving completely undone"; from *de* (Latin), "completely" + *linquere* (Latin), "leave undone"]

Definition:
a.   (*adjective*) Neglectful of a duty or obligation; seriously overdue.

Citizens who fail to vote out of indifference or laziness are **delinquent** in their civic duties.

"Pay your bills on time," mom advised. "It's not a good idea to let any of your accounts become **delinquent**."

b.   (*noun*) A person who fails to perform a duty; an offender.

The Family Court deals with juvenile **delinquents**, not adult offenders.

Related Form: (*noun*) delinquency

Synonyms: (*adjectives*) remiss, derelict, negligent; owing, outstanding, unsettled; (*nouns*) scofflaw; malefactor, wrongdoer

Antonyms: (*adjectives*) punctilious, scrupulous, dutiful, conscientious, meticulous; paid up

Phrases: dereliction of duty, in arrears

123. de-lude   *verb*   dĭ-lōōd´

[*deludere* (Latin), "play false"; from *de* (Latin), "away (i.e., from the truth)" + *ludere* (Latin), "play"]

Definition: To mislead or deceive.

Every year, clever swindlers and con artists **delude** thousands of credulous Americans out of their hard-earned savings.

"What they said was pure flattery," I thought. "If I took it seriously, I would only be **deluding** myself."

Related Forms: (*nouns*) deluder, delusion; (*adjectives*) deluded, delusive, delusory

Usage Note:

A *delusion* is a false belief that usually results from trickery, self-deception, or mental disease (e.g., "*delusions* of grandeur"). Do not confuse the word with *illusion*, which indicates a mistaken impression based on faulty perceptions or wishful thinking (e.g., "an optical *illusion*").

A magician, or illusionist, performing a trick.

Synonyms: (*verbs*) dupe, gull, cozen, hoodwink, trick, beguile

Phrases: a complete hoax, a clever scam, a con(fidence) game, a sting operation

124. de-mure   *adjective*   dĭ-myōōr´

[*demore* (Old French), "quiet"; from *demorer* (Old French), "linger"; from *de* (Latin), "completely" + *morari* (Latin), "delay"]

Definition: Modest and reserved in dress, manner, or behavior.

Though they are sisters, they are a study in contrasts: Anne so quiet and **demure**; Elizabeth so forceful and outspoken!

Related Forms: (*noun*) demureness; (*adverb*) demurely

160

Usage Notes:

a. Frequently, *demure* is used disparagingly to indicate false or affected modesty. In this sense, it is a synonym of *coy*.

b. As the example given above indicates, *demure* is usually reserved for young women. Men who exhibit similar characteristics would probably be called *proper* or *staid*.

c. Do not confuse the adjective *demure* (with an *e* at the end) with the verb *demur* (without an *e* at the end), which means "take exception to" or "object to."

Synonyms: (*adjectives*) sedate, prim, decorous, seemly, staid; diffident, shy, self-effacing; coy

Antonyms: (*adjectives*) bold, forward, immodest; assertive, aggressive, jaunty, bumptious

Phrases: a wallflower, a shrinking violet

125. de-noue-ment   *noun*   dā-nōō-män´

[*dénouement* (French), "an untying"; from *dé* (French), "un-" + *nouer* (French), "tie"]

Definition: The point at which the plot of a novel or drama is finally resolved; the outcome or solution of a complex sequence of events.

In the **denouement** of a Victorian novel, vice is usually punished and virtue rewarded.

Their impulsive, often blundering behavior has entangled them in a series of complicated problems whose **denouement** is far from clear.

Synonyms: (*nouns*) unraveling (of a plot), disentanglement, climax; final solution, final issue

126. des-ul-to-ry   *adjective*   dĕs´-əl-tô-rē

[*desultorius* (Latin), "relating to a jumper"; from *de* (Latin), "down" + *saltire* (Latin), "jump"]

Definition: Shifting from one thing to another without reason or purpose; haphazard or random.

The report on study habits indicated that fifteen minutes of concentrated effort produced better results than two hours of **desultory** labor.

Related Forms: (*noun*) desultoriness; (*adverb*) desultorily

Synonyms: (*adjectives*) fitful, erratic, spasmodic, intermittent; aimless, rambling; disconnected, unmethodical

Antonyms: (*adjectives*) constant, concentrated, steadfast; methodical, systematic, painstaking

Phrase: by fits and starts

161

127. de-vi-ate   *verb:* dē'-vē-āt   *noun:* dē'-vē-ĭt

[*deviare, deviatus* (Latin), "go off track"; from *de* (Latin), "away from" + *via* (Latin), "way, road"]

Definition:

a. (*verb*) To move away from, especially what is considered normal, right, or acceptable.

"I'm afraid I'll get lost," the driver said, "if I **deviate** from the route I was told to take."

In any society, there are those who adhere to the accepted code of behavior and those who **deviate** from it.

b. (*noun*) A person who differs markedly in behavior, belief, or attitude from what is accepted as normal or proper.

Most societies not only frown upon but also proscribe the behavior of various kinds of nonconformists and **deviates**.

Related Forms: (*nouns*) deviation, deviator; (*adjective*) deviant

Synonyms: (*verbs*) diverge, veer, swerve, stray, wander, ramble, digress; (*nouns*) nonconformist, maverick, oddball, heretic

Antonyms: (*verbs*) conform to, stick to, abide by, adhere to; (*nouns*) conformist, traditionalist

Maverick

The word *maverick* is derived from Samuel A. Maverick (1803–1870), a Texas cattleman who refused to brand his calves in accordance with common procedure. At first, the word *maverick* was applied to an unbranded calf that had strayed from the herd and thus could not be readily identified and sent back where it "belonged." Later, *maverick* came to mean an individual who does not follow the dictates of the majority, a political or social dissenter, one who refuses to conform to convention. Some synonyms for *maverick* follow: (*nouns*) a loner, individualist, insurgent; (*adjectives*) heterodox, recalcitrant, refractory.

128. de-void   *adjective*   dĭ-void´

[*devoide* (Middle English), "rid of"; from *desvuidier* (Old French), "get rid of"; from *des* (Old French), "completely" + *vuidier* (Old French), "empty"]

Definition: Empty; lacking in.

"They are so smug and self-satisfied!" I remarked. "Rarely have I encountered people so completely **devoid** of any awareness of their own imperfections."

That slogan may sound impressive, but it is totally **devoid** of meaning.

Synonyms: (*adjectives*) destitute (of), bereft (of), wanting (in), deficient (in), barren (in)

Antonyms: (*adjectives*) replete (with), fraught (with), saturated (with), full (of), teeming (with), bursting (with), stuffed (with)

129. de-vout   *adjective*   dĭ-vout´

[*de* (Latin), "completely" + *vovere, votus* (Latin), "vow"]

Definition: Deeply religious, earnest, or sincere.

Although they make no great show of their religion, they are **devout** believers in the teachings of their faith.

For more than 50 years, her allegiance to the cause of human rights has been truly **devout**.

Related Forms: (*verb*) devote; (*nouns*) devoutness, devotion, devotee; (*adjectives*) devoted, devotional; (*adverb*) devoutly

Synonyms: (*adjectives*) pious, faithful; reverent; ardent, zealous

Antonyms: (*adjectives*) irreligious, unreligious, unfaithful; irreverent; lukewarm, tepid

130. dex-ter-ous   *adjective*   dĕk´-strəs

[*dexter* (Latin), "(on the) right; skillful"]

Definition: Skillful in using one's hands or mind; clever.

Professional jugglers are among the most **dexterous** people on the face of the earth.

Any potentially explosive situation requires extremely **dexterous** and sensitive handling by all the parties concerned.

Related Forms: (*nouns*) dexterity, dexterousness; (*adverb*) dexterously

Usage Note:
Dexterous is sometimes spelled *dextrous*, but this is not the preferred form of the word.

Synonyms: (*adjectives*) handy, adroit, deft, adept, proficient

Antonyms: (*adjectives*) awkward, clumsy, gauche, inept, maladroit

A debate in the House of Commons about 1905, showing the seating arrangement. The party in power (here the Conservatives) sit to the right of the Speaker (the man in the wig on the throne); members of the opposition (*i.e.*, those not in the government) sit to his left.

A Curious Case of Linguistic Prejudice

Dexterous is one of several words which show that English has a curious preference for the right side. This probably stems, at least in part, from the fact that right-handed people have always outnumbered left-handed ones.

A number of other common English words display the same prejudice. For example, *sinister*, which means "ominous" or "evil-looking," is simply the Latin word for "left." Similarly, *gauche*, which means "clumsy" or "boorish," is in fact just the French word for "left." Finally, *adroit*, which means "clever" or "skillful," comes from a French phrase meaning "to the right."

This preference for the right may even be connected with the origin of some of our most common political terms. In medieval times, the most important guest at a banquet was seated in the most favored spot. This was to the right of the host. When parliaments and similar legislative bodies began to appear in Europe, the practice was carried over into politics. Accordingly, the dominant political group (almost always the conservative element) was seated on the right of the official head of the legislature. Liberal and radical groups sat on his left.

From this arrangement modern English derives such terms as *the right* (the conservative or traditionalist element in any political party or country) and *the left* (the more radical element). The expressions *right wing*, meaning "conservative," and *leftist*, meaning "radical," also come from the same source. Variations on this theme include *rightist*, *right winger*, *left wing*, and *left winger*.

Using the Words

Exercise I. Parts of Speech

Indicate the part of speech of each of the following words. In some cases, two answers are correct.

1. defer
2. demure
3. deviate
4. dexterous
5. defect
6. dapper
7. denouement
8. delinquent
9. delete

Exercise II. Words in Phrases

In each of the following groups, select the item that best expresses the meaning of the *italicized* word in the introductory phrase.

1. *defer* a decision
   a. withdraw   b. overrule   c. confirm   d. postpone

2. in a very *dejected* frame of mind
   a. aggressive   b. gloomy   c. playful   d. bizarre

3. *delinquent* behavior
   a. callow   b. remiss   c. evasive   d. puzzling

4. in a very *demure* outfit
   a. flashy   b. odd   c. staid   d. elegant

5. *desultory* reading
   a. dull   b. careful   c. banal   d. fitful

6. a truly *devout* follower of soap operas
   a. lukewarm   b. uninformed   c. ardent   d. sensitive

7. *deviate* from the straight and narrow
   a. veer   b. hale   c. infer   d. arise

Exercise III. Completing Sentences

Complete each of the following sentences or pairs of sentences by selecting the most appropriate word from the given group of words. Make any adjustments that are necessary to fit the words into the sentences properly.

dapper	delete	delinquent
delude	denouement	devoid
defect	dexterous	delineate

1. Though the idea looked good at first glance, I soon came to the conclusion that it was _____ of any real merit.

2. "The ending of this novel isn't very satisfactory," Paula observed. "The _____ just doesn't follow logically from the plot developments that lead up to it."

3. "How _____ you look!" mom exclaimed as I descended the stairs in my newly acquired finery. "You'll be the best-dressed young man at the dance!"

4. "Describing a character's outward appearance isn't enough to make the figure come alive," my creative-writing teacher told me. "You must also _____ his or her inner thoughts, feelings, and motivations.

5. It takes fairly _____ manipulation of the control strings to make a marionette's movements look smooth and natural.

6. I shortened some of the overly long sentences in my essay by _____ a few unnecessary words from each.

7. No one is perfect, but that doesn't mean we should completely ignore all of a person's _____.

8. "There is no point in _____ myself that I am a great artist," Walt said. "I am only a competent copyist."

Exercise IV.   Synonyms and Antonyms

A. In each of the following groups, select the **two** words that are most nearly **synonyms**.

1. a. accede b. retain c. allude d. acquiesce e. reject

2. a. shabby b. remiss c. respectful d. jubilant e. negligent

3. a. mediocre b. final c. natty d. spruce e. constant

4. a. accelerate b. swerve c. elate d. infect e. veer

5. a. leave b. concern c. depict d. injure e. portray

Now, for each pair of synonyms that you have selected, supply a word from the Basic Word List for this lesson (Words 116–130) that means **the same** or **almost the same** thing.

B. In each of the following, select the item that is most nearly **opposite** in meaning to the numbered word at the left.

1. delete   a. cancel b. harm c. encourage
              d. insert e. construe

2. dexterous   a. clever b. scholarly c. inept
              d. accurate e. bold

3. devoid   a. replete b. arbitrary c. wanting
              d. bleak e. destitute

4. defect   **a.** forsake **b.** elude **c.** complete
                   d. sketch **e.** adhere

5. desultory   **a.** sober **b.** concentrated **c.** expensive
                   d. merry **e.** awkward

Exercise V. Word Roundup

1. What is an *optical illusion*? Give an example of the phenomenon.

2. What is the difference between *devoted* and *addicted*? Use each in a sentence that clearly shows the difference.

3. In your own words, describe the kind of person indicated by each of the following phrases.

   a devoted mother   a devout Buddhist   a devotee of the arts

4. Explain the difference between the words in each of the following pairs.

   a. defective—deficient   **c.** delusion—illusion
   b. deferment—deference   **d.** demur—demure

5. What is a *leftist? a right winger?* Explain the story behind these expressions.

6. Give **three** examples of words that indicate the preference English seems to have for the right side.

7. Explain the meaning of each of the following phrases.

   a. down in the dumps   **e.** a con artist
   b. on top of the world   **f.** dereliction of duty
   c. a complete hoax   **g.** in arrears
   d. a sting operation   **h.** by fits and starts

Exercise VI. Framing Sentences

A. Use each of the following words in an original sentence.

1. dapper	2. delineate	7. denouement
2. delete	5. delinquent	8. desultory
3. delude	6. demure	9. devoid

B. Give a **noun** form of each of these words, and use it in an illustrative sentence.

1. dejected   2. dexterous   3. devout

C. Give an **adjective** form of each of these words, and use it in an illustrative sentence.

1. defect   2. defer   3. deviate

Completing Verbal Analogies

Analogy Question Type II. This is probably the most common type of analogy question used on standardized vocabulary tests. It looks more or less like this:

Type II

A   B

elm : tree =
a. llama : bird
b. hen : rooster
c. bison : animal

d. mammal : whale
e. tiger : ferocious

As you can see, in a Type-II analogy question, the student is given the two words in the key relationship (*A, B*). This pair of words is followed by five other pairs of words (*not* individual words!) labeled *a* through *e*. From this group, the student is to select the *pair of words* that will complete the analogy correctly.

Completing Type-II Analogies Correctly. There are two basic steps in the correct completion of Type-II analogy questions.

Step 1.   Look at the two words in the key pair (*A, B*), and determine the relationship between them. This is the same procedure that was used to complete Type-I analogies (see page 68).

In the sample analogy question given above, the word *elm* denotes a particular kind of tree. In other words, an elm is an example of a tree. For convenience, this relationship can be expressed as "*A* is an example of *B.*" This is the relationship that must appear on both sides of the equals sign if this particular analogy is to be correct.

A popular baseball player gives an on-the-spot interview to a reporter for a national magazine. A job as a journalist of one type or another is an excellent career objective for someone who uses words well.

Step 2. Inspect the five choices given, and determine which illustrates the same relationship as the key pair of words.

In the example given above, only Choice *c, bison : animal,* does this. A bison is an example of an animal, just as an elm is an example of a tree.

All the other choices do not illustrate the required relationship. A llama is not an example of a bird, nor is a hen an example of a rooster. Similarly, a mammal is not an example of a whale, though a whale is an example of a mammal. In other words, the two components of Choice *d* are given in the wrong order. Finally, both of the words in the key relationship (*A, B*) are nouns. Thus, *tiger : ferocious* is wrong because *ferocious* is an adjective, not a noun. Always remember to observe the parts of speech involved in the key relationship and the order in which its component parts appear. Doing this will help you eliminate many wrong choices quickly and efficiently.

Two Colons. On some standardized vocabulary tests (notably the Scholastic Aptitude Test) two colons (::) are used instead of the equals sign in the analogy questions. Thus, "elm : tree :: bison : animal" means exactly the same as "elm : tree = bison : animal." Both signs, of course, stand for the word *as.*

Exercise

The following items review what you have so far learned about analogy questions. Complete each.

Group A

1. **dexterous : clumsy** =
   a. copious : plentiful
   b. dapper : sloppy
   c. obese : culpable
   d. devoid : lacking
   e. affluent : agile

2. **corpulence : portly** =
   a. corroboration : contradictory
   b. criterion : saturated
   c. denouement : virtuous
   d. consensus : unanimous
   e. desultoriness : methodical

3. **orange : sphere** =
   a. grapefruit : ellipse
   b. round : cylinder
   c. rug : area
   d. diameter : waist
   e. wheel : circle

4. **creditable : praiseworthy** =
   a. pivotal : crucial
   b. sanguine : cynical
   c. delinquent : consummate
   d. demure : forward
   e. sporadic : gaunt

5. **harmonious : discord** =
   a. skill : inept
   b. devout : sincerity
   c. cursory : thoroughness
   d. delusion : trickery
   e. deferential : respect

6. **deviate : stray ::**
   a. delete : include
   b. adhere : defect
   c. hasten : defer
   d. curtail : enlarge
   e. delineate : depict

7. **devotion : faithful ::**
   a. intoxication : sober
   b. warmth : bleak
   c. mistaken : illusion
   d. indigence : penniless
   e. complacence :
      quarrelsome

8. **covert : overt ::**
   a. verbose : laconic
   b. tactful : diplomatic
   c. stealthy : naive
   d. ephemeral : transitory
   e. frank : candid

9. **hammer : tool ::**
   a. singer : soprano
   b. horse : cow
   c. typewriter : machine
   d. continent : Asia
   e. trunk : branch

10. **ambivalent : certainty ::**
    a. plausible : reliability
    b. inane : substance
    c. pathos : feeling
    d. manifest : openness
    e. fretful : concern

Working with Context Clues

Handling Sentence-Completion Exercises Successfully.   Study the following simple example of the kind of sentence-completion exercise that appears on standardized vocabulary tests:

When I told my landlord that I planned to _____ my apartment, he didn't seem too unhappy about my departure.

  a. clean   b. inspect   c. furnish   d. vacate   e. decorate

There are a number of simple steps involved in determining the answer to this or any other sentence-completion exercise you might encounter.

Step 1.   Read the sentence containing the blank carefully, and make sure you understand what it says.
   In the example given above, the sentence says two things. First, it tells you that the speaker ("I") informed the landlord of something. Secondly, it indicates the landlord's reaction to this information.

Step 2.   Determine what you are to do, and where the clue to the correct answer is likely to be.
   In the example given above, the part of the sentence indicating the landlord's reaction is complete. What you must do is finish the portion containing the speaker's initial statement.
   This means that you must figure out what the speaker said *on the basis of* the landlord's reaction. Thus, the wording of this reaction is likely to contain the clue that you are looking for.

Step 3. Isolate the clue.

In the example given above, look carefully at the landlord's reaction. It reads, "he didn't seem too unhappy about my departure."

Notice the words *about my departure*. These words don't tell you about the landlord's reaction; they tell you about what he was reacting to. In other words, they repeat or imply the gist of what the speaker ("I") said. This must have been something like "I'm moving out of the building" or "I'm giving up my apartment."

Now you know what the speaker initially said. You also know how to determine which word goes in the blank.

Step 4. Look at the five items labeled *a* through *e*, and choose the correct answer.

In the example given above, only one of the five items has anything to do with the idea of leaving. It is Choice *c*, *vacate*, which is, of course, the correct answer.

Step 5. Insert your answer into the blank, and reread the completed sentence silently. Check carefully to see that the whole thing "makes sense." If it doesn't, discard the answer you have chosen, and repeat Steps 1–4.

Here is what the example given above looks like when the correct answer is in place:

When I told the landlord that I planned to ___vacate___ my apartment, he didn't seem too unhappy about my departure.

Restatement Clues. The example given above contains a clue that more or less *repeats* the meaning of the missing word. This type of clue is called a **restatement clue**. It is the simplest and most obvious kind of clue used in sentence-completion exercises. As the example also suggests, a restatement clue is often simply a *synonym* or *near-synonym* of the missing word. Sometimes, it may even give a short *definition* of it.

Exercise

Complete each of the following by selecting the word that makes the best sense in the sentence as a whole. Indicate the clue or clues that led you to make this choice.

1. If you will supply the dishes for the picnic, I will _____ the food.

   a. devour b. enjoy c. cancel d. furnish e. inspect

2. People with _____ ideas are always thinking up new and different things to do, or say, or make.

   a. banal b. vague c. original d. simple e. antiquated

3. I had a feeling that our team would win, and my _____ proved correct.

   a. memory b. hunch c. information d. answer
   e. timing

4. Many substances that are well-known on earth are present on the sun in gaseous form—for example, iron, copper, and other _____ metals.

   a. strange **b.** costly **c.** unknown **d.** artificial
   e. familiar

5. "I'm willing to _____ your rude behavior," Lenny said, "if you're willing to ignore my nasty remarks about it."

   a. overlook **b.** criticize **c.** remember **d.** punish
   e. praise

Enriching the Lesson

Exercise I.   Borrowings from French

One of the words studied in this lesson is *denouement*, which English has borrowed more or less without change from French. A number of other French expressions that turn up in modern English are listed below. Define each. Then choose any **five**, and for each compose a short illustrative sentence.

1. ennui	11. macabre	21. sabotage
2. joie de vivre	12. nuance	22. de rigueur
3. mystique	13. tour de force	23. par excellence
4. fracas	14. nouveau riche	24. elite
5. éclat	15. charade	25. sortie
6. amour-propre	16. repertoire	26. timbre
7. rapprochement	17. volte-face	27. mot juste
8. queue	18. suave	28. rapport
9. avant-garde	19. souvenir	29. sang-froid
10. pièce de résistance	20. verve	30. repartée

Exercise II.   Anemic Expressions

A great many inexact or meaningless expressions turn up in the speech and writing of what might be called "lazy thinkers." Some of these items are descriptive adjectives like *lousy, swell*, and *fabulous*. Others are empty phrases like *or whatever, or something*, and *you know*.

What's wrong with these weak or "anemic" expressions should be obvious. They are too inexact, too nonspecific, too "fuzzy," to convey more than a vague impression of what the person using them has in mind.

Here's an example of a sentence containing such anemic expressions. Study it carefully.

The special effects in that movie were *out of this world*, but the acting was *awful*.

This sentence doesn't say very much, does it? To be sure, it tells the reader how the person who wrote it felt about certain aspects of the movie. Still, it doesn't make the reasons for these feelings very clear. What, for example, do you suppose the writer means by "awful" acting? special effects that are "out of this world"?

The reader really can't tell because the wording of the sentence is too imprecise, too unfocused. Instead of using more specific words whose meanings are clear and unambiguous, the writer has chosen empty expressions that convey nothing more than generalized emotions. Thus, the reader is left to guess at what the writer really had in mind.

Now look at the same sentence when it has been reworded in a more precise and meaningful way.

> The special effects in that movie were *incredibly lifelike and convincing.* Unfortunately, the acting was *too wooden and stylized to make me believe that the characters were real human beings.*

Now the passage really tells the reader something, not only about *how* the writer felt about the movie but *why.*

A number of sentences containing "anemic" expressions (printed in *italic* type) are given below. Substitute a more exact or meaningful expression for each italicized item. If you feel the sentence must be entirely rephrased in order to make it clearer, by all means rewrite it.

1. With a *terrific* quarterback, *dynamite* receivers, and a *super* defense, our team is sure to have a *fabulous* season.

2. Some of the paintings in the show were *gorgeous*; others were *blah*; and still others were *just plain awful.*

3. Though I admit that his last novel was *pretty lousy*, I still think the man is a *fantastic* writer.

4. The food at the party was *heavenly: yummy* shrimp and lobster, a *lovely* salad, and a *swell* dessert.

5. Rose spent most of her vacation shopping, sightseeing, *etc.*

6. Even though the weather that day was *rotten*, we had a *great* time at the fair.

7. All their *neat* plans for improving the gym *or whatever* fell through at the last moment.

Exercise III. Fused Phrases

The members of one group of English words were formed in a very curious way. Each is made up of a two- or three-word phrase that has been written as if it were one word. This phrase is usually of foreign origin, though in a number of cases it is just plain English. A good example of such "fused phrases" is the word *adroit*, which is simply a French phrase meaning "to the right" all run together.

Another is *alarm*, which comes from the Italian phrase *All'arme!*, meaning "To arms!"

Below are listed a number of other "fused phrases" used in present-day English. Define each. Then indicate the phrase from which the word comes, and translate it into English if it is of foreign origin.

1. debonair	7. nonplus	13. lagniappe
2. checkmate	8. metaphysics	14. puny
3. sinecure	9. akimbo	15. jeopardy
4. pedestal	10. apropos	16. orotund
5. legerdemain	11. pedigree	17. tantamount
6. namesake	12. vouchsafe	18. ado

Exercise IV. Expanding Your Word Power

The words listed below are not on the Basic Word List, but they were mentioned in passing in Lesson 12. All of them would make useful additions to your working vocabulary. Define each, give its etymology, list **two** synonyms and **two** antonyms (where possible), and use in a short illustrative sentence.

1. slovenly	6. hoodwink	11. intermittent
2. repudiate	7. jaunty	12. expunge
3. expedite	8. bumptious	13. digress
4. melancholy	9. systematic	14. tepid
5. scrupulous	10. dowdy	15. proficient

Lesson 13

---

131. **di-lap-i-dat-ed**   *adjective*   dĭ-lăp´-ə-dā-tĭd

[*dilapidare, dilapidatus* (Latin), "pull apart the stones; destroy"; from *dis* (Latin), "apart" + *lapis, lapidis* (Latin), "stone"]

Definition: Fallen into disrepair or partial ruin, usually through neglect.

"That part of the city has truly become a ghost town," Mark observed. "Only the rats now seem to inhabit what few **dilapidated** or burnt-out buildings still remain."

Related Forms: (*verb*) dilapidate; (*noun*) dilapidation

Synonyms: (*adjectives*) deteriorated, run-down, decaying, decrepit, rickety, ramshackle; dingy, seedy, sleazy

Antonyms: (*adjectives*) well kept up, well maintained, shipshape, unspoiled, undamaged

Phrases: in disrepair, go to seed, go to wrack and ruin, run into the ground, go to pot

132. **dil-a-tor-y**   *adjective*   dĭl´-ə-tôr-ē

[*dilatorius* (Latin), "causing delay"; from *differre, dilatus* (Latin), "delay"; from *dis* (Latin), "apart" + *ferre, latus* (Latin), "carry"]

Definition: Inclined to put things off; intended to postpone something.

Some people always pay their bills on time; others are as **dilatory** as snails.

Uncertain whether the Spanish were gods or not, the Aztec emperor Montezuma adopted a wait-and-see attitude toward them. In the end, this **dilatory** policy actually helped Cortés conquer Mexico.

Related Forms: (*noun*) dilatoriness; (*adverb*) dilatorily

Usage Note:
Do not confuse *dilatory* with the adjective *dilated*, which means "spread out" or "widened."

Synonyms: (*adjectives*) late, tardy, slow, behindhand, laggard, dawdling, procrastinating, sluggish, lackadaisical, lethargic, dilly-dallying, shilly-shallying, temporizing

Antonyms: (*adjectives*) prompt, punctual; speedy, swift, quick, fast, expeditious

Phrases: with alacrity, play a waiting game, drag one's heels, as slow as molasses in winter, play for time

175

133. dil-i-gent   *adjective*   dĭl´-ĭ-jĕnt

[*diligens, diligentis* (Latin), "loving; attentive"; from *dis* (Latin), "apart" + *legere* (Latin), "choose"]

Definition: Hardworking; thorough and persistent.

> Ann is a **diligent** student who devotes a lot of time and effort to her quest for academic excellence.

> They claim to have made a **diligent** search of the area, but I suspect that their efforts were no more than perfunctory.

Related Forms: (*noun*) diligence; (*adverb*) diligently

Synonyms: (*adjectives*) assiduous, sedulous, indefatigable

Antonyms: (*adjectives*) lazy, slothful, indolent; perfunctory, cursory

Phrases: take pains with, work like a beaver

134. dire   *adjective*   dīr

[*dirus* (Latin), "horrible, frightful"]

Definition:
a.   Dreadful or disastrous; bleak or cheerless.

> Even a limited confrontation between the superpowers is bound to have a **dire** effect on the rest of the world.

> Though this company's future looks a bit uncertain at present, your **dire** predictions for the coming year are far from justified.

b.   Urgent.

> As we use up the earth's fossil-fuel supplies, we are faced with an increasingly **dire** need to develop new energy resources.

Phrases: a dire fate, dire news, dire financial straits, a dire emergency

Related Forms: (*adjective*) direful; (*nouns*) direness, direfulness; (*adverbs*) direly, direfully

Synonyms: (*adjectives*) calamitous, fatal, woeful, grievous, horrendous; dismal, somber, gloomy; pressing, desperate, extreme

Antonyms: (*adjectives*) salutary, beneficial, salubrious; mild, gentle; inconsequential, insignificant

135. dis-com-fit   *verb*   dĭs-cŭm´-fĭt

[*desconfire, disconfit* (Old French), "rout"; from *dis* (Latin) "un-" + *com* (Latin), "together" + *facere, factus* (Latin), "do, make"]

Definition:
a.   To defeat or frustrate completely.

> Last night, Central High's Netnicks captured the state basketball championship by **discomfiting** the South High Slammers, 61–44.

The would-be burglars were thoroughly **discomfited** by the store's elaborate security system.

b. To perplex, confuse, or embarrass completely.

The sternness of his expression so **discomfited** me that I had difficulty replying to his question.

Related Form: (*noun*) discomfiture

Usage Note:

Do not confuse *discomfit* with *discomfort*. As a noun, *discomfort* indicates a feeling of uneasiness, uncomfortableness, or annoyance that is less severe and more generalized than pain. As a verb, it means "make mildly uneasy, uncomfortable, or annoyed."

Synonyms: (*verbs*) rout, trounce, drub; thwart, foil; baffle; nonplus, abash, disconcert, fluster

Antonyms: (*verbs*) lose to; reassure

---

136. dis-course   *noun:* dĭs´-côrs   *verb:* dĭs-côrs´

[*discursus* (Latin), "a running about; a conversation"; from *dis* (Latin), "in different directions" + *currere, cursus* (Latin), "run"]

Definition:

a. (*noun*) An oral exchange of ideas or conversation; a lengthy discussion, either written or spoken.

"Let your **discourse** with men of business be short and to the point," George Washington once advised.

My sister's last letter from abroad contained an amusing **discourse** on the problems of living in a foreign country.

In Puritan New England, a preacher would sometimes interrupt his Sunday **discourse** to chastise an inattentive member of the congregation.

b. (*verb*) To talk about or discuss at length.

She and I spent the afternoon casually **discoursing** on the state of the world and our ideas for improving it.

In a recent article in a national magazine, a noted sociologist **discoursed** ably and perceptively on the connection between drug abuse and crime.

Related Form: (*adjective*) discursive

Usage Note:

The adjective *discursive* means "rambling" or "digressive." Thus, a discursive style of writing is one that rambles aimlessly from one subject to another.

Synonyms: (*nouns*) treatise, dissertation; sermon, lecture, talk; colloquy; (*verbs*) enlarge (on), expand (on), expatiate (upon), descant (on)

Antonyms (All indicating brevity and conciseness of treatment): (*nouns*) summary, abstract, précis, synopsis; (*verbs*) summarize, synopsize, outline, sketch

137. dis-crim-i-nate   *verb*   dĭs-krĭm´-ə-nāt

[*discriminare, discriminatus* (Latin), "divide; distinguish," from *discrimen* (Latin), "distinction"]

Definition:

    a. To distinguish between two or more things, often by perceiving minute differences.

       Fine differences in markings or coloring often permit an expert birdwatcher to **discriminate** between two very similar species of birds.

       "In some cases," the psychiatrist observed, "the human mind may become so warped that it cannot **discriminate** between fact and fancy."

    b. To behave unfairly toward a person or group because of prejudice.

       Laws now forbid employers to **discriminate** against anyone on the basis of race, creed, color, or sex.

Related Forms: (*noun*) discrimination; (*adjectives*) discriminating, discriminatory, indiscriminate

Usage Note:

Discrimination may properly be used in both a favorable and an unfavorable sense. In its favorable sense, the word means "the ability to make fine or acute distinctions" or "the act of making such distinctions." This meaning occurs in such phrases as "showed little *discrimination* in their use of words." The adjective corresponding to this meaning is *discriminating*, as in "*discriminating* tastes."

    In its unfavorable sense, *discrimination* means "the practice of differentiating unfairly between individuals or groups because of prejudice." This meaning occurs in such phrases as "racial *discrimination*." The adjective corresponding to this meaning is *discriminatory*, as in "*discriminatory* practices."

Synonyms: (*verbs*) differentiate, discern; (*nouns*) perspicacity, acumen, perceptiveness, discernment; favoritism, bias, prejudice, bigotry

138. dis-par-age   *verb*   dĭs-păr´-ĭj

[*desparag(i)er* (Old French), "deprive a person of his or her rank; marry a person of inferior rank"; from *dis* (Latin) "not" + *par* (Latin), "equal"]

Definition: To speak slightingly of or undervalue.

       "I think your article on the basketball squad is eminently fair," I told Sandy. "It doesn't exaggerate the team's abilities, but it doesn't **disparage** them either."

Related Forms: (*noun*) disparagement; (*adjective*) disparaging; (*adverb*) disparagingly

Synonyms: (*verbs*) belittle, depreciate, derogate, decry, underrate, run down, minimize

Antonyms: exaggerate, magnify, increase, enhance; extol, laud, eulogize

139. dis-par-i-ty   *noun*   dĭs-păr′-ə-tē

[*disparitas* (Latin), "unlikeness"; from *dis* (Latin), "not" + *par* (Latin), "equal"]

Definition: Difference or inequality, as of age, character, or quality.

"Both students are the same age and have been in school for the same length of time," the teacher remarked. "Yet, there is a profound **disparity** in their individual reading skills and knowledge of math."

"The **disparity** between our growing energy needs and our dwindling fossil-fuel resources becomes more alarming each day," the official observed. "We must do everything in our power to close this gap."

Related Forms: (*adjective*) disparate; (*adverb*) disparately

Synonyms: (*nouns*) disproportion, dissimilarity, inconsistency

Antonyms: (*nouns*) parity, likeness, similarity, equality

Phrases: gap, the gender gap, a communications gap

140. dis-traught   *adjective*   dĭs-trôt′

[variant form of *distract* (Middle English), "distracted," from *distrahere, distractus* (Latin), "perplex"]

Definition: Deeply distressed or agitated.

All during that long night when little Angie was missing, I tried to calm and reassure her **distraught** parents.

At the news of her son's death in a car accident, Mrs. Bertelli became **distraught** with grief.

Synonyms: (*adjectives*) frantic, anguished, overwrought, hysterical, distracted, perturbed, upset

Antonyms: (*adjectives*) calm, collected, composed, impassive

141. di-vulge   *verb*   dĭ-vŭlj′

[*divulgare* (Latin), "spread among the people"; from *dis* (Latin), "abroad" + *vulgus* (Latin), "common people"]

Definition: To make known; to make public.

"I'm willing to tell the court what I have learned," the reporter declared, "but I refuse to **divulge** the names of my informants."

I couldn't prove my suspicions, so I didn't **divulge** them to anyone.

Related Form: (*noun*) divulgence

Synonyms: (*verbs*) reveal, disclose, impart

Antonyms: (*verbs*) conceal, hide

Phrases: go public with, betray a confidence, leak information to the press, plug security leaks, a shocking exposé

142. doc-ile   *adjective*   dŏs´-əl

[*docilis* (Latin), "teachable"; from *docere* (Latin), "teach"]

Definition: Easy to manage, teach, train or discipline.

"Some of my students are as **docile** as newborn lambs," the teacher remarked. "Others are as stubborn and headstrong as mules."

Related Forms: (*noun*) docility; (*adverb*) docilely

Synonyms: (*adjectives*) submissive, tractable, obedient, amenable, compliant

Antonyms: (*adjectives*) headstrong, willful, perverse, intractable, unmanageable, obdurate

143. dor-mant   *adjective*   dôr´-mənt

[*dormant* (French), "sleeping"; from *dormir* (French), "sleep"]

Definition: Inactive, as if in sleep; suspended in use, growth, or development.

The fact that the volcano is **dormant** does not mean that it is no longer capable of erupting.

After his talents had lain **dormant** for many years, he suddenly began to produce the great novels on which his reputation is based.

Related Form: (*noun*) dormancy

Synonyms: (*adjectives*) latent, passive, inert, quiescent, torpid

Antonyms: (*adjectives*) active, vigorous, vibrant; volatile, explosive; thriving, flourishing

Phrases: a latent talent, in a state of suspended animation

144. dras-tic   *adjective*   drăs´-tĭk

[*drastikos* (Greek), "active; efficient"; from *dran* (Greek), "do"]

Definition: Violently forceful and swift; extreme.

The problems of air and water pollution have become so severe and so pressing that they may require **drastic** measures to correct.

Defeat in the Civil War brought about **drastic** changes in the social structure of the South.

Phrases: a drastic remedy, drastic reforms

Related Form: (*adverb*) drastically

Synonyms: (*adjectives*) powerful, strong, rigorous, potent, thoroughgoing; severe, stern, draconian

Antonyms: (*adjectives*) weak, feeble, ineffectual, halfhearted; mild, gentle, restrained

145. du-plic-i-ty   *noun*   dōō-plĭs´-ĭ-tē *or* dyōō-plĭs´-ĭ-tē

[*duplicitas* (Latin), "deceit"; from *duo* (Latin), "two" + *plicare* (Latin), "fold"]

Definition: Deliberate deception in speech or conduct.

"Sandy tries to be honest and upright in all her dealings with other people," I remarked. "**Duplicity** simply has no place in her character."

Related Form: (*adjective*) duplicitous

Synonyms: (*nouns*) guile, deceit, trickery, dissimulation, chicanery, imposture, sharp practice, double-dealing

Antonyms: (*nouns*) honesty, integrity, uprightness, probity, plain dealing

Phrases: an artful dodge, a Judas kiss, under false colors, two-faced

A Judas Kiss

English has many colorful expressions that are concerned with duplicity or treachery. One of the most interesting of these is *a Judas kiss.*

As you may already know from reading the Bible, Judas Iscariot was the disciple who betrayed Jesus Christ to his enemies. The betrayal took place in the garden of Gethsemane outside Jerusalem the day before Christ was crucified. Jesus and some of his most trusted friends had gone there to meditate. Suddenly, Judas and a band of soldiers and ruffians appeared. As arranged in advance, Judas showed the soldiers which of the people in the garden was Jesus by kissing him lightly on the cheek. This was a customary greeting in those times. On the surface, Judas's kiss appeared to be a harmless act of friendship and affection. In reality, however, it was a signal telling the soldiers whom to seize and lead off to eventual death.

The details of Judas's treachery were recorded by several of the writers of the New Testament (for example, Matt. 26:29, Mark 14:45, Luke 22:47). It is from these Biblical sources that the phrase *a Judas kiss* has come into present-day English to indicate any act that on the surface looks kindly, affectionate, or courteous but in reality is quite the opposite.

Using the Words

Exercise I. Syllabication and Pronunciation

Syllabicate the following words correctly, and place the major stress mark(′) after the syllable that is accented when the word is pronounced. Two answers are correct in one instance.

1. dilapidated
2. dilatory
3. diligent
4. discourse
5. disparage
6. distraught
7. divulge
8. dormant
9. duplicity

Exercise II. Words Out of Context

In each of the following, select the item that best expresses the meaning of the numbered word at the left.

1. discomfit
   a. minimize b. soothe c. rout
   d. uncover

2. duplicity
   a. deceit b. promptness c. disrepair
   d. composure

3. dilapidated
   a. punctual b. run-down c. frantic
   d. obedient

4. dormant
   a. inactive b. cursory c. honest
   d. agitated

5. distraught
   a. amusingly clever b. extremely urgent
   c. deeply distressed d. surprisingly slow

6. drastic
   a. gentle b. willful c. severe d. lazy

7. divulge
   a. lessen b. absolve c. reveal
   d. blame

Exercise III. Completing Sentences

Complete each of the following sentences or pairs of sentences by selecting the most appropriate word from the given group of words. Make any adjustments that are necessary to fit the words into the sentences properly. Use each word only once.

discriminate   docile   disparage

diligent   disparity   divulge

discourse   dilatory   dire

1. "You're only supposed to present a brief, informal report at the meeting," my boss exclaimed, "not a learned scientific _____!"

2. "Don't expect them to do anything but _____ your abilities," my best friend warned me before my piano recital. "They never have a good word to say about anyone!"

3. "In 1900, there was a glaring _____ between the lifestyles of the 'haves' and the 'have-nots' of this country," the speaker said. "Fortunately, since then we have done much to close that appalling gap."

4. "I have some advice for our _____ coworkers in the shipping department," my supervisor said at the meeting. "Don't put off until tomorrow what you can do today!"

5. "At the end of the month, I found myself in _____ financial straits," Ed recalled bleakly. "Never before had I been in such an awful fix as far as money was concerned."

6. She is a _____ student whose hard work and dedication have been richly rewarded over the years.

7. "I believe it is wrong to _____ against people who are not exactly like ourselves," Sheila declared. "None of us should allow prejudice or bigotry to creep into our attitudes toward other human beings."

8. "Charlie Tompkins is much too _____ and easygoing to make an effective scoutmaster," Mr. Briggs remarked. "What we need is an energetic leader, not someone who can be led around by the nose with no trouble at all."

Exercise IV. Synonyms and Antonyms

Classify each of the following pairs of words as **S** for **synonyms** and **A** for **antonyms**.

1. discourse—lecture
2. diligent—lazy
3. praise—disparage
4. discrimination—prejudice
5. discomfit—fluster
6. conceal—divulge
7. headstrong—docile
8. calamitous—dire
9. disparity—similarity
10. deception—duplicity
11. dilatory—prompt
12. mild—drastic
13. dormant—latent
14. distraught—composed

Exercise V. Word Roundup

1. Explain what is meant by "a *discursive* writing style."
2. Explain the difference in meaning between the words in each of the following pairs.

   a. discomfit—discomfort   b. discriminating—discriminatory

3. Define the word *draconian*. What famous Greek lawgiver's name is embodied in this word? Why?

4. Explain the meaning of each of the following phrases.

   a. go to seed
   b. play a waiting game
   c. work like a beaver
   d. go public with

   e. drag one's heels
   f. run into the ground
   g. plug security leaks
   h. suspended animation

5. Explain what is meant by *a Judas kiss*.

6. In what famous 19th-century novel does the character called *the Artful Dodger* appear? Who is the author of this novel? What do you think the author was trying to suggest about the character by using this distinctive name?

Exercise VI.   Framing Sentences

A.   Use each of the following words in an original illustrative sentence.

1. dilatory
2. dire

3. dormant
4. distraught

5. divulge
6. duplicity

B.   Give a **noun** form of each of these words, and use it in an illustrative sentence.

1. dilapidated
2. discomfit
3. disparage

C.   Give an **adjective** form of each of these words, and use it in an illustrative sentence.

1. discourse
2. discriminate
3. disparity

D.   Give an **adverb** form of each of these words, and use it in an illustrative sentence.

1. diligent
2. docile
3. drastic

Peter Mark Roget

Peter Mark Roget (1779–1869), an English physician with an "insatiable thirst for knowledge and an appetite for work," was the father of a new kind of word book called a *thesaurus*. Unlike a dictionary, the words in a thesaurus are neither defined nor alphabetically arranged. Instead, they are presented in groups according to related ideas. Roget also devised a slide rule, attempted to perfect a calculating machine, invented and solved difficult chess problems, and founded a society for the diffusion of knowledge.

Dissecting the Words

1. The Latin prefix **de** is found at the beginning of a good many common English words. Among them are *defer, defect*, and most of the other basic words studied in Lesson 12. **De** has two primary meanings:

a. It may mean "away," "off," or "down," as in these words:

depart (literally, "go away")—to leave or deviate from

decapitate (literally, "take the head off")—to cut off the head

devolve (literally, "roll down")—to pass or transfer from one person to another

depress (literally, "press down")—to lower physically; to cause a lowering of mood or spirit

despoil (literally, "carry away or plunder")—to plunder or rob of by force

deter (literally, "frighten away")—to prevent or discourage

b. It may have a negative force roughly like "not" or "un-," as in these words:

dethrone (literally, "unthrone")—to remove from the throne

debunk (literally, "take the bunk out of")—to expose the falseness of unsound or exaggerated claims

demerit (literally, "not a merit; an unmerit")—a black mark usually involving the loss of some privilege or right

destabilize (literally, "unstabilize")—to upset the stability of

2. The Latin prefix **dis** is related to **de**. It occurs at the beginning of a number of words studied in Lesson 13, including *dispartiy* and *discriminate*. As with **de**, the prefix **dis** has two basic meanings:

a. It may mean "away from" or "apart," as in these words:

dispel (*dis*, "away" + *pel*, "drive")—to scatter or dissipate

dislodge (*dis*, "apart" + *lodge*, "place")—to remove from a place that has been occupied up until then

b. It may have a negative force meaning roughly "not" or "lack of," as in these words:

dissimilar (*dis*, "not" + *similar*)—not similar or alike

disinclined (*dis*, "not" + *inclined*)—not inclined

disintegrate (literally, "make not whole")—to deteriorate or rot away

disfranchise (*dis*, "not" + *franchise*)—to take the right to vote away from

disorder (*dis*, "lack of" + *order*)—confusion; lack of order

Note that **dis** becomes **di** before the letters *f, g, l, m,* and *v,* and sometimes these letters double. For example:

$$dis + fer = \textbf{differ}$$

The Latin root **cur** or **curs**, meaning "run," appears in one form or another in numerous English words. One of them is *discourse*, studied in Lesson 13. Here are a few other useful examples:

concur (literally, "run together")—to coincide; to agree

cursory—running over something hurriedly and superficially

curriculum—a course of study

precursor—a forerunner

discursive—passing from one subject to another in a rambling fashion

recur—to occur again

recourse—a turning to someone or something for help or protection

recurrent—happening again and again

concourse (literally, "a running together")—an assemblage; a place of
   meeting; an open space where several roads come together

courier (literally, "runner")—a messenger

Other words in which **cur(s)** appears include *excursion, occur, incur, current, currency,* and *course.*

Exercise

A. Complete the following activities relating to the prefixes *de* and *dis.*

1. Give the meaning of the following words containing the prefix *de.* Then choose any **five**, and, for each, compose a short illustrative sentence.

a. debar	e. denounce	i. deplete
b. demote	f. defer	j. depose
c. dejection	g. depreciate	k. decamp
d. delete	h. delinquent	l. decapitate

2. Define each of the following words, and show how its meaning is affected by the prefix *dis.*

a. disorganized	e. disqualify	i. disfranchise
b. disparity	f. discord	j. disinherit
c. dispraise	g. disenchant	k. disbar
d. disproportionate	h. disfigure	l. dismember

B. Now complete the following activities relating to the root *cur* or *curs.*

1. Give a synonym for each of the following words.

a. precursor	b. courier	c. discursive

2. With or without the aid of a dictionary, define the following words. Then use each in a short illustrative sentence.

a. recur	c. incur	e. recourse
b. excursion	d. recurrent	f. currency

Working with Context Clues

Review the "Working with Context Clues" section in Lesson 12 (pages 170–171) before you begin this section.

"Guideposts" to Restatement Clues. Sometimes the linking expressions present in a sentence-completion exercise can act as "guideposts" to the context clues you are looking for. In other words, these linking expressions can tip you off to the nature and location of the clue.

Let's look at the linking expressions that can do this for restatement clues. They include certain types of conjunctions (e.g., *and, or, both. . . and, not only. . . but also*), adverbs (e.g., *moreover, besides*), prepositional phrases (e.g., *in addition*), and related expressions (e.g., *that is*). Each in some way binds together two parallel or similar sentences or parts of a sentence. Usually, the clue is contained in one of these tied-together elements, and the blank appears in the other. The linking expression "points" to the clue by drawing your eye from the element containing the blank to the element to which it is tied. And, as you already know, this is the element that probably contains the clue.

Study the following simple example of a sentence-completion exercise. It contains both a restatement clue and a linking expression that points to this clue.

As both a hardworking businessman and an ＿＿＿＿＿＿ community leader, Joseph X. Laurelli has done much to promote the well-being of those who live in this town.

a. ignorant   b. ominous   c. energetic   d. ugly   e. apathetic

Notice that this sentence contains the phrase *both. . . and.* This is the type of conjunction that binds together parallel or similar parts of a sentence. In this case, it connects two parallel phrases, one of which contains the blank for the missing word.

An editor in a large publishing company prepares the text of a book for publication. Working for a publisher is an excellent career objective for someone who uses words well.

The presence of *both. . .and* in this situation tips you off to the type of clue you will find and its general location in the sentence. Since *both. . . and* connects parallel or similar sentence elements, you are probably going to find a restatement clue. Since, in this instance, it connects two parallel phrases, one of which contains the blank, you are probably going to find the clue in the other phrase, which is complete.

Look at the two phrases in question. They are "a hardworking businessman" and "an _____ community leader." Notice that each contains the indefinite article (*a, an*) and a noun (*businessman*) or noun phrase (*community leader*). Notice too that one of them contains an adjective (*hardworking*), but that the blank takes the place of a corresponding adjective in the other. This tells you that an adjective meaning something like *hardworking* is what goes in the blank.

Now look at the five words from which you are to choose the word that goes in the blank. Only one of them means anything even remotely like *hardworking*. It is Choice *c, energetic*. Clearly, this is the word that goes in the blank.

As you can see from this simple example, linking expressions can be very useful in dealing successfully with sentence-completion exercises.

Exercise

Complete each of the following by selecting the word that makes the best sense in the sentence (or group of sentences) as a whole. Indicate the clue or clues that led you to make your choice.

1. "My editor has foolishly _____ several important paragraphs from my article," the noted writer complained to his publisher. "In addition, the man has cut out all the footnotes!"

   a. buttressed b. deleted c. circumvented
   d. apprehended

2. "You have to work hard to get ahead in this company," my supervisor told me on my first day on the job. "Around here advancement only comes to those who are _____."

   a. dilatory b. dilapidated c. dormant d. diligent

3. The President of Trimark Toy Company is an able administrator, who can handle any problem with skill and _____.

   a. dexterity b. delinquency c. disparity d. duplicity

4. "Can you provide me with any solid proof of what you have just told me?" the lawyer asked. "If I had some _____ evidence, I might be able to help you."

   a. collaborating b. calumniating c. corroborating
   d. cajoling

5. Not only his _____ facial expression but also his discouraged tone of voice told me that he was feeling a little down in the dumps today.

   a. defective b. devout c. demure d. dejected

6. "I certainly looked a mess after romping around with my five-year-old nephew all afternoon," I recalled fondly. "My shirt-tails were hanging out, my hair was going in every imaginable direction, and my tie was all _____."

   a. ambivalent b. adverse c. articulate d. askew

7. As its title suggests, *Presidential* _____ is packed with amusing, often revealing stories involving the men who have held the first office in our land.

   a. *Anecdotes* b. *Devotions* c. *Anathemas* d. *Boycotts*

8. "I know your friend claims that his boss was guilty of serious wrongdoing while in public office," I replied. "But, so far he has done precious little to substantiate these charges and _____."

   a. criteria b. allegations c. discourses d. anomalies

9. I knew that she wanted me to give her an honest opinion of her performance at the recital. Still, I found it difficult to be _____ about my feelings without hurting hers.

   a. candid b. cynical c. brusque d. dapper

10. "Brevity is the soul of wit" simply means that a joke should be as _____ or succinct as humanly possible.

    a. banal b. academic c. concise d. bizarre

Enriching the Lesson

Exercise I. More Look-Alikes

As you know, English has a great many duos and even trios of words that look alike but mean quite different things. Some of these "look-alikes" were presented in Lesson 10 (page 135). Others are paired off below. With or without the aid of a dictionary, explain the difference in meaning between the members of each pair.

1.	emulate—simulate	11.	delegate—relegate
2.	faint—feint	12.	deprecate—depreciate
3.	resemble—dissemble	13.	allude—elude
4.	discrete—discreet	14.	envious—enviable
5.	boor—bore	15.	complaisant—complacent
6.	manners—mannerisms	16.	honorable—honorary
7.	capital—capitol	17.	authoritative—authoritarian
8.	aesthetic—ascetic	18.	imperial—imperious
9.	amend—emend	19.	allay—ally
10.	solid—stolid	20.	venal—venial

Now, choose any **five** of the pairs of words listed above. For each compose a set of **two** sentences, each of which illustrates the meaning of **one** of the words in the pair.

Exercise II. Biblical Expressions

One of the phrases mentioned in connection with *duplicity* (Word 145) in Lesson 13 is *a Judas kiss*. As you know, this phrase derives from an incident related in the New Testament of the Bible. The Bible has given English many other words and phrases like *a Judas kiss*. Some of these expressions are listed below. With or without the aid of a dictionary or other reference book, define or explain each. Then choose any **five**, and for each compose a short illustrative sentence.

1. see the handwriting on the wall
2. a shibboleth
3. apocryphal
4. a doubting Thomas
5. separate the sheep from the goats (*or* the wheat from the chaff)
6. a jeremiad
7. hide one's light under a bushel
8. a Good Samaritan
9. the salt of the earth
10. a Jonah
11. serve two masters
12. reap the whirlwind
13. a behemoth
14. turn the other cheek
15. apocalyptic
16. cast one's bread upon the waters
17. antediluvian
18. the promised land
19. manna from heaven
20. cast pearls before swine

Exercise III. A Verbal Diversion

A good many expressions that occur in present-day English utilize the names of foreign peoples with whom Americans may or may not have come into contact. Most of these expressions employ the foreign name quite literally. For example, the *French* in *French fried potatoes* simply indicates that the potatoes have been fried in a manner that is (or at some point was considered to be) typical of French cooking.

A few of these expressions, however, have an "extended" or "figurative" meaning that is not immediately revealed by the name of the foreign people employed. Some examples are listed below. With or without the aid of a dictionary or other reference book, define or explain each. Then choose any **five**, and for each compose a short illustrative sentence.

1. a Dutch uncle
2. Indian summer
3. a bohemian
4. a Dutch treat *or* go Dutch
5. get your Irish up
6. vandalism
7. put a little English on the ball
8. a Scotch verdict
9. Dutch courage
10. a Mexican standoff
11. French leave
12. get in Dutch with
13. Siamese twins
14. an Indian giver
15. a street Arab

190

Notice that some of the expressions listed above are not at all complimentary to the foreign peoples whose names appear in them. What do you think this says about how our language sometimes views foreigners?

Exercise IV. Ricochet Words

A **ricochet word** (sometimes called a **reduplicate word**) is a word consisting of two elements that are almost identical in form —for example, *dilly-dally* or *hurdy-gurdy*. The two elements in a ricochet word usually differ from one another only in a single vowel (e.g., *chitchat*) or consonant (e.g., *namby-pamby*). Sometimes they are separated from each other by a hyphen (e.g., *hocus-pocus*); sometimes they are not (e.g., *hubbub*).

There are several hundred ricochet words in use in present-day English. Some of them are listed below. With or without the aid of a dictionary define each.

1.	shilly-shally	12.	razzle-dazzle
2.	willy-nilly	13.	flimflam
3.	dilly-dally	14.	riffraff
4.	wishy-washy	15.	claptrap
5.	hoity-toity	16.	folderol
6.	harum-scarum	17.	tittle-tattle
7.	hanky-panky	18.	hubbub
8.	mishmash	19.	hurdy-gurdy
9.	voodoo	20.	hugger-mugger
10.	hobnob	21.	hodgepodge
11.	hocus-pocus	22.	helter-skelter

Choose any **five** of the items given above, and for each compose a short illustrative sentence.

Exercise V. Expanding Your Word Power

The words listed below are not on the Basic Word List, but they were mentioned in passing in Lesson 13. All of them would make useful additions to your working vocabulary. Define each, give its etymology, list **two** synonyms and **two** antonyms (where possible), and use in a short illustrative sentence.

1.	decrepit	6.	treatise	11.	impassive
2.	indefatigable	7.	perspicacity	12.	impart
3.	perfunctory	8.	bigotry	13.	tractable
4.	indolent	9.	depreciate	14.	feeble
5.	disconcert	10.	parity	15.	chicanery

Lesson 14

146. eclectic — 160. **enigma**

---

146. **ec-lec-tic**   *adjective and noun*   ĕ-klĕk´-tĭk
[*eklektikos* (Greek), "picked out"; from *ek* (Greek), "out of" + *legein* (Greek), "choose"]

Definition:
　　a. (*adjective*) Choosing what seems best from various sources.

　　　　Because of her **eclectic** teaching methods and "pick-and-choose" testing techniques, students enjoy Miss Curry's classes.

　　b.　(*noun*) One whose opinions and beliefs are drawn from various sources.

　　　　In a sense, St. Thomas Aquinas was an **eclectic** because he attempted to reconcile ancient Greek philosophy with Christian theology.

Phrases:　an eclectic philosopher, an eclectic style of architecture

Related Form:　(*noun*) eclecticism

Synonyms:　(*adjectives*) selective, synthesized

Antonyms:　(*adjectives*) uniform, monolithic

Phrase:　all of a piece

---

147. **ef-fete**   *adjective*   ĕ-fēt´ *or* ĭ-fēt´
[*effetus* (Latin), "worn out by childbearing"; from *ex* (Latin), "out" + *fetus* (Latin), "offspring"]

Definition:　Worn out or exhausted; marked by weakness, self-indulgence or decadence.

　　By late imperial times, centuries of soft living had turned the once hardy Roman people into an **effete** and indolent race.

Phrases:　an effete snob, an effete aristocrat, an effete society

Related Form:　(*noun*) effeteness

Usage Note:
　When used of males, the word *effete* often carries a sense of effeminacy or "unmanliness" with it.

Synonyms:　(*adjectives*) spent, burned-out; decadent; barren, sterile

Antonyms:　(*adjectives*) vigorous, energetic, dynamic; productive, fertile, flourishing, prolific

192

Edward Gibbon

The English historian Edward Gibbon (1737–1794) was the author of the multivolume *Decline and Fall of the Roman Empire*, a monumental study of the material decay and moral decline that brought about the collapse of a great civilization and turned a vigorous people into an effete and indolent race. The work, which begins with events in the second century A.D., covers almost 1300 years of history. Despite harsh criticism from some quarters, the book won Gibbon immediate acclaim as a historian and is still one of the most widely read historical studies of modern times.

148. ef-fi-ca-cious *adjective* ĕf-ə-kā´-shəs

[*efficax, efficacis* (Latin), "effective"; from *ex* (Latin), "out" + *facere, factus* (Latin), "do"]

Definition: Capable of producing the desired effect.

Afterschool detention seems to be an **efficacious** solution to the problem of student lateness.

Related Forms: (*nouns*) efficacy, efficaciousness; (*adverb*) efficaciously

Synonyms: (*adjectives*) effective, effectual, efficient, powerful, potent

Antonyms: (*adjectives*) ineffective, ineffectual, inefficient, unserviceable, useless, inadequate

149. ef-fron-ter-y *noun* ĕ-frŭn´-tə-rē

[*effronterie* (French), "shamelessness"; from *effrons, effrontis* (Latin), "barefaced"; from *ex* (Latin), "out" + *frons, frontis* (Latin), "forehead"]

Definition: Shameless boldness.

"You mean to tell me," I exclaimed in surprise, "that you had the **effrontery** to ask for a raise when your productivity has really fallen off lately?"

Synonyms: (*nouns*) audacity, impertinence, temerity, gall, nerve, cheek, chutzpah, presumption

Antonyms: (*nouns*) timidity, shyness, meekness, modesty, diffidence

Phrase: barefaced audacity

150. e-lic-it   *verb*   ĭ-lĭs´-ĭt

[*elicere, elicitus* (Latin), "draw out"; from *ex* (Latin), "out of" + *lacere* (Latin), "draw"]

Definition: To draw out or call forth.

Both sides in the dispute were so obviously biased that it was impossible to **elicit** a fair account of what had taken place.

Phrases: elicit a response, elicit the truth

Usage Note:

Do not confuse *elicit* with the adjective *illicit*, meaning "unlawful."

Synonyms: (*verbs*) evoke, prompt, extract, educe, produce

151. e-lite   *noun and adjective*   ĭ-lēt´ *or* ā-lēt´

[*élite* (French), "choice"; from *ex* (Latin), "out" + *legere, lectus* (Latin), "pick"]

Definition:

a.   (*noun*) A highly select group of superior individuals.

Membership in the National Honor Society indicates that a young person belongs to this country's academic **elite**.

b.   (*adjective*) Select; superior.

An **elite** corps of paratroopers, hand-picked for outstanding skill and bravery, made a surprise raid on the airfield and rescued the hostages being held there.

Related Forms: (*noun*) elitism; (*adjective*) elitist

A group of aristocrats, the elite of French society, attending a reception at Versailles during the reign of Napoleon III (1852–70).

Though *elite* is usually a favorable word, *elitist* and *elitism* are definitely not. These two words suggest undue pride in belonging to some supposedly superior group. They also imply an underlying belief in the domination of society by the people "on top." Thus, they indicate attitudes that are usually considered antidemocratic and antilibertarian. For this reason, these words are distinctly pejorative in tone.

Synonyms: (*nouns*) privileged class, privileged few, aristocracy, nobility, upper crust, cream of the crop, crème de la crème; (*adjectives*) choice, exclusive, first class, topnotch, top-drawer, A-one

Antonyms: (*nouns*) masses, common herd, proletariat, hoi polloi, rank and file, rabble, riffraff, dregs of society; (*adjective*) proletarian

152. e-ma-ci-at-ed   *adjective*   ē-mā´-shē-āt-ĭd

[*e* (Latin), "completely" + *maciare, maciatus* (Latin), "make lean"; from *macies* (Latin), "leanness"]

Definition: Wasted or reduced by starvation, disease, or the like.

The hollow eyes and shrunken cheeks of the **emaciated** children in the magazine ad were haunting reminders of our role in the fight against world hunger.

Nothing causes a checking account to look more **emaciated** than paying all the monthly bills.

Related Form: (*noun*) emaciation; (*verb*) emaciate

Synonyms: (*adjectives*) gaunt, haggard, shriveled, withered, skeletal, undernourished

Antonyms: (*adjectives*) fat, chubby, plump, corpulent, obese

153. em-a-nate   *verb*   ĕm´-ə-nāt

[*ex* (Latin), "out" + *manare, manatus* (Latin), "flow"]

Definition:
a. To flow out of.

When Coach Casey gives his pregame pep talk, the enthusiasm that **emanates** from him sparks the whole team.

b. To send forth.

Some radioactive substances can **emanate** dangerous radiation for many years.

Related Form: (*noun*) emanation

Synonyms: (*verbs*) flow from, proceed from, spring, originate, emerge; emit, project, give off, issue

Antonyms: (*verbs*) soak up, absorb, draw in, attract

154. em·bel·lish   *verb*   ĕm-bĕl´-ĭsh

[*embellir* (Old French), "beautify"; from *en* (Latin), "causing" + *bellus* (Latin), "beautiful"]

Definition: To decorate or enhance.

In the Victorian era, fashion designers **embellished** women's dresses with all sorts of frills and flounces.

"The facts will speak for themselves," my lawyer told me. You need not **embellish** them with elaborate explanations."

Related Form: (*noun*) embellishment

Usage Note:
Embellish is often used in the sense of adding fictitious details to a story or statement. When used in this way, the word is virtually a synonym of *fabricate* (Word 181). Thus, a story that has been *embellished* may be partially or totally untrue.

Synonyms: (*verbs*) adorn, dress up, spruce up, gussy up, garnish

Antonyms: (*verbs*) mar, deface, disfigure

155. em·i·nent   *adjective*   ĕm´-ə-nĕnt

[*eminens, eminentis* (Latin), "lofty"; from *ex* (Latin), "out" + *minere* (Latin), "stand; project"]

Definition:
a. High in rank; distinguished.

Who would have suspected that the modestly dressed, retiring woman was actually an **eminent** scientist of international reputation?

b. Outstanding; conspicuous.

Both students and teachers esteem Mr. Ortiz for his **eminent** fairness in evaluating student performance and ability.

Eminent among her sterling qualities of character are tact and consideration for others.

Related Forms: (*noun*) eminence; (*adverb*) eminently

Usage Notes:
a. The legal expression *eminent domain* indicates the right of a government to take over private property for public use (after paying a reasonable compensation for it, of course).

b. Do not confuse *eminent* with *imminent*, which means "threatening" or "impending."

c. *Your Eminence* is the proper phrase to employ when addressing a cardinal of the Roman Catholic Church.

Synonyms: (*adjectives*) prominent, renowned, illustrious; notable, great, noteworthy; remarkable, marked

Antonyms: (*adjectives*) obscure, lowly, undistinguished; unremarkable

196

156. em-pa-thy   *noun*   ĕm´-pə-<u>th</u>ē

[*empatheia* (Greek), "passion"; from *en* (Greek), "causing" + *pathos* (Greek), "suffering"]

Definition: A sympathetic understanding of, or identification with, the feelings, thoughts, and attitudes of someone or something else.

> Ellen's volunteer visits to the nursing home are motivated, not by a detached sense of duty, but by a genuine **empathy** for those who are lonely.

> So strong is my **empathy** with the poems of Robert Frost that I often feel as though I could have written them myself.

Related Forms: (*adjectives*) empathic, empathetic; (*verb*) empathize

Synonyms: (*nouns*) sympathy, compassion

Antonyms: (*nouns*) insensitivity, callousness, lack of understanding or appreciation

Phrases: the generation gap, a communications gap

157. em-u-late   *verb*   ĕm´-yə-lāt

[*aemulari, aemulatus* (Latin), "strive to excel"]

Definition: To try to equal or excel the excellence of.

> The old fable tells us to **emulate** the industry of the ant, so that we don't wind up empty-handed beggars like the improvident grasshopper.

Related Forms: (*nouns*) emulation, emulator

Synonyms: (*verbs*) imitate, match, rival, follow, mirror, take after

Phrases: follow in the footsteps of, follow the example of, model one's behavior on

158. en-clave   *noun*   ĕn´-klāv´ *or* än´-klāv

[*enclave* (Old French), "enclosure"; from *in* (Latin), "in" + *clavis* (Latin), "key"]

Definition:

a. A country or area lying wholly within the boundaries of another country or area.

> Though a completely independent state, Vatican City is no more than a tiny **enclave** in the heart of the great Italian capital city of Rome.

b. A separate group or community within a larger group or community.

> "All of us had dedicated our lives to the arts," I recalled. "For that reason, we thought of ourselves as an **enclave** of culture in a society concerned only with making money and having fun."

Synonyms: (*nouns*) enclosure, precinct

159. en-dem-ic   *adjective*   ĕn-dĕm´-ĭk

[*endémique* (French), "endemic"; from *endem(i)os* (Greek), "dwelling in a place"; from *en* (Greek), "in" + *demos* (Greek), "people"]

Definition: Peculiar to a particular locality or group of people.

Many diseases that are **endemic** to the tropics are entirely unknown in Alaska, Canada, or Siberia.

Phrases: an endemic plant or animal, an endemic disorder

Related Forms: (*adjectives*) endemical

Usage Note:
Though the use of *endemic* is normally restricted to diseases and plant–animal life, the word may occasionally be used figuratively in other contexts. For example, a problem may be said to be endemic to a particular profession, or racism endemic to a particular area or group.

Synonyms: (*adjectives*) indigenous, native

Antonyms: (*adjectives*) alien, extraneous, foreign

An Enigmatic Creature

In classical mythology, the sphinx was a monster having the head of a woman, the body of a lion, and the wings of an eagle. This female oddity was said to crouch on a block of stone outside the Greek city Thebes, where she confronted travelers with a riddle intended to stump them. The traveler who could not answer the riddle was killed. When Oedipus, a famous figure in Greek mythology, solved the riddle, the sphinx promptly killed herself. The ancient Egyptians constructed a colossal figure of a recumbant sphinx near the pyramids of Gizah (see photo).

Our modern word *sphinx* derives from this odd creature out of Greek myth. Today, the word is sometimes used to indicate a person who habitually asks unsolvable riddles, is engaged in mysterious actions, always wears an enigmatic facial expression (the proverbial "poker face"), or deliberately answers questions evasively.

160. e-nig-ma   *noun*   ĭ-nĭg´-mə

[*ainigma* (Greek), "riddle"; from *ainos* (Greek), "tale; story"]

Definition:

   a. An intentionally obscure statement; a riddle.

      Sometimes crossword-puzzle clues contain puns, **enigmas**, and other kinds of brainteasers, rather than straightforward hints to the words that are wanted.

   b. Someone or something that is puzzling or mysterious.

      Her consistently strange and unpredictable behavior has caused many people to regard her as a complete **enigma**.

      The unexpected death of a young person is one of life's most perplexing **enigmas**, especially for those who are the same age as the deceased.

Related Forms: (*adjectives*) enigmatic, enigmatical

Synonyms: (*nouns*) mystery, puzzle, conundrum, dilemma, brainteaser, mind-boggler

Phrases: a tough nut to crack, a complete question mark, terra incognita, a sealed (or closed) book

Using the Words

Exercise I. Parts of Speech

Indicate the part of speech of each of the following words. In one case, two answers are correct.

1. endemic	4. empathy	7. effrontery
2. enclave	5. enigma	8. elite
3. emulate	6. effete	9. efficacious

Exercise II. Words in Phrases

In each of the following groups, select the item that best expresses the meaning of the *italicized* word in the introductory phrase.

1. an *eclectic* style of architecture
    a. excellent b. selective c. efficacious d. modern
    e. popular

2. an *effete* snob
    a. greedy b. depressed c. inventive d. worn out
    e. outstanding

3. the *elite* of the entertainment world
    a. retired members b. fans c. rank and file d. superstars
    e. charlatans

4. a light *emanating* from the tunnel
   a. flashing   b. hurrying   c. blinking   d. radiating
   e. stolen

5. *endemic* to the North American continent
   a. related   b. averse   c. accustomed   d. extraneous
   e. native

6. *empathy* for her patient
   a. medical attention   b. compassion   c. fear   d. apathy
   e. financial support

7. a complete *enigma*
   a. puzzle   b. fool   c. success   d. failure   e. joke

8. an *eminent* historian
   a. elderly   b. obscure   c. renowned   d. retired   e. foreign

Exercise III.   Completing Sentences

Complete each of the following sentences or pairs of sentences by selecting the most appropriate word from the given group of words. Use each word only once. Make any adjustments that are necessary to fit the words into the sentences properly.

emaciated	enclave	empathy
elicit	eminent	efficacious
effrontery	embellish	emulate

1. "I was really only on a fishing expedition," the D.A. remarked. "I never expected my innocent question to _____ such an incriminating statement from the witness."

2. Though several workable solutions to the landfill problem were suggested at the meeting, Mrs. Brown's appeared to be the most _____.

3. My dad lost so much weight during his recent illness that for a while he looked positively _____.

4. Paris fashions are so popular that profit-minded New York designers take pains to _____ them.

5. He had the _____ to ask me for a recommendation despite the fact that I had just fired him for gross inefficiency.

6. "I know Monaco is an independent country," I replied. "Still, as far as territory goes, it is nothing more than a tiny _____ in the southeast corner of France."

7. One of the candidates running for the Senate is an _____ educator with a national reputation. The other is an obscure used-car salesman from Missoula.

8. "Your hat is decorated enough already," Glenda remarked. "You don't need to _____ it any further."

Exercise IV. Synonyms and Antonyms

A. In each of the following groups, select the **two** words that are most nearly **synonyms**.

1. a. spent   b. vigorous   c. inclement   d. burnt-out
2. a. audacity   b. temerity   c. timidity   d. callousness
3. a. evoke   b. illicit   c. produce   d. echo
4. a. puzzle   b. enclosure   c. mind-boggler   d. gall
5. a. sympathy   b. callousness   c. compassion   d. shyness

Now for each pair of synonyms that you have selected, supply a word from the Basic Word List in this lesson (Words 146–160) that means **the same** or **almost the same** thing.

B. In each of the following, select the item that is most nearly **opposite** in meaning to the numbered word at the left.

1. elite   a. hoi polloi   b. aristocracy   c. enclave
             d. affluence   e. modesty
2. emaciated   a. uniform   b. timid   c. corpulent
             d. haggard   e. barren
3. endemic   a. useless   b. native   c. fertile   d. alien
             e. puzzling
4. efficacious   a. selective   b. basic   c. exclusive
             d. potent   e. ineffective
5. embellish   a. fabricate   b. adorn   c. deface   d. emerge
             e. imitate

Exercise V. Word Roundup

1. Explain the difference in meaning between the words in each of the following pairs:

    a. imminent—eminent   b. illicit—elicit

2. With or without the aid of a dictionary, explain the meaning of each of the following phrases:

    a. hoi polloi   d. upper crust   g. a sealed book
    b. terra incognita   e. all of a piece   h. rank and file
    c. eminent   f. cream of the   i. generation
       domain   crop   gap

3. Who should be addressed as *Your Eminence*?

4. With or without the aid of a dictionary, explain the story behind each of the following expressions:

    a. sphinx   b. a poker face

Exercise VI. Framing Sentences

A. Use each of the following words in an original sentence.

1. eclectic
2. effete
3. elite

4. effrontery
5. endemic
6. elicit

7. enclave
8. empathize
9. enigmatic

B. Give a **noun** form of each of the following words, and use it in a short illustrative sentence.

1. embellish
2. emulate

3. eminent
4. emaciated

5. efficacious
6. emanate

Completing Verbal Analogies

"A Causes B."   Another word relationship that frequently appears in the analogy sections of standardized tests is "*A* necessarily causes *B*; *C* causes *D*." An example of an analogy question involving this relationship is given below. See if you can figure out the correct answer before you read the rest of this section.

starvation : emaciation ::
- **a.** moderation : burliness
- **b.** gluttony : obesity
- **c.** fasting : corpulence
- **d.** abstinence : stockiness
- **e.** dieting : rotundity

The answer is *b*. *Starvation* will necessarily produce bodily *emaciation*. In the same way, *gluttony* (that is, excessive overeating) will necessarily lead to *obesity*.

None of the other choices offered exhibits the same cause-effect relationship involved in the key pair of words. *Moderation* in the consumption of food has nothing to do with *burliness* (Choice *a*), nor does *abstinence* relate to *stockiness* (Choice *d*). Similarly, *fasting* does not produce *corpulence* (Choice *c*), and *dieting* does not lead to *rotundity* (Choice *e*).

Notice, however, that two of the wrong choices exhibit a relationship that involves the *opposite* of the relationship that is wanted. *Fasting* certainly does not produce *corpulence*, but it may lead to *emaciation*. Similarly, *dieting* does not lead to *rotundity*, but *rotundity* may make a person want to go on a *diet*. These items were both purposely included to make the selection of the correct answer more difficult.

"A Will Make a Person B."   A closely related form of the word relationship "*A* necessarily causes *B*" can conveniently be expressed as "*A* will make a person *B*; *C* will make a person *D*." Here is an example of an analogy question involving this relationship. Study it carefully.

practice : proficient ::
- **a.** interest : apathetic
- **b.** experience : talented
- **c.** study : knowledgeable
- **d.** wealth : wise
- **e.** famous : accomplishment

The answer is *c*. Continuous *practice* of a skill or art will make a person *proficient* at it. Similarly, continuous *study* of a subject will make a person *knowledgeable* about it.

None of the other choices exhibits this cause–effect relationship. *Interest* in something does not make a person *apathetic* about it (Choice *a*). *Experience* does not make a person *talented* because talent tends to be in-born (Choice *b*). The possession of *wealth* has nothing to do with how *wise* a person is (Choice *d*). Finally, the two words in Choice *e* come in the wrong order. In the key pair of words, the adjective (*proficient*) follows the noun (*practice*); in Choice *e*, however, the adjective (*famous*) precedes the noun (*accomplishment*).

"A Indicates the Extreme of B." Another common word relationship that appears on standardized vocabulary tests is "*A* indicates the extreme of *B*; *C* indicates the extreme of *D*." Here is an example of an analogy question involving this relationship. Study it carefully.

tiny : small ::
a. cold : frigid
b. tepid : lukewarm
c. economical : frugal
d. gigantic : large
e. drab : colorful

The answer is *d*. *Gigantic* indicates that something is *very large*, just as *tiny* indicates that it is *very small*.

None of the other choices exhibits this relationship. *Frigid* means *very cold*, but *cold* does not mean *very frigid* (Choice *a*). Similarly, *frugal* means *very economical*, but *economical* does not mean *very frugal* (Choice *c*). *Tepid* just means *lukewarm*, not *very lukewarm* (Choice *c*). And finally, *drab* does not mean *very colorful*; it means the *opposite* of *colorful* (Choice *e*).

Word Order.   The comments just made about Choices *a* and *c* point up an important consideration to bear in mind when answering analogy questions. It is this: Always make sure that the two words in the answer you select come *in the same order* as the two words in the key pair. If, for example, the key pair contains an adjective followed by a noun (or a strong word followed by a weak one), be certain that your answer also contains an adjective followed by a noun (or a strong word followed by a weak one). If not, you've made the wrong choice.

Teacher and students discuss a project in a journalism class. Teaching is an excellent career objective for someone who uses words well.

Exercise I

Complete the following analogies based on the word relationships studied in this lesson.

1. **relish : like ::**
   a. upset : outrage
   b. cherish : loathe
   c. leave : depart
   d. deter : abet
   e. abhor : dislike

2. **liquor : intoxication ::**
   a. food : obesity
   b. color : candor
   c. noise : blandness
   d. water : aridity
   e. sun : pallor

3. **distraught : upset ::**
   a. bleak : rosy
   b. simple : austere
   c. gaunt : thin
   d. modest : demure
   e. irritation : peevish

4. **enigma : puzzlement ::**
   a. confrontation : belligerent
   b. discomfiture : chagrin
   c. bickering : empathy
   d. enclave : dejection
   e. calumny : devotion

5. **disappointment : cynical ::**
   a. hardship : blithe
   b. insult : dormant
   c. failure : dexterous
   d. irritation : peevish
   e. pressure : calm

Exercise II

Compose **two** complete analogies based on the word relationship "A necessarily causes B" (or the related relationship "A will make a person B"), and **two** based on "A indicates the extreme of B."

Exercise III

Complete the following analogies.

1. **dexterous : gauche** = circumspect :
   (*clandestine, complacent, cogent, compatible, incautious*)

2. **alienate : estrange** = augment :
   (*atone, augur, appall, increase, curtail*)

3. **dilatory : promptness** = distraught :
   (*composure, energy, money, backbone, honesty*)

4. **dormancy : inactive** = dilapidation :
   (*impartial, rundown, dissimilar, biased, manageable*)

5. **opulent : rich** = exhausted :
   (*energetic, lazy, tired, prosperous, untidy*)

Working with Context Clues

Contrast Clues.   The second general type of context clue that you are like-ly to meet in the sentence-completion section of a standardized test may conveniently be called a **contrast clue**. As you already know, a restate-ment clue more or less repeats the meaning of the missing word. A con-trast clue, on the other hand, provides an *antonym* for, or a phrase that means the *opposite* of, the word that is wanted.

Study the following example of a sentence-completion exercise care-fully. It contains both a contrast clue and a linking expression that points to this clue.

"As you say, my view of the situation may be far too rosy," I admitted. "On the other hand, yours may be a bit too _____."

a. optimistic   b. scholarly   c. pious   d. concise   e. bleak

Notice the presence of the phrase *On the other hand* at the beginning of the second sentence. This is the kind of linking expression that binds together two contrasting or dissimilar sentences or sentence elements. In this case, it connects two complete sentences.

Thus, the words *On the other hand* tell you that you are about to read a sentence that in some way contrasts with the preceding sentence. In other words, the phrase pretty much tells you what kind of clue you are likely to find. It is a contrast clue.

But the phrase *On the other hand* also tells you something else. It tells you where to look for the clue. Since the blank for the missing word fol-lows (rather than precedes) the words *On the other hand*, you are likely to find your clue in the first sentence in the example.

Look at the first sentence. It tells you that the speaker ("I") has far too "rosy" a view of a particular situation. *Rosy*, of course, means "optimistic" or "confident." This implies that the person who is dealt with in the sec-ond sentence ("you") must have a view of the same situation that con-trasts with the speaker's view. In other words, it must in some way be "unrosy." Now you know the sense of the missing word.

Now look at the five words from which you are to select the item that goes in the blank. Only one of them means anything like "unrosy" or "unoptimistic." It is Choice *e, bleak*, which, as you learned in Lesson 7 (page 93), can mean "gloomy." This is clearly the missing word.

Exercise I

All the following sentence-completion exercises contain contrast clues. Complete each by selecting the word that makes the best sense in the sentence (or pair of sentences) as a whole. Indicate the clue or clues that led you to make your choice.

1. "This soda doesn't have any real orange juice in it," I re-marked. "Its flavor is completely _____."

    a. genuine   b. flat   c. artificial   d. normal   e. satisfying

2. Though it doesn't take a long time to demolish a building, it is certainly time-consuming to _____ one.

    a. photograph   b. visit   c. destroy   d. rent   e. erect

3. Candidate X is a member of a _____ New England family; Candidate Y, on the other hand, comes from a very humble background.

   a. indigent   b. prominent   c. affable   d. boisterous
   e. obscure

4. I was totally surprised by the outcome of the game, but my sister seemed to _____ our team to win from the opening buzzer.

   a. dare   b. encourage   c. want   d. expect   e. force

5. Some horses are headstrong and hard to manage; others are quite _____ and easy to ride.

   a. docile   b. boorish   c. belligerent   d. cantankerous
   e. agile

Exercise II

The following exercise reviews everything that you have learned about sentence-completion questions and context clues to this point. Complete each item in the exercise by selecting the word that makes the best sense in the sentence (or pair of sentences) as a whole. Indicate the clue or clues that led you to your choice.

1. I thought the movie was very _____, but my companion cried all through it.

   a. incoherent   b. realistic   c. timely   d. expensive
   e. amusing

2. "Something is wrong with the new toaster," dad observed. "Are you sure it is _____," mom asked in reply, "or are you simply unfamiliar with the proper way to operate it?"

   a. affluent   b. defective   c. captious   d. benign   e. cogent

3. One of the new employees is extremely hardworking and _____; the other doesn't seem to accomplish anything at all.

   a. productive   b. copious   c. desultory   d. cynical
   e. delinquent

4. The man is known as "The _____ of Elmsford" because most of the people who live in that town find his character and behavior completely baffling.

   a. Drunk   b. Bully   c. Enigma   d. Miser   e. Charlatan

5. Though I was brought up in a completely _____ part of the country, I find that life in the big city suits me to a tee.

   a. depressed   b. urban   c. barren   d. rural   e. new

Enriching the Lesson

Exercise I. Our Latin Heritage

A number of the English words studied in this lesson (e.g., *efficacious, enclave, emulate*) are based on Latin originals. English is rich in such Latin "borrowings." As a matter of fact, they make up a huge part of the vocabulary of present-day English.

A number of words and expressions borrowed or adapted from Latin (including medieval Latin) are listed below. With or without the aid of a dictionary, define each. Then choose any **five**, and for each compose a short illustrative sentence.

1. laborious	11. nugatory	21. lapse
2. unanimous	12. punitive	22. rapacious
3. magnanimous	13. obliterate	23. negotiate
4. puerile	14. ratify	24. superfluous
5. terminate	15. malevolent	25. provoke
6. mandate	16. nullify	26. quash
7. supersede	17. juxtapose	27. militate
8. raucous	18. regress	28. literate
9. nascent	19. minimal	29. notorious
10. jocose	20. malleable	30. reiterate

Exercise II. "Extreme" Words

The adjective *emaciated*, studied in this lesson, indicates extreme thinness. Its opposite, *obese*, noted in the synonyms under *emaciated*, indicates extreme fatness. English is rich in such "extreme" expressions. Do the following exercise involving a few of them.

The words in Column A refer to familiar emotions or traits of personality. The words in Column B refer to the same emotions or traits but in a more extreme or intense sense. Match each word in Column A with its related "extreme" word in Column B.

Column A	Column B
1. glad	a. solemn
2. restrained	b. adore
3. dislike	c. immaculate
4. serious	d. elated
5. like	e. distraught
6. clean	f. chaotic
7. wise	g. sagacious
8. forceful	h. austere
9. disorderly	i. overbearing
10. perturbed	j. detest
11. well-off	k. outrage
12. offend	l. opulent

Exercise III. Too Much of a Good Thing

The desire to excel is generally a healthy characteristic in a person. Experience, however, shows that it can easily go sour. Thus, under the "good" word *elite*, studied in this lesson, the negative words *elitist* and *elitism* also appear. Listed below are some other common English words that suggest a desire to be superior that is expressed in a negative or objectionable way. With or without the aid of a dictionary, define each. Then choose any **five**, and for each compose a short illustrative sentence.

1. snob	7. poseur	13. bumptious
2. moralistic	8. conceit	14. perfectionist
3. dogmatic	9. authoritarian	15. purist
4. sanctimonious	10. dilettante	16. self-righteous
5. labored	11. egocentric	17. narcissism
6. autocratic	12. preciosity	18. jingoism

Exercise IV. Forms of Direct Address

Under *eminent*, a word studied in this lesson, it was noted that *Your Eminence* is the proper phrase to use when addressing a cardinal of the Roman Catholic Church. English has a few other such phrases. They are all used when addressing royalty or persons holding certain positions in the government, the church, or the legal system. Six of these phrases are listed below. With or without the aid of a dictionary, name the person or group of people to whom each is properly applied. For example, *Your Eminence* is used of a *cardinal*.

1. Your Excellency	3. Your Grace	5. Your Honor
2. Your Highness	4. Your Holiness	6. Your Majesty

Exercise V. Expanding Your Word Power

The words listed below are not on the Basic Word List, but they were mentioned in passing in Lesson 14. All of them would make useful additions to your working vocabulary. Define each, give its etymology, list **two** synonyms and **two** antonyms (where possible), and use in a short illustrative sentence.

1. monolithic	6. diffidence	11. garnish
2. decadent	7. evoke	12. obscure
3. prolific	8. aristocratic	13. compassion
4. ineffectual	9. obese	14. indigenous
5. impertinence	10. originate	15. dilemma

Lesson 15

161. entice — 175. exigency

---

161. en-tice   *verb*   ĕn-tīs´

[*enticier* (Old French) "set on fire"; from *in* (Latin), "in" + *titio* (Latin), "firebrand"]

Definition: To lead on by arousing hope or desire.

Only the offer of a tremendous increase in salary could **entice** me into leaving my present job.

Related Forms: (*noun*) enticement; (*adjective*) enticing

Synonyms: (*verbs*) tempt, lure, allure, coax, inveigle, beguile, seduce

Antonyms: (*verbs*) repel, repulse, scare off, frighten away

Phrases: seductive charms, a beguiling manner, bait the hook, sweet-talk, soft-soap, rope into

162. en-treat   *verb*   ĕn-trēt´

[*entraitier* (Old French), "deal with; plead with"; from *en* (Old French), "in" + *traitier* (Old French), "deal, treat"]

Definition: To ask or petition earnestly.

The defense attorney **entreated** the jury to weigh *all* the evidence carefully and objectively before reaching a verdict.

Related Form: (*noun*) entreaty

Synonyms: (*verbs*) implore, beg, beseech, plead for, urge, importune, press for

Phrase: cap in hand

163. en-vis-age   *verb*   ĕn-vĭz´-ĭj

[*envisager* (French), "imagine"; from *en* (French), "in" + *visage* (French), "face"]

Definition: To have a mental image of something, especially when the thing does not yet exist; to conceive of.

I find it very difficult to **envisage** the kind of society that the Greek philosopher Plato once dreamt of creating.

From his writings it is clear that Thomas Jefferson **envisaged** an America made up of small independent farmers dedicated to hard work and egalitarian principles.

Synonyms: (*verbs*) envision, visualize, picture, imagine

164. ep-i-thet   *noun*   ĕp´-ə-thĕt

[*epitheton* (Greek), "an addition"; from *epi* (Greek), "on" + *tithenai* (Greek), "put, place"]

Definition:

   a. A word or phrase used to describe or characterize someone or something. (The expression need not be derogatory.)

      Some English kings, such as William the Conqueror and Richard the Lion-Hearted, are better known by their informal **epithets** than by their official titles.

      As John F. Kennedy once observed, the seemingly endless war of nerves between the United States and the Soviet Union has been given the curious **epithet** "cold."

   b. A term of abuse or contempt.

      When I discovered that my apartment had been burglarized, I couldn't help shouting a few choice **epithets** at the thieves.

Synonyms: (*nouns*) characterization designation, appellation, label, nickname, moniker, handle; curse, oath, obscenity

Phrases: badmouth someone, hurl brickbats at, mudslinging

165. e-qua-nim-i-ty *noun* ē-kwə-nĭm´-ə-tē *or* ĕk-wə-nĭm´-ə-tē

[*aequanimitas* (Latin), "evenness of temper"; from *aequus* (Latin), even; "equal" + *animus* (Latin), "mind"]

Definition: Calmness or evenness of temper.

   Only a true stoic, in the best sense of the term, could bear such reverses of fortune with dignity and **equanimity**.

Synonyms: (*nouns*) composure, self-composure, placidity, tranquility, serenity, sang-froid, unexcitability, imperturbability, unflappability, self-possession, nonchalance

Antonyms: (*nouns*) excitability, fretfulness, agitation, distress, hysteria

Phrases: mental (or emotional) stability, presence of mind

166. eq-ui-ta-ble   *adjective*   ĕk´-wə-tə-bəl

[*equitable* (French), "fair, just"; from *equite* (Old French), "justice"; from *aequus* (Latin), "even, equal"]

Definition: Fair or just.

   Most seniors were satisfied that the distribution of awards at graduation had been as **equitable** as possible.

Related Forms: (*adjective*) inequitable; (*adverb*) equitably; (*noun*) equity

Usage Note:

   Do not confuse *equitable* with *equable*, which means "unvarying" or "tranquil."

210

Synonyms: (*adjectives*) impartial, unbiased, evenhanded

Antonyms: (*adjectives*) unfair, unjust, biased, partial; unreasonable, lopsided, one-sided, uneven

167. er-u-dite   *adjective*   ĕr´-yŏŏ-dīt *or* ĕr´-ŏŏ-dīt

[*erudire, eruditus* (Latin), "take the roughness out of, polish"; from *e* (Latin), "out of" + *rudis* (Latin), "rough, rude"]

Definition: Deeply learned, especially in a specialized area.

Lord Chesterfield once advised his son never to appear more **erudite** than the people he was with.

Last night Professor Maurice Lenkowski presented an **erudite**, yet entertaining, lecture on the early history of aviation in this country.

Related Forms: (*noun*) erudition; (*adverb*) eruditely

Synonyms: (*adjectives*) scholarly, profound, knowledgeable, informed

Antonyms: (*adjectives*) ignorant, uninformed

Phrases: a savant, a pundit, a maven, a walking encyclopedia, highbrow, an ignoramus, lowbrow

168. es-o-ter-ic   *adjective*   ĕs-ə-tĕr´-ĭk

[*esoterikos* (Greek), "inner"; from *eso* (Greek), "within"]

Definition:

a. Understood by or intended for only a select few.

Only the members of the executive committee know all the **esoteric** rites involved in the initiation ceremonies of our fraternity.

b. Difficult to understand.

"When those two computer programmers began to talk shop, the conversation became awfully **esoteric**," Molly remarked. "Yes," I replied, "I wasn't even sure that they were still speaking English!"

Related Form: (*adverb*) esoterically

Synonyms: (*adjectives*) occult, secret, confidential, private; mysterious abstruse, recondite, arcane, incomprehensible, unfathomable, cryptic, inscrutable, impenetrable

Antonyms: (*adjectives*) popular, exoteric; intelligible, accessible, crystalclear, comprehensible

Phrases: not for public consumption, insiders, privileged information

Usage Note:

The adjective *exoteric*, derived from the Greek word for "external," has a number of meanings of which "less secret or confidential" (e.g., an *exoteric* rite") and "readily comprehensible" (e.g., an *exoteric* doctrine") are perhaps the most common.

169. eth-i-cal   *adjective*   ĕth´-ĭ-kəl

[*ethikos* (Greek), "moral"; from *ethos* (Greek), "moral custom"]

Definition: In accordance with accepted principles of right and wrong.

Although we cannot say outright that their sales techniques are illegal, we are prepared to argue that they are not **ethical**.

Related Forms: (*nouns*) ethicalness, ethicality, ethics, ethic, ethos; (*adjective*) unethical

Phrases: the Puritan work ethic, ethical drugs, the ethos of a people, the revolutionary ethos

Usage Notes:
   a. *Ethics* is the branch of philosophy concerned with the general nature of morals and the specific moral choices facing the individual. It is also sometimes called *moral philosophy*.

   b. An *ethic* is a principle of right or moral behavior, or a set of such principles. The phrase *Puritan work ethic* refers to the fundamental belief in the value of hard work that was a basic part of the Puritan outlook on life.

   c. An *ethos* is the set of fundamental attitudes, beliefs, and values that characterize a particular group or culture. Another word for this is *mores*, though today we would probably use *mind set* instead. *Ethos* also indicates a governing principle or central idea, as in the phrase "the revolutionary *ethos*."

   d. In such phrases as "*ethical* drugs," *ethical* indicates that the item is distributed solely through the medical profession.

Synonyms: (*adjectives*) moral, virtuous, honorable, decent, upright, honest, righteous, principled, correct, proper

Antonyms: (*adjectives*) unfair, unjust, immoral, unscrupulous, dishonorable, discreditable, unsportsmanlike, unprofessional

Phrases: fair play, a lack of principles, dirty pool, hit someone below the belt

170. eth-nic   *adjective*   ĕth´-nĭk

[*ethnikos* (Greek), "foreign"; from *ethnos* (Greek), "people, nation"]

Definition: Relating to a small but distinct social group within the population. (The group in question is usually distinguished from the rest of the population by its particular religious, racial, national, or cultural character.)

The population of "a pluralistic society" is made up of many different **ethnic** groups from many different parts of the world.

Phrases: ethnic food, ethnic pride, the ethnic vote

Related Forms: (*nouns*) ethnicity, ethnology

Usage Note:
Ethnic is sometimes used as a noun to indicate a member of a particular ethnic group. This usage, however, is decidedly informal.

An ethnologist at work in New Guinea. *Ethnology* is the science that deals with the individual cultures that make up the human family and their socioeconomic systems . It also concerns itself with the factors that bring about cultural growth and change.

171. eu-phe-mism   *noun*   yōo´-fɔ-mĭz əm

[*euphemismos* (Greek), "euphemism"; from *euphemia* (Greek), "use of good words"; from *eu* (Greek), "good, well" + *pheme* (Greek), "speech"]

Definition: The substitution of a relatively inoffensive term for one that is considered too harsh, unpleasant, or blunt.

If we know that a person has lied repeatedly, why we don't we say so, instead of using **euphemisms** like "stretched the truth"?

Related Form:'   (*adjective*) euphemistic

172. ex-ac-er-bate   *verb*   ĕg-zăs´-ēr-bāt *or* ĕk-săs´-ēr-bāt

[*exacerbare, exacerbatus* (Latin), "make harsh"; from *ex* (Latin), "completely" + *acerbus* (Latin), "harsh, bitter"]

Definition: To increase the bitterness or severity of; to irritate.

His stubborn refusal to follow the doctor's orders has done nothing but **exacerbate** his already serious medical problems.

"I don't think the proposal will do much to alleviate our present economic woes," the Senator remarked, "but it may **exacerbate** them."

Related Form: (*noun*) exacerbation

Synonyms: (*verbs*) aggravate, worsen, intensify

Antonyms: (*verbs*) lessen, moderate, temper, mitigate, mollify, allay, assuage, soothe, alleviate, palliate

Phrases: add fuel to the fire, stoke the flames, add insult to injury, rub salt in an open wound; pour oil on troubled waters

173. ex·alt   *verb*   ĕg-zôlt′ *or* ĭg-zôlt′

[*exaltare* (Latin), "lift up"; from *ex* (Latin), "out, up" + *altus* (Latin), "high"]

Definition: To elevate in power, position, character, or the like.

> The Old Testament tells us that righteousness **exalts** a people, but that evil debases it.

> From truly humble beginnings, Cardinal Woolsey rose to one of the most **exalted** positions in English politics.

Related Forms: (*adjective*) exalted; (*noun*) exaltation

Usage Note:
Do not confuse *exalt* with *exult*, which means "rejoice" or "feel a sense of joy or satisfaction over some success."

Synonyms: (*verbs*) ennoble, uplift, upgrade

Antonyms: (*verbs*) debase, degrade, demote, humble, abase

---

174. ex·em·pla·ry   *adjective*   ĕg-zĕm′-plə-rē *or* ĭg-zĕm′-plə-rē

[*exemplaire* (Old French), "model"; from *exemplum* (Latin), "example"]

Definition:
a.   Worthy of imitation.

> The Dean of Students congratulated the members of the senior class on their **exemplary** behavior at the prom.

b.   Serving as a model, illustration, or warning.

> "I plan to mete out **exemplary** punishment to a few of the mutineers," the general said. "That, I believe, will induce the rest to return to their duty without further resistance."

Related Form: (*noun*) exemplar

Synonyms: (*adjectives*) model, sterling; commendable, meritorious, laudable; (*nouns*) paragon, epitome, archetype, prototype

Phrases: ne plus ultra, beau idéal

Exemplar

An exemplar is a model that is worthy of imitation. For example, in medieval times, Sir Galahad (see illustration) was the exemplar of the knightly virtues, especially purity and nobility. *Exemplar* is also used to indicate both the original or archetype of something and a typical representative of it.

175. ex-i-gen-cy   *noun*   ĕk´-sə-jən-sē

[*exigens* (Latin), "demanding"; from *exigere, exactus* (Latin), "drive out; demand"]

Definition: A state of urgency or a situation demanding immediate attention; the pressing needs caused by such a crisis.

"The **exigencies** of the situation demand that we curtail all unnecessary expenditures immediately," the chairman of the board announced yesterday.

Related Forms: (*noun*) exigence; (*adjective*) exigent; (*adverb*) exigently

Usage Note:

As the illustrative sentence given above suggests, *exigency* is frequently used in the plural with the meaning "pressing needs" or "urgent requirements."

Synonyms: (*nouns*) emergency, crisis; needs, demands, requirements

Phrases: in a tight fix, in hot water, a hot spot, a troubleshooter

Using the Words

Exercise I. Syllabication and Pronunciation

Syllabicate the following words correctly, and place the major stress mark (′) after the syllable that is accented when the word is pronounced.

1. esoteric
2. ethnic
3. euphemism
4. epithet
5. erudite
6. exacerbate
7. exigency
8. entice
9. ethical

Exercise II. Words Out of Context

In each of the following groups, select the item that best expresses the meaning of the numbered word at the left.

1. entice   a. repel b. tilt c. force d. exist e. tempt

2. esoteric   a. intoxicated b. agitated c. unfair d. incomprehensible e. interesting

3. envisage   a. feature b. deceive c. forget d. offer e. visualize

4. ethical   a. morally correct b. mildly amusing c. clearly wrong d. emotionally stable e. deeply learned

5. exacerbate   a. alleviate b. intensify c. urge d. imagine e. humble

6. entreat   **a.** coddle   **b.** repulse   **c.** beg   **d.** downgrade
                e. clarify

7. exalt   **a.** rejoice   **b.** uplift   **c.** question   **d.** pursue
                e. upset

Exercise III. Completing Sentences

Complete each of the following sentences or pairs of sentences by selecting the most appropriate word from the given group of words. Use each word only once. Make any adjustments that are necessary to fit the words into the sentences properly.

exemplary	equitable	erudite
equanimity	euphemism	epithet
entice	exigencies	ethnic

1. "It is one thing to offer constructive criticism of me and my administration," the President remarked. "It is quite another to shower us with empty _____ and meaningless verbal abuse."

2. *Pass away* is a common _____ for *die*.

3. The _____ of an overloaded business schedule prevented my dad from taking his annual vacation last year.

4. "Emma is an _____ employee," the letter of recommendation read, "whose performance over the years might well serve as a model for any budding young secretary."

5. Though Renaissance history is only a hobby with him, he is as _____ in the subject as any professional scholar.

6. Though I think of myself as an ordinary American, my family is of Polish origin, and I am proud of my _____ heritage.

7. "Someone who is wise will try to bear even the most appalling misfortune with _____," he observed. "Someone who is silly will be devastated by the slightest setback."

8. Joe seems satisfied that his present salary arrangements are _____, but I don't think they're at all fair.

Exercise IV. Synonyms and Antonyms

Classify each of the following pairs of words as **S** for **synonyms** or **A** for **antonyms**.

1. ethical—immoral
2. alleviate—exacerbate
3. debase—exalt
4. implore—entreat
5. lure—entice
6. esoteric—abstruse
7. uninformed—erudite
8. equanimity—excitability
9. unfair—equitable
10. envisage—picture

Exercise V. Word Roundup

1. With or without the aid of a dictionary, define each of the following colorful expressions.

   a. soft-soap
   b. badmouth someone
   c. hit below the belt
   d. mudslinging

   e. rub salt in an open wound
   f. pour oil on troubled waters
   g. ne plus ultra
   h. in hot water

2. Explain the difference between the items in each of the following word pairs.

   a. equitable—equable   b. exalt—exult

3. What is a *savant*? a *pundit*? an *ignoramus*? What do *highbrow* and *lowbrow* mean?

4. What is *privileged information*? Who might *insiders* be?

5. Name a *hot spot* in the world today. What does a *troubleshooter* do?

6. Both *moniker* and *handle* are slang expressions. What do they mean?

7. Define or explain each of the following:

   a. the Puritan work ethic
   b. moral philosophy

   c. the ethos of a people
   d. ethical drugs

8. With what does the science of *ethnology* concern itself? What does an *ethnologist* do?

9. What does the phrase *a pluralistic society* mean? What relationship does it have to *a melting pot*?

10. What is a *paragon*? the *epitome* of gracious living?

11. Define the expression *beau idéal*. From what foreign language does it come?

Exercise VI. Framing Sentences

A. Use each of the following words in an original sentence.

1. equanimity
2. equitable
3. envisage

4. ethical
5. epithet
6. esoteric

7. exemplary
8. exigency
9. exacerbate

B. Give a **noun** form of each of these words, and use it in a short illustrative sentence.

1. entreat
2. erudite

3. entice
4. ethnic

C. Give an **adjective** form of each of these words, and use it in a short illustrative sentence.

1. exalt

2. euphemism

Dissecting the Words

1. The Latin prefix **e, ex**, and its Greek counterpart, **ec, ex**, are among the most common word elements used in English. They appear in several words studied in Lessons 14 and 15, including *eclectic, elicit, effete*, and *exalt*.

The primary meanings of **e, ec, ex** are "out (of)" and "away (from)." These meanings occur in the following common English words:

expel (*ex*, "out" + *pel*, "drive")—to drive out

erupt (*e*, "out" + *rupt*, "break")—to break out

eject (*e*, "out" + *ject*, "throw")—to throw out

expire (*ex*, "out" + *pire*, "breathe")—to breathe one's last; to come to an end

efface (*ex*, "out" or "away" + *face*)—to erase; to make indistinct by rubbing

excise (*ex*, "out" or "away" + *cise*, "cut")—to cut out or remove

exegesis (*ex*, "out" + *hegeisthai*, "lead")—a critical explanation, interpretation, or analysis, especially of a part of the Bible

expropriate (*ex*, "away from" + *proprius*, "one's own" + *ate*, "make")—to deprive of what is rightfully one's own, especially for public use

exorcise (*ex*, "away" + *horos*, "oath")—to expel an evil spirit by means of a spell or magical incantation

Note that in some words like *efface, ex* becomes **ef** before an *f*.

Other meanings of *e, ex* include "up," as in *exalt* ("to lift up") and "completely," as in *efficacious* ("completely capable of producing the desired effect") and *execute* ("to perform completely").

Other common words containing the prefix *e, ec, ex* include *excavation, exhale, emigrate, excerpt* (all from Latin), and *eclipse* (from Greek).

Archeologists excavating an Indian village on the Snake River in the state of Washington.

2. The formative prefix **en** occurs in several words studied in Lesson 15, including *envisage* (Word 163). This prefix comes from the Latin word element *in*. It is called "formative" because it serves to transform nouns and adjectives into verbs that take objects. For example, when *en* is prefixed to the noun *courage*, the result is the verb *encourage*, meaning "to inspire with courage." When it is attached to the adjective *noble*, it produces the verb *ennoble*, meaning "to make noble or elevate in dignity."

Note that *en* becomes **em** before the letters *b*, *p*, and sometimes *m*, as in the words *empower* and *emboss*.

Root

The Latin root **fac**, **fic**, **fact**, **fect**, all meaning "do" or "make," appeared in the word *efficacious*, studied in Lesson 14. This root and its derivatives occur in countless common English words, including:

benefactor—one who does good

facile—easy to do

feat—a great deed

factual—pertaining to facts ("things done"); real

edifice—a building or structure

feasible—capable of being done; workable

facilitate—to help in getting something done

Other common words containing this root and its derivatives are *infect*, *effect*, *affect*, *perfect*, and *confection*.

Suffix

The Latin root *fac, fic, fact, fect* also gives English the suffix **fy**, which appears in such words as *clarify* and *exemplify*. Note that the attachment of *fy* to a root results in a word with a sense of action or performance. For example:

beautify—to make beautiful

amplify—(literally, "make wide")—to enlarge

ratify—to make valid

pacify—to make quiet or set at peace

terrify—to make to feel terror

edify—to enlighten

codify—to arrange in a code; to systematize

magnify—to enlarge or increase

deify—to worship or revere as a god

glorify—to exalt, to make more glorious than is actually the case

rectify—to correct

villify—to defame or denigrate

falsify—to misrepresent; to counterfeit

signify—to mean or betoken

A. With or without the aid of a dictionary, select the word that best answers the following questions relating to the prefix *e, ec, ex.*

1. Which of the following might be *eclipsed*?
   a. a luminary b. a contingency c. an extension

2. Which of the following might be *excised*?
   a. a mendicant b. an abrogation c. a paragraph

3. Which of the following might be *eclectic*?
   a. an encomium b. an anthology c. an ovation

4. Which of the following might be *effaced* by time?
   a. capitulations b. recollections c. denouements

B. With or without the aid of a dictionary, define each of the following words. Then show how the prefix *e, ec, ex* affects its overall meaning.

1. emanate
2. exegesis
3. elicit
4. efficacious
5. exacerbate
6. exalt

C. Attach the formative prefix *en* to each of the following nouns or adjectives, and define the resulting combination. Then choose any **five**, and for each compose a short illustrative sentence.

1. dear
2. shrine
3. feeble
4. crust
5. trap
6. compass
7. circle
8. gulf
9. vision
10. rich
11. throne
12. danger

D. With or without the aid of a dictionary, complete each of the following exercises relating to the root *fac, fic, fact, fect.*

1. Define each of the following English words containing a form of *fac.* Then choose any **five**, and for each compose a short illustrative sentence.

   a. facsimile
   b. edifice
   c. factotum
   d. feasible
   e. facilitate
   f. factor
   g. infection
   h. faction
   i. faculty
   j. feat
   k. benefactor
   l. facile

2. What is the difference in meaning between *affect* and *effect*? Use each in a short illustrative sentence.

3. The expressions *ipso facto* (Latin) and *fait accompli* (French) both stem from the Latin root *fac.* Explain what each means.

E. Form an English verb from each of the following English or Latin words by adding the suffix *fy.* Then define the resulting combination.

1. humid
2. pretty
3. null
4. identity
5. solid
6. person
7. verse
8. magnum ("great")
9. verus ("true")

Working with Context Clues

Review the "Working with Context Clues" section in Lesson 14 (page 205) before you begin the following material.

"Guideposts" to Contrast Clues.   Just as some linking expressions act as "guideposts" to the presence and location of restatement clues in sentence-completion exercises, so other linking expressions signal contrast clues. One such expression, *on the other hand*, was examined in Lesson 14 (page 205). Others include certain conjunctions (e.g., *but, however, though, although, even though, still*), adverbs (e.g., *not, unfortunately*), prepositions (e.g, *despite*), prepositional phrases (e.g., *in spite of*), and similar contrasting expressions (e.g., *some . . . others*).

Each of these items in some way binds together two contrasting or dissimilar sentences or sentence elements. Usually, the clue is contained in one of these contrasting elements, and the blank appears in the other. The linking expression "points" to the contrast clue by making the reader keenly aware of the difference between the element containing the blank and the element to which it is tied.

Study the following example of a sentence-completion exercise carefully. It contains both a contrast clue and a linking expression that points to this clue.

> "A person has to have a strong stomach to work in a funeral parlor or morgue," I observed. "Handling corpses is not a job for the _____."
>
> a. enigmatic   b. squeamish   c. indigent   d. ambitious   e. callous

Read over the two sentences carefully. The first informs you that work in a funeral parlor or morgue requires persons with a certain kind of temperament. The second says that such work is *not* for people with another kind of temperament. You are to specify what the second kind of temperament is by filling in the blank.

Thus, the word *not* in the second sentence indicates that these two sentences present contrasting information. In other words, it is your "guidepost" to the type of clue that you are likely to find, and that is a contrast clue.

But the word *not* does something else as well. It tells you where to look for your contrast clue. Since the blank is in the same sentence as the word *not*, you are likely to find your clue in the other sentence.

Look at this sentence. It indicates that work in a funeral parlor or morgue is only for people who have strong stomachs. Clearly, the phrase "has to have a strong stomach" is your clue. If work in a funeral parlor or morgue requires people with strong stomachs, then such work is clearly *not* for people who *don't* have strong stomachs. Now you know the sense of the word that goes in the blank. It means, roughly, "without a strong stomach."

Now look at the five items from which you are to select the word that goes in the blank. Only one of them means anything like "without a strong stomach." It is Choice *b, squeamish*, which means "easily nauseated, disgusted, or offended" or "overly sensitive." This is clearly the word that goes in the blank.

None of the other choices fits the situation as outlined above. Note, however, Choice *e, callous*, which, as you know, means "insensitive"—the opposite of the word you are looking for. It was intentionally included to confuse you and make selecting the right answer more difficult.

Exercise I

The following sentence-completion exercises contain contrast clues and linking expressions that point to these clues. Complete each exercise by selecting the word that makes the best sense in the sentence (or pair of sentences) as a whole. Indicate the clue or clues that led you to make your choice.

1. "Though the proposal before us would alleviate some of our financial problems," I observed at the last board meeting," it would unfortunately _____ others."

   a. boycott b. allay c. construe d. exacerbate e. delude

2. "Mom became hysterical when she heard that I'd been in a car accident," Jeff recalled. "Dad, on the other hand, received the news with total _____."

   a. equanimity b. duplicity c. consensus d. ambience e. blight

3. "'They claim to have offered a completely _____ settlement to the dispute," my boss said. "In point of fact, however, the terms of the deal are grossly unfair to our side."

   a. aesthetic b. bombastic c. circuitous d. delinquent e. equitable

4. "I'm trying to help you—not _____ you!" I exclaimed in annoyance.

   a. employ b. rescue c. hinder d. notice e. assist

5. "I'm perfectly willing to go along with any sales technique that I believe to be _____," the chairman of the board remarked. "But I refuse to condone selling practices that are dishonest, misleading, or illegal."

   a. erudite b. efficacious c. esoteric d. eclectic e. ethical

Exercise II

The following exercise reviews everything you have learned about sentence-completion questions and context clues to this point. Complete each item in the exercise by selecting the word that makes the best sense in the sentence (or pair of sentences) as a whole. Indicate the clue or clues that led you to your choice.

1. Though the results of any Presidential election are simply a matter of record, the reasons for them are quite often purely a matter of _____.

   a. conjecture b. aesthetics c. coherence d. empathy e. logic

2. "I'm willing to tell you what I know about the matter," she remarked, "but I can't _____ the names of my sources."

   a. elicit b. conceal c. censor d. divulge e. assimilate

3. Some 19th-century aristocrats lived amid extraordinarily
   _____ surroundings; others, however, had long since
   been reduced to complete poverty.

   a. adverse b. effete c. opulent d. austere e. bleak

4. It is one thing to be brave in the face of unavoidable danger. It
   is quite another to be _____ or to take unnecessary risks
   with your life.

   a. boorish b. foolhardy c. diligent d. immoral
   e. cynical

5. The old-time "medicine show" was notorious for its quacks
   and _____, all hawking spurious remedies for the ills of
   mankind.

   a. executives b. advocates c. bureaucrats d. charlatans
   e. connoisseurs

Enriching the Lesson

Exercise I. Words Ending in (o)logy

One of the items discussed in Lesson 15 was the term *ethnology*.
This term contains the element *logy*, which comes from the Greek
word *logos*, meaning "word." *Logy* and its related form *ology* have
several meanings, one of which is "the study of" or "the science
of." This meaning appears in many scientific and philosophical
terms used in present-day English. These include *biology*, the
study of life, and *etymology*, the study of word origins.

   Listed below are a number of other English words ending in *logy*
or *ology*. Some of these words use these elements in their primary
sense of "the science (study) of"; others employ them in different
meanings. With or without the aid of a dictionary, define each of
the words on the list. Then indicate what *logy* or *ology* means in
that particular word.

1. ornithology	11. cosmology	21. philology
2. theology	12. penology	22. tautology
3. ecology	13. sociology	23. toxicology
4. physiology	14. astrology	24. ophthalmology
5. terminology	15. pathology	25. entomology
6. archeology	16. trilogy	26. osteology
7. paleontology	17. geology	27. chronology
8. ontology	18. anthropology	28. tetralogy
9. teleology	19. phraseology	29. parasitology
10. psychology	20. mythology	30. methodology

Exercise II. Euphemisms: Sugarcoating the Pill

If you called your overweight friends *fat*, they would undoubtedly be offended; if you called them *pleasantly plump*, they would probably smile and feel flattered. A discreet person who wishes to be candid and yet not have such frankness cause offense will often find it desirable to substitute a **euphemism** (Word 171) to sugarcoat the harsh facts.

Euphemisms were a fetish in the Victorian era. Propriety then decreed that one should avoid referring to certain parts of the body by their natural or common names. Little Nell might well have swooned at the mention of such "coarse" words as *belly* and *corsets*, or even *legs*. In writing, the epithet *damned* appeared as

The death of Little Nell, the heroine of Charles Dickens's novel *The Old Curiosity Shop* (1841).

d--d. Shakespeare's plays were published in bowdlerized editions, purged of words deemed to be obscene or unrefined, and thus objectionable. Understandably, the adjective *Victorian* has become synonymous with prudishness and exaggerated genteelism.

Although we are much less likely than the Victorians to be squeamish about the "facts of life," we are still given to verbal evasions of reality. For example, a clerical assistant in an office may try to enhance his job by calling himself a "junior executive."

This "word game" has spread into many other areas. Since the existence of poverty in our society is an unwelcome fact, we may choose to refer to poor people as "disadvantaged," or "underprivileged," or "in the lower-income brackets." Elderly people are "senior citizens." Charity has become "welfare assistance." A mistake in spelling may be presented as an "orthographic irregularity."

Governmental officials and military leaders are certainly not beyond retreating into euphemisms. A breakdown in services resulting from inefficiency has been called an "organizational disruption." A military retreat after a crushing defeat may be termed a "rearrangement of forces." In some countries, assassinations of political enemies are referred to as "necessary liquidations."

At this point, a word of warning is in order. Although we may laugh at such flabby and sometimes dishonest evasions of reality, we should also realize that there *are* occasions when euphemisms and genteelisms can serve a useful purpose. They may be used to spare the feelings of people under severe strain, or to soften harsh or gross realities which for some reason we are not prepared to face at a given time. Certainly, no harm is done if euphemisms are used selectively and with good judgment under such circumstances to raise the level of courtesy and consideration for others. But the key word is *selectively*. If we use euphemisms indiscriminately in place of plain, homely words, our language may become at best overrefined, and at worst obscure and even ludicrous.

A. Below are two lists of corresponding words or expressions. Those in Column A are "Euphemistic or Genteel"; in Column B, "Realistic or Natural." In what context, or under what circumstances might each of these expressions be appropriately used? Give examples of such usage.

Column A *Euphemistic or Genteel*	Column B *Realistic or Natural*
perspire	sweat
odor	smell
expectorate	spit
cinema	movies
financially embarrassed	broke
exaggerate	lie
boutique	shop
retire for the night	go to bed
deceased	dead

B. Each of the following expressions is sometimes used euphemistically as a substitute for a more familiar, down-to-earth term. Give a "blunt" equivalent in each case.

1. mortician
2. protective custody
3. hair supplementation
4. billiard academy
5. gratuity
6. cocktail lounge
7. termination of employment
8. tonsorial parlor
9. figure control
10. pugilistic encounter

Exercise III. Expanding Your Word Power

The words listed below are not on the Basic Word List, but they were mentioned in passing in Lesson 15. All of them would make useful additions to your working vocabulary. Define each, give its etymology, list **two** synonyms and **two** antonyms (where possible), and use in a short illustrative sentence.

1. inveigle
2. repel
3. importune
4. envision
5. designation
6. stability
7. literate
8. composure
9. confidential
10. allay
11. cryptic
12. crisis
13. abase
14. commendable
15. hysteria

Lesson 16

---

176. ex-o-dus   *noun*   ĕk´-sə-dəs

[*exodos* (Greek), "a going out"; from *ex* (Greek), "out" + *hodos* (Greek), "road, way"]

Definition: A departure, usually of large numbers of people.

Religious persecution is one of the main reasons for the continuing **exodus** of minority groups from Soviet-bloc countries.

During the summer, "sun-worshippers" begin their weekly **exodus** from the city around 3:00 p.m. on Friday afternoon.

Synonyms: (*nouns*) flight, escape, migration, emigration, hegira

Antonyms: (*nouns*) arrival, influx, immigration

Moses, by Michelangelo

Flight School

In both Latin and English, the second book of the Old Testament of the Bible is called Exodus. It recounts the departure of the Israelites (under the leadership of Moses) from Egypt during the time of the pharaohs, about 1260 B.C. The word *exodus* is actually Greek in origin, but the title of the Old Testament book helped it come into English. This is just one of the ways in which the Bible has influenced the growth of our vocabulary. Refer to page 190 for other examples.

In Arabic, the prophet Mohammed's departure from Mecca in A.D. 622 is called "Al Hijrat," which means "The Flight." The event is important in the Moslem world because it is regarded as the beginning of the Moslem era. It has some importance in the English-speaking world as well. That is because it gave modern English a new word for "flight" or "exodus." The word is **hegira**, which is pronounced hĭ-jī´-rə or hĕj´-ər-ə.

177. ex·o·tic   *adjective*   ĕg-zŏt´-ĭk

[*exotikos* (Greek), "foreign"; from *exo* (Greek), "outside"]

Definition: Foreign; charmingly unfamiliar or strikingly unusual.

"Australia is a fascinating continent full of strange and **exotic** wildlife," my Canadian friend remarked.

Phrases: an exotic plant, exotic foods

Synonyms: (*adjectives*) alien; striking, extraordinary

Antonyms: (*adjectives*) native, indigenous, endemic; commonplace, familiar, ordinary

178. ex·pe·di·ent   *adjective and noun*   ĕk-spē´-dē-ĕnt

[*expediens, expedientis*, "freeing, disentangling"; from *ex* (Latin), "out of" + *pes, pedis* (Latin), "foot"]

Definition:

a. (*adjective*) Advantageous to one's interest or purpose.

"In solving this problem, we cannot simply do whatever is **expedient**," I protested. "We must make sure that the course of action we adopt is also ethical."

b. (*noun*) An emergency course of action; a means to an end.

"We can overcome our present financial problems in a number of ways," the personnel manager remarked. "Cutting back on the staff is by no means the only **expedient** open to us."

Related Forms: (*noun*) expediency; (*adjective*) inexpedient

Synonyms: (*adjectives*) convenient, opportune, timely, practical; (*nouns*) device, scheme, design, stratagem, maneuver, stopgap

Antonyms: (*adjectives*) disadvantageous, unserviceable, unsuitable

179. ex·ploit   *verb:* ĕk-sploit´   *noun:* ĕk´-sploit

[*exploit, explait* (Old French), "achievement"; from *ex* (Latin), "out" + *plicare* (Latin), "fold"]

Definition:

a. (*verb*) To use to the greatest possible advantage, often selfishly.

Working conditions have come a long way since the "bad old days," when it was customary to **exploit** the labor of children.

b. (*noun*) A brilliant or heroic deed.

Because he took such pride in his wartime **exploits**, we thought it fitting to bury my grandfather in his army uniform.

Related Forms: (*nouns*) exploitation, exploiter; (*adjective*) exploitable

Synonyms: (*verbs*) capitalize on, cash in on, make the most of, take advantage of; (*nouns*) feat, heroics, coup, tour de force, derring-do

227

180. ex-pound   *verb*   ĕk-spound´ *or* ĭk-spound´

[*espo(u)ndre* (Old French), "put forth"; from *ex* (Latin), "out" + *ponere* (Latin), "put, place"]

Definition: To explain in detail.

> In an influential book published in 1936, the English economist J. M. Keynes **expounded** his epoch-making theory of the causes of economic collapse.

> I spent most of the evening listening to her **expound** her views on all sorts of interesting topics.

Related Forms: (*nouns*) exposition, exponent; (*adjective*) expository

Synonyms: (*verbs*) clarify, elucidate, explicate, delineate (Word 121)

Antonyms: (*verbs*) summarize, abstract, précis, synopsize

Phrases: air one's views, in a nutshell, a thumbnail sketch

Exposition and Expository Writing

Basically, the word *exposition* refers to the setting forth of meaning or intent in a clear and intelligible way. Nonetheless, the word has several technical usages that are worth knowing about. For example, to musicians, *exposition* indicates the opening section of a sonata or fugue, where the various musical themes that will be developed are first introduced. To dramatists, the word indicates the part of a play where the chief characters and overall theme are first presented. And to producers of public entertainments, it indicates a public exhibition of recent artistic or industrial developments.

Expository writing is the technical term for the kind of writing that is designed to set forth ideas or describe people and events in straightforward intelligible English. This is essentially the kind of writing that is necessary in all sorts of everyday situations. For example, a book review, a newspaper article, a business letter, and a chapter in a textbook all involve expository writing of one kind or another. Students, of course, are familiar with expository writing from the compositions, reports, and term papers that they do for school courses.

181. fab-ri-cate   *verb*   făb´-rĭ-kāt

[*fabricari, fabricatus* (Latin), "make, build"]

Definition:

   a.   To assemble or construct from separate parts.

> Philosophers have been **fabricating** new theories of the universe for thousands of years.

   b.   To make up with the intention of deceiving.

> "I don't believe that your account of the incident has any basis in fact," mom said. "I think you **fabricated** it in order to avoid my displeasure."

Related Forms: (*nouns*) fabrication, fabricator; (*verb*) prefabricate

Prefabricate refers to a manufacturing process in which standardized parts or sections are mass-produced for shipment and assembly elsewhere. Thus, a prefabricated house is constructed out of ready-made sections that were manufactured in another place.

Synonyms: (*verbs*) produce, devise, manufacture, concoct, contrive, come up with, cook up

Phrases: a trumped-up charge; coin an excuse; make up out of whole cloth

182. fa-ce-tious   *adjective*   fə-sē´-shəs

[*facetieux* (Old French), "joking"; from *facetia* (Latin), "joke, jest"]

Definition: Not meant seriously; playful or humorous.

"Be careful what you say to him," I warned my sister. "He is so sensitive that he takes even a **facetious** remark to heart."

I didn't pay any attention to what he said because I could see that he was being **facetious**.

Related Forms: (*noun*) facetiousness; (*adverb*) facetiously

Synonyms: (*adjectives*) waggish, whimsical, joking, comic, frivolous, droll

Antonyms: (*adjectives*) serious, grave, solemn, sober, earnest, humorless

Phrases: a tongue-in-cheek remark, joshing, kidding; for real

183. fac-sim-i-le   *noun and adjective*   făk-sĭm´-ə-lē

[*fac simile* (Latin), "make (it) the same"; from *facere* (Latin), "do, make" + *similis, simile* (Latin), "same"]

Definition:

a. (*noun*) An exact copy.

Modern artbooks often contain surprisingly accurate full-color **facsimiles** of the paintings they discuss.

b. (*adjective*) Reproduced exactly.

Usually, a Xerox is in every respect a **facsimile** copy of the original from which it was made.

Synonyms: (*nouns*) replica, reproduction, duplicate

Phrases: a carbon copy, a chip off the old block; a mirror image

184. fal-la-cy   *noun*   făl´-ə-sē

[*fallacia* (Latin), "deceit, trick"; from *fallere* (Latin), "deceive"]

Definition:

a. Faulty reasoning; an error in logic.

"It shouldn't be too hard to shoot holes in his argument," I observed. "After all, the **fallacies** it contains are as plain as day."

b. A false or mistaken notion.

It's a **fallacy** to assume that all redheaded people have quick tempers.

Related Forms: (*adjective*) fallacious; (*noun*) fallaciousness

Synonyms: (*nouns*) mistake, flaw, fault, defect (Word 117), solecism

185. fath-om   *noun and verb*   făth´-əm

[*faethm* (Old English), "the distance between two outstretched arms"]

Definition:

a. (*noun*) A unit of length roughly equal to six feet and used primarily in the measurement of marine depths.

It might be difficult to raise a famous wreck like the *Titanic* because its remains lie under hundreds of **fathoms** of water.

b. (*verb*) To get to the bottom of; to understand.

For as long as human beings have been able to think, they have attempted to **fathom** the mysteries of the universe.

Related Forms: (*adjectives*) fathomable, unfathomable, fathomless

Synonyms: (*verbs*) sound, plumb, probe, delve, penetrate; ferret out, root out; divine, grasp, comprehend

186. **fat-u-ous**   *adjective*   făch´-ōo-wəs

[*fatuus* (Latin), "silly, foolish"]

Definition: Unconsciously foolish, stupid, or absurd.

It was such a **fatuous** remark that I almost burst out laughing when I heard it.

Phrases: a fatuous expression on one's face, a fatuous monarch

Related Forms: (*nouns*) fatuousness, fatuity

Synonyms: (*adjectives*) inane, vacuous, vapid, nonsensical, laughable, silly, ridiculous, ludicrous; wacky, goofy

Antonyms: (*adjectives*) sensible, intelligent, perceptive; acute, incisive; judicious

187. **fea-si-ble**   *adjective*   fē´-zə-bəl

[*faisible* (Old French), "workable"; from *facere* (Latin), "do, make"]

Definition: Possible; both doable and workable.

"I would really like to invite everyone I know to my party," LeVar remarked. "Unfortunately, that idea just isn't **feasible** because my home is too small to hold all my friends."

Phrases: a feasible solution, a feasible plan, a feasible proposal

Related Forms: (*adjective*) unfeasible; (*nouns*) feasibility; feasibleness

Synonyms: (*adjectives*) practicable, practical, usable, realistic

Antonyms: (*adjectives*) impossible, unworkable, impracticable, impractical

Phrases: within the realm of possibility, out of the question

A Useful Distinction

Practicable indicates that something is capable of being done. *Practical* indicates that it is not only capable of being done but also sensible or worthwhile. Thus, it may be practicable to travel to and from the office by pogo stick, but the idea certainly doesn't sound practical.

231

Feint

A *feint* (pronounced fānt) is a misleading attack against a false target designed to draw the defense away from the real objective, and so make it easier to take. Though the word was originally a military term, it is frequently used today in sports (e.g., boxing) and other areas to indicate any kind of misleading movement or strategy. Do not confuse *feint* with *faint*, which as a verb means "swoon" and as an adjective means "indistinct."

188. feign   *verb*   fān

[*feindre* (Old French), "pretend"; from *fingere* (Latin), "shape, form"]

Definition: To pretend or give a false appearance of.

"He wasn't really sick," I said. "He just **feigned** illness in order to get out of school early."

Phrases: feign sleep, feign authorship of, feign knowledge of

Related Forms: (*adjective*) feigned; (*noun*) feint

Synonyms: (*verbs*) fake, sham, simulate

Phrases: sail under false colors, pass oneself off as, pose as; a wolf in sheep's clothing, a humbug, an ignis fatuus; the real McCoy

189. fe-lic-i-tous   *adjective*   fĭ-lĭs′-ĭ-təs *or* fə-lĭs′-ə-təs

[*felicity* + *ous*; from *felicitas* (Latin), "happiness"; from *felix, felicis* (Latin), "happy"]

Definition: Agreeably suited to the purpose or occasion; aptly or gracefully expressed.

"I know you don't consider yourself much of a diplomat," mom told me. "Still, I think you handled that very delicate problem in a truly **felicitous** manner."

"Perhaps the phrasing of your letter isn't particularly **felicitous**," I said, "but the sentiments you express are indeed appropriate."

Related Forms: (*nouns*) felicity, felicitousness; (*adverb*) felicitously; (*verb*) felicitate

Synonyms: (*adjectives*) appropriate, suitable, fitting, apropos, apposite, apt; graceful, agreeable, seemly, becoming; well-chosen, well-put

Antonyms: (*adjectives*) graceless, unseemly, unbecoming, unsuitable; awkward, inept

Phrases: to the point, on target, ad rem; wide of the mark

190. fet-ish   *noun*   fĕt´-ĭsh *or* fē´-tĭsh

[*feitiço* (Portuguese), "charm"; from *facere, factus* (Latin), "do, make"]

Definition:

   a. An object believed among primitive peoples to have magical powers.

   > Down in the main square, a wrinkled old peasant woman sold charms and **fetishes** to ward off the evil eye.

   b. An object of unreasonably excessive attention or reverence.

   > It is one thing to be concerned about discipline; it is quite another to make a **fetish** of it.

Synonyms: (*nouns*) charm, amulet, talisman; fixation, obsession (Word 283), preoccupation, compulsion

Phrases: an idée fixe, a hang-up; get a complex about; a monomaniac; a sacred cow

Using the Words

Exercise I. Parts of Speech

Indicate the part of speech of each of the following words. In some cases, two answers are correct.

1. exotic
2. facsimile
3. expound
4. exploit
5. expedient
6. fabricate
7. fathom
8. exodus
9. feasible

Exercise II. Words in Phrases

In each of the following groups select the item that best expresses the meaning of the *italicized* word in the introductory phrase.

1. *feign* illness
    a. cure b. prevent c. investigate d. pretend e. cause

2. *fatuous* comments
    a. perceptive b. interesting c. silly d. appropriate
    e. surprising

3. a *felicitous* remark
    a. well-known b. well-worn c. well-heeled d. well-fed
    e. well-chosen

4. *exotic* dishes
    a. delightfully unfamiliar   b. outrageously expensive
    c. unusually sweet   d. woefully inadequate
    e. moderately priced

5. will do whatever is *expedient*
   a. fashionable b. advantageous c. easy d. enjoyable
   e. correct

6. *expound* a theory
   a. attack b. demolish c. improve d. investigate
   e. explain

7. *facsimile* copies of the document
   a. secondhand b. forged c. newly discovered d. exact
   e. famous

Exercise III. Completing Sentences

Complete each of the following sentences or pairs of sentences by selecting the most appropriate word from the given group of words. Use each word only once. Make any adjustments that are necessary to fit the words into the sentences properly.

fallacy	fabricate	feasible
fathom	facetious	feign
exodus	exploit	fetish

1. "He is not interested in solving this problem quickly and intelligently," I said. "He is only interested in _____ the difficulties it has created to his own advantage."

2. "Let's get out of here," Sy said after we'd been in the museum only ten minutes. "All these strange idols and _____ give me the creeps!"

3. In *The Art of the Possible*, Golda Meir suggests that politics and diplomacy have one thing in common. They are both concerned with what is _____ rather than with what is ideal.

4. Fortunately, we were able to _____ a replacement for the missing article from a few short press releases and some government statistics.

5. "I've puzzled about it for days," mom told dad, "but I still can't _____ the motives behind young Tom's strange behavior lately."

6. The blatant anti-Semitism of the Nazi regime was wholly responsible for the tremendous _____ of Jews from Germany in the 1930's.

7. "Your conclusion isn't valid," I remarked, "because the argument leading up to it contains an obvious _____."

8. "This is a serious conversation," Jane protested. "Why do you insist on disrupting it by constantly making _____ remarks?"

Exercise IV.   Synonyms and Antonyms

A. In each of the following groups, select the two words that are most nearly **synonyms**.

1. **a.** overwhelm **b.** clarify **c.** imagine **d.** elucidate
   e. manufacture

2. **a.** devise **b.** escape **c.** concoct **d.** stumble
   e. pretend

3. **a.** solution **b.** duplicate **c.** salary **d.** problem
   e. copy

4. **a.** charm **b.** hobby **c.** guilt **d.** profession **e.** amulet

5. **a.** migrate **b.** understand **c.** comprehend **d.** create
   e. summarize

Now, for each pair of synonyms, supply a word from the Basic Word List for Lesson 16 (Words 176–190) that means the **same** or **almost the same** thing.

B. In each of the following, select the item that is most nearly **opposite** in meaning to the numbered word at the left.

1. fatuous   **a.** honest **b.** brave **o.** intelligent
              d. wealthy **e.** famous

2. feasible   **a.** unworkable **b.** unknown **c.** unseen
              d. unfaithful **e.** unavoidable

3. facetious   **a.** awkward **b.** usable **c.** ridiculous
              d. commonplace **e.** serious

4. exodus   **a.** scheme **b.** arrival **c.** flaw **d.** lie
              e. copy

5. exotic   **a.** convenient **b.** sensible **c.** mistaken
              d. native **e.** comic

Exercise V.   Word Roundup

1. Explain the difference between the words in each of the following pairs.

   a. feint—faint   **b.** practical—practicable

2. What is a *hegira*? From what foreign language does the word come, and to what historical event did it originally refer?

3. Define each of the following words.
   a. solecism   **c.** humbug   **e.** monomaniac
   b. coup   **d.** heroics   **f.** exposition

4. Explain the meaning of each of the following colorful phrases.
   a. in a nutshell   **d.** a carbon copy
   b. a tongue-in-cheek remark   **e.** a tour de force
   c. deeds of derring-do   **f.** an idée fixe

Exercise VI. Framing Sentences

A. Use each of the following words in an original sentence that clearly illustrates its meaning.

1. exodus	4. exploit	7. fatuous
2. exotic	5. expound	8. felicitous
3. expedient	6. facsimile	9. fetish

B. Give an **adjective** form of each of these words, and use it in an original sentence.

1. fallacy   2. feign   3. fathom

C. Give a **noun** form of each of these words, and use it in an original sentence.

1. feasible   2. fabricate   3. facetious

Completing Verbal Analogies

"A Is Primarily Concerned with B." Another word relationship that frequently appears in the analogy sections of standardized vocabulary tests is "A is primarily concerned with B; C is primarily concerned with D." Here is an example of an analogy question involving this relationship. Try to determine the correct answer before you go on to read the explanation of it.

veterinarian : animals =
a. druggist : addicts
b. psychology : mind
c. disputes : arbitrator
d. warden : prisoners
e. theologian : angels

The answer is *d.* A *warden* is primarily concerned with *prisoners*, just as a *veterinarian* is primarily concerned with *animals*.

None of the other choices exhibits the same relationship as the key pair of words. A *druggist* is not primarily concerned with *addicts* (Choice *a*), nor is a *theologian* primarily concerned with *angels* (Choice *e*). Though an *arbitrator* is certainly concerned with *disputes* (Choice *c*), *disputes* are not concerned with *arbitrators*. In other words, the two items in the pair come in the wrong order. Finally, *psychology* is indeed concerned with the *mind* (Choice *b*), but the items in the pair are not parallel to the items in the key pair. *Psychology* indicates a science, not a person (as *veterinarian* does), and *mind* indicates a human faculty, not a type of creature (as *animals* does). Both Choices *b* and *c* were intentionally included to confuse the student and make the selection of the right answer more difficult.

"A Is a Part of B." Another word relationship that appears in the analogy sections of standardized tests is "A is a part of B; C is a part of D." Here is an example of an analogy question involving this relationship. Try to determine the correct answer before you read the explanation of it.

rung : ladder =
a. cauldron : kettle
b. saddle : stirrup
c. apartment : room
d. match : lighter
e. step : staircase

The answer is *e*. A *step* is part of a *staircase*, just as a *rung* is part of a *ladder*.

None of the other choices exhibits the same relationship. A *cauldron* is not part of a *kettle* (Choice *a*); it is a kind of kettle. In other words, the two words means roughly the same thing. A *saddle* is not part of a *stirrup* (Choice *b*), though a stirrup is part of a saddle. Similarly, an apartment is not part of a *room* (Choice *c*), though a room is part of an apartment or may even be an apartment. In other words, the items in Choice *b* and *c* come in the wrong order. Finally, a *match* is not part of a *lighter* (Choice *d*), though it serves the same function as a lighter. In other words, these items are complementary, since they indicate two different ways of producing a flame.

Parallelism. In the explanation of the example under "*A* is primarily concerned with *B*," it was pointed out that the items in the answer you select should always be as parallel as possible to the items in the key pair. If they are not, you have probably made the wrong choice and should reconsider your answer.

Exercise I

Complete each of the following analogies based on the word relationships "*A* is primarily concerned with *B*" and "*A* is a part of *B*."

1. **chapter : novel =**
   a. pen : pencil
   b. dictionary : word
   c. essay : composition
   d. act : drama
   e. paragraph : sentence

2. **dentist : teeth =**
   a. ornithologist : ears
   b. surgeon : bruises
   c. ophthalmologist : eyes
   d. feet : chiropodist
   e. pharmacy : medicine

3. **deck : ship =**
   a. church : pew
   b. field : meadow
   c. chair : table
   d. bookcase : shelf
   e. floor : house

4. **legislator : lawmaking =**
   a. lawfulness : judge
   b. citizen : law-abiding
   c. criminal : lawbreaker
   d. lawsuit : attorney
   e. police officer : law enforcement

5. **astronomy : stars =**
   a. archeologist : antiquities
   b. zoology : animals
   c. archery : buildings
   d. philatelist : coins
   e. insects : entomology

6. **county : state =**
   a. tree : forest
   b. hive : bee
   c. voyage : trip
   d. continent : peninsula
   e. mare : stallion

Compose **two** complete analogies involving the word relationship "*A* is primarily concerned with *B*" and **two** involving "*A* is a part of *B*."

Exercise III

The following items review what you have so far learned about analogy questions. Complete each.

1. **augment : increase** :: horrify :
   (arbitrate, appall, condone, atone, deviate)

2. **circuitous : direct** :: skimpy :
   (culpable, scant, devoid, copious, deferential)

3. **failure : chagrin** :: success :
   (disgust, puzzlement, elation, apathy, frustration)

4. **cantankerous : affability** :: disgruntled :
   (ability, wisdom, courage, honesty, contentment)

5. **like : adore** :: dislike :
   (loathe, lithe, lathe, loath, lath)

Working with Context Clues

Inference Clues. The third general type of context clue you are likely to meet in the sentence-completion sections of standardized vocabulary tests is an **inference clue**. In an inference clue, the whole situation outlined in the sentence or pair of sentences suggests the sense of the word that goes in the blank. For that reason, the reader must *infer* the word that is wanted, often by recognizing familiar situations, drawing on past knowledge and experience, or applying simple logic. As you can see, an inference clue is a broader and more indirect type of hint than a restatement clue or a contrast clue.

Here is an example of a sentence-completion exercise that involves an inference clue. Try to determine the correct answer before you read the explanation of it given below.

> Ninety-year-old Annie Blakeley's *The Lowing Herd Winds Slowly O'er the Lea* presents the reader with a touching picture of life in _____ Kansas at the turn of the 20th century.
>
> **a.** industrialized **b.** rural **c.** maritime **d.** urban **e.** colonial

The answer is *b. rural.* Here's why.

The position of the blank indicates that you are looking for a descriptive adjective. A quick check of the five choices you are offered confirms this impression. Now you know what you need.

But you know something else as well. The blank appears immediately before the word *Kansas.* This suggests that Kansas will be of some value in determining the word that goes in the blank.

Now read the entire sentence carefully to determine what else it offers in the way of clues to the correct choice. The sentence concerns the content of a novel or memoir by a woman who grew up in Kansas around 1900. This suggests that the title of the book will be of some help in ascertaining the correct choice. It also suggests that the part of the country mentioned (Kansas) and the time frame indicated (at the turn of the 20th century) may also be of some use.

Now you know where the clues are likely to be. Notice that an understanding of the sense of the sentence and the application of simple logic were the governing factors in isolating the probable clues.

Reread the title of the 90-year-old woman's book carefully. It evokes a picture that immediately eliminates three of the five choices as the correct answer.

And what is that picture? It is a picture of a herd of cows moving slowly through a meadow. *Low* means the same thing as *moo*, so you know you are dealing with a herd of cows. *Lea* is an old poetic word for *meadow*.

Now, in what sort of a setting would you be likely to find a herd of cows crossing a meadow? Certainly not in an *industrialized* area (Choice *a*) or an *urban* center (Choice *d*) or even a *maritime* community (Choice *c*). These three items are clearly wrong, and you are down to two possibilities because cows would be found in both a *rural* and a *colonial* setting (Choices *b* and *e*).

To determine which of the two remaining possibilities is correct, think about each in regard to the part of the country mentioned (Kansas) and the time frame indicated (around 1900). Kansas was primarily an agricultural area at the turn of the century, so *rural* (Choice *b*) seems to fit. However, Kansas was never one of the 13 colonies and, by 1900, had long since become a full-fledged member of the Union. Clearly, *colonial* (Choice *e*) won't work, so *rural* (Choice *b*) must be the correct answer. And, of course, it is.

Notice that determining the correct answer to this sentence-completion exercise depended on a combination of utilizing the whole context, recognizing familiar situations, drawing on past knowledge, and applying simple logic. These are essentially the ingredients that go into the successful solution of the type of sentence-completion exercise that involves an inference clue.

Exercise I

The following sentence-completion exercises contain inference clues. Complete each by selecting the word that makes the best sense in the sentence (or pair of sentences) as a whole. Indicate the clue or clues that led you to make your choice.

1. Henry II, Richard I, and several other medieval English _____ spent more of their time in France than in England.

   a. queens b. nights c. bishops d. merchants e. kings

2. As my knock failed to _____ any response, I tried the door. Unfortunately, it was locked, and I wasn't able to get in.

   a. abet b. fabricate c. elicit d. buttress e. curtail

3. The movie *Panic in Needle Park* paints a grim, uncompromising portrait of the everyday life of a _____ living in New York City.

   a. heroin addict b. used-car salesman c. deep-sea diver
   d. visiting dignitary e. dairy farmer

4. Only a thoroughly _____ person could look at real suffering without batting an eye or feeling the least twinge of conscience.

   a. compassionate b. boisterous c. dapper d. callous
   e. benign

5. "The man who builds a factory builds a temple," President Calvin Coolidge once said, "and the man who works in that factory in a sense _____ there."

   a. sleeps b. worships c. eats d. plays e. entertains

Exercise II

The following exercises review everything you have learned about sentence-completion questions and context clues to this point. Complete each item in the exercise by selecting the word that makes the best sense in the sentence (or pair of sentences) as a whole. Indicate the clue or clues that led you to make your choice.

1. It takes years of experiences "in the trenches" to turn a _____ young rookie, fresh out of the Police Academy, into a seasoned, street-smart veteran.

   a. emaciated b. affable c. callow d. distraught
   e. brusque

2. "We haven't a moment to lose," the President declared. "We must take _____ action to settle this dispute, once and for all."

   a. cautious b. prompt c. future d. little e. dilatory

3. I like visiting small towns and rural villages from time to time, but the big city is my _____ home.

   a. permanent   b. original   c. temporary   d. former
   e. accidental

4. The model's hands were soft and well cared for; the construction worker's were a mass of knots and _____.

   a. discourses   b. epithets   c. buttresses   d. aggregates
   e. calluses

5. The radio, the television set, and other modern forms of mass _____ were entirely unknown at the beginning of the 20th century.

   a. hysteria   b. employment   c. transportation   d. murder
   e. communication

Enriching the Lesson

Exercise I.   Loan Words from Faraway Places

The inclusion of the word *exotic* in Lesson 16 brings to mind the fact that some of the vocabulary of present-day English comes from very striking and unusual sources. Listed below are a number of these unusual loan words. With or without the aid of a dictionary, define each and tell where it comes from. Then choose any **five**, and for each compose an original sentence.

1. kowtow	8. taboo	15. juggernaut
2. amuck	9. loot	16. paradise
3. tycoon	10. mogul	17. mumbo jumbo
4. powwow	11. tariff	18. mufti
5. zombie	12. pariah	19. voodoo
6. thug	13. totem	20. nadir
7. boomerang	14. caucus	21. oasis

Exercise II.   The Language of Logic

One of the words studied in Lesson 16 is *fallacy*, which is a technical term in the language of logic. Below are listed some other words and expressions used in the study of logic. With or without the aid of a dictionary, define each.

1. logic	6. induction
2. syllogism	7. deduction
3. major premise	8. valid
4. minor premise	9. invalid
5. conclusion	10. pathetic fallacy

Exercise III. "Die-Hards"

Lesson 16 includes the word *fathom*, which might be termed a "die-hard" in the sense that it goes back, practically without change, to Old English. Old English, you will recall, represents the earliest stage of our language. It was used in England in the period before the Norman Conquest of 1066.

"Die-hards" like *fathom* make up an important and sizable segment of the vocabulary of present-day English. A few examples of other "die-hard" expressions are listed below. With or without the aid of a dictionary, define each.

1. mirth	6. threat	11. quench
2. seethe	7. spurn	12. forbear
3. din	8. fret	13. mood
4. slough	9. mete (*verb*)	14. beckon
5. quell	10. swarthy	15. hurdle

Exercise IV. The Language of the Mind

Fetish, studied in Lesson 16, is frequently used in connection with psychology, which is the science that deals with the workings of the mind and with human behavior. The 20th century has witnessed major developments in the science of psychology, and in recent years there has been great popular interest in it. As a result, many psychological terms have filtered down into everyday speech and writing.

Listed below are a number of terms and expressions drawn from the language of psychology. With or without the aid of a dictionary, define each.

1. neurotic	6. split personality	11. introvert
2. psychosomatic	7. maladjustment	12. extrovert
3. paranoid	8. psychic	13. schizoid
4. subconscious	9. complex	14. hypochrondriac
5. extrasensory	10. psychotic	15. burnout

Exercise V. Expanding Your Word Power

The words listed below are not on the Basic Word List, but they were mentioned in passing in Lesson 16. All of them would make useful additions to your working vocabulary. Define each, give its etymology, list **two** synonyms and **two** antonyms (where possible), and use in a short illustrative sentence.

1. influx	6. synopsis	11. replica
2. preoccupation	7. explicate	12. solecism
3. stratagem	8. devise	13. delve
4. talisman	9. earnest	14. simulate
5. feat	10. whimsical	15. apposite

Lesson 17

191. **fiasco** — 205. **futile**

---

191. **fi-as-co**   *noun*   fē-ăs′kō

[*fiasco* (Italian), "flask; failure"]

Definition: A complete and ridiculous failure.

In no time at all, poor planning turned what should have been a sure-fire success into a total **fiasco**.

Synonyms: (*nouns*) disaster, debacle, mess, bomb, flop

Antonyms: (*nouns*) triumph, success, hit

Phrases: go over like a lead balloon, a flash in the pan, a feather in one's cap, come off with flying colors

192. **fick-le**   *adjective*   fĭk′-əl

[*ficol* (Old English), "false, deceitful"]

Definition: Likely to change for no apparent reason; inconstant.

"I wouldn't count too heavily on such windfalls happening again," I remarked. "After all, Lady Luck is notoriously **fickle**."

The taste of the general public is so **fickle** that what is fashionable today is likely to be outdated tomorrow.

Related Forms: (*noun*) fickleness; (*adjective*) fickle-minded

Phrases: fickle weather, fickle fortune, fickle affections

Synonyms: (*adjectives*) changeable, capricious, unstable, mercurial, erratic, variable, flighty, fitful, volatile

Antonyms: (*adjectives*) steadfast, constant, immutable, steady

Phrase: blow hot and cold

193. **filch**   *verb*   fĭlch

[*filchen* (Middle English), "take as booty"; from *fylcian* (Old English), "draw up in battle array"; from *gefylce* (Old English), "band of men"]

Definition: To steal slyly, especially small things.

Two of the youngsters acted as decoys, while a third attempted to **filch** a couple of apples from the unguarded bin.

Synonyms: (*verbs*) pilfer, purloin, shoplift, pinch, rip off, snatch, heist, swipe

194. fi-nesse   *noun and verb*   fĭ-nĕs´ ,

[*finesse* (French), "delicacy"; from *fin* (French), "fine"]

Definition:

 a. (*noun*) Skill, delicacy, or subtlety in doing something or handling a situation.

> For over an hour, the two brilliant conversationalists traded verbal blows with all the **finesse** of expert swordsmen.

 b. (*verb*) To accomplish by subtle or skillful maneuvering.

> "He's a clever man who has managed to **finesse** himself into a very important position in this company," my boss remarked.

Synonyms: (*nouns*) artfulness, craftiness, shrewdness, adroitness, dexterity, facility, savoir-faire, know-how, savvy; (*verbs*) maneuver, contrive, finagle, manipulate

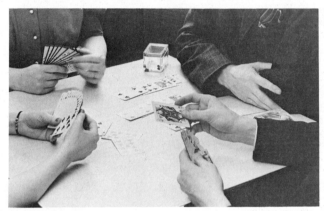

In addition to its normal uses, *finesse* is a technical term in the card game bridge. As a bridge term, it refers to an attempt to take a trick with a low card while holding a much higher card in the same suit. The point of doing this is either to take the trick as cheaply as possible or to induce your opponent to play an intermediate card that you can then top.

195. fla-grant   *adjective*   flā´-grǝnt

[*flagrans, flagrantis* (Latin), "burning, blazing" from *flagrare* (Latin), "burn"]

Definition: Extremely and deliberately conspicuous; glaring.

> Some people were satisfied, even pleased, with the outcome of the trial; others branded it a **flagrant** miscarriage of justice.

Related Forms: (*nouns*) flagrancy, flagrance; (*adverb*) flagrantly

Synonyms: (*adjectives*) shocking, gross, rank, heinous (Word 222), atrocious, scandalous, disgraceful, brazen, egregious, arrant

Antonyms: (*adjectives*) negligible, insignificant, minor

Phrases: caught red-handed, in flagrante delicto

196. flaunt   *verb*   flônt

[Origin unknown; possibly akin to *flanta* (Norwegian), "gad about," and *flana* (Old Norse), "rush headlong"]

Definition: To show off in a conspicuous or offensive way.

Some people would try to downplay the fact that they're living on easy street, but he **flaunts** his wealth in an exceedingly offensive way.

Synonyms: (*verbs*) display, parade, exhibit, draw attention to, sport, spotlight

Antonyms: (*verbs*) hide, conceal, screen, cover up; downplay, soft-pedal, deemphasize

197. flout   *verb*   flout

[*flouten* (Middle English), "play the flute"; from *flauter* (Old French), "play the flute," and *flaute* (Old French), "flute"]

Definition: To treat openly with scorn or contempt.

Tony **flouted** the school dress code by appearing in class in a ragged pair of blue jeans and an old sweat shirt.

Usage Note:

Be careful not to confuse *flout* with its look-alike *flaunt* (Word No. 196). Though these two words are sometimes considered to be synonyms in *nonstandard* English, they are quite different and should be kept separate.

Synonyms: (*verbs*) mock, scoff at, jeer at, deride, disparage, ridicule, sneer at, defy

Antonyms: (*verbs*) respect, observe, abide by; esteem, venerate, honor

Phrases: laugh up one's sleeve at, poke fun at

198. fluc-tu-ate   *verb*   flŭk´-choo-āt

[*fluctuare, fluctuatus* (Latin), "move like a wave"; from *fluere* (Latin), "flow"]

Definition: To change continually from one position to another.

Since the moon lacks an atmosphere, temperatures on the surface of that heavenly body **fluctuate** wildly.

As the tide of battle shifted repeatedly from one side to the other, we found ourselves **fluctuating** between elation and despair.

Related Forms: (*nouns*) fluctuation, flux

Phrases: fluctuating interest rates, fluctuating popularity

Synonyms: (*verbs*) waver, vacillate, oscillate, seesaw

Phrases: in a constant state of flux, ups and downs, ebb and flow, a checkered career

199. foi·ble   *noun*   foi´-bəl

[*foible* (obsolete French), "weak"]

Definition: A minor, often amusing, fault or weakness in character.

"I agree that the candidate's strong points are indeed admirable," I replied. "It is his **foibles** that I find laughable."

Usage Note:
When certain types of foibles become too pronounced, they may develop into *obsessions* (Word 283) or *phobias* (Word 301). For example, a concern for punctuality may become an obsession, or a dislike of cats a phobia.

Synonyms: (*nouns*) frailty, failing, flaw, defect (Word 117), shortcoming, idiosyncrasy, peculiarity, oddity, quirk, eccentricity, crotchet

Antonyms: (*nouns*) forte, strong point, long suit

200. fore·stall   *verb*   fôr-stôl´

[*foresteall* (Old English), "highway robbery"; from *fore* (Old English), "in front of" + *steall* (Old English), "position"]

Definition: To secure an advantage or prevent a loss by previous action.

The President tried to **forestall** the impending defeat of his legislative program by drumming up popular support for it on national TV.

Synonyms: (*verbs*) hinder, thwart (Word 376), frustrate, preclude, obviate, prevent, ward off, fend off, stave off, anticipate

Phrases: take precautionary measures, nip in the bud, cut off at the pass, steal a march on, beat to the draw, preventive medicine, a pre-emptive strike

201. for·mi·da·ble   *adjective*   fôr´-mĭ-də-bəl

[*formidabilis, formidabile* (Latin), "causing fear"; from *formido* (Latin), "terror, dread"]

Definition:
   a.   Arousing fear or admiration because of the unusual size or superiority of the thing involved.

The accused mobster entered the courtroom with a **formidable** array of lawyers and other legal advisers.

   b.   Difficult to do because of the size of the job involved.

The **formidable** task of cleaning up after the tornado could not have been accomplished without the cooperation of the entire community.

Phrases: a formidable opponent, a formidable intellect, a formidable memory, a formidable accomplishment

Related Forms: (*nouns*) formidability, formidableness

246

Synonyms: (*adjectives*) awesome, redoubtable, alarming, frightening, terrifying, horrifying; mind-boggling, impressive; huge, tremendous

Antonyms: (*adjectives*) unimpressive; inconsequential, insignificant, paltry, puny, negligible; simple, easy, undemanding

202. for-tu-i-tous   *adjective*   fôr-tōō´-ĭ-təs *or* fôr-tyōō´-ĭ-təs

[*fortuitus* (Latin), "accidental"; from *fors, fortis* (Latin), "chance"]

Definition: Occurring by chance or accident.

Quite by chance I bumped into her on the street one day, and the results of that **fortuitous** meeting have changed the whole course of my life.

Related Forms: (*nouns*) fortuitousness, fortuity; (*adverb*) fortuitously

Usage Note:

Be careful not to confuse *fortuitous* with *fortunate*. *Fortuitous* means "accidental" or "happening by chance." The consequences of a fortuitous occurrence can be either fortunate or unfortunate, though the word tends to suggest that they are good rather than bad. *Fortunate*, on the other hand, simply means "lucky" or "happy," and the consequences of a fortunate development are always good. In other words, *fortuitous* refers to the way something happened, while *fortunate* refers to its results.

Synonyms: (*adjectives*) accidental, unplanned, inadvertent, casual, adventitious; unforeseen, unexpected, unanticipated

Antonyms: (*adjectives*) intentional, planned, deliberate, premeditated

Phrases: a fluke, a windfall, a chance occurrence

203. fru-gal   *adjective*   frōō´-gəl

[*frugalis* (Latin), "economical"; from *frux, frugis* (Latin), "fruit, produce"]

Definition:

a. Thrifty or economical in the use of money.

"Inflation has really put a dent in my buying power this year," I thought. "If I'm going to make ends meet, I'll have to be more **frugal**."

b. Involving little expense; meager.

Surprisingly, the **frugal** meal we got from the old peasant woman was more satisfying than many a banquet I'd attended.

Related Forms: (*nouns*) frugality, frugalness; (*adverb*) frugally

Synonyms: (*adjectives*) sparing, careful, prudent, provident; scanty, skimpy, paltry; stingy, parsimonious, penurious, niggardly, tightfisted, penny-pinching

Antonyms: (*adjectives*) lavish, extravagant, prodigal, improvident

Phrases: a skinflint, penny-wise and pound-foolish

204. **ful-some**   *adjective*   fŏŏl′-səm

[*fulsom* (Middle English), "loathsome"; from *full*, "excess" + *some*, "characterized by"]

Definition: Excessive and, for that reason, offensive to good taste and obviously insincere.

> "We know you're trying to curry favor with the boss," the note read. "Still, must you greet every last one of his bright ideas with such **fulsome** and obvious flattery?"

Related Forms: (*noun*) fulsomeness; (*adverb*) fulsomely

Synonyms: (*adjectives*) inordinate, extravagant, gross, immoderate, overdone; repulsive, disgusting, nauseating, odious, loathsome; vulgar, crass, tasteless

Antonyms: (*adjectives*) modest, understated, muted, subdued, toned down, quiet

Phrases: ad nauseam, in poor taste

205. **fu-tile**   *adjective*   fyŏŏ′-əl *or* fyŏŏ′-tīl

[*futilis, futile* (Latin), "leaky; worthless"]

Definition: Incapable of producing the desired result; unsuccessful or ineffective.

> Though the lifeguard made a heroic attempt to save the drowning woman's life, his efforts unfortunately proved **futile**.

Related Forms: (*nouns*) futility, futileness; (*adverb*) futilely

Synonyms: (*adjectives*) vain, fruitless, unavailing, idle, ineffectual, bootless, pointless, useless

Antonyms: (*adjectives*) effective, effectual, efficacious (Word 148), successful

Phrases: to no purpose, all for naught, carry coals to Newcastle

Carry Coals to Newcastle

The expression *carry coals to Newcastle* means "do something that is superfluous or unnecessary" or "supply something that is already abundant." Newcastle upon Tyne in northern England, the Newcastle of the expression, has long been the center of coal mining, so there is no need to import coal as it is already plentiful in the area.

Using the Words

Exercise I. Syllabication and Pronunciation

Syllabicate the following words correctly, and place the major stress mark (′) after the syllable that is accented when the word is pronounced.

1. fiasco	4. flagrant	7. foible
2. fickle	5. frugal	8. formidable
3. finesse	6. fluctuate	9. fortuitous

Exercise II. Words Out of Context

In each of the following groups, select the item that best expresses the meaning of the numbered word at the left.

1. fickle   a. respectful   b. changeable   c. modest   d. idle

2. flagrant   a. quiet   b. prudent   c. vain   d. gross

3. flaunt   a. show off   b. steal   c. frustrate   d. laugh at

4. flout   a. cover up   b. lavish   c. sneer at   d. waver

5. forestall   a. emphasize   b. observe   c. alarm   d. prevent

6. fortuitous   a. impressive   b. wasteful   c. accidental   d. fruitless

7. fulsome   a. loathsome   b. generous   c. simple   d. unstable

Exercise III. Completing Sentences

Complete each of the following sentences by selecting the most appropriate word from the given group of words. Use each word only once. Make any adjustments that are necessary to fit the words into the sentences properly.

finesse	frugal	fluctuate
futile	fiasco	forestall
foible	filching	formidable

1. Prices for consumer goods _____ in accordance with the ups and downs of the economy.

2. Though the young boxer doesn't look particularly impressive in his street clothes, he is a _____ opponent once he's in the ring.

3. I admire someone who can handle a delicate social situation with tact and _____.

4. Curiously, a play that "bombs" in London is a hit, while one that "bombs" on Broadway is a _____.

5. My personality isn't all of a piece; it's a mixture of strengths and weaknesses, fortes and _____.

6. She is a _____ homemaker who delights in comparison shopping and bargain hunting.

7. Someone who starts off _____ pennies may end up stealing millions.

8. The police recaptured one of the fugitives in a matter of hours, but their efforts to retake the other proved _____.

Exercise IV. Synonyms and Antonyms

Classify each of the following pairs of words as **S** for **synonyms** or **A** for **antonyms**.

1. flagrant—glaring
2. shortcoming—foible
3. flaunt—conceal
4. formidable—awesome
5. success—fiasco
6. flout—respect
7. capricious—fickle
8. lavish—frugal
9. finesse—dexterity
10. effective—futile
11. fluctuate—vacillate
12. thwart—forestall
13. fortuitous—premeditated
14. pilfer—filch

Exercise V. Word Roundup

1. Explain the difference between the items in each of the following pairs.

   a. flout—flaunt
   b. fortuitous—fortunate

2. With or without the aid of a dictionary, define each of the following colloquial or slang expressions.

   a. a heist
   b. to soft-pedal
   c. a windfall
   d. a fluke
   e. a skinflint
   f. a flop

3. With or without the aid of a dictionary, explain the meaning of each of the following colorful phrases.

   a. blow hot and cold
   b. caught red-handed
   c. laugh up one's sleeve at
   d. a checkered career
   e. go over like a lead balloon
   f. a person's long suit
   g. steal a march on
   h. carry coals to Newcastle
   i. a flash in the pan
   j. penny-wise and pound-foolish

4. Explain the meaning of the following Latin phrases commonly used in present-day English.

    a. ad nauseam   **b.** (in) flagrante delicto

5. Explain what *finesse* means in bridge.

Exercise VI. Framing Sentences

A. Use each of the following words in an original illustrative sentence.

1. fiasco	4. flaunt	7. fortuitous
2. filch	5. flout	8. forestall
3. finesse	6. foible	9. fulsome

B. Give a **noun** form of each of the following words, and use it in an original illustrative sentence.

1. fickle	3. fluctuate	5. frugal
2. flagrant	4. formidable	6. futile

Dissecting the Words

Prefixes

1. The Old English prefix **fore**, meaning "before," "earlier," "in advance," or "in front of," appears in the word *forestall*, studied in this lesson. Following are some other common English words in which it occurs. In each case, note how the prefix contributes to the overall meaning of the word in which it appears.

forewarn (*fore*, "before" + *warn*)—to warn in advance

forecast (*fore*, "in advance" + *cast*)—to predict; a prediction

foresee (*fore*, "before" + *see*)—to see or know beforehand

forebear (*fore*, "before" + *bear* (Old English), "a being, person")—an ancestor

forebode (*fore*, "in advance" + *bode*)—to indicate the likelihood of; portend. (Note that *forebode* usually implies that what is coming is bad rather than good.)

foreshadow (*fore*, "beforehand" + *shadow*)—to indicate or suggest beforehand

Other common English words containing the prefix *fore* include *foretaste, forefather, foreword, forerunner*, and *foretell*.

2. Do not confuse the prefix *fore* with the Old English look-alike prefix **for** (without an *e*). *For* means "away, off" or "completely, utterly." It appears in a number of common English words, including:

forgo (*for*, "completely away" + *go*)—to abstain from completely; to do totally without *forlorn* (*for*, "completely" + *lorn*, "abandoned")—wretched and pitiful; nearly hopeless

forbear (*for*, "completely away" + *bear*)—to refrain completely from

forsake (*for*, "completely" + *sake*, "deny, reject")—to leave or desert completely

Other modern English words in which the prefix *for* appears are *forbid* and *forswear*.

Root

The Latin root **flu** or **fluct**, meaning "flow," is found in the word *fluctuate*, studied in this lesson. Here are some other common English words in which the root appears.

affluent (literally, "flowing toward")—wealthy, well-to-do

confluence (literally, "a flowing together")—the junction of two rivers

flux—a constant change or flow

fluent—easily flowing; effortless, polished, or graceful

influx (literally, "a flowing in")—the arrival of great numbers of something

superfluous (literally, "flowing over and above")—superabundant, excessive, extra. Noun: *superfluity*

mellifluous (literally, "flowing with honey")—very sweet and smooth; honeyed

Exercise

1. On the basis of your knowledge of the prefix *fore*, tell what each of the following compound words means:

   a. foreword
   b. forefront
   c. foremost
   d. foreshorten
   e. foresight
   f. forehand

2. With or without the aid of a dictionary, define each of the following words containing the prefix *for*. Explain how the prefix contributes to the overall meaning of the word.

   a. forlorn
   b. forbearance
   d. forswear

3. For each of the following definitions, supply an English word that contains either the prefix *fore* or the prefix *for*. In some instances, two answers are possible.

   a. an ancestor
   b. do totally without
   c. predict
   d. warn in advance
   e. see beforehand
   f. completely wretched

4. Define each of the following words, and use it in an original illustrative sentence.

   a. affluent
   b. fusion
   c. influx
   d. superfluous
   e. fluent
   f. influential

Working with Context Clues

Two-Word Omissions. So far you have been dealing with sentence-completion exercises containing only one blank. The sentence-completion sections of most standardized vocabulary tests, however, contain a good many items involving the omission of *two* words, not one. These two-word omissions work in exactly the same way as one-word omissions; they are just more challenging.

Study the following example of a typical two-word omission. Try to determine the correct answer before reading the explanation of it given below.

Florida Fats and the other _____ of McDuffy's Billiard Academy come from every walk of life. You are unlikely to find a more _____ crew assembled under any other roof in town.

a. quadrupeds . . . elegant   c. denizens . . . motley
b. employees . . . uniform   d. proprietors . . . aristocratic

The best way to begin dealing with this example is to determine the parts of speech of the missing words. From the position of the blanks, you seem to need a noun in the first and an adjective in the second.

Notice that the noun you need forms part of the subject of the first sentence. This suggests that it may form part of the subject of the entire passage. Accordingly, read the passage carefully to determine what it is about. It concerns the kind of people who can be found in a pool hall called McDuffy's Billiard Academy. This is confirmed by the phrase *crew assembled under any . . . roof* in the second sentence and the personal name *Florida Fats* in the first. Now you know that the noun you need means something like "customers," or possibly "employees."

Run your eye down the first item in each of the four lettered choices. Eliminate any choice that does not fit in with your conclusion about the meaning of the first missing word. Choices *b* and *c* seem to work. *Employees* (Choice *b*) dovetails neatly with what you think may go in the first blank. So does *denizens* (Choice *c*), which means "inhabitants" or "residents." Choices *a* and *d*, however, don't agree with your ideas, so they can be eliminated. A *quadruped* (Choice *a*) is a four-legged animal, not a person; *proprietors* (Choice *d*) indicates the owners of a business, not its customers or employees.

DVLCE·ET·DECORVM·EST·PRO·PATRIA·MORI
ARLINGTON · MEMORIAL · AMPHITHEATER
ANNO·DOMINI·MCMXV

Though officially a "dead" language, Latin is still used in the modern world. For instance, carved over the entrance to the Amphitheater of Arlington National Cemetery in Virginia is the Roman poet Horace's simple but unforgettable line about patriotism, "It is satisfying and fitting to die for one's country."

Now you are down to two possibilities. However, you'll need more information before you can decide which of the two is correct. Accordingly, move on to consider the second blank, for which you need an adjective.

Notice that the missing adjective modifies the word *crew*. This suggests that it in some way describes the nature or character of the people who can be found at McDuffy's. Carefully reread the entire passage to determine what it has to say about this matter.

The passage says that the crew at McDuffy's *comes from every walk of life*. This suggests that the adjective you need means something like "extremely varied" or "richly diverse."

Run your eye over the second item in Choices *b* and *c*, your two remaining possibilities for the correct answer. *Uniform* (Choice *b*) does not agree with your conclusion about the meaning of the adjective you need, since the word means the opposite of *varied* or *diverse*. For that reason, it can be eliminated.

Motley in Choice *c*, however, does fit since it does mean "richly diverse" or "extremely varied." Choice *c*, therefore, must be the correct answer, and, of course, it is.

One final point: Notice that two-word omissions work on exactly the same kinds of context clues as one-word omissions. In the example given above, one of the hints was essentially a restatement clue since *crew* and *denizens* mean more or less the same thing. The other was an inference clue since *motley* is implied by the phrase *come from every walk of life*.

Exercise

Choose the pair of words that best complete the meaning of each of the following passages. Indicate the clue or clues that led you to make your choice.

1. Thoroughly _____ by their team's unexpected success against Elk Grove, the _____ students of Twin Lakes High carried the victorious squad triumphantly around the basketball court on their shoulders.

   a. bored . . . disinterested   c. depressed . . . crestfallen
   b. elated . . . jubilant   d. dismayed . . . terrified

2. The _____ of the night air was suddenly shattered by the _____ strains of canned music blaring from the radio of a passing automobile. Once the car had gone, however, peace was restored.

   a. chill . . . boisterous   c. density . . . delicate
   b. dampness . . . muted   d. tranquility . . . raucous

3. The soldiers who fell in the engagement were _____ in a portion of the battlefield on which they had fought. Though the spot where they were laid to rest was not technically "hallowed ground," it was considered appropriate because they had in effect _____ it with their blood.

   a. interred . . . consecrated   c. decorated . . . sullied
   b. wounded . . . protected   d. assembled . . . nurtured

4. High winds fanned the flames, and, in no time at all, the
_____ had spread to a nearby tire factory. Clouds of
thick black smoke billowed up into the sky, and the acrid
_____ of burning rubber filled the air.

   a. avalanche...odor   c. innundation...aroma
   b. conflagration...stench   d. drought...scent

5. A person has to expect a little bumping and pushing in a
crowded bus. It just isn't possible to avoid _____
another passenger when the aisle is so _____ people.

   a. maiming...glutted with   c. jostling...congested with
   b. effacing...devoid of   d. tackling...clear of

Enriching the Lesson

Exercise I. Our Italian Heritage

Lesson 17 includes *fiasco*, a word borrowed without change from
Italian. Listed below are a number of other Italian words and
phrases that are commonly used in present-day English. With or
without the aid of a dictionary, define each expression as it is used
in Modern English.

1. torso	8. quarantine	15. manifesto
2. imbroglio	9. libretto	16. solo
3. sotto voce	10. studio	17. scenario
4. vendetta	11. graffiti	18. vista
5. tempo	12. motto	19. cognoscenti
6. squadron	13. salvo	20. gala
7. prima donna	14. incognito	21. virtuoso

Exercise II. Money Talks

The presence of *frugal* in Lesson 17 brings to mind the fact that
Modern English includes an impressive array of expressions relating to business, finance, and economics. A few of these items are
listed below. With or without the aid of a dictionary or other
reference book (*e.g.*, an economics textbook), define each.

1. depression	8. surplus	15. deficit
2. recession	9. monetary policy	16. monopoly
3. inflation	10. market economy	17. bull market
4. deflation	11. economic climate	18. national debt
5. boom	12. private sector	19. windfall profits
6. asset	13. free enterprise	20. liability
7. gross national product	14. medium of exchange	21. prime interest rate

Exercise III.   A Verbal Diversion

Since sports and games play so important a role in our daily lives, it is only natural that many colorful terms and expressions have "spilled over" from the sports world into the everyday language. A few examples of this phenomenon are given below. With or without the aid of a dictionary, define or explain each. Then indicate the sport from which the expression comes.

1. pinch-hit for
2. put on an all-court press
3. par for the course
4. parry a blow
5. a gambit
6. have an ace up one's sleeve
7. kick off a campaign
8. a Monday morning quarterback
9. a goal-line stand
10. stymied
11. hotdog (verb)
12. a stalemate
13. a front-runner
14. showboating
15. a long shot
16. start out with two strikes against you

Exercise IV.   Expanding Your Word Power

The words listed below are not on the Basic Word List, but they were mentioned in passing in Lesson 17. All of them would make useful additions to your working vocabulary. Define each, give its etymology, list **two** synonyms and **two** antonyms (where possible), and use in a short illustrative sentence.

1. debacle
2. erratic
3. steadfast
4. purloin
5. maneuver
6. egregious
7. defy
8. oscillate
9. forte
10. quirk
11. preclude
12. redoubtable
13. inadvertent
14. prodigal
15. inordinate

Lesson 18

206. gape — 220. harbinger

---

206. **gape**   *verb*   gāp
[*gapa* (Old Norse), "open the mouth; stare"]

Definition: To stare open-mouthed in amazement; to open wide.

Astonished motorists **gaped** in disbelief as a crippled helicopter attempted to land in the middle of the freeway.

Meteorites sometimes crash into the Earth with sufficient force and violence to produce **gaping** craters in the landscape.

Related Forms: (*noun*) gap; (*adverb*) agape

Synonyms: (*verbs*) gawk (at); goggle (at), rubberneck, ogle; yawn

Antonyms: (*verbs*) purse (the lips), pucker (the mouth), furrow (the brow)

207. **gar-ble**   *verb*   gär´-bəl
[*garbellare* (Old Italian), "sift"; from *g(h)arbala* (Arabic), "he selected"; possibly from *cribellum* (Late Latin), "sieve"]

Definition: To distort in such a way as to make unintelligible.

"My secretary **garbled** your message so badly," I told my aunt, "that I couldn't even make out who had called."

Phrases: a garbled quotation, garble instructions

Synonyms: (*verbs*) scramble, jumble, confuse, mangle, mutilate, butcher, misrepresent, misquote, misreport

Phrases: take something out of context, get something wrong; get something straight, set the record straight

208. **gloat**   *verb*   glōt
[Origin uncertain; possibly *glotta* (Old Norse), "grin"]

Definition: To regard with excessive or malicious satisfaction.

"I know it really isn't worthy of me," I thought gleefully. "Still, I can't help **gloating** just a little over my archrival's abrupt dismissal from my true love's affections."

Synonyms: (*verbs*) revel (in), delight (in), relish, crow (over), exult (in), glory (in)

Phrases: lord it over, rub it in

An elephant boy uses a goad to control the movements of his charge.

209. goad *noun and verb* gōd

[*gad* (Old English), "spearhead"]

Definition:

    a. (*noun*) A long pointed stick used for driving animals; anything that spurs a person on.

        Customarily, Indian elephant boys use short wooden **goads** to control and direct the movements of their huge charges.

        Simple financial necessity is often the **goad** that prompts a composer or painter to produce new material.

    b. (*verb*) To drive or urge on.

        Try as he might, he could not **goad** me into doing something that I knew in my heart was foolish.

Synonyms: (*nouns*) prod, spur, stimulus, incentive, inducement; (*verbs*) prod, spur, propel, hound, impel, incite, provoke, egg on

Antonyms: (*nouns*) restraint, curb, check, deterrent; (*verbs*) restrain, curb, check, deter, impede

Phrases: needle someone, fire up an audience, whip up enthusiasm

210. graph-ic *adjective* grăf´-ĭk

[*graphikos* (Greek), "able to draw or paint"; from *graphein* (Greek), "draw, paint"]

Definition:

    a. Relating to a drawn or pictorial representation; visual.

        Messages posted on our refrigerator door have become quite eye-catching since my sister began majoring in **graphic** arts.

    b. Giving a clear and effective picture; vivid.

        The book contains a **graphic** and hair-raising account of the seizure of the U.S. embassy in Iran.

Related Forms: (*nouns*) graph, graphics; (*adverb*) graphically

Synonyms: (*adjectives*) pictorial, diagrammatic; striking, tellling, lively, lifelike, realistic, true-to-life, picturesque

Antonyms: (*adjectives*) sketchy, vague; unrealistic; colorless, bloodless, anemic, pallid, bland

Graphs and Graphics

There is a whole family of terms and expressions related to the adjective *graphic*, studied in this lesson. For example, a *graph* as you probably already know, is a line drawing or similar pictorial device used to represent numerical (or other abstract) relationships. The word is constantly used (both as a noun and as a verb) in mathematics and the other arts and sciences. For example, your math teacher may ask you to graph the equation $2x + y = 16$, or your history textbook may contain a graph showing unemployment in the United States during the Great Depression. Graphs, of course, are also widely used in business and other fields as convenient devices for representing abstract relationships in concrete and eye-catching ways.

A *graphic* (plural *graphics*) is similar to a graph, but broader in meaning. To business people and commercial artists, it indicates a picture, chart, or similar device that is designed to illustrate something. To computer experts, it refers to a diagram that the computer generates on the screen (or CRT).

Graphics has several meanings. To architects and engineers, it refers to the art of making technical drawings according to strict mathematical rules. To commercial artists, it indicates the art of making graphic illustrations. And to computer experts, it means the process by which a computer displays a graphic on the screen.

Finally, the *graphic arts* are any of the visual arts that involve applying lines to a two-dimensional surface. Thus, drawing, lettering, photography, and printing are all examples of the graphic arts.

A *gratuity* is a tip, usually in the form of money, given in thanks for a service. Waiters and waitresses (like the one shown in this photo) customarily receive gratuities in this country.

211. **gra-tu-i-tous**   *adjective*   grə-tōō´-ĭ-təs *or* grə-tyōō´-ĭ-təs

[*gratuitus* (Latin), "given as a favor"; from *gratia* (Latin), "favor"]

Definition:

   a. Freely given; done without recompense.

      She gives people a great deal of **gratuitous** service, simply because she likes them.

   b. Uncalled-for; unjustified.

      After treating them so well, we were deeply offended by their **gratuitous** insults.

Related Forms: (*nouns*) gratuitousness, gratuity; (*adjective and adverb*) gratis; (*adverb*) gratuitously

Synonyms: (*adjectives*) free, complimentary, voluntary, unsolicited; unwarranted, unfounded, groundless, baseless

Phrases: on the house, free of charge, a freebie; foot the bill for

212. **gre-ga-ri-ous**   *adjective*   grĭ-gâr´-ē-əs

[*gregarius* (Latin), "belonging to a herd or flock"; from *grex, gregis* (Latin), "herd"]

Definition:

   a. Tending to form or move in a herd or other group; social.

      Prehistoric peoples banded together into tribes, not only for mutual protection, but also to satisfy their **gregarious** instinct.

   b. Enjoying the company of others; sociable.

      Extroverts are by nature **gregarious**; they are usually unhappy if they are forced to be alone.

Related Forms: (*noun*) gregariousness; (*adverb*) gregariously

Synonyms: (*adjectives*) outgoing, extroverted, friendly, companionable, affable, genial

Antonyms: (*adjectives*) antisocial, misanthropic, unsociable, unfriendly, withdrawn, reserved, detached, aloof, introverted

Phrases: esprit de corps, birds of a feather, a social butterfly; live in an ivory tower, a loner

260

213. **gri·mace**   *noun and verb*   grĭm′-ĭs *or* grĭ-mās′

[*grimache* (Old French), "grimace"; related to *grima* (Old English), "mask; fear" and ultimately of Germanic origin]

Definition:

a. (*noun*) A twisted facial expression indicating pain, disgust, or disapproval.

> The **grimace** on her face told me more eloquently than words could have that she disapproved of my decision.

b. (*verb*) To contort the features of the face in order to indicate pain, disgust, or disapproval.

> When the doctor jabbed me with that long needle, I involuntarily **grimaced** in pain.

Synonyms: (*nouns and verbs*) frown, scowl, glower, glare, wince

Antonyms: (*nouns and verbs*) smile, grin; (*verb*) beam

Phrases: make a (wry) face, make faces, screw up one's face; grin from ear to ear, grin like a Cheshire cat

214. **grope**   *verb*   grōp

[*grop(i)en* (Middle English), "grope"; from *grapian* (Old English), "grasp"]

Definition: To feel around uncertainly for.

> When the lights suddenly went out, I **groped** my way down the stairs with the aid of a pocket lighter.

> There was a momentary pause in the conversation as I **groped** for an answer to her unexpected question.

Phrases: grope for the telephone, grope for a clue

Synonyms: (*verbs*) fumble (for), poke around (for), hunt (for), cast about (for), fish around (for), look (for), flounder around (for)

Phrases: pick one's way through; send out a feeler, send up a trial balloon, see how the land lies, see which way the wind is blowing

215. **gru·el·ing**   *adjective*   grōō′-ə-lĭng

[Origin uncertain; possibly *gruel* (obsolete English), "punish" + *ing*]

Definition: Extremely demanding and exhausting.

> With four minutes left to play, a glorious but **grueling** eighty-yard drive put the winning points on the board for the Rams.

Synonyms: (*adjectives*) taxing, draining, fatiguing, wearying, tiring, arduous, intense

Antonyms: (*adjectives*) easy, simple, enjoyable, relaxing, invigorating

216. grue-some   *adjective*   groo´-səm

[*grue* (obsolete English), "shudder" + *some*, "characterized by"]

Definition: Causing great shock, horror, and repugnance.

The **gruesome** sight of maimed and burned people was enough to disillusion me forever about the so-called "glories" of war.

Phrases: a gruesome murder, the gruesome details

Related Forms: (*noun*) gruesomeness; (*adverb*) gruesomely

Synonyms: (*adjectives*) horrifying, horrible, monstrous, hideous, grisly, ghastly, macabre, grotesque, lurid

Antonyms: (*adjectives*) pleasant, lovely, delightful, agreeable, attractive, charming, engaging, pleasurable

217. gul-li-ble   *adjective*   gŭl´-ə-bəl

[*gull* (English), "cheat, dupe" + *ible*]

Definition: Easily cheated or deceived.

No matter how much protective legislation we pass, there will probably always be **gullible** consumers for swindlers and con artists to prey on.

Related Forms: (*noun*) gullibility; (*noun and verb*) gull

Synonyms: (*adjectives*) credulous, naive, ingenuous, unsuspecting, exploitable, trusting, unwary, green

Antonyms: (*adjectives*) skeptical, incredulous, dubious, wary, cautious, circumspect

Phrases: a patsy, a soft touch, a sitting duck, a pigeon; born yesterday, still wet behind the ears; pull the wool over someone's eyes, take someone for a ride; jive; caveat emptor

218. hag-gard   *adjective*   hăg´-ērd

[*hagard* (Old French), "wild," used of a female hawk in falconry]

Definition: Worn and exhausted from anxiety, disease, hunger, or fatigue.

As soon as I saw how **haggard** his face looked, I began to realize just how much he had been through recently.

Related Form: (*noun*) haggardness

Usage Note:

As the example above indicates, *haggard* usually refers to the face or facial expression. It suggests thinness, worry, or weariness, and implies severe mental or physical distress.

Synonyms: (*adjectives*) careworn, drawn, gaunt, wasted, hollow-eyed, drained, wan, cadaverous, pinched

Antonyms: (*adjectives*) rosy, florid, ruddy, rubicund, glowing, radiant

The Trojan Horse

The story of the Trojan Horse, as told in Homer's *Odyssey* and Virgil's *Aeneid*, is a classic example of guile and gullibility. The Greek army besieging Troy was unable to break into the city. The wily Greeks thereupon built a huge statue of a horse and left it outside the city walls. Armed Greek soldiers were concealed inside the hollow structure. Then the Greeks pretended to depart. The jubilant Trojans regarded the statue as a parting gift from a defeated foe and, despite warnings (Cassandra remarked, "I fear the Greeks, even when bearing gifts"), dragged the "gift horse" into the city. At night the Greek soldiers crept out of the horse and opened the city's gates to their comrades. In this way, the city of Troy was taken.

219. ha-rangue   *noun and verb*   hə-răng´

[*harenga* (Medieval Latin), "public address"]

Definition:

    a. (*noun*) A long, emotional public address designed to arouse strong feelings or spur the audience on to action; a similar piece of writing.

        Suddenly a young man rushed onto the stage and began to deliver one of the most intemperate **harangues** I have ever heard.

    b. (*verb*) To deliver a harangue.

        It's a truly frightening experience to watch old film clips of Adolf Hitler **haranguing** his followers at the Nuremberg rallies of the 1930's.

Synonyms: (*nouns*) tirade, diatribe, philippic, denunciation; (*verbs*) rant, hold forth, pontificate

Phrases: rant and rave, get up on a soapbox, ride a hobbyhorse

220. **har-bin-ger**   *noun and verb*   här´-bĭn-jər

[*herbergere, herbengar* (Middle English), "person sent to prepare lodgings"; from *herberge* (Old French but of Germanic origin), "lodging." Originally, a harbinger was a servant or messenger sent on ahead to prepare lodging and entertainment for traveling royal or titled persons.]

Definition:
  a. (*noun*) A forerunner.

> Wild geese flying south from Canada are **harbingers** of winter.

> The brutal conflict over Kansas and Nebraska in the 1850's turned out to be a modest **harbinger** of a much bloodier struggle in the 1860's.

  b. (*verb*) To herald the approach of.

> To most people's minds, the appearance of crocuses **harbingers** the return of spring.

> I hope tonight's easy victory over Elk Grove **harbingers** success in our bid for the state basketball championship.

Synonyms: (*nouns*) precursor, herald; omen, sign, portent; (*verbs*) presage, foreshadow, prefigure, augur, signal; usher in

Phrases: a point man, an advance man

Using the Words

Exercise I. Parts of Speech

Indicate the part of speech of each of the following words. In some cases, two answers are correct.

1. gape
2. garble
3. goad
4. gratuitous
5. grimace
6. grope
7. gullible
8. harangue
9. harbinger

Exercise II. Words in Phrases

In each of the following groups, select the item that best expresses the meaning of the *italicized* word in the introductory phrase.

1. *gratuitous* criticisms
   a. perceptive b. unexpected c. mindless d. uncalled-for

2. a very *gregarious* young lady
   a. erudite b. outgoing c. beautiful d. obese

3. the *gruesome* details
   a. vague b. sigificant c. horrible d. minor

4. a *grueling* test
   a. surprise b. written c. brief d. draining

5. *grope* for a name
   a. rush b. call c. send d. fumble

6. a *haggard* expression
   a. careworn b. felicitous c. trite d. foreign

7. *grimaced* in reply
   a. nodded b. winked c. scowled d. laughed

Exercise III. Completing Sentences

Complete each of the following sentences or pairs of sentences by selecting the most appropriate word from the given group of words. Use each word only once. Make any adjustments that are necessary to fit the words into the sentences properly.

gloat	gaping	harbinger
graphic	haggard	gullible
harangue	goad	garbled

1. It made me dizzy to lean over the edge of the precipice and peer down into the _____ abyss below.

2. The report contained such a _____ and misleading account of my activities that at first I didn't recognize them.

3. Even though their crowing may embarrass you a little, your parents do have some right to _____ over your successes.

4. Fear and confusion may _____ a perfectly rational person into behaving in a most irrational way.

5. The article gave such a _____ description of the catastrophe that I could almost see it occurring before my eyes.

6. Only a thoroughly _____ person would be taken in by the absurd claims of some TV commercials.

7. "The man's no statesman," I declared. "He's a rabble-rouser who uses his official position as a soapbox from which to _____ a captive and reluctant audience."

8. In my family, opening day at the ballpark, not the advent of warmer weather, is the _____ of summer.

Exercise IV. Synonyms and Antonyms

A. In each of the following groups, select the **two** words that are most nearly **synonyms.**

1. a. unwarranted b. unplanned c. uncontrolled
   d. unjustified e. unnamed

2. a. rant b. scramble c. douse d. spur e. jumble

3. a. peasant **b.** knight **c.** herald **d.** forerunner
  e. merchant

4. a. grisly **b.** wary **c.** ghastly **d.** lazy **e.** sketchy

5. a. chubby **b.** gaunt **c.** stately **d.** radiant **e.** cadaverous

Now, for each pair of synonyms you have selected, supply a
word from the Basic Word List for Lesson 18 (Words 206–220) that
means **the same** or **almost the same** thing.

B. In each of the following, select the item that is most nearly
opposite in meaning to the numbered word at the left.

1. goad   **a.** grin **b.** mangle **c.** rave **d.** restrain
        e. prod

2. gullible   **a.** energetic **b.** disinterested **c.** skeptical
        d. friendly **e.** frightening

3. grueling   **a.** fulfilling **b.** undemanding **c.** striking
        d. unrewarding **e.** fatiguing

4. gregarious **a.** naive **b.** genial **c.** monstrous **d.** aloof
        e. ruddy

5. grimace   **a.** smile **b.** yawn **c.** cough **d.** nod
        e. scowl

Exercise V. Framing Sentences

A. Use each of the following words in an original illustrative
sentence.

1. gape	**4.** goad	**7.** grueling
2. garble	**5.** grimace	**8.** harangue
3. gloat	**6.** grope	**9.** harbinger

B. Give a **noun** form of each of the following words, and use it in
an original illustrative sentence.

1. gullible   **2.** gregarious   **3.** haggard

C. Give an **adverb** form of each of the following words, and use it
in an original illustrative sentence.

1. graphic   **2.** gruesome   **3.** gratuitous

Exercise VI. Word Roundup

1. With or without the aid of a dictionary, explain what the
  following phrases mean.

   a. live in an ivory tower   **d.** wet behind the ears
   b. get up on a soapbox   **e.** see how the land lies
   c. pull the wool over   **f.** grin like a Cheshire
       someone's eyes   cat

2. With or without the aid of a dictionary, define each of the following colorful terms.

   a. rubberneck   c. social butterfly   e. freebie
   b. gadfly   d. sitting duck   f. birds of a feather

3. Explain what each of the following means.

   a. a graph   c. graphics
   b. a graphic   d. the graphic arts

4. Define the following foreign expressions used in present-day English.

   a. gratis   b. esprit de corps   c. caveat emptor

5. What is an *extrovert*? How does one differ from an *introvert*?

6. Recount the story of the Trojan Horse.

Completing Verbal Analogies

"If Something Is A, a Person Can B It." Another common word relationship that occurs in the analogy sections of standardized tests involves a state or action that is stipulated by the meaning of a given word. This relationship can be expressed in abstract terms as, "If something is *A*, a person can *B* it; if something is *C*, a person can *D* it."

Here is an example of an analogy question involving this relationship. Try to determine the correct answer before reading the explanation of it given below.

tangible : touch ::
   a. susceptible : doubt   d. pliant : enjoy
   b. affable : speak   e. mutable : show
   c. portable : carry

The answer is *c*. If something is *tangible*, a person can *touch* it. Similarly, if something is *portable*, a person can *carry* it.

"If Something Is A, a Person Cannot B It." A related word relationship involves a state or action that is precluded by the meaning of a given word. This word relationship can be expressed in abstract terms as, "If something is *A*, a person cannot *B* it; if something is *C*, a person cannot *D* it."

Here is an example of an analogy involving this relationship. Try to figure out the correct answer before reading the explanation of it given below.

immutable : change ::
   a. insurgent : raise   d. inscrutable : see
   b. inadvertent : tame   e. indelible : erase
   c. irrevocable : examine

The answer is *e*. If something is *immutable*, a person cannot *change* it. Similarly, if something is *indelible*, a person cannot *erase* it.

One Final Note. The two word relationships examined in this section may apply to people as well as things. In that case, they may be expressed in abstract terms as "If someone is *A*, a person can(not) *B* him/her."

Complete each of the following analogies based on the word relationships "If something is *A*, a person can *B* it" and "If something is *A*, a person cannot *B* it."

1. **illegible : read =**
   a. invisible : see
   b. inaudible : taste
   c. innumerable : avoid
   d. immobile : touch
   e. inflammable : imagine

2. **edible : eat =**
   a. notable : forget
   b. feasible : scare
   c. pliable : bend
   d. execrable : relish
   e. stable : shift

3. **gullible : hoodwink =**
   a. reliable : mistrust
   b. affable : reject
   c. culpable : reward
   d. sensible : mislead
   e. tractable : control

4. **insuperable : overcome =**
   a. unquenchable : swallow
   b. invincible : choose
   c. inscrutable : raise
   d. indomitable : tame
   e. infallible : duplicate

Exercise II

Compose **one** complete analogy based on the word relationship "If something is *A*, a person can *B* it" and **one** based on the word relationship "If something is *A*, a person cannot *B* it."

Exercise III

The following items review what you have so far learned about analogy questions. Complete each.

1. **treachery : revulsion** :: courage :
   (despair, horror, admiration, boredom, indifference)

2. **poignant : sadden** :: droll :
   (appall, enlighten, exhaust, puzzle, amuse)

3. **nimble : ungainly** :: blithe :
   (facetious, lithe, exotic, morose, gratuitous)

4. **philosopher : truth** :: aesthete :
   (beauty, research, money, fame, controversy)

5. **prong : fork** :: spoke :
   (headlight, wheel, pedal, handlebar, brake)

6. **interest : absorption** :: joy :
   (sadness, exultation, amazement, attention, apathy)

7. **apple : fruit** :: potato :
   (vegetable, mineral, animal, metal, product)

8. **affluent : indigent** :: eminent :
   (notable, genial, obscure, heinous, defective)

9. **epigram : witty** :: cliché :
   (prolix, hackneyed, piquant, rational, novel)

10. **diminutive : puny** :: mammoth :
    (specious, dapper, emaciated, gigantic, haggard)

Working with Context Clues

More About Two-Word Omissions. Study the following example of a typical two-word omission. Try to determine the correct answer before reading the explanation of it given below.

Though a(n) _____ master might deal kindly and generously with the slaves he owned, a cruel one would usually _____ his.

a. brutal. . .exploit
b. enlightened. . .coddle

c. humane. . .maltreat
d. affluent. . .emancipate

The answer is *c. humane. . .maltreat.* Here's why.

The word *though* at the beginning of the example should immediately suggest to you that the sentence will present contrasting information of some kind. It should also tip you off to the kind of clue you are likely to find —a contrast clue.

Bearing this in mind, read the sentence carefully to determine how the words that go in the blanks contribute to its meaning. The sentence does indeed present contrasting information. It says that one kind of master treated his slaves in one way, but another kind of master treated his differently. You are to supply an adjective that reveals the character of the first type of master and a verb that indicates how the second treated his slaves. To help you do this, you have been told how the first type of master behaved (*deal. . .generously*) and what the second was like (*cruel*).

You now have enough information to begin completing the sentence correctly. Accordingly, consider the first blank, for which you need an adjective that describes a person's character or personality. You know that the second type of master was cruel. This suggests that the first type was "uncruel"—that is, "kind." This conclusion is backed up by the statement that the first type treated his slaves *kindly and generously.*

Run your eye down the first item in each of the four lettered choices. Eliminate any choice that does not agree with your conclusion about the character of the first type of master. Choices *b (enlightened)* and *c (humane)* dovetail with it, so they can stay. Choice *a (brutal),* however, does not and can confidently be eliminated. Similarly, Choice *d (affluent)* has nothing to do with kindness or cruelty, so it can be discarded as well.

Now you have reduced the likely possibilities for the correct answer to two. Still, you can't tell which is actually right without more help. Accordingly, turn to the second blank, for which you need a verb indicating behavior.

You know that the first type of master treats his slaves kindly and generously. This suggests that the second type of master treats his *unkindly or meanly*. This conclusion, of course, also follows from the fact that the second type of master is known to be cruel.

In light of this new conclusion, consider the second item in Choices *b* and *c*, your two remaining possibilities for the correct answer. Choice *b* reads *coddle*, which does not agree with your ideas about how the cruel master treated his slaves. *Coddle* means "treat too indulgently," not "treat badly." Accordingly, Choice *b* can be eliminated.

Choice *c*, however, reads *maltreat*, which fits in nicely with what you think belongs in the blank. Clearly, then, Choice *c* is the correct answer, simply because none of the other choices produces a sensible or meaningful statement when it is inserted into the sentence.

Exercise

Complete each of the following two-word omissions by selecting the pair of words that make the best sense in the passage as a whole. Indicate the clue or clues that led you to make your choice.

1. While those who agreed with the speaker signified their _____ by applauding vigorously, those who disagreed with him _____ loudly.

   a. puzzlement...whispered   c. loathing...booed
   b. approval...jeered   d. indifference...clapped

2. "If you want to get ahead in this company, you must work hard," the supervisor told the new employee. "Around here, _____ only comes to those who are _____."

   a. advancement...diligent   c. preferment...indolent
   b. exhaustion...relaxed   d. dismissal...industrious

3. Some people really enjoy doing all the tiresome and time-consuming chores associated with housework, but to me such _____ is truly _____.

   a. labor...attractive   c. apathy...foreign
   b. speculation...foolish   d. drudgery...repugnant

4. Once our fossil-fuel reserves are exhausted, they are gone forever. For that reason, we should try to _____ our use of these precious resources so that they are not _____ too quickly.

   a. accelerate...replaced   c. modify...increased
   b. curtail...depleted   d. expand...consumed

5. "A treat for all ages," the review read, "this little volume combines the _____ of a scholar with the skill and creativity of an expert _____."

   a. ignorance...painter   c. erudition...storyteller
   b. wisdom...novice   d. affluence...surgeon

Enriching the Lesson

Exercise I. More Classical Contributions to English

The geography, history, and mythology of the classical world have contributed much to the richness and variety of modern English. Below are listed a few more examples of this remarkable heritage. Tell what each of the items means, and explain its connection with classical Greece or Rome. Then choose any **five** of the expressions, and, for each, compose an original illustrative sentence.

1. a mausoleum
2. an odyssey
3. chimerical
4. hector someone
5. a nestor
6. caught between Scylla and Charybdis
7. meander
8. a maecenas
9. a thespian
10. a nemesis
11. pile Pelion on Ossa
12. open a Pandora's box
13. a xanthippe
14. pander to
15. stentorian
16. a mentor
17. a platonic relationship
18. leave no stone unturned

Exercise II. Expressions Old and New

A. Below are listed a number of expressions that are frequently used in present-day English. With or without the aid of a dictionary, define each. Then choose any **three**, and, for each, compose an original illustrative sentence.

1. hit pay dirt
2. in the limelight
3. out of kilter
4. a Johnny-come-lately
5. buy a pig in a poke
6. the pecking order
7. moonlight as a cabbie
8. old hat
9. a backhanded compliment
10. wear one's heart on one's sleeve
11. swallow one's pride
12. jump the gun
13. reach for the moon
14. get wind of
15. open a can of worms
16. a bull in a china shop
17. roll out the red carpet
18. a rule of thumb
19. fly off the handle
20. keep one's nose to the grindstone

B. Below are listed ten expressions that you are likely to encounter in a newspaper or on radio or TV. None of them, probably, would have been used, or even understood, a few generations ago. With or without the aid of a dictionary, tell what each means. Then choose any **three**, and, for each, compose an original illustrative sentence.

1. keep one's options open
2. a counterculture
3. follow a game plan
4. make a value judgment
5. a polarized community
6. hands-on operations
7. a lifestyle
8. prime time
9. a ballpark estimate
10. a paraprofessional

Exercise III. Soul Language

One of the items mentioned in passing in Lesson 18 (page 262) was the word *jive. Jive* probably originated in a special brand of American English called Soul. Soul was developed by black people after the Civil War to express their unique needs, aspirations, experiences, and lifestyle. Though Soul more or less springs from everyday American English, new words were introduced and old words were given new and different meanings, thus producing a separate and distinct kind of English.

Many of the linguistic innovations of Soul have become popular in the majority white culture and seem to have found a lasting place for themselves in the American language. A few such expressions are listed below. Find out what they mean, both in Soul and in everyday American English. Note: To do this, you may have to do some digging in specialized reference books or compare notes with friends, relatives, or classmates.

1. cool	6. busted	11. heavy
2. dude	7. stash	12. stuff
3. bread	8. jive	13. smooth
4. heat	9. uptight	14. do your thing
5. sting	10. foxy	15. okee-dokee

Exercise IV. Expanding Your Word Power

The words listed below are not on the Basic Word List, but they were mentioned in passing in Lesson 18. All of them would make useful additions to your working vocabulary. Define each, give its etymology, list **two** synonyms and **two** antonyms (where possible), and use in a short illustrative sentence.

1. mutilate	6. anemic	11. florid
2. revel	7. introverted	12. diatribe
3. incentive	8. lurid	13. pontificate
4. incite	9. invigorate	14. gratuity
5. impede	10. dubious	15. portent

Lesson 19

---

221. **haugh-ty**   *adjective*   hô´-tē

[*haut* (Old French), "high," from *altus* (Latin), "high"]

Definition: Scornfully superior and aloof.

I know I wasn't born with a silver spoon in my mouth, but that's no reason for a **haughty** salesclerk to treat me as if I had just crawled out of the woodwork.

Their **haughty** manner proclaimed more eloquently than words could have that they could never associate with an obscure nobody like me.

Phrases: a haughty aristocrat, a haughty manner

Related Forms: (*nouns*) haughtiness, hauteur; (*adverb*) haughtily

Synonyms: (*adjectives*) supercilious, disdainful, contemptuous, snooty, condescending, patronizing; proud, arrogant

Antonyms: (*adjectives*) modest, diffident, unassuming, unpretentious, meek; servile, fawning, obsequious (Word 282)

Phrases: as proud as a peacock, look down one's nose at, get up on one's high horse

222. **hei-nous**   *adjective*   hā´-nəs

[*haineus* (Old French), "hateful," from *haine* (Old French), "hatred"]

Definition: Grossly wicked or vile.

We found it hard to believe that our mild-mannered neighbor had actually committed the **heinous** crime of which he was accused.

For ancient Greeks and Romans, throwing away one's shield and fleeing from the battlefield was the most **heinous** act of cowardice a soldier could commit.

Phrases: a heinous offense, a heinous act of treason

Related Forms: (*noun*) heinousness; (*adverb*) heinously

Synonyms: (*adjectives*) diabolic, villainous, nefarious, monstrous, infamous; odious, reprehensible, abominable, loathsome, atrocious, despicable, abhorrent, execrable

Antonyms: (*adjectives*) laudable, commendable, meritorious, estimable, admirable

Phrases: moral turpitude, a venial sin, a mortal sin

223. **ig-no-min-y** *noun* ĭg´-nə-mĭn-ē

[*ignominia* (Latin), "removal of one's good name"; from *in* (Latin), "un-, not" + *nomen, nominis* (Latin), "name"]

Definition: Dishonor or disgrace usually resulting from some sort of shameful conduct.

He was indeed a changed young man after he had suffered the **ignominy** of expulsion from West Point for conduct unbecoming an officer and a gentleman.

Related Forms: (*adjective*) ignominious; (*adverb*) ignominiously

Synonyms: (*nouns*) humiliation, degradation; disrepute, opprobrium, odium, infamy, obloquy

Antonyms: (*nouns*) esteem, acclaim, honor, admiration, glory, fame

Phrases: be under a cloud, be in bad odor, a blot on the escutcheon

224. **il-lic-it** *adjective* ĭ-lĭs´-ĭt

[*ill*, a form of *in* (Latin), "not" + *licitus* (Latin), "allowed"]

Definition: Unlawful, illegal.

Each year, part of the American tax-dollar goes toward stemming the flood of **illicit** narcotics pouring into the country.

Related Forms: (*noun*) illicitness; (*adverb*) illicitly; (*adjective*) licit

Synonyms: (*adjectives*) unauthorized, unsanctioned; banned, forbidden, proscribed, outlawed; under-the-counter, under-the-table

Antonyms: (*adjectives*) legal, lawful, authorized, sanctioned; permissible, admissible, allowable, legitimate

Phrases: contraband goods, the black market, get in by the back door, a wildcat strike, off limits; go by the book

225. **im-mac-u-late** *adjective* ĭ-măk´-yə-lĭt

[*im*, a form of *in* (Latin), "un-, not" + *maculatus* (Latin), "blemished"]

Definition: Entirely free of stain, blemish, fault, or error; spotless.

Despite the heat and dirt of a summer day in the city, my mother managed to keep her clothing absolutely **immaculate**.

He was a brilliant statesman whose record remained **immaculate** throughout a long career in public office.

Related Forms: (*noun*) immaculateness; (*adverb*) immaculately

Synonyms: (*adjectives*) unsoiled, unsullied, untarnished, undefiled; flawless, impeccable, unimpeachable, irreproachable

Antonyms: (*adjectives*) stained, spotted, blemished, sullied, tarnished

Phrases: spick-and-span, lily-white, simon-pure, pure as the driven snow

Police and U.S. Treasury agents close down a bar during Prohibition.

The Black Market

Black Market is the popular term for the illegal sale and purchase of various kinds of commodities in violation of official restrictions, such as price controls and rationing. The expression is also applied to the place where such transactions are carried out. Today, there are black markets for a whole host of commodities ranging from automobiles and guns to cigarettes and drugs. Black-market operations are also common in the exchange of foreign and domestic currency, especially in countries where the government has set the official exchange rate too high. During the Prohibition Era in the United States (1920–1933), when the manufacture and sale of alcohol was illegal, *bootlegging* became a highly lucrative business. Bootlegging, which is the illegal sale of alcohol, was essentially a black-market operation under a different name.

226. im-mu-ni-ty *noun* ĭ-myōō´-nĭ-tē

[*immunis* (Latin), "exempt from service"; from *in* (Latin), "not" + *munia* (Latin), "duty, tax"]

Definition: Exemption from something, especially a disease.

Many people are fortunate enough to possess a natural **immunity** to certain diseases.

Though we all long for security in life, none of us can acquire total **immunity** from the hazards and misfortunes of the human condition.

Related Forms: (*verb*) immunize; (*noun*) immunization; (*adjective*) immune

Phrases: immune from prosecution; immune to reason; the immunization procedure

Synonyms: (*nouns*) impunity, insusceptibility; freedom, exclusion, release, protection, safety; dispensation, amnesty

Phrases: handle with kid gloves, preferential treatment, with impunity, get off with a slap on the wrist, go scot-free

227. im-mu-ta-ble   *adjective*   ĭ-my͞oo´-tə-bəl

[*im*, a form of *in* (Latin), "not" + *mutare, mutatus* (Latin), "change" + *abilis, abile* (Latin), "able to"]

Definition: Not subject to change or modification.

"Our legal system is not an **immutable** institution," the Chief Justice observed. "Like all else, it grows, develops, and changes over time."

Despite a series of unforeseen setbacks and failures, her faith in her own abilities remained **immutable**.

Related Forms: (*nouns*) immutability, immutableness, mutability; (*adjective*) mutable; (*adverb*) immutably

Synonyms: (*adjectives*) unchangeable, changeless, constant, fixed, invariable, unalterable, permanent; resolute, steadfast, unwavering, inflexible, rigid

Antonyms: (*adjectives*) changeable, alterable, variable; fickle, erratic, capricious, mercurial

Phrases: as constant as the northern star, as solid as the Rock of Gibraltar; a house built on sand

228. im-passe   *noun*   ĭm´-păs

[*impasse* (French), "dead end"; from *in* (French), "not" + *passer, passé* (French), "pass"]

Definition: A deadlock or dead end.

"Since we have reached an **impasse** in these negotiations," the union official asked the representative of management, "why don't we adjourn for the night?"

Related Forms: (*adjective*) impassable; (*nouns*) impassability, impassableness

Synonyms: (*nouns*) stalemate, cul-de-sac, standstill, dilemma

Phrases: lead up a blind alley, paint oneself into a corner, in a fix, in a bind, a Catch-22 situation, come to a screeching (grinding) halt, a stand-off, on the horns of a dilemma

A Catch-22 Situation

A *Catch-22 situation* is a difficult problem for which the different solutions that seem to be possible are logically invalid. The expression comes from *Catch-22*, the title of a novel by Joseph Heller, an American novelist who was born in 1923 (see photo). The hero of *Catch-22* faces many such situations throughout the course of the novel.

229. im-ped-i-ment   *noun*   ĭm-pĕd´-ə-mĕnt

[*impedimentum* (Latin), "obstacle"; from *impedire* (Latin), "get under foot or in the way"; from *in* (Latin), "in (the way of)" + *pes, pedis* (Latin), "foot"]

Definition: A hindrance or obstruction.

An inability to communicate in Standard English is usually an insuperable **impediment** to getting a good job in our society.

Phrase: a speech impediment

Related Forms: (*verb*) impede; (*noun*) impedimenta

Synonyms: (*nouns*) encumbrance; obstacle, handicap, barrier, bar

Antonyms: (*nouns*) aid, help, assistance

Phrases: a stumbling block, a fly in the ointment, a bottleneck, without let or hindrance, pull oneself up by one's bootstraps

230. im-per-vi-ous   *adjective*   ĭm-pĕr´-vē-əs

[*im*, a form of *in* (Latin), "not" + *per* (Latin), "through" + *via* (Latin), "road, way"]

Definition: Incapable of being penetrated or affected.

Cloth raincoats are usually treated with chemicals to make them **impervious** to water.

"I know a stoic is supposed to be **impervious** to pain," he said, "but if you needle one long enough, he'll react."

Related Form: (*noun*) imperviousness; (*adjective*) pervious

Synonyms: (*adjectives*) impenetrable, impermeable; unresponsive, unreceptive, unamenable, closed (to)

Antonyms: (*adjectives*) penetrable, permeable, responsive, receptive, amenable (to), open (to), susceptible (to)

Phrases: proof against, hermetically sealed, vacuum-packed; stonewall someone; a closed society, a closed mind

231. im-pla-ca-ble   *adjective*   ĭm-plăk´-ə-bəl

[*im*, a form of *in* (Latin), "not" + *placare* (Latin), "calm, soothe" + *abilis, abile* (Latin), "able to"]

Definition: Incapable of being pacified or appeased; inflexible.

An **implacable** foe of slavery, William Lloyd Garrison took an uncompromising stand in favor of its abolition as early as 1831.

"The man frightens me," she observed, "because his approach to the administration of justice is so **implacably** heartless and mechanical."

Phrases: an implacable disease, implacable wrath

Related Forms: (*nouns*) implacableness, implacability; (*adverb*) implacably

Synonyms: (*adjectives*) unappeasable, unrelenting, unforgiving, relentless, inexorable, remorseless, unbending, obdurate, adamant, merciless

Antonyms: (*adjectives*) conciliatory, compassionate, understanding, merciful, forbearing

232. im-plic-it   *adjective*   ĭm-plĭs´-ĭt

[*implicitus* (Latin), "entangled, involved"; from *in* (Latin), "in" + *plicare, plicatus* (Latin), "fold"]

Definition:
   a. Understood, implied.

> In almost any contract, there are **implicit** duties and obligations which must be fulfilled even though they are not expressed in so many words.

   b. Absolute, unquestioning.

> He is the type of officer who expects **implicit** obedience from the troops under his command. When he gives an order, he assumes that it will be carried out.

Related Forms: (*adverb*) implicitly; (*nouns*) implicitness, implication; (*verb*) imply

Synonyms: (*adjectives*) inferred, inherent; tacit, unspoken; complete, unqualified, unconditional

Antonyms: (*adjectives*) explicit, specific, express

Phrases: take something for granted, categorically deny something, on a person's express orders

233. im-pugn   *verb*   ĭm-pyo͞on´

[*in* (Latin), "against" + *pugnare* (Latin), "fight"]

Definition: To call into question; to cast doubt on.

> "Before you **impugn** the man's motives for doing what he did," I said, "you'd better make certain that you can back up your suspicions with hard evidence."

Phrases: impugn a person's veracity or honor, impugn a claim

Related Forms: (*noun*) impugnment

Synonyms: (*verbs*) question, query, challenge, deny, gainsay, dispute, malign

Antonyms: (*verbs*) vindicate, acquit, exonerate, exculpate; justify, rationalize; defend, champion, vouch for; affirm, verify, substantiate, confirm, corroborate

Phrases: cast aspersions on, run down, take exception to, badmouth someone, hurl brickbats at; backbiting; stick up for, an apologist

234. in-car-cer-ate   *verb*   ĭn-kär′-sə-rāt

[*incarcerare, incarceratus* (Latin), "imprison"; from *in* (Latin), "in" + *carcer* (Latin), "prison"]

Definition: To put in jail or otherwise confine.

In a democratic society like ours, people may freely express their opinions without fear of being **incarcerated** for doing so.

In the Victorian era, fashionable ladies thought nothing of **incarcerating** their waists in tight corsets in order to achieve a chic "hourglass" figure.

Related Form: (*noun*) incarceration

Synonyms: (*verbs*) jail, imprison, intern; cage, immure, constrain, constrict

Antonyms: (*verbs*) liberate, emancipate, set free, release

Phrases: mew up, coop up, keep under lock and key, keep under wraps, a shut-in

235. in-cense   *verb*   ĭn-sĕns′

[*incendere, incensus* (Latin), "set on fire, enrage"; from *in* (Latin), "in, on" + *candere* (Latin), "glow"]

Definition: To make violently angry.

"You rarely give me cause to become angry," dad said, "but this time your behavior has truly **incensed** me."

Incensed at the outrageous treatment they were receiving from unsympathetic foreign governors, the native population rose in revolt.

Related Form: (*adjective*) incendiary

Synonyms: (*verbs*) enrage, infuriate, enflame, provoke, incite

Antonyms: (*verbs*) soothe, calm, pacify, mollify, appease, placate

Phrases: see red, make one's blood boil, raise the hackles on one's neck, get under one's skin; a thorn in one's side

A Thai dancer burns incense before a performance. As a noun, *incense* (pronounced ĭn′-sĕns) indicates an aromatic gum or wood that produces a pleasant aroma when burned. Incense is often used in religious ceremonies.

Using the Words

Exercise I.   Syllabication and Pronunciation

Syllabicate the following words correctly, and place the major stress mark (′) after the syllable that is accented when the word in pronounced.

1. heinous
2. ignominy
3. illicit
4. impediment
5. immunity
6. immutable
7. impugn
8. incarcerate
9. impasse

Exercise II.   Words Out of Context

In each of the following groups, select the item that best expresses the meaning of the numbered word at the left.

1. illicit
   a. illiterate   b. illustrious   c. illegible
   d. illogical   e. illegal

2. immaculate
   a. harmless   b. spotless   c. timeless
   d. shameless   e. pointless

3. impasse
   a. solution   b. viewpoint   c. mistake
   d. deadlock   e. tunnel

4. implicit
   a. villainous   b. constant   c. implied
   d. legitimate   e. modest

5. impervious
   a. shocked by   b. closed to   c. fond of
   d. eager for   e. undecided about

6. implacable
   a. costly   b. outlawed   c. unspoken
   d. diabolic   e. relentless

7. incense
   a. enrage   b. puzzle   c. frighten   d. bore
   e. elate

Exercise III.   Completing Sentences

Complete each of the following sentences by selecting the most appropriate word from the given group of words. Use each word only once.

impugn	incarcerate	impediment
heinous	incense	immutable
immunity	ignominy	haughty

1. According to the Greek philosopher Heraclitus, the only _____ law of nature is, paradoxically, that everything changes.

280

2. Somehow or other, the convicted murderer managed to escape from the maximum-security prison in which he had been _____.

3. Once the leader's integrity had been _____, his authority began to be challenged as well.

4. It wasn't the misfortune of losing the tennis match that mortified me so much as the _____ of being defeated by a mere beginner.

5. Few crimes have been so monstrous and inhuman as Adolf Hitler's _____ scheme to exterminate millions of innocent people in grisly death camps.

6. With a sneer of contempt and a flick of his fingers, the _____ young man disdainfully dismissed both me and my suggestion from his mind.

7. No matter how carefully we try to protect ourselves, none of us ever achieves complete _____ from sickness and disease.

8. Fear of failure can often become a formidable _____ to success because it inhibits the mind and paralyzes the will.

Exercise IV. Synonyms and Antonyms

Classify each of the following pairs of words as **S** for **synonyms** or **A** for **antonyms**.

1. anger—incense
2. impervious—receptive
3. illicit—legal
4. immaculate—flawless
5. ignominy—disgrace
6. meek—haughty
7. heinous—loathsome
8. impediment—obstacle
9. fixed—immutable
10. defend—impugn
11. incarcerate—liberate
12. standstill—impasse
13. implacable—unrelenting
14. explicit—implicit

Exercise V. Word Roundup

1. With or without the aid of a dictionary, explain the difference in meaning between the words in each of the following pairs.

   a. illicit—elicit
   b. impugn—impute
   c. impassable—impassive
   d. venal—venial

2. With or without the aid of a dictionary, explain what each of the following expressions means.

   a. impedimenta
   b. an apologist
   c. a shut-in
   d. a bottleneck
   e. stonewall someone
   f. badmouth someone

3. With or without the aid of a dictionary, explain what each of the following colorful phrases means.

a. look down one's nose at
b. be under a cloud
c. go by the book
d. see red
e. paint oneself into a corner
f. go scot-free
g. get up on one's high horse
h. handle with kid gloves

4. Define each of the following, and explain where it came from.

a. a Catch-22 situation
b. simon-pure

Exercise VI. Framing Sentences

A. Use each of the following words in an original sentence.

1. impugn
2. impasse
3. incense
4. immutable
5. implacable
6. impervious

B. Give a **noun** form of each of the following words, and use it in an original sentence.

1. incarcerate
2. heinous
3. haughty

C. Give a **verb** form related to each of the following words, and use it in an original sentence.

1. immunity
2. impediment
3. implicit

D. Give an **adverb** form of each of the following words, and use it in an original sentence.

1. illicit
2. immaculate
3. ignominy

Dissecting the Words

Prefixes

1. The Latin prefix **in** appears in a great many common English words. Basically, this prefix has two quite distinct meanings:

a. "Not," as in these words:

indefensible (*in*, "not" + *defensible*)—not capable of being defended, justified, or excused

invalidate (*in*, "not" + *validate*)—to nullify

inactivity (*in*, "not" + *activity*)—a lack of activity; idleness

inadvertently (*in*, "not" + *advertently*)—accidentally or unintentionally

When *in* has the meaning "not," it negates the sense of the word to which it is attached. In this regard, it functions in exactly the same way as the other negative prefixes used in modern English—*non, un,* and *a(n)*.

b. "In, into, within," as in these words:

incarnate (*in*, "into" + *caro, carnis* [Latin], "flesh")—to invest with bodily form and nature

inauguration (*in*, "in" + *augur*)—a formal beginning or introduction

incarcerate (*in*, "into" + *carcer* [Latin], "prison"]—to put in prison

Note: In a few English words, *in* acts as an intensive, with the general meaning "very" or "completely." This use of the prefix occurs, for example, in the word *incandescent*, which means "glowing very bright."

2. The prefix *in* has several variant forms which are used when the word to which *in* is attached begins with a particular consonant, as follows:

a. The form **ig** is used in a few English words starting with *n*. For example:

ignoble (*ig*, "not" + *noble*)—base or lowborn; dishonorable

ignominy (*ig*, "not" + *nomen, nominis* [Latin], "name")—great personal shame usually stemming from some kind of disgraceful conduct

b. The form **il** is used before words beginning with an *l*. For example:

illogical (*il*, "not" + *logical*)—not logical

illuminate (*il*, "in" + *lumen, luminis* [Latin], "light")—to light up. Noun: *illumination*

c. The form **im** is used before a word beginning with an *m* or a *p*. For example:

immoral (*im*, "not" + *moral*)—not in accord with the accepted moral code

immerse (*im*, "not" + *mergere, mersus* [Latin], "dip")—to submerge or absorb completely

impure (*im*, "not" + *pure*)—not pure

impede (*in*, "in" + *pes, pedis* [Latin], "foot")—to hinder or obstruct

d. The form **ir** is used before a word beginning with an *r*. For example:

irreverent (*ir*, "not" + *reverent*)—lacking in sufficient respect for

irrigate (*ir*, "in" + *rigare, rigatus* [Latin], "bring water")—to supply with water; to wash out with water or another fluid

Roots

1. The Latin word **via**, which appears in the word *impervious*, studied in this lesson, means "road" or "way." Other common English words in which *via* appears as a root element include:

viaduct (*via*, "road" + *ducere, ductus* [Latin], "lead")—a bridge supporting a road or railroad over a valley or another (rail)road

deviate (*de* [Latin], "away" + *via*, "road, way" + *ate*, an English verb-forming suffix)—to turn or move away from. Noun: *deviation*

devious (*de* [Latin], "away" + *via*, "road, way" + *ous*, "characterized by")—not straightforward; roundabout or shifty. Noun: *deviousness*

convey (*cum* [Latin], "with" + *via*, "road, way")—to transmit or transport. Noun: *conveyance*—a vehicle; the act of transporting something

By itself, the Latin word *via* is used in English as a preposition with the meaning "by way of." For example, "I drove to Chicago *via* Buffalo."

2.   The Latin root **nomin** means "name." It appears in a number of common English words, including *ignominy*, studied in this lesson. Other English words in which it is used are:

nominal (*nomen, nominis*, "name" + *alis* [Latin], "relating to")—existing in name only; insignificantly small

nominate (*nomen, nominis*, "name" + *ate*, an English verb-forming suffix)—to propose for some office, responsibility, or honor. Noun: *nomination*

denomination (*de* [Latin], "completely" + *nomen, nominis*, "name" + *ation* [Latin], "state or process of"—the name of a specific group or class; an organized religious group

misnomer (*minus* [Latin], "less, wrong" + *nomen, nominis*, "name")—an error in naming something; a name inappropriately applied to something

3.   The parallel Greek word-building element usually appears in English as **onym** or **onomy**. Like *nomin*, these word elements mean "name." They appear in a number of very familiar English words, including *synonym, antonym,* and *homonym*. Other English words in which they are used are:

pseudonym (*pseudes* [Greek], "false" + *onoma, onuma,* [Greek], "name")—an assumed name

anonymous (*an* [Greek], "without" + *onoma, onuma,* [Greek], "name" + *ous* [Latin] "characterized by")—of unknown authorship. Noun: *anonymity*

onomatopoeia (*onoma, onuma,* [Greek], "name" + *poiein* [Greek], "make")—the formation of a word that imitates the sound of the thing it designates; for example, *hiss* or *buzz*

It is a little known fact that Charlotte Bronte (1816–1855), the author of *Jane Eyre*, produced many of her works under the masculine pseudonym Currer Bell.

Exercise

1. For each of the following definitions, give an English word that contains the prefix *in* or one of its variants. Consult a dictionary if necessary.

    a. base or lowborn
    b. not capable of variation
    c. not able to be defended
    d. not in motion
    e. lacking sufficient respect

    f. not valid
    g. showing no emotion
    h. spotlessly clean
    i. not logical
    j. nullify

2. Change each of the following positive words to its negative form by adding the prefix *in* or one of its variants. Consult a dictionary if necessary.

    a. apt
    b. reversible
    c. excusable
    d. solvent
    e. contestible

    f. pious
    g. redeemable
    h. justifiable
    i. reducible
    j. adequate

3. With or without the aid of a dictionary, define each of the following words and use it in a short illustrative sentence.

    a. nomenclature
    b. pseudonym
    c. nominate
    d. conveyance
    e. devious

    f. convoy
    g. deviate
    h. misnomer
    i. viaduct
    j. anonymity

Working with Context Clues

More About Two-Word Omissions.   Carefully study the following example of a fairly difficult two-word omission. Try to determine the correct answer before you read the explanation of it given below.

Because a medieval castle was primarily a fortress, it was built more for _____ than for _____.

a. decoration. . .usefulness
b. aggression. . .belligerence

c. pageantry. . .protection
d. defense. . .comfort

The correct answer is *d. defense. . .comfort,* as the following explanation clearly indicates.

Notice the brevity of the sentence contained in the example. It is only 17 words long. This suggests that some kind of inference clue will play a large part in determining the correct answer. Notice too the word *Because.* It suggests that you are dealing with a cause-and-effect relationship. Finally, notice the phrase *more for. . . than for* toward the end of the sentence. It indicates that two contrasting words go in the blanks.

Bearing these considerations in mind, reread the sentence carefully to find out what you are to do and how you can go about doing it. The sentence says that a medieval castle was by nature a certain type of build-

A view of the fortress at Carcassonne, France, one of the few surviving examples of a medieval walled city.

ing, and that this defined the purpose it served. You are to explain what that purpose was, based upon the information the sentence gives about the nature of a castle.

And what was the nature of a castle? The sentence says it was *primarily a fortress*. As you know, a fortress can be used for several purposes. It can serve as a refuge, or as a prison, or as a means of holding rebellious subjects in line. This suggests that the word that goes in the first blank means something like "protection" or "security," or some related idea.

Now run your eye down the first item in each of the four lettered choices. Eliminate any choice that does not conform to your conclusion about the general meaning of the word that goes in the first blank.

Choices *a (decoration)* and *c (pageantry)* do not agree with your conclusion, so they can safely be eliminated. Choices *b (aggression)* and *d (defense)*, however, do, so you still have some thinking to do before you can make the correct choice.

At this point, recall what was said about the implication of the phrase *more for . . . than for*. It suggests that two *contrasting* words go in the blanks.

Accordingly, consider Choices *b* and *c* from this angle. Choice *b (aggression . . . belligerence)* does not contain contrasting nouns, so it can be eliminated. Choice *a (defense . . . comfort)*, however, does, so it must be the correct answer. And, of course, it is.

Exercise

Complete each of the following two-word omissions by selecting the pair of words that make the best sense in the passage as a whole. Indicate the clue or clues that led you to make your choice.

1. Horseback riding is not only a pleasurable form of exercise, it is a(n) _____ one as well. In the days before the advent of the automobile, it was a universally accepted truism that the best tonic for the inside of a human being was the _____ of a horse.

    a. pointless . . . topside
    b. healthy . . . outside
    c. unusual . . . underside
    d. outmoded . . . backside

2. It may have taken all the intellectual _____ of a visionary to think up such a radically new solution to an old problem, but it took all the mental _____ of a shrewd and practical politician to get it through Congress.

   a. asperity. . . authenticity   c. audacity. . . acumen
   b. atrophy. . . perspicacity   d. alacrity. . . adversity

3. I was in a terrible _____, out of which I couldn't gracefully extract myself. Either I hurt him by being _____ about my feelings, or I hurt myself by misrepresenting them.

   a. deadlock. . . biased   c. quandary. . . dishonest
   b. predicament. . . candid   d. dilemma. . . erratic

4. "On a job interview, always put your best foot forward," my guidance counselor advised me. "_____ the positive, downplay the _____, and don't mess with Mister In-Between!"

   a. Delete. . . favorable   c. Embellish. . . affirmative
   b. Accentuate. . . negative   d. Curtail. . . pejorative

5. The earthquake had more or less reduced our house to a pile of worthless rubble. Nonetheless, we picked carefully through the _____, trying to _____ items of value. Unfortunately, very little could be saved.

   a. debris. . . salvage   c. chaos. . . divulge
   b. anarchy. . . corroborate   d. impasse. . . fathom

Enriching the Lesson

Exercise I. The Vocabulary of Social Change

Many expressions used today are associated with movements for social or cultural change. The words that make up these expressions have usually been around for a long time, but they are now being used in a sense that gives them a new significance and relevancy. The following exercise is designed to help you improve your knowledge of a few of these terms.

A. *Causes Galore.* Our national history in recent years has been marked by many special "causes" and reform movements. The terms connected with a few of these movements are listed below. With or without the aid of a dictionary or other reference book, define each.

1. consumerism   4. feminism   7. elitism
2. environmentalists   5. local autonomy   8. regionalism
3. urban renewal   6. libertarianism   9. welfarism

B. *The Struggle for Racial Equality.* Listed below are a number of terms and expressions associated with the struggle for racial equality. One of them, *lily-white*, was mentioned in passing in Lesson 19. With or without the aid of a dictionary or other reference book, define each.

1. racism
2. second-class citizenship
3. black power
4. segregation
5. integration
6. multi-racial society
7. stereotype
8. backlash
9. lily-white
10. pluralism
11. Uncle Tom
12. affirmative action

Exercise II. The Heritage of Literature

A. *Contributions Old and New.* Modern English has borrowed a surprising number of words and phrases from the works of famous and not-so-famous authors. Two of these expressions, *Catch-22* and *simon-pure*, were mentioned in Lesson 19. A few more are listed below. With or without the aid of a dictionary or other reference book, define each. Then give the source of the expression.

1. quixotic
2. a Pollyanna
3. gargantuan
4. a Babbitt
5. braggadocio
6. a Scrooge
7. serendipity
8. a rodomontade
9. a quark
10. bite the hand that feeds you
11. a termagant
12. a yahoo
13. utopian
14. a ragamuffin
15. an Ugly Duckling

Sir Thomas More (1478–1535) was a great English statesman, humanist, and martyr. Which of the words listed in Part A of Exercise II on this page did he contribute to the English language?

B. *William Shakespeare.* The works of William Shakespeare (1564–1616) have had a remarkable impact on the English language, including its vocabulary. Listed below are a number of familiar expressions that all derive in one way or another from Shakespeare's plays. With or without the aid of a dictionary or other reference book, define each as it is used in present-day English. Then give the name of the play from which the expression comes.

1. salad days
2. a pound of flesh
3. the milk of human kindness
4. a benedict
5. the primrose path
6. sleep in Abraham's bosom
7. mum's the word
8. hoist by one's own petard

Exercise III. A Verbal Diversion

One of the interesting English expressions mentioned in passing in Lesson 19 was *see red*, meaning "become very angry." English has a number of other useful terms and expressions employing the adjective *red*. Some of them are listed below. With or without the aid of a dictionary, define or explain each. Then choose any **five**, and, for each, compose an original illustrative sentence.

1. a red-letter day
2. a red herring
3. caught red-handed
4. a redneck
5. to paint the town red
6. in the red
7. to red-pencil
8. to roll out the red carpet
9. red tape
10. to redline

Exercise IV. Expanding Your Word Power

The words listed below are not on the Basic Word List, but they were mentioned in passing, in one form or another, in Lesson 19. All of them would make useful additions to your working vocabulary. Define each, give its etymology, list **two** synonyms and **two** antonyms (where possible), and use in a short illustrative sentence.

1. condescend
2. nefarious
3. turpitude
4. sully
5. impunity
6. dispensation
7. unimpeachable
8. encumber
9. obdurate
10. gainsay
11. rationalize
12. constrain
13. acclaim
14. mollify
15. query

Lesson 20

236. inception — 250. justify

---

236. in-cep-tion   *noun*   ĭn-sĕp´-shən

[*inceptio, inceptionis* (Latin), "beginning"; from *incipere, inceptus* (Latin), "begin"; from *in* (Latin), "in, on" + *capere* (Latin), "take"]

Definition: The beginning of something.

"I have been an active member of our local bowling association," grand-dad proudly boasted, "since its **inception** thirty years ago."

At the time of its **inception**, politicians always predict that great things will come of a new government program, but these high hopes are rarely ever fully realized.

Related Forms: (*adjective*) incipient; (*nouns*) incipience, incipiency

Synonyms: (*nouns*) commencement, inauguration, initiation, outset, kickoff, origin, onset, outbreak, debut, opening

Antonyms: (*nouns*) conclusion, finale, wind-up, finish, termination, close, completion, consummation, culmination, climax, denouement (Word 125)

Phrases: the opening gun, the starting lineup; from soup to nuts; the alpha and omega

---

237. in-di-gent   *adjective*   ĭn´-dĭ-jənt

[*indigens, indigentis* (Latin), "lacking, needing"]

Definition: Impoverished; needy.

The Wall Street Crash of 1929 left many a wealthy speculator as **indigent** as the proverbial church mouse.

Though the federal government does much to help the **indigent**, private charities play no little part in seeing to their welfare.

Related Form: (*noun*) indigence

Usage Note:
Be careful not to confuse *indigent* with either *indigenous*, meaning "native to," or *indignant*, meaning "irate" or "incensed."

Synonyms: (*adjectives*) destitute, impecunious, penniless, poverty-stricken

Antonyms: (*adjectives*) rich, wealthy, affluent (Word 17), well-to-do, well-off, well-heeled

Phrases: down in the heels, on the rocks, as poor as a church mouse; keep the wolf from the door, make ends meet, down and out

Thomas Alva Edison (1847–1931), the "Wizard of Menlo Park," was one of the most ingenious inventors ever produced by the United States.

238. in-gen-ious   *adjective*   ĭn-jēn´-yəs

[*ingenieux* (French), "clever"; from *ingenium* (Latin), "inborn talent"]

Definition: Showing remarkable originality, imagination, inventiveness, or skill; clever.

In 1793, Eli Whitney invented the cotton gin, an **ingenious** device for separating the seeds from the fiber quickly and easily.

Related Forms: (*nouns*) ingeniousness, ingenuity; (*adverb*) ingeniously

Usage Note:
Be careful not to confuse *ingenious* with *ingenuous* (note the first *u*), meaning "artless and unsophisticated" or "open and frank."

Synonyms: (*adjectives*) brilliant, inventive, creative, imaginative, talented; shrewd, cunning, crafty, astute; masterly, Daedalian

Antonyms: (*adjectives*) unimaginative, uninventive, unremarkable, unoriginal, pedestrian

239. in-her-ent   *adjective*   ĭn-hîr´-ĕnt

[*inhaerens, inhaerentis* (Latin), "sticking to"; from *in* (Latin), "in, on" + *haerere* (Latin), "stick, adhere"]

Definition: Existing as a natural or essential part of.

Most Americans firmly believe that the advantages **inherent** in a democratic form of government far outweigh the drawbacks that such a system usually entails.

Related Forms: (*adverb*) inherently; (*verb*) inhere; (*noun*) inherence

Synonyms: (*adjectives*) intrinsic, implicit, essential, internal, inner, fundamental, built-in, immanent, organic, natural, innate

Antonyms: (*adjectives*) extrinsic, external, extraneous, outside, foreign, alien; incidental, adventitious

Phrases: in the blood, to the manner born; a congenital defect

240. in-no-va-tion   *noun*   ĭn-ə-vā´-shən

[*innovare, innovatus* (Latin), "renew, alter"; from *in* (Latin), "completely" + *novus* (Latin), "new"]

Definition: Something new; a change.

In our eagerness to modernize American life, we must not assume that all **innovations** are necessarily practical and constructive.

Related Forms: (*noun*) innovator; (*verb*) innovate; (*adjective*) innovative

Usage Notes:
    a.   Do not use the word *new* to qualify *innovation* because the word *new* is redundant.

    b.   *Innovation* is often followed by the preposition *in*, as in the phrase "make innovations *in* the school curriculum."

Synonyms: (*nouns*) novelty, alteration, new wrinkle

Phrases: give something a new look, give something a face-lift, cosmetic alterations, the avant-garde, a neologism (or neoterism), coin a word

241. in-sti-gate   *verb*   ĭn´-stĭ-gāt

[*instigare, instigatus* (Latin), "spur on"; from *in* (Latin), "in, on" + *stigare* (Latin), "goad, spur"]

Definition: To stir up or urge on.

Troublemakers in the crowd attempted to **instigate** a riot, but fortunately their efforts proved unsuccessful.

Related Forms: (*nouns*) instigation, instigator

Synonyms: (*verbs*) provoke, incite, foment, generate, touch off, start

Antonyms: (*verbs*) quell, quash, squelch, suppress, stop; allay, pacify

Phrases: put the kibosh on; an agent provocateur; a stormy petrel

242. in-su-per-a-ble   *adjective*   ĭn-soo´-pĕr-ə-bəl

[*insuperabilis, insuperabile* (Latin), "unconquerable" from *in* (Latin), "not" + *superare* (Latin), "conquer" + *abilis, abile* (Latin), "able to"]

Definition: Incapable of being overcome.

"Much as I'd love to play shortstop for the Yanks, my age is an **insuperable** barrier to realizing any such dream," granddad remarked.

Phrases: insuperable obstacles, insuperable difficulties

Related Forms: (*nouns*) insuperability, insuperableness

Synonyms: (*adjectives*) insurmountable, overwhelming, invincible, unconquerable, indomitable

Antonyms: (*adjectives*) surmountable, conquerable, vincible

292

243. in·ter·vene   *verb*   ĭn-tĕr-vēn´

[*intervenire* (Latin), "come between"; from *inter* (Latin), "between" + *venire* (Latin), "come"]

Definition: To come between; to involve oneself in.

The decades that **intervened** between the two world wars of the 20th century were a period of turmoil, blunders, and missed opportunities.

However benevolent your intentions, you may do more harm than good if you **intervene** in other people's quarrels.

Related Forms: (*nouns*) intervention, interventionism

Synonyms: (*verbs*) separate; interfere, meddle, intrude, interpose; kibitz

Phrases: an interloper; horn in on, poke one's nose into, put one's oar in, put one's two cents' worth in; in the interim; sandwiched in between

A Russian tank patrols the streets of Kabul, Afghanistan. Recently the Soviet Union intervened in the civil war raging in that country.

Interventionism

Interventionism is a term that is often used these days in discussions of international politics to describe the behavior of one country in regard to the other countries of the world, especially the smaller, weaker, and less stable ones. What the term indicates is an intentional government policy of interfering in the domestic affairs of another sovereign nation. The implication, of course, is that such a policy is undertaken for purely selfish reasons or in order to achieve some advantage over one's enemies. Accordingly, the tone of the word is decidedly negative.

244. in-trep-id   *adjective*   ĭn-trĕp´-id

[*intrepidus* (Latin), "fearless"; from *in* (Latin), "not" + *trepidus* (Latin), "frightened, alarmed"]

Definition: Fearless and bold.

The rows of white gravestones in Arlington Cemetery are poignant reminders of the **intrepid** men and women who gave their lives in defense of this country.

"In carrying out new programs," the legislator remarked, "we need people who are **intrepid** enough to take a few risks, even with their lives and reputations."

Related Forms: (*nouns*) intrepidity, intrepidness; (*adverb*) intrepidly

Synonyms: (*adjectives*) valiant, daring, courageous, gallant, gutsy, stout-hearted, lion-hearted, audacious, valorous, heroic

Antonyms: (*adjectives*) cowardly, craven, timorous, pusillanimous

245. in-veigh   *verb*   ĭn-vā´

[*invehere* (Latin), "carry in, attack"; from *in* (Latin), "in" + *vehere* (Latin), "carry"]

Definition: To protest bitterly or vehemently.

When the train ground to a halt yet again, one passenger began to **inveigh** angrily against the transit system and the people who ran it.

Related Form: (*noun*) invective

Usage Note:
Do not confuse *inveigh* with *inveigle*, which means "to obtain by flattery or deceit."

Synonyms: (*verbs*) rail against, fulminate against, denounce, berate, decry, lambaste

Antonyms: (*verbs*) praise, commend, extol, laud

Phrases: jump down someone's throat, give someone a tongue-lashing

246. i-ro-ny   *noun*   ī´-rə-nē

[*eironeia* (Greek), "pretended ignorance"; from *eirein* (Greek), "say"]

Definition: Incongruity between what might be expected and what actually happens.

It was one of life's little **ironies** that a man who had condemned so many others to the gallows should himself die by the noose.

Related Forms: (*adjectives*) ironic, ironical; (*adverb*) ironically

Synonyms: (*nouns*) contradiction, paradox

Phrases: a backhanded compliment, damn with faint praise

Mark Antony (Marlon Brando) delivers the funeral oration in a recent film version of Shakespeare's *Julius Caesar*.

Verbal and Dramatic Irony

Verbal irony refers to the use of words to convey the opposite of their literal meaning. For example, a person who uses expressions of praise in order to scold someone else is employing verbal irony. The device is frequently used to achieve a humorous, sarcastic, or dramatic effect. One of the most famous examples of the use of verbal irony to achieve a dramatic effect occurs in Shakespeare's *Julius Caesar*. In his funeral oration over Caesar's body, Mark Antony repeatedly characterizes Brutus and the other conspirators as "honorable men" who did Rome a service by murdering Caesar when, of course, he intends his audience to understand that they were quite the opposite.

Dramatic irony is a related device used in plays and similar material. The term indicates an incongruity between the significance of an action on the stage and the literal meaning of the words or speeches that accompany it. The audience, of course, perceives this incongruity, but the characters in the play do not. For example, Lady Macbeth's effusive greeting of King Duncan in Shakespeare's *Macbeth* is painfully ironic because the audience knows that she and her husband plan to murder the old monarch that night. King Duncan is unaware of this, so he takes the lady's words at face value and blithely walks into the trap. To Duncan, Lady Macbeth appears to be the quintessence of hospitality; to the audience, she is more like a spider luring a fly into its web.

247. jeop-ard-ize   *verb*   jĕp´-ẽr-dīz

[*jeu parti* (Old French), a game in which the chances of winning or losing are equal; from *jeu* (French), "game" + *parti* (French), "divided"]

Definition: To endanger.

> High-school students who settle for mediocre grades when they could be doing better are **jeopardizing** their chances of being accepted by the college of their choice.

Related Form: (*noun*) jeopardy

Usage Note:

> The legal expression *double jeopardy* refers to putting a person on trial for the same crime twice. Under our system of law, this is of course illegal.

Synonyms: (*verbs*) risk, hazard, imperil, compromise, gamble with

Antonyms: (*verbs*) protect, shield, safeguard, defend; improve, better

Phrases: sail too near the wind, fly too close to the sun, tempt fate

248. jet-ti-son   *verb*   jĕt´-ĭ-sən *or* jĕt´-ĭ-zən

[*getteson(e)* (Old French), "a throwing overboard"; from *jacere, jactus* (Latin), "throw"]

Definition: To throw overboard; to discard.

> The crew of the sinking freighter **jettisoned** most of the cargo in a desperate effort to keep the ship afloat.

> In our eagerness to improve the quality of life in America, we should not be too quick to **jettison** old ideas simply because they are old.

Synonyms: (*verbs*) dump, throw out, junk, abandon, toss out

Antonyms: (*verbs*) conserve, preserve, keep, hold on to, retain

Phrases: flotsam and jetsam, give something the deep-six

249. ju-di-cious   *adjective*   jōō-dĭsh´-əs

[*judicieux* (French), "wise"; from *judicium* (Latin), "judgment"]

Definition: Having or exhibiting sound judgment.

> Thanks to my broker's **judicious** advice, I refrained from making what turned out to be a very unsound investment.

Related Forms: (*noun*) judiciousness; (*adverb*) judiciously; (*adjective*) injudicious

Usage Note:

> Be careful not to confuse the adjective *judicious*, meaning "having or showing sound judgment," with the related adjective *judicial*. The latter means "relating to a court, the administration of justice, or the office of a judge." For example, the *judicial* system is the court system.

296

Similarly, *judicial review* is the constitutional principle that gives the Supreme Court the right to cancel any legislative or executive act that the justices sitting on that court consider unconstitutional.

Phrases: a judicious choice of words, a judicious mixture of elements

Synonyms: (*adjectives*) prudent, astute, discriminating, discerning, sagacious, sage, shrewd

Antonyms: unwise, imprudent, foolish, rash, unsound

250. jus-ti-fy   *verb*   jŭs'-tə-fī

[*justificare* (Latin), "do justice to"; from *justus, justi* (Latin), "just" + *facere* (Latin), "do, make"]

Definition: To show to be just, right, valid, or free of blame.

"You may be able to **justify** your anger at Bill," I replied, "but you were quite wrong to hit him."

The excellent quality of the coat clearly **justifies** its high price.

Related Forms: (*adjective*) justifiable; (*adverb*) justifiably; (*nouns*) justification, justifiability, justifiableness

Synonyms: (*verbs*) defend, vindicate, show just cause for, give good reasons for

Using the Words

Exercise I. Parts of Speech

Indicate the part of speech of each of the following words.

1. indigent
2. innovation
3. insuperable
4. intrepid
5. inveigh
6. irony
7. jettison
8. judicious
9. justify

Exercise II. Words in Phrases

In each of the following groups, select the item that best expresses the meaning of the *italicized* expression in the introductory phrase.

1. *jeopardize* one's chances of success
   a. insure b. endanger c. calculate d. doubt
   e. enhance

2. a *judicious* choice of words
   a. surprising b. silly c. novel d. painful e. prudent

3. *inveigh against* injustice
   a. champion b. ignore c. denounce d. report
   e. improve

4. an *ingenious* scheme to make money
   a. clever b. unworkable c. costly d. problematic
   e. dangerous

5. full of *inherent* problems and defects
   a. built-in b. minor c. unexpected d. knotty
   e. temporary

6. since its *inception*
   a. demise b. graduation c. marriage d. inauguration
   e. dismissal

7. "*justify* the ways of God to man"
   a. criticize b. divulge c. vindicate d. deplore
   e. conceal

Exercise III.   Completing Sentences

Complete each of the following sentences or pairs of sentences by selecting the most appropriate word from the given group of words. Use each word only once.

intrepid	intervene	indigent
instigate	jettison	irony
innovation	inveigh	insuperable

1. The old man's ragged clothing and emaciated body told me instantly that he was totally _____.

2. Often a(n) _____ that seems bold and inventive when it is first introduced is soon taken for granted.

3. "I will never concede defeat," I told myself, "no matter how _____ the odds against me appear to be."

4. The old adage, "Don't throw the baby out with the bath water," cautions us against inadvertently _____ the good with the bad.

5. There is an unmistakable _____ in the fact that the steps the dictator took to insure his own safety proved his undoing.

6. "It is one thing to be _____," my best friend observed when I tried to ride a horse I couldn't handle. "It is quite another to be foolhardy."

7. "Are you the troublemaker who _____ the food fight in the cafeteria today?" the dean asked me angrily.

8. Though I didn't start to write my report until two weeks after I had completed my research, I used the time that _____ to plan it out.

Exercise IV. Synonyms and Antonyms

A. In each of the following groups, select the **two** words that are most nearly **synonymous**.

1. a. clever b. prominent c. mature d. inventive
2. a. baffle b. provoke c. foment d. divulge
3. a. inaudible b. insurmountable c. inconceivable
   d. invincible
4. a. interfere b. conclude c. meddle d. devise
5. a. abandon b. discard c. retain d. increase

   Now, for each pair of synonyms that you have selected, supply a word from the Basic Word List for this lesson (Words 236–250) that means **the same** or **almost the same** thing.

B. In each of the following, select the item that is most nearly **opposite** in meaning to the numbered word at the left.

1. judicious a. illegal b. wealthy c. unwise d. novel
   e. expert
2. inception a. articulation b. fabrication c. inauguration
   d. collaboration e. termination
3. indigent a. dejected b. coarse c. blithe d. eminent
   e. affluent
4. intrepid a. slovenly b. treacherous c. ignorant
   d. cowardly e. cruel
5. jeopardize a. protect b. yield c. claim d. delay
   e. encounter

Exercise V. Word Roundup

1. Explain the difference in meaning between the items in each of the following pairs of words.
   a. indigent—indigenous   c. ingenious—ingenuous
   b. inveigh—inveigle   d. judicious—judicial
2. With or without a dictionary, define each of the following French expressions commonly used in modern English.
   a. agent provocateur   b. tour de force   c. avant-garde
3. With or without the aid of a dictionary, explain what each of the following means.
   a. a backhanded compliment   c. a congenital defect
   b. cosmetic alterations   d. to the manner born
4. Define or explain the following legal expressions.
   a. judicial review   b. double jeopardy

5. Define each of the following colorful expressions.

   a. keep the wolf from the door   **b.** jump down someone's throat

Exercise VI.   Framing Sentences

A. Use each of the following words in an original sentence.

1. inception   **3.** insuperable   **5.** inveigh
2. indigent   **4.** intrepid   **6.** jettison

B. Give a **noun** form of each of the following words, and use it in a short illustrative sentence.

1. instigate   **2.** intervene   **3.** jeopardize

C. Give an **adjective** form of each of the following words, and use it in a short illustrative sentence.

1. innovation   **2.** irony   **3.** justify

D. Give an **adverb** form of each of the following words, and use it in a short illustrative sentence.

1. ingenious   **2.** judicious   **3.** inhere

Completing Verbal Analogies

"A Is by Definition a Person Who B's."   Another word relationship that frequently appears in the analogy questions on standardized vocabulary tests may be expressed as "*A* is by definition a person who *B*'s; *C* is by definition a person who *D*'s." Following is an example of an analogy question involving this relationship. Try to determine the correct answer before reading the explanation of it given below.

   fugitive : flee =
   a. critic : censor   **d.** doctor : operate
   b. spectator : observe   **e.** tyrant : prosecute
   c. advertiser : conceal

   The answer is *b*. A *spectator* is by definition someone who *observes*, just as a *fugitive* is by definition someone who *flees*.
   None of the other choices exhibits the same relationship as the key pair of words. A *critic* (Choice *a*) may praise or censure, but he or she does not *censor*. Similarly, a *tyrant* (Choice *e*) usually persecutes people, but he does not by definition *prosecute* them. (That is the job of someone like a district attorney.) Though a surgeon by definition *operates* on his or her patients, a *doctor* (Choice *d*), the more general term for someone in the medical profession, is not by definition associated with such a procedure. (For Choice *d* to be correct, it would have to read either *surgeon : operate* or *doctor : heal*.) Finally, an advertiser (Choice *c*) makes a product or service more widely known; he or she does not *conceal* it.
   Note: A related form of this word relationship may be expressed as "*A* is by definition someone who is *B*; *C* is by definition someone who is *D*." For example, *hero : valorous = knight : chivalrous*.

"The Tone of A is B." Another useful word relationship may be expressed as "The tone of *A* is *B*; the tone of *C* is *D*." Here is an example of an analogy question involving this relationship. Try to determine the correct answer before reading the explanation of it given below.

salubrious : favorable =
a. munificent : unfavorable
b. pernicious : favorable
c. deleterious : unfavorable
d. inimical : favorable
e. beneficial : unfavorable

The answer is *c*. The tone of *deleterious* is decidedly negative or *unfavorable*, just as the tone of *salubrious*, its antonym, is positive or *favorable*.

All of the other choices are clearly wrong. The tone of both *munificent* (Choice *a*) and *beneficial* (Choice *e*) is *favorable*, not unfavorable. Similarly, the tone of *pernicious* (Choice *b*) and *inimical* (Choice *d*) is *unfavorable, not favorable*.

Exercise I

Complete each of the following analogies based on the word relationships "*A* is a person who *B*'s" and "The tone of *A* is *B*."

1. **circumspect : favorable ::**
   a. opinionated : favorable
   b. rash : unfavorable
   c. cumbersome : favorable
   d. splendid : unfavorable
   e. erratic : favorable

2. **thief : steal ::**
   a. hoard : miser
   b. refugee : asylum
   c. researcher : investigator
   d. mendicant : beg
   e. monarch : usurp

3. **activist : militant ::**
   a. mourner : doleful
   b. proprietor : incessant
   c. accomplice : dominant
   d. peacemaker : belligerent
   e. coward : intrepid

4. **arbitrator : mediate ::**
   a. prophet : eavesdrop
   b. mason : slaughter
   c. parish : rector
   d. counselor : advise
   e. warden : prisoner

5. **murmur : low ::**
   a. mumble : clear
   b. jeer : gladden
   c. screech : piercing
   d. rasping : whine
   e. bellow : melodious

Exercise II

Compose **two** complete analogies based on the word relationship "*A* is by definition a person who *B*'s" and **two** based on "The tone of *A* is *B*." In your original analogies, use at least **two** words from the Basic Word List for Lessons 1–20 (Words 1–250).

The following items review what you have so far learned about analogy questions. Complete each.

1. **abet : encourage** = thwart :
   (connive, frustrate, abhor, forbear, defend)

2. **intrepid : craven** = laudable :
   (praiseworthy, illicit, reprehensible, timely, indigent)

3. **effrontery : audacious** = fickleness :
   (capricious, felicitous, adamant, fortuitous, haggard)

4. **haughty : humility** = effete :
   (duplicity, effrontery, credibility, equanimity, vitality)

5. **impervious : penetrate** = implacable :
   (grimace, justify, appease, impugn, filch)

Working with Context Clues

By now you have enough familiarity with the two-word omissions that appear on standardized tests to handle them without further guidance. Accordingly, the remaining "Working with Context Clues" sections of this book will concentrate on providing you with enough practice in dealing with two-word omissions for you to tackle those that actually appear on standardized tests with skill and confidence. In trying to apply the knowledge you now possess to practical situations, remember one important principle: Always isolate the context clues before you attempt to choose the right answer.

Exercise

Complete each of the following two-word omissions by selecting the pair of words that make the best sense in the passage as a whole. Indicate the clue or clues that led you to make your choice.

1. During the _____, the carnage had been horrendous. Where the fighting had been the fiercest, the _____ were piled three deep.

   a. snowstorm . . . drifts   c. war . . . supplies
   b. battle . . . bodies   d. game . . . spectators

2. Over the years, consumer prices have soared, while the purchasing power of the dollar has _____. If the cost of living continues to _____, the value of our money must surely shrink even more.

   a. increased . . . dwindle   c. dwindled . . . increase
   b. increased . . . increase   d. dwindled . . . dwindle

3. People who aren't grossly overweight don't normally need to go on particularly stringent _____ to lose unwanted pounds. People who have become _____, however, must usually restrict their intake of food severely in order to shed the excess tonnage.

   a. diets...obese
   b. fads...alienated
   c. vacations...exhausted
   d. programs...emaciated

4. Some Senators _____ the proposal and in the warmest terms exhorted their colleagues to pass the measure. Others disliked the idea and just as vehemently _____ its adoption.

   a. criticized...agitated for
   b. favored...inveighed against
   c. approved of...fought for
   d. ignored...denounced

5. Though I am perfectly willing to give praise where I feel praise is due, I refuse to _____ an action that I consider _____.

   a. condone...laudable
   b. amend...defective
   c. abhor...heinous
   d. commend...despicable

6. After romping around with my six-year-old nephew all afternoon, I had become woefully _____. My trousers were rumpled, my shirttails were hanging out, and my tie was all _____.

   a. disheveled...askew
   b. disreputable...awry
   c. garrulous...timid
   d. lamentable...orderly

7. "I think we can ascribe her popularity chiefly to her natural _____," I observed. "In the same way, we can _____ his failure to make many friends to his cold and distant manner."

   a. aloofness...assign
   b. rudeness...credit
   c. warmth...defer
   d. affability...attribute

8. "Those who circumvent the law are often as _____ as those who actually break it," the lawyer said. "The seriousness of such an offense is not mitigated by the fact that technically no _____ has been committed."

   a. crass...violation
   b. vulnerable...atrocity
   c. culpable...crime
   d. susceptible...feat

9. Mozart was a precocious youngster who wrote his first _____ at the age of eleven. Though he was never as _____ a composer of theater music as some of his contemporaries, his output in this area was by no means negligible.

   a. novel...intrepid
   b. opera...prolific
   c. play...barren
   d. comedy...fulsome

10. Since her objections to my proposal were clearly _____,
I thought that she was being _____. After all, if she had
been serious, her comments would have had more substance
to them.

a. plausible . . . seemly   c. inaudible . . . forthright
b. genial . . . meddlesome   d. frivolous . . . facetious

Enriching the Lesson

Exercise I.   Coining Words

Coinage of English words goes on all the time. When a new development occurs—in politics, science, business, entertainment, or whatever—and if current language has no suitable words to define or describe it, a new word will probably be devised, or an old word or old words in combination will be adapted to meet the need. If the coinage is vivid, or picturesque, or pointedly fitting, it catches on and may enjoy some degree of permanence.

Consider the word *conglomerate*. This is by no means a newcomer to English, having been used for centuries to refer to a certain type of rock composed of fragments. It *is* new, however, in its application to a recently developed type of business combination.

The nuclear age has given birth to the word *brinkmanship* (*brink + manship*), linguistically structured like *horsemanship*, *penmanship*, and *salesmanship*, to describe a certain type of strategy used in international politics. It suggests the act of creating a potentially explosive international situation and pushing it to the very "brink" (of war) so as to intimidate other nations and force them to make concessions.

In the 1950's, the novelist Jack Kerouac used the common word *beat* in a new phrase, *beat generation*, to identify members of the disillusioned generation following World War II who developed a new lifestyle of nonconformity and free-wheeling self-expression and social criticism.

Other more or less recent coinages include: *take-home pay, astronaut, brainwash, telethon, skyjackers, miniskirt,* and *print-out*. Other coinages go far back into the history of our language.

Listed below are a number of expressions which are more or less recent coinages. With or without the aid of a dictionary or other reference book, define each. Then choose any **five**, and, for each, compose a short illustrative sentence.

1. urbanologist
2. superstar
3. cybernetics
4. automation
5. consumer advocate
6. environmentalist
7. astronaut
8. supersonic
9. brainwash
10. unisex
11. paraprofessional
12. laser
13. programmer
14. brunch
15. quasar

During the 1950's, Jack Kerouac (1922–1969) was as much the "apostle of the beat generation" in prose as Allen Ginsberg was in poetry. A native of Lowell, Massachusetts, Kerouac roamed through the United States and Mexico for a number of years investigating the "beatnik" subculture. He published a series of novels that drew upon his travels and reflected his restless pursuit of new experience and sensation. These include *The Town and the City* (1950), *On the Road* (1957), *The Dharma Bums* (1958), and *Big Sur* (1962).

16. generalist
17. Kremlinologist
18. miniskirt
19. superdome
20. Astroturf
21. megalopolis
22. astrodynamics

23. prime time
24. play-off
25. motorcade
26. aquacade
27. telethon
28. cheeseburger
29. motel

30. minibike
31. laundromat
32. skyjack
33. stagflation
34. litterbug
35. bikini
36. camper

Exercise II. Expanding Your Word Power

The words listed below are not on the Basic Word List, but they were mentioned in one form or another in Lesson 20. All of them would make useful additions to your working vocabulary. Define each, give its etymology, list **two** synonyms and **two** antonyms (where possible), and use in a short illustrative sentence.

1. culminate
2. impecunious
3. immanent
4. adventitious
5. indomitable

6. fulminate
7. compromise
8. suppress
9. hazard
10. sagacious

11. vindicate
12. timorous
13. interpose
14. generate
15. conserve

Review

Exercise I. Syllabication and Pronunciation

Syllabicate the following words correctly and place the major stress mark (′) after the syllable that is accented when the word is pronounced. Two answers are correct in some instances.

1. construe	6. emanate	11. grimace
2. corroborate	7. esoteric	12. gullible
3. defect	8. expedient	13. harangue
4. deviate	9. fetish	14. inveigh
5. eclectic	10. futile	15. justify

Exercise II. Parts of Speech

Indicate the part of speech of each of the following words. In some cases, two answers are correct.

1. consensus	6. discourse	11. finesse
2. consummate	7. epithet	12. heinous
3. counsel	8. forestall	13. impasse
4. curtail	9. fickle	14. impugn
5. dire	10. filch	15. irony

Exercise III. Words Out of Context

In each of the following groups, select the lettered item that best expresses the meaning of the numbered word at the left.

1. devoid — a. saturated b. angry c. empty d. foolish e. clumsy

2. efficacious — a. effective b. inadequate c. extravagant d. recent e. lethargic

3. fabricate — a. remove b. concoct c. conceal d. destroy e. consider

4. facsimile — a. oath b. treachery c. skill d. duplicate e. fortune

5. garble — a. distort b. clarify c. report d. sing e. control

6. goad — a. suppose b. curb c. investigate d. enjoy e. prod

7. haggard — a. sunny b. wealthy c. gaunt d. fat

8. instigate   a. snoop   b. foment   c. explore   d. yawn
                           e. complain

9. illicit   a. invincible   b. illiterate   c. interminable
                           d. illegal   e. inflexible

10. jettison   a. beautify   b. discard   c. preserve   d. order

Exercise IV. Completing Sentences

Complete each of the following sentences by selecting the most appropriate word from the given group of words.

Group A

exacerbate	foibles	flagrant
grueling	criterion	dcleted

1. Though I admire the candidate's strong points, I find his _____ laughable.

2. In my haste to cut my essay down to size, I accidentally _____ some essential information.

3. "Though the proposal will certainly solve some of our economic problems," the Senator remarked, "it will unfortunately _____ others."

4. A 26-mile marathon is a _____ test of any runner's strength and endurance, no matter how well prepared he or she may be.

5. Though the defense attorney was overjoyed by the outcome of the trial, the prosecutor branded it a _____ miscarriage of justice.

Group B

fiasco	ethnic	innovation
jeopardize	gaped	dilatory

6. Having to pay a sizable fine on some overdue library books has taught me not to be so _____ in the future.

7. Many of the minority groups that have come to the United States have managed to preserve their _____ identities while at the same time becoming full-fledged Americans.

8. A combination of poor planning and bad luck turned what should have been a sure-fire success into an utter _____.

9. "Pursuing such a risky and ill-considered course of action now," I observed, "will surely _____ all that we have so far succeeded in achieving."

10. Observers on the shore _____ open-mouthed in horror as the stricken vessel slowly sank beneath the turbulent waters of the storm-tossed sea.

Exercise V. Words in Phrases

In each of the following groups, select the item that means the same as the *italicized* word in the introductory phrase.

1. a *crucial* moment
    a. comical   b. pivotal   c. sad   d. boring   e. wasted

2. a group of *demure* young women
    a. bold   b. pretty   c. secretive   d. arrogant   e. modest

3. a *diligent* worker
    a. hardworking   b. new   c. pleasant   d. foreign
    e. bright

4. *fatuous* remarks
    a. perceptive   b. inane   c. amusing   d. brief   e. loud

5. *fluctuate* in popularity
    a. seesaw   b. continue   c. increase   d. remain
    e. decline

6. *elicit* a response
    a. make up   b. repeat   c. call forth   d. ignore
    e. strike out

7. *formidable* opposition to the proposal
    a. negligible   b. unexpected   c. reluctant   d. awesome
    e. recent

8. *embellish* the facts
    a. investigate   b. report   c. conceal   d. reveal
    e. improve upon

9. the *gruesome* details
    a. relevant   b. horrible   c. minor   d. important
    e. unknown

10. all kinds of *ingenious* devices
    a. clever   b. unworkable   c. costly   d. practicable
    e. dangerous

Exercise VI. Related Forms

A. Give a **noun** form of each of the following words.

| 1. cynical | 3. ethical | 5. haughty |
| 2. dormant | 4. frugal | 6. intervene |

B. Give a **verb** form of each of these words.

1. empathy   2. immunity   3. impediment

C. Give an **adjective** form of each of these words.

1. enigma   2. fallacy   3. euphemism

D. Give an **adverb** form of each of these words.

1. drastic   2. graphic   3. ignominy

Exercise VII. Synonyms and Antonyms

Classify each of the following pairs of words as **S** for **synonyms** or **A** for **antonyms**.

1. dapper—slovenly
2. dejected—crestfallen
3. corpulent—skinny
4. eminent—obscure
5. divulge—reveal

6. fathom—comprehend
7. feign—pretend
8. harbinger—forerunner
9. indigent—affluent
10. intrepid—timorous

Exercise VIII. Framing Sentences

Use each of the following words in a short illustrative sentence of your own devising.

1. cursory
2. copious
3. dexterous
4. disparage
5. emaciated

6. emulate
7. erudite
8. elite
9. feasible
10. gloat

11. gregarious
12. inception
13. incarcerate
14. innovation
15. judicious

Exercise IX. Word Roundup

1. Explain the difference between the words in each of the following pairs.

   a. flout—flaunt
   b. indigent—indigenous
   c. demur—demure
   d. credibility—credence
   e. discomfit—discomfort

   f. counsel—council
   g. exalt—exult
   h. feint—faint
   i. fortuitous—fortunate
   j. deferment—deference

2. Define each of the following terms.

   a. a gadfly
   b. a windfall
   c. a fluke
   d. to stonewall
   e. to rubberneck
   f. to soft-soap

3. Explain the meaning of each of the following colorful phrases.

   a. down in the dumps
   b. strike while the iron is hot
   c. pour oil on troubled waters
   d. paint oneself into a corner
   e. keep the wolf from one's door
   f. drag one's heels
   g. live in an ivory tower
   h. still wet behind the ears
   i. see red
   j. pull the wool over someone's eyes

4. Explain the meaning of each of the following foreign expressions used in present-day English, and tell what language it comes from.

   a. idée fixe
   b. hoi polloi
   c. impedimenta
   d. esprit de corps
   e. ad nauseam
   f. tour de force

5. Explain why you would be *flattered* or *insulted* if you were described as each of the following:

   a. an ignoramus   c. a connoisseur   e. a patsy
   b. a greenhorn   d. a dapper Dan   f. an opportunist

Exercise X. Etymology

1. For each of the following definitions, supply an English word that begins with the Latin prefix *co, col, com, con,* or *cor.*

   a. fight against   c. stick together   e. eat away
   b. fall down   d. build or erect   f. work together
       completely

2. Define each of the following words beginning with the Latin prefix *de* or the Latin prefix *dis.*

   a. dispel   c. depose   e. disinherit
   b. denounce   d. dismember   f. demerit

3. Form a verb from each of the following English words by adding the suffix *(i)fy.* Then define the resulting combination.

   a. null   c. identity   e. beauty
   b. person   d. solid   f. terror

4. List and define **three** English words containing the Latin root *flu* or *fluct.* What does this root mean?

5. Change each of the following positive words to its negative form by adding the Latin prefix *in* or one of its variants. Then define the resulting combination.

   a. reverent   c. moral   e. noble
   b. validate   d. logical   f. excusable

Lesson 21

---

251. ku-dos   *noun*   kyōō´-dŏs *or* kōō´-dōz

[*kudos* (Greek), "fame, glory"; originally English university slang but popularized in the United States some years ago by *Time* magazine]

Definition: The prestige or acclaim that results from some noteworthy achievement or position.

An "unsung hero" is a person whose achievements have never been accorded the **kudos** they deserve.

Usage Note:
Since *kudos* is singular, it takes a singular verb. *Kudo* (without the *s*) is sometimes mistakenly used as the singular, but it is not considered correct.

Synonyms: (*nouns*) glory, honor, acclamation, credit, recognition, renown; accolade, plaudit

Antonyms: (*nouns*) odium, opprobrium, obloquy, contempt, disdain

Accolade

During the Middle Ages, an *accolade* was the ceremony in which a king or other overlord conferred knighthood upon a deserving subject. During part of this elaborate ceremony, usually conducted in the presence of the notables of the land, the king officially elevated the subject to the rank of knight by embracing him around (*ad* [Latin]) the neck (*collum* [Latin]) and tapping him lightly on the shoulder with the flat of a sword. The ceremony still survives in countries (e.g., Great Britain) that have a titled nobility or where knighthood is customarily bestowed as an official token of thanks for outstanding personal service to the nation. It is from this connection with knighthood that the word *accolade* has now come to mean not only the formal bestowal of important honors and awards but also the simple granting of praise or approval.

Queen Elizabeth II makes a deserving subject a knight.

311

252. lack-a-dai-si-cal   *adjective*   lăk-ə-dā´-zĭ-kəl

[*lackaday* (obsolete English), "Woe is me," an archaic expression of sorrow or regret derived from *Alack* (= Woe) *the day*]

Definition: Sorely lacking in spirit, energy, or purpose.

"No matter how bright a youngster is," the child psychologist observed, "a **lackadaisical** attitude toward studying will result in poor grades."

Related Forms: (*noun*) lackadaisicalness; (*adverb*) lackadaisically

Synonyms: (*adjectives*) lethargic, listless, sluggish, torpid, indolent, lazy, supine, slothful; blase, nonchalant, indifferent; perfunctory

Antonyms: (*adjectives*) energetic, vigorous, dynamic, spirited, animated

Phrases: a devil-may-care attitude, a fainéant administration, a drone

253. leg-a-cy   *noun*   lĕg´-ə-sē

[*legatia* (Medieval Latin), "office of deputy; bequest"; from *legare, legatus* (Latin), "send as a deputy; bequeath"]

Definition: Something left to a person in a will; something handed down from the past.

In her will, grandmother left me a sizable cash **legacy**, which I have wisely used to further my education.

It is our duty to preserve and augment the **legacy** of freedom that we have received from earlier generations of Americans.

Synonyms: (*nouns*) bequest, inheritance, endowment; present, gift

Phrases: a family heirloom, a hand-me-down

254. li-a-bil-i-ty   *noun*   lī-ə-bĭl´-ə-tē

[*ligare, ligatus* (Latin), "tie, bind" + *abilis, abile* (Latin), "able to" + *itas, itatis* (Latin), "state or condition of"]

Definition:
   a.   A debt or obligation, especially of a financial nature.

"When we balanced this company's assets against its **liabilities**," the executive remarked, "we found that we had turned a handsome profit this year."

   b.   A hindrance or handicap.

Sometimes the traits of character that make people successful in the business world can prove to be **liabilities** in their personal lives.

My failure to learn how to type in high school later proved to be a **liability** when I applied for a secretarial position at a large Chicago firm.

Related Form: (*adjective*) liable

Synonyms: (*nouns*) indebtedness, debit, minus; disadvantage, draw-back, obstacle

Antonyms: (*nouns*) asset, plus, advantage

Phrases: have an albatross around one's neck, have a cross to bear, have a millstone around one's neck, a stumbling block

255. li-bel   *noun and verb*   lī′-bəl

[*libellus* (Latin), "little book, petition"; from *liber* (Latin), "book"]

Definition:
   a. (*noun*) A public statement or picture that damages a person by falsely impugning his or her character, motives, or actions, or by unjustly exposing the person to public censure or ridicule.

> "The laws of this land do not shield public figures from just criticism," the lawyer remarked, "but they do protect them against **libel**."

   b. (*verb*) To slander publicly.

> "Reliable witnesses can prove beyond the shadow of a doubt that the defendant has scurrilously **libeled** my client," the prosecutor told the jury.

Related Form: (*adjective*) libelous

Synonyms: (*nouns*) calumny, slander; (*verbs*) calumniate, defame, traduce, badmouth

Antonyms: (*verbs*) whitewash, gloss over, cover up

Phrases: hurl brickbats at, do a hatchet job on, drag someone's name through the mud; defamation of character; character assassination; a muckraker

256. lit-i-ga-tion   *noun*   lĭt-ĭ-gā′-shən

[*litigare, litigatus* (Latin), "sue"; from *lis, litis* (Latin), "lawsuit" + *agere, actus* (Latin), "bring, incite"]

Definition: Legal action; a lawsuit.

> "You are perfectly free to take your case to court," the lawyer told her client, "but if you do, the matter may be tied up in **litigation** for years."

Related Forms: (*noun*) litigant; (*adjective*) litigious; (*verb*) litigate

Usage Notes:
   a. *Litigation* usually indicates that a civil, as opposed to a criminal, action is involved.

   b. *Litigious* means "given to engaging in lawsuits" or, more broadly, "quarrelsome, pugnacious."

Synonyms: (*noun phrase*) legal proceedings

Phrases: initiate legal proceedings against, bring an action against, file suit against, press charges against, go to court over, bring to book

257. lu-cid   *adjective*   lo͞o′-sĭd

[*lucidus* (Latin), "clear, bright"; from *lucere* (Latin), "shine"]

Definition: Clear and intelligible to the understanding; mentally competent.

The speaker gave such a **lucid** explanation of the complicated medical procedure that even a non-professional like me could understand it.

Though George III was declared permanently insane in 1810, he occasionally had brief periods when he was quite **lucid**.

Related Forms: (*nouns*) lucidity, lucidness; (*adverb*) lucidly

Synonyms: (*adjectives*) crystal-clear, understandable, comprehensible; sane, rational

Antonyms: (*adjectives*) unintelligible, confused, puzzling; ambiguous, equivocal; mad, insane, irrational

Phrase: (non) compos mentis

258. lu-cra-tive   *adjective*   lo͞o′-krə-tĭv

[*lucrativus* (Latin), "profitable"; from *lucrum* (Latin), "profit, gain"]

Definition: Profitable.

"Running a popular pizza parlor may not be the most elevated occupation in the world," he replied, "but it certainly is **lucrative**."

Elizabethan opposition to the growth of Spanish power in Europe and the Americas proved far more **lucrative** than originally anticipated.

Related Forms: (*nouns*) lucrativeness, lucre

Synonyms: (*adjectives*) gainful, remunerative, rewarding, worthwhile; productive, fruitful, advantageous

Antonyms: (*adjectives*) unprofitable, unrewarding, unremunerative; unproductive, barren

Phrase: the profit motive

259. lurk   *verb*   lûrk′

[*lurka* (Old Norse), "sneak away slowly"]

Definition: To sneak; to lie hidden or in wait.

The police officer stopped to question the seedy-looking man who had been **lurking** around the corner drugstore for hours.

Who would have imagined that such a subtle thought could **lurk** in that innocent-looking head!

Synonyms: (*verbs*) skulk, prowl, slink, loiter

Phrases: a prowler, a stalking-horse

Filthy Lucre

Lucre, meaning "monetary profit or gain," has a decidedly negative connotation, perhaps because its most common use occurs in the phrase *filthy lucre*, which is derived from the New Testament. In his first letter to his disciple Timothy, the apostle Paul mentions that a bishop should not be "greedy of filthy lucre" (1 Timothy 3:2). In this context, *filthy* means "sordid" or "dishonorable," and Paul is saying that a bishop should not be open to bribes and other questionable ways of acquiring money. Accordingly, the phrase *filthy lucre* has come to be a highly contemptuous synonym for "ill-gotten gains," though it is also sometimes applied to people who are simply overly interested in making and amassing money, whatever their means.

St. Paul

260. lush   *adjective*   lŭsh´

[*lusch* (Middle English), "lax, soft"]

Definition:

  a. Luxuriant, plentiful; luxurious, opulent.

      Someone who has never been in the tropics can scarcely imagine the diversity and density of the **lush** jungle vegetation.

      Lush Piersian carpets gave the room an atmosphere of opulence and luxury that it would not otherwise have possessed.

  b. Overelaborate or overripe.

      What a contrast between George Orwell's lean, understated prose and the **lush**, overblown style of some of his contemporaries!

Phrases: lush farmland, lush surroundings, a lush orchestral texture

Related Forms: (*noun*) lushness; (*adverb*) lushly

Synonyms: (*adjectives*) dense, thriving, flourishing, profuse, lavish, prodigal, extravagant; ornate, sumptuous

Antonyms: (*adjectives*) simple, restrained, spartan; bleak, barren

261. mal-a-prop-ism   *noun*   mãl´-ə-prŏp-ĭz-əm

[*mal'a propros* (French), "out of place, inappropriate"]

Definition: An unconscious and usually ludicrous misuse of a word.

In one of his typical **malapropisms**, my super informed me on the hottest day of the year that he didn't mind the heat so much as the humility.

Synonyms: (*nouns*) flub, gaffe, solecism

Phrases: a play on words, a pun, an Irish bull, a spoonerism

262. mal-ice   *noun*   mãl´-ĭs

[*malitia* (Latin), "wickedness"; from *malus* (Latin), "bad, evil"]

Definition: A desire to cause harm or suffering; deep-seated ill will.

In a famous passage in his Second Inaugural Address (1865), Abraham Lincoln suggested that national unity could never be restored if the defeated South were treated with **malice** rather than magnanimity.

Phrase: malice aforethought

Related Forms: (*adjective*) malicious; (*noun*) maliciousness

Synonyms: (*nouns*) malevolence, spite, rancor, animosity, vindictiveness, malignity, enmity, resentment

Antonyms: (*nouns*) benevolence, beneficence, good will, generosity, charity, magnanimity

263. mam-moth   *noun and adjective*   mãm´-əth

[*mammot'* (Russian), "a mammoth"]

Definition:
a.   (*noun*) An extinct form of elephant; a giant or colossus.

During the Ice Age, woolly **mammoths** and other huge elephant-like creatures were common in much of North America.

According to legend, Paul Bunyan, America's most celebrated lumberjack, was a **mammoth** of a man, whose proudest possession was a gigantic blue ox named Babe.

b.   (*adjective*) Gigantic.

The popular British singing group capped off its tour of the United States with a **mammoth** rock concert at Yankee Stadium.

Synonyms: (*nouns*) mastodon, behemoth; (*adjectives*) colossal, titanic, vast, gargantuan, enormous, monstrous, prodigious, stupendous

Antonyms: (*adjectives*) minute, minuscule, diminutive, Lilliputian, microscopic, tiny

The English actress Mary Boland as Mrs. Malaprop in Richard Brinsley Sheridan's comedy *The Rivals*.

Malapropisms, Irish Bulls, and Puns

The 18th-century Anglo-Irish playwright Richard Brinsley Sheridan (1751–1816) took the French phrase *mal à propos*, meaning "out of place" or "inappropriate," as the basis for the name of one of his most inspired comic creations, Mrs. Malaprop in *The Rivals* (1775). Mrs. Malaprop's most outstanding quality is her propensity to confuse words in a way that yields unintentionally comic effects. For example, she says, "I would have her instructed in geometry [i.e., geography] that she might know something of the boundaries of contagious [i.e., contiguous] countries" and "He is as headstrong as an allegory on the banks of the Nile." Such incongruous misusages, dubbed *malapropisms* in the lady's honor, are scattered like buckshot throughout *The Rivals*.

More recently, comedian Jimmy Durante and movie mogul Sam Goldwyn achieved a certain amount of notoriety for their malapropisms. Goldwyn, for example, was "credited" with such inspired verbal gaffes as "An oral contract is not worth the paper it is written on" and "I'll answer you with a definite maybe." This kind of self-contradictory statement is sometimes called an *Irish bull*. One of the most successful TV characters of our time, Archie Bunker of "All in the Family" and "Archie's Place," is also strongly identified with malapropisms.

Finally, it has been said that a *pun* (an intentionally comic play on words) is a "deliberate" or "controlled" malapropism. If you analyze a typical pun, you will see that this is true.

Larger Than Life

Modern English is rich in interesting expressions that indicate tremendous size. One of the most useful of these is *colossal*, which comes from the Greek word *kolossos* and its Latin equivalent, *colossus*. To the ancient Greeks and Romans, a kolossos or colossus was a gigantic statue. For example, the Colossus of Rhodes, one of the "Seven Wonders" of classical antiquity, was a gigantic statue erected about 280 B.C. by the inhabitants of Rhodes, an island republic off what is now southwest Turkey, to commemorate their deliverance from a siege. The statue, which represented the sun god Helios, the patron deity of the republic, was made entirely of bronze and rose to a height of 105 feet. It is from this connection with one of the most famous tourist attractions of the ancient world that we get our words *colossus*, meaning "anything of great size or impressiveness," and *colossal*, meaning "immense."

Our word *coliseum* also comes from the same source. It is a variant of the Latin word *Colosseum*, the name of the huge sports stadium that the Flavian emperors built in Rome about A.D. 80 (see photo). It is interesting to note, however, that many modern coliseums are not, strictly speaking, colosseums in the ancient sense, because they are not open-air structures and were not primarily designed for sporting events.

Another useful expression relating to great size is *gargantuan*, which comes from the title of a famous novel by François Rabelais (1494?–1553), a French comic writer who lived during the Renaissance. Gargantua, the hero of this book, is described by Rabelais as a giant with enormous vitality and unlimited appetites. Accordingly, the English adjective *gargantuan* usually suggests an enormous capacity for food and pleasure, as in the phrase "a *gargantuan* appetite."

The 18th-century English satirist Jonathan Swift (1667–1745) also contributed two interesting "size" words to our vocabulary. Lemuel Gulliver, the hero of Swift's classic novel, *Gulliver's Travels*, visits the kingdom of Lilliput, where the inhabitants are only six inches tall and everything else is correspondingly small. On a later voyage, he travels to the land of Brobdingnag, where everything is gigantic. Swift's description of Gulliver's adventures in these two fantastic places was so memorable that soon the adjectives *Lilliputian*, meaning "extremely small in size or outlook," and *Brobdingnagian*, meaning "gigantic and correspondingly gross or boorish," had found permanent places in the vocabulary of English.

264. **man-da-to-ry**   *adjective*   măn´-də-tôr-ē

[*mandatum* (Latin), "command + *orius* (Latin), "having the effect of"; from *manus* (Latin), "hand" + *dare, datus* (Latin), "give, place"]

Definition: Required, obligatory.

> In this state, attendance at school is **mandatory** for children between the ages of six and seventeen.

Related Form: (*noun and verb*) mandate

Phrases: a mandatory life sentence, the mandate of the court, mandated services, a mandated territory, a writ of mandamus

Usage Notes:

  a. In politics, the word *mandate* is sometimes used to express the authorization which the voters have presumably given to public officials by electing them. The following sentence illustrates this use of the word:

> "The overwhelming victory I have won," the Governor-elect said, is a clear **mandate** to carry out my program."

  b. After World War I, the League of Nations used the term *mandate* to describe a colonial territory that had been taken from one of the defeated belligerents and assigned to the administrative control of one of the victors. For example, Great Britain had a mandate over Palestine, which formerly belonged to the Turkish Empire. Under the UN, *trusteeship* is used for much the same arrangement.

Synonyms: (*adjectives*) compulsory, requisite; imperative

Antonyms: (*adjectives*) optional, discretionary, voluntary

Phrases: de rigueur, an elective course

265. **me-di-um**   *noun*   mē´-dē-əm

[*medium* (Latin), "the middle," from *medius* (Latin), "middle"]

Definition: The means by which some goal is achieved or the person through whom it is realized.

> Modern-day activists advocate strong political action as the most effective **medium** of social change.

> Carlos was the **medium** through whom we made our views known to the Student Council.

Usage Notes:

  a. Among those involved in the occult, a medium is a person who is believed to have the power to communicate with the dead.

  b. The plural of *medium* is *media*. In recent years, this plural form has come to be used to refer collectively to our modern means of mass communication, particularly newspapers and radio-TV. Note: Since *media* is a plural form, it takes a *plural* verb, though some modern authorities sanction the use of the singular.

Synonyms: (*nouns*) agency, channel, vehicle

Using the Words

Exercise I. Syllabication and Pronunciation

Syllabicate the following words correctly, and place the major stress mark (') after the syllable that is accented when the word is pronounced.

1. kudos
2. lackadaisical
3. liability
4. lucid
5. lucrative
6. malice
7. mammoth
8. mandatory
9. medium

Exercise II. Words Out of Context

In each of the following groups, select the item that best expresses the meaning of the numbered word at the left.

1. kudos
   a. lawsuit b. glory c. agency
   d. calumny e. inheritance

2. lackadaisical
   a. obscure b. unrewarding c. energetic
   d. obligatory e. lethargic

3. lucrative
   a. daily b. intelligible c. eager
   d. profitable e. average

4. malice
   a. charity b. sensitivity c. animosity
   d. indifference e. idleness

5. liability
   a. refuge b. advantage c. environment
   d. commencement e. drawback

6. mammoth
   a. gigantic b. kindly c. optional
   d. shabby e. evil

7. libel
   a. murder b. slander c. famine
   d. chaos e. disaster

Exercise III. Completing Sentences

Complete each of the following sentences by selecting the most appropriate word from the given group of words. Use each word only once.

lucid   legacy   mandatory

litigation   malapropism   lush

lurk   libel   medium

1. Deteriorating climatic conditions eventually transformed what had been a _____ tropical paradise into a barren and inhospitable wasteland.

2. Though slavery has long since passed from the scene, the _____ of guilt and fear it left behind still affects our national life.

3. Fortunately, we were able to avoid a great deal of costly _____ by settling the dispute out of court.

4. Though he worked in a variety of materials, stone was the _____ through which Michelangelo preferred to express his artistic ideas.

5. Her prose is as _____ and direct as mine is muddled and digressive.

6. Who can ever accurately predict what evil schemes _____ like sneak thieves in the dark recesses of a criminally insane person's mind?

7. The Senator's command of English is so uncertain that his public utterances are full of bizarre _____ like "make a bee dive for the door" and "the boy who cried, '*Woof*'!"

8. Though high-school students are no longer required to study Latin and Greek, English is still a _____ subject.

Exercise IV.   Synonyms and Antonyms

Classify each of the following pairs of words as **S** for **synonyms** or **A** for **antonyms**.

1. lush—opulent
2. lackadaisical—energetic
3. libel—slander
4. skulk—lurk
5. liability—asset
6. channel—medium
7. litigation—lawsuit
8. lucrative—unprofitable
9. lucid—unintelligible
10. compulsory—mandatory
11. kudos—acclaim
12. benevolence—malice
13. legacy—bequest
14. diminutive—mammoth

Exercise V.   Word Roundup

1. Give the plural of *medium*, explain how it is used in contemporary English, and use it in a short illustrative sentence.

2. Explain the story behind each of the following expressions.

   a. accolade
   b. filthy lucre
   c. Lilliputian
   d. gargantuan

3. With or without the aid of a dictionary, define each of the following.

   a. a drone
   b. a hand-me-down
   c. a muckraker
   d. a stalking-horse

4. What is a *mandate*?

5. With or without the aid of a dictionary, explain what each of the following means.

   a. an elective course
   b. a family heirloom

   c. defamation of character
   d. malice aforethought

6. With the help of a dictionary, define each of the following foreign phrases used in modern English.

   a. non compos mentis
   b. de rigueur

7. Define each of the following expressions.

   a. a pun
   b. a spoonerism

   c. an Irish bull
   d. a malapropism

Exercise VI.   Framing Sentences

A. Use each of the following words in an original illustrative sentence.

1. kudos	3. lurk	5. mammoth
2. legacy	4. malapropism	6. medium

B. Give a **noun** form of each of the following words, and use it in an original illustrative sentence.

1. lush
2. mandatory
3. lucrative

C. Give an **adjective** form of each of these words, and use it in an original illustrative sentence.

1. litigation
2. libel
3. liability

D. Give an **adverb** form of each of these words, and use it in an original illustrative sentence.

1. lucid
2. malice
3. lackadaisical

Dissecting the Words

Prefix

The Latin prefix **inter**, meaning "between" or "among," occurs in a great many English words, including *intervene*, studied in Lesson 20. Here are a few other useful English words in which it appears:

interpose (*inter*, "between" + *ponere, positus* [Latin], "place")—to place between, to come between

interject (*inter*, "between" + *jacere, jactus* [Latin], "throw")—to thrust abruptly between. Noun: *interjection*

intermediary (*inter*, "between" + *medius* [Latin], "middle")—a go-between

interstice (*inter*, "between" + *sistere, status* [Latin], "cause to stand")—a space between two things *intersperse* (*inter*, "among" + *spargere, sparsus* [Latin], "scatter")—to scatter or distribute among other things

interrogate (*inter*, "between" + *rogare, rogatus* [Latin], "ask")—to question formally. Nouns: *interrogation* and *interrogator*

intersect (*inter*, "between" + *secare, sectus* [Latin], "cut")—to cut across or through. Noun: *intersection*

intercept (*inter*, "between" + *capere, captus* [Latin], "seize")—to stop or interrupt the intended progress of. Noun: *interception*

Do not confuse the prefix **inter** with the prefix **in** when the latter occurs before the syllable **ter**. For example, the word *interminable* begins with what looks like the prefix **inter** but is in fact the prefix **in** (meaning "not") followed by the word *terminable* (meaning "capable of being ended" or "having an end").

Roots

1. The Latin and French roots **mal(e)** have a number of meanings: (*1*) "bad, badly"; (*2*) "evil, ill"; and (*3*) "abnormal, abnormally." These word elements occur in many common English words, including *malice*, studied in Lesson 21. For example:

malefactor (*male*, "evil" + *facere, factus* [Latin], "do")—a person who commits a crime or other offense

malevolent (*male*, "evil, ill" + *volens, volentis* [Latin], "wishing")—showing ill will; having an evil influence. Noun: *malevolence*

maladroit (*mal*, "ill, badly" + *adroit* [French], "skillful")—clumsy or inept

malodorous (*mal*, "badly" + *odor* [Latin], "smell")—foul smelling

malign (*mal*, "evil" + *gignere, genitus* [Latin], "bear, bring forth")—to speak evil or ill of

malaise (*mal*, "ill" + *aise* [French], "comfort, ease")—a vague, undefined feeling of illness or discomfort

malformation (*mal*, "abnormal" + *formation*)—an abnormal structure or formation

Other words that contain the word element **mal(e)** include *malcontent*, *malpractice*, *malfunction*, *malediction*, *malignant*, and *malnutrition*.

2. The Latin word element **ben(e)** indicates the opposite of *mal(e)*; that is, "good" or "well." It occurs in several useful English words, including *benign*, studied in Lesson 6. Here are a few others in which it appears.

benefactor (*bene*, "good" + *facere, factus* [Latin], "do")—a person who confers some kind of good on another. Nouns: *benefactress, benefaction*

benediction (*bene*, "good, well" + *dicere, dictus* [Latin], "say")—a blessing

benevolent (*bene*, "good, well" + *volens, volentis* [Latin], "wishing")—kindly and generous. Noun: *benevolence*

benign (*bene*, "well" + *genus* [Latin], "born"; from *gignere, genitus* [Latin], "bear, bring forth")—gentle and mild; beneficial; not dangerous. Noun: *benignity*

Other words in which **ben(e)** appears include *benefit, beneficial, beneficiary, benefice, beneficent,* and *benignant.*

3. The Latin and Greek word element **gen** or **gene** has a number of meanings: (*1*) "give birth"; (*2*) "born" and; (*3*) "race or kind." Among the many words in which this element appears is *ingenious,* studied in Lesson 20. Here are a few others.

genesis ([Greek], "beginning")—the origin of something. Adjective: *genetic*

generate (*genus* [Latin], "birth" + *ate* [from Latin *-atus*], "make")—to produce or bring into being. Noun: *generation*

genocide (*genos* [Greek], "race" + *caedere, caesus* [Latin], "kill")—the systematic destruction of a racial or cultural group

genealogy (*genea* [Greek], "family, kin" + *logy* [Greek], "study, science") —a record of the ancestry of a person or family; the study of family ancestry; lineage or descent. Adjective: *genealogical*

generic (*genus, generis* [Latin], "kind, sort")—characteristic of an entire group or class

progeny (*pro* [Latin], "forward" + *gignere, genitus* [Latin], "beget")— offspring, descendents

Other words in which **gen(e)** appears include *gentle, genteel, gentile, gender, general, generous, genre, congenial, heterogeneous, indigenous,* and *primogeniture.*

Exercise

1. Add the prefix *inter* to each of the following words. Then define the new word that results, and explain how *inter* contributes to its meaning.

    a. cede   **c.** denominational   **e.** marry
    b. collegiate   **d.** lock   **f.** national

2. With or without the aid of a dictionary, define each of the following words. Then choose any **five**, and, for each, compose a short illustrative sentence.

    a. intercession   **c.** interloper   **e.** interval
    b. intermittent   **d.** interlude   **f.** interpolate

3. For each of the following definitions, supply a word beginning with the root *mal(e).*

    a. a vague feeling of discomfort   **d.** clumsy or inept
    b. a lawbreaker   **e.** to speak ill or evil of
    c. foul-smelling   **f.** ill will or spite

4. For each of the following definitions, supply a word beginning with the root *ben(e).*

    a. a blessing   **c.** an heir
    b. gentle and mild   **d.** advantageous

5. With or without the aid of a dictionary, explain what each of the following words means.

a. engender   d. genus   g. genesis
b. degenerate e. ingenuous   h. congenial
c. homogeneous f. heterogeneous i. progeny

Working with Context Clues

With or without the aid of a dictionary, complete each of the following two-word omissions by selecting the pair of words that make the best sense in the passage as a whole. Indicate the clue or clues that led you to make your choice.

1. One of the most hotly contested Presidential _____ in American history took place in 1968. Public opinion polls even went so far as to suggest that none of the candidates would obtain a majority of votes in the Electoral College. If that happened, the long and costly process would end in a _____.

a. races...victory   c. appointments...treaty
b. decisions...stand-off d. elections...deadlock

2. Few people would make a minor disagreement the excuse for _____ a close friendship. For example, my cousin and I _____ all the time, but we never cease to be friends, even while we're arguing.

a. usurping...dissent   c. commencing...agree
b. terminating...squabble d. ending...work

3. "We could no longer sit idly by while a gross injustice went uncorrected," she recalled. "For that reason, we joined a group of _____ reformers actively trying to get the situation _____."

a. militant...rectified   c. lackadaisical...deferred
b. incorrigible...ignored   d. idealistic...exacerbated

4. "The general's death-defying feats of _____ in the recent war certainly deserve our approbation," the article declared. "But, by the same token, his wanton acts of cruelty merit our severest _____."

a. cowardice...umbrage   c. charity...kudos
b. gallantry...censure   d. bravery...apathy

5. The old adage "Time heals all wounds" recognizes the fact that human beings are both _____ and _____.

a. sensitive...implacable c. cowardly...arrogant
b. brash...cantankerous   d. vulnerable...resilient

6. In A.D. 267, a band of barbarous Heruli raided the ancient Greek religious center of Delphi. For several days they _____ the town and _____ its temples. Then they rode off laden with booty.

   a. observed...studied
   b. repaired...refurbished
   c. pillaged...desecrated
   d. occupied...dedicated

7. Tony's general attitude toward people is so _____ that he has _____ absolutely everybody who knows him. If he didn't walk around with such a huge chip in his shoulder, he might have a few friends.

   a. benevolent...provoked
   b. adverse...exhilarated
   c. belligerent...alienated
   d. amicable...repelled

8. Some people always stick up their noses at food they're not accustomed to, but I'm not at all _____ to trying something new. Still, experience has taught me to be _____ of such dubious delicacies as chocolate-covered ants, and I usually "look before I leap," so to speak.

   a. disinclined...heedless
   b. averse...wary
   c. rash...negligible
   d. impervious...fond

9. Office workers usually lead relatively _____ lives between nine and five. For that reason, many a "desk jockey" finds a weekly trip to the gym a(n) _____ way to keep fit.

   a. prosaic...pernicious
   b. stationary...poor
   c. covert...gratuitous
   d. sedentary...efficacious

10. First she measured out the flour, sugar, and other _____ she would use in her cookies. Then she carefully _____ them all into a stiff dough.

    a. fetishes...garbled
    b. ingredients...blended
    c. elements...jettisoned
    d. impediments...merged

Enriching the Lesson

Exercise I.   More Words from Literary Sources

A few useful expressions derived from the names or works of famous and not-so-famous authors are listed below. With or without the aid of a dictionary or other reference book, define each.

1. Machiavellian	6. Rabelaisian	11. Barmecidal
2. a Lothario	7. a Frankenstein	12. Pecksniffery
3. namby-pamby	8. a pamphlet	13. euphuism
4. a Tartuffe	9. a gal Friday	14. a Micawber
5. tilt at windmills	10. a Simon Legree	15. a panjandrum

Exercise II.   Russian Loan Words in English

For the first time in this book, you have studied a word derived from Russian. That word, of course, is *mammoth*. Listed below are a number of other English words that have been borrowed from Russian. With or without the aid of a dictionary, define each.

1. pogrom	4. ukase	7. czar
2. knout	5. steppe	8. samovar
3. intelligentsia	6. tundra	9. vodka

Many of the Russian words that English has taken over in recent years have to do with the theory and practice of communism. This is scarcely surprising, in view of the fact that communism, whether perceived as a promise or a menace, has become an important factor in the modern world.

A few of the more common Russian words of this type are given below. With or without the aid of a dictionary, define each. Note, however, that you may have to consult an unabridged dictionary for some of them.

10. commissar	12. tovarish	14. kulak
11. troika	13. apparatchik	15. soviet

Exercise III.   Plurals in *A*

A number of useful English words form their plurals in the same way as *medium* (Word 265) does. A few of these items are listed below. With or without the aid of a dictionary, define each and give its plural form.

1. addendum	3. agendum	5. bacterium
2. erratum	4. datum	6. stratum

Exercise IV.   Expanding Your Word Power

The words listed below are not on the Basic Word List, but they were mentioned in one form or another in Lesson 21. All of them would make useful additions to your working vocabulary. Define each, give its etymology, list **two** synonyms and **two** antonyms (where possible), and use in a short illustrative sentence.

1. disdain	6. traduce	11. enmity
2. supine	7. rational	12. diminutive
3. equivocal	8. sumptuous	13. remuneration
4. endowment	9. skulk	14. imperative
5. liable	10. solecism	15. vehicle

Lesson 22

---

266. **mer-ce-nar-y**   *noun and adjective*   mûr´-sə-nĕr-ē

[*mercenarius* (Latin), "hired, paid" from *merces* (Latin), "wages, salary"]

Definition:
a. (*noun*) A hireling, especially a hired professional soldier.

The Roman army of Republican times was essentially a citizen militia, though foreign **mercenaries** were sometimes used as auxiliary troops.

b. (*adjective*) Motivated solely by a desire for material gain.

Once the war had been won, the victors laid aside the high-minded ideals for which they had fought and became embroiled in a deplorably **mercenary** squabble over the spoils.

Related Form: (*noun*) mercenariness

Synonyms: (*nouns*) hired hand, soldier of fortune, condottiere; (*adjectives*) greedy, avaricious, acquisitive, grasping, rapacious

Antonyms: (*adjectives*) altruistic, disinterested

267. **moot**   *adjective and verb*   mo͞ot

[*mot* (Old English), "a meeting for discussion"]

Definition:
a. (*adjective*) Debatable and therefore unresolved.

The seemingly incontestable right that a person has to direct his or her own life becomes a **moot** point when it interferes with the rights of others.

b. (*verb*) To bring up for discussion.

"I rejected the idea when it was first **mooted** years ago," the Governor said, "and I haven't regretted my decision yet."

Phrases: a moot question, a moot court

Usage Note:
A *moot court* is a mock court in which law students try hypothetical cases in order to obtain experience "under fire."

Synonyms: (*adjectives*) arguable, disputable; questionable, doubtful; (*verbs*) broach, raise, pose, put forward

Antonyms: (*adjectives*) incontrovertible, indisputable, irrefutable

Phrases: a Gordian knot, a foregone conclusion

268. mo-rass   *noun*   mə-răs′ *or* mô-răs′

[*moeras* (Dutch), "marsh"; from *maresc, mareis* (Old French), "swamp"; of Germanic origin and related to *mersc, merisc* (Old English), "marsh"]

Definition: A swamp or bog; a confused or degrading situation that is difficult to get out of.

> Heavy rains had transformed the unpaved road into a miniature **morass**, and we were soon up to our knees in mud.

> "Our once great city," the candidate complained, "is slowly sinking into a **morass** of waste, corruption, and decay."

Synonyms: (*nouns*) quagmire, marsh, fen

269. mot-ley   *noun and adjective*   mŏt′-lē

[Origin uncertain; perhaps from *mot* (Old English), "speck"]

Definition:

a. (*noun*) A kind of multicolored cloth; a garment made from this cloth, especially the costume worn by a court jester or clown.

> Shakespeare's players were a versatile crew; even the great tragic actor Richard Burbage donned **motley** now and then.

b. (*adjective*) Multicolored; diverse or varied.

> In no time at all, she turned a **motley** assortment of leftovers into an elegant and tasty dinner.

> As W. S. Maugham once observed, the human personality is a **motley** collection of strengths and weaknesses, foibles and fortes.

Related Forms: (*adjective*) mottled; (*verb*) mottle

Synonyms: (*adjectives*) polychrome, polychromatic, piebald; variegated, heterogeneous, miscellaneous

Antonyms: (*adjectives*) monochrome, monochromatic; monolithic, homogeneous, uniform

Phrases: a pluralistic society, a diversified economy, a checkered career

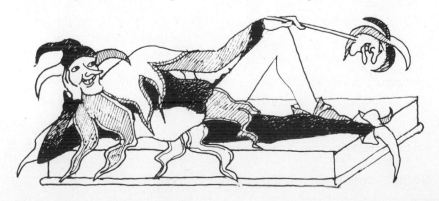

270. mun-dane   *adjective*   mŭn-dān′ *or* mŭn′-dān

[*mundanus* (Latin), "relating to the world"; from *mundus* (Latin), "world"]

Definition: Worldly (as opposed to spiritual); humdrum or everyday.

"May I interrupt this esoteric discussion of interpersonal relationships," I asked, "and turn your attention to more **mundane** matters—like what's for dinner?"

Most people I know are too busy dealing with such **mundane** concerns as paying off the mortgage or meeting deadlines at the office to have much time for abstruse philosophical speculation.

Related Form: (*adverb*) mundanely

Synonyms: (*adjectives*) earthly, terrestrial; secular, temporal; material, physical; ordinary, prosaic, routine, commonplace, banal (Word 55)

Antonyms: (*adjectives*) celestial, heavenly, cosmic; unworldly, spiritual; metaphysical, transcendental; extraordinary, unique

Phrases: worldly goods, worldly wisdom; a man of the world

271. myr-i-ad   *adjective*   mîr′-ē-əd

[*murias, muriadis* (Greek), "ten thousand"; from *murios* (Greek), "countless"]

Definition: Countless, innumerable.

During the Great Blackout of 1966, the **myriad** lights by which New York is normally illuminated at night suddenly all went out.

Can any one man or woman reasonably be expected to deal with the **myriad** problems and predicaments that now face a President of the United States?

Usage Note:
Occasionally, *myriad* is used in older writing as a noun; for example in the phrases "a *myriad* of stars" and "a *myriad* of possibilities." In such cases, the word means "a vast number" or "a great multitude."

Synonyms: (*adjectives*) multitudinous, multifarious, manifold, infinite

Antonyms: (*adjectives*) finite, limited

272. nar-cis-sis-tic   *adjective*   när-sə-sĭs′-tĭk

[*Narcissus,* see caption on page 331 + *istic* (from Greek *istikos*), "like"]

Definition: Dominated by an excessive love or admiration of oneself.

"Is a constant need to admire oneself in the mirror a sign that a person is developing a **narcissistic** personality?" I asked.

Narcissistic tendencies can perhaps be excused as an inevitable phase in a teenager's struggle to achieve an identity, but they are alarming in an adult.

Related Forms: (*nouns*) narcissism, narcissist

Synonyms: (*adjectives*) egotistic(al), egoistic, egomaniacal, self-centered, conceited, vain

Antonyms: (*adjectives*) self-deprecating, self-deprecatory, self-critical, self-destructive

Phrase: amour-propre

Narcissus and Narcissism

Narcissism is a psychological term derived from the ancient Greek mythological figure of Narcissus. Narcissus was a beautiful young man who steadfastly refused to fall in love with anyone, including the lovely mountain nymph Echo. As a punishment for this attitude, the gods made Narcissus fall in love with his own reflection in a mountain pool. Since he was unable to consummate this love, Narcissus pined away with grief. Eventually, he was transformed into the white or yellowish flower that we know by the name of narcissus. Echo, by the way, also pined away from unrequited love until all that was left of her was her voice, which, as you may suspect, was the first echo.

People who suffer from narcissism have exalted feelings of self-importance, personal success, and attractiveness. They generally feel a strong need to be the center of attention. They are dominated by fantasies of gaining great wealth and power, displaying dazzling creative talents, and achieving ideal love relationships. Of course, all people share symptoms of this type, but in the *narcissist* they become dominant to the point where reality blurs into fantasy. Accordingly, the narcissist is typically preoccupied with his or her own needs and feelings and shows little or no capacity to relate constructively and warmly to other people.

Adapted in part from *Psychology for You*, by Sol Gordon (New York: William H. Sadlier, Inc., 1983), page 59.

273. neb-u-lous   *adjective*   nĕb´-yə-ləs

[*nebulosus* (Latin), "cloudy, misty"; from *nebula* (Latin), "cloud"]

Definition: Hazy, vague, or indistinct.

His ideas on how to solve our economic woes are much too **nebulous** for us to act on with any confidence of success.

Elected officials must be very careful about their behavior because the line between what the public considers proper and what it doesn't is often extremely **nebulous**.

Phrases: a nebulous recollection of an event, nebulous fears and suspicions

Related Forms: (*nouns*) nebulousness, nebulosity, nebula

Synonyms: (*adjectives*) amorphous, opaque, shapeless, fuzzy, indefinite

Antonyms: (*adjectives*) clear, distinct, well-defined, unambiguous

Nebulae

In astronomy, *nebula* (plural, *nebulae*) is the name given to a discrete mass of matter and gases that appears in the sky. Sometimes these formations are illuminated; sometimes they are not. They also have several different shapes. Some are cloudlike or spiral-shaped. Others are long, irregular veils or thin hazes stretched across the sky. Still others look something like planets because they consist of an outer envelope of gassy material completely surrounding a star. Though our galaxy, the Milky Way, contains a number of nebulae, other important examples of the formation can be found outside it. One nebula is even thought to be a separate galaxy of its own. This is the Great Spiral Nebula of Andromeda (shown at the left).

274. neg-li-gi-ble   *adjective*   nĕg´-lĭ-jə-bəl

[*negligere* (Latin), "ignore" + *abilis, abile* (Latin), "able to"]

Definition: Too small to be significant.

Though the product does indeed contain a **negligible** amount of a harmful chemical, it poses absolutely no threat to anyone's health.

"Since events in the Soviet bloc have stirred up so much controversy lately," the Senator remarked, "their influence on the outcome of this election will probably not be **negligible**."

Related Forms: (*nouns*) negligibility, negligibleness

Synonyms: (*adjectives*) insignificant, inconsequential, trivial, piddling, trifling, nugatory

Antonyms: (*adjectives*) significant, considerable; telling, meaningful; critical, crucial, pivotal

Phrases: small potatoes, trivia

275. nep-o-tism   *noun*   nep´-ə-tĭz-əm

[*nepotismo* (Italian), "favoritism to nephews"; from *nepote* (Italian), "nephew"; from *nepos, nepotis* (Latin), "nephew; descendant"]

Definition: Unwarranted favoritism shown to relatives or friends by someone in high office.

"If your brother-in-law is really the best available candidate for the job you have to offer," I told my boss, "no one will accuse you of **nepotism**."

Some **nepotism** is unavoidable in a small, family-run business, such as a mom-and-pop candy store.

Related Forms: (*noun*) nepotist; (*adjectives*) nepotistic(al)

Synonyms: (*nouns*) partisanship, bias, partiality, patronage

Alexander VI

Cesare Borgia

During the Middle Ages and Renaissance, the rulers of the Roman Catholic Church were occasionally accused of showing special consideration for their nephews and other relatives when making appointments to high ecclesiastical office, such as the cardinalate. For example, Pope Alexander VI (1492–1503) was notorious for the blatant favoritism he showed to his relatives Cesare (1475–1507) and Lucrezia (1480–1519) Borgia. Needless to say, Alexander's case was unusual, even for those somewhat lax times, and one should not conclude that nepotism is either typical of or confined to the Roman Catholic Church.

276. no-mad-ic   *adjective*   nō-măd′-ĭk

[*nomas, nomadis* (Greek), "wanderer in search of pasturage" (from *nemein* [Greek], "pasture") + *ikos* (Greek), "pertaining to"]

Definition: Wandering, roving.

About 5000 B.C., the peoples of the Near East began to make the transition from the **nomadic** existence of a hunter to the more settled life of a farmer.

Related Form: (*noun*) nomad

Phrase: urban nomads

Synonyms: (*adjectives*) itinerant, migratory, peripatetic

Antonyms: (*adjectives*) settled, fixed, stationary

Phrases: footloose and fancy free; a fly-by-night operation, a roving reporter, a Peripatetic philosopher, a migrant farm worker; wanderlust

Aristotle

The Peripatetics

The *Peripatetic* school of ancient Greek philosophy owed its name in part to the unusual teaching habits of its founder, the famous philosopher Aristotle of Stagira (384–322 B.C.). Aristotle, a pupil of Plato, preferred to teach or lecture while walking about rather than while sitting or standing still. (His students, of course, would follow him as he moved around.) One of his favorite places for doing this kind of nomadic pedagogy was a covered walkway called the Peripatos ("Walkabout"), which formed part of a gymnasium in Athens called the Lukeion or Lyceum. Accordingly, the school of philosophy that Aristotle founded came to be called *peripatetikos*—that is, "the one founded in the Peripatos."

Initially, the members of the Peripatetic school were almost exclusively students or followers of Aristotle and his empirical approach to philosophy. These men spent most of their time writing commentaries on Aristotle's works, attempting to refine his philosophic system, or composing specialized treatises on the natural sciences. Later, however, some of the Peripatetics developed more independent lines of philosophic thought.

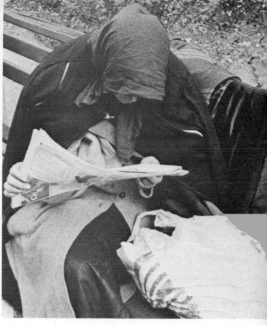

Urban Nomads

Pathetic reminders of our dim nomadic past, bag ladies (like the one in this photo) and other homeless persons now roam the streets of some of our largest cities.

277 nom·i·nal   *adjective*   nŏm´-ə-nəl

[*nominalis* (Latin), "relating to a name"; from *nomen, nominis* (Latin), "name"]

Definition:
a. Existing in name only.

 Since the Prime Minister actually directs the British government, the reigning monarch is really only the **nominal** head of state.

b. Insignificantly small.

 Most government-funded medical centers charge only **nominal** fees so that even the poorest member of the community can afford their services.

Phrases: a nominal Christian, nominal representation on the board

Related Forms: (*adverb*) nominally; (*nouns*) nominalism, nominalist

Synonyms: (*adjectives*) titular; token, symbolic; trifling, inconsequential

Antonyms: (*adjectives*) real, actual; exorbitant, excessive

Phrase: a puppet ruler

278. nos·tal·gia   *noun*   nŏ-stăl´-jə *or* nə-stăl´-jə

[*nostos* (Greek), "a return home" + *algos* (Greek), "pain"; actually a learned translation of *Heimweh* (German), "homesickness"]

Definition: A longing to return to a sentimentalized past; homesickness.

 Around Christmas, I always get a feeling of **nostalgia** for the days of my youth and the friends I grew up with.

Related Form: (*adjective*) nostalgic

Synonyms: (*nouns*) yearning, pining, hankering; wistfulness, sadness, sentimentality, sorrow, regret; lonesomeness

279. nov·ice   *noun*   nŏv′-ĭs

[*novicius* (Medieval Latin), "probationary member of a religious order"; from *novus* (Latin), "new"]

Definition:
    a. A person who has just entered a religious order on a probationary basis.

        Many **novices** find their first days in a religious community difficult, but usually they become accustomed to the lifestyle relatively quickly.

    b. A beginner of any kind.

        Show jumping is an aspect of the art of horseback riding that an experienced rider can tackle, but not a **novice**.

        "He's such a consummate master of the art of politics that he makes even a seasoned veteran look like a **novice**," I remarked.

Related Form: (*noun*) novitiate

Usage Note:
    Occasionally novice is used as an adjective before another noun or a noun phrase; for example, "a *novice* swimmer."

Synonyms: (*nouns*) postulant; neophyte, tyro, fledgling, trainee, rookie, probationer, greenhorn, tenderfoot

Antonyms: (*nouns*) expert, pro, veteran, old hand, past master, virtuoso

Phrases: still wet behind the ears; a babe in the woods, a freshman Congressman, a black belt in karate

280. nu·ance   *noun*   n(y)o͞o-äns′   *or*   n(y)o͞o′-äns

[*nuance* (French), "shade, hue"; from *nubes* (Latin), "cloud"]

Definition: A slight or subtle variation in meaning, expression, tone, feeling, color, or the like.

    Two synonyms are never exactly alike because **nuances** of tone or applicability make each of the words unique.

    Music can sometimes express a **nuance** of mood or feeling that would be difficult to put into words.

    Her colorful outfit contained every imaginable **nuance** of red—from the palest pink to the deepest burgundy.

    We may hope that our friends will understand the **nuances** of feeling implied in our words, but we shouldn't expect them to be mind-readers.

Synonyms: (*nouns*) subtlety, nicety, overtone, gradation, refinement, delicacy

Phrases: read between the lines, read the small print; a fine point

Using the Words

Exercise I. Parts of Speech

Indicate the part of speech of each of the following words. In some cases, two answers are correct.

1. mercenary
2. moot
3. motley
4. mundane
5. myriad
6. nebulous
7. nepotism
8. nominal
9. nuance

Exercise II. Words in Phrases

In each of the following groups, select the item that best expresses the meaning of the *italicized* word in the introductory phrase.

1. at a *nominal* cost to the consumer
   a. guaranteed b. token c. sizable d. fair

2. *nebulous* plans
   a. radical b. detailed c. costly d. vague

3. *mundane* pursuits
   a. commonplace b. sensible c. odd d. interesting

4. a *motley* group
   a. snobbish b. penniless c. enthusiastic d. diverse

5. for purely *mercenary* reasons
   a. practical b. monetary c. social d. personal

6. *nuances* of tone and shading
   a. subtleties b. theories c. uses d. problems

7. the *myriad* leaves on an oak
   a. edible b. uniform c. countless d. colorful

Exercise III. Completing Sentences

Complete each of the following sentences by selecting the most appropriate word from the given group of words. Use each word only once.

narcissistic	nepotism	nuance
novice	negligible	morass
nostalgia	nomadic	moot

1. Understandably, many of those who suffered through the hard economic times of the 1930's don't remember that particular era with much _____.

2. "Twenty-five dollars may be a _____ amount of money to you," I replied, "but it's sizable to me."

3. Whether or not Lincoln could have bound up the nation's wounds by being merciful is a _____ question, simply because he was assassinated before he got the chance to try.

4. Since most people cannot resist sneaking a peek at their reflections in a plate-glass window, is it fair to say that human beings generally have a _____ streak in them?

5. Trying to work my way through the _____ of complicated paperwork involved in the project was like trying to swim through shark-infested custard.

6. "Once you have mastered the basics of the game and can play with some degree of skill and confidence," my instructor said, "you will cease to be a _____."

7. I chose the _____ life of a traveling salesman simply because I felt too tied down by a nine-to-five office job.

8. "The appointment of your son to the job may have been based solely on merit," I told the Mayor, "but your critics will surely see it as _____."

Exercise IV. Synonyms and Antonyms

A. In each of the following groups, select the **two** words that are most nearly **synonymous**.

1. a. precipice   b. quagmire   c. grove   d. bog

2. a. conceited   b. affluent   c. vengeful   d. egotistic

3. a. prosaic   b. humdrum   c. gullible   d. slovenly

4. a. biased   b. infinite   c. hazy   d. vague

5. a. ace   b. greenhorn   c. tenderfoot   d. hillbilly

Now, for each pair of synonyms that you have selected, supply a word from the Basic Word List for Lesson 22 (Words 266–280) that means **the same** or **almost the same** thing.

B. In each of the following, select the item that is most nearly **opposite** in meaning to the numbered word at the left.

1. moot   a. incredible   b. invaluable   c. interminable
                 d. insoluble   e. indisputable

2. nomadic   a. pleasant   b. itinerant   c. awkward
                 d. stationary   e. theatrical

3. motley   a. trite   b. uniform   c. charitable
                 d. ambiguous   e. miscellaneous

4. nominal   a. exorbitant   b. genial   c. abject
                 d. prompt   e. human

5. mercenary   a. arduous   b. aggressive   c. altruistic
                 d. arbitrary   e. ambitious

338

Exercise V. Word Roundup

1. With or without the aid of a dictionary, explain the meaning of each of the following terms indicating kinds of people.

   a. a soldier of fortune
   b. a free-lance writer
   c. a puppet ruler
   d. a roving reporter
   e. a Peripatetic philosopher
   f. a man of the world
   g. a freshman Senator
   h. an urban nomad
   i. a migrant farm worker
   j. a nominal Christian

2. With or without the aid of a dictionary, explain the meaning of each of the following expressions indicating things.

   a. a moot court
   b. a fly-by-night operation
   c. a client state
   d. a checkered career
   e. a diversified economy
   f. a pluralistic society

3. What is *a Gordian knot*? Tell the story behind the phrase.

4. With or without the aid of a dictionary, explain what each of the following foreign expressions means, and tell what language it comes from.

   a. condottiere   b. amour-propre   c. wanderlust

5. With or without the aid of a dictionary, explain the meaning of each of the following colorful English expressions.

   a. wet behind the ears
   b. read between the lines
   c. small potatoes
   d. a babe in the woods

6. Tell the story of Echo and Narcissus. How does this story relate to the meaning of the psychological term *narcissism*? What is a *narcissist*?

7. What is *the spoils system*? *the merit system*? How do the two systems differ?

8. What is *a nebula*? In what science is this term used?

Exercise VI. Framing Sentences

A. Use each of the following words in an original illustrative sentence.

1. mercenary
2. moot
3. morass
4. myriad
5. mundane
6. motley
7. nominal
8. novice
9. nuance

B. Give a **noun** form for each of the following words, and use it in an original illustrative sentence.

1. narcissistic   2. nomadic   3. negligible

C. Give an **adjective** form for each of these words, and use it in an original illustrative sentence.

1. nostalgia   2. nepotism   3. nebula

Completing Verbal Analogies

By now you should be familiar enough with how verbal analogies work to handle them on your own. Accordingly, the remaining "Completing Verbal Analogies" sections of this book will concentrate on providing you with ample practice in dealing with them. That way, you will acquire the skill and confidence needed to tackle those that actually appear on standardized vocabulary tests. However, since many of the word relationships that you will meet, both in the remaining analogy sections in this book and on standardized tests, will be new to you, in the sense that you have not formally studied them, bear one important principle in mind: Always identify the relationship between the words in the key or given pair before you attempt to choose your answer.

Exercise

Complete each of the following analogies.

Group A

1. **momentous : trivial =**
   a. opportune : negligible
   b. year : decade
   c. temporary : ephemeral
   d. moot : nomadic
   e. significant : inconsequential

2. **ship : nautical =**
   a. subterranean : tunnel
   b. helicopter : lunar
   c. automobile : terrestrial
   d. horse : marine
   e. skateboard : celestial

3. **philatelist : stamps =**
   a. spendthrift : profits
   b. numismatist : coins
   c. charity : philanthropist
   d. speculation : philosopher
   e. astrologer : books

4. **behemoth : puny =**
   a. mammoth : massive
   b. gargantuan : carnivore
   c. mastodon : huge
   d. leviathan : minuscule
   e. colossus : gigantic

5. **cat : feline =**
   a. equine : horse
   b. cow : bovine
   c. rooster : hen
   d. dog : mongrel
   e. sheep : amphibian

Group B

1. **callow : experience ::**
   a. predatory : intelligence
   b. pensive : aplomb
   c. petulant : imagination
   d. self-esteem : narcissistic
   e. provincial : sophistication

2. **lax : stringent ::**
   a. circuitous : straight
   b. errant : nightly
   c. nominal : meritorious
   d. decadent : motley
   e. nebulous : hazy

3. **pickpocket : filch ::**
   a. cutthroat : deface
   b. spendthrift : hoard
   c. daredevil : lurk
   d. spoilsport : incarcerate
   e. scofflaw : flout

4. **avarice : grasping ::**
   a. humility : bare-knuckled
   b. liability : tight-fisted
   c. nepotism : light-fingered
   d. generosity : open-handed
   e. nostalgia : double-jointed

5. **palace : opulence ::**
   a. mansion : austerity
   b. shack : affluence
   c. hovel : indigence
   d. cottage : luxury
   e. skyscraper : poverty

Working with Context Clues

Complete each of the following two-word omissions by selecting the pair of words that make the best sense in the passage as a whole. If necessary, consult a dictionary for the meaning of any word with which you are not familiar.

1. A _____ government will prove workable only so long as its members are able to transcend party differences. As soon as they become entangled in factional disputes, however, the partnership will begin to _____.

   a. dictatorial. . . revive
   b. coalition. . . collapse
   c. democratic. . . emerge
   d. motley. . . progress

2. "We've got enough proof here to _____ a dozen smugglers," the D.A. gleefully remarked. "But the most incriminating piece of evidence is clearly the kilo of _____ drugs found in the suspect's suitcase."

   a. convict. . . contraband
   b. exonerate. . . illicit
   c. incarcerate. . . mundane
   d. discomfit. . . ethical

3. Only the sound of my footsteps echoing through the empty hallway disturbed the sepulchral _____ in which the deserted office building was enveloped. "It's as quiet as a _____ in here at night," I thought.

   a. atmosphere. . . parade
   b. shroud. . . subway
   c. silence. . . tomb
   d. glow. . . cemetery

4. For a minor infraction of the rules of a hockey game, the _____ player is relegated to the penalty box, or "sin bin," for two minutes. For a more serious _____, he is put there for five.

   a. offending. . . violation
   b. defending. . . calumny
   c. offensive. . . fiasco
   d. defensive. . . fallacy

5. "The flamboyant _____ of the peacock has always struck me as overly ostentatious," the ornithologist remarked. "By contrast, the peahen looks too _____ in her somber browns and greys."

   a. personality...diligent   **c.** posture...dapper
   b. plumage...dowdy   **d.** pedigree...demure

6. "If you always act cautiously, you should be able to _____ many of life's snares and pitfalls," dad advised. "Still, some difficulties cannot be avoided, even by the most _____ behavior."

   a. surmount...lackadaisical **c.** forestall...dilatory
   b. emulate...judicious   **d.** elude...circumspect

7. His lies and fabrications sounded so much like the truth that I was completely taken in by them. If they hadn't seemed so _____, I don't think I would have been _____ quite so easily.

   a. nebulous...deluded   **c.** dubious...exploited
   b. believable...hoodwinked **d.** ingenious...alluded

8. "An _____ is supposed to _____ the commission of a crime," the burglar growled at his sidekick. (The latter had just set off the alarm system of the bank the pair were robbing.) "But all _you_ can seem to do is make this job more difficult."

   a. arbiter...abet   **c.** accomplice...facilitate
   b. aesthete...hamper   **d.** advocate...impede

9. "They're asking far too much for this _____ merchandise," mom said. "I'd be a fool to pay such a(n) _____ price for goods that are so badly made."

   a. shoddy...exorbitant   **c.** defective...negligible
   b. bogus...nominal   **d.** exemplary...equitable

10. Over the years, the _____ of our patrons and sponsors has kept the wolf from our door more than once. Without their generous support, I don't know how our little theater group would have _____ disaster.

   a. apathy...confronted   **c.** liberality...averted
   b. fickleness...exploited   **d.** malice...courted

11. If my secretary had been more _____ about keeping the files in order, I wouldn't have had any trouble locating the correspondence I needed. But they proved to be in such disarray that the task proved to be most _____.

   a. scrupulous...irksome   **c.** remiss...foul
   b. officious...inopportune **d.** nonchalant...ominous

Enriching the Lesson

Exercise I. Our German Heritage

Modern German has contributed a number of useful words to the vocabulary of present-day English. One such expression, *wanderlust*, was mentioned in passing in Lesson 22. A few others are listed below. With or without the aid of a dictionary, define each. Then choose any **three**, and, for each, compose a short illustrative sentence.

1. strafe
2. ersatz
3. leitmotif
4. wunderkind
5. blitz(krieg)
6. putsch
7. seminar
8. flak
9. kitsch

Exercise II. The Clothes We Wear

One of the meanings noted for the word *motley*, studied in this lesson, was "a kind of multicolored cloth or a garment made from this material." This brings to mind the fact that there is a great deal of interesting history involved in the names of some of our most familiar fabrics and articles of clothing.

Listed below are the names of some common fabrics or articles of wearing apparel. With or without the aid of a dictionary or other reference book, identify each, and explain where the name comes from.

1. raglan
2. jeans
3. knickerbockers
4. mackintosh
5. Levi's
6. muslin
7. madras
8. lisle
9. dungarees
10. Stetson
11. cardigan
12. denim
13. calico
14. oxfords
15. fedora

Exercise III. Words from the Sciences

One of the items mentioned in passing in Lesson 22 was the term *nebula*, which comes from the science of astronomy. This brings to mind the fact that a good many scientific terms have been borrowed for use in a broad social sense. A few such expressions are listed below. With or without the aid of a dictionary, define each as it is used in the sciences and as it is used in more everyday situations. Then choose any **three**, and, for each, compose an original illustrative sentence.

1. catalyst
2. polarize
3. hybrid
4. eclipse
5. erosion
6. symbiosis
7. parasite
8. inertia
9. satellite

343

Exercise IV. What's in a Name?

Listed below are a number of expressions for different kinds of names. With or without the aid of a dictionary, define each. Then choose any **four**, and, for each, compose an original illustrative sentence.

1. epithet	6. sobriquet	11. pen name
2. surname	7. misnomer	12. nickname
3. alias	8. appellation	13. pseudonym
4. stage name	9. moniker	14. patronymic
5. honorific	10. toponym	15. diminutive

Exercise V. Number Words

Earlier in this lesson it was noted that *myriad* (Word 271) comes directly from the Greek term meaning "ten thousand." The English word, however, has lost this precise numerical denotation and is used to suggest (connote) the idea of "a very large number."

There are many other words in English derived from specific numbers. Some of them are listed below. Identify the number in each case. Then tell what the word means in present-day usage. In some cases, the original number meaning has been retained. In others, an entirely new meaning has been assumed. Try to account for the change. An unabridged dictionary will help.

1. millennium	8. Pentecostal	15. decathlon
2. quintet	9. trivial	16. monogamy
3. decade	10. unique	17. monopoly
4. centurion	11. triumvirate	18. pentathlon
5. septuagenarian	12. pentagon	19. decimal
6. bicentennial	13. trilogy	20. quadruped
7. trio	14. monolithic	21. decimate

Exercise VI. Expanding Your Word Power

The words listed below are not on the Basic Word List, but they were mentioned in one form or another in Lesson 22. All of them would make useful additions to your working vocabulary. Define each, give its etymology, list **two** synonyms and **two** antonyms (where possible), and use in a short illustrative sentence.

1. altruistic	6. egotistical	11. itinerant
2. incontrovertible	7. opaque	12. titular
3. fledgling	8. finite	13. partisan
4. temporal	9. nugatory	14. wistful
5. manifold	10. patronage	15. refinement

Lesson 23

281. obscene — 295. pensive

281. ob-scene   *adjective*   ŏb-sēn´ *or* əb-sēn´

[*obsc(o)enus* (Latin), "foul, repugnant"; probably from *ob* (Latin), "on account of" + *sc(a)enum* (Latin), "dirt, filth"]

Definition: Offensive to accepted standards of decency; repulsive.

"Your ideas are as crude and offensive," I exclaimed in disgust, "as the **obscene** language in which you express them!"

Though the music to that song is charming, the lyrics verge on the **obscene**.

Phrases: an obscene gesture, an obscene dance, an obscene picture

Related Forms: (*noun*) obscenity, (*adverb*) obscenely

Synonyms: (*adjectives*) indecent, lewd, salacious, smutty, bawdy, scatological, pornographic; risqué, suggestive; vulgar, crude, coarse; disgusting, abominable, reprehensible, loathsome

Antonyms: (*adjectives*) decent, refined, modest; laudable, meritorious

Phrases: not fit for mixed company, an X-rated film, an off-color joke

282. ob-se-qui-ous   *adjective*   ŏb-sē´-kwē-əs

[*ob* (Latin), "to, toward" + *sequi* (Latin), "follow, yield" + *osus* (Latin), "characterized by, full of"]

Definition: Excessively submissive to another person's wishes or ideas, often for purely self-interested reasons.

During imperial times, the Roman Senate was little more than a collection of **obsequious** yes men, intent on preserving their own lives by gratifying the Emperor's every whim.

At an autocrat's court, free speech is usually replaced by the **obsequious** twaddle of self-seeking toadies and flunkies.

Related Forms: (*nouns*) obsequiousness, obsequy; (*adverb*) obsequiously

Usage Note:
The noun *obsequy*, usually used in the plural, means "a funeral rite."

Synonyms: (*adjectives*) servile, fawning, subservient, groveling, mealy-mouthed, sycophantic, unctuous, compliant, deferential

Antonyms: (*adjectives*) independent; frank, candid, outspoken; self-assertive, aggressive, bumptious

Phrases: a yes man, a rubber stamp; toe the line, knuckle under to

283. **ob-ses-sion** *noun* ŏb-sĕsh´-ən *or* əb-sĕsh´-ən

[*ob* (Latin), "on" + *sedere, sessus* (Latin), "sit"]

Definition: An irrational preoccupation with an idea or feeling that usually results in severe anxiety.

Fear of falling victim to some dread disease can become such an **obsession** that it actually drives a person into a nervous breakdown.

Related Forms: (*verb*) obsess; (*adjective*) obsessive

Phrases: obsessed by a sense of one's own importance, obsessed with an idea, an obsessive need for reassurance

Synonyms: (*nouns*) compulsion, fixation, mania, phobia, hang-up

Phrases: an idée fixe; have a one-track mind; have a bee in one's bonnet, have an ax to grind, ride a hobbyhorse; a perfectionist, a monomaniac, a paranoiac, a megalomaniac, a compulsive gambler

Have a Bee in One's Bonnet

The colloquial expression *have a bee in one's bonnet* means "have some fixed idea or obsession that other people find odd or eccentric."

284. **ob-so-lete** *adjective* ŏb-sə-lēt´ *or* ŏb´-sə-lēt

[*obsolescere, obsoletus* (Latin), "grow old; wear out"]

Definition: No longer in use; outmoded.

"I'm interested in the present-day meaning of the word," I exclaimed, "not in one that has been **obsolete** for over 200 years!"

The automobile made many older forms of land transportation, such as the horse and buggy, **obsolete** almost overnight.

Phrases: an obsolete expression, obsolete equipment, an obsolete idea

Related Forms: (*nouns*) obsolescence, obsoleteness; (*adjective*) obsolescent

Usage Note:

Be careful to distinguish between *obsolete*, which indicates that something has already become outmoded, and *obsolescent*, which indicates that it is still in the process of becoming antiquated.

346

Synonyms: (*adjectives*) old-fashioned, antiquated, dated, out-of-date, passé, old hat, superannuated; archaic, defunct, extinct

Antonyms: (*adjectives*) up-to-date, new, novel, fresh, newfangled, avant-garde, ultramodern

Phrases: behind the times, past one's prime; a discontinued model, a has-been, a thing of the past; au courant, dernier cri, still on the drawing board, hot off the presses

285. of-fi-cious   *adjective*   ə-fĭsh´-əs

[*officiosus* (Latin), "dutiful"; from *officium* (Latin), "duty, obligation"]

Definition: Excessively forward in offering unwanted or unnecessary help or advice; meddlesome.

> "I'm not going to get this job done any faster," I objected, "just because you shout unnecessary instructions at me and otherwise make an **officious** nuisance of yourself."

Related Forms: (*noun*) officiousness; (*adverb*) officiously

Usage Note:
Be careful to distinguish between *officious* and *official*, which, as an adjective, means "authoritative" or "formal" and, as a noun, means "a person in authority." Of course, an official may be officious (annoyingly meddlesome), but the two words are not related in meaning.

Synonyms: (*adjectives*) intrusive; prying, nosy; forward, pushy, bossy; importunate

Phrases: a busybody, a gadfly, a self-appointed watchdog of the government

286. om-i-nous   *adjective*   ŏm´-ə-nəs

[*ominosus* (Latin), "ill-omened"; from *omen, ominis* (Latin), "sign, portent" + *osus* (Latin), "full of"]

Definition: Foreshadowing evil; menacing or threatening.

> The **ominous** silence that greeted the proposal presented by one of the members clearly foretold the plan's eventual defeat.

> If we had paid some attention to the **ominous** sounds coming from the engine, we would have not been so surprised when the car stopped dead in the middle of nowhere.

Phrases: an ominous pause, ominous clouds

Related Forms: (*nouns*) ominousness, omen; (*adverb*) ominously

Synonyms: (*adjectives*) portentous, ill-omened, foreboding, untoward, unpromising, sinister

Antonyms: (*adjectives*) lucky, happy, felicitous (Word 189), auspicious, propitious

Phrases: a bird of ill omen

287. op-por-tune   *adjective*   ŏp-ĕr-tōon´ *or* ŏp-ĕr-tyōon´

[*opportunus* (Latin), "suitable, favorable"; from the phrase *ob portum veniens* (Latin), "coming (*i.e.*, blowing) toward the harbor"; from *ob* (Latin), "to, toward" + *portus* (Latin), "harbor"]

Definition: Suitable, appropriate, or timely.

Someone with a natural sense of timing can usually select the most **opportune** moment to ask his or her boss for a raise.

Related Forms: (*nouns*) opportunity, opportunism, opportunist; (*adjectives*) inopportune, opportunistic

Usage Note:
An *opportunist* is a person who takes advantage of events to further his or her own purposes, regardless of the principles involved. Similarly, *opportunism* is the policy or practice of letting circumstance, rather than principle, dictate a person's behavior or course of action.

Synonyms: (*adjectives*) convenient, seasonable, apt, fitting, propitious, fit, auspicious, advantageous

Antonyms: (*adjectives*) inappropriate, untimely, unsuitable, ill-timed, inconvenient, inauspicious

Phrases: a timeserver, take time by the forelock

288. os-ten-si-ble   *adjective*   ŏ-stĕn´-sə-bəl

[*ostensibilis* (Medieval Latin), "apparent"; from *ob* (Latin), "before, out in front" + *tendere, tensus* (Latin), "stretch" + *abilis, abile* (Latin), "able to"]

Definition: Apparent or professed.

Though a commendable concern for the average wage earner's welfare was the **ostensible** reason for the candidate's proposal, I suspect that his real motives were more self-serving.

Related Form: (*adverb*) ostensibly

Synonyms: (*adjectives*) purported, alleged, avowed, nominal (Word 277), supposed, reputed, evident, manifest

Antonyms: (*adjectives*) true, real, actual, authentic (Word 50), genuine

289. os-tra-cize   *verb*   ŏs´-trə-sīz

[*ostrakizein* (Greek), "banish"; from *ostrakon* (Greek), "potsherd; shell"]

Definition: To banish or exclude from a group; to shun.

Once the details of his scandalous behavior became public knowledge, he found himself **ostracized** by the entire community.

Will the day ever come when Americans finally agree to **ostracize** industrial pollution of the environment, once and for all?

Related Form: (*noun*) ostracism

Synonyms: (*verbs*) expel, exile; blacklist, blackball, snub; boycott (Word 67); bar, repudiate, reject; proscribe, outlaw

Antonyms: (*verbs*) accept, welcome, embrace; associate with

Phrases: give someone the cold shoulder, cut someone dead, drum out of the army, send someone to Coventry; a pariah

Ostraka from the marketplace in Athens. Among the names that appear on these broken bits of pottery are Aristeides and Themistokles.

Ostracism

In the ancient Greek city of Athens, it became customary to banish any citizen who was considered to be dangerous to the welfare of the state. Just who should be banished was decided by voting. On the day that the vote was taken, each citizen scratched the name of the person he wished to banish on a bit of broken pottery and deposited this curious ballot in one of the official voting urns set up for the purpose. These broken pieces of crockery were called *ostraka* (singular, *ostrakon*) in Greek. They were used as ballots because great numbers of them lay scattered about the marketplace (or *agora*), where the voting took place. Once all the ballots had been cast, the officials supervising the voting sorted them out. The man who received the largest number of votes was banished from Athenian territory, usually for a period of ten years. The voting was declared invalid, however, if fewer than 6000 votes (total) were cast.

The first *ostracism*, as the Greeks called this curious "unpopularity poll," took place in 487 B.C. and the last about 416 B.C.. By the way, many famous Athenians, including Themistokles and Aristeides "the Just," two of Athens's greatest generals and statesmen, were the victims of ostracism, and no particular shame or disgrace was attached to it. In fact, ostracism became such a useful political tool that a number of other Greek city-states adopted it. In Syracuse, the institution was called *petalism*, because the names were written on olive leaves (*petala*), not potsherds.

290. pan-de-mo-ni-um   *noun*   păn-də-mō´-nē-əm

[*pas, pan* (Greek), "all" + *daimon* (Greek), "(evil) spirit; deity." For further details, see the caption and illustration on next page.]

Definition: General disorder, confusion, noise, and commotion.

When the veridct of the jury was announced, **pandemonium** broke loose in the courtroom.

The trading floor of the Commodities Exchange was a scene of unbelievable **pandemonium**, unlike anything I had ever witnessed before.

Related Form: (*adjective*) pandemoniac

Synonyms: (*nouns*) chaos, bedlam, turmoil, tumult, din, cacophony, hubbub, hullaballoo, ruckus, racket, rumpus

Antonyms: (*nouns*) order, silence, calm, tranquility, placidity, repose, peace

Phrases: raise a hue and cry, a three-ring circus, a brouhaha

291. par-a-dox   *noun*   păr´-ə-dŏks

[*paradoxos* (Greek), "incredible"; from *para* (Greek), "beyond" + *doxa* (Greek), "thought, opinion, expectation"]

Definition:
  a. A seemingly self-contradictory statement that, on closer examination, proves worthy of belief.

At some time in our lives, all of us discover the truth of the ancient **paradox** that by giving freely to others, we gain more for ourselves.

  b. Someone or something that is full of contradictions and inconsistencies.

That terrible instruments of war should in fact prove useful as guardians of the peace is one of the **paradoxes** of modern life.

Related Forms: (*adjective*) paradoxical; (*adverb*) paradoxically

Synonyms: (*nouns*) riddle, enigma, anomaly

Phrases: caught on the horns of a dilemma, a Gordian knot, an oxymoron, a contradiction in terms

Some Famous Paradoxes

Whosoever shall exalt himself shall be abased; and he that shall humble himself shall be exalted.   —The Bible

There are two tragedies in life: one is not getting what you want; the other is finding it.   —Oscar Wilde

Pandaemonium, by the 19th-century French illustrator Gustave Doré.

Pandemonium

The word *pandemonium* was originally coined by the English poet John Milton (1608–1674) as the name of the capital city of Hell, where much of the action of Milton's great epic poem *Paradise Lost* (1667) takes place. The following extract from this poem shows how Milton originally used the word also and how he spelled it:

> The rest were all
> Far to the inland retir'd, about the walls
> Of Pandaemonium, city and proud seat
> Of Lucifer. . . .
> *Paradise Lost*, X, 422–425

Milton also used the word as the name of the palace of Lucifer (or Satan), the ruler of Hell.

Later, the word came to mean Hell itself and, finally (now shorn of its capital letter and second *a*), any place that was like Hell—that is, any scene of wild commotion, general disorder, and noise. This more "extended" meaning is normally what the word denotes in present-day English.

292. par-a-phrase *verb and noun* păr´-ə-frāz

[*paraphrazein* (Greek), "restate"; from *para* (Greek), "alongside" + *phrazein* (Greek), "show, tell"]

Definition:

   a. (*verb*) To restate in other words or another form, often in order to clarify meaning or avoid difficulties.

        She didn't quote the passage verbatim; she **paraphrased** it.

   b. A restatement in other words or another form.

        Some of the most famous passages in Shakespeare's plays turn out to be loose **paraphrases** of Holinshed's *Chronicles* or North's translation of Plutarch.

Related Forms: (*adjective*) paraphrastic; (*noun*) paraphrasis

Usage Note:

Do not confuse the adjective *paraphrastic*, meaning "in the nature of a paraphrase," with the look-alike adjective *periphrastic*, which means "circumlocutory" or "roundabout."

Synonyms: (*verbs*) reword, rephrase; (*nouns*) rewording, rephrasing, free rendering, version

Antonyms: (*verbs*) quote, duplicate, reproduce; (*noun*) quotation

Phrase: a word-for-word (or literal) translation

293. pa-ro-chi-al *adjective* pə-rō´-kē-əl

[*parochia* (Latin), "parish" + *alis, ale* (Latin), "relating to"; from *paroikos* (Greek), "neighbor, Christian"; from *para* (Greek), "alongside" + *oikos* (Greek), "house"]

Definition:

   a. Located in, or supported by, a parish (a type of ecclesiatical district).

        The Roman Catholic Church maintains a system of **parochial** schools that provide students with religious instruction in addition to their regular academic education.

   b. Restricted in scope or range; narrow or limited.

        I found it hard to believe that a person who had read and traveled so extensively should have such a **parochial** outlook on life.

Related Form: (*noun*) parochialism

Usage Note:

When used of a school or school system, *parochial* is confined to establishments maintained by the Roman Catholic Church. Though other religious organizations certainly maintain schools of their own, these institutions are not normally referred to as parochial schools.

Synonyms: (*adjectives*) local, regional, district; narrow-minded, insular, provincial, hidebound, myopic

Antonyms: (*adjectives*) broad-minded, cosmopolitan, liberal

Phrase: wear blinders (or blinkers)

294. par-o-dy   *noun and verb*   păr´-ə-dē

[*paroidia* (Greek), "burlesque poem"; from *para* (Greek), "alongside; subsidiary to" + *oide* (Greek), "song, poem"]

Definition:

    a. (*noun*) A comic imitation of the style, form, or content of a serious piece of work.

        The pages of *Mad* magazine and *The National Lampoon* often contain amusing **parodies** of popular TV shows and films.

    b. (*noun*) A performance that is so bad as to constitute a mockery of the thing it is intended to represent.

        "You may call trying an innocent man on a trumped-up charge before a packed jury a trial," she replied. "I call it a **parody** of justice."

    c. (*verb*) To imitate in a mocking or unworthy way.

        Her ability to **parody** the words and gestures of prominent Americans makes her an excellent comic impressionist.

        Despite empty pronouncements about "freedom" and "justice," the government of that country does nothing more than **parody** the principles of democracy.

Related Form: (*noun*) parodist

Synonyms: (*nouns*) spoof, take-off, lampoon, caricature, burlesque, travesty, satire; (*verbs*) spoof, lampoon, satirize, mock, ridicule

Caricature

A *caricature* is a distorted representation of a person in which a characteristic physical feature, mannerism, or other peculiarity is exaggerated in order to produce a comic effect. Often certain physical features provide the focus of the caricature. Other times, the subject's style, attitudes, or ideas are the central feature, as the accompanying cartoon of Theodore Roosevelt reveals. By the way, a caricature need not be a drawing; it may also take the form of a written composition.

295. **pen-sive**   *adjective*   pĕn´-sĭv

[*pensif, pensive* (French), "thoughtful"; from *penser* (French), "think"]

Definition: Immersed in deep, often melancholy, thought.

Usually, Mary is overflowing with good cheer, but today she is rather **pensive** and withdrawn.

Related Forms: (*noun*) pensiveness; (*adverb*) pensively

Synonyms: (*adjectives*) meditative, reflective, contemplative, introspective; sad, melancholy, wistful, heavy-hearted, mournful, doleful

Antonyms: (*adjectives*) light-hearted, blithe, cheerful, gay, mirthful, merry, jocund

Phrases: mull over, ruminate on, be lost in thought

Using the Words

Exercise I. Syllabication and Pronunciation

Syllabicate the following words correctly, and place the major stress mark (´) after the syllable that is accented when the word is pronounced. Two answers are correct in one instance.

1. obsequious
2. obsolete
3. officious
4. ostensible
5. pandemonium
6. paradox
7. paraphrase
8. parochial
9. pensive

Exercise II. Words Out of Context

In each of the following groups, select the item that best expresses the meaning of the numbered word at the left.

1. obsequious   **a.** lively   **b.** courteous   **c.** deferential   **d.** vague   **e.** profitable

2. obsolete   **a.** required   **b.** insignificant   **c.** daring   **d.** costly   **e.** outmoded

3. officious   **a.** meddlesome   **b.** changeable   **c.** gigantic   **d.** exciting   **e.** clever

4. ostensible   **a.** outrageous   **b.** economical   **c.** graphic   **d.** apparent   **e.** luxurious

5. ostracize   **a.** steal   **b.** shun   **c.** seal   **d.** sham   **e.** stun

6. paradox   **a.** enigma   **b.** consensus   **c.** anathema   **d.** kudos   **e.** facsimile

7. paraphrase **a.** recall **b.** return **c.** repulse **d.** renew
   e. restate

8. pensive **a.** theoretical **b.** crucial **c.** disorderly
   d. contemplative **e.** foolhardy

Exercise III. Completing Sentences

Complete each of the following sentences by selecting the most appropriate word from the given group of words. Use each word only once. Make any adjustments that are necessary to fit the words into the sentences properly.

parody	pensive	ostracize
obsession	opportune	parochial
ominous	pandemonium	obscene

1. Today, films containing _____ language or nudity are usually given an "X" rating in order to alert potential viewers to the sensitive nature of the material presented.

2. Since I was desperately in need of funds, mom's check arrived at a most _____ moment.

3. *Omlet, the Great Dane* is both an amusing _____ of Shakespeare's *Hamlet* and an irreverent commentary on recent American politics.

4. Some of my friends went to public school; others attended private or _____ schools.

5. Somehow or another, the speaker managed to make herself heard above the _____ that reigned in the convention hall.

6. It is one thing to be concerned about punctuality; it is quite another to allow it to become a(n) _____.

7. One sight of the _____ black clouds rolling in from the west, and I knew we were in for a storm.

Exercise IV. Synonyms and Antonyms

Classify each of the following pairs of words as **S** for **synonyms** or **A** for **antonyms**.

1. bedlam—pandemonium
2. fixation—obsession
3. ominous—auspicious
4. ostensible—alleged
5. newfangled—obsolete
6. parody—lampoon
7. paraphrase—quote
8. cosmopolitan—parochial
9. obscene—smutty
10. blithe—pensive
11. ostracize—blackball
12. opportune—timely

1. With or without the aid of a dictionary, explain what each of the following means.

    a. a yes man
    b. a megalomaniac
    c. a monomaniac
    d. a has-been
    e. an opportunist
    f. a paranoiac
    g. a timeserver
    h. a perfectionist

2. With or without the aid of a dictionary, define each of the following colorful idiomatic expressions.

    a. raise a hue and cry
    b. knuckle under to
    c. wear blinders
        (or blinkers)
    d. give someone the
        cold shoulder
    e. take time by the forelock
    f. have a one-track mind

3. Explain what each of the following means. Consult a dictionary if necessary.

    a. a Gordian knot
    b. an off-color joke
    c. a rubber stamp
    d. an X-rated film

4. The following expressions have been borrowed from French. What does each mean?

    a. avant-garde   b. idée fixe   c. au courant

5. Explain the difference between the items in each of the following pairs of words.

    a. obsolete—obsolescent   b. officious—official

6. Explain the story behind the word *ostracize*. From what foreign language does it come? Name two famous statesmen who were subjected to ostracism.

Exercise VI.   Framing Sentences

A. Use each of the following words in an original illustrative sentence.

1. obsequious
2. obsolete
3. obsession
4. opportune
5. pandemonium
6. paraphrase
7. parochial
8. parody
9. pensive

B. Give a **noun** form of each of the following words, and use it in an original illustrative sentence.

1. obscene   2. ostracize   3. officious

C. Give an **adverb** form of each of these words, and use it in an original illustrative sentence.

1. ostensible   2. paradox   3. ominous

Dissecting the Words

Prefixes

1. The Latin prefix **ob** occurs, in one form or another, in a great many common English words, including *obsequious, obsession,* and *obscene,* all of which were studied in Lesson 23. This prefix has a variety of meanings, depending upon how it is used in the word in which it appears. These meanings include:

a. "To, toward," as in these words:

objective (*ob,* "to, toward" + *jacere, jactus* [Latin], "throw")—(*noun*) an aim or goal; (*adjective*) real or actual; uninfluenced by personal feeling or prejudice

obverse (*ob,* "to, toward" + *vertere, versus* [Latin], "turn")—the part of something that is turned toward the viewer; the front

b. "Against, in opposition to," as in these words:

obstacle (*ob,* "against" + *stare, status* [Latin], "stand")—someone or something that is in a person's way

obloquy (*ob,* "against" + *loqui* [Latin], "speak")—abuse; the discredit resulting from such abuse

obstruct (*ob,* "against" + *struere, structus* [Latin], "pile up")—to block, hinder, or impede. Noun: *obstruction*

obtuse (*ob,* "against" + *tundere, tu(n)sus* [Latin], "beat")—dull or blunt

c. "In front of, before," as in these words:

obsess (*ob,* "in front of, before" + *sedere, sessus* [Latin], "sit")—to haunt, harass, or bedevil. Noun: *obsession*

obstetrics (*ob,* "in front of" + *stare, status* [Latin], "stand"; in Latin a midwife was called an *obstetrix,* literally, "a woman who stands before [the bed]")—the branch of medicine dealing with care of women before, during, and just after childbirth. Adjective: *obstetric.* Noun: *obstetrician*

d. "Down, over," as in this word:

obituary (*ob,* "down, over" + *ire, itus* [Latin], "go")—a death notice

e. "Out of, away from," as in this word:

obliterate (*ob,* "out of, away from" + *littera* [Latin], "letter" + *atus* [Latin], "make, do"; in Latin the verb for "delete" was *oblitterare*)—to do away with completely. Noun: *obliteration*

f. "Completely," as in these words:

obdurate (*ob,* "completely" + *durare, duratus* [Latin], "harden")—unyielding, inflexible, or intractable

obfuscate (*ob,* "completely" + *fuscare, fuscatus* [Latin], "darken")—to darken, muddy, or confuse. Noun: *obfuscation*

oblong (*ob,* "completely" + *longus* [Latin], "long")—having one dimension (length or width) much longer than the other

2. The prefix **ob** changes form, depending upon the first letter of the root to which it is attached. These changes include the following:

a. *Ob* becomes **o** before *m*, as in this word:

   omit (*ob*, "away from" + *mittere, missus* [Latin], "send")—to leave out. Noun: *omission*

b. *Ob* becomes **oc** before *c*, as in these words:

   occident (*ob*, "down" + *cadere, casus* [Latin], "fall, go")—the west (because that is where the sun sets). Adjective: *occidental*

   occlude (*ob*, "completely" + *claudere, clausus* [Latin], "close")—to cause to close; to shut in, out, or off. Noun: *occlusion*

   occult (*ob*, "completely" + *cul(t)*, a Latin root meaning "conceal")—secret, beyond the understanding of most people

c. *Ob* becomes **of** before an *f*, as in these words:

   offend (*ob*, "against" + *fendere, fensus* [Latin], "strike")—to insult or outrage. Noun: *offense*. Adjective: *offensive*

   offer (*ob*, "to, toward" + *ferre* [Latin], "bring")—to put forward or present. Noun: *offering*

   Note, however, that *ob* remains unchanged in the word *obfuscate*, studied above.

d. *Ob* becomes **op** before *p*, as in these words:

   oppose (*ob*, "against" + *ponere, positus* [Latin], "put")—to combat or resist. Nouns: *opposition, opponent*. Adjective: *opposite*

   oppress (*ob*, "against" + *premere, pressus* [Latin], "press")—to weigh heavily on; to persecute. Adjective: *oppressive*

   opprobrium (*ob*, "against" + *probum* [Latin], "reproach")—the disgrace that arises from shameful behavior. Adjective: *opprobrious*

3. The Greek prefix **par(a)** appears in a number of useful English words, including *paradox, paraphrase, parochial,* and *parody,* all of which were studied in Lesson 23. This prefix has a number of meanings, including:

a. "Alongside, by the side of, beside," as in these words:

   parable (*parabola* [Greek], "comparison"; from *para*, "beside" + *ballein*, "throw")—a simple story of everyday life illustrating a moral or religous principle. Related noun: *parabola*

   paradigm (*paradeigma* [Greek], "model; from *para*, "alongside" + *deiknunai*, "show, exhibit")—an example or model

   paragon (*parakone* [Medieval Greek], "whetstone"; from *para*, "alongside" + *akonan*, "sharpen")—a model or pattern of excellence

   paraprofessional (*para*, "alongside"+ *professional*)—a person who is not a member of a given profession but who helps those who are

   parapsychology (*para*, "alongside" + *psychology*)—the study of phenomena that cannot be explained by known natural laws—for example, mental telepathy

   Other words in which this meaning of *para* is used include *paraplegia, paragraph, parameter, parasite,* and *parenthesis.*

b. "Beyond," as in these words:

paralogism (para, "beyond" + *logos* [Greek], "logic")—faulty or illogical reasoning

paranoia (*paranoos* [Greek], "demented"; from *para*, "beyond" + *nous*, "mind")—a mental illness characterized by delusions of being persecuted or being greater than one is. Adjective: *paranoid*. Noun: *paranoiac*

paraphernalia (*para*, "beyond" + *pherne* [Greek], "dowry")—the gear or equipment used in some activity; one's personal belongings

c. "Wrongly, harmfully," as in this word:

paralysis (*paraluein* [Greek], "disable"; from *para*, "wrongfully" + *luein*, "loosen, release")—loss or impairment of the ability to move or feel; a general stoppage of activity. Verb: *paralyze*

d. "Completely," as in this word:

paroxysm (*paroxusmos* [Greek], "irritation, stimulation"; from *para*, "completely, very" + *oxunein*, "whet, sharpen")—a sudden outburst of feeling or emotion (*e.g.*, laughter)

Note that in a few military words, such as *paratrooper*, the element *para* is not the Greek prefix but a shortened form of the word *parachute*.

Exercise

1. With or without the aid of a dictionary, define each of the following words containing the Latin prefix *ob*, and explain what the prefix means in that particular word. Then choose any **five** of the words, and, for each, compose an original illustrative sentence.

   a. obliterate
   b. oblong
   c. obloquy
   d. obviate
   e. obstruct
   f. obverse
   g. obituary
   h. obnoxious
   i. obsess
   j. obdurate
   k. obtuse
   l. obtrude

2. With or without the aid of a dictionary, define each of the following words containing the Greek prefix *para*, and explain what the prefix means in that particular word. Then choose any **five** of the words, and, for each, compose an original illustrative sentence.

   a. paranoid
   b. parabola
   c. paralyze
   d. parasite
   e. paraphernalia
   f. paroxysm
   g. parameter
   h. paraplegic
   i. paragon

3. Add the prefix *para* to each of the following English words, define the resulting combination, and explain how *para* has altered the meaning of the original word.

   a. military
   b. psychology
   c. medical
   d. professional

Working with Context Clues

Complete each of the following two-word omissions by selecting the pair of words that make the best sense in the passage as a whole. If necessary, consult a dictionary for the meaning of any word with which you are not familiar.

1. As he grew older, the Senator began to long for a life of undisturbed _____ in some quiet _____ far from the storms and stresses of the political arena.

   a. pandemonium. . . enclave
   b. litigation. . . asylum
   c. activity. . . impasse
   d. repose. . . haven

2. "As long as you listen to your advisors, you won't run any real risk of losing this election," the campaign manager told the candidate. "If you _____ them, however, you may _____ your chances of winning."

   a. ignore. . . jeopardize
   b. alienate. . . justify
   c. emulate. . . curtail
   d. heed. . . damage

3. As the storm _____ in intensity, the normally calm waters of the lake became more and more turbulent. Strong gusts of wind slapped at our sails, and our tiny craft was _____ about like a ping-pong ball in an electric blender.

   a. fluctuated. . . enticed
   b. diminished. . . coerced
   c. increased. . . buffeted
   d. augmented. . . lurked

4. Just before the wedding of Prince Charles and Lady Diana Spencer, most of Europe's remaining royalty _____ on London. Once it was over, they _____ as quickly as they had come.

   a. converged. . . departed
   b. adjourned. . . abdicated
   c. deferred. . . deleted
   d. jettisoned. . . intervened

5. It isn't wise to give very young children _____ that will break easily. Until they have learned to handle fragile items gingerly, they should be supplied with _____ playthings.

   a. dolls. . . flimsy
   b. clothes. . . compatible
   c. toys. . . durable
   d. pets. . . complicated

6. A tremendous explosion ripped through the building, reducing it to a pile of smoking _____ and shattering windows for blocks around. Great showers of sparks shot out in every direction, _____ small fires all over the area.

   a. jetsam. . . extinguishing
   b. debris. . . forestalling
   c. rubble. . . igniting
   d. incense. . . fabricating

7. "It took me months of _____ effort to extricate this company from the financial _____ in which I found it,"

he said smugly. "If I hadn't worked like a dog, the firm would still be in economic hot water."

a. occasional...morass
b. diligent...mess
c. persistent...exodus
d. futile...fiasco

8. Alexander the Great was an implacable foe of the Persians as long as they posed a _____ to Greek security. Once he had averted the danger by conquering them, however, he proved to be their most steadfast _____.

a. question...enemy
b. solution...ally
c. problem...rival
d. threat...champion

9. I had hoped that one of the _____ would make a few novel observations during the course of those TV debates that were aired just before the election. All I got, however, were the same tired old _____ that politicians have been mouthing for decades.

a. candidates...platitudes
b. reporters... malapropisms
c. moderators...fallacies
d. spectators... euphemisms

10. "I haven't had time to give your report more than a _____ glance," my boss told me. "However, I plan to _____ it carefully before we actually sit down to discuss it."

a. cursory...scrutinize
b. gratuitous...parody
c. nominal...libel
d. quick...disregard

Enriching the Lesson

Exercise I.   More of Our Greek Heritage

A number of the words studied in Lesson 23, including *ostracize* and *paradox*, are derived with very little change from Greek. Some other useful English words derived from Greek prototypes are listed below. With or without the aid of a dictionary, define each, and give its etymology. Then choose any **five** of the words, and, for each, compose an original illustrative sentence.

1. protagonist	11. polyglot	21. myth
2. spasmodic	12. toxic	22. heterogeneous
3. psychotic	13. xenophobic	23. lyric
4. tyrannical	14. phantasm	24. schism
5. polemic	15. litany	25. tragedy
6. lethargy	16. autochthonous	26. tautology
7. therapeutic	17. panoply	27. phlegmatic
8. mimic	18. metaphoric	28. kaleidoscope
9. rhetoric	19. mosaic	29. category
10. calisthenics	20. kinetic	30. periphery

Exercise II. Ecclesiastically Speaking

English is rich in words and phrases relating to the church or the clergy. One such expression, *parochial*, was studied in Lesson 23. A few others are listed below. With or without the aid of a dictionary or other reference book, define each, and give its etymology. Then choose any **five** of the items, and, for each, compose an original illustrative sentence.

1. sacrilege	6. pastoral	11. canonical
2. sacrament	7. liturgy	12. Pentecostal
3. prelate	8. ecumenical	13. theology
4. laity	9. diocese	14. rite
5. ecclesiastical	10. monastic	15. episcopal

Exercise III. Manias

A *mania* is an exaggerated or hampering obsession, a dominating preoccupation or craving that often leads to unbalanced or irrational behavior. The word *mania* forms part of many compound words that indicate particular kinds of behavior patterns. A few of these words are listed below. With or without the aid of a dictionary or other reference book, define each, and give its etymology.

1. pyromania	3. kleptomania	5. egomania
2. bibliomania	4. dipsomania	6. megalomania

Exercise IV. Expanding Your Word Power

The words listed below are not on the Basic Word List, but they were mentioned in passing, in one form or another, in Lesson 23. All of them would make useful additions to your working vocabulary. Define each, give its etymology, list **two** synonyms and **two** antonyms (where possible), and use in a short illustrative sentence.

1. salacious	6. omen	11. insular
2. unctuous	7. untimely	12. satire
3. compulsive	8. purport	13. duplicate
4. defunct	9. exile	14. portentous
5. intrusive	10. tumult	15. introspective

Lesson 24

---

296. pe-remp-to-ry   *adjective*   pə-rĕmp´-tə-rē

[*peremptorius* (Latin), "final"; from *per* (Latin), "completely" + *emere, emptus* (Latin), "buy, obtain" + *orius* (Latin), "characterized by"]

Definition:
- **a.** Having the nature of a command in that it does not allow discussion, contradiction, or refusal.

  Good supervisors soon learn that they can get more cooperation from those under them by making polite requests than by issuing **peremptory** orders.

- **b.** Determined, resolute.

  "Though we are always ready to settle our differences with other countries peacefully," the official said, "we are not afraid to make **peremptory** use of force when necessary."

- **c.** Offensively dictatorial.

  Though his manner is **peremptory** with those below him in the office hierarchy, it is obsequious with those higher up.

Related Forms: (*noun*) peremptoriness; (*adverb*) peremptorily

Synonyms: (*adjectives*) binding, obligatory, mandatory, prescriptive; categorical, unconditional, positive, emphatic, concerted; despotic, tyrannical, high-handed

Antonyms: (*adjectives*) tentative, contingent, provisional; irresolute, indecisive, hesitant; mild, unassuming, diffident

---

297. per-jure   *verb*   pĕr´-jûr

[*per* (Latin), "through; harmfully, falsely" + *jurare* (Latin), "swear"]

Definition: To lie deliberately while under oath to tell the truth.

Though there are minor inconsistencies in their testimony, there is no evidence that any of the witnesses actually **perjured** himself.

I described my reaction to his performance at the recital as favorably as I could without actually **perjuring** myself.

Related Forms: (*nouns*) perjury, perjurer; (*adjective*) perjurious

Phrases: commit perjury, perjured testimony

Synonyms: (*verbs and phrasal verbs*) bear false witness, give false testimony, forswear, prevaricate

298. per-me-ate   *verb*   pĕr´-mē-āt

[*permeare, permeatus* (Latin), "pass through"; from *per* (Latin), "through" + *meare, meatus* (Latin), "go, pass"]

Definition: To spread through; to penetrate.

Noxious fumes from the industrial accident so **permeated** the atmosphere that scores of people living nearby had to be evacuated from their homes.

"Do you think," she asked, "that present-day society is **permeated** by a loss of faith in established institutions?"

Related Forms: (*nouns*) permeation, permeability; (*adjectives*) permeable, impermeable

Synonyms: (*verbs*) pervade, infiltrate, diffuse, saturate, impregnate, imbue, filter into, seep through, soak through

Phrase: infiltrate enemy lines

299. per-ni-cious   *adjective*   pĕr-nish´-əs

[*perniciosus* (Latin), "destructive"; from *per* (Latin), "completely" + *nex, necis* (Latin), "violent death" + *osus* (Latin), "full of"]

Definition: Highly injurious or harmful.

Despite mounting medical evidence concerning the **pernicious** effects of cigarette smoking, many people categorically refuse to give up the habit.

Phrases: a pernicious influence, a pernicious practice

Related Forms: (*noun*) perniciousness; (*adverb*) perniciously

Synonyms: (*adjectives*) deleterious, detrimental, malignant, baneful, ruinous, destructive

Antonyms: (*adjectives*) wholesome, beneficial, salutary, salubrious

300. per-se-vere   *verb*   pĕr-sə-vîr´

[*perseverare* (Latin), "persist"; from *per* (Latin), "thoroughly" + *severus* (Latin), "serious, in earnest"]

Definition: To continue steadfastly despite obstacles or discouragment.

The old saying, "If at first you don't succeed, try, try again," encourages all of us to **persevere** in whatever we undertake.

Related Forms: (*noun*) perseverance; (*adjective*) persevering

Synonyms: (*verbs*) persist, endure, plug away at

Antonyms: (*verbs*) quit, desist, give up on, abandon

Phrases: stick something out, stop at nothing to achieve a goal, stick to one's guns; throw in the towel

364

301. pho·bi·a   *noun*   fō´-bē-ə

[*phobos* (Greek), "fear, flight" + *-ia* (Greek), "state of"]

Definition: An intense irrational fear of something; any strong aversion.

She attributed her pronounced **phobia** for dogs to the fact that she was nipped on the finger by an overly defensive collie when she was a child.

The legislator warned that we must not allow our natural concern for security to develop into an obsessive **phobia** for foreigners.

Related Form: (*adjective*) phobic

Usage Note:

Phobia often appears in compound words indicating particular kinds of fears or aversions. For example, *claustrophobia* (*claustrum* [Latin], "enclosed place" + *phobia*) is the proper term for an irrational fear of small, tightly enclosed places. The related word element *-phobe*, meaning "one who fears or dislikes," also appears in such words. For example, a *Francophobe* is a person who dislikes the French and all things relating to them. Note that *-phobe* is only used as a combining form, not as an independent word.

    The Greek suffixes *-philia*, meaning "a liking or attraction for," and *-phil(e)* or *-philiac*, meaning "one who has a liking for or is attracted to," are the "antonyms" of *phobia* and *-phobe*. For example, a philosopher is someone who loves (*philos* [Greek], "loving, liking") the truth (*sophia* [Greek], "truth"). Similarly, *necrophilia* is the technical name for a morbid attraction to dead bodies (*necros* [Greek], "corpse"). Note that *-philia*, *-phil(e)*, and *-philiae* are only used as combining forms, not as independent words.

Synonyms: (*nouns*) dread (of), horror (of), aversion (to), distaste (for), abhorrence (of), antipathy (for), loathing (for)

Antonyms: (*nouns*) liking (for), taste (for), partiality (for), fondness (for), affinity (for), predilection (for)

Phrases: have a soft spot in one's heart for; have no stomach for

302. pla·gia·rism   *noun*   plā´-jə-rĭz-əm

[*plagiarius* (Latin), "kidnapper"; from *plaga* (Latin), "net"]

Definition: The use of another person's writings or ideas as one's own without acknowledging their source.

"No one is going to accuse you of **plagiarism**," the editor told the fledgling author, "just because a couple of paragraphs in a very long novel are vaguely reminiscent of Hemingway."

Far from being a "retelling" of one of O. Henry's best-loved short stories, as the author claims, the work is an outright **plagiarism**.

Related Forms: (*verb*) plagiarize; (*nouns*) plagiary, plagiarist, plagiarizer

Synonyms: (*nouns*) theft, piracy

Phrases: literary piracy, an infringement of copyright, a crib

303. plain·tive   *adjective*   plān´-tĭv

[*plaintif, plaintive* (Old French), "sorrowful"; from *plangere, planctus* (Latin), "lament"]

Definition: Sorrowful or melancholy; mournful.

She closed her recital with a **plaintive** little Scottish ditty entitled "The Exile's Lament."

The **plaintive** moaning of a distant foghorn accorded well with the regret I felt in my heart at leaving that fair city forever.

Related Forms: (*nouns*) plaint, plaintiveness; (*adverb*) plaintively

Phrases: the plaintive tones of an oboe, the plaintive cry of an orphan

Synonyms: (*adjectives*) doleful, dolorous, disconsolate, lachrymose, wistful, heartbroken, tearful, lugubrious

Antonyms: (*adjectives*) merry, jocund, cheerful, light-hearted

Phrase: shed crocodile tears

Jeremiah

Jeremiad

In modern English, a long, involved lament is sometimes called a *jeremiad*. This word has an interesting origin. It is based on the name Jeremiah. Jeremiah (*ca.* 628–586 B.C.), as you may recall, was one of the major prophets of the Old Testament and the author, among other things, of a book of moving poems mourning the destruction of Jerusalem by the Babylonians. As a result, Jeremiah became associated with the elegiac mood, and this in turn gave rise to the use of a word based on his name for any kind of lengthy lament or tale of woe.

304. pleth-o-ra   *noun*   plĕth´-ə-rə

[*plethora* (Greek), "fullness"; from *plethein* (Greek), "be full"]

Definition: Superabundance or excess.

As usual, we got a **plethora** of advice about what to do but precious little help doing it.

Phrases: a plethora of ideas, a plethora of letters, a plethora of food and drink

Synonyms: (*nouns*) profusion, welter, superfluity, glut, surplus, surfeit, deluge, avalanche

Antonyms: (*nouns*) scarcity, paucity, dearth, shortage, lack, want

Phrases: give something short shrift, a shortfall

In 1750, the poet Thomas Gray (1716–1771) published one of the most poignant poems in the English language, "Elegy Written in a Country Churchyard."

305. poign-ant   *adjective*   poin´-yənt

[*poignant*, present participle of *poindre* (Old French), "sting"; from *pungere* (Latin), "puncture, sting"]

Definition: Keenly touching or moving.

Though the play was essentially a comedy, it nevertheless contained a **poignant** moment or two.

"Few people can imagine," the old woman observed, "just how **poignant** a feeling it is for me to revisit the scenes of my childhood and summon up again the vanished faces of those with whom I spent it."

Related Forms: (*nouns*) poignancy, poignance; (*adverb*) poignantly

Synonyms: (*adjectives*) heartbreaking, tender, heart-rending, wistful, affecting, melancholy, elegiac, bittersweet

Antonyms: (*adjectives*) unaffecting; bland, vapid, insipid

367

306. pre-car-i-ous   *adjective*   prĭ-kâr´-ē-əs

[*precarius* (Latin), "dependent upon prayer or entreaty"; from *prex, precis* (Latin), "prayer, entreaty" + *arius* (Latin), "relating to"]

Definition: Dangerously insecure, unstable, or uncertain.

Some of the firefighters battled the blaze from a **precarious** perch atop a mobile crane called a "cherry picker."

Even with the help of modern life-support systems, a premature baby's hold on life is often **precarious**.

Related Forms: (*noun*) precariousness; (*adverb*) precariously

Synonyms: (*adjectives*) perilous, hazardous, risky, treacherous; dubious, touch-and-go, ticklish, touchy, delicate

Antonyms: (*adjectives*) safe, secure, stable, firm, certain, impregnable

Phrases: skate on thin ice, walk a tightrope, hang by a thread, out on a limb, a sword of Damocles

307. pre-co-cious   *adjective*   prĭ-kō´-shəs

[*praecox, praecocis* (Latin), "ripening before its time"; from *prae* (Latin), "before" + *coquere, coctus* (Latin), "cook, boil"]

Definition: Developing unusually early.

Wolfgang Amadeus Mozart was a **precocious** youngster who wrote his first opera at the age of eleven.

Given the kinds of tools the Egyptians had to work with, raising the pyramids constituted an extraordinarily **precocious** feat of engineering.

Related Forms: (*nouns*) precociousness, precocity; (*adverb*) precociously

Phrases: at a precocious age, a precocious achievement

Synonyms: (*adjectives*) forward, gifted; advanced; premature

Antonyms: (*adjectives*) backward, retarded; underdeveloped; laggard

Phrases: a child prodigy; a late bloomer

308. pred-a-to-ry   *adjective*   prĕd´-ə-tô-rē

[*praedari, praedatus* (Latin), "plunder, pillage" + *orius* (Latin), "characterized by"; from *praeda* (Latin), "booty"]

Definition: Preying on, plundering, or piratical.

Though many other **predatory** creatures prefer to hunt at night, lions and leopards are active during the daytime.

Karl Marx viewed capitalists as an essentially **predatory** class of people because he felt that they lived off the labor of others.

Related Forms: (*nouns*) predator, predatoriness

Predators like this mountain lion still inhabit the less settled areas of the Western United States, where they prey on deer, horses, cattle, and other animals.

Synonyms: (*adjectives*) marauding, pillaging, looting; rapacious, voracious, avaricious, extortionate

Phrases; prey on, despoil the land of its resources, pirate a novel, a harpy, cannibalize a manuscript

309. pre-lude *noun* prā′-lōod *or* prĕl′-yōod
[*prae* (Latin), "before" + *ludere, lusus* (Latin), "play"]

Definition: An introductory piece of music; anything that precedes or introduces something else.

The **prelude** to the third act of Verdi's *La Traviata* is one of the most poignant pieces of music I have ever heard.

In Winston Churchill's view, the rearmament of Germany in the 1930s could only be construed as the **prelude** to aggression.

Synonyms: (*nouns*) overture, prologue, preface, curtain raiser

Antonyms: (*nouns*) postlude, epilogue, aftermath, sequel

Phrases: lay the groundwork for, a dress rehearsal

310. pre-mise   *noun and verb*   prĕm´-ĭs

[*prae* (Latin), "before, ahead" + *mittere, missus* (Latin), "send"]

Definition:

　a.　(*noun*) A statement upon which an argument is based or from which a conclusion is drawn.

　　Your suggestion that you be given the lead in the school play is based on the totally unrealistic **premise** that you are the most talented actor available.

　b.　(*verb*) To state or assume as the basis for something else; to offer in advance as an explanation of, or introduction to, something else.

　　Much of the judge's thinking is **premised** on the proposition that, in the eyes of the law, all people are equal.

　　"Let me **premise** my remarks tonight," the speaker said, "with a bit of personal history that will explain why I feel so strongly about certain subjects."

Usage Note:

When used in the plural, *premise* also indicates a building or residence, including the land upon which it stands or which is immediately adjacent to it. This use of the word occurs in such phrases as "vacate the *premises*" and "on the *premises*."

Synonyms:　(*nouns*) proposition, axiom, thesis, hypothesis, assumption; (*verbs*) preface, introduce; posit, predicate; presuppose

Using the Words

Exercise I.　Parts of Speech

Indicate the part of speech of each of the following words. In one case, two answers are correct.

1.　peremptory	4.　plethora	7.　predatory
2.　pernicious	5.　poignant	8.　prelude
3.　plagiarism	6.　precocious	9.　premise

Exercise II.　Words in Phrases

In each of the following groups, select the item that best expresses the meaning of the *italicized* word in the introductory phrase.

1.　a *peremptory* tone of voice
　　a. hopeful　b. dictatorial　c. jubilant　d. discouraged

2.　now *permeates* our system of justice
　　a. makes better　b. investigates　c. spreads through
　　d. ignores

3. a *pernicious* influence on society
   a. harmful   b. lasting   c. superficial   d. wholesome

4. *persevere* despite all obstacles
   a. die out   b. carry on   c. pull down   d. give up

5. the *plaintive* notes of an oboe
   a. merry   b. melodious   c. majestic   d. mournful

6. a *plethora* of problems
   a. shortage   b. creator   c. deluge   d. solver

7. a *poignant* memory
   a. bittersweet   b. remarkable   c. vague   d. amusing

8. *predatory* bands of Vikings
   a. enormous   b. unexpected   c. friendly   d. piratical

Exercise III.   Completing Sentences

Complete each of the following sentences by selecting the most appropriate word from the given group of words. Use each word only once. Make any adjustments that are necessary to fit the words into the sentences properly.

perjure	precarious	persevere
pernicious	precocious	prelude
premise	phobia	plagiarism

1. My most recent acquisition is a two-record set of overtures and _____ to famous Italian operas.

2. "With a great team like the Islanders breathing down our necks," the Rangers' star goalie observed, "our hold on first place in the Patrick Division can only be described as _____."

3. Over the years, her childhood fear of the dark developed into a serious and debilitating _____.

4. The judge instructed the jury to disregard the witness's testimony after the D.A. proved that the man had _____ himself while on the stand.

5. "Your conclusion is clearly invalid," I replied, "simply because it is based on a false _____."

6. She was a gifted youngster who started to go to college at the _____ age of 15.

7. Though the United States subscribes to an international system of copyright laws designed to protect writers from _____ and other forms of literary piracy, the Soviet Union does not.

Exercise IV. Synonyms and Antonyms

A. In each of the following groups, select the **two** words that are most nearly **synonyms**.

1. a. pervade b. esteem c. saturate d. blemish e. resolve
2. a. intelligence b. reward c. aversion d. antipathy
   e. fondness
3. a. unassuming b. piratical c. sensible d. tarnished
   e. plundering
4. a. treacherous b. wistful c. melancholy d. feminine
   e. obvious
5. a. glut b. request c. scarcity d. honor e. profusion

Now, for each pair of synonyms you have selected, supply a word from the Basic Word List for Lesson 24 (Words 296–310) that means **the same** or **almost the same** thing.

B. In each of the following, select the item that is most nearly **opposite** in meaning to the numbered word at the left.

1. persevere   a. cling b. repair c. quit d. increase
                  e. steal

2. plaintive   a. wooden b. merry c. puzzling d. silent
                  e. thoughtful

3. prelude   a. anathema b. epilogue c. facsimile
                  d. euphemism e. impasse

4. pernicious   a. wholesome b. partial c. ruinous
                  d. shabby e. tentative

5. precarious   a. delicate b. envious c. pompous
                  d. illegal e. secure

Exercise V. Word Roundup

1. The expression *a peremptory challenge* is frequently used in the courtroom. What does it mean?
2. What is *claustrophobia*? a *Francophobe*?
3. Define a *jeremiad*. What is the origin of this word?
4. With or without the aid of a dictionary, define each of the following colorful idiomatic expressions.

   a. throw in the towel   c. skate on thin ice
   b. stick to one's guns   d. shed crocodile tears

5. With or without the aid of a dictionary, define each of the following useful terms.

   a. a child prodigy   c. a late bloomer
   b. a shortfall   d. a curtain raiser

Exercise VI. Framing Sentences

A. Use each of the following words in an original sentence.

1. peremptory	5. phobia	9. poignant
2. permeate	6. plagiarize	10. precocious
3. pernicious	7. plaintive	11. prelude
4. precarious	8. plethora	12. premise

B. Give a **noun** form of each of the following words, and use it in an original illustrative sentence.

1. persevere   2. predatory   3. perjure

Completing Verbal Analogies

Complete each of the following analogies.

Group A

1. **durable : long life ::**
   a. unison : great variety
   b. elite : great wisdom
   c. impecunious : great wealth
   d. prodigious : great size
   e. capricious : great reliability

2. **veer : away ::**
   a. inflate : down
   b. revert : back
   c. compress : apart
   d. proceed : sideways
   e. decline : forward

3. **rabbit : burrow ::**
   a. lion : den
   b. horse : lair
   c. nest : bird
   d. cow : bovine
   e. dog : manger

4. **kindle : extinguish ::**
   a. jeopardize : hazard
   b. instigate : repress
   c. parody : ostracize
   d. perjure : prevaricate
   e. allot : spare

5. **plod : slow ::**
   a. browse : fast
   b. dash : slow
   c. scurry : fast
   d. dawdle : fast
   e. sprint : slow

Group B

6. **fruitless : result =**
   a. heartless : skill
   b. tactless : merit
   c. value : priceless
   d. tireless : energy
   e. aimless : purpose

7. **sweater : attire =**
   a. sword : weapon
   b. horse : tether
   c. scavenger : jackal
   d. will : legacy
   e. mammoth : fetish

8. **thin : gaunt =**
   a. clear : cryptic
   b. lush : nebulous
   c. haughty : meek
   d. big : mammoth
   e. ominous : pensive

9. **officious : unfavorable =**
   a. obsequious : favorable
   b. astute : unfavorable
   c. precocious : favorable
   d. lucrative : unfavorable
   e. narcissistic : favorable

10. **scoff : contempt =**
    a. vex : enjoyment
    b. rue : sorrow
    c. happiness : elate
    d. lament : levity
    e. meditate : anger

Working with Context Clues

Complete each of the following two-word omissions by selecting the pair of words that make the best sense in the passage as a whole. If necessary, consult a dictionary for the meaning of any word with which you are not familiar. Indicate the clue or clues that led you to choose your answer.

1. At one point in last night's hockey game, home-team fans became so angry with the referee that they began to _____ him with refuse. Programs, paper cups, and even a dead fish _____ through the air and landed at his feet.

   a. singe...gushed
   b. pelt...hurtled
   c. coddle...trickled
   d. shower...plodded

2. Since I was the only one in the crowd who had actually seen the accident happen, the police officer decided to _____ me first. I tried to _____ each of his queries as truthfully and accurately as possible.

   a. arrest...rebuff
   b. interrogate...frame
   c. question...answer
   d. charge...recompense

3. When I was very young, I _____ a life of adventure and excitement. Now that I'm middle-aged, however, I am perfectly content with my rather _____ existence.

   a. yearned for...humdrum
   b. abstained from... arduous
   c. indulged in...hazardous
   d. brooded about... complicated

4. Strong winds fanned the flames, and the _____ quickly spread to adjacent buildings. Though the firefighters worked hard to _____ its progress, the blaze soon engulfed the entire block.

   a. holocaust. . .facilitate
   b. conflagration. . .retard
   c. avalanche. . .impede
   d. deluge. . .ignore

5. The old adage that "clothes often _____ the man" simply means that a person's _____ is frequently a kind of public statement about his or her personality or position in life.

   a. impoverish. . .gait
   b. suit. . .visage
   c. conceal. . .demeanor
   d. proclaim. . .attire

6. At first, I was perfectly content to do the rather menial _____ that my job entailed; but as time went on, I became thoroughly _____ with such undemanding and often unpleasant assignments.

   a. hours. . .elated
   b. duties. . .satisfied
   c. tasks. . .disgruntled
   d. wages. . .obsessed

7. "That rock group's strange antics, _____ costumes, and weird songs really don't impress me," Clara remarked. "Frankly, I prefer _____ who are more conventional."

   a. outlandish. . .musicians
   b. whimsical. . .spectators
   c. melancholy. . .specialists
   d. bizarre. . .novelists

8. The speaker did not _____ many examples to back up her argument, but those she did provide were extremely well chosen. A larger but less _____ selection of illustrations would probably not have made such a powerful impression on the audience.

   a. devise. . .inane
   b. entertain. . .ungainly
   c. assemble. . .outdated
   d. cite. . .judicious

9. "Though I'd spent all my life on a farm, I didn't think I'd have any real trouble adjusting to city life," Ann said. "Making the _____ to a(n) _____ environment, however, proved far more difficult than I had imagined."

   a. regression. . .maritime
   b. adaptation. . .rural
   c. transition. . .urban
   d. detour. . .colonial

10. Acquiring a foreign language can be a particularly _____ chore because it involves so much _____. If a person didn't have to learn almost everything by rote, the task would be a good deal less arduous.

   a. exasperating. . .reading
   b. onerous. . .memorizing
   c. tiresome. . .writing
   d. tedious. . .speaking

Enriching the Lesson

Exercise I. Common Phobias

It is a rare human being indeed who does not have some kind of personal anxiety or phobia. Listed below are the technical terms for a number of these peculiarities. With or without the aid of an unabridged dictionary, define each and give its etymology. Then choose any **five**, and, for each, compose an original illustrative sentence.

1. ailurophobia
2. monophobia
3. hydrophobia
4. acrophobia
5. agoraphobia
6. xenophobia
7. gynephobia
8. nyctophobia
9. Anglophobia
10. bibliophobia
11. triskaidekaphobia
12. cynophobia
13. arachnephobia
14. keraunophobia
15. ophidiophobia

Exercise II. Words Based on *Philos*

English has a group of words based on the Greek root **philos**, meaning "loving" or "dear." A number of these expressions are listed below. With or without the aid of a dictionary, define each, and give its etymology.

1. philosophy
2. philatelist
3. Francophile
4. hemophilia
5. philanthropy
6. philology
7. philharmonic
8. discophile
9. Anglophile
10. philander

Exercise III. A Verbal Diversion

Modern English contains a good many adjectives that refer to members of the animal kingdom. Some of these words are sometimes applied to individual human beings to indicate that they are the possessors of whatever characteristics are associated with that particular animal. A few of these adjectives are listed below. With or without the aid of a dictionary, define each, or name the animal to which it refers. Also give any figurative or "extended" meanings the word may have.

1. feline
2. canine
3. equine
4. bovine
5. leonine
6. vulpine
7. lupine
8. leporine
9. ovine
10. elephantine
11. porcine
12. pavonine
13. serpentine
14. ursine
15. simian
16. taurine
17. piscine
18. anserine

Exercise IV. Colorful Phrases

A number of colorful phrases usually employed in a figurative or metaphorical sense are listed below. With or without the aid of a dictionary or other reference book, define or explain each. Then choose any **five**, and, for each, compose an original illustrative sentence.

1. look a gift horse in the mouth
2. a dog in the manger
3. lose face
4. rob Peter to pay Paul
5. call someone on the carpet
6. rest on one's laurels
7. a snake in the grass
8. put all one's eggs in one basket
9. split hairs
10. pocket one's pride
11. pay through the nose for
12. fly off the handle
13. in a nutshell
14. live from hand to mouth
15. buy a pig in a poke
16. put something on a back burner

Exercise V. Expanding Your Word Power

The words listed below are not on the Basic Word List, but they were mentioned in one form or another in Lesson 24. All of them would make useful additions to your working vocabulary. Define each, give its etymology, list **two** synonyms and **two** antonyms (where possible), and use in a short illustrative sentence.

1. contingent
2. categorical
3. despotic
4. imbue
5. salubrious
6. desist
7. affinity
8. lugubrious
9. surfeit
10. elegiac
11. impregnable
12. pillage
13. aftermath
14. hypothesis
15. posit

Lesson 25

---

311. pre-rog-a-tive   *noun*   prĭ-rŏg´-ə-tĭv

[*praerogativus* (Latin), "asked to vote first"; from *prae* (Latin), "before" + *rogare*, *rogatus* (Latin), "ask"]

Definition: A special right or privilege that belongs to a person or group by virtue of rank, position, or the like.

In republican Rome, election to the consulship came to be the special **prerogative** of a tiny group of noble families belonging to the senatorial order.

Synonyms: (*nouns*) perquisite, advantage, benefit, birthright

312. pro-bi-ty   *noun*   prō´-bə-tē

[*probitas* (Latin), "honesty, uprightness"; from *probus* (Latin), "honest, upright, virtuous" + *-itas, -itatis* (Latin), "state of"]

Definition: Unquestionable honesty or uprightness.

True **probity** is not just the absence of deceit; it is a positive passion for behaving honorably and speaking the truth.

"The **probity** of his financial dealings has been called into question," I replied, "not their profitableness."

Synonyms: (*nouns*) integrity, rectitude, ethicality, righteousness, honorableness, decency

Antonyms: (*nouns*) unscrupulousness, underhandedness, shadiness, knavery, chicanery, skulduggery

Phrases: a man or woman of principle, sharp practice, moral fiber

313. pro-cras-ti-nate   *verb*   prō-krăs´-tə-nāt

[*procrastinare, procrastinatus* (Latin), "put off until tomorrow"; from *pro* (Latin), "forward" + *cras* (Latin), "tomorrow"]

Definition: To delay action.

"We must do something about the problem now," the Congresswoman declared. "The longer we **procrastinate**, the worse the situation will become."

Related Forms: (*nouns*) procrastination, procrastinator

378

Synonyms: (*verbs*) postpone, shilly-shally, dilly-dally, temporize, stall

Antonyms: (*verbs and phrases*) act (on), take action (on), settle, decide, dispose of, take care of

Phrases: play a waiting game, table (or shelve) a bill, put something on ice (or in cold storage), mark time, keep in a holding pattern, drag one's feet about, let something hang fire

314. pro-di-gious *adjective* prə-dĭj´-əs

[*prodigium* (Latin), "omen, marvel" + *osus* (Latin), "full of"]

Definition: Extraordinary in size or extent; marvelous.

Cleaning up after the flood was such a **prodigious** task that everyone in the town was needed to complete it.

Lord Macaulay, the English historian and essayist, had such a **prodigious** memory that he had a clear recollection of every book he had ever read.

Phrases: a prodigious appetite, a prodigious effort

Related Forms: (*nouns*) prodigiousness, prodigy; (*adverb*) prodigiously

Synonyms: (*adjectives*) tremendous, stupendous, mammoth (Word 263), vast, gargantuan, immense, massive, enormous; phenomenal, fabulous, incredible, wondrous

Antonyms: (*adjectives*) puny, tiny, minute, trivial, minuscule, negligible, infinitesimal; unexceptional, undistinguished, unimpressive, mediocre

Phrases: a herculean task, a gargantuan appetite

315. pro-lif-er-ate *verb* prō-lĭf´-ə-rāt

[*proles, prolis* (Latin), "offspring" + *ferre* (Latin), "bear" + *ate*, English verb-forming suffix]

Definition: To increase rapidly in size or abundance.

In this city, fast-food shops like McDonald's and Wendy's have **proliferated** at a tremendous rate in recent years.

It was almost a law of ancient Roman historical writing that where the facts were few, fictions **proliferated**.

Recently, the United States and the Soviet Union have negotiated a treaty designed to prevent the uncontrolled **proliferation** of some types of nuclear weaponry.

Related Forms: (*noun*) proliferation; (*adjective*) prolific

Synonyms: (*verbs*) burgeon, snowball, mushroom, thrive, multiply, spread, prosper, flourish, expand, escalate, accelerate

Antonyms: (*verbs*) decline, diminish, wane, taper off, decrease, peter out, subside, dwindle

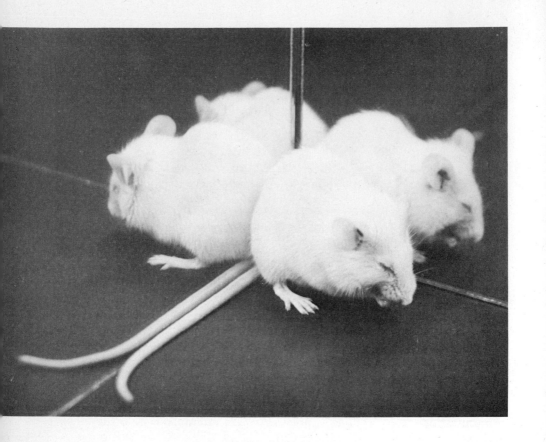

Clones and Cloning

The word *clone* (a derivative of the Greek *klon*, meaning "twig") comes from modern biological theory but has been popularized to a degree by both the social sciences and science fiction. A *clone* is a group of organisms (plants or animals) that come from a single parent and that receive exactly the same genetic makeup. Thus, all the members of the clone are, in effect, identical copies of one another. Indeed, they may be regarded, in a sense, as aspects of the same individual.

Cloning (the production of clones) has been associated thus far mainly with plants, by such processes as grafting and budding. Hence the derivation from the word for "twig." However, the process has also been used successfully with mice (see photo), and there is at least the theoretical possibility of using new techniques to produce clones of the higher animals, including humans. Science fiction writers have already given us stories about whole communities made up of genetically identical persons derived from the development of a single egg cell. Such a grouping would presumably be the ultimate in homogeneity and absence of social conflicts. Sociologists have speculated about the possibility of population planning based on these techniques.

Is the prospect of human clones a promise or a nightmare? This is a question you will have to answer for yourself. Meanwhile, the word *clone*, once used by biological specialists, is bound to come into more widespread use.

316. prom-ul-gate   *verb*   prŏm´-əl-gāt

[*promulgare, promulgatus* (Latin), "publish"; possibly from *pro* (Latin), "before, in front of" + *vulgus* (Latin), "common people, crowd"]

Definition: To announce officially, as a law or decree.

What good will it do to **promulgate** new reforms if we lack the resouces and the will to make them a reality?

Related Forms: (*nouns*) promulgation, promulgator

Synonyms: (*verbs*) proclaim, decree, broadcast, publish, disseminate

Antonyms: (*verbs*) conceal, keep secret

Phrases: issue a ukase, speak ex cathedra

317. pro-pen-si-ty   *noun*   prə-pĕn´-sə-tē

[*propendere, propensus* (Latin), "be inclined to" + *-itas, -itatis* (Latin), "state of"; from *pro* (Latin), "in the direction of" + *pendere* (Latin), "lean, hang"]

Definition: A natural tendency or inclination.

Someone who has a **propensity** for saying the wrong thing at the wrong time might be described as a victim of foot-in-mouth disease.

Synonyms: (*nouns*) penchant (for), proclivity (toward), capacity (for), predilection (for), bent (for), gift (for), genius (for), preference (for), fondness (for)

Antonyms: (*nouns*) aversion (to), repugnance (for), disinclination (to), antipathy (to); immunity (to)

Phrases: accident-prone, be allergic to something

318. pro-pi-ti-ate   *verb*   prō-pĭsh´-ē-āt

[*propitiare, propitiatus* (Latin), "appease"; from *propitius* (Latin), "favorable" + *-are, -atus* (Latin), a verb-forming suffix roughly meaning "make"]

Definition: To appease or pacify.

Before they set out, the hunters of the Ice Age performed ceremonies designed to **propitiate** the spirits of the animals they would slay.

Try as I might, I could not **propitiate** my wrathful father for having wrecked the family car.

Related Forms: (*nouns*) propitiation, propitiator; (*adjective*) propitiatory

Synonyms: (*verbs*) mollify, placate, conciliate

Antonyms: (*verbs*) antagonize, alienate (Word 21), exasperate, vex, anger, annoy, incense (Word 235)

Phrases: pour oil on troubled waters, hold out an olive branch, make one's peace with, defuse a situation, a scapegoat (Word 356)

319. pro-tract-ed   *adjective*   prō-trăk´-tĭd

[*protrahere, protractus* (Latin), "prolong, extend"; from *pro* (Latin), "forth, out" + *trahere, tractus* (Latin), "drag, draw"]

Definition: Extended or prolonged excessively.

Three great military blunders were responsible for turning World War I into a **protracted** struggle that neither side could win without outside help.

Related Forms: (*verb*) protract; (*nouns*) protraction, protractor

Synonyms: (*adjectives*) drawn-out, elongated; interminable, endless, long-winded

Antonyms: (*adjectives*) contracted, compressed, truncated, brief, fore-shortened, curtailed

---

320. prow-ess   *noun*   prou´-ĭs

[*proesse* (Old French), "valor"; from *prou* (Old French), "brave"]

Definition: Superior courage, ability, or skill.

In World War I, Sergeant Alvin York of Tennessee received this country's highest decorations for his extraordinary feats of **prowess** on the battlefields of France.

Annie Oakley's **prowess** with a rifle became legendary, even in her own time.

Synonyms: (*nouns*) valor, gallantry, daring, bravery, intrepidity; mettle, pluck; expertise, facility, proficiency

Antonyms: (*nouns*) cowardice, timidity; incompetence, ineptitude

Phrases: feats of derring-do, a tour de force, a paladin

---

321. pseu-do-nym   *noun*   sōō´-də-nĭm

[*pseudonumos* (Greek), "having a false name"; from *pseudes* (Greek), "false" + *onuma, onoma* (Greek), "name"]

Definition: A fictitious name assumed by an author.

"Mark Twain," the **pseudonym** of Samuel Langhorne Clemens, is actually a Mississippi riverboat expression relating to the measurement of water depths.

Since the Victorians didn't think it "proper" for a lady to write novels, many women published their works under masculine **pseudonyms**.

Related Form: (*adjective*) pseudonymous

Synonyms: (*nouns and noun phrases*) pen name, nom de plume, alias

George Sand

Mark Twain

Voltaire

George Eliot

Each of the famous authors pictured on this page wrote under a **pseudonym**. Find out their real names.

322. purge   *verb and noun*   pûrj

[*purgare* (Latin), "cleanse"; from *purus* (Latin), "pure" + *agere* (Latin), "lead, do, make"]

Definition:
> a. (*verb*) To cleanse or purify, especially to rid a group of undesirable elements.
>
>> "The only way you can **purge** yourself of a charge of contempt," the judge admonished the refractory witness, "is to begin cooperating with this court."
>>
>> On the bloody "Night of the Long Knives," June 26, 1934, Adolf Hitler **purged** the Nazi Party of anyone who might threaten his position as absolute master of Germany.
>
> b. (*noun*) A medicine that cleanses; the elimination of undesirable elements from a group.
>
>> Until relatively recent times, doctors frequently used strong **purges** designed to cure illness by removing impurities from the body.
>>
>> During the bloody **purges** of the 1930's, Josef Stalin "liquidated" all opposition to his rule, ideas, and methods.

Related Forms: (*nouns*) purgation, purgatory, purgative; (*adjective*) purgatorial; (*verb*) expurgate

Synonyms: (*verbs*) flush out; eject, expel, liquidate, exterminate, weed out; expiate, clear; (*nouns*) physic, laxative; pogrom

Phrases: wipe the slate clean, make a clean sweep of, a witch-hunt, a catharsis

Usage Note:
A *pogrom* (from the Russian phrase meaning "like thunder") is an organized massacre or persecution of a minority group, especially the Jews.

323. pu-sil-lan-i-mous   *adjective*   pyōō-sə-lăn´-ə-məs

[*pusillus* (Latin), "very small or weak" + *animus* (Latin), "soul, spirit"]

Definition: Contemptibly cowardly or mean-spirited.

> Most people regarded the government's attempt to avert a war by buying off the aggressor as not only shameful but **pusillanimous** as well.
>
> He characterizes his behavior during the recent crisis as circumspect; I call it **pusillanimous**.

Related Forms: (*noun*) pusillanimity; (*adverb*) pusillanimously

Synonyms: (*adjectives*) timid, timorous, frightened, fearful, spineless, gutless, lily-livered, faint-hearted

Antonyms: (*adjectives*) bold, daring, intrepid, courageous, spirited, dynamic, forceful

Phrases: have spunk; afraid of one's own shadow

A portrait of Dante Alighicri by Domenico di Francesco

Purgatory

In Roman Catholic theology, the term *Purgatory* indicates a temporary condition or state of the soul in the afterlife. It is in Purgatory that the souls of those who have died in grace and are eventually destined to enter Heaven are purged (through suffering) of whatever spiritual impurities still remain. The nature and length of this suffering varies, and the punishment is different from that of the souls in Hell. One of the most interesting descriptions of Purgatory is contained in the *Purgatorio* (Purgatory), which is the second part of the medieval Italian poet Dante Alighieri's long epic poem on salvation, *La Commedia Divina* (The Divine Comedy). It is from its connection with the theology of the afterlife that the modern English word *purgatory* (with a small *p*) has taken on the extended meaning of "any place or condition of prolonged misery and suffering."

---

324. quell   *verb*   kwĕl

[*cwellan* (Old English), "kill"]

Definition: To bring to an end, usually by force; to quiet or pacify.

When the handful of police officers who were on the scene were unable to **quell** the riot, reinforcements were called in.

A few kind words is often all it takes to **quell** a child's fears and soothe his or her anguished spirit.

Synonyms: (*verbs*) suppress, extinguish, subdue, stamp out, quash, squelch, crush, put down; silence, calm, allay, assuage

Antonyms: (*verbs*) instigate (Word 241), foment, provoke, incite, kindle; enflame, arouse, stir up

Phrases: put the kibosh on, incite to riot, an agent provocateur, a peacemaker

385

Pablo Picasso's famous painting of Don Quixote and Sancho Panza

325. quix·ot·ic   *adjective*   kwĭk-sŏt′-ĭk

[After Don Quixote, the main character in the Renaissance Spanish writer Miguel de Cervantes's famous novel of the same name]

Definition: High-minded but impractical.

The 1920's saw the passage of several important pieces of federal legislation, including a **quixotic** scheme to prohibit the sale and use of alcohol.

Related Form: (*adverb*) quixotically

Usage Note:
Quixotic has an alternate form, *quixotical*, but this is not the preferred form of the word.

Synonyms: (*adjectives*) idealistic, visionary, fanciful, unrealistic, utopian, chimerical

Antonyms: (*adjectives*) realistic, practical, down-to-earth

Phrases: have one's head in the clouds, a pie-in-the-sky proposal

Using the Words

Exercise I. Syllabication and Pronunciation

Syllabicate the following words correctly, and place the major stress mark (′) after the syllable that is accented when the word is pronounced.

1. prerogative
2. probity
3. proliferate
4. promulgate
5. propitiate
6. prowess
7. pseudonym
8. pusillanimous
9. quixotic

Exercise II.   Words Out of Context

In each of the following groups, select the item that best expresses the meaning of the numbered word at the left.

1. probity
   a. blandness b. knavery c. skill
   d. integrity e. hostility

2. prodigious
   a. immense b. timely c. offensive
   d. demure e. eager

3. prowess
   a. prejudice b. valor c. arrogance
   d. courtesy e. wisdom

4. promulgate
   a. disguise b. contradict c. foretell
   d. understand e. proclaim

5. purge
   a. purify b. mystify c. edify
   d. sanctify e. horrify

6. propitiate
   a. judge b. bolster c. pacify d. honor
   e. investigate

7. pusillanimous
   a. rude b. biased c. expensive
   d. cowardly e. ugly

8. quixotic
   a. practical but costly
   b. sensible but difficult
   c. inexpensive but worthless
   d. feasible but foolish
   e. high-minded but impractical

Exercise III.   Completing Sentences

Complete each of the following sentences by selecting the most appropriate word from the given group of words. Use each word only once. Make any adjustments that are necessary to fit the words into the sentences properly.

quell	proliferate	procrastinate
protracted	propensity	quixotic
prerogative	promulgate	pseudonym

1. The old adage "Don't put off until tomorrow what you can do today " warns all of us not to _____.

2. When she said that I "tended to view the world through rose-colored glasses," she simply meant that I had a _____ for looking on the bright side of things.

3. Though the insurrection ultimately proved unsuccessful, the government was hard pressed to _____ it.

4. Though it was the _____ of the Head of the Senate in ancient Rome to give his opinion first, no other special privilege seems to have attached to the office.

5. I wonder why Eric Blair (1903–1950) chose to publish his novels and essays under the _____ George Orwell.

6. As long as more and more Americans turn to home computers for entertainment, video games will continue to _____.

7. Mismanagement turned what should have been a quick and easy victory into a _____ struggle that ended in stalemate.

Exercise IV. Synonyms and Antonyms

Classify each of the following pairs of words as **S** for **synonyms** or **A** for **antonyms**.

1. promulgate—proclaim
2. propensity—aversion
3. utopian—quixotic
4. privilege—prerogative
5. stupendous—prodigious
6. prowess—intrepidity
7. intrepid—pusillanimous
8. liquidate—purge
9. procrastinate—act
10. multiply—proliferate
11. propitiate—appease
12. protracted—compressed
13. unscrupulousness—probity
14. squelch—quell

Exercise V. Word Roundup

1. With or without the aid of a dictionary, define each of the following foreign expressions used in present-day English, and tell what language it comes from.

   a. alias
   b. ex cathedra
   c. nom de plume
   d. agent provocateur
   e. nom de guerre
   f. tour de force

2. With or without the aid of a dictionary or other reference book, name the person who used each of the following *pseudonyms*.

   a. Mark Twain
   b. O. Henry
   c. Molière
   d. Voltaire
   e. George Eliot
   f. Saki

3. Explain the story behind each of the following interesting English words.

   a. chimerical
   b. utopian
   c. quixotic

4. With or without the aid of a dictionary, define each of the following words.

   a. paladin
   b. clone
   c. scapegoat
   d. catharsis
   e. spunk
   f. protractor

5. With or without the aid of a dictionary, explain the meaning of each of the following phrases.

   a. a pie-in-the-sky proposal
   b. sharp practice
   c. table a bill
   d. a witch-hunt

Exercise VI. Framing Sentences

A. Use each of the following words in an original illustrative sentence.

1. prerogative
2. probity
3. propensity
4. protracted
5. prowess
6. pseudonym
7. purge
8. quell
9. quixotic

B. Give a **noun** form of each of the following words, and use it in an original illustrative sentence.

1. procrastinate
2. prodigious
3. proliferate
4. propitiate
5. promulgate
6. pusillanimous

Dissecting the Words

1. The Latin prefix **per** occurs in a great many common English words, including *peremptory, perjure,* and *permeate,* which were all studied in Lesson 24. As with many of the other word elements studied in this book, **per** has a number of meanings:

a. "Through" or "throughout," as in these words:

percolate (*per*, "through" + *colare, colatus* [Latin], "seep")—to seep or filter slowly through. Noun: *percolator*

perforate (*per*, "through" + *forare, foratus* [Latin], "bore")—to punch or pierce small holes in. Noun: *perforation*

perennial (*per*, "throughout" + *annus* [Latin], "year")—lasting throughout the year or through many years; recurring

permanent (*per*, "throughout" + *manens, manentis* [Latin], "remaining")—fixed, lasting, or unchanging. Noun: *permanence*

perambulate (*per*, "through" + *ambulare, ambulatus* [Latin], "walk")—to roam or stroll about, especially to inspect something.

pervade (*per*, "through" + *vadere* [Latin], "go")—to spread through. Adjective: *pervasive*

perspire (*per*, "through" + *spirare* [Latin], "breathe")—to sweat.

perspicacious (*per*, "through" + *specere, spectus* [Latin], "look, see")—acutely perceptive. Noun: *perspicacity*

b. "Thoroughly" or "completely," as in these words:

perfect (*per*, "completely" + *facere, factus* [Latin], "do")—(*adjective)* complete or flawless; (*verb*) to bring to completion or perfection

permutation (*per*, "completely" + *mutare, mutatus* [Latin], "change")—a complete change or transformation

perpetrate (*per*, "completely" + *patrare, patratus* [Latin], "bring about or do with the authority of a father")—to carry out, perform, or commit. Nouns: *perpetration, perpetrator*

perplex (*per*, "completely" + *plectere, plexus* [Latin], "weave, entwine")—to puzzle or bewilder. Noun: *perplexity*

pertinacious (*per*, "thoroughly" + *tenere* [Latin], "hold")—holding firmly to some purpose or belief despite all obstacles. Noun: *pertinacity*

perturb (*per*, "thoroughly" + *turbare* [Latin], "throw into disorder")—to disturb or upset greatly. Noun: *perturbation*

c.   "Very," as in these words:

persist (*per*, "very" + *sistere* [Latin], "stand firm")—to continue; to hold firmly to some course or purpose. Noun: *persistence*. Adjective: *persistent*

perfervid (*per*, "very" + *fervidus* [Latin], "eager")—extremely eager; impassioned or zealous

percussion (*per*, "very hard" + *quatere, quassus* [Latin], "strike")—the violent collision of two bodies or the sound that such a collision makes

d.   "Away," as in these words:

perdition (*per*, "away" + *dare, datus* [Latin], "give")—eternal damnation; utter ruin

peregrination (*per*, "away" + *ager, agri* [Latin], "field")—a journey from place to place

perfidy (*per*, "away" + *fides* [Latin], "faith")—treachery. Adjective: *perfidious*

perish (*per*, "away" + *ire, itus* [Latin], "go")—to pass away, die, or disappear. Noun: *perishables*

Per also occurs as an independent word with the general meaning "by" in a number of phrases that modern English has borrowed from Latin, including:

per annum—annually   *per se*—by itself
per capita—by the head   *per diem*—by the day

2.   The prefix **pre** (from Latin *prae*) occurs in a great many common English words, including *premise* and *prerogative*, studied in Lessons 24 and 25. **Pre** means "before, in front of, or ahead of in time, position, or importance," as these words show:

preamble (*prae*, "before" + *ambulare* [Latin], "walk")—an introductory statement or event

prearrange (*pre* + *arrange*)—to arrange ahead of time. Noun: *prearrangement*

precaution (*pre* + *caution*)—an action taken in advance to prevent a possible difficulty or danger. Adjective: *precautionary*

precede (*prae*, "before" + *cedere* [Latin], "go")—to come before in time or position. Nouns: *precedence, precedent*

preclude (*prae*, "before" + *claudere* [Latin], "close")—to prevent by previous action or by virtue of a previous situation

precursor (*prae*, "before" + *currere, cursus* [Latin], "run")—a forerunner *predict* (*prae*, "before" + *dicere, dictus* [Latin], "say, tell")—to foretell or prophesy. Noun: *prediction*

predilection (*prae*, "before" + *diligere, dilectus* [Latin], "choose, prefer") —a preference

predominate (*prae*, "before" + *dominare, dominatus* [Latin], "rule over")—to prevail over or dominate totally. Adjective: *predominant*

pre-empt (*prae*, "before" + *emere, emptus* [Latin], "buy")—to gain possession of by advance action. Adjective: *pre-emptive*. Noun: *pre-emption*

preface (*prae*, "before" + *fari, fatus* [Latin], "speak")—(*noun*) an introductory statement or essay; (*verb*) to introduce

prehistoric (*pre* + *historic*)—belonging to the period before written history. Noun: *prehistory*

premature (*prae*, "before" + *maturus* [Latin], "ripe")—unexpectedly early in development; coming too soon

premeditate (*pre* + *meditate*)—to plan, arrange, or deliberate in advance. Noun: *premeditation*

premonition (*prae*, "before" + *monere, monitus* [Latin], "warn")—an advance warning or foreboding

preoccupy (*pre* + *occupy*)—to absorb completly or to the exclusion of all else. Noun: *preoccupation*

preponderate (*prae*, "before" + *ponderare, ponderatus* [Latin], "weigh") —to be greater in power, force, or importance than all others. Noun: *preponderance*. Adjective: *preponderant*

presage (*prae*, "before" + *sagire* [Latin], "perceive")—(*verb*) to warn of in advance; (*noun*) an omen or portent

presentiment (*prae*, "before" + *sentire* [Latin], "feel, perceive")—a premonition or foreboding

preside (*prae*, "before" + *sedere, sessus* [Latin], "sit")—to be head of or have authority over. Nouns: *president, presidency*

presume (*prae*, "before" + *sumere* [Latin], "take")—to suppose to be true, to take for granted; to be overbold. Adjectives: *presumptuous, presumptive*

prevail (*prae*, "before" + *valere* [Latin], "be strong")—to triumph over or win out against; to be in force, use, or effect. Adjective: *prevalent*

Note that **prae**, the Latin spelling of this prefix, is retained in a few words that relate to Roman history, notably *praetor* and *praenomen*.

3. The Latin prefix **pro** also occurs in numerous English words, including *procrastinate* and *propensity*, studied in Lesson 25. It, too, has a number of meanings:

a. "Forward," "forth," or "in public," as in these words:

proceed (*pro*, "forward" + *cedere* [Latin], "go")—to move forward or onward. Nouns: *proceedings, proceeds, process, procession, procedure*

proclaim (*pro*, "in public" + *clamare* [Latin], "cry out")—to announce or declare openly or officially. Noun: *proclamation*

The Chimaera

The *Chimaera* (from the Greek word *chimaira*, meaning "nanny goat") was a fabulous monster that, according to Homer, had the head of a lion, the body of a goat, and the tail of a dragon. It was the offspring of Typhon, the monstrous son of Gaea, and was born in Lycia in what is now southwest Turkey. (Typhon also fathered a number of other equally monstrous creatures, including Echidna, Cerberus, the Hydra, and the Sphinx.) The Chimaera was eventually killed by the Greek hero Bellerophon with the aid of his winged horse Pegasus. It is from this colorful creature out of Greek mythology that modern English gets the words *chimera* (pronounced kī-mîr´-ə), meaning "a wild and foolish fancy" or "a highly improbable and incongruous scheme," and *chimerical* (pronounced kī-mîr´-ə-kəl), meaning "given to unrealistic fantasies" or "wildly improbable."

produce (*pro*, "forth" + *ducere* [Latin], "lead")—(*verb*) to bring forth or yield; (*noun*) products, especially farm products. Adjective: *productive*

profess (*pro*, "in public" + *fateri, fassus* [Latin], "acknowledge")—to affirm openly; to claim. Noun: *professor, profession*

profuse (*pro*, "forth" + *fundere, fu(n)sus* [Latin], "pour")—plentiful, extravagant. Noun: *profusion*

progress (*pro*, "forward" + *gredi, gressus* [Latin], "step, move")—(*noun*) forward movement; (*verb*) move forward. Noun: *progression.*

promote (*pro*, "forward" + *movere, motus* [Latin], "move")—to raise or advance to a higher rank or degree; to contribute to the advancement or success of. Nouns: *promotion, promoter*

propel (*pro*, "forward" + *pellere* [Latin], "drive")—to cause to move forward. Nouns: *propulsion, propeller*

propose (*pro*, "forward" + *ponere, positus* [Latin], "put")—to put forward for consideration. Nouns: *proposal, proposition*

proscribe (*pro*, "in public" + *scribere* [Latin], "write")—to outlaw or condemn. Noun: *proscription*

b. "Away," as in these words:

   prodigal (*pro*, "away" + *agere* [Latin], "drive" + *alis* [Latin], "relating to")—(*adjective*) recklessly wasteful; (*noun*) a spendthrift. Noun: *prodigality*

   profligate (*pro*, "down and away" + *fligare, fligatus* [Latin], "strike")—dissolute, wasteful

c. "For" or "on behalf of," as in this word:

   procure (*pro*, "on behalf of" + *curare* [Latin], "take care of")—to acquire or obtain, often for another person. Noun: *procurement*

d. "Before," as in this word:

   profane (*pro*, "before, in front of" + *fanum* [Latin], "temple, sanctuary"; for the Romans, things done before [i.e., outside] a temple were neither sacred nor elevated)—(*adjective*) nonreligious, secular; vulgar, coarse; blasphemous; (*verb*) to treat with irreverence or otherwise abuse. Noun: *profanity*

e. "In favor of," as in this word:

   pro-revolutionary (*pro*, "in favor of" + *revolutionary*)—in favor of revolution

Pro also appears as an independent word with the general meaning "for" or "for the sake of" in a few phrases that English has borrowed from Latin, including:

pro forma—purely as a matter of form
pro tem(pore)—for the time being

4. The Greek prefix **pro**, meaning "in front of," before," or "forward," also occurs in a few useful English words, including:

prologue (*pro*, "before" + *legein* [Greek], "say")—an introduction to a play; an introductory act or event

proboscis (*pro*, "in front" + *boskein* [Greek], "feed")—the long tubular nose of an elephant or similar animal

problem (*pro*, "forward" + *ballein* [Greek], "throw")—a difficulty. Adjective: *problematic(al)*

proem (*pro*, "before" + *oime* [Greek], "song")—a short introduction or preface

prognosis (*pro*, "before" + *gignoskein* [Greek], "know")—a prediction of the probable course or outcome of something. Verb: *prognosticate*

Exercise

1. With or without the aid of a dictionary, define each of the following words using the Latin prefix *per*, and explain what the prefix means in that particular word. Then choose any **three** of the words, and for each compose an illustrative sentence.

   a. pervade   c. perpetrate   e. persist
   b. perspicacious   d. pertinacious   f. perish

2. For each of the following definitions, supply an English word beginning with the Latin prefix *pre*. (Note: in some cases more than one answer may be correct.)

    a. come before in time or position
    b. foretell or prophesy
    c. developing or occurring too early
    d. an advance warning or foreboding

3. With or without the aid of a dictionary, define each of the following words using the Latin prefix *pro*, and explain what the prefix means in that particular word. Then choose any **three** of the words, and for each compose an original illustrative sentence.

    a. proclaim   **c.** produce   **e.** profane
    b. propose   **d.** prodigal   **f.** pro-Marxist

4. For each of the following definitions, supply an English word beginning with the Greek prefix *pro*.

    a. the long tubular nose of an elephant
    b. the introductory scene of a play
    c. a difficulty or puzzle
    d. a prediction of the probable course or outcome of

5. Explain the meaning of each of the following Latin phrases commonly used in English. Then choose any **two**, and for each compose an original illustrative sentence. Consult a dictionary as necessary.

    a. per capita   **c.** per diem   **e.** pro forma
    b. per annum   **d.** per se   **f.** pro tem(pore)

Bowdlerize

In 1807 and 1818, an Englishman named Thomas Bowdler brought out a 10-volume edition of the works of Shakespeare in which "those words [were] omitted which [could not] with propriety be read aloud in a family." He called his edition *The Family Shakespeare*. Actually, much of the editing work on this project appears to have been done by Bowdler's sister Henrietta Maria (Harriet), but she didn't want her involvement in the matter made public "for propriety's sake." It is from the activities of Thomas Bowdler and his sister that modern English gets the verb *bowdlerize* (pronounced bōd´-lə-rīz), which means "expurgate or censor a literary work."

William Shakespeare

Working with Context Clues

Complete each of the following two-word omissions by selecting the pair of words that make the best sense in the passage as a whole. If necessary, consult a dictionary for the meaning of any word with which you are not familiar.

1. "Her methods are hardly what I'd call _____, but they do get results," the sales manager said of his star sales-woman. "If she took a more traditional approach, our profits might not be so _____."

   a. dynamic...disheartening   c. orthodox...substantial
   b. quaint...marginal   d. controversial...poor

2. The book is full of amusing stories involving people who were _____ at the time. One of these witty little _____ tells how a world-famous actress used garlic to discourage a flirtatious leading man.

   a. wealthy...epithets   c. eminent...pseudonyms
   b. prominent...anecdotes   d. crucial...impasses

3. "It isn't _____ to spend more than you make," I observed. "Only a fool would allow expenses to _____ income."

   a. foolish...outstrip   c. abnormal...impugn
   b. wise...augment   d. prudent...exceed

4. When prices go up, the value of our money _____. The higher the cost of living climbs, the more deeply inflation erodes away the purchasing power of the _____.

   a. increases...penny   c. persists...quarter
   b. decreases...dollar   d. revives...dime

5. Where the soil is _____, various kinds of fruits and vegetables abound; where it is worn out, little more than weeds can _____.

   a. fertile...prosper   c. barren...proliferate
   b. lush...wither   d. inhospitable...flourish

6. "Look on the bright side of things," _____ said to me in his most paternal tones. "Don't think of these old suits as hand-me-downs; think of them as family _____."

   a. dad...heirlooms   c. Uncle Al...crests
   b. sis...members   d. mom...legacies

7. The referee who _____ a hockey game and the _____ who presides over a court of law are very much alike in function.

   a. participates in...juror   c. plays in...prosecutor
   b. rules over...defendant   d. officiates at...judge

Enriching the Lesson

Exercise I. Our Latin Heritage

A number of the English words studied in this Lesson (e.g., *probity* and *pusillanimous*) are based on Latin originals. As you have already discovered in Lessons 9 (page 125) and 14 (page 207), English is rich in such Latin borrowings. A few more examples of this heritage are listed below. With or without the aid of a dictionary, define each of the items listed and give its etymology. Then choose any **five**, and for each compose an original illustrative sentence.

1. abjure	11. rabid	21. molest
2. juvenile	12. juncture	22. neutrality
3. latent	13. lethal	23. purport
4. opacity	14. magnate	24. enumerate
5. mendacious	15. luminous	25. mute
6. obtrude	16. nocturnal	26. putative
7. longevity	17. orifice	27. pulverize
8. oscillate	18. maturate	28. recluse
9. motivate	19. proxy	29. rancid
10. orbit	20. putrid	30. ordinance

Exercise II. Verbal Pollution—the Ecology of Words

Recently, the National Council of Teachers of English gave its annual "Obfuscation Award" to a former press secretary of a national political figure. He was "honored" in this way for having sought to mislead the public over a period of years with garbled and spurious news releases. The citation hailed him as a master of dissembling, whose specialty was not so much the outright misstatement of facts as the use of words to obscure the truth, give distorted impressions, and create unwarranted associations. In short, a sort of verbal pollution.

There is nothing unique about this. There are far too many examples of verbal pollution in the nation today, threatening our linguistic ecology. Euphemisms of various types are widely employed to disguise the true nature of what is happening, both here and abroad, in both civilian and military affairs. Never before has so much been obfuscated with such fogbanks of nebulous word fallout.

This is not to say the misuse of language is necessarily more rampant today than in earlier eras. Dissembling has always been with us. But technological advances, above all TV, have greatly increased the potency of the communications media and have resulted in massive ecological disturbances in the area of language and understanding.

You know that TV announcers, especially in urban regions, give an "Air Pollution Index" in connection with each weather report. It has been suggested that it might not be a bad idea to supplement this with a "Word Pollution Index" to indicate just how badly our news sources are being fouled up by deliberate or inadvertent misuse of language.

Look for examples of deliberate misuse of words that threaten the wholesomeness of our verbal ecology. You may find them in statements of public figures, advertisements, speeches, publicity releases, newspaper editorials, columns, textbooks, classroom lectures, academic pronouncements, and many other sources. You may even find that you are guilty of this kind of verbal pollution once in a while.

1. With or without the aid of a dictionary, define each of the following words as used in the preceding selection.

a. obfuscation	f. unwarranted	k. nebulous
b. spurious	g. distort	l. linguistic
c. dissemble	h. unique	m. inadvertent
d. pollution	i. potency	n. supplement
e. ecology	j. fallout	o. civilian

2. Read each of the following examples of the "art of dissembling in language," and then explain what is really being said. Note: In one case, nothing at all is probably being said.

   a. My previous statements are now inoperative.

   b. The downtrend in the economic indices may be reflected in a certain amount of drying up of employment opportunities.

   c. You can take X cigarettes out of the country, but you can't take the country out of X cigarettes.

   d. The inevitable tradeoff for needed industrial development may be a temporary raising of impurity levels in the atmosphere.

Exercise III. Expanding Your Word Power

The words listed below are not on the Basic Word List, but they were mentioned in one form or another in Lesson 25. All of them would make useful additions to your working vocabulary. Define each, give its etymology, list **two** synonyms and **two** antonyms (where possible), and use in a short illustrative sentence.

1. perquisite	6. disseminate	11. expurgate
2. skulduggery	7. proclivity	12. eject
3. temporize	8. rectitude	13. expiate
4. prodigy	9. truncate	14. quash
5. burgeon	10. mettle	15. utopian

Lesson 26

---

326. raze   *verb*   rāz

[*radere, rasus* (Latin), "scrape, shave"]

Definition: To level to the ground; to blot out or demolish.

The atomic bomb that was dropped on Hiroshima in 1945 **razed** almost every building in the city.

Before work on the new shopping mall could begin, a group of shabby old tenements occupying the site had to be **razed**.

Usage Note:
Be careful not to confuse *raze* with its look-alike, *raise*, which means "erect" or "lift up," the opposite of what *raze* means.

Synonyms: (*verbs*) flatten, gut, fell, obliterate, eradicate, efface, tear down, dismantle, knock down, devastate

Antonyms: (*verbs*) raise, erect, set up, build

Phrases: lay waste to, reduce to a pile of rubble

327. re-cal-ci-trant   *adjective and noun*   rĭ-kăl′-sĭ-trĕnt

[*recalcitrans, recalcitrantis* (Latin), "kicking backwards" (used of a horse); from *re* (Latin), "back(wards)" + *calx, calcis* (Latin), "heel"]

Definition:
a.   (*adjective*) Stubbornly resistant to reason or authority.

Though a handful of **recalcitrant** delegates made a last-ditch effort to kill the bill, the measure was eventually passed.

b.   (*noun*) A perverse or wayward person.

"Cell Block R," the warden explained, "houses a group of **recalcitrants** who have so far resisted every effort we have made to rehabilitate them."

Phrases: a recalcitrant child, a recalcitrant animal, a recalcitrant motor

Related Form: (*noun*) recalcitrance

Synonyms: (*adjectives*) obstinate, perverse, intractable, unyielding, contrary, rebellious, defiant, uncooperative, contumacious, pigheaded, ornery

Antonyms: (*adjectives*) compliant, complaisant, acquiescent, tractable, cooperative, docile, amenable, accommodating, willing

Phrases: be at odds with, a die-hard, as stubborn as a mule

328. re-cant   *verb*   rĭ-kănt′

[*re* (Latin), "back" + *cantare* (Latin), "sing, chant"]

Definition: To withdraw formally or publicly.

The theory that the earth moves around the sun was so opposed to accepted thinking during the Renaissance that many a scientist of the time was forced to **recant** his belief in it.

Related Form: (*noun*) recantation

Synonyms: (*verbs*) disown, renounce, retract, repudiate, disavow, abjure

Antonyms: (*verbs*) affirm, reaffirm, aver; hold fast to, cleave to, adhere to

Phrase: eat one's words

329. re-cip-ro-cate   *verb*   rĭ-sĭp′-rə-kāt

[*reciprocare, reciprocatus* (Latin), "move back and forth"; possibly from *recus* (Latin), "backwards" + *procus* (Latin), "forwards"]

Definition: To give in return for, or in response to, something already given.

Can you blame me for being bitter when a supposed friend **reciprocated** my confidence with betrayal and slander?

Phrases: reciprocal assistance, a reciprocal relationship

Related Forms: (*nouns*) reciprocation, reciprocity; (*adjective*) reciprocal

Usage Notes:

a.   A *reciprocal trade agreement* is one in which two or more nations "swap" favors or concessions of more or less equal value. The principle involved in such an agreement is termed *reciprocity.*

b.   In mathematics, a *reciprocal* is the quotient of a quantity divided into 1. For example, the reciprocal of 7 is $1/7$.

Synonyms: (*verbs*) exchange, repay, requite, reimburse, recompense, interchange

Phrases: tit for tat, pay back in kind

330. re-crim-i-na-tion   *noun*   rĭ-krĭm-ə-nā′-shən

[*re* (Latin), "back" + *crimen, criminis* (Latin), "charge, accusation" + *are, atus* (Latin), a verb-forming suffix roughly meaning "make"]

Definition: The act of answering one accusation with another; a bitter reply.

Although I have been deeply wounded by their totally unfounded accusations, I am not going to reply to them with ugly and pointless **recriminations**.

Related Forms: (*verb*) recriminate; (*adjective*) recriminatory

Synonyms: (*nouns*) countercharge, counteraccusation, retort

331. **re-dun-dant**   *adjective*   rĭ-dŭn´-dĕnt

[*redundans, redundantis* (Latin), "overflowing"; from *re* (Latin), "back" + *unda* (Latin), "wave"]

Definition: Unnecessarily repetitive or superfluous; more than what is normally considered adequate or necessary.

> When Marlo harshly demanded that I "return back" the book she had lent me, she was being not only discourteous but **redundant** as well.

> In a way, the phrase "pizza pie" is **redundant** because, in Italian, *pizza* means "a type of pie."

Related Forms: (*nouns*) redundancy, redundance

Usage Note:

The English verb *redound* comes from the same Latin word elements as *redundant*, but the two words are not related in meaning. *Redundant*, as you know, means "repetitive"; *redound* means "have as a consequence" or "contribute to."

Synonyms: (*adjectives*) verbose, prolix, pleonastic, wordy, tautological; superabundant, excessive

Antonyms: (*adjectives*) succinct, laconic, terse; insufficient, scarce

The principle of *redundancy* is built into spacecraft, so that there are more than enough safeguards or "back-up" systems to keep the machine operating if the main system goes out.

332. re-lent   *verb*   rĭ-lĕnt´

[*re* (Latin), "completely; very" + *lentare* (Latin), "soften"]

Definition: To become less harsh or severe; to let up or slacken.

At first I was determined to see justice done, but her eloquent appeal for compassion and understanding touched my heart, and I **relented**.

When the wind and rain finally **relented**, I went outside to inspect the damage the storm had done.

Related Forms: (*adjective*) relentless; (*noun*) relentlessness

Synonyms: (*verbs*) yield, moderate, soften

Antonyms: (*verbs*) harden, stiffen, be adamant

Phrase: temper the wind to the shorn lamb

333. rem-i-nis-cence   *noun*   rĕm-ə-nĭs´-ĕns

[*reminiscens, reminiscentia* (Latin), "remembering"; from *re* (Latin) + *mens, mentis* (Latin), "mind"]

Definition: The act of recalling the past; a memory.

Grandmother's **reminiscences** of her youth may seem trivial to an outsider, but, as a family member, I know how precious they are to her.

Related Forms: (*adjective*) reminiscent; (*verb*) reminisce

Usage Notes:
a. The adjective *reminiscent*, meaning "suggestive," is normally followed by the preposition *of*. For example, the lyrics of a pop song may be *reminiscent of* one of Shakespeare's sonnets or a poem by John Keats.

b. The plural noun *reminiscences* is often used to indicate the narrated recollections that a person has published in book or essay form. These are also sometimes called *memoirs*.

Synonyms: (*nouns*) recollection, remembrance; memoir

Phrases: a flashback, dwell on the past, relive the past, total recall, déjà vu

Déjà Vu

"Somehow I had the feeling that I had been in that old house before, and that I was familiar with many of its contents, even though I was well aware that I could not possibly have entered it on any previous occasion."

Many of us have had the kind of strange experience suggested by this statement. Psychologists refer to it by the term *déjà vu* (dā-zhä-vōō). This comes from French and means literally "already seen." The psychological reasons for such an illusion are not entirely clear, and indeed may differ widely from one case to another.

Déjà vu is also used to characterize something (e.g., a film) that is supposed to be original but is actually trite and reminiscent of other works.

334. re-morse *noun* rĭ-môrs′

[*re* (Latin), "back; very" + *mordere, morsus* (Latin), "bite"]

Definition: Anguish, self-reproach or bitter regret for wrongdoing.

Feeling **remorse** for your thoughtlessness cannot undo the harm you have done, but it may prevent you from doing the same thing again.

The great American poet Emily Dickinson once wrote that "**remorse** is memory awake."

Related Forms: (*adjectives*) remorseful, remorseless; (*nouns*) remorselessness; (*adverbs*) remorsefully, remorselessly

Synonyms: (*nouns*) regretfulness, shame, contrition, sorrow, repentance, penitence

Antonyms: (*nouns*) callousness, indifference, unconcern, impenitence

Phrases: wear sackcloth and ashes, a twinge (or pang) of conscience, the prick of conscience, have a heart of stone

Emily Dickinson

Emily Dickinson lived most of her life in Amherst, Massachusetts, where she was born in 1830. Her lawyer father raised her in the strict Puritan tradition that was characteristic of New England in the 19th century. After 1853, she gradually became a recluse, possibly as the result of an unhappy love affair. The secluded life that she led became her chief source of inspiration as a poet and resulted in over 1000 poems of great poignancy and beauty. Many of her brief, delicate lyrics, full of startling imagery, concern nature, love, death, and immortality. Only seven of them were published during her lifetime, and the extent of her literary output—sometimes scribbled on odd bits of paper or the backs of old envelopes—was not discovered until after her death. Indeed, her recognition as a poet of immense stature did not even begin until the publication of the first collected edition of her works four years after her death in 1886. Since that time, her remarkable achievement has exerted a tremendous influence on modern American writers. (For further details consult *Emily Dickinson: An Interpretive Biography*, by T. H. Johnson.)

335. ren-e-gade   *noun and adjective*   rĕn´-ə-gād

[*renegado* (Spanish), "turncoat"; from *re* (Latin), "again; very" + *negare, negatus* (Latin), "deny"]

Definition:

    a.   A person who deserts one cause or group for another.

> One of history's most celebrated **renegades** is a Roman emperor by the name of Julian, who gave up Christianity when he came to the throne.

> Neither threats nor "sweet talk" succeeded in luring back a few of the **renegades** who had gone over to the opposition just before the crucial vote was to be taken.

    b.   (*adjective*) Disloyal or traitorous.

> To many of the white settlers in the Southwest, Geronimo was just another **renegade** Apache; but to his own people, he was a patriot.

> Recently the terms *boll weevils* and *gypsy moths* were applied to a group of **renegade** Southern Democrats who supported Republican President Ronald Reagan against their own party.

Related Form: (*verb*) renege

Synonyms: (*nouns*) turncoat, traitor, defector, deserter, apostate; (*adjectives*) recreant, perfidious

Antonyms: (*noun*) loyalist; (*adjectives*) loyal, staunch, true-blue, reliable

Phrases: a volte-face, do an about-face

Usage Note:

During the American Revolution the *Loyalists* (note the *L*), also called *Tories*, were the colonists who opposed independence and supported the British cause. Most of the Loyalists were large landowners, Crown officials, and members of the clergy, though other groups were also represented. The Loyalists were most numerous in the far South (Georgia and South Carolina) and in the Middle Atlantic region (New York and Pennsylvania). After the revolution was over, a great many Loyalists moved permanently to Canada, the West Indies, or England.

336. re-per-cus-sion   *noun*   rĕ-pĕr-kŭsh´-ən

[*re* (Latin), "back; very" + *per* (Latin), "through; very" + *cutere, cussus* (Latin), "strike (hard)"]

Definition: An indirect effect or result produced by an event or action.

> The recent "energy crisis" has had major **repercussions** in many areas of modern American life.

> It is difficult to convince most people that baby-care habits in the United States have serious **repercussions** in "third-world" nations, but they do.

Synonyms: (*nouns*) aftereffect, aftermath, reverberation, backlash

337. re-plen-ish   *verb*   rĭ-plĕn´-ĭsh

[*re* (Latin), "back; very" + *plenus* (Latin), "full"]

Definition: To refill or provide a new supply of.

Just before I run out of my favorite snack food, I **replenish** my supply.

When I am most deeply discouraged, their optimism and confidence seem to **replenish** my faith in my own abilities.

Related Forms: (*nouns*) replenishment, repletion; (*adjective*) replete

Usage Notes:

a. The noun *repletion* indicates a state of excessive fullness.

b. The adjective *replete*, meaning "abundantly supplied," is followed by the preposition *with*—for example, an essay *replete with* glaring grammatical errors.

Synonyms: (*verbs*) restock, renew, replace

Antonyms: (*verbs*) deplete, use up, empty, exhaust

Phrase: devoid of

338. re-pris-al   *noun*   rĭ-prī´-zəl

[*reprisaille* (Medieval French), "retaliation"; from *reprehendere, reprehensus* (Latin), "seize, recover"]

Definition: Retaliation in kind for injuries received.

The Soviet Union expelled two of our diplomats in **reprisal** for our expulsion of two of theirs.

The Nazi occupiers of France usually replied to damage done by the Resistance Movement by taking **reprisals** on the civilian population of the country.

Synonyms: (*nouns*) retribution, requital, vengeance, revenge

Phrases: a vendetta; a quid pro quo; an eye for an eye, a tooth for a tooth; get a dose of one's own medicine

339. re-scind   *verb*   rĭ-sĭnd´

[*re* (Latin), "back; very" + *scindere* (Latin), "cut"]

Definition: To cancel or withdraw.

As soon as I received an acceptance from the college of my choice, I **rescinded** the applications I had filed at other colleges.

When my boss saw that there was no practical way to carry out her orders, she **rescinded** them.

Phrases: rescind a law, rescind a contract, rescind an agreement, rescind a regulation

Related Forms: (*nouns*) rescindment, rescission

Synonyms: (*verbs*) revoke, repeal, retract, recall, abrogate, annul, nullify, countermand, invalidate

Antonyms: (*verbs*) affirm, confirm, enforce, endorse, uphold, ratify, underwrite

Phrase: null and void

340. re-sil-i-ent   *adjective*   rĭ-zĭl´-yĕnt

[*resiliens, resilientis* (Latin), "leaping back"; from *re* (Latin), "back" + *salire* (Latin), "jump, leap, spring"]

Definition:

a. Springy or flexible; able to resume its original shape.

   Astroturf is a tough but **resilient** material that is ideal for long-term use as a playing surface in professional sports.

b. Able to recover quickly from sickness, change, or misfortune.

   Scarlett O'Hara's remarkable recovery from the disasters of the Civil War was chiefly due to her **resilient** spirit and indomitable will.

Related Forms: (*nouns*) resilience, resiliency

Synonyms: (*adjectives*) pliable, supple, malleable, buoyant

Antonyms: (*adjectives*) inflexible, rigid, stiff, obdurate, adamant

Phrase: roll with the punches

Using the Words

Exercise I. Parts of Speech

Indicate the part of speech of each of the following words. In some cases, two answers are correct.

1. recalcitrant
2. recant
3. redundant
4. reminiscence
5. renegade
6. repercussion
7. reprisal
8. rescind
9. resilient

Exercise II. Words in Phrases

In each of the following groups, select the item that best expresses the meaning of the *italicized* word in the introductory phrase.

1. a *recalcitrant* student
   a. foreign b. brilliant c. perverse d. young e. polite

2. *recant* his beliefs
   a. discuss b. distort c. disclose d. discover e. disavow

3. exchange *recriminations*
   a. pleasantries   b. countercharges   c. anecdotes   d. jokes
   e. addresses

4. when she finally *relented*
   a. yielded   b. arrived   c. complained   d. answered
   e. finished

5. felt no *remorse*
   a. loneliness   b. animosity   c. hunger   d. regret
   e. desire

6. a *renegade* politician
   a. fledgling   b. turncoat   c. freshman   d. veteran
   e. expert

7. the *repercussions* of an event
   a. memories   b. reports   c. details   d. causes   e. effects

8. *reprisal* for an attack
   a. retaliation   b. need   c. plan   d. occasion   e. weapon

Exercise III. Completing Sentences

Complete each of the following sentences by selecting the most
appropriate word from the given group of words. Use each word
only once. Make any adjustments that are necessary to fit the
words into the sentences properly.

reciprocate	raze	recalcitrant
replenish	resilient	redundant
recrimination	rescind	reminiscence

1. As part of the Mayor's urban renewal program, a group of run-
   down inner-city buildings was _____ and replaced by
   an ultramodern civic center.

2. To my mind, the name *Rio Grande River* is slightly _____
   because the word *river* appears twice, once in English and
   once in Spanish.

3. About a week after the Elsons had me over for dinner, I
   _____ the kindness by inviting them to lunch.

4. When the legislators realized that the law they had passed
   simply couldn't be enforced, they _____ it.

5. Though we can replace some of the natural resources we have
   used up, we cannot _____ our dwindling supplies of
   fossil fuels.

6. As its name indicates, *Recollections of My Youth* contains the
   author's _____ of her girlhood and the people she grew
   up with.

7. People who are _____ are able to "bounce back" quickly and easily from unexpected failures or defeats.

Exercise IV. Synonyms and Antonyms

A. In each of the following groups, select the **two** words that are most nearly **synonymous**.

1. a. defector b. advocate c. beggar d. deserter
2. a. wordy b. pleasant c. verbose d. relevant
3. a. reply b. renounce c. retract d. report
4. a. proposal b. hunch c. recollection d. memory
5. a. pride b. contrition c. stature d. repentance

Now, for each pair of synonyms that you have selected, supply a word from the Basic Word List for Lesson 26 (Words 326–340) that means **the same** or **almost the same** thing.

B. In each of the following groups, select the item that is most nearly **opposite** in meaning to the numbered word at the left.

1. replenish a. exhaust b. avoid c. restock d. contain e. repel
2. raze a. allay b. consider c. defer d. smolder e. erect
3. rescind a. ravage b. rival c. ratify d. ruffle e. repudiate
4. recalcitrant a. wordy b. accommodating c. gorgeous d. affluent e. knowledgeable
5. relent a. collapse b. wander c. lend d. stiffen e. protrude

Exercise V. Word Roundup

1. Explain the difference between *raze* and *raise*.
2. What is a *reciprocal trade agreement*?
3. Explain what is meant by the *principle of redundancy* as applied to space equipment.
4. Tell what preposition usually follows each of these words:

   a. replete   b. reminiscent

5. With or without the aid of a dictionary, define the following words.

   a. a die-hard   c. overkill   e. ricochet
   b. a Loyalist   d. reciprocity   f. a flashback

6. With or without the aid of a dictionary, explain what each of the following colorful expressions means.

a. eat one's words
b. be at odds with
c. give tit for tat
d. temper the wind to the shorn lamb
e. wear sackcloth and ashes
f. turn a blind eye to
g. roll with the punches
h. lay waste to

7. With or without the aid of a dictionary, define each of the following foreign expressions used in present-day English, and tell what language it comes from.

a. quid pro quo
b. volte-face
c. vendetta
d. déjà vu

Exercise VI. Framing Sentences

A. Use each of the following words in an original illustrative sentence.

1. raze
2. recrimination
3. recalcitrant
4. remorse
5. replenish
6. reprisal
7. renegade
8. repercussion
9. rescind

B. Give a **noun** form of each of the following words, and use it in an original illustrative sentence.

1. recant
2. resilient
3. redundant

C. Give an **adjective** form of each of the following words, and use it in an original illustrative sentence.

1. reciprocate
2. relent
3. reminiscence

The principle of redundancy has also been applied to nuclear weaponry, as this cartoon suggests. The word *overkill*, used in the cartoon, is found in some of the latest dictionaries. How would you define it?

Sanders in the *Milwaukee Journal*

Completing Verbal Analogies

Complete each of the following analogies.

Group A

1. **frugal : bountiful =**
   a. oblique : slanting
   b. timid : audacious
   c. churlish : expensive
   d. willful : garish
   e. resilient : flexible

2. **sequel : after =**
   a. residue : behind
   b. proximity : beneath
   c. avalanche : between
   d. intrigue : beyond
   e. postlude : before

3. **busybody : meddlesome =**
   a. grouch : genial
   b. advocate : perverse
   c. spendthrift : prodigal
   d. hero : coward
   e. faithful : renegade

4. **purge : oust =**
   a. pulverize : cement
   b. instill : remove
   c. bolster : delay
   d. reminisce : relent
   e. replenish : refill

5. **raze : down =**
   a. quell : up
   b. instigate : down
   c. erect : up
   d. exalt : down
   e. demolish : up

Group B

6. **hero : gallantry ::**
   a. bully : remorse
   b. prodigy : reprisal
   c. mendicant : levity
   d. renegade : disloyalty
   e. pusillanimous : coward

7. **rant : bombastic ::**
   a. exhort : dilatory
   b. whine : mellifluous
   c. inveigh : vitriolic
   d. champion : noncommital
   e. poignant : melodrama

8. **bovine : sluggish ::**
   a. porcine : pig
   b. horse : equine
   c. feline : awkward
   d. mammoth : mastodon
   e. elephantine : huge

9. **reprehensible : condemnation ::**
   a. meritorious : approbation
   b. intrinsic : commiseration
   c. precocious : recrimination
   d. nominal : expiation
   e. elongation : protracted

10. **author : pseudonym ::**
    a. stage name : actress
    b. criminal : alias
    c. poet : playwright
    d. peasant : honorific
    e. nickname : sister

Working with Context Clues

Complete each of the following two-word omissions by selecting the pair of words that make the best sense in the passage as a whole. If necessary, consult a dictionary for the meaning of any word with which you are not familiar. Indicate the clue or clues that led you to choose your answer.

1. I know that an injection of Novocain doesn't normally inflict a great deal of _____. Still, the mere thought of the dentist's _____ is enough to make me wince in imaginary discomfort.

    a. delight . . . scalpel   c. hurt . . . hammer
    b. pain . . . needle   d. pleasure . . . chair

2. Laura is a(n) _____ worker who always does what her boss tells her to do. Tom, on the other hand, is both lazy and _____.

    a. proficient . . . prudent   c. awkward . . . amenable
    b. vigorous . . . vigilant   d. industrious . . . insubordinate

3. An experienced worker doesn't normally have much trouble handling his or her _____; a _____, however, will usually flounder around until he or she learns the ropes.

    a. boss . . . connoisseur   c. job . . . beginner
    b. knowledge . . . fledgling   d. money . . . veteran

4. At first, our troops clearly had the upper hand, but enemy reinforcements suddenly appeared and turned our easy victory into a complete _____. Most of our soldiers were killed, though a small _____ did manage to escape.

    a. rout . . . remnant   c. success . . . portion
    b. defeat . . . majority   d. fiasco . . . dearth

5. The earliest inhabitants of North America led _____ lives. They were constantly on the move in pursuit of the big-game animals that made up the greater part of their diet. This endless _____ for food eventually took them to all parts of the continent.

    a. sedentary . . . need   c. nomadic . . . quest
    b. pampered . . . desire   d. stationary . . . search

6. "I'm more than happy to shop at any _____ that is owned by reputable businessmen," I observed, "but I refuse to _____ an establishment that is run by people who are out to cheat me."

    a. library . . . divulge   c. airport . . . boycott
    b. store . . . patronize   d. intersection . . . assist

7. "If we are to win this election," the Senator remarked, "we must put aside our private _____ and present a united front. Those who heed this advice will be helping our cause; those who _____ it can only hurt us."

    a. quarrels...ignore   **c.** feuds...countenance
    b. lives...revere   **d.** goals...expedite

8. Most of the adults seemed to find Kal's Kiddie Karnival a bit of a bore, but their children were _____. Though the grownups had clearly had enough halfway through the performance, the youngsters' appetites for the kind of fare Kal served up were by no means _____ when the show was over.

    a. enhanced...accentuated   **c.** impeded...absolved
    b. enthralled...satiated   **d.** excised...extenuated

9. Some of my _____ are the epitome of _____ splendor; others always look as though they have slept in their clothes.

    a. possessions...culinary   **c.** goals...military
    b. achievements...nautical   **d.** friends...sartorial

10. "The passage is far too _____ to quote verbatim," I said. "To get it down to the size you need, you'll have to _____ part of it."

    a. long...delete   **c.** short...reiterate
    b. wordy...augment   **d.** brief...condense

Enriching the Lesson

Exercise I.   Adjectives Derived from Proper Names

If a poet or dramatist were described as *Shakespearean,* you would certainly interpret this as a very high compliment. It suggests immediately all the qualities that we associate with Shakespeare—vivid characterization, insight into human motivation, evocative use of language, and so forth. In short, the name *Shakespeare* carries so many clearly understood associations that it can serve as a useful adjective.

    There are a good many other names, drawn from various cultures and different periods of history, that have been converted into adjectives. In each case, of course, the adjective suggests the qualities and accomplishments for which a particular person is famous. The words are commonly, but not always, used in a favorable or complimentary sense.

    Terms of this type can be a useful part of your vocabulary. You are bound to run across some of them in your reading, and you can often introduce them into your own speech and writing to express forcefully a particular aspect of meaning that you have in mind.

Each of the words listed below is derived directly from the name of a famous person. In each case, identify the person whose name is involved. Incidentally, some of these forms may not appear in your dictionary. In that case, you may want to refer to an encyclopedia or other reference work to pin down the source of the word and the person to whom it refers.

1. Byronic
2. Keynesian
3. Chaucerian
4. Joycean
5. Marxist
6. Aristotelian
7. Edwardian
8. Kafkaesque
9. Jeffersonian
10. Elizabethan
11. Platonic
12. Thomistic
13. Dickensian
14. Mosaic
15. Napoleonic
16. Socratic
17. Freudian
18. Machiavellian
19. Shavian
20. Darwinian
21. Rabelaisian

Drawing by Ed Fisher; © 1975 The New Yorker Magazine, Inc.

"Ho, ho, ho! Ah, Monsieur Rabelais, there's just no word to describe that earthy humor of yours."

Exercise II. Our Celtic Heritage

Modern English contains a number of expressions drawn from Irish, Welsh, and Scottish Gaelic, the chief modern representatives of the Celtic branch of the Indo-European family of languages. A few of these items are listed below. With or without the aid of a dictionary, define each.

1. shamrock
2. banshee
3. crag
4. clan
5. brogue
6. leprechaun
7. plaid
8. slogan
9. bog

Hundreds of the expressions used in Modern English are of French origin. You have already met some of these items in Lessons 3 and 12 and elsewhere in this book. A few more are listed below. With or without the aid of a dictionary, define each. Then choose any **five**, and, for each, compose an original illustrative sentence.

1. communiqué
2. etiquette
3. morale
4. protégé
5. entrée
6. vis-à-vis
7. flair
8. plateau
9. reservoir
10. encore
11. penchant
12. genre
13. ensemble
14. tête-à-tête
15. liaison

Exercise IV. Expanding Your Word Power

The words listed below are not on the Basic Word List, but they were mentioned, in one form or another, in Lesson 26. All of them would make useful additions to your working vocabulary. Define each, give its etymology, list **two** synonyms and **two** antonyms (where possible), and use in a short illustrative sentence.

1. dismantle
2. devastate
3. contumacious
4. verbose
5. requite
6. retort
7. tautology
8. contrite
9. memoir
10. buoyant
11. deplete
12. backlash
13. underwrite
14. malleable
15. apostate

Lesson 27

---

341. ret-i-cent   *adjective*   rĕt´-ĭ-sənt

[*reticens, reticentis* (Latin), "keeping silent"; from *re* (Latin), "very; completely" + *tacere, tacitus* (Latin), "keep silent"]

Definition: Disinclined to speak out; reserved or restrained.

> Though he is usually willing to talk about a wide range of general subjects, he is curiously **reticent** about his personal life.

> I've always felt that a person who is **reticent** about his or her private life may have something to hide.

> Understandably, diplomats must be **reticent** people, simply because what they say publicly may adversely affect delicate and complicated negotiations.

Related Forms: (*noun*) reticence

Synonyms: (*adjectives*) taciturn, tight-lipped, uncommunicative, close-mouthed, hesitant

Antonyms: (*adjectives*) voluble, prolix, garrulous, loquacious, talkative

Phrases: run off at the mouth; mum's the word

342. re-tri-bu-tion   *noun*   rĕt-rə-byōō´-shən

[*re* (Latin), "back" + *tribuere, tributus* (Latin), "pay" + *tio, tionis* (Latin), a noun-forming suffix roughly meaning "state or act of"]

Definition: Just payment for something else, especially a punishment.

> Most ancient peoples looked upon plagues, famines, and other natural disasters as forms of divine **retribution** for human sin.

> "I believe you all know just what kind of **retribution** you can expect if you willingly collaborate with the enemy," the leader of the resistance movement warned the crowd.

> "Can any society that thinks of justice exclusively in terms of **retribution** be considered 'enlightened'?" the lawyer asked.

Related Forms: (*adjectives*) retributive, retributory

Phrases: retributive justice, in retribution for

Synonyms: (*nouns*) requital, recompense, redress, compensation, satisfaction, retaliation, reprisal (Word 338), restitution, vengeance, revenge

Phrase: one's just deserts

The Four Horsemen
of the Apocalypse

In the Book of Revelations (sometimes called the Apocalypse) in the New Testament, St. John the Divine describes four horsemen who issue from four seals on a closed book. These figures are usually interpreted as forms of divine retribution for human sin. They consist of pestilence (on a white horse), war (on a red horse), famine (on a black horse), and death (on a "pale" horse). Though the calamities represented by this grisly group appear regularly throughout history as the result of natural or manmade causes, St. John regards them as the instruments of God's judgment on a wayward and iniquitous human race. In the 1920's, the phrase "the four horsemen (of the Apocalypse)" was applied to a group of invincible Notre Dame football players who exacted the appropriate revenge on any opponent that attempted to score against the Fighting Irish. The Spanish novelist Vincente Blasco Ibáñez (1867–1928) called his most famous novel *The Four Horsemen of the Apocalypse (Los cuatro jinentes del Apocalipsis*, 1916).

The Four Horsemen of the Apocalypse, by Albrecht Dürer.

---

343. **ret-ro-ac-tive**   *adjective*   rĕt-rō-ăk´-tĭv

[*retre* (Latin), "back" + *agere, actus* (Latin), "drive, lead"]

Definition: Applying or referring to a period prior to enactment.

Though I didn't actually receive my salary increase until the middle of February, it was **retroactive** to the first of the year.

Phrases: a retroactive order, a retroactive law, a retroactive tax hike

Related Form: (*adverb*) retroactively

Synonym: (*adjective*) retrospective

Phrases: an ex post facto law, an a priori argument

Usage Notes:
   a. An *ex post facto law* is one that imposes a punishment on an action that was not punishable or illegal at the time it was committed. Such laws are, of course, unconstitutional in the United States.

   b. An *a priori argument* is one in which the conclusion is deduced from a theory or hypothesis that has been stated in advance, rather than from experiment, experience, or fact.

344. **re-ver-ber-ate**   *verb*   rĭ-vûr´-bə-rāt

[*re* (Latin), "back; again" + *verberare, verberatus* (Latin), "whip, lash"; from *verber* (Latin), "a whip"]

Definition: To echo over and over again; to resound.

The majestic chords of the organ **reverberated** from the walls of the cathedral as the funeral cortege began its slow journey down the center aisle.

Lincoln's call for volunteers to fight to preserve the Union **reverberated** through the Northern states.

Related Forms: (*noun*) reverberation; (*adjective*) reverberant

Synonyms: (*verbs*) rebound, recoil, bounce back, snap back; resonate, rumble, boom, thunder

Phrase: the recoil of a rifle

345. **re-vere**   *verb*   rĭ-vîr

[*re* (Latin), "very; completely" + *vereri* (Latin), "respect"]

Definition: To hold in great awe, esteem, or respect.

People of all ages, races, and backgrounds **revere** the memory of Martin Luther King and his fight for human dignity.

Even though the old man was in no way related to the little orphan, she **revered** him as a father.

The old sage was **revered** for the wisdom of his advice and the probity of his behavior.

Related Forms: (*noun*) reverence; (*adjectives*) reverent, reverential

Usage Note:
Reverend (with a capital *R*) is regularly used to address a Protestant minister or priest. *Rev.* is the usual abbreviation of the word.

Synonyms: (*verbs*) venerate, cherish, idolize, esteem, admire, honor

Antonyms: (*verbs*) ridicule, revile, execrate, disparage, belittle, denigrate

Phrases: hero worship, put someone on a pedestal

346. **rit-u-al**   *noun*   rĭch´-o͞o-əl

[*ritus* (Latin), "ceremony" + *alis, ale* (Latin), "pertaining to; like"]

Definition: A prescribed form or order for some kind of ceremony; something that is regularly and faithfully practiced.

Much of the religion of the ancient Romans involved carrying out elaborate **rituals** designed to propitiate the gods and elicit their support.

Pledging allegiance to the flag can become an empty **ritual** if we fail to think of the meaning behind the words and gestures involved in it.

The coronation of Queen Elizabeth II at Westminister Abbey, June 2, 1953. The crowning of an English monarch is an impressive ritual full of pomp and pageantry.

Related Forms: (*nouns*) rite, ritualism; (*adjective*) ritualistic; (*adverb*) ritually

Usage Note:
Ritual is sometimes used as an adjective. In that case, it means "ceremonial" or "having the nature of a ritual." Examples of this use of the word include "pay a *ritual* call on a sick aunt" and "a *ritual* murder."

Synonyms: (*nouns*) liturgy, ceremony, formalities, service, ceremonial

Phrase: stand on ceremony

347. ru-di-ment *noun* rōō´-də-mĕnt

[*rudimentum* (Latin), "beginning, first attempt"; from *rudis* (Latin), "rough, raw"]

Definition: A basic principle, element, or skill.

Any good teacher will tell you that you must master the **rudiments** of a subject before you can proceed to its fine points.

Anyone who has the slightest acquaintance with the **rudiments** of economics will see that we cannot solve our financial problems simply by borrowing more and more money.

Related Forms: (*adjectives*) rudimentary, rudimental

Synonyms: (*nouns*) basics, fundamentals, ABC's, first principles

Phrases: a primer of behavioral psychology, start out on the right foot, in an embryonic stage of development

417

348. ru-mi-nate   *verb*   rōō´-mə-nāt

[*ruminare, ruminatus* (Latin), "chew the cud; ponder"; from *rumen, ruminis* (Latin), "throat, gullet"]

Definition:

    a. To chew cud. (In this sense, the word is applied to cows and other ruminants.)

        The barn was full of dairy cows contentedly **ruminating** in their stalls.

    b. To ponder at length; to turn over in one's mind.

        In the corner of the garden stood a copy of Rodin's great statue of "The Thinker," forever **ruminating** on the problems of the world.

Related Forms: (*adjective*) ruminative; (*noun and adjective*) ruminant

Ruminant

A *ruminant* is an animal that chews a cud, which is a wad of partially digested food that has been regurgitated into the mouth. Sheep, goats, cattle, oxen, deer (*e.g.*, the whitetail buck shown at the right), camels, and giraffes are all ruminants.

Synonyms: (*verbs*) masticate; mull over, reflect upon, deliberate, muse on, cogitate

Phrase: put on one's thinking cap

349. ruse   *noun*   rōōz

[*ruse* (Old French), "trick, stratagem"; ultimately from *recusare* (Latin), "reject, drive back"]

Definition: An action or device designed to confuse or mislead.

    After ten long years of fruitless fighting, the Greeks finally captured Troy by resorting to a **ruse**.

    Many a wily criminal has been trapped by an even more clever **ruse**.

Synonyms: (*nouns*) stratagem, ploy, subterfuge, artifice, gimmick, trick

Phrase: a red herring

350. sab-o-tage   *verb and noun*   săb´-ə-täzh

[*saboter* (French), "throw a wooden shoe into; botch"; from *sabot* (French), "a kind of wooden shoe." Supposedly, disgruntled French and Belgian factory workers threw their wooden shoes into the machinery owned by the company they worked for in order to cause damage and delay.]

Definition:

a. (*verb*) To hamper, injure, or destroy maliciously or stealthily.

Members of the resistance movement tried unsuccessfully to **sabotage** an enemy munitions factory outside their native town.

Sensing that they would be left out in the cold if the two nations actually signed a peace treaty, the terrorists did everything they could to **sabotage** the negotiations.

b. (*noun*) Malicious damage, destruction, or hindrance of something.

The inhabitants of that country could express their opposition to the ruthless military regime under which they lived only through **sabotage** and subversion.

Related Form: (*noun*) saboteur

Synonyms: (*verbs*) subvert, undermine, disrupt, hamstring, wreck, damage; (*nouns*) subversion, treachery

Phrases: throw a monkey wrench into the works, stab someone in the back, gum up the works, fifth column, a job action

Fifth Column

The term *fifth column* originated during the Spanish Civil War in the 1930's. In 1936, the insurgent (rebel) forces had an army composed of four distinct columns or units driving on Madrid (below). The insurgent commander, General Emilio Mola, predicted victory because, he said, he had a "fifth column" of secret sympathizers within the city, ready to engage in espionage and sabotage against the defenders. Today, the term *fifth column* is used to indicate a subversive or traitorous element within any type of organization.

351. sac-ri-le-gious *adjective* săk-rə-lē´-jəs *or* sak-rə-lĭ´-jəs

[*sacrilegus* (Latin), "one who steals sacred things"; from *sacer, sacri* (Latin), "holy, sacred" + *legere* (Latin), "gather"]

Definition: Wickedly disrespectful of sacred or revered things.

In 17th-century New England it was considered **sacrilegious** to read any book but the Bible on Sunday.

In the eyes of most Americans, those who burn or spit on our flag are guilty of an intolerably **sacrilegious** act.

Related Forms: (*noun*) sacrilege; (*adverb*) sacrilegiously

Usage Note:
Sacrilege indicates the criminal abuse or misuse of something that is considered holy or sacred. Since the tone of the word is very strong, *sacrilege* is normally reserved for actions that are really reprehensible— for example, desecrating a cemetery or vandalizing a church or synagogue. Nonetheless, the word is occasionally used in a "light" or semi-humorous context. For example, "he regarded my attempt to sit in his favorite chair as tantamount to *sacrilege*."

Synonyms: (*adjectives*) impious, blasphemous, ungodly, unholy, wicked, sinful, immoral, reprobate, irreverent, iconoclastic

Antonyms: (*adjectives*) pious, reverent, godly, devout

Phrases: accused of blasphemy, blaspheme (against), a blasphemer, an iconoclast

352. sa-li-ent *noun and adjective* sā´-lē-ĕnt *or* sā´-lyĕnt

[*saliens, salientis* (Latin), "jumping, leaping"; from *salire, saltus* (Latin), "jump, leap"]

Definition:
a. (*noun*) An outward projection in a military position; anything that protrudes beyond its surroundings.

The long Allied struggle to push back the **salient** that the Nazis had created in Belgium in 1944 is popularly known as "The Battle of the Bulge."

Peninsulas can be defined as **salients** of land protruding into the sea.

b. (*adjective*) Prominent or conspicuous.

The newspaper article contained a brief synopsis of the **salient** points in the President's address.

Huge chalk cliffs projecting into the sea are the **salient** feature of the landscape around Dover.

Fairmindedness is probably the most **salient** quality of her personality.

Phrases: a salient trait, the salient details

Related Forms: (*noun*) salience; (*adverb*) saliently; (*verb*) sally

Synonyms: (*nouns*) protuberance, protrusion, bulge, bump; (*adjectives*) outstanding, noticeable, striking, pronounced

Antonyms: (*nouns*) dent, depression, trough, cavity, hole, dip; (*adjectives*) inconspicuous, unobtrusive

Phrases: keep a low profile, in high relief

353. sanc-ti-mo-ni-ous   *adjective*   săngk-tə-mō´-nē-əs

[*santimonia* (Latin), "holiness"; from *sanctus* [Latin], "holy"]

Definition: Making a great but insincere show of being holy or righteous, usually for the purpose of impressing others.

> The **sanctimonious** manner in which they flaunt their faith makes me suspect that, deep down, they aren't very religious.

> I have always admired the woman because she is high-minded without being **sanctimonious** and tenderhearted without being sentimental.

Related Forms: (*noun*) sanctimony; (*adverb*) sanctimoniously

Synonyms: (*adjectives*) hypocritical, pietistic, self-righteous, canting, pompous, insincere, holier-than-thou, simon-pure

Antonyms: (*adjectives*) heartfelt, sincere

Phrase: a stuffed shirt

354. san-guine   *adjective*   săng´-gwĭn

[*sanguineus* (Latin), "bloody; blood-red"; from *sanguis* (Latin), "blood"]

Definition:

a. Reddish or ruddy.

> My uncle was a large man with a **sanguine** complexion that radiated good health and good cheer.

b. Cheerfully confident or optimistic.

> "Given the depressed state of the economy," I replied, "your **sanguine** assessment of this company's future doesn't appear to be very realistic."

Related Forms: (*nouns*) sanguinity, sanguineness; (*adverb*) sanguinely

Usage Note:
Be careful not to confuse *sanguine* with *sanguinary*, which means "bloodthirsty" or "murderous."

Synonyms: (*adjectives*) rosy, rubicund; florid, flushed, glowing; buoyant, sunny, bright, hopeful

Antonyms: (*adjectives*) pale, pallid, wan; pessimistic, despondent, bleak (Word 61), gloomy, glum

Phrases: a Pollyanna; a prophet of doom

355. sat-el-lite *noun and adjective* săt´-əl-īt

[*satelles, satellitis* (Latin), "attendant"; possibly from *satnal* (Etruscan), "guard"]

Definition:

a. (*noun*) A natural or artificial body revolving around a celestial body of larger size.

> The Earth has only one natural **satellite**, the Moon.

> Manmade **satellites** positioned above the Atlantic and Pacific oceans make a global system of telecommunications possible.

b. (*noun*) A country that is under the domination or influence of a larger power.

> Although nominally independent, many Eastern European countries have long since become mere **satellites** of the Soviet Union.

c. (*adjective*) Dependent.

> Multinational corporations consisting of a number of **satellite** companies under the direct control of the parent organization exert a tremendous influence on today's economy.

Synonyms: (*nouns*) spacecraft, Sputnik; appendage, protectorate, client; (*adjectives*) subordinate, subject

Antonyms: (*nouns*) hegemony, dominion; (*adjectives*) dominant, parent, predominant, principal, governing

Phrases: a sphere of influence, a client state; a mother country, a parent organization

A weather forecaster checks a satellite photo of the Earth. Artificial satellites stationed above the Earth help scientists predict our weather with speed and accuracy.

Using the Words

Exercise I.   Syllabication and Pronunciation

Syllabicate the following words correctly, and place the major stress mark (´) after the syllable that is stressed when the word is pronounced.

1. reticent
2. retroactive
3. reverberate
4. ritual
5. ruminate
6. sabotage
7. sacrilegious
8. sanctimonious·
9. satellite

Exercise II.   Words Out of Context

In each of the following groups, select the item that best expresses the meaning of the numbered word at the left.

1. reticent
   a. colorful b. needy c. fortunate
   d. tremendous e. reserved

2. reverberate
   a. honor b. recall c. echo d. question
   e. ponder

3. ritual
   a. garment b. ceremony c. weapon
   d. development e. profession

4. sabotage
   a. consider b. forecast c. scorn
   d. wreck e. improve

5. sacrilegious
   a. judicious b. obscure c. impious
   d. stubborn e. garish

6. salient
   a. elaborate b. workable c. prominent
   d. unexpected e. costly ʼ

7. sanguine
   a. optimistic b. wordy c. useful
   d. treacherous e. bleak

8. satellite
   a. utensil b. principle c. texture
   d. appendage e. focus

Exercise III.   Completing Sentences

Complete each of the following sentences by selecting the most appropriate word from the given group of words.

revere	retroactive	reverberate
sanctimonious	satellite	ruminate
retribution	rudiment	ruse

1. A novice swimmer is someone who is just learning the _____ of the art.

2. Though the man was scorned and laughed at in his own lifetime, he is greatly _____ today.

3. Since the general couldn't take the enemy town by direct assault, he tried to capture it by a _____.

4. Though ordinary Greeks didn't give the nature of reality a second thought, professional philosophers like Plato and Aristotle spent their lives _____ on the matter.

5. Knowing what I do about repression in the Soviet Union, I found the Russian exchange student's criticisms of government regulation in the United States offensively _____.

6. My rent didn't actually go up until March, but the increase was _____ to the first of the year.

7. Though many of his contemporaries looked upon the destruction of Pompeii as an act of divine _____, Pliny the Elder saw it as a purely natural phenomenon unconnected with questions of reward and punishment.

Exercise IV.   Synonyms and Antonyms

Classify each of the following pairs of words as **S** for **synonyms** or **A** for **antonyms**.

1. undermine—sabotage
2. revere—revile
3. ponder—ruminate
4. reverberate—resound
5. sacrilegious—reverent
6. sanctimonious—self-righteous
7. retribution—reprisal
8. subject—satellite
9. fundamentals—rudiments
10. reticent—talkative
11. ritual—rite
12. ruse—stratagem
13. pessimistic—sanguine
14. salient—inconspicuous

Exercise V.   Word Roundup

1. Explain the difference in meaning between *sanguine* and *sanguinary*.

2. To whom is the title *Reverend* properly applied?

3. What kind of animal is referred to as a *ruminant*? Give two examples of animals that are ruminants.

4. With or without the aid of a dictionary, explain what each of the following means:

   a. an iconoclast
   b. a saboteur
   c. a stuffed shirt
   d. a fifth columnist

5. With or without the aid of a dictionary, explain the meaning of the following phrases:

   a. an ex post facto law
   b. an a priori argument

c. hero worship
d. a Latin primer
e. a red herring

f. a job action
g. a client state
h. a sphere of influence

6. With or without the aid of a dictionary, explain what each of the following colorful expressions means:

a. run off at the mouth
b. stand on ceremony

c. keep a low profile
d. stab someone in the back

Exercise VI. Framing Sentences

A. Use each of the following words in an original illustrative sentence.

1. retroactive
2. ritual
3. ruminate

4. ruse
5. sabotage
6. salient

7. sanctimonious
8. sanguine
9. satellite

B. Give a **noun** form of each of the following words, and use it in an original illustrative sentence.

1. reticent
2. reverberate
3. sacrilegious

C. Give an **adjective** form of each of these words, and use it in an original illustrative sentence.

1. rudiment
2. revere
3. retribution

Dissecting the Words

Prefixes

1. The Latin prefix **re** appears in a great many common English words, including *revere* and *reticent*, studied in Lesson 27. This prefix has a number of different meanings, depending upon how it is used in the word in which it appears. These meanings include:

a. "Back, backward(s)," or "behind," as in these words:

revert (re "back" + *vertere, versus* [Latin], "turn")—to return to a previous condition, subject, or practice. Noun: *reversion*

recede (re, "back" + *cedere, cessus* [Latin], "go")—to move back. Noun: *recession*

retract (re, "back" + *trahere, tractus* [Latin], "draw, drag")—to take back something that has been said, offered, or published. Noun: *retraction*

remain (re, + *manere, mansus* [Latin], "stay")— to continue without change. Noun: *remainder*

relinquish (re, "behind" + *linquere, liqui* [Latin], "leave")—to give up or yield

relic (*re*, "behind" + *linquere, liqui* [Latin], "leave")—something that has survived the passage of time; an artifact of the past

b. "Again" or "repeatedly," as in these words:

redo (*re*,"again" + *do*)—to do over

revive (*re*, "again" + *vivere, victus* [Latin], "live")—to impart new life to. Noun: *revival*

c. "Very" or "completely," as in this word:

revile (*re*, "very, completely" + *vilis, vile* [Latin], "vile")—to denounce or scorn

Occasionally **re** appears as **red**, especially before a vowel. This happens, for example, in the following word:

redeem (*red* "back; again" + *emere, emptus* [Latin], "buy")—to rescue or recover. Noun: *redemption*

2. The Latin prefix **retro** is related to **re**. Like **re**, it means "back, backward(s), or behind." It appears in the following useful English words:

retrocede (*retro*, "back" + *cedere, cessus* [Latin], "go")—to go back or recede. Noun: *retrocession*

retrograde (*retro*, "back, backwards" + *gradi, gressus* [Latin], "walk, step")—moving backwards; reverting to an earlier condition; inverted or reversed; contrary or opposed to

retrogress (*retro*, "back, backwards" + *gradi, gressus* [Latin], "walk, step")—to move or go backwards; to return to an earlier, inferior, or less complicated state. Noun: *retrogression*

retrospect (*retro*, "back" + *specere, spectus* [Latin], "look")—a survey or review of the past. Adjective: *retrospective*

retroversion (*retro*, "back" + *vertere, versus* [Latin], "turn")—a turning or tilting backwards

Roots

1. The Latin root **sacr** or **secr**, meaning "holy" or "sacred," appears in a a number of useful English words, including *sacrilegious*, studied in Lesson 27. For example:

consecrate (*con*, a form of *cum* [Latin], "very; completely" + *sacrare, sacratus* [Latin], "make holy")—to set apart as holy. Noun: *consecration*

desecrate (*de* [Latin], "away from; un-" + *sacrare, sacratus* [Latin], "make holy")—to abuse or violate the sanctity of. Noun: *desecration*

sacrament (*sacramentum* [Latin], "a holy oath or binding obligation")—one of the seven sacred rites of the Christian church; a sacred symbol or bond. Adjective: *sacramental*

sacristy (*sacristia* [Latin], "holy place"—a room in a church for housing sacred vessels and vestments

sacrifice (*sacer, sacri* [Latin], "holy, sacred" + *facere, factus* [Latin], "make")—(*verb*) to offer to a deity as homage or in atonement for sin; to forfeit something of value for something else of greater value; (*noun*) an offering to a deity; the forfeiture of something valuable for something else of greater value. Adjective: *sacrificial*

2. The Latin root **sanct** is related to **sacr** or **secr**. It also means "holy" or "sacred." Here are a few common words in which this root appears.

sanctify (*sanctus* [Latin], "holy" + *facere, factus* [Latin], "make")—to consecrate; to give religious approval to

sanctity (*sanctus* [Latin], "holy" + *itas, itatis* [Latin], "state of")—holiness, godliness, or saintliness

sanctuary (*sanctuarium* [Latin], "a holy place")—the most holy part of a sacred place; a place of asylum or refuge

sanction (*sanctio, sanctionis* [Latin], "an ordaining")—(*verb*) to authorize or approve; (*noun*) authorization or approval; a measure adopted to coerce a nation or other entity into observing the law

Note the following word in which both **sacr** and **sanct** appear:

sacrosanct—sacred and inviolable

Sacrosanct may sometimes be used ironically to suggest an undeserved immunity from questioning or attack. For example, your father may observe that a particular way of doing a job at his office is sacrosanct.

Exercise

1. With or without the aid of a dictionary, define each of the following words, and explain what the prefix *re* means in that particular word.

   a. reactionary   c. recompense   e. retrench
   b. revive   d. revere   f. relinquish

2. For each of the following definitions, supply an English word using the prefix *retro*. Two answers are correct in some instances.

   a. a review of the past   c. moving backwards
   b. return to an earlier state   d. a turning or tilting
                                   backwards

3. With or without the aid of a dictionary, define each of the following words using the root *sacr* or *secr*. Then choose any **three**, and, for each, compose an original illustrative sentence.

   a. desecrate   c. sacrifice   e. sacrilegious
   b. consecrate   d. sacrament   f. sacristy

4. For each of the following definitions, supply an English word employing the Latin root *sanct*. Then use each in an original illustrative sentence.

   a. authorize   b. refuge   c. holiness

5. With or without the aid of a dictionary, explain what each of the following means.

   a. a sacrifice hit   c. a sacred cow
   b. an inner sanctum   d. in re

Working with Context Clues

Complete each of the following two-word omissions by selecting the pair of words that make the best sense in the passage as a whole. If necessary, consult a dictionary for the meaning of any word with which you are unfamiliar. Indicate the clue or clues that led you to choose your answer.

1. Though human beings are neither _____ nor _____, they can certainly use what they do know to avoid making foolish or unnecessary mistakes.

    a. diffident...supercilious
    b. omniscient...infallible
    c. altruistic...malevolent
    d. pliable...invulnerable

2. During the long years that the painter struggled to _____ fame, his talents never failed him. Once he had actually achieved the public _____ that he sought, however, they began to desert him.

    a. attain...esteem
    b. comprise...nonchalance
    c. suppress...ignominy
    d. ascertain...kudos

3. "The thinner I got, the more _____ I felt," Kathy remarked about the negative side effects of her excessive dieting. "After a while, I became so _____ that I had absolutely no energy at all."

    a. commotion...limpid
    b. decrepit...copious
    c. listless...emaciated
    d. omnipotent...active

4. "My years in the foreign service have taught me to be as _____ as possible," the veteran diplomat observed facetiously. "These days, turning up one's nose at another country's national dish, no matter how _____, might just trigger an international incident."

    a. suave...chaotic
    b. recalcitrant...costly
    c. compatible...sanguine
    d. omnivorous...unpalatable

5. "Silence is golden," I jokingly remarked to my _____ friend. "It is better to give than to receive," he _____ in reply.

    a. clandestine...lamented
    b. garrulous...quipped
    c. tacit...gloated
    d. abstemious...ruminated

6. I might not be so _____ about suggesting improvements at the office if my boss were more _____ to constructive criticism. But I keep such ideas to myself because he seems to resent my advice.

    a. bovine...implacable
    b. zealous...magnanimous
    c. reticent...receptive
    d. exuberant...immune

7. I didn't _____ the dispute between my two closest friends because I thought that outside interference would aggravate, rather than _____, the situation.

   a. disparage . . . whet
   c. concur in . . . loll
   b. intervene in . . . alleviate
   d. elucidate . . . rescind

8. "Since these are only _____ of the Declaration of Independence," the clerk said, "the price we're asking for them is a great deal _____ than what the real thing would cost."

   a. anathemas . . . higher
   c. impasses . . . firmer
   b. facsimiles . . . lower
   d. fiascos . . . nearer

9. "Using a(n) _____ has caused me an unexpected problem," the famous novelist remarked. "Most people only know me by my pen name. So, if I introduce myself by my real name, I'm likely to be regarded as a _____."

   a. epitaph . . . nonentity
   c. legacy . . . foreigner
   b. prelude . . . VIP
   d. pseudonym . . . nobody

10. The man's cold and distant attitude toward other people clearly betrayed his deep-rooted _____ for the human race. No one who genuinely liked human beings would constantly have preferred to remain so _____ from them.

   a. relish . . . solicitous
   c. anguish . . . prone
   b. disdain . . . aloof
   d. obsession . . . callous

Enriching the Lesson

Exercise I. Myth and Ritual

In this lesson, we have introduced *ritual* (Word 346), meaning a prescribed way of doing things in order to satisfy some standard of a religious, intellectual, or emotional nature. Students of society and of literature have emphasized that the rituals practiced by any group of people are closely tied up with their *myths*.

The word *myth* (from the Greek *mythos*, "tale or story") is a word with many levels of meaning that has found new applications in recent years. In the most familiar and traditional sense, the word refers to an anonymous (usually ancient) story reflecting primitive beliefs and purporting to explain the mysteries of the natural universe. Thus, we have myths of the creation of the world, of the origin of a particular group of people, of heroes and gods, of cosmic catastrophes and miraculous redemptions.

The word *myth* is sometimes used in a rather pejorative sense. It suggests a belief that many people accept but that has no basis in fact and may lead to wrong and harmful judgments. Thus, we may say that writers such as James Baldwin and Ralph Ellison have devoted themselves to shattering racist *myths* about black people.

This has provided the basis for the word *demythologize*, which means "to strip away an accretion of legend and sentiment and to get to the hard facts underneath." We speak of historians who have sought to *demythologize* such revered figures as George Washington and John F. Kennedy. (Of course, there is always the danger that the "demythologizer," in seeking to be rigorously critical and "scientific," may be propagating new myths.)

In more recent theory, a *myth* is thought of not as a sort of harmless (or harmful) fairy tale but rather as a symbolic projection of a people's collective values. It is a way of expressing, in a communal or instinctive fashion, how a group of people feels about life and what its ultimate values are. The rituals associated with the myth —whether religious, patriotic, aesthetic, or whatever—are a means of expressing group loyalty and acceptance of a common body of tradition.

A myth, in this extended meaning, may be embodied in a work of art that strikes some very deep chord in the collective consciousness of the group. In this sense, Hamlet, Oedipus, Captain Ahab, and Moby Dick are all *mythic* figures embodied in literary creations. Whether or not they are literally "true" is beside the point. They are *mythically* true.

A sociologist might define a myth as the imaginative interpretation of social reality. In other words, it is a way of looking at the experience of the group and of making it satisfying and familiar in common human terms. It may have great value in promoting a feeling of solidarity and in helping the group to defend itself and to survive. Indeed, it has been said that there is no successful and long-lasting grouping of human beings that does not have its accepted mythology.

The great psychologist Carl Jung, a colleague and then a rival of Sigmund Freud, built his interpretation of human nature and behavior on myths. The accepted myths of the group, as Jung saw it, represent *archetypes* of the human psyche or mind. An *archetype* in this sense is a basic pattern or theme of life experience to which special details may be added to make a story. There is, for example, the archetype of the struggle between a hero and a monster, which may represent symbolically man's never-ending fight against the hostile forces of nature that seek to destroy him. Virtually all cultures of which we have any knowledge seem to possess some variation of this mythical archetype.

Modern anthropologists (*anthropology* is the "science of man") undertake, among other things, the comparative study of the mythologies of different societal groups. Much attention is given to the mythologies of "primitive" (that is, "technologically underdeveloped") groups and to the rituals connected with them. However, anthropologists such as Margaret Mead have been quick to emphasize that the mythological traditions of such peoples are not necessarily more "fanciful" or "childlike" than the mythologies of people who consider themselves "highly developed."

A. The preceding discussion contained all of the following words. With or without the aid of a dictionary, define each.

1. traditional	11. projection	21. prescribed
2. purport	12. ultimate	22. propagate
3. cosmic	13. aesthetic	23. extended
4. catastrophe	14. colleague	24. collective
5. redemption	15. solidarity	25. symbolic
6. accretion	16. societal	26. primitive
7. demythologize	17. fanciful	27. embody
8. rigorous	18. anthropology	28. comparative
9. anonymous	19. archetype	29. psyche
10. communal	20. racist	30. technological

B. With or without the aid of an encyclopedia, dictionary, or other reference book, identify each of the following mythic figures.

1. Balder (Norse)	6. Marduk (Babylonian)
2. Quetzalcoatl (Mexican)	7. Prometheus (Greek)
3. Osiris (Egyptian)	8. Romulus (Roman)
4. Cú Chulainn (Irish)	9. Paul Bunyan (American)
5. Shiva (Hindu)	10. Siegfried (German)

Exercise II. A Verbal Diversion

The inclusion of *reticent* in Lesson 27 brings to mind the fact that modern English contains a good many compound adjectives that involve parts of the human body. A few of these items are listed below. With or without the aid of a dictionary, define each. Then choose any **five**, and, for each, compose an original illustrative sentence.

1. silver-tongued	6. openhanded	11. light-fingered
2. tightlipped	7. thin-skinned	12. tightfisted
3. hard-nosed	8. sharp-tongued	13. lightheaded
4. flatfooted	9. close-mouthed	14. wide-eyed
5. hotheaded	10. open-faced	15. hot-blooded

Exercise III. Expanding Your Word Power

The words listed below are not on the Basic Word List, but they were mentioned, in one form or another, in Lesson 27. All of them would make useful additions to your working vocabulary. Define each, give its etymology, list **two** synonyms and **two** antonyms (where possible), and use in a short illustrative sentence.

1. prolix	6. liturgy	11. reprobate
2. cogitate	7. embryonic	12. cant
3. retaliate	8. ploy	13. hypocrite
4. retrospective	9. hamstring	14. wan
5. recoil	10. blaspheme	15. hegemony

Lesson 28

---

356. scape·goat *noun* skāp´-gōt

[*(e)scape* + *goat*; an English translation of *ez-ozel* (Hebrew), "goat that escapes," from the allusion in Leviticus 16:8 to a goat that was let loose to perish in the wilderness after the Jewish High Priest had symbolically placed the sins of the Jewish people on its head]

Definition: Someone or something that is innocently made to bear the blame or punishment for the sins or misdeeds of others.

> "I can understand why *you* don't want to take the blame for this fiasco," I said, "but why are you trying to make *me* the **scapegoat**?"

> Making the Jews the **scapegoat** for the ills of Germany was part and parcel of Hitler's malevolent scheme to become master of Europe.

Synonyms: (*nouns*) victim, butt, target, patsy

Phrases: a whipping boy, a fall guy; pin the blame on; a witch-hunt

357. schism *noun* sĭz´-əm *or* skĭz´-əm

[*schisma* (Greek), "cleft, division"; from *schizein* (Greek), "split"]

Definition: A split or division within the ranks of an organization.

> The split in the Roman Catholic Church that lasted from 1378 to 1417 is usually referred to as the "Great **Schism**."

> The 20th century has witnessed an ever widening **schism** between popular and so-called "serious" music.

Related Form: (*noun and adjective*) schismatic

Synonyms: (*nouns*) breach, break, cleft, rupture, rift, cleavage

Antonyms: (*nouns*) merger, fusion, union, amalgamation

Phrases: a falling-out among friends, a splinter group, a separatist movement; a fusion ticket

358. scru·ti·nize *verb* skrōō´-tĭ-nīz

[*scrutinium* (Latin), "search" (from *scrutari* [Latin], "search closely") + *ize*]

Definition: To examine closely or critically.

> I reread my essay carefully, **scrutinizing** it for errors that I had over-looked before.

Related Forms: (*noun*) scrutiny; (*adjective*) inscrutable

Synonyms: (*verbs*) peruse, study, inspect, pore over; critique

Antonyms: (*verbs*) gloss over, skip over, scan

Phrases: eyeball something; give something a lick and a promise

359. sec-u-lar   *adjective*   sĕk´-yə-lər

[*saecularis, saeculare* (Latin), "coming once in an age"; from *saeculum* (Latin), "lifetime, age, century"]

Definition: Not religious; pertaining to worldly (as opposed to spiritual) matters; pertaining to the state.

> The program presented at last night's concert contained a fine blend of sacred and **secular** music.

> It should come as no surprise to anyone that members of the clergy have **secular** concerns and interests just like everyone else.

> During the Middle Ages, a person convicted of a crime in a religious court was sometimes handed over to the **secular** authorities for punishment.

Phrases: secular studies, the secular clergy, secular humanism

Related Forms: (*verb*) secularize; (*nouns*) secularism, secularization

Synonyms: (*adjectives*) temporal, mundane (Word 270)

Antonyms: (*adjectives*) sacred, divine; spiritual; ecclesiastical, religious

The Secular Games

In ancient Rome, gladiatorial shows, chariot races (like the one from the film *Ben Hur* shown below), and other sporting events honoring the gods were given at irregular intervals. These entertainments, which lasted three days, were called the *secular games*, principally because they were supposed to be celebrated only once in a person's lifetime (*saeculum* in Latin). Theatrical entertainments, banquets, and the recitation of hymns specially composed for the occasion were also featured. One of these hymns has come down to us from antiquity. It is the "Secular Hymn" (*Carmen Saeculare*) composed by the Roman poet Quintus Horatius Flaccus (better known as Horace) for the secular games given by the Emperor Augustus about 13 B.C.

360. se-nile   *adjective*   sē´-nīl *or* sĕn´-ĭl

[*senilis, senile* (Latin), "relating to an old man"; from *senex, senis* (Latin), "old; old man"]

Definition: Showing the signs of old age, especially advanced mental or physical deterioration.

> "I may be getting on in years," granddad said at his retirement party, "but I'm not **senile** yet."

> By A.D. 450, the once vigorous Roman Empire had become decidedly **senile**.

Related Forms: (*nouns*) senility, senescence; (*adjective*) senescent

Usage Notes:
  a. *Senescent* and *senescence* indicate that someone or something is in the process of becoming old; *senile*, on the other hand, indicates that he, she, or it has already reached that stage.

  b. *Senile dementia* is the technical term for the abnormally rapid deterioration of the mental and emotional faculties that sometimes comes with advanced age.

Synonyms: (*adjectives*) aged, decrepit, doddering, feeble-minded, infirm, superannuated, obsolescent

Antonyms: (*adjectives*) youthful, adolescent, juvenile, infantile

Phrase: the science of gerontology

361. sol-ace   *noun and verb*   sŏl´-ĭs

[*solacium* (Latin), "comfort"; from *solari* (Latin), "console"]

Definition:
  a. (*noun*) Comfort or consolation in sorrow, distress, or misfortune.

> While waiting to be executed for treason, the Roman statesman Boethius sought **solace** from personal misfortune in the composition of one of the world's greatest spiritual works, *The Consolation of Philosophy*.

> It is the duty of a friend to offer congratulations in times of triumph, encouragement in times of trial, and **solace** in times of distress.

  b. (*verb*) To comfort or console.

> In his or her own way, everyone who attended the funeral tried to **console** the grieving widow.

Phrase: give solace to

Synonyms: (*nouns*) succor, sympathy, commiseration, condolence, cheer; (*verbs*) succor, soothe, reassure

Antonyms: (*verbs*) vex, aggravate, badger, worry, upset, alarm

Phrases: cold comfort; give someone a boost (*or* a lift), a letter of condolence

434

A group of senior citizens enjoying some of the fruits of retirement.

Some "Seniors" You Should Know

The English word *senior* comes from the same Latin root as *senile*. Modern English contains a good many useful expressions involving the word *senior*. For instance, a *senior citizen* is a person who has reached or gone beyond the age of retirement from a job. That age is, of course, 65 at present. A *senior high school* is a high school that usually comprises Grades 10 through 12. It is the counterpart of a *junior high school*, which consists of Grades 7 through 9 exclusively. A *senior* is a student in his or her last year of high school or college, or a person who is over the retirement age. *Seniority* indicates a privileged status attained by virtue of long service in a company, institution, or other organization. The privileges that seniority brings include preferential treatment in regard to promotions and choice of work shift. The phrase *seniority rule* refers to the custom by which members of Congress choose their committee assignments according to their length of service in the House or Senate. By the way, the word *senate* is also related to *senile*. Originally, it referred to a group of old men who acted as the advisers to a king or other ruler. Now, of course, it is used of the highest law-making body in the land, regardless of the age or sex of its members. *Senatorial courtesy* refers to the custom of refusing to confirm a Presidential appointment when both Senators from the prospective appointee's state or the senior Senator in the President's party oppose the idea.

362. sor-did   *adjective*   sôr´-dĭd

[*sordidus* (Latin), "filthy"; from *sordere, sorditus* (Latin), "be filthy" and *sordes, sordis* (Latin), "filth"]

Definition:
a. Filthy and mean.

Despite the great wealth and abundance this country has to offer, some Americans still live and die in **sordid** and depressing slum conditions.

b. Morally degrading or reprehensible.

The country was dumbfounded as, little by little, the **sordid** details of the scandal came to light.

Disgusted with what he considered the **sordid** materialism of his countrymen, the French painter Paul Gauguin fled to Tahiti to live close to nature.

Phrases: a sordid crime, sordid motives

Related Form: (*noun*) sordidness

Synonyms: (*adjectives*) foul, wretched, gross, sleazy, squalid; vile, shameful, dishonorable; crass

Antonyms: (*adjectives*) splendid, opulent, luxurious; admirable, meritorious, praiseworthy; noble, lofty

Phrases: a slumlord, urban blight

363. stam-i-na   *noun*   stăm´-ĭ-nə *or* stăm´-ə-nə

[*stamina*, the plural of *stamen, staminis* (Latin), "thread, fiber." Originally, the *stamina* were believed to be the threads of life spun by the Fates at a person's birth. These determined how long a person would live and, by extension, how much staying power he or she had.]

Definition: Endurance; the moral or physical strength required to withstand hardships or overcome obstacles.

A runner needs a great deal of determination, as well as remarkable physical **stamina**, to complete a 26-mile marathon.

Do you think that present-day Americans display the same amount of mental, moral, and physical **stamina** as the early pioneers?

I agree that the candidate is a brilliant person, but I'm not sure that he has the **stamina** to serve effectively in the most trying job in the world.

Synonyms: (*nouns*) fortitude, perseverance, guts, grit, mettle, staying power, energy, vitality

Antonyms: (*nouns*) weakness, infirmity, debility, frailty, fragility, lack of strength, impotence

Phrases: intestinal fortitude; run out of steam

The Fates

In Greek mythology, the Fates (*Moirai*) were three sisters who were believed to determine a person's life span by spinning and cutting a slender thread that represented time. (This thread was called a *stamen* in Latin.) Clotho ("Spinner") spun the thread, Lachesis ("Allotter") measured it, and Atropos ("Inflexible") cut it. The Romans called these divinities the *Parcae*, and they are known as the *Norns* in Norse myth. One of the most interesting representations of the Norns occurs in the prologue to Richard Wagner's great music drama, *Twilight of the Gods* (*Götterdämmerung*), which was first performed in Germany in 1876.

The Fates, by Michelangelo

---

364. ster-e-o-type *noun and verb* stĕr´-ē-ə-tīp *or* stîr´-ē-ə-tīp
[*stéréotype* (French), "a kind of plate used in printing"]

Definition:
    a. A conventional, usually oversimplified, conception or representation of something.

        Though we all have some tendency to think in **stereotypes**, Archie Bunker seems to have perfected the habit.

        In recent years, the women's movement has done much to demolish the sexist **stereotypes** of a bygone age.

    b. To force into a uniform, and usually oversimplified, mold; to develop a fixed and unvarying idea about.

        The various groups that make up our population are composed of all kinds of people; it would be foolish, therefore, to try to **stereotype** any one element of the population on the basis of race, religion, or ethnic background.

Related Forms: (*adjectives*) stereotypic(al), stereotyped

Synonyms: (*noun*) cliche; (*verbs*) classify, generalize about, typecast, pigeonhole, categorize

Phrase: force of habit

365. stig·ma·tize   *verb*   stĭg′-mə-tīz

[*stigmatizein* (Greek), "brand, mark"; from *stigma, stigmata* (Greek), "mark, brand, tattoo"]

Definition: To brand or characterize as blemished or disgraceful.

Stigmatized as a traitor by his fellow Americans, Benedict Arnold spent the last years of his life in exile in England.

Related Forms: (*nouns*) stigma, stigmata, astigmatism; (*adjective*) stigmatic

Usage Notes:

   a.   A *stigma* is a mark or token of infamy, disgrace, or reproach. For example, Edgar Allan Poe bore the *stigma* of having been expelled from West Point.

   b.   *Astigmatism* is a condition in which the eye does not focus properly. Glasses can usually correct this problem.

Synonyms: (*verbs*) denounce, condemn, decry, discredit, disparage, belittle; label, impute

Antonyms: (*verbs*) whitewash; compliment, extol

Stigmata

In Roman Catholicism, the term *stigmata* (the plural of *stigma*) is used to designate the impressions or marks that the Crown of Thorns and the nails left on the body of Christ during His crucifixion. Devout Roman Catholics believe that replicas of these marks have by divine favor appeared miraculously on the bodies of certain saintly men and women, including St. Francis of Assisi, on whose body the stigmata are said to have been impressed by a seraph with six wings.

366. stip-u-late   *verb*   stĭp´-yə-lāt

[*stipulari, stipulatus* (Latin), "make a specific demand for some condition in an agreement"]

Definition: To specify or demand as a condition for agreement; to guarantee or affirm.

> One of the clauses in the contract **stipulates** that the agreement may be canceled if the price of oil drops below a certain level.

> The lawyer for the defense **stipulated** that her client had employed the witness as a private investigator on numerous occasions.

Phrases: stipulate a price, stipulate the manner of payment

Related Form: (*noun*) stipulation

Synonyms: (*verbs*) require, contract, provide for

Phrases: a proviso, a must, a sine qua non; with no strings attached

---

367. strat-e-gy   *noun*   străt´-ə-jē

[*strategia* (Greek), "generalship"; from *strategos* (Greek), "general"; from *stratos* (Greek), "army" + *agein* (Greek), "lead"]

Definition:
  a. An overall plan of action designed to achieve a specific goal.

> "The **strategy** by which we hope to win this war," the general said, "employs guerrilla tactics and avoids set battles."

> Only a person with a broad knowledge of politics, social conditions, and popular attitudes throughout the country can effectively plan the **strategy** of a Presidential campaign.

  b. The science of planning and directing such an operation.

> Among the subjects I studied at West Point were **strategy** and tactics.

Related Forms: (*nouns*) strategist, stratagem; (*adjective*) strategic

Phrases: a strategic withdrawal, at strategic points, strategic bombing

Usage Notes:
  a. *Strategy* is sometimes used to perform the function of an adjective; for example, in the phrase "a *strategy* meeting."

  b. Do not confuse *strategy* with *stratagem*. A *stratagem* is a specific scheme or device employed to gain some advantage over an opponent. In other words, it is a *tactic*. *Strategy*, on the other hand, refers to the broad, overall plan of operation.

  c. The use of *strategy* is not confined to military operations; the word may properly be applied to business, politics, sports, or other areas of life in which planning is essential.

Synonyms: (*nouns*) plan, blueprint, program, policy, approach, scenario

Phrases: a game plan; operational tactics; the science of logistics

368. **stri-dent**   *adjective*   strīd´-ĕnt

[*stridens, stridentis* (Latin), "loud and harsh"; from *stridere* (Latin), "make a loud, harsh noise"]

Definition: Loud and harsh in sound.

On the corner a man shouting at the top of his lungs in a very **strident** voice was haranguing a throng of idle passers-by.

As election day got closer and closer, the tone of his political oratory became more and more **strident**.

Related Forms: (*nouns*) stridence, stridency; (*adverb*) stridently

Synonyms: (*adjectives*) grating, shrill, raucous, dissonant, cacophonous, jarring

Antonyms: (*adjectives*) mellifluous, euphonious, melodious, dulcet

369. **sur-veil-lance**   *noun*   sər-vā´-ləns

[*sur* (French), "over, on" + *veiller* (French), "watch" + *ance* (French), "state or act of"]

Definition: Close observation of a person or group considered suspicious; a continuous watch for the purpose of direction or control.

Throughout the period that the terrorist thought he had gone undetected, he was actually under close **surveillance** by the CIA.

The disputed territory was kept under strict UN **surveillance** until peace was restored to the area.

Observers on the ground keep close **surveillance** on air traffic at a busy international airport by means of various electronic devices, including radar.

Synonyms: (*nouns*) watch, monitoring, supervision, vigilance

Phrases: a police stakeout, tail (*or* put a tail on) a suspect, keep tabs (*or* an eye) on, industrial espionage

370. **syn-drome**   *noun*   sĭn´-drōm

[*sundrome* (Greek), "combination"; from *sun* (Greek), "together" + *dramein* (Greek), "run"]

Definition: A group of traits, symptoms, or signs that collectively characterize a disease or social condition.

A high temperature, a yellowish complexion, and a general feeling of overwhelming fatigue are characteristic of the mononucleosis **syndrome**.

The conference sought to develop effective strategies to combat the **syndrome** of violence, crime, and drug abuse that afflicts our society.

Synonym: (*noun*) complex

Using the Words

Exercise I. Parts of Speech

Indicate the part of speech of each of the following words. In some cases, two answers are correct.

1. schism
2. scrutinize
3. senilc
4. solace
5. stamina
6. stereotype
7. strident
8. surveillance
9. syndrome

Exercise II. Words in Phrases

In each of the following groups, select the item that best expresses the meaning of the *italicized* word in the introductory phrase.

1. a *schism* in the ranks
   a. traitor b. movement c. spy d. split

2. *scrutinized* the report
   a. ignored b. examined c. delivered d. questioned

3. *secular* pursuits
   a. religious b. scholarly c. typical d. worldly

4. slowly becoming *senile*
   a. feeble-minded b. tight-lipped c. iron-clad
   d. open-handed

5. sought *solace* in her scholarly activities
   a. payment b. glory c. knowledge d. comfort

6. *sordid* motives
   a. unclear b. shameful c. puzzling d. lofty

7. has no *stamina*
   a. money b. evidence c. staying power d. job

8. a *strident* voice
   a. shrill b. soft c. clear d. deep

Exercise III. Completing Sentences

Complete each of the following sentences by selecting the appropriate word from the given group of words.

stipulate	syndrome	scapegoat
strident	strategy	stereotype
stigmatize	sordid	surveillance

1. One of the clauses in the contract _____ that employees are to be allowed ten "sick days" a year.

2. The courts have placed strict limits on secret monitoring of telephone conversations and other forms of electronic _____.

3. He is clever at devising temporary measures to prevent his company from going bankrupt, but he seems incapable of developing a long-term financial _____.

4. "Instead of looking for a _____ to saddle with the blame for this mess," I asked, "why don't you admit your own responsibility for it?"

5. "Though the official must, of course, bear the burden of guilt for what he has done," Angela observed, "we should not allow his misdeeds to _____ innocent members of his family."

6. The fact that we throw away so much edible food is evidence of the _____ of wastefulness that seems to afflict modern American life.

7. Though we tend to regard racial and ethnic _____ as relatively modern phenomena, we should not forget that the ancient world thought in such clichés as well.

Exercise IV.   Synonyms and Antonyms

A. In each of the following groups, select the **two** words that are most nearly **synonymous**.

1. a. brand b. reply c. intrude d. condemn
2. a. consider b. inspect c. examine d. support
3. a. plan b. blueprint c. essay d. novel
4. a. modern b. sleazy c. affluent d. squalid
5. a. endurance b. fortitude c. memory d. plight

Now, for each pair of synonyms you have selected, supply a word from the Basic Word List for Lesson 28 (Words 356–370) that means the **same** or **almost the same** thing.

B. In each of the following, select the item that is most nearly **opposite** in meaning to the numbered word at the left.

1. secular a. financial b. scientific c. athletic d. political e. sacred

2. senile a. lush b. wealthy c. abrupt d. youthful e. kindly

3. strident a. mellifluous b. obscure c. hurried d. docile e. raucous

4. schism a. crusade b. development c. fusion d. rupture e. prologue

5. solace a. pay b. upset c. study d. answer e. burn

Exercise V.　Word Roundup

1. Give the origin of the word *scapegoat*.
2. With what is each of the following sciences concerned?

   a. gerontology　　　　　　b. logistics

3. Explain the difference in meaning between the words in each of the following pairs:

   a. senile—senescent　　　b. obsolete—obsolescent

4. Name the Fates, and explain how they were thought to determine a person's life span.
5. With or without the aid of a dictionary, define each of the following expressions:

   a. a whipping boy　　　　d. a slumlord
   b. a splinter group　　　　e. a game plan
   c. a senior citizen　　　　f. a stakeout

6. With or without the aid of a dictionary, explain what each of the following terms means:

   a. seniority　　　　　　　c. astigmatism
   b. merger　　　　　　　　d. espionage

7. With or without the aid of a dictionary, define each of the following foreign expressions used in present-day English, and tell what language it comes from.

   a. sine qua non　　b. scenario　　　c. proviso

8. With or without the aid of a dictionary or other reference book, explain what is meant by each of the following colorful phrases:

   a. to pigeonhole something　c. to eyeball something
   b. to give something a lick　d. to put a tail on
   　　and a promise　　　　　　someone

Exercise VI.　Framing Sentences

A. Use each of the following words in an original illustrative sentence.

1. scapegoat　　　3. solace　　　　5. surveillance
2. secular　　　　4. stamina　　　6. syndrome

B. Give a **noun** form of each of the following words, and use it in an original illustrative sentence.

1. scrutinize　　　3. sordid　　　　5. stipulate
2. senile　　　　4. stigmatize　　6. strident

C. Give an **adjective** form of each of the following words, and use it in an original illustrative sentence.

1. schism　　　　　2. stereotype　　　3. strategy

443

Completing Verbal Analogies

Complete each of the following analogies.

1. **gibberish : meaning ::**
   a. bombast : padding
   b. clarity : exhortation
   c. innuendo : subtlety
   d. drivel : substance
   e. stamina : endurance

2. **vitriolic : acid ::**
   a. petulant : wine
   b. decadent : water
   c. unctuous : oil
   d. sordid : milk
   e. secular : soda

3. **expurgate : censor ::**
   a. persevere : lie
   b. embezzle : steal
   c. desecrate : cheat
   d. award : rob
   e. solace : murder

4. **dapper : slovenly ::**
   a. shrewd : astute
   b. quixotic : feasibility
   c. coward : pusillanimous
   d. mellifluous : strident
   e. precarious : perch

5. **hypocrite : sanctimonious ::**
   a. showoff : ostentatious
   b. glutton : abstinent
   c. avarice : miser
   d. drunkard : winsome
   e. infantile : senile

6. **egregious : mountain =**
   a. punctilious : pigsty
   b. grandiose : foxhole
   c. dispassionate : toadstool
   d. precocious : mousetrap
   e. inconsequential : molehill

7. **asymmetrical : balance =**
   a. anomalous : function
   b. frog : amphibian
   c. satellite : autonomous
   d. amorphous : shape
   e. axiom : theorem

8. **dowdy : appearance =**
   a. abstemious : background
   b. gauche : behavior
   c. sedentary : age
   d. debonair : build
   e. prodigious : color

9. **fox : fur =**
   a. giraffe : gist
   b. monkey : simian
   c. ruminant : gnu
   d. parrot : plumage
   e. colt : foal

Working with Context Clues

Complete each of the following two-word omissions by selecting the pair of words that make the best sense in the passage as a whole. If necessary, consult a dictionary for the meaning of any word with which you are not familiar. Indicate the clue or clues that led you to choose your answer.

1. He was thrown out of the club for constantly _____ writing paper and other small items from the supply room. According to club rules, that type of petty theft constitutes valid grounds for _____.

    a. ordering...acceptance c. requesting...election
    b. pilfering...promotion   d. filching...expulsion

2. Today Paul Bunyan isn't remembered for what he thought or said. No, his gigantic size and extraordinary _____ of strength are the things that have made him _____.

    a. tests...repugnant   c. acts...unknown
    b. feats...immortal   d. lack...repellent

3. Does the old saying, "Nothing _____, nothing gained," mean that someone who expects to be well _____ for his or her efforts must be prepared to take a few risks?

    a. planned...educated   c. ventured...rewarded
    b. accomplished...timed   d. needed...paid

4. Her _____ are just average, but she has exploited them to the fullest. He, on the other hand, was given great natural abilities, but he has _____ them on trifles.

    a. talents...squandered   c. ideas...questioned
    b. relatives...exhausted   d. needs...employed

5. The _____ statistics contained in the article certainly impaired its effectiveness. If the author had made sure that his figures were correct, his argument would have been more _____.

    a. accurate...revealing   c. erroneous...convincing
    b. questionable...exorbitant d. recent...complete

6. "We deeply regret that conditions in our public transportation system have become so _____," the official declared. "Still, people must try to put up with this deplorable _____ until the city has had time to correct it."

    a. intolerable...situation   c. incongruous...journey
    b. inalienable...arrangement d. ineffable...problem

Enriching the Lesson

Exercise I.   Fairness in Language

One of the most basic complaints of supporters of the women's movement today is that there are sexist attitudes embedded in our language that tend to belittle and degrade women. They call attention, for example, to usages such as the following:

- The use of the masculine pronoun in contexts that should apply to women fully as much as to men. For example, we may say, "Each of us should do *his* best to serve *his* community." Does this imply that men are the pivotal figures in society and that the role of women is inferior and inconsequential? Perhaps there is no such idea in the mind of the speaker or writer, but it may still be true that the constant use of this kind of expression reflects and reinforces sexist attitudes, if only on an unconscious level. It may be argued that English, unlike some other languages, doesn't have an equivalent for *he* and *his* that applies to both sexes and that we must live with this peculiarity of our language. The answer is that one can usually get around the snag with just a little ingenuity. For example, "All of us should do *our* best to serve *our* community."

- The use of *Mrs.* and *Miss* as terms of address for married and unmarried women, respectively. The term *Mr.* applies to men, whether married or not. Does this imply, perhaps, that a woman has no real identity aside from her marital status— that is, her relationship to men? Supporters of the women's movement recommend the title *Ms.* for all women, and this form has been quite widely adopted.

- The use of such expressions as *chairman, Congressman, foreman, spokesman,* and *anchorman* to indicate positions of authority and importance. It is often said that the *man* part of such terms is simply a convention of language, with no sexist intent. However, feminists and their supporters assert that such expressions derive from a period when male dominance was taken for granted and that it is time to root them out. Suggested substitutes, such as *Congressperson* and *chairperson,* seem rather strange at first, but with continued use, they begin to sound quite normal.

- The tendency to specify the sex of a doctor, lawyer, or some other professional person who happens to be a woman. One may say, for example, "I am being treated by a lady dentist." Would you say, "I am being treated by a man dentist"? Or (even more ridiculous) by a "gentleman dentist"? Surely, sex is irrelevant to professional qualifications, and the specification that a dentist is a woman is male-oriented and patronizing, if not insulting. Incidentally, the use of *lady* is frowned upon by many feminists because it suggests a delicate and sheltered creature, probably of the "upper classes," who must be kept apart from the gross realities of real life. The more down-to-earth term *woman*—the exact equivalent of *man*—is much preferred.

You may not be inclined to accept fully all such criticisms of our language habits. However, it is hard to deny that there *are* many conventions of English usage that reflect a male-dominated society, and that it is high time to make some changes that reflect the status and attitudes of women in our own time.

Listed below are some words and phrases commonly used in connection with the women's movement. Define each.

1. sexism	9. stigma	17. denigrate
2. feminism	10. male chauvinism	18. conformity
3. stereotype	11. taboo	19. liberation
4. feminine mystique	12. consciousness-raising	20. male supremacy
5. conventions	13. grievance	21. dependence
6. frustration	14. fulfillment	22. domestic
7. discrimination	15. identity	23. monogamy
8. equal rights	16. career-oriented	24. confrontation

Exercise II. "Sound" Words

Lesson 28 includes the word *strident*, which refers to sound. A number of other useful "sound" words are listed below. With or without the aid of a dictionary, define each, and give its etymology. Then choose any **five**, and, for each, compose an original illustrative sentence.

1. vociferate	6. sibilant	11. purl
2. rasping	7. shrill	12. dulcet
3. sonorous	8. tremulous	13. snarl
4. bleat	9. keen (*verb*)	14. discordant
5. quaver	10. stentorian	15. clangorous

Exercise III. Expanding Your Word Power

The words listed below are not on the Basic Word List, but they were mentioned, in one form or another, in Lesson 28. All of them would make useful additions to your working vocabulary. Define each, give its etymology, list **two** synonyms and **two** antonyms (where possible), and use in a short illustrative sentence.

1. cleft	6. succor	11. scan
2. fuse	7. squalid	12. vigilance
3. critique	8. debilitate	13. euphonious
4. scrutiny	9. categorize	14. monitor
5. superannuated	10. denounce	15. civil

Lesson 29

371. **tacit** — 385. **venal**

---

371. tac-it   *adjective*   tăs´-ĭt

[*tacitus* (Latin), "silent"; from *tacere* (Latin), "be silent"]

Definition: Unspoken; implied or inferred.

Her friendly smile of recognition was a **tacit** invitation to join the little group of admirers surrounding her.

When my proposal was returned without comment of any kind, I took it as **tacit** approval to proceed.

"Don't you think that anybody who neglects to vote is in a way giving **tacit** support to the enemies of democracy?" she asked.

Though we were still angry with each other, we had a **tacit** agreement not to let our feelings show while our parents were present.

Phrases: a tacit assumption, tacit consent, a tacit warning, a tacit arrangement

Related Forms: (*noun*) tacitness; (*adverb*) tacitly

Synonyms: (*adjectives*) understood, implicit, wordless, unexpressed, unvoiced

Antonyms: (*adjectives*) explicit, express, expressed, specific

Phrase: a silent partner

372. tac-i-turn   *adjective*   tăs´-ə-tûrn

[*taciturnus* (Latin), "silent"; from *tacere, tacitus* (Latin), "be silent"]

Definition: Habitually untalkative.

My uncle is a **taciturn** man who rarely utters more than a word or two at a time.

Some of my friends are as talkative as magpies; others are definitely on the **taciturn** side.

Jim is such a **taciturn** fellow that I sometimes forget he is even in the room.

Related Forms: (*noun*) taciturnity; (*adverb*) taciturnly

Synonyms: (*adjectives*) close-mouthed, tight-lipped, laconic, reserved, uncommunicative, reticent (Word 341)

Antonyms: (*adjectives*) talkative, loquacious, garrulous, prolix, voluble

Phrases: economy of words, give someone the silent treatment, a silent butler

373. **tan-gi-ble**   *adjective*   tăn´-jə-bəl

[*tangibilis, tangibile* (Late Latin), "able to be touched"; from *tangere* (Latin), "touch"]

Definition: Capable of being touched; real or concrete.

"Your suspicions may indeed be justified," the D.A. remarked, "but until you can come up with some **tangible** evidence to support them, my hands are tied."

One **tangible** result of the policy was a slow but steady decline in the annual rate of inflation.

Phrases: a tangible reward, a tangible benefit, a tangible gain, tangible assets

Related Forms: (*nouns*) tangibility, tangibleness; (*adverb*) tangibly; (*adjective*) intangible

Usage Notes:
a. The legal term *tangible assets* refers to possessions that are capable of being valued in money or can be turned into cash. Similarly, the related term *tangibles* indicates material assets or property.

b. *Intangible* means "not capable of being perceived, identified, or defined precisely." In other words, something that is intangible is *elusive*. The plural noun *intangibles* refers to things that cannot be perceived or identified, especially what cannot be perceived by the senses. For example, a person's influence on the course of events is an intangible.

Synonyms: (*adjectives*) perceptible, discernible, palpable; material, actual, physical, solid

Antonyms: (*adjectives*) imperceptible, insubstantial, immaterial, untouchable; nebulous, hazy, vague

374. **ten-a-ble**   *adjective*   tĕn´-ə-bəl

[*tenable* (Old French), "capable of being held"; from *tenere* (Latin), "hold"]

Definition: Capable of being defended or maintained.

When the general realized that his forward positions were no longer **tenable**, he ordered an immediate withdrawal to more defensible ground.

Modern scientific research has shown that many 19th-century theories about the origins of language are no longer **tenable**.

Phrases: a tenable argument, a tenable idea, a tenable assumption

Related Forms: (*nouns*) tenableness, tenability; (*adverb*) tenably; (*adjective*) untenable

Synonyms: (*adjectives*) defensible, defendable, maintainable; irrefutable, incontestable, unassailable; plausible, believable, credible

Antonyms: (*adjectives*) indefensible, insupportable, unmaintainable; flawed, faulty; specious, implausible, questionable

375. ten-ta-tive   *adjective*   těn´-tə-tǐv

[*tentativus* (Medieval Latin), "provisional"; from *tentare, tentatus* (Latin), "try, attempt"]

Definition: In the nature of an experiment or trial; uncertain.

"We have made **tentative** plans to go to the shore next weekend," Randy reported, "but we will call off the trip if the weather turns bad."

A sort of **tentative**, almost apologetic smile spread over his face when I told him that I wasn't angry at him for making a first-class mess of the project.

Phrases: a tentative arrangement, tentative acceptance, a tentative schedule

Related Forms: (*noun*) tentativeness; (*adverb*) tentatively

Usage Note:
Occasionally *tentative* is used as a noun with the meaning "an experiment."

Synonyms: (*adjectives*) provisional, contingent, probationary, interim; experimental, exploratory; hesitant, unsure, doubtful; iffy

Antonyms: (*adjectives*) definite, settled, certain, finalized

Phrases: send up a trial balloon, a pilot program, subject to change, contingency plans, buy something on approval; finalize one's plans

376. thwart   *verb*   thwôrt

[*thwerr, thwert* (Old Norse), "oblique; across"]

Definition: To block or frustrate.

In 1978, a Fascist attempt to take over the Spanish government and set up a military dictatorship was **thwarted** by the prompt and energetic actions of King Juan Carlos.

Our opponents' alert defense **thwarted** our efforts to score on a surprise end sweep.

"Watching too much TV has a tendency to **thwart** the natural growth of a child's reading abilities," the noted educator remarked.

Related Form: (*preposition*) athwart

Usage Note:
Athwart is an old preposition that mean "across" or "crosswise." It sometimes occurs in older writing or literature; for example, in the phrase "a log lying *athwart* my path."

Synonyms: (*verbs*) foil, baffle (Word 54), neutralize, defeat, stymie, cripple; impede, inhibit

Antonyms: (*verbs*) promote, aid, help, abet (Word 2), encourage, advance, foster

Phrases: short-circuit something, nip something in the bud, take the wind out of someone's sails, clip someone's wings

450

377. tran-quil   *adjective*   trăn′-kwĭl
[*tranquillus* (Latin), "quiet"]

Definition: Peaceful and quiet; free of mental agitation.

After years of living amid the noise and hubbub of the city, we were delighted to discover the **tranquil** atmosphere of that sleepy country town.

At first I was almost hysterical with rage, but as I grew more **tranquil**, I began to perceive that the situation was not as bad as it seemed.

"Now that I have retired from the storms and stresses of the political arena," the ex-Senator remarked, "my heart has become as **tranquil** as a country churchyard on an autumn afternoon."

Related Forms: (*nouns*) tranquility, tranquilness, tranquilizer; (*verb*) tranquilize

Phrase: domestic tranquility

Usage Note:
A *tranquilizer* is a drug that lessens anxiety or tension in a person or animal. Valium, Librium, and Triavil, for example, are commonly used tranquilizers.

Synonyms: (*adjectives*) calm, serene, placid; cool, composed, self-possessed, unexcited, unperturbed; impassive, dispassionate

Antonyms: (*adjectives*) turbulent (Word 380), tumultuous, stormy, tempestuous, raucous; distraught, agitated, troubled, upset

Phrase: keep one's cool

378. trau-mat-ic   *adjective*   trô-măt′-ĭk *or* trou-măt′-ĭk
[*trauma* (Greek), "wound" + *ikos* (Greek), "relating to"]

Definition: So shocking as to produce a lasting psychological effect.

"Being lost in the woods for almost a day," Fred recalled, "was one of the most **traumatic** experiences of my childhood."

The sudden death or assassination of a great political leader usually has a **traumatic** effect on his or her followers.

The aftermath of the Civil War was probably as **traumatic** for most Southerners, black and white, as the war itself had been.

Related Forms: (*nouns*) trauma, traumatism; (*verb*) traumatize

Usage Note:
In medicine, *trauma* indicates a wound produced by sudden physical injury. In psychology, it refers to an emotional shock that produces substantial and lasting psychological damage. The plural of the word is either *traumas* or *traumata*.

Synonyms: (*adjectives*) shocking, paralyzing, jolting

Antonyms: (*adjectives*) beneficial, salutary, salubrious; uplifting, inspirational

379. trench-ant   *adjective*   trĕn´-chĕnt

[*trenchant* (Old French), "cutting"; from *trenchier* (Old French), "cut"]

Definition: Perceptive and forceful; cutting.

"Today's newspaper contains one of the most **trenchant** letters to the editor that I have ever read," Estelle observed.

Dorothy Parker once dismissed an actress's performance of a certain role with the **trenchant** comment that she had run "the emotional gamut from A to B."

Phrases: a trenchant reply, a trenchant pen, a trenchant imagination, a trenchant argument, a trenchant writer

Related Forms: (*noun*) trenchancy; (*adverb*) trenchantly

Synonyms: (*adjectives*) incisive, keen, acute; effective, cogent; caustic, mordant, biting

Antonyms: (*adjectives*) bland, pallid; obtuse, vacuous, vapid, inane

380. tur-bu-lent   *adjective*   tûr´-byə-lĕnt

[*turbulentus* (Latin), "stormy"; from *turba* (Latin), "turmoil, confusion"]

Definition: Violently agitated or disturbed; restless or unruly.

During a storm the normally calm waters of the lake become so **turbulent** that a small boat may easily founder.

He is well informed and has many interesting ideas, but his **turbulent** nature infuriates the people around him.

The years between 1789 and 1815 were a **turbulent** era in the history of Europe.

Related Forms: (*noun*) turbulence; (*adverb*) turbulently

Usage Note:

Do not confuse *turbulent* with the related adjective *turbid*, which means "muddy," "unclear," or "confused."

Synonyms: (*adjectives*) stormy, troubled, tumultuous, tempestuous

Antonyms: (*adjectives*) calm, peaceful, placid, tranquil (Word 377)

381. u-biq-ui-tous   *adjective*   yōō-bik´-wə-təs

[*ubiquitas* (Latin), "state of being everywhere"; from *ubique* (Latin), "everywhere"]

Definition: Being or seeming to be everywhere.

"I almost get the impression that Harry is **ubiquitous**," Roseann remarked. "No matter where or when there's a party, Harry's present."

Nowadays nothing seems to escape the **ubiquitous** eye of the TV camera.

Related Forms: (*nouns*) ubiquity, ubiquitousness

Mechanics make repairs on a jet engine. The word *turbulence* is often used by pilots and other people connected with airplanes to indicate a highly irregular atmospheric condition produced by rapid changes in the speed and direction of the wind and the presence of up and down air currents.

Synonyms: (*adjectives*) omnipresent, pervasive, universal, ever-present

Antonyms: (*adjectives*) rare, scarce

Phrases: in short supply, as scarce as hen's teeth

382. ur-bane   *adjective*   ûr-bān´

[*urbanus* (Latin), "belonging to a city; refined"; from *urbs, urbis* (Latin), "city"]

Definition: Refined, elegant, and sophisticated in manner or style.

The American novelist Edith Wharton (1862–1937) usually wrote about the **urbane** gentlemen and elegant ladies who made up New York's social elite in the last quarter of the 19th century.

If these negotiations are to be successful, we need less emotionalism and more of the calm, **urbane** manner of a diplomat.

Related Forms: (*noun*) urbanity; (*adverb*) urbanely

Usage Note:
Be careful not to confuse *urbane* with its look-alike *urban*, which means "relating to, or characteristic of, the city." Synonyms of *urban* include *metropolitan* and *citified*.

Synonyms: (*adjectives*) suave, cosmopolitan, polished, genteel, smooth, bland, courtly, well-bred

Antonyms: (*adjectives*) crude, boorish, rude, discourteous, ill-bred, gauche

453

383. u·surp   *verb*   yōō-sûrp′ *or* yōō-zûrp′

[*usurpare* (Latin), "take possession of something simply by using or occupying it";
from *usu* (Latin), "by use" + *rapere, raptus* (Latin), "seize"]

Definition: To seize a power, office, function, or the like without any legal right to do so.

> In 1399, the Earl of Hereford **usurped** the English throne and set in motion a train of events that led to civil war 56 years later.

> The legislators resisted the Governor's attempts to **usurp** powers specifically granted to them by the state constitution.

Related Forms: (*nouns*) usurpation, usurper

Synonyms: (*verbs*) expropriate, arrogate; encroach, infringe; supplant, supersede

Phrases: a coup d'état, steal someone's thunder, steal the show, upstage someone, make inroads into

---

384. va·ga·ry   *noun*   vā′-gə-rē *or* və-gâr′-ē

[*vagari* (Latin), "wander"; from *vagus* (Latin), "meandering"]

Definition: A bizarre or eccentric idea, action, or condition.

> Any decision to drop out of school and hitchhike around the country is far too serious to be dismissed as a mere adolescent **vagary**.

> Making a success of a small business connected with one of our beaches or resorts is unavoidably dependent on the **vagaries** of the weather.

> "Say what you will," Steve remarked, "there's just no accounting for the **vagaries** of fashion."

Synonyms: (*nouns*) whim, caprice, peculiarity, quirk, crotchet, oddity, eccentricity

Phrases: a passing fancy, a maggot in the brain, a fad, without rhyme or reason

---

385. ve·nal   *adjective*   vē′-nəl

[*venalis* (Latin), "for sale"; from *venum* (Latin), "sale"]

Definition: Open to, or marked by, bribery or corruption.

> Although President Ulysses S. Grant was personally incorruptible, he surrounded himself with **venal** politicians and financiers whose scandalous dealings rocked the nation.

> Gaius Verres, Governor of Sicily between 73 and 71 B.C., headed up one of the most **venal** and extortionate administrations ever imposed on a Roman province.

Related Form: (*noun*) venality

Do not confuse *venal* with *venial* (note the *i*), which means "not serious enough to merit severe criticism" or "pardonable." For example, theologians speak of "a *venial* (minor) sin."

Synonyms: (*adjectives*) corruptible, bribeable, mercenary (Word 266)

Antonyms: (*adjectives*) incorruptible, scrupulous, honest, upright

Phrases: on the take, grease someone's palm

Using the Words

Exercise I.   Syllabication and Pronunciation

Syllabicate the following words correctly, and place the major stress mark (´) after the syllable that is accented when the word is pronounced. Two answers are correct in one instance.

1. taciturn
2. tangible
3. tentative
4. traumatic
5. turbulent
6. ubiquitous
7. urbane
8. vagary
9. venal

Exercise II.   Words Out of Context

In each of the following groups, select the item that best expresses the meaning of the numbered word at the left.

1. tacit
   a. laconic   b. implicit   c. general
   d. valuable   e. doubtful

2. taciturn
   a. unprofitable   b. unspoken   c. unlikely
   d. uncommunicative   e. unfortunate

3. tenable
   a. calm   b. worthless   c. experimental
   d. biting   e. defendable

4. traumatic
   a. banal   b. wealthy   c. shocking
   d. faithful   e. reliable

5. trenchant
   a. incisive   b. specific   c. muddy
   d. provisional   e. inane

6. turbulent
   a. sunny   b. cool   c. humid   d. rainy
   e. stormy

7. urbane
   a. prominent   b. final   c. suave   d. affluent
   e. metropolitan

8. venal
   a. minor   b. corruptible   c. raucous
   d. sharp   e. beneficial

Exercise III. Completing Sentences

Complete each of the following sentences by selecting the most appropriate word from the given group of words.

thwart	tentative	tranquil
tangible	vagary	traumatic
ubiquitous	venal	usurp

1. Camels may be a rare sight in the United States, but in the Sahara they are _____.

2. Farmers don't lead _____ lives, free of cares and worries; they are involved in a tough and competitive business.

3. "Since my vacation plans were only _____ anyway," the busy executive remarked, "I didn't mind changing them at the last minute."

4. Far from abetting his starry-eyed scheme to run off and join a traveling circus, I did everything in my power to _____ it.

5. The plot of the novel concerns an evil nobleman's attempt to murder a young king and _____ his throne.

6. Since stock prices fluctuate for all kinds of unexpected reasons, it is often difficult to account for the _____ of the market.

7. Though recent political polls indicate that support for Candidate X has declined considerably, they also show that Candidate Y has made _____ gains in popularity.

Exercise IV. Synonyms and Antonyms

Classify each of the following pairs of words as **S** for **synonyms** or **A** for **antonyms**.

1. thwart—foil
2. trenchant—obtuse
3. usurp—seize
4. incorruptible—venal
5. loquacious—taciturn
6. defensible—tenable
7. tentative—provisional
8. tempestuous—tranquil
9. traumatic—paralyzing
10. boorish—urbane
11. quirk—vagary
12. tacit—explicit
13. tangible—concrete
14. turbulent—placid

Exercise V. Word Roundup

1. Explain the difference between the words in each of the following pairs.

   a. venal—venial

   b. urban—urbane

2. Define each of the following foreign expressions used in present-day English and tell what language it comes from.

    a. gauche   b. coup d'état

3. With or without the aid of the dictionary, explain what each of the following means.

    a. a silent partner   e. tangible assets
    b. a silent butler   f. contingency plans
    c. a pilot program   g. a maggot in the brain
    d. a tranquilizer   h. domestic tranquility

4. With or without the aid of a dictionary, explain what each of the following colorful expressions means.

    a. upstage someone   e. nip in the bud
    b. on the take   f. buy on approval
    c. keep one's cool   g. give someone the silent
    d. send up a trial balloon   treatment

Exercise VI. Framing Sentences

A. Use each of the following words in an original illustrative sentence.

1. tacit	4. tentative	7. trenchant
2. tangible	5. tranquil	8. ubiquitous
3. tenable	6. thwart	9. vagary

B. Give a **noun** form of each of the following words, and use it in an original illustrative sentence.

1. taciturn	3. turbulent	5. usurp
2. traumatic	4. urbane	6. venal

Dissecting the Words

Prefix

The Latin prefix **sub** or one of its variants appears in a great many common English words, including *subvert*, mentioned earlier in this book. This prefix has a number of meanings, including:

a. "Under, below, or beneath," as in these words:

    subbasement—a story or floor below the main basement of a building

    subjugate—(*sub* + *jugum* [Latin], "yoke")—to conquer or subdue. Noun: *subjugation*

    subliminal (*sub* + *limen, liminis* [Latin], "threshold")—below the level of conscious perception. Noun: *sublimation*

    submerge (*sub* + *mergere* [Latin], "plunge")—to thrust fully under, or cover with, water; to hide from view *subordinate* (*sub* + *ordinare, ordinatus* [Latin], "arrange in order")—(*adjective*) secondary; (*noun*) a person who is inferior in rank or status to another person; (*verb*) to make inferior to. Noun: *subordination*

subpoena (Latin for "under penalty")—(*noun*) a legal document requiring a person to appear in a court to give testimony; (*verb*) to order or serve such a document

substratum (*sub* + *sternere, stratus* [Latin], "lie flat")—an underlying layer; the foundation or groundwork for something

subsume (*sub* + *sumere* [Latin], "take up")—to place in a more comprehensive category or under a more general heading

b. "Secondary in rank," as in these words:

subcommittee—a subordinate committee composed of some of the members of a larger committee

subculture—a distinct cultural group within the main culture

subdivide—to divide a part of something into smaller parts. Noun: *subdivision*

sublet—to rent property from someone who is himself or herself renting it from the owner

c. "Away" or "after," as in these words:

subdue (*sub*, "away" + *ducere, ductus* [Latin], "lead")—to conquer or defeat

subsequent (*sub*, "after" + *sequens, sequentis* [Latin], "following")—coming after something in time or position

d. "Down," as in these words:

subside (*sub* + *sidere* [Latin], "settle")—to sink, decrease, or abate

subsidy (*sub* + *sidere* [Latin], "settle")—financial assistance. Verb: *subsidize*

e. "Up from under," as in this word:

subsist (*sub* + *sistere* [Latin], "cause to stand")—to live or exist. (Note that this verb is often followed by the prepositions *on* or *by*.) Noun: *subsistance*

f. "Secretly," as in this word:

suborn (*sub* + *ornare* [Latin], "equip")—to induce a person to commit a wrong or illegal act. Noun: *subornation*

g. "Somewhat less than," as in these words:

subhuman—not fully human

subtropical—relating to areas adjacent to the tropics

Note that **sub** becomes **suc, suf, sug, sum, sup**, or **sur** before *c, f, g, m, p,* or *r,* respectively. **Sub** also sometimes becomes **sus** before *c, p,* or *t.* The process by which this happens is called *assimilation* (see page 55). Here are a few words illustrating these changes:

succumb (*sub*, "under" + *cingere, cinctus* [Latin], "gird")—to yield or submit to; to give in to *suffice* (*sub* + *facere* [Latin], "do, make")—to meet present needs; to be equal to the intended task or function

suggest (*sub*, "underneath" + *genere, gestus* [Latin], "carry")—to offer for consideration. Adjective: *suggestive*

summon (*sub*, "secretly" + *monere* [Latin], "warn, remind")—to send for or request. Noun: *summons*

supplant (*sub*, "up from under" + *planta* [Latin], "sole of the foot")—to take the place of; to oust

surreptitious (*sub*, "secretly" + *rapere* [Latin], "seize")—performed in secret or by stealth

susceptible (*sub*, "up from under" + *capere, captus* [Latin], "take")—readily subject to or influenced by. Noun: *susceptibility*

suspend (*sub*, "up from under" + *pendere* [Latin], "hang")—to hang up; to bar temporarily from a privilege or position

sustain (*sub*, "up from under" + *tenere* [Latin], "hold")—to maintain, support, or prolong; to affirm the validity of. Noun: *sustenance*

Roots

1. The Latin root **ten** (also spelled **tain** and **tin**) means "hold." It is used in a number of common English words, including *tenable*, studied in Lesson 29. Here are a few more useful words in which it appears:

retain (*re* [Latin], "back" + *tenere* [Latin], "hold")—to keep or hold back; to keep in mind or remember. Adjective: *retentive*. Noun: *retention*

maintain (*manu* [Latin], "by hand" + *tenere* [Latin], "hold")—to carry on or continue; to preserve or keep up. Noun: *maintenance*

sustenance (*sub* [Latin], "up from under" + *tenere* [Latin], "hold")—support for life or health, especially food or a means of livelihood

tenacity (*tenacitas* [Latin], "perseverance")—persistence or perseverance. Adjective: *tenacious*

pertinent (*per* [Latin], "thoroughly" + *tenens, tenentis* [Latin], "holding")—relevant. Noun: *pertinency*. Verb: *pertain*

detain (*de* [Latin], "away" + *tenere* [Latin], "hold")—to delay; to hold in custody. Noun: *detention*

tenet (literally "he, she, or it holds")—a belief or doctrine held by a person or group

2. The Latin root **tang, tact**, meaning "touch," is the source of the word *tangible*, studied in Lesson 29. Other useful English words in which this root appears are given below. As these words indicate, **tang, tact** has a number of variant forms, including **tig, tag, ting**, and **tain**.

tact (*tactus* [Latin], "sense of touch")—the ability to do or say the kindest or most appropriate thing. Adjectives: *tactful, tactless*

tactile (*tactus* [Latin], "sense of touch" + *ilis, ile* [Latin], "pertaining to")—perceptible to the sense of touch; used for feeling

tangent (*tangens, tangentis* [Latin], "touching")—a line touching but not intersecting another line. Phrase: *go off at* (or *on*) *a tangent*

tangential—merely touching or only superficially connected with

contiguous (*cum* [Latin], "with" + *tangere* [Latin], "touch")—having the same edge or boundary as something else; adjacent. Noun: *contiguity*

contingent (*cum* [Latin], "with" + *tangens, tangentis* [Latin], "touching") —dependent on events or developments that have not yet occurred; possible. (Note that this adjective is often followed by the prepositions *on* or *upon*.) Noun: *contingency*

contagious (*cum* [Latin], "with" + *tagio, tagionis* [Latin],, "pollution by touch")—transmitted by direct contact. Noun: *contagion*

attain (*ad* [Latin], "to, as far as" + *tangere* [Latin], "touch, reach")—to gain, reach, or accomplish. Noun: *attainment*

Exercise

1. With or without the aid of a dictionary, define the following words using the Latin prefix *sub*, and explain what the prefix means in each.

   a. subjugate
   b. subsequent
   c. subdivide
   d. subsist
   e. suborn
   f. subpoena
   g. subtitle
   h. subsidy
   i. subhuman

2. With or without the aid of a dictionary, explain the meaning of each of the following phrases involving an *italicized* word derived from the Latin root *ten*.

   a. a *retentive* memory
   b. a *tenacious* grip
   c. have *tenure*
   d. a *retainer* fee

3. With or without the aid of a dictionary, define each of the following words using the Latin root *tang, tact* (or one of its variants).

   a. tactful
   b. attainment
   c. contagious
   d. tactile
   e. tangential
   f. contingency
   g. contiguous
   h. intangibles
   i. tactless

Walter W. Skeat

To Walter W. Skeat (1853–1912) goes the credit for creating a general interest in linguistics in both England and the United States. In 1878, Skeat became Professor of Anglo-Saxon at Cambridge, a post he retained for the rest of his life. His most important work was probably *The Etymological Dictionary of the English Language*, which first appeared in 1882. It has been said that Skeat contributed more to a sound knowledge of English linguistics than any other scholar of his time.

Working with Context Clues

Complete each of the following two-word omissions by selecting the pair of words that make the best sense in the passage as a whole.

1. For days after the fire, the acrid _____ of burnt rubber hung in the air. It _____ everything, even getting into my freshly laundered shirts.

   a. smell. . .propitiated c. aroma. . .perjured
   b. stench. . .permeated d. fragrance. . .purged

2. A group of carefree four-year-olds _____ happily on the lawn, while from the adjacent patio their _____, like beneficent goddesses, made sure no harm came to them as they played.

   a. reposed. . .fathers c. frolicked. . .mothers
   b. collaborated. . .sisters d. battled. . .aunts

3. Their _____ display of emotion struck a _____ note that was totally out of keeping with the otherwise restrained and tasteful proceedings.

   a. mawkish. . .harmonious c. blatant. . .mellifluous
   b. impassive. . .inauspicious d. maudlin. . .discordant

4. We can go ahead with this project as soon as we have the _____ to finance it. Unfortunately, however, it must remain _____ as long as we lack those funds.

   a. staff. . .tentative c. time. . .active
   b. money. . .dormant d. backing. . .stable

5. You'll usually win a debate if your arguments are valid and convincing. If your position is _____, however, you'll eventually be forced to concede _____.

   a. bona fide. . .interest c. glib. . .support
   b. dubious. . .skill d. untenable. . .defeat

6. Most dictators don't just address their audiences; they _____ them. Their words are not meant to soothe or enlighten; they are designed to _____ the listener to violence and hatred.

   a. probe. . .insulate c. thwart. . .reconcile
   b. harangue. . .incite d. usurp. . .prod

7. I really appreciated the _____ that my grandmother left me in her will. Since, however, I couldn't thank her personally for her kindness, I decided to show my _____ by using her gift as wisely as possible.

   a. gift. . .indifference c. legacy. . .gratitude
   b. advice. . .clumsiness d. heirloom. . .disdain

8. "I hate to complain," the bored princess remarked to the court _____, "but as long as you're pulling things out of a hat, couldn't you come up with something nourishing? I'm hungry, and bouquets of fake flowers aren't particularly _____."

   a. magician. . . nutritious   c. jester. . . tangible
   b. clerk. . . pedestrian   d. physician. . . ordinary

9. On a clear day, I usually take a _____ stroll through the park after school. When a storm is _____, however, I hurry home.

   a. grueling. . . bellowing   c. leisurely. . . imminent
   b. lax. . . eminent   d. lethargic. . . unlikely

10. Some parts of the President's program were warmly received by Congress and passed without a fuss. Others produced a tremendous _____, and the _____ that they caused still hasn't died down.

   a. abyss. . . impediment   c. oblivion. . . armistice
   b. backlash. . . commotion   d. fiasco. . . opus

Enriching the Lesson

Exercise I. Is There a Doctor in the House?

The word *trauma*, studied in this lesson, now has a wide range of applications, but its first use was in medical science. This is just one example of how medical terminology yields words of general application to enrich and enlarge the vocabulary resources of English. A few other words of this type are listed below. With or without the aid of a dictionary, define each, and give its etymology.

1. diagnosis	6. convalescence	11. fatal
2. symptom	7. psychosomatic	12. prognosis
3. therapy	8. organic	13. inoculate
4. pathology	9. epidemic	14. hysteria
5. aggravate	10. debilitate	15. cancerous

   Now complete each of the following sentences by selecting the right word from the list of words given above.

1. My point is that if we borrow money to meet our immediate obligations, we will only _____ our long-range problems.

2. His style of oratory, which you evidently admire so much, seems to depend on building up emotion to the point of _____.

3. The crisis has been overcome; the immediate danger is past. Now begins the long period of _____.

4. It is our collective task in the years ahead to clear the social organism of the _____ growth of racial, ethnic, and religious prejudice.

5. This neighborhood has been going downhill rapidly, and it shows all the _____ of developing into a full-fledged slum.

6. It is difficult to predict how such a simple and isolated society will react to a(n) _____ of ideas and resources from the outside world.

Exercise II. Some "Tricky" Words

Some English words are very deceptive. They seem to mean one thing but actually mean something else. Anyone, therefore, trying to guess at their proper meaning on the basis of their appearance is likely to go far afield.

Below is a list of such "tricky" words that merit your close attention. First indicate what you think each of these words means, based on the way it looks. Then, with or without the aid of a dictionary, define each. Finally, choose any **five** of the words, and, for each, compose an original illustrative sentence.

1. scarify	6. fulsome	11. adventitious
2. histrionic	7. enjoin	12. momentum
3. quizzical	8. officious	13. egress
4. noisome	9. contentious	14. bombination
5. querulous	10. meretricious	15. irenic

Exercise III. Expanding Your Word Power

The words listed below are not on the Basic Word List, but they were mentioned in passing in Lesson 29. All of them would make useful additions to your working vocabulary. Define each, give its etymology, list **two** synonyms and **two** antonyms (where possible), and use in an original illustrative sentence.

1. provisional	6. neutralize	11. omnipresent
2. voluble	7. serene	12. cosmopolitan
3. palpable	8. raucous	13. arrogate
4. refute	9. inspiration	14. crotchet
5. interim	10. mordant	15. upright

Lesson 30

---

386. ve-neer   *noun and verb*   və-nēr´

[*Furnier* (German), "veneer"; from *fournir* (French), "furnish"]

Definition:
  a. (*noun*) A thin layer of fine material put on the surface of something in order to make it more attractive or cover defects; a deceptively attractive outward appearance.

> The table was made of inexpensive pine that had been covered with a thin **veneer** of fine walnut.

> Beneath the **veneer** of sophistication and urbanity, I recognized the amoral opportunist I had known so long ago.

  b. (*verb*) To cover something with a veneer of fine material.

> Aluminum siding is one of the most popular materials with which modern Americans **veneer** their houses.

Synonyms: (*nouns*) facing, façade, coating, gloss, sheen, overlay, varnish, lacquer, glaze; (*verbs*) overlay, laminate, whitewash, glaze, gild; mask, screen

Phrases: a false façade, a false front

387. ven-er-a-ble   *adjective*   vĕn´-ēr-ə-bəl

[*venerabilis, venerabile* (Latin), "revered"; from *venerari, veneratus* (Latin), "revere" + *abilis, abile* (Latin), "able to"]

Definition: Worthy of reverence or respect because of character, position, age, or religious or historical associations.

> Though he had retired from public life many years before, the **venerable** old statesman was still consulted on matters of national concern.

> I am glad to see that yet another **venerable** old building in this city has been declared a landmark.

> "The **venerable** oak trees that line the broad avenue to the big house," the guide said, "have seen a good deal of Southern history played out beneath them."

Related Forms: (*nouns*) venerableness, venerability, veneration; (*verb*) venerate

Usage Note:
Venerable is used as a title of respect for anyone who has achieved the first degree of sainthood in the Roman Catholic Church; for example, the *Venerable* Bede.

Synonyms: (*adjectives*) time-honored, revered, esteemed, august, eminent, hallowed, hoary

Antonyms: (*adjectives*) spurned, scorned, reviled

Phrases: as old as the hills, hallowed ground, hallowed halls, an elder statesman

The Venerable Bede

One of the most important historians of the Old English period was a Benedictine monk whom we now call the Venerable Bede (673?–735). Bede spent the whole of his adult life in the monasteries of Wearmouth and Jarrow in northern England. One of the most learned men of his time, he wrote treatises on all sorts of theological, historical, and scientific subjects. His most famous work is *The Ecclesiastical History of the English Nation.* Originally written in Latin but soon translated into Old English, this book contains a full and reliable account of the growth of Christianity in England and the flowering of Anglo-Saxon culture. It is still an indispensable source for the history of England between 597 and 731. Bede was named a Doctor of the Church in 1899.

388. ve-rac-i-ty   *noun*   və-răs′-ə-tē

[*veracitas* (Medieval Latin), "truth"; from *verax, veracis* (Latin), "true"]

Definition: Habitual adherence to the truth; accuracy.

My judgment may be open to question, but I have told you the facts as I know them, so you have no reason to doubt my **veracity**.

The 18th-century English poet Thomas Gray once wrote that any fool could compose a valuable book if he would only put down what he had heard or seen with **veracity**.

Phrases: unshakable veracity, the veracity of a witness

Related Forms: (*adjective*) veracious; (*noun*) veraciousness

Synonyms: (*nouns*) truthfulness, honesty, integrity, reliability, credibility; authenticity, genuineness

Antonyms: (*nouns*) dishonesty, falsity, spuriousness, deceptiveness; untrustworthiness

Phrase: in vino veritas

389. ver-sa-tile   *adjective*   vûr´-sə-təl *or* vûr´-sə-tīl

[*versatilis, versatile* (Latin), "revolving"; from *versare* (Latin), "turn" + *abilis, abile* (Latin), "able to"]

Definition: Capable of doing many things or serving many functions.

A truly **versatile** actor or actress is at home in many different types of theater, from tragedy and drama to comedy and farce.

"This company produces a **versatile** line of products designed for a wide range of uses in the home and office," the President of Amerprod Corporation boasted.

Phrases: a versatile basketball player, a versatile speaker, a versatile painter, a versatile garment, a versatile material

Related Forms: (*nouns*) versatility, versatileness

Synonyms: (*adjectives*) all-around, all-purpose, many-sided, multi-purpose; flexible, adaptable, resourceful

Antonyms: (*adjectives*) single-purpose; unadaptable, unresourceful

Phrases: all-purpose flour, an all-around athlete, all-purpose wear, a utility infielder

390. ve-to   *noun and verb*   vē´-tō

[*veto* (Latin), "I forbid"; from *vetare* (Latin), "forbid"]

Definition:

a. (*noun*) The right or power of the chief executive to reject measures approved by the legislative body; any authoritative prohibition.

"Even if the legislation is approved by both houses of Congress," the Senator observed, "a Presidential **veto** is sure to prevent it from becoming law."

The Principal's **veto** put a quick end to Student Council plans for setting up a senior smoking lounge next to the cafeteria.

b. (*verb*) To prevent a bill from becoming law by exercising the right of veto; to prohibit or reject.

Though the British monarch still possesses the power to **veto** bills passed by Parliament, no king or queen has actually exercised the right since the reign of Queen Anne (1702–1714).

I had planned to hitchhike across the country this summer, but my parents **vetoed** the idea.

Phrases: a pocket veto, the veto power, a veto message

Synonyms: (*nouns*) rejection, refusal, interdiction; (*verbs*) kill, quash, turn down, forbid, interdict, rule out

Antonyms: (*nouns*) approval, consent, sanction; (*verbs*) approve, ratify, sanction

Phrases: turn thumbs down to, say nix to; give something one's blessing, give something the green light (*or* go-ahead)

An American President signs a bill into law. The President has the right to veto legislation passed by Congress and return it (with a statement of his objections) to the house in which it originated. The bill can then be re-passed over the President's veto by a two-thirds vote of both houses of Congress.

391. vie   *verb*   vī

[*envier* (Old French), "challenge"; from *invitare* (Latin), "invite"]

Definition: To struggle for superiority with; to contend with.

Having recovered from a crushing defeat in World War II, Japan now **vies** with the world's leading manufacturing countries for control of the electronics and computer market.

Three teams are now **vying** with one another for possession of first place in the American League East.

Synonyms: (*verbs*) compete, contest

Phrases: neck and neck; nolo contendere

392. vin-dic-tive   *adjective*   vĭn-dĭk´-tĭv

[*vindicta* (Latin), "vengeance" + *ivus*, a Latin suffix roughly meaning "tending toward" or "performing"]

Definition: Inclined to seek revenge; intended to inflict pain or harm.

Though I am by no means a **vindictive** person, I sometimes find it very difficult not to retaliate for a particularly nasty insult.

Related Forms: (*noun*) vindictiveness; (*adverb*) vindictively

Synonyms: (*adjectives*) vengeful, revengeful, retaliatory, malevolent, spiteful, hostile

Antonyms: (*adjectives*) magnanimous, forgiving, conciliatory

Phrases: bear a grudge; bury the hatchet; let bygones be bygones

467

393. **vi-ti-ate**   *verb*   vĭsh´-ē-āt

[*vitiare, vitiatus* (Latin), "injure"; from *vitium* (Latin), "defect, flaw"]

Definition: To impair the quality, force, or value of; to debase.

Even though the effect of the article was somewhat **vitiated** by erroneous statistics and garbled quotations, the point it was making was sound.

"Be careful," the elder statesman told the would-be Presidential candidate. "Every time you make a wrong choice or take a questionable stand, you **vitiate** your influence in the party."

Related Form: (*noun*) vitiation

Synonyms: (*verbs*) mar, poison, taint, contaminate, reduce, lower, lessen, weaken, depreciate, dilute, tarnish

Antonyms: (*verbs*) strengthen, buttress (Word 73), bolster, reinforce, promote, brace

Phrase: feet of clay

Feet of Clay

One of the most interesting expressions that present-day English has derived from the Bible is *feet of clay*. The expression comes from the Old Testament Book of Daniel. Nebuchadnezzar II (605–562 B.C.), the conqueror-king of Babylon, was troubled by a bad dream in which he saw a statue of himself. The Bible describes this statue as follows: "This image's head was of fine gold, its chest and arms of silver, its stomach and thighs of brass, its legs of iron, and its feet partly of iron and partly of clay." In the dream, a stone thrown by some unseen supernatural force (*i.e.*, God) hits the feet of the statue and causes it to collapse and smash to smithereens on the pavement. Daniel explains that this is a vision of the eventual destruction of Nebuchadnezzar's kingdom as the result of some fatal flaw (the feet of clay) in one of his successors. By extension, the expression *feet of clay* has now come to mean "*any* fatal personal flaw that proves to be a person's undoing."

394. vol·a·tile   *adjective*   vŏl´-ə-təl

[*volare, volatus* (Latin), "fly" + *ilis, ile* (Latin), "tending to"]

Definition:

    a.   Evaporating readily at normal temperatures or pressure levels.

       Gases such as argon and helium are not very active chemically, but ammonia is extremely **volatile**.

    b.   Changeable and potentially explosive.

       "I feel as though we're sitting on a powder keg," the diplomat confessed in reference to the **volatile** situation in that troubled area of the world.

       I think that "having a short fuse" aptly describes his **volatile** temperament.

Related Forms: (*nouns*) volatility, volatileness

Synonyms: (*adjectives*) volcanic, heated, supercharged; mecurial, erratic

Antonyms: (*adjectives*) stable, static, constant, settled; stagnant, torpid, sluggish, inert, quiescent, dormant; phlegmatic

Phrases: a short fuse, a hot spot

395. wane   *verb and noun*   wān

[*wanen* (Middle English), "decrease"; from *wanian* (Old English), "diminish"]

Definition:

    a.   (*verb*) To decrease gradually in size, extent, power, or intensity.

       During the 19th century it was literally true that the sun did not set nor the full moon **wane** on the British Empire.

       As their infatuation with one another **waned**, they found themselves making excuses for not getting together as often as before.

    b.   (*noun*) A gradual decline or decrease.

       "If the President's popularity continues on the **wane**," the Senator remarked, "he may well lose the next election."

Usage Note:

Be careful not to confuse the verb *wane* with the adjective *wan* (pronounced wŏn), which means "pale or colorless." Two other words with which *wane* is sometimes confused are *wain* (a large heavy cart used in farming) and *vane* (a device for showing the direction of the wind).

Synonyms: (*verbs*) slacken, subside, dim, diminish, abate, taper off, ebb, fade, peter out, dwindle; (*nouns*) diminution, weakening, falling-off, fading

Antonyms: (*verbs*) wax, increase, intensify, grow, swell, mushroom, expand, augment; (*nouns*) increase, augmentation, growth, expansion, increment, addition, accretion

Phrases: an ebb tide, a recessional

396. wrath   *noun*   răth

[*wraeththu* (Old English), "anger"; from *wrath* (Old English), "angry"]

Definition: Intense anger.

"My father's **wrath** will know no bounds when he sees the damage I have done to the family car," Shelly moaned.

In a blistering tirade, the old prophet called down the **wrath** of God on those who had offended against His laws.

The easternmost tip of Cuba was the first populated area to feel the **wrath** of Hurricane Zelda.

Related Forms: (*adjective*) wrathful; (*noun*) wrathfulness

Usage Note:
Be careful not to confuse the noun *wrath* with its look-alike, *wraith* (pronounced rāth), which means "a specter or apparition."

Synonyms: (*nouns*) rage, fury, indignation, ire, choler, spleen

Antonyms: (*nouns*) favor, blessing, approval, pleasure

Phrase: in high dudgeon

397. yoke   *noun and verb*   yōk

[*geoc* (Old English), "yoke"]

Definition:

a. (*noun*) A wooden frame joining a pair of oxen or other draft animals together at the neck; any form or symbol of bondage or subjection.

    The barn had been turned into a museum of all kinds of old-fashioned implements and devices used in farming, including flails, **yokes**, and other interesting items.

    In 1776, the 13 American colonies cast off their **yoke** of subjection and declared themselves free and independent of Great Britain.

b. (*verb*) To join or bond together.

    Many of the pioneers crossed the Great Plains in Conestoga wagons drawn by pairs of oxen **yoked** together at the neck.

    A remarkable collaboration in the composition of light operas and other kinds of musical entertainments has forever **yoked** the names *Gilbert* and *Sullivan*.

Phrases: a yoke of oxen, the yoke of oppression

Usage Note:
In the phrase *a yoke of oxen*, sometimes encountered in older literature, the word *yoke* means "pair."

Synonyms: (*nouns*) harness, collar, oxbow; (*verbs*) hitch, link, harness, couple, unite

Antonyms: (*verbs*) sunder, separate, disconnect, dissociate, detach, split, divide

Conestoga wagons drawn by "yokes" of oxen brought the early pioneers into the fertile farmlands of the Great Plains.

398. **zany**   *noun and adjective*   zā´-nē

[*zanni* (Italian), "buffoon," a variant of *Gianni* (Italian), "Johnny," the pet form of *Giovanni* (Italian), "John," the name of the clownish servant in early Italian comedies]

Definition:

    a.   (*noun*) A comical person given to outlandish behavior; a buffoon.

      It disturbed me to watch a person of such taste and intelligence assuming the role of a vulgar **zany**.

    b.   (*adjective*) Ludicrously comic, bizarre, or absurd.

      I still enjoy watching the **zany** antics of old-time movie clowns like the Marx Brothers or Abbott and Costello.

      Whenever a party starts to get dull, you can count on their **zany** behavior to liven things up.

Related Form: (*noun*) zaniness

Synonyms: (*nouns*) clown, fool, prankster; (*adjectives*) ridiculous, laughable, hilarious, ludicrous, inane; wacky, goofy, loony

Antonyms: (*adjectives*) sensible, serious, proper, staid, sober

Phrases: play the fool; high jinks; a straight man

399. **zeal**   *noun*   zēl

[*zelos* (Greek), "fervor, enthusiasm"]

Definition: Enthusiastic devotion to something; fervor.

"In our **zeal** to improve the quality of life in the United States," the speaker declared, "let us not blindly discard old ideas and institutions simply because they are old."

Related Forms: (*nouns*) zealot, zealotry; (*adjective*) zealous; (*adverb*) zealously

Synonyms: (*nouns*) ardor, gusto, eagerness, passion, intensity, alacrity, vigor, enthusiasm, relish, keenness, rapture, ecstasy

Antonyms: (*nouns*) apathy (Word 32), indifference, listlessness, unconcern, nonchalance

Phrase: gung ho

Zealot

The Zealots were a group of fervently devout Jews who organized themselves into a sort of political party or "action group" during the reign of Herod the Great, King of Judaea (37–4 B.C.). They derived their name from their unswerving devotion to orthodox Judaism as prescribed by the Torah, the scroll containing the first five books of the Bible. (The Torah was used for instruction during services at a synagogue.) The Zealots opposed the secularizing tendencies of Herod and other contemporary Jewish leaders. They also detested the Romans, who controlled Palestine at the time, and frequently caused minor revolts and other problems for them. After a large-scale Jewish revolt was put down in A.D. 70, a group of Zealots fled to Masada, a fortress atop an impregnable rock formation overlooking the Dead Sea. There they held out against the Romans for several years. When the Romans were on the point of taking the place, the Zealots chose to kill themselves rather than submit to the hated foreign overlords. It is from the activities of this 1st-century religious group that present-day English has derived the word *zealot*, meaning "anyone excessively or fanatically committed to some cause, idea, or belief."

Masada

400. ze-nith *noun* zē´-nĭth

[*zenit* (Old Spanish), "apex"; from *samt ar-ra's* (Arabic), "way over the head"]

Definition:

a. The point of a celestial sphere that is directly above the observer and vertically opposite the extreme point below.

> We knew that it was close to noon because the sun was almost at its **zenith**.

b. The highest point or state of something.

> Historians agree that Rome reached the **zenith** of her power during the reigns of the "Five Good Emperors" in the 2nd century of the Christian era.

> "If I am indeed at the **zenith** of my creative powers now," the world-famous author ruefully thought to himself, "there is no place for me to go from here but down."

Synonyms: (*nouns*) summit, apex, apogee, peak, acme, culmination, climax, pinnacle

Antonyms: (*nouns*) nadir, perigee

Using the Words

Exercise I. Parts of Speech

Indicate the part of speech of each of the following words. In some cases, two answers are correct.

1. veneer
2. veracity
3. versatile
4. veto
5. vie
6. vindictive
7. volatile
8. wane
9. zany

Exercise II. Words in Phrases

In each of the following, select the item that best expresses the meaning of the *italicized* word in the introductory phrase.

1. a *veneer* of respectability
   a. façade b. wealth c. goal d. lack e. history
2. a *vindictive* attitude
   a. puzzling b. foolish c. healthy d. modern e. spiteful
3. a very *volatile* situation
   a. heartwarming b. explosive c. curious d. ordinary
   e. stable
4. *vitiate* the effect of the speech
   a. analyze b. confirm c. impair d. measure e. assess

5. a *yoke* around their necks
   a. jewel   b. oxbow   c. medal   d. sign   e. scarf

6. a *zany* thing to do
   a. sensible   b. costly   c. sad   d. ridiculous   e. thoughtful

7. the *zeal* of her followers
   a. fervor   b. age   c. intelligence   d. background
   e. number

Exercise III.   Completing Sentences

Complete each of the following sentences by selecting the appropriate word from the given group of words. Use each word only once.

zenith	vie	veracity
veto	venerable	yoke
wane	versatile	wrath

1. Toward the end of his life the champion wrestler's fabulous strength _____ to the point where he could hardly walk.

2. All through high school, Laura and Peter _____ energetically for first place in their class.

3. "Only a trial in a court of law can establish the _____ of the charges leveled at my client," the lawyer remarked.

4. A utility infielder has to be a _____ player because he is a "jack-of-all-trades" on the baseball diamond.

5. Though Spain had been at the _____ of her power during the 16th century, the 17th century saw the beginning of a long, slow decline in the country's fortunes.

6. The school I went to was a _____ old institution with a long and cherished history of outstanding accomplishment in the field of secondary education.

7. The countless religious ceremonies that the ancient Romans performed during the year were designed to gain the favor of the gods and turn away their _____.

8. "The President is still trying to decide whether to sign or _____ that bill," the aide reported.

Exercise IV.   Synonyms and Antonyms

A. In each of the following groups, select the **two** words that are most nearly **synonymous**.

1. a. hallowed   b. emaciated   c. revered   d. dilapidated

2. a. equitable   b. flexible   c. culpable   d. adaptable

3. **a.** complain **b.** compete **c.** contend **d.** confer

4. **a.** mar **b.** collect **c.** repeal **d.** impair

5. **a.** rage **b.** fury **c.** terror **d.** delight

Now, for each pair of synonyms you have selected, supply a word from the Basic Word List for Lesson 30 (Words 386–400) that means **the same** or **almost the same** thing.

B. In each of the following, select the item that is most nearly **opposite** in meaning to the numbered word at the left.

1. veto   **a.** boycott **b.** sanction **c.** permeate
   d. compete **e.** rescind

2. veracity   **a.** antiquity **b.** immunity **c.** sincerity
   d. equanimity **e.** falsity

3. wane   **a.** buff **b.** polish **c.** wax **d.** varnish
   e. glaze

4. zany   **a.** obvious **b.** weird **c.** expensive **d.** sensible
   e. ruthless

5. zenith   **a.** nadir **b.** anathema **c.** kudos **d.** plethora
   e. consensus

Exercise V. Word Roundup

1. Explain the difference in meaning between the words in each of the following pairs:

   a. wan—wane   **b.** wrath—wraith

2. What is *a pocket veto*?

3. Who were the *Zealots*, and how are they connected with the present-day meaning of the word *zealot*?

4. With or without the aid of a dictionary or other reference book, define each of the following:

   a. a hot spot   **d.** an ebb tide
   b. a recessional   **e.** a short fuse
   c. high jinks   **f.** an elder statesman

5. With or without the aid of a dictionary or other reference book, explain what each of the following means:

   a. in high dudgeon **b.** neck and neck **c.** gung ho

6. With or without the aid of a dictionary or other reference book, explain the meaning of each of the following colorful expressions:

   a. bear a grudge against   **d.** turn the other cheek
   b. turn thumbs down to   **e.** hit rock bottom
   c. bury the hatchet   **f.** give something the green
                                          light

Exercise VI. Framing Sentences

A. Use each of the following words in an original sentence.
sentence.

1. veneer
2. venerable
3. veto
4. vie
5. vitiate
6. wane
7. yoke
8. zany
9. zealous

B. Give a **noun** form of each of these words, and use it in an original illustrative sentence.

1. versatile
2. vindictive
3. volatile

C. Give an **adjective** form of each of these words, and use it in an original illustrative sentence.

1. veracity
2. wrath
3. zeal

Completing Verbal Analogies

Complete the following analogies.

Group A

1. **lawyer : legal =**
   a. nautical : naval
   b. policeman : criminal
   c. athlete : intellectual
   d. chef : culinary
   e. wraith : wrath

2. **deluge : water =**
   a. avalanche : wind
   b. holocaust : fire
   c. hurricane : ice
   d. snow : tornado
   e. blizzard : air

3. **sponge : impervious =**
   a. glass : brittle
   b. wall : rigid
   c. umbrella : porous
   d. belt : pliable
   e. circuitous : detour

4. **sword : brandish =**
   a. string : kite
   b. flag : wave
   c. inflate : deflate
   d. airplane : train
   e. unfurl : banner

5. **malevolent : unfavorable =**
   a. deft : favorable
   b. undaunted : unfavorable
   c. unfavorable : officious
   d. ominous : favorable
   e. scrupulous : unfavorable

Group B

6. **pinnacle : high ::**
   a. strait : wide
   b. plateau : steep
   c. haven : level
   d. abyss : deep
   e. flat : mountain

476

7. **bear : hibernate ::**
   - a. horse : mare
   - b. yoke : ox
   - c. scavenger : jackal
   - d. cow : ruminate
   - e. camel : giraffe

8. **fathom : depth ::**
   - a. width : meter
   - b. bushel : height
   - c. knot : speed
   - d. inch : yard
   - e. length : breadth

9. **small : infinitesimal ::**
   - a. large : small
   - b. poor : beggar
   - c. big : colossal
   - d. wide : deep
   - e. mansion : opulent

10. **poignant : sadden ::**
    - a. nondescript : whet
    - b. droll : amuse
    - c. frighten : zany
    - d. comfort : solace
    - e. innocuous : appall

Working with Context Clues

Complete each of the following two-word omissions by selecting the pair of words that make the best sense in the passage as a whole. If necessary, consult a dictionary for the meaning of any word with which you are not familiar. Indicate the clue or clues that led you to choose your answer.

1. Elected officials cannot be too careful about their behavior while in office. If they become _____ about matters of right and wrong, they may do things that the average citizen does not consider _____. Such mistakes could cost the offender his or her job.

   - a. solicitous...seemly
   - b. obsessed...prodigal
   - c. blasé...ethical
   - d. resolute...indiscriminate

2. Some of my friends have remarkably _____ memories from which nothing ever seems to escape. Unfortunately, I've been blessed with a memory that is as _____ as a sieve.

   - a. staid...durable
   - b. retentive...porous
   - c. ample...volatile
   - d. devoid...prodigious

3. A dreadful disease had reduced my friend to a pale shadow of her former self. For that reason, I did not at first recognize the _____ figure that lay in the bed before me. Indeed, it took me some time to find the happy, carefree girl that I had once known in the drawn and _____ face that I was now looking at.

   - a. cryptic...jaunty
   - b. ravaged...disarming
   - c. gaunt...haggard
   - d. stinted...fervent

4. Though they never seem to think alike on any subject, there isn't the slightest hint of _____ between them. I find that somewhat surprising. Usually two people whose views _____ so much dislike one another intensely.

a. persecution...abut
b. enmity...diverge
c. impunity...encroach
d. doctrine...nullify

5. For a while the politician stood high in public favor, but then his reputation suddenly _____ to earth. One day he was basking in the sunshine of popular approval; the next he was _____ under the yoke of universal disfavor.

a. plummeted...chafing
b. wavered...beaming
c. parried...wallowing
d. belittled...rankling

6. "My ability to hold this job will pretty much depend on the answer to one _____ question," I thought. "Will I prove to be hardworking and reliable or _____ and irresponsible?"

a. pivotal...shiftless
b. whimsical...personable
c. impending...tractable
d. vital...dexterous

7. "I certainly don't view the upcoming exam with any _____," I asserted confidently. "Still, it's a serious matter, and I'm not treating it with undue _____, either."

a. gallantry...vitality
b. nausea...interest
c. curtness...vexation
d. trepidation...levity

8. "The charges that have been leveled at my client are totally _____," the defense attorney told the jury in her opening statement. "Far from proving his guilt, the evidence that will be presented at this trial will clearly and unmistakably _____ his complete innocence."

a. unfounded...confirm
b. solvent...obliterate
c. naive...disclaim
d. rational...disprove

9. "You don't need to address issues that will clearly have no effect on the outcome of this election," the campaign manager told the candidate. "But it is _____ for you to take a firm stand on those that may prove _____."

a. tedious...bland
b. degrading...reciprocal
c. gratifying...pallid
d. imperative...crucial

10. "My critics claim that my support for human rights has never been anything but halfhearted," the Senator remarked. "However, the record clearly shows that I have been _____ in my commitment to this great cause. Indeed, I pride myself on the fact that I have never _____ or wavered in my allegiance to it."

a. offhand...malingered
b. steadfast...faltered
c. inert...adapted
d. negligent...loitered

Enriching the Lesson

Exercise I. Misusing Words: A Look Back

In earlier lessons we have referred to various ways of using language that are usually considered weak or ineffective, even if they are not flatly wrong. These "language flaws" may be classified under the following headings:

Clichés (= **C**)
Malapropisms (= **M**)
Euphemisms (= **E**)
Inappropriate Connotation (= **I**)
Gobbledygook (= **G**)

At this point, you will do well to review the sections in which these concepts are analyzed and illustrated. You will note that most of these flaws are matters of *degree*. For example, it would be extremely difficult to avoid clichés entirely, and there is no point in attempting to do so, but a piece of writing that is saturated with clichés is likely to be weak, boring, and even ridiculous. Similarly, a limited amount of euphemism in speech or writing may serve a good purpose, but beyond a certain point it almost always turns sour.

When you are confident that you have refreshed your recollection of these ideas, do the following exercise.

Each of the following sentences illustrates one of the language flaws listed above. Apply the correct identifying letter in each case. Then try your hand at rephrasing each statement in more acceptable form. (In some cases, you may be able to fit a sentence into more than one category. This really doesn't make too much difference, as long as you see what has gone wrong.)

1. *From a furniture store advertisement:* We sell the cheapest furniture in town.

2. *Sign in government office:* Illumination by electrical facilities is hereby required to be extinguished on these premises promptly upon the termination of daily activities prior to the vacating of the area.

3. We were all required to take cover during the stimulated air raid.

4. What a terrific bed! No sooner had I hit the hay than I was in the arms of Morpheus, and I slept like a top all night.

5. Alaska and Rhode Island are respectfully the largest and smallest of the 50 states.

6. He is world famous as an interpreter of Bach's music and as an organ freak.

7. Receiving the full weight of the enemy attack, the troops of the 5th Division broke and scampered to the rear at full speed.

8. It is the established policy of this company to extend full cooperation to its employees in assisting them to qualify for more responsible positions within the existing organizational framework of the enterprise.

9. When I saw that the doors were open, I made a bee dive for the exit.

10. The Nazis attempted to solve their minority problems by a policy of selective elimination of population elements considered undesirable.

11. Dr. Bellman is considered an outstanding maven in the field of cancer research.

12. With her exquisite features, magnificent eyes, flawless complexion, and long, golden hair, she was perhaps the cutest girl I have ever seen.

13. Having made every mistake in the book, I found myself behind the well-known eight ball and was in the depths of despair.

14. Is it any wonder that the country is in trouble when the administration has flaunted all the laws of sound financial management!

15. We worked like dogs to make our social function a rousing success.

16. At this point in time, we hope to finalize the agreement, with full confidence that profits will be maximized and that the bottom line will be a source of satisfaction to all concerned.

17. Our gridiron heroes looked none the worse for wear after a grueling workout in preparation for the annual classic against State.

Exercise II. Expanding Your Word Power

The words listed below are not on the Basic Word List, but they were mentioned in passing, in one form or another, in Lesson 30. All of them would make useful additions to your working vocabulary. Define each, give its etymology, list **two** synonyms and **two** antonyms (where possible), and use in an original illustrative sentence.

1. façade	6. ire	11. dilute
2. august	7. spiteful	12. nadir
3. deceptive	8. taint	13. hoary
4. resourceful	9. static	14. detach
5. interdict	10. increment	15. ecstasy

Review

Exercise I. Syllabication and Pronunciation

Syllabicate the following words correctly, and place the major stress mark (′) after the syllable that is accented when the word is pronounced.

1. legacy	6. precocious	11. stereotype
2. mercenary	7. propitiate	12. taciturn
3. nepotism	8. redundant	13. tentative
4. ostensible	9. resilient	14. venerable
5. permeate	10. retribution	15. veto

Exercise II. Parts of Speech

Indicate the part of speech of each of the following words. In some cases, two answers are correct.

1. libel	6. parody	11. sacrilegious
2. mammoth	7. peremptory	12. satellite
3. morass	8. pusillanimous	13. surveillance
4. narcissistic	9. recant	14. tacit
5. paraphrase	10. remorse	15. yoke

Exercise III. Words Out of Context

In each of the following groups, select the lettered item that best expresses the meaning of the numbered word at the left.

1. kudos — a. lawsuit b. glory c. agency d. falsehood e. inheritance

2. nebulous — a. tasty b. crazy c. lazy d. hazy e. daisy

3. obscene — a. foolhardy b. crucial c. outmoded d. frugal e. smutty

4. plaintive — a. majestic b. malicious c. melodious d. merry e. mournful

5. prowess — a. wisdom b. significance c. valor d. arrogance e. terror

6. rescind — a. repeal b. repeat c. repel d. reply e. reprove

7. ruse   a. fiasco   b. impasse   c. exodus
                  d. stratagem   e. enigma

8. solace   a. interest   b. comfort   c. schedule
                  d. report   e. ally

9. trenchant   a. experimental   b. profitable   c. fortunate
                  d. hazardous   e. incisive

10. vie   a. complete   b. complain   c. compete
                  d. compose   e. comply

Exercise IV.   Words in Phrases

In each of the following groups, select the lettered item that best expresses the meaning of the *italicized* word in the introductory phrase.

1. a *lucrative* business venture
    a. reprehensible   b. profitable   c. risky   d. clandestine
    e. expensive

2. *nomadic* tribes
    a. primitive   b. indigent   c. numerous   d. superstitious
    e. wandering

3. an *ominous* development
    a. disturbing   b. recent   c. puzzling   d. sudden
    e. pleasing

4. a *pernicious* influence
    a. pivotal   b. salubrious   c. curious   d. detrimental
    e. welcome

5. *promulgate* a law
    a. retract   b. support   c. announce   d. oppose
    e. amend

6. a group of *renegade* Republicans
    a. loyal   b. elderly   c. turncoat   d. eminent   e. junior

7. a *sanctimonious* pronouncement
    a. pie-in-the-sky   b. holier-than-thou   c. devil-may-care
    d. fly-by-night   e. hand-me-down

8. *scrutinize* a report
    a. write   b. suggest   c. ignore   d. type   e. study

9. *tangible* evidence
    a. hidden   b. questionable   c. new   d. fabricated
    e. concrete

10. a *vindictive* attitude
    a. retaliatory   b. benign   c. disinterested   d. strange
    e. foolish

Exercise V. Completing Sentences

Complete each of the following sentences or pairs of sentences by selecting the most appropriate word from the given group of words. Use each word only once. Make any adjustments that are necessary to fit the words into the sentences properly.

Group A

relent	procrastinate	negligible
pensive	scapegoat	phobia

1. "Why are you so _____ today?" I asked. "Do you have something weighing on your mind?"

2. "Don't postpone your research until the last minute," my professor cautioned me. "Students who _____ usually can't get their term papers done on time."

3. "Though I'm perfectly willing to take the blame for my own mistakes," I replied angrily, "I'm not about to let you make me the _____ for yours."

4. By then the hurricane had pretty much blown itself out, and damage in the area was _____.

5. Over the years, her childhood fear of heights developed into a serious and debilitating _____.

Group B

stamina	volatile	lush
usurp	reminisce	pandemonium

6. It is hard to believe that such a bleak and barren wasteland had once been a _____ tropical paradise.

7. In an interesting article called "Strolling Down Memory Lane," a world-famous actress _____ about life in the theater over 50 years ago.

8. The kind of physical, mental, and emotional _____ a runner needs to complete a 26-mile marathon can justly be called "true grit."

9. In Shakespeare's *Richard III*, the villainous Duke of Gloucester has his royal nephew murdered in the Tower of London and then _____ his throne.

10. "We're sitting on a volcano that is ready to erupt," the official remarked in reference to the _____ situation in that turbulent part of the world.

Exercise VI. Synonyms and Antonyms

Classify each of the following pairs of words as **S** for **synonyms** or **A** for **antonyms**.

1. lackadaisical—energetic
2. nominal—token
3. fixation—obsession
4. prelude—aftermath
5. quell—foment
6. undermine—sabotage
7. raze—erect
8. schism—rift
9. pervasive—ubiquitous
10. zenith—nadir

Exercise VII. Framing Sentences

Use each of the following words in an original illustrative sentence.

1. mandatory
2. motley
3. novice
4. opportune
5. poignant
6. purge
7. replenish
8. ritual
9. salient
10. strident
11. sordid
12. thwart
13. vagary
14. veneer
15. zeal

Exercise VIII. Related Forms

A. Give a **noun** form of each of the following words.

1. perjure
2. prodigious
3. reciprocate
4. predatory
5. ostracize
6. versatile

B. Give a **verb** form of each of the following words.

1. plagiarism
2. tranquil
3. traumatic

C. Give an **adjective** form of each of the following words.

1. rudiment
2. strategy
3. nostalgia

D. Give an **adverb** form of each of the following words.

1. malice
2. paradox
3. lucid

Exercise IX. Word Roundup

1. Explain the difference between the words in each of the following pairs.

   a. obsolete—obsolescent
   b. officious—official
   c. senile—senescent
   d. venal—venial
   e. urban—urbane
   f. turbid—turbulent
   g. wrath—wraith
   h. wan—wane

2. Define each of the following.

   a. a muckraker
   b. a drone
   c. a timeserver
   d. a clone
   e. a has-been
   f. a gadfly

3. Explain the meaning of each of the following expressions.

a. a whipping boy
b. an elective course
c. a maggot in the brain
d. a checkered career
e. hero worship
f. a splinter group
g. sphere of influence
h. feet of clay
i. an urban nomad
j. tangible assets

4. Explain what each of the following colorful phrases means.

a. wet behind the ears
b. eat one's words
c. bury the hatchet
d. keep a low profile
e. send up a trial balloon
f. shed crocodile tears
g. throw in the towel
h. put a tail on someone
i. in high dudgeon
j. give someone the cold shoulder

5. Define each of the following foreign expressions used in present-day English, and tell what language it comes from.

a. idée fixe
b. vendetta
c. non compos mentis
d. scenario
e. wanderlust
f. sine qua non
g. amour-propre
h. coup d'état
i. quid pro quo

6. Explain the story behind each of the following.

a. Lilliputian
b. gargantuan
c. utopian
d. quixotic
e. chimerical
f. zealot

Exercise X. Etymology

1. Define each of the following words utilizing the Latin prefix *inter*.

a. intercede
b. interact
c. interlude
d. interloper
e. intercept
f. interim

2. Define each of the following words utilizing the Latin prefix *ob*, and explain what the prefix means in that particular word.

a. obverse
b. obituary
c. obtuse
d. obliterate
e. obsess
f. obdurate

3. Define each of the following expressions utilizing the Latin preposition *per*.

a. per annum
b. per capita
c. per se

4. For each of the following definitions, supply an English word using the Latin root *sanct*.

a. authorize
b. refuge
c. holiness

5. Define each of the following words utilizing the Latin root *tang, tact* or one of its variants.

a. tactful
b. contagious
c. tangential
d. attainment
e. contiguous
f. contingency

Cumulative Review

1. **abdicate** — 400. **zenith**

Exercise I.   Syllabication and Pronunciation

Syllabicate each of the following words properly, and place the major stress mark (´) after the syllable that is accented when the word is pronounced. In one case, two answers are correct.

1. academic	11. credibility	21. lucrative
2. aggregate	12. deviate	22. nostalgia
3. anecdote	13. duplicity	23. ostensible
4. anomaly	14. eminent	24. precarious
5. atrocity	15. epithet	25. procrastinate
6. bizarre	16. feasible	26. reprisal
7. bravado	17. formidable	27. sacrilegious
8. cantankerous	18. gregarious	28. stipulate
9. circuitous	19. heinous	29. vagary
10. confrontation	20. intervene	30. vindictive

Exercise II.   Parts of Speech

Indicate the part of speech of each of the following words. In many cases, two answers are correct.

1. abject	11. consummate	21. mammoth
2. advocate	12. delinquent	22. mercenary
3. anachronism	13. discourse	23. obsequious
4. array	14. eclectic	24. premise
5. atrophy	15. esoteric	25. prowess
6. benign	16. expedient	26. renegade
7. boorish	17. finesse	27. salient
8. buttress	18. harangue	28. stereotype
9. censor	19. incarcerate	29. taciturn
10. compatible	20. jettison	30. yoke

Exercise III.   Words Out of Context

In each of the following groups, select the lettered item that best expresses the meaning of the numbered word at the left.

1. abet   a. deplore   b. conclude   c. assist   d. refine
   e. hamper

2. agenda   a. failure   b. battle   c. omen   d. environment
   e. schedule

3. anarchy   a. chaos   b. poverty   c. throwback   d. prejudice
   e. curse

4. apprehend   a. accuse   b. catch   c. protect   d. invade
     e. release

5. augment   a. increase   b. scorn   c. curtail   d. expiate
     e. compensate

6. bicker   a. esteem   b. measure   c. provide   d. relax
     e. squabble

7. boisterous   a. bloated   b. dismal   c. friendly   d. rowdy
     e. suspicious

8. candid   a. learned   b. costly   c. frank   d. sour
     e. tactful

9. charlatan   a. officer   b. employee   c. fraud   d. baker
     e. relative

10. condone   a. point at   b. flinch at   c. aim at   d. rail at
     e. wink at

11. culpable   a. in unison   b. at fault   c. off guard
     d. on target   e. by heart

12. devout   a. casual   b. ignorant   c. eccentric   d. ardent
     e. polite

13. dormant   a. inactive   b. cursory   c. frantic   d. decrepit
     e. obedient

14. emaciated   a. gaunt   b. gigantic   c. gleeful   d. gingerly
     e. gracious

15. exacerbate   a. alleviate   b. incur   c. intensify   d. confuse
     e. humble

16. feign   a. cure   b. pretend   c. honor   d. cause
     e. investigate

17. fiasco   a. development   b. effect   c. reason   d. attempt
     e. failure

18. garble   a. distort   b. revise   c. allow   d. concede
     e. embellish

19. impasse   a. solution   b. tunnel   c. error   d. deadlock
     e. viewpoint

20. ingenious   a. expensive   b. modern   c. frank   d. clever
     e. dangerous

21. mandatory   a. grasping   b. lethargic   c. required
     d. masculine   e. profitable

22. moot   a. debatable   b. snobbish   c. radical   d. diverse
     e. monetary

23. parody   a. saloon   b. monsoon   c. pontoon   d. lampoon
     e. dragoon

24. pernicious   a. welcome   b. eternal   c. fragile   d. economical
     e. harmful

25. prerogative   a. privilege   b. facility   c. antipathy
     d. circumstance   e. requirement

26. rescind   a. reply   b. repeal   c. reprove   d. repel   e. repeat

27. retribution   **a.** hostility   **b.** discord   **c.** pestilence
                        d. vengeance   **e.** calamity

28. senile   **a.** open-handed   **b.** tight-lipped   **c.** feeble-minded
                        d. hot-blooded   **e.** thin-skinned

29. ubiquitous   **a.** incisive   **b.** omnipresent   **c.** vacuous
                        d. provisional   **e.** specific

30. veracity   **a.** endurance   **b.** wisdom   **c.** truthfulness
                        d. determination   **e.** agility

Exercise IV. Completing Sentences

Complete each of the following sentences by selecting the most appropriate word from the given group of words. Make any adjustments that are necessary to fit the words into the sentences properly.

Group A

distraught	accede	ignominy
incense	pseudonym	brash

1. Though most of the committee readily _____ to my request for additional funds, a few members stubbornly refused to countenance the unexpected expenditure.

2. "He is a _____ young man," the general observed sourly, "whose reckless and precipitate actions almost cost us the battle."

3. Though one of the women received the news of the accident with remarkable composure, the other became _____ with grief and worry.

4. Though most writers publish their works under their own names, a few prefer to use _____.

5. I could tell from the loud voices and angry words issuing from my boss's office that something had really _____ him.

Group B

cajole	innovation	inherent
enigma	affluent	replenish

6. The fact that I have grown up in a(n) _____ suburb does not mean that I am unaware of conditions in the inner-city slums.

7. Though we all desire to improve life in the United States, we should not blindly accept every _____ that comes along simply because it is new.

8. A little sweet-talk is usually a sure-fire means of _____ someone into doing what you want done.

9. When I realized that we were running out of potato chips, I made a hurried trip to the corner grocery store to _____ our supply.

10. Just who is being described in Sir Edward Elgar's _____ *Variations* has puzzled music lovers for close to a century now.

Group C

euphemism	sabotage	ethnic
anathema	caustic	lurk

11. He is so malicious that if he cannot control the organization, he may try to _____ or otherwise hinder its operations.

12. After the nightmarish experience I had in the park last fall, I began to imagine muggers and purse-snatchers _____ behind every tree or bush I passed.

13. When he said, "One man's meat is another man's poison," he simply meant that what one person likes may be _____ to somebody else.

14. In order to spare the feelings of relatives, funeral directors usually resort to _____ like "the loved one" or "the dear departed" when speaking of the person who has died.

15. She has a sharp tongue and a(n) _____ wit that she uses with great skill and imagination in her televised movie reviews.

Group D

collaborate	arbitrate	fathom
myriad	surveillance	secular

16. When the contract negotiations broke down, both labor and management agreed to call in an impartial third party to _____ the dispute.

17. One of the verses in my favorite sea chanty begins, "Five _____ deep my father lies; his bones are coral made."

18. For almost 20 years, Gilbert and Sullivan _____ on a series of world-famous light operas, including *H.M.S. Pinafore* and *The Yeoman of the Guard.*

19. The facets of the human personality are as _____ as the stars in a summer sky or the sands on a tropical beach.

20. Though members of the clergy must devote most of their time to their clerical duties, they are usually able to pursue _____ interests that have little or no bearing on their profession.

Group E

obsession	construe	fortuitous
connoisseur	traumatic	augur

21. Although he has been looking forward to retirement, he found the change in his lifestyle a disturbing, even a(n) _____ experience.

22. I have no objection to a person having a keen interest in bridge, but I am afraid that the game has become almost a(n) _____ with you.

23. When Albert Einstein remarked that God does not play dice with the universe, he meant that developments in nature are not purely _____.

24. Since I didn't know how to _____ her unexpected remark, I asked my best friend what he made of it.

25. We might describe a "promising development" as something that _____ well for success or victory in the future.

Group F

harbinger	grope	venerable
phobia	devoid	baffle

26. What began as a mere distaste for subway travel has developed into a full-blown _____ that makes even a short trip an agonizing experience.

27. That school is a _____ institution that has seen generations of students pass through its hallowed portals.

28. The proposal may look good at first glance, but if you study it carefully, you will see that it is _____ of any real merit.

29. Suddenly awakened by the insistent ringing of the telephone, I _____ around sleepily for the receiver.

30. Ordinary detectives may be _____ by a particularly ingenious crime, but the redoubtable Hercule Poirot is never stumped.

Exercise V. Words in Phrases

In each of the following groups, select the lettered item that best expresses the meaning of the *italicized* word in the introductory phrase.

1. completely *absolved* the defendant
   a. ignored   b. convicted   c. reproached   d. arrested
   e. acquitted

2. *adjourned* the meeting
   a. planned   b. suspended   c. attended   d. approved   e. opened

3. their *ambivalent* attitude
   a. scholarly   b. laudable   c. narrow-minded   d. contradictory
   e. discourteous

4. an *articulate* proponent of the plan
   a. long-standing   b. unexpected   c. well-known   d. eloquent
   e. self-appointed

5. seek *asylum* in the United States
   a. justice   b. refuge   c. wealth   d. fame   e. revenge

6. solely motivated by *avarice*
   a. hatred   b. fear   c. greed   d. ambition   e. jealousy

7. a *brusque* reply
   a. curt   b. pompous   c. interesting   d. amusing   e. silly

8. an outright *calumny*
   a. joke   b. disaster   c. blunder   d. refusal   e. falsehood

9. *clandestine* meetings
   a. unexpected   b. welcome   c. noisy   d. secret   e. important

10. an interesting *conjecture*
    a. fact   b. development   c. guess   d. book   e. history

11. my *corpulent* uncle
    a. portly   b. elderly   c. stately   d. wealthy   e. surly

12. *defer* a decision
    a. withdraw   b. overrule   c. ignore   d. confirm   e. postpone

13. *diligent* students
    a. recalcitrant   b. indolent   c. knowledgeable   d. indefatigable
    e. talented

14. the *elite* of the entertainment world
    a. retired members   b. fans   c. rank and file   d. superstars
    e. has-beens

15. bore the news with *equanimity*
    a. assistance   b. composure   c. indifference   d. reluctance
    e. hysteria

16. *expound* a theory
    a. attack   b. verify   c. explain   d. demolish   e. ignore

17. *filch* an apple
    a. steal   b. polish   c. eat   d. grow   e. buy

18. a *grueling* race
    a. downhill   b. contested   c. brief   d. draining   e. surprising

19. *impugned* my motives
    a. cast doubt on   b. threw light on   c. paid attention to
    d. gave evidence of   e. took comfort in

20. "*justify* the ways of God to man"
    a. criticize   b. vindicate   c. divulge   d. deplore   e. report

21. a *lucid* account
    a. muddled   b. long   c. funny   d. brief   e. clear

22. at a *nominal* cost to the consumer
    a. guaranteed   b. legal   c. token   d. sizable   e. fair

23. in a *pensive* mood
    a. puzzling   b. thoughtful   c. elated   d. friendly   e. obstinate

24. a *peremptory* tone of voice
    a. hopeful   b. dictatorial   c. jubilant   d. discouraged
    e. plaintive

25. *promulgate* a law
    a. announce   b. oppose   c. circumvent   d. advocate
    e. propose

26. felt no *remorse*
    a. loneliness   b. animosity   c. hunger   d. regret   e. desire

27. a mere *satellite* of the Soviet Union
    a. enemy   b. friend   c. aim   d. dependency   e. citizen

28. *scrutinize* the faces on the platform
    a. ignore   b. examine   c. draw   d. memorize   e. remember

29. *tangible* results
    a. insignificant   b. costly   c. unexpected   d. negative
    e. concrete

30. the *volatile* situation in that part of the world
    a. heartwarming b. curious c. explosive d. tranquil
    e. recent

Exercise VI.   Synonyms and Antonyms

Classify each of the following pairs of words as **S** for **synonyms** or **A** for **antonyms**.

1. abhor—relish
2. amiable—affable
3. alienate—estrange
4. apathy—enthusiasm
5. astute—obtuse
6. belligerent—hostile
7. boycott—patronize
8. catholic—parochial
9. habitual—chronic
10. complacent—smug
11. truncate—curtail
12. dapper—slovenly
13. praise—disparage
14. endemic—native
15. ignorant—erudite
16. exploit—feat
17. fluctuate—vacillate
18. smile—grimace
19. explicit—implicit
20. inception—inauguration
21. liability—asset
22. nebulous—vague
23. bedlam—pandemonium
24. plaintive—mournful
25. quell—foment
26. raze—erect
27. ruse—stratagem
28. strident—mellifluous
29. foil—thwart
30. nadir—zenith

Exercise VII.   Related Forms

A. Give a **noun** form of each of the following words.

1. abdicate
2. agile
3. allege
4. banal
5. bombastic
6. corroborate
7. emulate
8. entice
9. futile
10. jeopardize
11. nomadic
12. prodigious
13. redundant
14. usurp
15. versatile

B. Give an **adjective** form of each of the following words.

1. coerce
2. bureaucracy
3. defect
4. disparity
5. rudiment
6. strategy

C. Give an **adverb** form of each of the following words.

1. arbitrary
2. circumspect
3. facetious
4. graphic
5. malice
6. paradox

D. Give a **verb** form of each of the following words.

1. authentic
2. impediment
3. plagiarism

Exercise VIII.   Look-Alikes

Explain the difference in meaning between the words in each of the following pairs.

1. loath—loathe
2. averse—adverse
3. aesthetic—ascetic
4. callous—callow
5. forbear—forebear
6. flout—flaunt

7. indigent—indigenous	10. exalt—exult	13. urban—urbane
8. demur—demure	11. official—officious	14. venal—venial
9. discomfit—discomfort	12. turbid—turbulent	15. wan—wane

Exercise IX.   Framing Sentences

Compose an original illustrative sentence for each of the following words.

Group A

1. abstain	6. crucial	11. lackadaisical
2. amnesty	7. divulge	12. ominous
3. austere	8. ethical	13. purge
4. bleak	9. foible	14. revere
5. censure	10. immunity	15. tranquil

Group B

16. affectation	21. delineate	26. motley
17. appall	22. effrontery	27. perjure
18. avid	23. exodus	28. reciprocate
19. bungle	24. goad	29. scapegoat
20. concise	25. judicious	30. veto

Exercise X.   Word Roundup

1.   Define each of the following words.

a. teetotaler	f. windfall	k. timeserver
b. academician	g. rubberneck	l. has-been
c. claptrap	h. fluke	m. clone
d. aesthete	i. dilettante	n. gadfly
e. mannerism	j. greenhorn	o. muckraker

2.   Explain what each of the following phrases means.

a. academic freedom	f. Judas kiss
b. halcyon days	g. mirror image
c. red tape	h. hero worship
d. devil's advocate	i. feet of clay
e. credibility gap	j. splinter group

3.   Explain what each of the following colorful idioms means.

a. live high off the hog	f. live in an ivory tower
b. rest on one's laurels	g. pour oil on troubled waters
c. put on airs	h. bury the hatchet
d. see red	i. throw in the towel
e. paint oneself into a corner	j. shed crocodile tears

4.   Explain the story behind each of the following words.

a. boycott	c. jeremiad	e. quixotic
b. comstockery	d. malapropism	f. zealot

5.   Explain the meaning of each of the following foreign expressions used in present-day English, and tell what language it comes from.

a. milieu	d. vendetta
b. impedimenta	e. coup d'état
c. tour de force	f. quid pro quo

Index

a, an (Greek prefix), 55
a, plurals in, 327
abbreviations, 155
abstemious, 29
academic freedom, 30
academic question, 30
academy, academician, 30
accolade, 311
acculturation, 65
acronyms, 155–156
acute/chronic, 119
ad (Latin prefix), 55
adjective, definition of, 2
adverb, definition of, 3
affluent society, 41
Afrikaans, 15, 95
ag, act (Latin root), 79
amateur, 141
ambi (Latin prefix), 100
American English, 17, 19
amphi (Greek prefix), 100
analogies, verbal
  A causes *B*, 202
  A denotes lack of *B*, 112
  A indicates extreme of *B*, 203
  A indicates state of being *B*, 134
  A is example of *B*, 168
  A is part of *B*, 236
  A is person who *B*'s, 300
  A is primarily concerned with *B*, 236
  A means opposite of *B*, 88
  A means same as *B*, 68
  A will make a person *B*, 200–203
  definition of, 45
  If something is *A*, a person can(not) *B*

it, 267
  key or given relationship, 68
  parallelism in, 237
  tone of *A* is *B*, 301
  two colons, use of, 169
  Type I, 68
  Type II, 168–169
  word order in, 203
anarchism, anarchist, 51
anemic expressions, 172–173
animals, 92, 376
antonym, definition of, 3
Apocalypse, Four Horsemen of the, 415
apprehensive, apprehension, 61
a priori argument, 415
Arabic, 14
arbiter elegantiae, 62
arch (Greek root), 55; (English word) 56, (Greek prefix) 56
ascetic/aesthetic, 40
askance/askew/awry, 64
assimilation, 55, 65
astigmatism, 438
athwart, 450
Atonement, Day of (Yom Kippur), 72
auspicious, 75
auto, autos (Greek root), 78
averse/adverse, 38

baneful/banal, 83
be (Germanic prefix), 100
Bede, the Venerable, 465
bee in one's bonnet, have a, 346
bellicose/belligerent, 84
ben, bene (Latin root),

323–324
Bible, expressions drawn from, 190
black market, 275
blends, 47
body, parts of the, 431
bona fide, 76
boor/bore/Boer, 95
bootlegging, 275
bowdlerize, 394
Boycott, Charles C., 96
brinkmanship, 130
brisk/brusque, 97
Brobdingnagian, 318

callow/callous/callus, 106
candidate, 107
careers for word buffs
  copywriter, 89
  editor, 187
  journalist, 168
  teacher, 203
caricature, 353
Catch-22 situation, 276
Catholic/catholic, 109
ced, ceed (Latin root), 35
Celtic, borrowings from, 412
censor, censorship, 116
chic, 157
Chimaera, chimerical, 392
chron, chrono (Greek root), 123
chutzpah, 81
circu, circum (Latin prefix), 123
claptrap, 95
classical contributions to English, 102, 271
clichés, 91–92
clone, cloning, 380
clothing, words indicating, 343
coherence, 127
coining words, 304–305